D1084325

FISCAL CHALLENGES

Fiscal Challenges: An Interdisciplinary Approach to Budget Policy brings together leading experts from a range of disciplines to explore the problems of budget policy. The authors, including top economists, political scientists, historians, psychologists, and legal scholars, together provide a unique, multidisciplinary introduction to the subject. In addition to an in-depth analysis of congressional budget procedures and the economics of federal deficits and debt, *Fiscal Challenges* explores important recent developments in budget policy at the state level and in the European Union. The goal of the volume is to offer readers wide-ranging perspectives on the many different academic disciplines and perspectives that bear on the evaluation of budgetary procedures and their reform.

Elizabeth Garrett is the Sydney M. Irmas Professor of Public Interest Law, Legal Ethics, Political Science, and Policy, Planning, and Development at the University of Southern California. She is also the Co-Director of the USC-Caltech Center for the Study of Law and Politics.

Elizabeth A. Graddy is a professor of public policy and political science at the University of Southern California and the Senior Associate Dean of Faculty and Academic Affairs in the University of Southern California School of Policy, Planning, and Development.

Howell E. Jackson is the James S. Reid, Jr., Professor of Law at Harvard University. His research interests include financial regulation, consumer protection, and federal budget policy.

FISCAL CHALLENGES

AN INTERDISCIPLINARY APPROACH TO BUDGET POLICY

Edited by

ELIZABETH GARRETT
University of Southern California Gould School of Law

ELIZABETH A. GRADDY
University of Southern California School of Policy,
Planning, and Development

HOWELL E. JACKSON
Harvard Law School

CAMBRIDGE
UNIVERSITY PRESS

CAMBRIDGE UNIVERSITY PRESS

Cambridge, New York, Melbourne, Madrid, Cape Town, Singapore, São Paulo, Delhi

Cambridge University Press
32 Avenue of the Americas, New York, NY 10013-2473, USA

www.cambridge.org
Information on this title: www.cambridge.org/9780521877312

First published 2008

Printed in the United States of America

A catalog record for this publication is available from the British Library.

Library of Congress Cataloging in Publication Data

Fiscal challenges : an interdisciplinary approach to budget policy / edited by
Elizabeth Garrett, Elizabeth A. Graddy, Howell E. Jackson.
    p.   cm.
Includes bibliographical references and index.
ISBN 978-0-521-87731-2 (hardback)
1. Budget – United States.   I. Garrett, Elizabeth, 1963–   II. Graddy, Elizabeth A., 1950–
III. Jackson, Howell E.   IV. Title.
HJ2051.F483   2008
352.4′80973 – dc22   2007027738

ISBN   978-0-521-87731-2 hardback

Contents

Preface   *page* vii

Contributors   xi

PART ONE: THE LAW AND POLITICS OF FISCAL POLICY

Introduction   1

1 The Congressional Budget Process   4
   William G. Dauster

2 Budget Gimmicks   39
   Cheryl D. Block

3 Transparency in the U.S. Budget Process   68
   Elizabeth Garrett and Adrian Vermeule

4 European Experiences with Fiscal Rules and Institutions   103
   Jürgen von Hagen

Part One Bibliography   130

PART TWO: UNDERSTANDING FEDERAL DEFICITS AND PUBLIC DEBT

Introduction   139

5 Economic Perspectives on Federal Deficits and Debt   141
   Michael J. Boskin

6 Counting the Ways: The Structure of Federal Spending   185
   Howell E. Jackson

7 Starving the Beast: The Political Psychology of Budget Deficits   221
   Jonathan Baron and Edward J. McCaffery

Part Two Bibliography   242

PART THREE: BUDGETING AND FISCAL CONSTRAINTS AT THE STATE LEVEL

Introduction   249

8   Budgetary Arrangements in the 50 States: In Search of Model
    Practices   251
    Juliet Ann Musso, Elizabeth A. Graddy, and Jennifer Bravo Grizard

9   The Calculus of Constraint: A Critical Review of State Fiscal
    Institutions   271
    Tracy M. Gordon

10 When Does the Ballot Box Limit the Budget? Politics and Spending
    Limits in California, Colorado, Utah, and Washington   290
    Thad Kousser, Mathew D. McCubbins, and Kaj Rozga

Part Three Bibliography   322

PART FOUR: INTERGOVERNMENTAL ASPECTS OF BUDGET POLICY

Introduction   329

11 Dysfunctional or Optimal Institutions? State Debt Limitations, the
    Structure of State and Local Governments, and the Finance of
    American Infrastructure   331
    John Joseph Wallis and Barry R. Weingast

12 Federal–State Budgetary Interactions   366
    David A. Super

Part Four Bibliography   396

PART FIVE: JUDICIAL POWERS AND BUDGET POLICY

Introduction   399

13 New Property, Entrenchment, and the Fiscal Constitution   401
    John Harrison

14 Courts, Constitutions, and Public Finance: Some Recent
    Experiences from the States   418
    Richard Briffault

Part Five Bibliography   446

Index   451

Preface

How should the government spend society's limited resources? What rules and procedures should legislative bodies and executive officers follow in making spending decisions? To what extent should the government limit itself to spending that can be financed through current taxes, and to what extent should the government rely on the issuance of public debt that will impose financial burdens on future generations? How can we tell if the government's deficits are too high and its public debts too large? What role can and should the general public play in monitoring or defining fiscal priorities? To what extent can constitutional or quasi-constitutional constraints on budget-making procedures improve a country's fiscal decisions? Can we depend on the judiciary to enforce constitutional or other restraints on fiscal policies?

These are deep and difficult questions, and no single academic discipline can provide complete answers. Undoubtedly, economics offers important insights into the implications of annual deficits and the accumulation of public debts. But one must also be versed in the study of political science and the behavior of complicated organizations such as legislative bodies in order to understand the impact and potential consequences of budgetary rules and procedures. The processes whereby the general public forms opinions about matters of public finance – rational and otherwise – also have a place in the study of budget policy. Even some knowledge of the principles of financial accounting is necessary in order to evaluate how the country's financial condition might best be summarized and communicated to broader audiences.

But theoretical understanding alone will never be sufficient to guide sound decision making on such matters. One must have an appreciation of the manner in which budgetary procedures have actually evolved in practice. A process as byzantine as the congressional budget procedures of the federal government can only be understood as an amalgamation of more than a century of innovations and reforms. Historical perspective is also valuable to understand the efficacy and likely ramification of budgetary policies. Over the years, reformers have adopted many procedures designed to rationalize the spending decisions across various governmental functions or constrain overall levels of spending. With surprising consistency, these reforms have failed to work as originally intended. To the extent that one envisions a role for the courts in policing budgetary outcomes – as, for example, may be the case for proponents of constitutional amendments requiring a balanced budget – consideration of the success of the courts in fulfilling similar functions in the past could be illuminating. Those who seek to make recommendations for future budgetary reforms without some appreciation of the lessons of the past proceed at their own peril.

Finally, a comparative perspective on experiences with budgetary reforms in other contexts can deepen our understanding of budget policy. Within our own country, the states have experimented with a host of budgetary reforms stretching back over many decades, and they offer a body of evidence that is potentially susceptible to useful empirical analysis. International comparative studies are also of potential interest to the serious student of budget policy. Recent developments in the European Union, where member states have in theory agreed to abide by specific fiscal guidelines, are an especially fruitful source of comparative study.

Our not unambitious goal in constructing this volume is to introduce the readers to these many different perspectives of fiscal policies. We have assembled a number of the world's most prominent scholars on budget policy and invited them to address the topic of a variety of disciplinary perspectives. Our authors include leading experts in economics, political science, congressional budget procedures, legal studies, public behavioral economics, governmental accounting, economic history, European fiscal affairs, state budgetary procedures, and federal–state fiscal relations. We have also attempted to provide methodological diversity, including theorists as well as practitioners, econometric empiricists as well as psychological experimentalists. Some chapters take a historical perspective on the evolution of budget policy, while others are chiefly concerned with issues of current policy. While the volume does not purport to offer the last word on any of these perspectives, we hope to provide readers with useful entry points on most of the major disciplinary perspectives relevant to the study of budget policy.

We also hope that this volume will stimulate greater teaching of budget policy in colleges and graduate schools as well as more research and scholarship on the subject. To facilitate classroom discussions, we include at the end of each chapter a series of questions and comments. In connection with the preparation of this volume, the editors also commissioned a series of 32 briefing papers setting forth literature reviews on various aspects of budget policy and including extensive bibliographies. These briefing papers, which were prepared by students at Harvard Law School, are available online at http://www.law.harvard.edu/faculty/hjackson/budget.php. The papers will be updated in the spring of 2008 and periodically thereafter.

Finally, we owe thanks to many people who helped make this volume possible. Many of the chapters in this volume were initially presented at a conference held at the USC Gould School of Law and sponsored by the USC-Caltech Center for the Study of Law and Politics, the USC School of Policy, Planning, and Development through a grant from the James Irvine Foundation, and Harvard Law School. Betsey Hawkins provided expert administrative guidance at that conference and was invaluable in coordinating many months of work on the manuscript. Without her tireless work and good humor, this book would not have been possible. We appreciate the research assistance of the following students: Christopher Craig ('07) and Robert Porter ('08) of Harvard Law School as well as Jeffrey R. Makin ('07), Brent Tubbs ('07), Meegan Maczek ('08), Jennifer Wiegley ('08), Derek Lazzaro ('09), and Daniel Schwartz ('09) at USC Gould School of Law. We also appreciate the support we received from John Berger at Cambridge University Press.

Elizabeth Garrett
Elizabeth A. Graddy
Howell E. Jackson

Contributors

Jonathan Baron is Professor of Psychology at the University of Pennsylvania, where he teaches Judgments and Decisions and Behavioral Law and Economics. Baron is the author of several books, including *Thinking and Deciding* (1988, 1994, 2000, 2008), a widely used textbook, and he is Editor of the journal *Judgment and Decision Making*. He is a Fellow of the American Association for the Advancement of Science and of the Association for Psychological Science.

Cheryl D. Block recently joined the faculty at Washington University in St. Louis as a Professor of Law after many years on the faculty at the George Washington University Law School.

Michael J. Boskin is the T. M. Friedman Professor of Economics and Hoover Institution Senior Fellow at Stanford University. He is also Research Associate, National Bureau of Economic Research. An advisor to governments and businesses globally, Dr. Boskin also serves on several corporate and philanthropic boards of directors. He served as Chairman of the President's Council of Economic Advisers (CEA) from 1989 to 1993.

Richard Briffault is the Joseph P. Chamberlain Professor of Legislation at Columbia Law School, where he also is the Director of Columbia's Legislative Drafting Research Fund. His primary areas of research, teaching, and writing are state and local government law, election law, and property.

William G. Dauster is Deputy Staff Director and General Counsel for the U.S. Senate Finance Committee. He has served on Senate and White House staffs since 1986, including periods as Deputy Assistant to the President for Economic Policy and Deputy Director of the National Economic Council during the Clinton administration, as well as Democratic Staff Director for the Senate Budget Committee and the Senate Labor and Human Resources Committee. He has written three editions of a book called *Budget Process Law Annotated*.

Elizabeth Garrett is the Sydney M. Irmas Professor of Public Interest Law, Legal Ethics, Political Science, and Policy, Planning, and Development at the University of Southern California. She is also the Co-Director of the USC-Caltech Center for the Study of Law and Politics (CSLP). She serves on the Board of Directors of the Initiative and Referendum Institute at USC. President George W. Bush appointed her to serve on the nine-member bipartisan Tax Reform Panel that released its final report in November 2005. Her primary scholarly interests are legislative process, direct democracy, the federal budget process, study of democratic institutions, statutory interpretation, administrative law, and tax policy. She is the coauthor of the fourth edition of the leading casebook on legislation and statutory interpretation, *Cases and Materials on Legislation: Statutes and the Creation of Public Policy*, and of the second edition of *Legislation and Statutory Interpretation*. She is the author of many articles and book chapters analyzing campaign finance laws, courts and political parties, various congressional procedures, judicial review of regulatory statutes, the initiative process, and the California recall. Before entering academia, she clerked for Justice Thurgood Marshall on the U.S. Supreme Court, and she served as legal counsel and legislative director for Senator David L. Boren (D-Okla.).

Tracy M. Gordon is an assistant professor in the School of Public Policy at the University of Maryland and an adjunct Fellow at the Public Policy Institute of California. Her research interests are state and local public finance, urban economics, and political economy. She holds a Ph.D. in public policy with a concurrent M.A. in economics from the University of California, Berkeley.

Elizabeth A. Graddy is a professor of public policy and political science at USC and the Senior Associate Dean of Faculty and Academic Affairs in its School of Policy, Planning, and Development. Her research focuses on the private-sector role in public functions, how industry and organizational structure affect performance, and how information asymmetry and uncertainty affect institutional design and effectiveness. These interests have led to numerous publications addressing the performance of public and private institutional arrangements, including private provision of public services, state budgetary processes, tort liability laws, licensing boards and regulatory outcomes, and hospital industry structure and performance. Her current work focuses on public–private alliances providing public services, community foundations and local governance, and state healthcare regulation. Professor Graddy is a past public member and vice president of the California State Board of Podiatric Medicine. She received her doctorate from Carnegie Mellon University.

Jennifer Bravo Grizard is a Master of Public Policy graduate of the University of Southern California, School of Policy, Planning, and Development.

John Harrison is the David Lurton Massee, Jr., Professor of Law and the Henry L. and Grace Doherty Charitable Foundation Professor at the University of Virginia. His teaching subjects include constitutional history, federal courts, remedies, corporations, civil procedure, legislation, and property.

Howell E. Jackson is the James S. Reid, Jr., Professor of Law at Harvard Law School. His research interests include financial regulation, international finance, consumer protection, federal budget policy, and Social Security reform. Professor Jackson has served as a consultant to the United States Treasury Department, the United Nations Development Program, and the World Bank/International Monetary Fund. He is a member of the National Academy on Social Insurance, a trustee of the College Retirement Equities Fund (CREF) and its affiliated TIAA-CREF investment companies, a member of the panel of outside scholars for the NBER Retirement Research Center, and a senior editor for the Cambridge University Press series on International Corporate Law and Financial Regulation. Professor Jackson frequently testifies before Congress and consults with government agencies on issues of financial regulation. He is the coauthor of *Analytical Methods for Lawyers and Regulation of Financial Institutions* and the author of numerous scholarly articles. Before joining the Harvard Law School faculty in 1989, Professor Jackson was a law clerk for Associate Justice Thurgood Marshall and practiced law in Washington, D.C. Professor Jackson received juris doctor and master of business administration degrees from Harvard University in 1982 and a bachelor of arts degree from Brown University in 1976.

Thad Kousser is an associate professor of political science at the University of California, San Diego. His general research interests include legislative politics, policy making, and political regulation. His publications include work on the initiative process, term limits, reapportionment, campaign finance laws, the blanket primary, healthcare policy, and European Parliament elections.

Edward J. McCaffery is the Robert C. Packard Trustee Chair in Law, Political Science and Economics at the University of Southern California and Visiting Professor of Law and Economics at the California Institute of Technology. The author of many articles and several books, he recently coedited *Behavioral Public Finance* (Russell Sage Press) with Joel Slemrod.

Mathew D. McCubbins is the Chancellor's Associates Chair VIII in the Department of Political Science at the University of California, San Diego. He is the coauthor of six books. He is also editor or coeditor of eight additional books and has authored more than 90 scientific entries, with one winning the 1986 Congressional Quarterly Prize for best article on legislative politics and another winning the 2005 APSA SPPQ Award.

Juliet Ann Musso is an associate professor of public policy at the University of Southern California School of Policy, Planning, and Development. She has expertise in federalism and urban political economy, with specific research interests in intergovernmental fiscal policy, local institutional reform, and community governance.

Kaj Rozga is a graduate of the University of California, San Diego.

David A. Super is a professor of law at the University of Maryland School of Law. Before joining the faculty at the University of Maryland, Professor Super served as general counsel to the Center on Budget and Policy Priorities.

Adrian Vermeule is a Professor of Law at Harvard Law School. He was a professor at the University of Chicago Law School from 1998 to 2006. His interests include legislation and legislative process, administrative law, and constitutional law.

Jürgen von Hagen is a professor of economics at the University of Bonn and a Research Fellow of CEPR, London. He previously taught at Indiana University and the University of Mannheim, Germany. Von Hagen has been a consultant to the IMF, the World Bank, the Interamerican Development Bank, the European Central Bank, and numerous national governments.

John Joseph Wallis is a professor of economics, University of Maryland, and a National Fellow, Hoover Institution, Stanford University. His primary fields of research are the economic history of American government and the political economy of government promotion or retardation of economic development.

Barry R. Weingast is a senior Fellow at the Hoover Institution as well as the Ward C. Krebs Family Professor in the Department of Political Science at Stanford University. He is also a professor of economics, by courtesy, at the university. He was a Fellow at the Center for Advanced Study in the Behavioral Sciences from 1993 to 1994. Weingast is an expert in political economy and public policy, the political foundation of markets and economic reform, U.S. politics, and regulation.

PART ONE

THE LAW AND POLITICS OF FISCAL POLICY

The United States Constitution places the power of the purse in the legislature's domain: Article I, §9, cl. 7 specifies that "No Money shall be drawn from the Treasury, but in Consequence of Appropriations made by Law." Thus, the founders entrusted the federal government's most important power to the most politically accountable branch, the U.S. Congress. Congress not only sets the amount of money appropriated to executive branch agencies and other government activities, but it also directs how that total is to be spent by enacting directives in appropriations laws.[1] Congress has not always handled its budgetary authority responsibly, which can result in an abdication of its power to the executive branch. In some cases, legislators fail to meet constitutional obligations because they wish to avoid blame for potentially unpopular decisions; in other cases, congressional inaction may be due to collective action problems inherent in entities made up of many individuals often pursuing different objectives.

In Chapter 1, William Dauster describes the evolution of the congressional budget process with a particular emphasis on the modern era, beginning with the adoption of the Congressional Budget and Impoundment Control Act of 1974. He describes what has been called the "fiscal Constitution"[2] because of its importance in the American political process. Over the past 30 years, Congress has adopted a series of institutional reforms, including enactment of framework laws that structure the deliberative process in committees and on the floor and creation of the Congressional Budget Office to provide lawmakers more professional expertise. Framework legislation "creates rules that structure congressional lawmaking; these laws establish internal procedures that will shape legislative deliberation and voting with respect to certain laws or decisions

---

[1] See Kate Stith, *Congress' Power of the Purse*, 97 YALE L.J. 1343, 1345 (1988), terming the two powers "a Principle of the Public Fisc" and a "Principle of Appropriations Control."
[2] Kenneth W. Dam, *The American Fiscal Constitution*, 44 U. CHI. L. REV. 271 (1977).

in the future."[3] The congressional budget process is the archetypical framework law, and it affects a substantial portion of Congress' legislative business.

The evolving framework shaping the congressional budget process is designed to achieve several objectives. First, it serves as a *coordination device* to govern the actions of the dozens of committees in both chambers that are involved in spending or raising money. Second, the framework may serve *symbolic purposes*, particularly when the public is concerned about growing deficits, to saliently demonstrate to voters that lawmakers are fiscally responsible. Third, at least some parts of the budget framework are intended to serve as a *precommitment device* to make it harder for lawmakers to engage in deficit spending. Fourth, the budget process also has shifted the *balance of political power* in important ways, as Dauster discusses in his chapter. Not only did Congress hope to regain power that it had ceded to the executive branch, but the framework also works to shift power internally from long-serving committee leaders to party leaders. Some of these changes in power were intended by those adopting budget rules, but some may have been unforeseen at the time of enactment.

Cheryl D. Block builds on Dauster's comprehensive description of the congressional budget framework to describe how strategic political actors manipulate these rules to achieve their goals. In Chapter 2, she describes a bagful of tricks that lawmakers and interest groups use to ensure that programs important to them continue to receive federal support even during times that Congress claims to be pursuing spending restraint. Not only do these games undermine fiscal discipline, but they can also threaten rational decision making because the information that lawmakers rely on is not accurate or complete. Moreover, policymakers may choose to construct federal programs in particular ways merely to comply with budget rules, and these structures may not be the most efficient or equitable way to deliver benefits. Examples of the effect of budget gimmicks are legion, and Block illustrates her analysis with provisions enacted by both Republican and Democratic Congresses. When it comes to budget games, the players come from both sides of the aisle and seem able to discover ways around even the most complicated of rules.[4]

Lawmakers resort to budget gimmicks because they want to enact new policies even when the legislative environment is shaped to constrain them. Their reelection is dependent in part on their record of achievement on issues that matter to voters, and many voters prefer policies that cost the federal government money to policies designed to cut the deficit. Even voters who favor smaller government and spending restraint would often prefer that programs

---

[3] Elizabeth Garrett, *The Purposes of Framework Legislation*, 14 J. Contemp. Legal Iss. 717, 718 (2005).
[4] Not surprisingly, games occur at the state level as well. See Richard Briffault, *Balancing Acts: The Reality Behind State Balanced Budget Amendments* (1996).

benefiting them and their families stay off the cutting block and perhaps even receive more resources. In addition, lawmakers know that their reelection is crucially related to their ability to raise money for campaigns. A large part of that financial support comes from organized interest groups that expect lawmakers to help them pursue their top priorities. In some cases, the objectives of interest groups may not align with the general welfare.

Elizabeth Garrett and Adrian Vermeule tackle this tension between accountability to voters and accountability to organized interest groups in their chapter on transparency in budgeting decision making. They reach the counterintuitive conclusion in Chapter 3 that broad and immediate disclosure of deliberation on budget matters may not be desirable because it disproportionately advantages organized interests rather than the unorganized and dispersed public. They also compare the kind of deliberation that occurs in public with that possible in more private venues. They recommend a different sort of framework for budget transparency, not only to apply to congressional entities but also to executive branch advisory committees and interbranch budget summits.

In the final chapter of this section, we turn to a comparative analysis of budget institutions. Jürgen von Hagen describes the experience in the European Union, which confronts the challenge of controlling deficit spending in a context different from that of the United States. Not only is Europe characterized by parliamentary systems, but the EU is seeking to impose a framework on countries that have long histories of autonomy in fiscal policy. The federated European system is vastly different from the federal system in the United States, and thus it poses different challenges for the designers of budget institutions. Comparative studies like von Hagen's provide insight into the larger issues of institutional design; for example, the EU had the advantage in the 1990s that it could severely punish nations that did not adhere to fiscal objectives because it could deny them entry to the European Monetary Union. The effect of such a penalty on the behavior of EU countries during this time illuminates the challenges for the U.S. system and now for the EU, where the punishment for defection from budget objectives is largely political. This chapter is only the first kind of comparative analysis we will provide; Part III's comprehensive analysis of state budgetary structures allows a different sort of comparison to the federal process.

1 The Congressional Budget Process

William G. Dauster

I. HOW IT EVOLVED

"Money is power," wrote President Andrew Jackson in an 1833 veto message.[1] More than anything else, that equation explains how budgets work. America's congressional budget process evolved from efforts to grasp and disperse that power. This chapter recounts the evolution of the process and then discusses how it works – focusing particularly on the president's budget, Congress' budget resolution, authorizations and appropriations, and the budget reconciliation process.

A. The Founders

America's founders gave Congress the power over money to provide a check on the president. Article I, Section 9 of the Constitution states the following: "No Money shall be drawn from the Treasury, but in Consequence of Appropriations made by Law." The founders learned from their study of English history that it was important to separate the power to control the government's money from the power to run the government. They felt that enhancing the legislature's money powers would help to preserve the rights of the people. James Madison summarized the English experience when he wrote in the *Federalist Papers*, concerning the House of Representatives:

> They, in a word, hold the purse – that powerful instrument by which we behold, in the history of the British Constitution, an infant and humble representation of the people gradually enlarging the sphere of its activity and importance, and finally reducing, as far as it seems to have wished, all the overgrown prerogatives of the other branches of the government. This power over the purse may, in

---

[1] Andrew Jackson, pocket veto message (Dec. 4, 1833), *in* SEN. J. 20, 30 (Dec. 5, 1833).

William G. Dauster is Deputy Staff Director and General Counsel for the U. S. Senate Finance Committee.

fact, be regarded as the most complete and effectual weapon with which any constitution can arm the immediate representatives of the people, for obtaining a redress of every grievance, and for carrying into effect every just and salutary measure.[2]

B. The Ways and Means and Finance Committees

The English Parliament's struggle for power with the king culminated in the English Civil War in the 1640s. The forces aligned with Parliament prevailed, and Parliament wrested the power of the purse exclusively to itself. As part of that process, in 1641, the Parliament formed its Committee on Ways and Means, giving it the power to determine tax policy.

America's House of Representatives formed a Ways and Means Committee early on and patterned it on its parliamentary forbearer.[3] After a period of legislating through ad hoc committees, the Senate followed suit in 1816 with its Committee on Finance.[4] In these early days, the Ways and Means and Finance Committees held nearly plenary jurisdiction over fiscal policy. They handled both taxes and spending. That may have been the last time that America had a simple congressional budget process. Of course, America was simpler then, too. Our first appropriation act fit on a single page.[5] Today, funding the government each year can take a dozen separate laws, each often spanning hundreds of pages.

C. The Appropriations Committees

The increased fiscal demands of the American Civil War demonstrated the power of the two money committees. For the first time, the government spent more than $1 billion in one year. In the wake of the war, Congress sought to disperse that power, separating the power to spend from the power to tax. To oversee spending, the House created the Appropriations Committee in 1865, and the Senate followed suit in 1867.[6] The House Ways and Means and Senate Finance Committees retained their jurisdiction over taxes.

---

[2] James Madison, THE FEDERALIST No. 58, at 359 (Clinton Rossiter ed., 1961).

[3] *See* Donald R. Kennon and Rebecca M. Rogers , THE COMMITTEE ON WAYS AND MEANS: A BICENTENNIAL HISTORY: 1789–1989, at 6 (1989) (H. Doc. 244, 100th Cong., 2d Sess.).

[4] *See* Staff of S. Comm. on Finance, 97th Cong., HISTORY OF THE COMMITTEE ON FINANCE 14–18 (1981).

[5] *See* H.R. 32, 1st Cong., 1st Sess. (1789) (An Act Making Appropriations for the Service of the Present Year), *reprinted in* 4 DOCUMENTARY HISTORY OF THE FIRST FEDERAL CONGRESS OF THE UNITED STATES OF AMERICA 49 (Charlene Bangs Bickford and Helen E. Veit eds., 1986).

[6] *See* Staff of S. Comm. on Appropriations, 109th Cong., UNITED STATES SENATE COMMITTEE ON APPROPRIATIONS; 138TH ANNIVERSARY; 1867–2005, at 4–5 (2005); Allen Schick, LEGISLATION, APPROPRIATIONS, AND BUDGETS: THE DEVELOPMENT OF SPENDING DECISION-MAKING IN CONGRESS (May 1984) (CRS rep. no. 84-106).

Appropriations bills provided the authority for the Treasury to disburse money to run the government. These must-pass bills provided vehicles on which some sought to enact unrelated changes in law. Beginning in the 1830s in the House and in 1850 in the Senate, Congress adopted rules that further divided the spending power.[7] Under those rules, appropriations bills merely funded existing programs and "carr[ied] out the provisions of some existing law."[8] The rules prohibited these bills from creating new programs. Other committees – called "authorizing" or "legislative" committees – worked on legislation creating ("authorizing") new programs, revising ("reauthorizing") old ones, and terminating programs that ceased to serve their purposes. The authorizing committees reported legislation to authorize levels of spending subject to later appropriations. Authorizing legislation did not in itself allow money to leave the Treasury.

In the wake of the increased fiscal demands of World War I, Congress sought to rationalize the executive branch's budget process by enacting the Budget and Accounting Act of 1921.[9] That law created the Bureau of the Budget (the forerunner of today's Office of Management and Budget, or OMB), created the General Accounting Office (GAO, forerunner of today's Government Account- ability Office) independent of the executive, and required the president to sub- mit budgets to Congress every year.

D. The Congressional Budget Act

Beginning particularly with the New Deal programs of the 1930s – notably Social Security – and continuing with the Great Society programs of the 1960s – notably Medicare and Medicaid – authorizing committees came to report leg- islation that obligated the government to make payments, *not* subject to annual appropriations, to beneficiaries who met specified requirements. This spend- ing – called an "entitlement," "mandatory spending," or "direct spending" – grew to increasingly large portions of the federal budget by the 1970s. Enti- tlement spending surpassed appropriated spending in 1975.[10] The appropria- tions process thus ceased to oversee the broad sweep of federal spending. Since the formation of the Appropriations Committees, Congress had dispersed the powers of taxing and spending among several committees, without any single committee to oversee the bottom-line effect of Congress' actions on the deficit, and the growth of entitlement spending only increased this fragmentation of responsibility.

---

[7] The process was not a linear one. The late 19th century and early 20th century saw several revisions of these processes, as powers shifted between authorizers and appropriators.
[8] Senate Rule XXX (Dec. 19, 1850).
[9] Pub. L. No. 67-13, 42 Stat. 20 (codified as amended in scattered sections of 31 U.S.C.).
[10] *See* Congressional Budget Office, THE BUDGET AND ECONOMIC OUTLOOK: FISCAL YEARS 2007 TO 2016, at 144 (2006).

The early 1970s also saw a constitutional confrontation between the Congress and the Nixon administration over the president's power to refuse to spend money that Congress had by law directed the president to spend. President Nixon claimed the power not to spend – to "impound" – these funds. Congress asserted its traditional power of the purse. When courts addressed lawsuits raising these issues, they tended to deny that the president has either constitutional or statutory authority to decline to spend the funds.[11]

Congress addressed this impoundment crisis, and also the problem of not having one entity or a coordinated process to examine the fiscal bottom line, in the Congressional Budget and Impoundment Control Act of 1974.[12] Title X of the act solved the impoundment confrontation through a legislative compromise. Congress granted the president the power to defer spending money for a limited time, unless one house of Congress passed a resolution – a "legislative veto" – disapproving the deferral. On the other hand, Congress deprived the president of the power to cancel or "rescind" funds, unless Congress also passed a rescission bill canceling the funds. In 1983, the Supreme Court ruled legislative vetoes of the sort used by the Impoundment Control Act unconstitutional because such a veto was a legislative act that needed to meet the constitutional requirements of bicameralism and presentment.[13] After that case, stopping a presidential deferral took the vote of both houses of Congress, most probably by a two-thirds vote to overcome a veto, instead of merely a majority vote of one house of Congress through a legislative veto. Consequently, Congress has rarely acted on deferrals.

The first nine titles of the 1974 Budget Act proved more significant than its impoundment provisions; they created new congressional institutions and added new congressional procedures. The Budget Act created Budget Committees to join the other committees in each house of Congress. The Budget Act also created the Congressional Budget Office (CBO) to provide Congress with its own, neutral source of information independent of the president's Office of Management and Budget.

In addition, the Budget Act created fast-track legislative vehicles to consider fiscal policy. First came the concurrent resolution on the budget, or budget resolution. The budget resolution provided rules for Congress that constituted an overall blueprint for the nation's fiscal policy. As a concurrent resolution, the budget resolution was not presented to the president for signature or veto. The

---

[11] *See, e.g., Train v. Campaign Clean Water, Inc.,* 420 U.S. 136 (1975); *Train v. City of New York,* 420 U.S. 35 (1975); *Commonwealth of Pennsylvania v. Lynn,* 501 F.2d 848 (D.C. Cir. 1974); *State Highway Comm'n of Missouri v. Volpe,* 479 F.2d 1099 (8th Cir. 1973).

[12] *See* Pub. L. No. 93-344, 88 Stat. 297 (1974) (codified as amended at 2 U.S.C. §§ 601–688).

[13] The Supreme Court held legislative vetoes unconstitutional in *I.N.S. v. Chadha,* 462 U.S. 919 (1983). Applying *Chadha,* the Court of Appeals in *City of New Haven, Conn. v. United States,* 809 F. 2d 900 (D.C. Cir. 1987), struck down Section 1013 of the Impoundment Control Act regarding deferrals.

House of Representatives considered the budget resolution as it did almost all legislation, under rules specific to the particular legislation under consideration that restricted debate and amendment. In contrast, the Senate found the fast-track procedures governing the budget resolution most unusual. Normally, the Senate's rules ensured senators the right to speak as long as they wanted. Thus ordinarily senators could engage in extended debate – or a "filibuster" – unless 60 senators voted to bring debate to a close.[14] Because the Budget Act created special procedures to limit debate on the budget resolution, however, senators could not wage a filibuster against it. A simple majority of senators voting could determine what amendments the Senate would adopt, and a simple majority could pass the resolution. Thus, the Budget Act's processes increased the power of the majority party, especially in the Senate, which could use the act's fast-track process to advance its agenda with fewer delays.

Participants in the federal budget process initially underestimated the potential power of the budget resolution. They failed completely, however, to foresee the power of a second fast-track procedure created by the Budget Act called "reconciliation." The Budget Act originally provided for two budget resolutions: The first would advise, and the second, passed closer to the start of the fiscal year, would bind. The Budget Act provided that the second budget resolution could instruct committees of Congress to reconcile laws passed within their jurisdiction to the new budget priorities of the second budget resolution. The idea was that the reconciliation bill would merely clean up changes that occurred over the summer between the two budget resolutions.

The reconciliation process did not turn out to be quite as modest as the drafters of the Budget Act had intended. Rather, it became a fast-track, coordinated vehicle of great power to change permanent law affecting spending and taxes. In years when the budget resolution contained reconciliation instructions, the authorizing committees instructed were required to report changes in law within their jurisdictions to modify spending or taxes by the overall amount that the resolution instructed. As with the budget resolution, the Senate considered the reconciliation bill under fast-track procedures unusual for that body.

The experience under the Congressional Budget Act divides into four eras. Between enactment of the Congressional Budget Act and the beginning of the use of the reconciliation process, 1974 to 1980, the congressional budget process was neutral as to the fiscal result. Congress could enforce the fiscal policy that it created. But that process did not point toward balancing the budget or expanding the deficit. And the tools that Congress used to enforce its fiscal policy were relatively weak, lacking supermajority requirements or use of the fast-track reconciliation process to change permanent law.

---

[14] *See* Standing Rules of the Senate, Rule XXII(2) (the cloture rule).

Beginning with the first use of reconciliation in 1980 and extending through 1996, the congressional budget process experienced a second period in which the process was biased toward deficit reduction. The Senate parliamentarian advised during this period that the Senate could not use reconciliation for legislation that worsened the deficit. And in 1985, Congress changed the law to require 60 votes in the Senate to get around many budget rules.

The third period began with the parliamentarian's reinterpretation of the reconciliation process in 1996 and extended through 2007. As a result of that reinterpretation, reconciliation became generally available for budget-related policy change, regardless of whether it improved or worsened the nation's fiscal balance. And the congressional budget process returned to one that was neutral as to the fiscal result. This time, however, Congress had relatively strong tools to enforce its fiscal policy – supermajority hurdles and fast-track reconciliation legislation.

Finally, Congress began the fourth era in 2007, returning to fiscal discipline by adopting a budget resolution that tightened pay-as-you-go rules and restricted reconciliation to deficit reduction once again.

E. Budgeting to Reduce the Deficit

The Congress first enacted a reconciliation bill reported by the Budget Committee in 1980. In 1981, in an effort to enact President Reagan's first budget, the budget resolution included reconciliation instructions for years beyond the first fiscal year covered by the resolution, extending the reach of the reconciliation vehicle to more-permanent changes in law. Congress thus converted the reconciliation process from a short-term measure to recalibrate actions that Congress took in the most recent summer to a long-term measure to change permanent law. This expansion of reconciliation further enhanced the power of the congressional budget process and the Budget Committees, at the expense of other committees in Congress.

After 1981, reconciliation became a regular feature of most budget resolutions, and Congress has accomplished most significant deficit reduction through the reconciliation process. Congress also enacted many other legislative items as part of reconciliation legislation, taking advantage of reconciliation's limits on debate and amendment. For example, the 1981 reconciliation act included substantial legislative matter regarding federal housing programs. Reconciliation bills have included provisions ranging from lawn mower standards to the maximum speed limit (for cars, not lawn mowers). The power of reconciliation thus attracted much matter not strictly related to the budget. In response to this "extraneous" matter, in 1985 the Senate adopted the Byrd Rule,[15] named after its sponsor, Democratic Leader Robert C. Byrd (W. Va.). At

---

[15] Congressional Budget Act § 313, 2 U.S.C. § 644.

the pain of requiring a 60-vote waiver in the Senate, the Byrd Rule prohibited including items without budgetary effect.

Meanwhile, in the mid-1980s, the nation was running deficits in excess of 5 percent of the gross domestic product, rates not seen since the World War II era. President Reagan's 1981 tax cuts lowered the share of the gross domestic product that the federal government collected in taxes from 20.2 percent in 1981 (a record high shared with 1969) to 18.0 percent in 1984. The government did not, however, reduce spending during the same period. Total federal outlays accounted for 22.9 percent of the economy in 1981 and rose marginally to 23.0 percent by 1984. In 1983, OMB Director David Stockman warned that failing to act on the budget would produce $200 billion deficits "as far as the eye can see."[16] In reaction to these deficits, Congress turned in 1985 to a new procedure, called Gramm-Rudman-Hollings, designed to ensure that the budget process worked toward a balanced budget.[17] Named after its three principal sponsors, Senators Phil Gramm, Warren Rudman, and Ernest Hollings, Gramm-Rudman-Hollings directed the budget process toward a particular policy goal. With Gramm-Rudman-Hollings, the nation explicitly adopted the fiscal policy of a balanced budget.

Gramm-Rudman-Hollings established a series of deficit targets leading gradually to a balanced budget in the fifth year. If the government failed to cause the projected deficit to fall within $10 billion of the required target, then the law required the president to order across-the-board cuts – called "sequesters" – to bring the deficit down to the target amount. This sequestration was not as draconian as it could have been because Gramm-Rudman-Hollings exempted the vast majority of entitlement programs from these cuts.

As originally enacted, Gramm-Rudman-Hollings called for the CBO to make one estimate of the deficit and the president's OMB to make another. To the extent that the two estimates differed, the law directed the GAO to average the two estimates and issue a final report that would bind the president. This provision set the stage for a constitutional challenge of the new process. In 1986, the Supreme Court ruled that Gramm-Rudman-Hollings violated the Constitution's doctrine of separation of powers.[18] The court reasoned that the law allowed a congressional actor – the GAO – to direct the president how to execute the laws, whereas the Constitution provides that "[t]he executive Power shall be vested in [the] President of the United States of America."[19]

---

[16] Helen Dewar, *Stockman Issues Blunt Warning; Budget Agreement Called Vital*, WASH. POST, Apr. 19, 1983, at A1.

[17] The Balanced Budget and Emergency Deficit Control Act of 1985, Pub. L. No. 99-177, tit. II, 99 Stat. 1037, 1038 (1985), *amended by* the Balanced Budget and Emergency Deficit Control Reaffirmation Act of 1987, Pub. L. No. 100-119, tit. I-II, 101 Stat. 754 (1987), *and largely repealed by* Budget Enforcement Act of 1990, Pub. L. No. 101-508, tit. XIII, 104 Stat. 1388, 1388-573–1388-630 (1990) (codified as amended at 2 U.S.C. §§ 900–922).

[18] *Bowsher v. Synar*, 478 U.S. 714, 721–734 (1986).

[19] U.S. Const. art. II, § 1, cl. 1.

In addition to its sequester system, Gramm-Rudman-Hollings also bolstered the procedural obstacles to violating the Congressional Budget Act – called "points of order." The Gramm-Rudman-Hollings law increased to 60 votes in the Senate the number of votes required to evade a variety of budget levels. This change vastly increased the number of occasions on which the Senate would need 60 votes to pass legislation. Budget Act points of order became instant filibusters, allowing senators to impose a supermajority requirement on the Senate without having to spend the hours to mount a true filibuster. Representative David Obey would later remark in exasperation: "The Senate rules say you can't do anything, short of going to the bathroom, without 60-vote approval."[20]

The Supreme Court's decision striking down the enforcement mechanism of Gramm-Rudman-Hollings required a congressional response to keep the process viable. After the Democrats took back control of the Senate in 1986, fiscally conservative Democrats sought a tool to bring President Reagan to the negotiating table with Congress to work out a deal to reduce the deficit. At the same time, Republican members of Congress sought to control the size of government and the amount of congressional spending. These fiscally conservative groups joined together to enact legislation restoring the automatic trigger on Gramm-Rudman-Hollings in a constitutional way by giving final estimating authority to the president's OMB.

Gramm-Rudman-Hollings can claim some credit for the drop in the deficit from $221 billion in 1986 to $150 billion in 1987, but in 1990, the last year in which the law's deficit targets governed, the deficit rose back to $221 billion, exactly where it started under Gramm-Rudman-Hollings.[21] Thus, at best, over its lifetime, Gramm-Rudman-Hollings prevented further growth in the deficit. In practice, the president and Congress complied with Gramm-Rudman-Hollings only through the use of unrealistically optimistic economic assumptions, shifts of spending from the budget year into another, and other "myopic budgeting"[22] techniques that improved appearances in the current budget year but did not improve the long-run picture. As the government focused on avoiding the particular year's impending fiscal crisis, it did not solve the deficit problem for ensuing years.

As 1990 approached, the task of reaching the fiscal year 1991 deficit targets again appeared overwhelming. Officials from the first Bush administration and the bipartisan congressional leadership met in a series of budget summit meetings stretching from March through September 1990, some of them at Andrews Air Force Base outside Washington, D.C. In the end, they produced

[20] *The Final Word*, Congress Daily, May 18, 1992.
[21] *See* Congressional Budget Office, *supra* note 10, at 140.
[22] 1 The Balanced Budget Amendment: Hearings Before the House Comm. on the Budget, 102d Cong., 2d Sess. 151–152 (1992) (serial no. 42) (statement of CBO Director Robert Reischauer). *See* Cheryl Block's discussion of the devices that actors in the budget process have used to subvert the budget process, in Chapter 2 of this volume.

a package that reduced the deficit by $482 billion over five years.[23] They also agreed to a set of procedures to make sure that the deficit reduction happened – the Budget Enforcement Act of 1990.[24] The Budget Enforcement Act abandoned fixed deficit targets in all but name. The targets continued as floating goals that the law automatically adjusted for 1992 and 1993, and then allowed the president to adjust for 1994 and 1995 (which President Clinton did). The deficit targets never again bound decision makers; Gramm-Rudman-Hollings was dead.

Instead of regulating the *effect* of government's fiscal policy – the deficit – the Budget Enforcement Act regulated the *cause* of deficits – government spending and tax cuts. The Budget Enforcement Act preserved sequesters in two separate environments. The law set up a series of caps on annually appropriated spending. Sequesters cut appropriated spending down to the levels of the caps when the government enacted spending bills that caused appropriations to exceed them. The law also set up a procedure that would allow for flexibility to adjust the caps in emergencies.[25]

All budget actions other than appropriated spending (and Social Security, which the law took off budget) fell into the second system created by the 1990 law. Under new "pay-as-you-go" or "PAYGO" rules, the sum of all spending and tax legislation outside of appropriation bills could not worsen the deficit. If tax-cutting or spending legislation from authorizing committees (typically, entitlement programs) worsened the deficit for a fiscal year, the law required the president to order a sequester in certain entitlement programs at the end of the year to make up the breach.

The Budget Enforcement Act measured the effects of legislation based on estimates made at the time of the legislation's enactment, so it held Congress and the president responsible only for the budgetary effects that they could foresee. Some disparaged this system as "no-fault budgeting," as the law did not hold the government responsible for the actual results it produced.[26] Advocates of the 1990 law, however, noted that it focused accountability on the portion of the system responsible for breaking the rules.

The Budget Enforcement Act broadened the myopic one-year focus of Gramm-Rudman-Hollings to a five-year budget window. The law lengthened the coverage of budget resolutions from three to five years, and it expanded the

---

[23] Robert Keith, Deficit Impact of Reconciliation Legislation Enacted in 1990, 1993, and 1997 (Sept. 21, 2005) (CRS rep. no. RS22098).

[24] Pub. L. No. 101-508, tit. XIII, 104 Stat. 1388, 1388-573–1388-630 (1990) (codified as amended in scattered sections of 2 U.S.C., 15 U.S.C. § 1022, 31 U.S.C §§ 1105, 1341, 1342).

[25] *See* William G. Dauster, *Budget Emergencies*, 18 J. Legis. 249 (spring 1992); James V. Saturno, Emergency Spending: Statutory and Congressional Rules (May 11, 2005) (CRS rep. no. RS21035).

[26] Alan Fram, *Washington Today: Whatever Happened to Gramm-Rudman?* Associated Press, Nov. 29, 1991 (quoting Allen Schick of the University of Maryland).

focus of several points of order from a single year to the first five fiscal years. Consequently, Congress could no longer easily evade the law by shifting expenditures or taxes from one year into an adjacent year, or by starting programs up in the year after the budget year.

In the first year of the Clinton administration, the government once again achieved a major deficit-reduction package of $433 billion,[27] but this one with only Democratic votes, including the vice president's, to break the tie – something made possible by the fast-track rules for reconciliation that eliminated any threat of a filibuster. As called for in President Clinton's first budget message, the fiscal year 1994 budget resolution extended the multiyear focus from five years to ten years. As revised further in the fiscal year 1995[28] and 1996[29] budget resolutions, a pay-as-you-go provision required deficit neutrality in taxes and entitlement spending in the first year, the first five years, and the second five years in order to avoid a point of order requiring 60 votes to waive.

F. Budgeting to Worsen the Deficit

Thanks in part to President Clinton's budget policy, Republicans regained control of the Senate in 1995. The new majority leader changed the Senate parliamentarian, the officer who advises the presiding officer how to rule on points of order. Following the new parliamentarian's advice, in 1996, the Senate created a controversial precedent that allowed the majority to use reconciliation bills for tax cuts and spending that increased the deficit.[30] Thus began the Budget Act's third era. Since 1996, Congress has enacted several major laws using the fast-track reconciliation process. In 1996, the Republican Congress used the reconciliation process to enact a sweeping welfare reform bill.[31] And, in 1997, Congress used the reconciliation process to enact a tax cut bill that added to the deficit by $80 billion over five years.[32] That same year, Congress also enacted a spending reduction bill that cut spending by $198 billion.[33]

During the George W. Bush administration, reconciliation has played a key role in cutting taxes, but less in cutting spending. If one puts aside annual appropriations and considers the five pieces of legislation that had the largest effect on the budget during the Bush administration, three of the five were

---

[27] See Keith, *supra* note 23.

[28] See H.R. Con. Res. 218, 103d Cong., 2d Sess., § 23 (1994).

[29] See H.R. Con. Res. 67, 104th Cong., 1st Sess., § 202 (1995).

[30] See 142 Cong. Rec. S5415-20 (daily ed., May 21, 1996); *id.* at S5516 (daily ed., May 23, 1996); Bill Dauster, *The Day the Senate Died: Budget Measure Weakens Minority*, Roll Call, May 30, 1996, at 5, *reprinted in* 142 Cong. Rec. S6135 (daily ed., June 12, 1996); Bill Dauster, *The Monster That Ate the United States Senate*, 18 Pub. Budgeting & Fin. 87 (summer 1998).

[31] See Personal Responsibility and Work Opportunity Reconciliation Act of 1996, Pub. L. No. 104-193, 110 Stat. 2105 (1996).

[32] See Taxpayer Relief Act of 1997, Pub. L. No. 105-34, 111 Stat. 788 (1997).

[33] See Balanced Budget Act of 1997, Pub. L. No. 105-33, 111 Stat. 251 (1997).

tax-cut bills enacted by using the reconciliation process.[34] The reconciliation process in particular has helped to make the Congressional Budget Act the most significant change in Senate procedure since it adopted the cloture rule in 1917. To facilitate the operation of the new reconciliation era, in 2003 the Republican Congress revised the pay-as-you-go rules to create an exception for anything that Congress included in the budget resolution.[35] So if Congress provided for a tax cut in the budget, then Congress did not need to pay for it. This left the pay-as-you-go discipline, as one wag put it, as a pure pay-as-*you*-go discipline – not a pay-as-*we*-go discipline – as it only worked to discourage initiatives that the majority party chose not to include in its budget resolution. Once again, this change enhanced the power of the majority party and leadership at the expense of other senators.

The era of budgeting to worsen the deficit came to an end with the 2006 elections and restored Democratic majorities in both Houses of Congress. In 2007, Congress adopted a budget resolution that restored a strict pay-as-you-go rule and a prohibition on using reconciliation to worsen the deficit.[36]

The congressional budget process that this history bequeaths to us resembles a coral reef; it has become the way it is through decades and centuries of evolution. Layer upon layer of budget-process reforms have built their homes one on top of another, none digging up the prior structure to start anew. Rather than alter the prerogatives of existing participants, each new budget-process reform has added more participants with new duties to the process. The process continues to change to this day.

The resulting congressional budget process is quite complex and decentralized. No individual would have designed a process to look the way that ours does. Some feel that the founders wanted in the Constitution to create a fiscal system that would be so complicated that the government would find it difficult to interfere with the private sector's free market.[37] If these theorists are right,

---

[34] *See* Economic Growth and Tax Relief Reconciliation Act of 2001, Pub. L. No. 107-16, 115 Stat. 38 (2001) ($1.3 trillion over ten years); Jobs and Growth Tax Relief Reconciliation Act of 2003, Pub. L. No. 108-27, 117 Stat. 752 (2003) ($350 billion); Tax Increase Prevention and Reconciliation Act of 2005, Pub. L. No. 109-222 (2006) ($70 billion). Another was a tax cut passed without reconciliation. *See* Working Families Tax Relief Act of 2004, Pub. L. No. 108-311, 118 Stat. 1166 (2004) ($146 billion). The nontax law among the five largest Bush laws was the Medicare Prescription Drug, Improvement, and Modernization Act of 2003, Pub. L. No. 108-173, 117 Stat. 2066 (2003), which increased the deficit by $395 billion and did not employ the reconciliation process. Congress also enacted another spending reduction bill using the reconciliation process in 2006. *See* Deficit Reduction Act of 2005, Pub. L. No. 109-171, 120 Stat. 4 (2006), although this law – at $50 billion over ten years – was smaller than all of the aforementioned bills.

[35] *See* H.R. Con. Res. 95, 108th Cong., 1st Sess., §§ 505 (2003). The baseline assumption in section 505(a)(5)(A) creates the loophole.

[36] *See* S. Con. Res. 21, 110th Cong., 1st Sess. § 201-202 (2007).

[37] This is a tenet of the Public Choice economists. *See, e.g.*, James M. Buchanan and Gordon Tullock, THE CALCULUS OF CONSENT: LOGICAL FOUNDATIONS OF CONSTITUTIONAL DEMOCRACY (1962).

then Congress has surely created a budget process complicated enough to make the founders proud.

But since 1996, budget actors have reshaped the congressional budget process. They have increased the power of the congressional budget process to streamline congressional lawmaking. It has thus become the main tool for implementing the majority party's fiscal policy. The congressional budget process has expanded and usurped much of the rest of Congress. The power of those involved in the budget process – the Budget Committees and the congressional leadership – has been enhanced at the cost of other senators' rights to debate and amend. But the founders and the generations of senators who created the filibuster intended it to be hard for Congress to make laws. This difficulty helped determined minorities to defend their rights. The more-efficient budget process has allowed Congress more easily to enact fiscal policy. The jury is still out on whether that is a good development for our political system.

II. THE PRESIDENT'S BUDGET

So, how does this mess work in practice? Let's look at a typical budget cycle. It starts with formulation of the president's budget.[38] Like seeds buried in the ground, ideas for the budget often start buried deep in the agencies of the executive branch of the federal government. Fittingly for the agricultural analogy, they begin in spring, as program officers in government agencies begin to assemble material for the president's budget submission. But budget ideas take some time to germinate; they will break through to see the light of day (if at all) only as part of the president's budget in the following February. And that February presidential budget will address the fiscal year beginning that October 1. So the budget cycle begins about a year and a half before the budget year that it addresses.

Think of OMB as the farmer overseeing the process. Soon after sending the previous presidential budget to Congress in February, OMB begins to work on the following year. In March or April, OMB begins the process (fertilizes the fields?) by issuing its spring planning guidance to executive branch agencies. The guidance outlines the administration's program priorities and overall funding levels. Departmental officials then typically build their budgets from the bottom up. In June or July, OMB distributes to executive agencies circular A-11, giving the agencies detailed instructions on how to submit budget data and materials. The June 2006 circular A-11 spanned 809 pages.

In September, in line with a specific OMB deadline, the agencies make their budget submissions to OMB. From then until late November, OMB conducts

---

[38] For explanations of the presidential budget process, *see, e.g.*, Office of Management and Budget, Circular A-11; Preparation, Submission, and Execution of the Budget, § 10 (2006); Office of Management and Budget, Analytical Perspectives, Budget of the United States Government, Fiscal Year 2007, at 375–396 (2006).

its fall review of the agency budget proposals in light of the president's priorities, program performance, and how much money fiscal policy allows them to use. The staff raise issues and present options to the OMB director and other senior OMB officials for their decisions. Based on these decisions, OMB comes up with a complete recommendation for a set of proposals to include in the president's budget. And, in late November, OMB briefs the president and senior White House advisors on proposed budget policies, and the president and senior White House aides make their changes to the proposals.

After that, in what is called the "passback," OMB passes the White House decisions back to the agencies. OMB usually informs all the executive agencies at the same time about the decisions on their budget requests. From then until the deadline for getting papers to the printer in early January, agencies appeal the White House decisions on their budgets to OMB and the president. Most times, the OMB director resolves differences with the agency head. But when the director and agency head cannot work things out, they and White House staff present the remaining issues to the president for a decision. Finally, in January, agencies prepare and OMB reviews congressional budget justification materials. These budget justification materials help to explain agency budget requests to congressional committees and subcommittees.

The Government Printing Office prints the budget in several large paperback volumes. Since fiscal year 1992, OMB has presented the budget in four $8\frac{1}{2}$- by 11-inch volumes, usually ranging from 300 to 1,300 pages each. The *Budget of the United States Government* volume contains the president's budget message, the president's budget and management priorities, and budget overviews by agency. The *Analytical Perspectives* volume contains discussions of specified subject areas, economic and accounting analyses, information on federal receipts and collections, analyses of federal spending, information on federal borrowing and debt, and baseline or current-services estimates. The *Historical Tables* volume provides data on budget numbers going back generally to 1940. The *Appendix* volume contains detailed information on the various appropriations and funds that constitute the budget and provides the working document for the Appropriations Committees.

On the first Monday in February, the president transmits the budget to the Congress.[39] OMB staff bring boxes of the president's budget to various committees of Congress and congressional offices. But delivery of the president's budget recommendations is not the end of the process, just another beginning. Unlike other parliamentary democracies, the United States government does

---

[39] *See* 31 U.S.C. § 1105(a). Sometimes delays in enacting the previous year's budget force this submission to come later. In years when a new president takes office on January 20, the new White House staff submits an abbreviated budget document later in the spring. *See* Robert Keith, Submission of the President's Budget in Transition Years (July 31, 2001) (CRS rep. no. RS20752).

not adopt or reject the president's budget, as such.[40] Rather, Congress fashions its own budget, which may or may not follow the president's budget. Congress can and often does treat the president's budget as just so many suggestions.

III. THE BUDGET RESOLUTION

After the president has submitted the executive branch's budget request, the House and Senate Budget Committees take the stage.[41] Early on the day that the president releases the budget, the OMB director typically holds a press conference to tout its benefits. But before the day is out, the chairs and ranking minority members of the House and Senate Budget Committees usually will have their press conferences, as well, reacting to the budget. Reaction tends to break along party lines. Rarely do the messages agree.

A. Hearings

The House and Senate Budget Committees begin holding hearings early in the year. The director of CBO – Congress's own, nonpartisan budget agency – sets the scene by presenting its *Budget and Economic Outlook* report to the Budget Committees, usually in January. The OMB director and the secretary of the Treasury lead off the administration's testimony, followed by other members of the president's cabinet. The Budget Committees frequently invite outside experts, as well.

And while the Budget Committees conduct their hearings, other committees of Congress also conduct hearings on the president's budget. While the Budget Committee will be the first to react to the president's budget, these other committees will later make the changes in law that implement fiscal policy. The Budget Act and the Budget Committees thus invite the committees with spending jurisdiction to submit their "views and estimates" of the president's budget to the Budget Committees within six weeks after the president submits it. Budget Committee staff then review the views and estimates.

B. Drafting the Budget Resolution

The Budget Committees then begin formulating the budget resolution. The budget resolution serves several purposes. It provides a vehicle for Congress to

---

[40] See Jürgen von Hagen's discussion of the differing budget procedures in the European Union in Chapter 4 of this volume.

[41] For explanations of the congressional budget process, *see, e.g.*, Staff of S. Comm. on the Budget, 105th Cong., The Congressional Budget Process; An Explanation (1998); Robert Keith and Allen Schick, Introduction to the Federal Budget Process (2004) (CRS rep. no. 98-721); Alan S. Frumin, Riddick's Senate Procedure 502–642 (1992); and William G. Dauster, Budget Process Law Annotated (1993).

Table 1.1. Budget functions

Function number	Function
Function 050	National Defense
Function 150	International Affairs
Function 250	General Science, Space, and Technology
Function 270	Energy
Function 300	Natural Resources and Environment
Function 350	Agriculture
Function 370	Commerce and Housing Credit
Function 400	Transportation
Function 450	Community and Regional Development
Function 500	Education, Training, Employment, and Social Services
Function 550	Health
Function 570	Medicare
Function 600	Income Security
Function 650	Social Security
Function 700	Veterans Benefits and Services
Function 750	Administration of Justice
Function 800	General Government
Function 900	Net Interest
Function 920	Allowances
Function 950	Undistributed Offsetting Receipts

debate the nation's fiscal policy early in the year, before most legislation makes its way through the legislative process. It also provides an opportunity to look at the big picture, the total effect of Congress's many fiscal actions, all at one time.

The mammoth presidential budget dwarfs the modest congressional budget resolution. In contrast to the 2,500 or so pages and four volumes of the president's budget, the budget resolution generally fills only 35 to 50 5- by 9-inch pages. The budget resolution paints with a broad brush, not with the detail of the president's submission. Traditionally, budget numbers do not generally address amounts smaller than $100 million – an amount that budget staff fondly call "point one," for one-tenth of a billion. Out of deference to the other committees of jurisdiction, the Budget Committee addresses only broad "functional categories" of government actions. (See Table 1.1 – Budget Functions.) And even the budget resolution's numbers in these functional categories do not bind the other committees of Congress. The budget resolution draws an overall blueprint for the nation's fiscal policy. Other legislation enacted later in the year will fill in the detail and actually give the executive branch the authority to spend money and raise taxes.

The budget resolution is a concurrent resolution, and thus Congress does not present it to the president for signature or veto. Congress adopts the budget resolution as an exercise of its constitutional authority to set its own rules.

Congress adopts the budget resolution to clear a procedural path for the later bills that will fund the government.

C. Constraining Other Committees

The budget resolution has three binding procedural consequences. Section V of this chapter will discuss in detail one of the key consequences – that, in many years, the budget resolution triggers the fast-track reconciliation process. Second, the resolution gives every committee with spending jurisdiction its allocation of spending for the year, gives the revenue committees a floor on revenues, and gives the Congress, as a whole, overall caps on spending. These levels provide the basis for points of order, many requiring the votes of 60 senators to waive, which any single representative or senator can raise to enforce the government's fiscal policy.[42] The House of Representatives, through its Rules Committee, often passes a special rule for the consideration of a specific bill that waives all Budget Act points of order. Thus, when the House adopts the rule to structure the debate and voting on a particular piece of legislation, it also often eliminates any possibility of a representative raising this sort of objection to provisions in it. But in the Senate, the threat that a senator may raise a point of order and thus force proponents to get 60 out of the Senate's 100 votes gives the Budget Act procedures much of their power. For example, of 54 points of order that senators raised enforcing the 2004 budget resolution, the Senate defeated motions to waive on 53 of 54 occasions.[43] Thus the budget resolution helps to stop legislation that does not comport with the budget resolution's blueprint and helps to advance legislation that does. Points of order also appear to protect tax bills and spending bills from amendment on the Senate floor – including amendments that do not worsen the deficit – and the points of order thereby enhance the power of the committees with jurisdiction over those bills at the expense of individual senators.[44]

Section IV of this chapter will address the way that the Appropriations Committees respond to the budget's allocation to those committees. For authorizing committees, the budget resolution's allocation constrains the amount of new direct spending that they may create. To avoid procedural obstacles requiring 60 votes on the Senate floor, an authorizing committee must keep the sum of direct spending within its jurisdiction below the allocation given it in the budget resolution. The budget resolution often will allocate – or "crosswalk" – to authorizing committees the baseline level of spending, that is, the level of

---

[42] For a listing of Budget Act points of order, *see, e.g.*, James V. Saturno, POINTS OF ORDER IN THE CONGRESSIONAL BUDGET PROCESS (May 19, 2005) (CRS rep. no. 97-865).

[43] *See* Staff of S. Comm. on the Budget, 108th Cong., BUDGET BULLETIN, Sept. 17, 2003, at 2.

[44] *See* Marsha Jean Simon, *The Real Rules of the Budget Game: Minority Fiscal Decision Making in the United States Senate* (June 2005) (unpublished Ph.D. dissertation, Massachusetts Institute of Technology).

spending that would occur if Congress made no change in law. When the budget resolution does this, an authorizing committee that wishes to increase direct spending has to come up with offsetting spending reductions to avoid a point of order. To avoid this point of order, a committee cannot use new tax revenues as an offset for new spending, unless the budget resolution specifically provides for it through language called a "reserve fund."

Furthermore, another procedural objection – the pay-as-you-go point of order – also requiring 60 votes to waive, lies in the Senate against direct spending or tax legislation that, taken together with other direct spending and tax legislation enacted to date, would increase the deficit for certain time periods up to ten years away.[45]

D. Changing the Budget Process

Third, under what some call the Budget Act's "elastic clause," a budget resolution may "set forth such other matters, and require such other procedures, relating to the budget, as may be appropriate to carry out the purposes of [the Budget] Act."[46] Those purposes are rather broad, although the Senate parliamentarian requires that these new procedures not loosen budgetary enforcement. So budget resolutions have created a number of budget-process procedures and sometimes created new points of order. In doing so, Congress uses the budget resolution to further expand the congressional budget process.

For example, a number of budget resolutions have created overall caps on the amount of money that the Senate could appropriate in a year. Once again, 60-vote points of order enforced these caps in the Senate. Budget resolutions have also created "firewalls" between defense and nondefense appropriated spending – in effect, subcaps – to protect parts of the budget, and budget resolutions have provided mechanisms for increasing the caps. Budget resolutions have limited the amount of appropriations that Congress could provide in advance of the coming fiscal year. And budget resolutions have sought to limit emergency exceptions to the overall appropriation caps in the Senate, especially for domestic appropriations.

In many of these instances, the budget resolution creates a budget-process provision that functions much like a section of the Budget Act itself. But Congress adopts these changes to its own rules by using the fast-track budget resolution process, and thus avoids extended debate or involvement of the executive branch. The majority party can thus change the rules that govern the Senate more easily by using the budget process than it could by amending the Standing Rules of the Senate. And thus the budget process here again enhances the power of the majority party's leadership.

---

[45] *See* S. Con. Res. 21, 110th Cong., 1st Sess., § 201.
[46] Congressional Budget Act § 301(b)(4), 2 U.S.C. § 632(b)(4).

E. Considering the Budget Resolution

In March or April, the chair of the Budget Committee, in consultation with committee members, usually drafts an initial proposal – or "chairman's mark" – for the budget resolution. The chair attempts to broker a resolution geared as much as possible to the chair's policy goals while still achieving the necessary majorities in the Budget Committee and on the floor of the Senate or House. The Budget Committee holds a meeting or series of meetings – called a "markup" – to consider and often to amend the chairman's mark.

Each house of Congress next takes up the budget resolution. The House of Representatives considers the budget resolution as it does almost all legislation, under rules that restrict debate and amendment. But the procedures for considering a budget resolution are exceptions to the usual rule in the Senate. Because the Budget Act limits debate on the budget resolution, senators cannot wage a filibuster against it. In the budget resolution, Congress has a train that can move. The Congressional Budget Act therefore expedites Congress's making of fiscal policy and enhances the power of the majority party. The Budget Act limits debate on the budget resolution to ten hours plus up to four hours for debate on economic goals and priorities in the House of Representatives, and up to 50 hours (including debate on economic goals and priorities) in the Senate. The Budget Act divides time equally between the majority and minority parties in both houses.

Generally, not just in the budget context, amendments must be germane in the House, but senators usually have a right to offer amendments on any subject. This freedom to change the subject usually limits the power of the Senate majority leader to set the Senate's agenda. But with respect to budget resolutions, the Budget Act requires amendments to be germane. And the Senate's standards for what are germane are narrower than merely sticking to the subject matter of the underlying bill – what in Senate procedure is called "relevance." In the budget arena, an amendment is germane only if it strikes a provision, changes a number or date, states purely precatory language (such as findings or a sense of the Congress) within the jurisdiction of the Budget Committee, or otherwise does not add any new subject matter. Thus, what a majority of the Budget Committee reports to the floor determines the allowable subject matter for amendments. This limitation thus reduces the power of senators in the minority party and senators who do not sit on the Budget Committee.

The Budget Act limits time to debate amendments in the Senate. Both managers, however, can yield time from the time under their control on the resolution, so debate on an amendment can, and often does, take more than the time allowed under the statute. All of this amendment time comes out of the total 50 hours on the resolution, so neither manager has a guarantee to have 25 hours to use.

Once the Senate has exhausted or yielded back the 50 hours of debate, senators still may seek recognition and offer amendments. The Senate votes on these amendments (or motions or points of order in relation to those amendments) in rapid succession without debate – or, customarily, by unanimous consent, with two minutes of debate equally divided. Senators call this process "vote-a-rama," and many senators find it disagreeable. Allowing senators to offer amendments after time has expired, however, protects the rights of senators in the minority party, who might otherwise lose their right to offer amendments.

When the conference committee on the budget resolution finishes its work, the Budget Act limits debate on the conference report to not more than five hours in the House of Representatives and ten hours in the Senate.

Through these various time limits, the Budget Act provides that a simple majority of senators voting can determine which amendments the Senate will adopt, and a simple majority can pass the resolution. As a result, budget resolutions have come to advance the majority party's fiscal policy. And thus they tend to be rather divisive exercises. In recent times, most budget resolutions have passed with slim majorities and little support from the minority party; and in some years Congress is unable to reach bicameral agreement on any concurrent resolution.[47] Thus, in the past 15 years, the congressional budget process has not led to consensus.

IV. AUTHORIZATIONS AND APPROPRIATIONS

A. Appropriations Bills

After the budget resolution gives the Appropriations Committees their overall allocation of spending authority, the Appropriations Committees subdivide that allocation among their subcommittees (see Table 1.2 – Appropriations Subcommittees).[48] These subdivisions – or "302(b) allocations" – in turn constrain these subcommittees as they begin to mark up their separate appropriations bills. When an appropriations bill is pending, any member may raise a point of order under the Budget Act against a bill that would exceed this subcommittee allocation. Considering the significant effect that these subdivisions have on the allocation of the nation's resources, it is noteworthy that just the

---

[47] From 1992 to 2007, only one budget resolution received more than 55 votes on final passage. In 2007 (fiscal year 2008), the vote was 52-40; in 2006 there was no budget resolution; in 2005, the vote was 52–47; in 2004 there was no resolution; in 2003, the vote was 51–50; in 2002, there was no resolution; in 2001, the vote was 53–47; in 2000, the vote was 50–48; in 1999, the vote was 54–44; in 1998, there was no resolution; 1997 was the exception with a vote of 76–22; in 1996, the vote was 53–46; in 1995, the vote was 54–46; in 1994, the vote was 53–46; in 1993, the vote was 55–45; and, in 1992, the vote was 52–41.

[48] For explanations of the appropriations process, *see, e.g.*, Staff of S. Comm. on Appropriations, *supra* note 6, at 25–30; FRUMIN, *supra* note 41, at 150–213.

Table 1.2. Appropriations subcommittees in 2007

Agriculture, Rural Development, Food and Drug Administration, and Related Agencies
Commerce, Justice, Science and Related Agencies
Defense
Energy and Water Development
Financial Services and General Government
Homeland Security
Interior, Environment, and Related Agencies
Labor, Health and Human Services, Education, and Related Agencies
Legislative Branch
Military Construction, Veterans Affairs, and Related Agencies
State, Foreign Operations, and Related Programs
Transportation, Housing and Urban Development, and Related Agencies

28 senators on the Senate Appropriations Committee and the 66 representatives on the House Appropriations Committee, rather than the Congress as a whole, make these subdivisions. Indeed, the chairs of the two Appropriations Committees, with the support of the majority of their committees (15 senators and 34 representatives) play a dominant role in formulating the subdivisions. As initial membership on the committee is determined by support from the party leadership (particularly in the House Republican and Senate Democratic caucuses) and seniority (particularly in the Senate Republican caucus), more senior members and members aligned with caucus leadership have disproportionate influence in this process.

The Appropriations subcommittees then traditionally exercise a great deal of autonomy in formulating the separate appropriations bills. In particular, the chairs of the Appropriations subcommittees have substantial influence in assembling those bills. Their power and secretiveness have caused some to call these chairs the "college of cardinals."[49] The House traditionally originates appropriation acts. The House views that prerogative as a subset of the constitutional requirement that all revenue measures originate in the House even though the Constitution's Origination Clause does not mention appropriations. The Senate Appropriations Committee traditionally amends the House-passed bill. As they formulate the appropriations bills, the cardinals and their senior staff – called simply "clerks"[50] – take into account requests for appropriations submitted by other members of Congress, particularly those of other Appropriations Committee members and congressional leaders.

---

[49] *See, e.g.*, Richard Munson, The Cardinals of Capitol Hill; The Men and Women Who Control Government Spending (1993).

[50] The clerks are relatively powerful staffers who serve as full committee or subcommittee staff directors. They also historically have been a relatively long-serving group. In the 140-year history of the Senate Appropriations Committee, just 16 men have served as staff director of the full committee. *See* Staff of S. Comm. on Appropriations, *supra* note 6, at 219.

Appropriations bills, and the committee reports that accompany them, can designate funds for particular purposes – "earmark" funds – to respond to these requests. Earmarking has been increasing,[51] leading some to call for reform to limit the use of earmarks or bring more transparency to the process through aggressive disclosure. In August of 2007, Congress passed legislation requiring some disclosure.[52]

These appropriations bills provide the authority for federal agencies to incur financial obligations in the course of running the government, and for the Treasury to pay off the obligations. Through these bills, Congress annually chooses how to spend money. They thus are called "discretionary spending" – in contrast to direct spending, which takes place whether Congress takes any further action or not. Appropriations bills fund most of the things that people think about when they think about the government. For example, appropriations bills fund the interstate highway system and the FBI. They fund the Army and medical research at the National Institutes of Health.

B. Authorizations of Appropriations and Legislation on Appropriations

House and Senate rules require that Congress has to enact a law creating a program – an authorization law – before Congress can appropriate money for a program. The rules intend that authorization laws create, extend, or modify federal programs. And the rules intend that appropriations bills fund existing programs but do not legislatively create new programs. An authorizing bill can authorize a specific dollar amount to be appropriated; this is called a "definite authorization." Or an authorizing bill can authorize "such sums as are necessary"; this is called an "indefinite authorization." The levels included in authorization laws provide guidance to the Appropriations Committees on what would be an appropriate level of funding for appropriations bills to provide to the program. But the Appropriations Committees may provide less than the amounts authorized without incurring any procedural penalty.

Authorizations may be permanent or they may cover only specified fiscal years. When an authorization for a set number of years expires, Congress may choose to extend the life of the program by passing another authorization bill – a "reauthorization." Unless specifically prohibited by law, Congress also may extend a program simply by providing additional appropriations. When appropriations fund a program after its authorization has expired, this is called an "unauthorized appropriation."

House rules allow a member to raise a point of order against an appropriation that lacks an authorization. When the House of Representatives initially

---

[51] See CRS Appropriations Team, Earmarks in Appropriation Acts: FY1994, FY1996, FY1998, FY2000, FY2002, FY2004, FY2005 (Jan. 26, 2006).
[52] See Honest Leadership and Open Government Act of 2007, S.1, 110th Cong., 1st Sess., § 521 (2007).

considers a bill, it sometimes will remove unauthorized appropriations. The House, however, generally considers legislation subject to rules passed specifically for the bill at hand. And the House Rules Committee typically reports a rule that waives points of order against unauthorized appropriations that are contained in an appropriations bill conference agreement. The Senate has an even more limited prohibition against considering unauthorized appropriations. Congress increasingly has failed to reauthorize programs. As a result, appropriations bills have in effect taken on more of the function traditionally accomplished by authorizing bills. And appropriators regularly use their power over the purse to influence the substantive details of programs – authorized or not – and thus get around the bifurcated authorization and appropriation process. These practices have shifted power to the Appropriations Committees and the leadership.

Even though appropriations bills (unlike budget resolutions and reconciliation bills) are subject to filibuster, senators see them as "must-do" bills, unlike most other legislation. Thus, appropriations bills provide a tempting vehicle for members seeking to enact substantive proposals. Senate rules, however, prohibit including in appropriations bills provisions creating new programs – often called "riders." Rule XVI of the Standing Rules of the Senate prohibits, among other things, legislating on an appropriations bill.[53] If a senator offers an amendment that "proposes general legislation," then any other senator may raise a point of order against the amendment. If the presiding officer sustains the point of order, the amendment falls. The rule provides no process to waive the point of order. A senator may appeal the ruling of the chair, but overturning the chair can create a precedent weakening the rule.[54] If the House already has included legislation in the bill to which the amendment might possibly be germane, then an avenue is available for a senator to get an amendment added to the bill.[55] Some recent majority leaders have tried to avoid such amendments by moving to consider a Senate-reported appropriations bill, as opposed to the traditional House bill with Senate amendments.[56] As well, senators will sometimes seek a two-thirds vote to suspend rule XVI to allow consideration of their amendment, but these efforts rarely succeed.[57] It is thus difficult to amend appropriations bills with new legislative matters. Nonetheless, legislation often finds its way into appropriations bills.

The appropriators race to finish these bills before October 1, the beginning of the fiscal year. Increasingly, the appropriators have relied on omnibus

[53] *See* Senate Standing Rule XVI(4).　　　　[54] *See* Frumin, *supra* note 41, at 208–209.

[55] *Id.* at 164–171, 1507–1508.

[56] *See* 146 Cong. Rec. S4172-77 (daily ed., May 18, 2000) (remarks of Sens. Feingold and Wellstone).

[57] *See, e.g.,* 151 Cong. Rec. S10,072-73 (daily ed., Sept. 15, 2005) (motion by Sen. Lieberman); *id.* at S10,006 (daily ed., Sept. 14, 2005) (motion by Sen. Dorgan); 149 Cong. Rec. S13,435 (daily ed., Oct. 29, 2003) (motion by Sen. Dorgan); *id.* at S13,352-57 (daily ed., Oct. 28, 2003) (motion by Sen. Lugar).

appropriations bills to keep the government going, without enacting all the separate appropriations bills.[58] This process also reduces the opportunities for members of Congress to offer amendments and to vote on the nation's fiscal policy. Thus the trend toward omnibus appropriations bills increases the power of Appropriations Committee members and leadership, while depriving other members of their ability to affect the legislation. These omnibus bills also reduce the accountability of members for the decisions that the bills include, as the member can characterize the vote on the bill as a vote to keep the government running, and the member's political challenger will have a more difficult time characterizing the vote as one on a particular item in the bill. And because the bill contains so many items, the member is less likely to learn about or focus on particular items and is more likely to vote to support the leadership.

C. Authorizing Committees

The other committees with spending jurisdiction – the "authorizing" or "legislative" committees – work on legislation of two sorts. As previously discussed, authorizing committees can report legislation that authorizes spending subject to later appropriations. This kind of legislation does not allow money to leave the Treasury, and thus it does not constitute the final congressional action on spending for those programs.

But authorizing committees also write legislation that creates entitlements for beneficiaries who meet specific qualifications. This type of legislation – entitlement, mandatory spending, or direct spending – now accounts for most federal spending. The government's largest entitlements are Social Security, Medicare (health care for seniors and people with disabilities), and Medicaid (health care for the poorest seniors, people with disabilities, children, and parents).

The budget resolution's allocations constrain the creation of new entitlement spending. But what about existing entitlement spending? What constrains its continued growth? The preferred budget-process tool for addressing existing entitlement spending is the reconciliation process, to which we turn next. Setting the stage for this powerful fast-track procedure to enact legislation is one of the main procedural consequences of the budget resolution.

V. RECONCILIATION

A budget resolution can create a fast-track bill – a reconciliation bill – to make certain types of changes in law.[59] The budget resolution – a concurrent

---

[58] *See, e.g.*, Robert Keith, Omnibus Appropriations Acts: Overview of Recent Practices (Apr. 27, 2005) (CRS rep. no. RL32473).

[59] For an explanation of the reconciliation process, *see, e.g.*, Robert Keith and Bill Heniff Jr., The Budget Reconciliation Process: House and Senate Procedures (2005) (CRS rep. no. RL33030).

resolution that Congress does not present to the president and therefore cannot have legislative effect – only makes changes to Congress' internal rules. On the other hand, a reconciliation bill – a bill that Congress does present to the president for signature or veto – can change permanent law. Because the Congressional Budget Act limits debate on reconciliation bills, the majority party can use the process to enact laws on the subjects covered by the reconciliation bill. Reconciliation bills thus have become the dominant means for Congress to make fiscal policy.

A. The Scope of Reconciliation Instructions

Budget resolutions create a reconciliation bill by instructing committees of Congress to recommend changes in law. Budget resolutions may contain reconciliation instructions to authorizing committees to change three things: direct spending law, tax law, and the statutory debt limit. The budget resolution may create up to three reconciliation bills in any fiscal year, one for each of these three purposes.[60] A single budget resolution cannot, however, create more than one reconciliation bill for any of these three purposes. Thus once the Senate has considered one spending reconciliation bill, a second bill could not address spending and still retain its special status as a reconciliation bill.

A budget resolution may, however, instruct committees to report out spending and tax changes together in one reconciliation bill. When the budget resolution instructs a single committee to recommend both spending and tax changes within its jurisdiction, the Budget Act allows that committee to shift up to a fifth of the total amount the committee was instructed to achieve from spending to taxes, or vice versa. Because to some extent this rule makes outlays and revenues fungible, some call it the "fungibility rule." As a practical matter, this rule applies most significantly to the Ways and Means and Finance Committees, which have jurisdiction over revenue matters generally. The revenue committees thus are able to move more legislation through the reconciliation process than other committees. For an example of the fungibility rule's application, take the case of a budget resolution that instructs a committee to achieve $3 million in outlay reductions and $7 million in revenue increases, for a total of $10 million in deficit reduction. By virtue of this rule, that committee permissibly could achieve outlay reductions as low as $1 million ($3 million minus 20 percent of $10 million, or $2 million), as long as it achieved a total of at least $10 million in deficit reduction by also achieving at least $9 million in revenue increases. Alternatively, the committee could achieve revenue increases as low as $5 million ($7 million minus 20 percent of $10 million, or $2 million), as long as it achieved a total of at least $10 million in deficit reduction by also achieving outlay reductions of at least $5 million. The fungibility rule does not allow shifting between spending and taxes when the budget resolution has

---

[60] *See* 142 Cong. Rec. S5415-20 (daily ed., May 21, 1996); *id.* at S5516 (daily ed., May 23, 1996).

instructed just spending changes or just tax changes, even if the committee's jurisdiction includes both spending and taxes.

The budget resolution can determine only the total amount of the change, the type of change, and the time period for the change. The budget resolution's reconciliation instructions may not require that the reporting committee achieve its savings from certain types of programs or raise its revenues in specific ways.[61] The Budget Act spells out that budget resolutions may specify changes in budget authority, entitlement authority, credit authority, revenues, the statutory limit on the public debt, or any combination of these, including a direction to achieve "deficit reduction."[62] And budget resolutions also have instructed committees to achieve changes in outlays and other categories of spending. Budget resolutions may not make reconciliation instructions for changes in authorization subject to appropriations. No limitations apply to the number of years that reconciliation instructions may cover.

B. Committee Responses to Reconciliation Instructions

If a budget resolution makes reconciliation instructions to just one committee in each house – for example, just to the Senate Finance Committee and House Ways and Means Committee to change tax law – then that committee reports reconciliation legislation directly to its house. If, however, a budget resolution makes reconciliation instructions to more than one committee, then each of those committees submits recommendations to the Budget Committee of its house. The Budget Committee cannot make any substantive changes to those recommendations, but must package up all the recommendations that it receives and report them out to its house as a single reconciliation bill.

If a committee fails to comply with the budget resolution's reconciliation instructions, in the House, the Rules Committee can make it so that the House can consider amendments to achieve changes specified by the reconciliation instructions. And in such a case it is in order during Senate consideration of the reconciliation bill for any senator to offer a motion to recommit the reconciliation bill with instructions to report back forthwith with an amendment – which need not be germane – that achieves those savings.[63] Thus, failure to comply causes the offending committee to lose the protection of the requirement that amendments be germane and may mean that another senator will write the offending committee's provisions on the floor.

---

[61] *See* 128 Cong. Rec. S5506 (May 19, 1982) (inquiries of Sen. Dole); 131 Cong. Rec. S5863 (May 9, 1985) (inquiry of Sen. Helms regarding amendment by Sen. Bradley).

[62] Congressional Budget Act § 310(a), 2 U.S.C. § 641(a). An instruction to achieve deficit reduction would allow the committee instructed to cut spending or raise taxes in any combination within the committee's jurisdiction.

[63] *See* Frumin, *supra* note 41, at 628; 127 Cong. Rec. 12,692 (June 17, 1981).

If a committee submits its reconciliation recommendations to the Budget Committee after the deadline that the budget resolution sets for submitting recommendations to the Budget Committee, and the Budget Committee nonetheless includes the tardy committee's reconciliation recommendations in the reconciliation legislation that it reports, no extraordinary remedy is available to respond to the failure of the committee to comply with the deadline.[64] And if many instructed committees choose to delay weeks beyond the deadline, and the Budget Committee then reports a reconciliation bill, it still will receive the protections of a reconciliation bill.

The reconciliation process thus can combine legislative work products from disparate committees into one vehicle, a process unusual in the Senate. Senators and representatives then can vote for the overall bill and the idea of deficit reduction while disavowing particular parts of the larger compromise. As well, the bill allows advocates of one area of spending to see that others will share in the sacrifice that they are making for the common good. The reconciliation bill also allows advocates for certain programs to deflect the blame for cutting the program onto the budget resolution and the larger reconciliation process.

The resulting bill often becomes something of a behemoth. The text of the bill often spans hundreds of printed pages.[65] And as the bill often covers multiple subjects and jurisdictions, members of Congress have difficulty mastering its content. Moreover, it can be very difficult for voters, outside groups, and the media to determine all the details of the bill before members vote on it, and it may be challenging to understand all of the legislation even after it passes. Thus, the omnibus reconciliation bill's effect on legislative electoral accountability is likely not to be positive, although the ability to enact various parts of compromises simultaneously and without significant threat of delay in the Senate may have other positive benefits for the legislative process.

The Budget Act limits debate on the reconciliation bill in the Senate to 20 hours, a short time for a matter of this consequence. The Budget Act then applies to reconciliation bills all the other restrictions that the act applies to budget resolutions. Thus amendments must be germane; senators may debate amendments only for limited amounts of time; at the end of the 20 hours of debate senators may engage in a vote-a-rama; and senators may debate the

---

[64] *See* 135 Cong. Rec. S12,589 (daily ed. Oct. 4, 1989) (statement of Budget Committee Chair Sasser); *cf.* 141 Cong. Rec. S14,135 (daily ed., Sept. 22, 1995) (statement of Budget Committee Chair Domenici asserting Budget Committee discretion to report late).

[65] For example, the final printed version of the Balanced Budget Act of 1997 (BBA), Pub. L. No. 105-33, 111 Stat. 251 (1997), was 537 pages; the Personal Responsibility and Work Opportunity Reconciliation Act of 1996, Pub. L. No. 104-193, 110 Stat. 2105 (1996), was 251 pages; and the Deficit Reduction Act of 2005, Pub. L. No. 109-171, 120 Stat. 4 (2006), was 181 pages. To their credit (at least in this respect), some recent reconciliation bills have been relatively shorter. The Jobs and Growth Tax Relief Reconciliation Act of 2003, Pub. L. No. 108-27, 117 Stat. 752 (2003), was 17 pages; and the Tax Increase Prevention and Reconciliation Act of 2005, Pub. L. No. 109-222, 120 Stat. 345 (2006), was 29 pages.

conference report for no more than ten hours. These restrictions bind all the more in the context of a large reconciliation bill.

C. The Byrd Rule's Limits on Reconciliation

The reconciliation process thus has the power to force a high volume of legislative product through the sausage works.[66] As long as a preponderance of this product has a budgetary impact, a reconciliation bill may contain non-budgetary amendments to substantive law and still be protected under the Budget Act.[67] The Byrd Rule[68] serves as something of a check on that product. The Byrd Rule stands at the intersection between the desire to expedite fiscal policy widely shared among jurisdictions and the dangers of reconciliation's tight restrictions on debate and amendment. This tension inherent in the reconciliation process remains unresolved.

The Byrd Rule provides something of an antidote to the omnibus nature of the reconciliation bill. The Byrd Rule allows the Senate to remove from a reconciliation bill language that the rule defines as "extraneous."[69] Under the Byrd Rule, during consideration of a reconciliation bill, any senator may raise a point of order against extraneous language in the bill or an amendment. The senator who raises the point of order gets to define what language is in question. If the chair sustains the point of order, the language thus found to be extraneous "shall be deemed stricken from the bill and may not be offered as an amendment from the floor."[70] Moreover, a senator may raise a point of order against a provision of an amendment, and need not raise a point of order against the entire amendment. Thus in its effect, the Byrd Rule operates differently from most other points of order. Points of order generally can bring down an entire bill or amendment. The Byrd Rule, however, can excise specific language and leave the rest of the bill or amendment to go along its merry way. This different effect makes it easier for senators to employ the Byrd Rule than most other points of order, as the senator raising the point of order need confront only the constituency defending the offending language, not those defending the entire bill – who usually include the Senate leadership and the committee chair.

---

[66] People often attribute to Chancellor Otto von Bismarck this warning: "If you like laws and sausages, you should never watch either one being made." *See* RESPECTFULLY QUOTED: A DICTIONARY OF QUOTATIONS, no. 996 (1989).

[67] *See* 127 Cong. Rec. S6664 (daily ed. June 22, 1981) (statement of Majority Leader Baker).

[68] *See* Congressional Budget Act § 313, 2 U.S.C. § 644.

[69] *See id.*; *see generally* Robert Keith, THE BUDGET RECONCILIATION PROCESS: THE SENATE'S "BYRD RULE" (Apr. 7, 2005) (CRS rep. no. RL30862).

[70] Congressional Budget Act § 313(a), 2 U.S.C. § 644(a); *see also* 131 Cong. Rec. S14,034 (daily ed., Oct. 24, 1985) (during debate on the amendment that would later become the Byrd Rule, Senators Byrd and Johnston discussed what language the operation of the rule would strike).

Before the presiding officer has ruled on a point of order, any senator may move to waive the point of order. To waive the point of order, 60 senators must vote in favor of the motion. Thus a minority of the Senate may use the Byrd Rule to delete language from the bill. The Byrd Rule gives the minority party one of its few opportunities to affect the outcome of the reconciliation process. The minority party may not have the votes to add items to the bill, but the Byrd Rule can give the minority party the power to take some items out of the bill. The Byrd Rule thus provides one of the few aspects of the congressional budget process that aids the minority party. As a result, challenges under the Byrd Rule provide some of the few moments of drama in the reconciliation process as it is applied.

The Byrd Rule defines six classes of language as "extraneous."[71] Note that this analysis is distinct from whether an amendment is "germane" or "relevant." First, language that has no budgetary effect is extraneous. Nonbinding sense-of-the-Senate language provides a clear example.[72] Similarly, budget-process language that in itself does not change the deficit also flunks this test.[73] A provision is not extraneous under this test if it has a budgetary effect and decreases exactly offset increases. Provisions that have budgetary effects that the CBO cannot estimate do not necessarily violate the subsection.

A provision is not extraneous under this test if the provision provides one of the "terms and conditions under which outlays are made or revenues are required to be collected."[74] Examples of terms and conditions include mechanisms to enforce changes in outlays or revenues, and procedures for collecting outlays or revenues. The parliamentarian tries not to let drafters use this "terms and conditions" language as an artifice to attach language that would otherwise be extraneous. The language setting forth the terms and conditions must deal with the same issue as does the language that produces the change in outlays or revenues and must have a logical link to that language. The parliamentarian analyzes language with a view to whether inclusion of the language would be an abuse of the fast-track procedures under reconciliation. The parliamentarian asks why language asserted to be a term or condition is integral to the change in outlays or revenues, why it is essential or necessary to achieving the change in outlays or revenues. In this analysis, the parliamentarian strictly scrutinizes provisions that authorize appropriations or change the terms under which appropriations are authorized, as well as reporting requirements.

The second group of provisions that offend the Byrd Rule are provisions that worsen the deficit, if the committee reporting the provision has failed to achieve its reconciliation instructions. Like Mary Poppins, most committees

---

[71] *See* Congressional Budget Act § 313(b), 2 U.S.C. § 644(b).

[72] *See* 141 Cong. Rec. S16,016 (daily ed., Oct. 27, 1995).

[73] *See* 139 Cong. Rec. S7920 (daily ed., June 24, 1993); *id.* at S7921 (daily ed. June 24, 1993).

[74] Congressional Budget Act § 313(b)(1)(A), 2 U.S.C. § 644(b)(1)(A).

believe that "a spoonful of sugar helps the medicine go down."[75] Legislative drafters thus will often include "sweeteners" that help to secure support for the legislation. In reconciliation, where instructions often require distasteful cuts in programs, these sweeteners often involve increased spending and program expansions. The Budget Act allows this sort of thing, so long as the totality of the committee's work product meets its instructions. Thus the Byrd Rule encourages committee compliance, so that a committee's sweeteners will not become subject to excision with a Byrd Rule point of order.

The third group of provisions that offend the Byrd Rule are provisions that are not in the jurisdiction of the committee that reported the provisions as part of its recommendation. This part of the Byrd Rule provides a useful protection against the overly aggressive committee that tries to take advantage of the fast-track reconciliation process and omnibus nature of the bill to slip through changes in another committee's jurisdiction that the other committee's leadership would, in the normal course of legislation, be able to stop. The rule provides an exception if the provision is an integral part of a larger piece within the reporting committee's jurisdiction, and the provision sets forth the procedure to carry out substantive provisions within the reporting committee's jurisdiction. And the rule provides another exception if the provision states an exception to, or a special application of, a general provision that is within the reporting committee's jurisdiction.

The fourth Byrd Rule test provides much of the ambiguity in the rule. Under this test, a provision is extraneous if it produces budgetary changes that "are merely incidental to the non-budgetary components of the provision."[76] The parliamentarian has not laid down any bright-line test on how to interpret this language, and the parliamentarian reserves the right to consider each individual case on its merits. The drafters of this subparagraph wished to prohibit provisions in which policy changes plainly overwhelmed deficit changes. For example, a nationwide abortion prohibition might marginally reduce government spending, but it would constitute a much more significant policy change than budgetary action. The application of this subparagraph, however, has ranged wider than such plain cases.

Here are two examples: The chair did not sustain a point of order raised against a provision regarding requirements for the domestic content of cigarettes that the CBO estimated would reduce outlays (when taken together with other provisions in the same section) by $29 million over five years.[77] The chair sustained a point of order against a provision that the maker of the point of order characterized as "a $2 billion blank check for one State" and that a senator said "would require the Secretary of Health and Human Services to

---

[75] Robert B. Sherman, "A Spoonful of Sugar," in *Mary Poppins* (The Walt Disney Co., 1964).

[76] Congressional Budget Act § 313(b)(1)(D), 2 U.S.C. § 644(b)(1)(D).

[77] *See* 139 Cong. Rec. S10,675-78 (daily ed., Aug. 6, 1993).

approve the privatization of all Federal and State health and human services benefit programs in the State of Texas."[78]

The Senate parliamentarian has advised that his office begins its analysis by scrutinizing a provision for any "nonbudgetary components." This analysis is linked to that under the first Byrd Rule test. If a component produces no change in outlays or revenues or the terms and conditions by which the government obtains outlays or revenues, then the component is non-budgetary. In other words, if a component would violate the first Byrd Rule test if it stood alone as a provision, then it contributes to a violation of this test when viewed in conjunction with other components. Once the parliamentarian has identified a non-budgetary component, he then weighs that component or that and other non-budgetary components against the budgetary components, asking whether the latter are "merely incidental" to the former. The parliamentarian's analysis does not end with a simple components test.

Budgetary effect, without more, does not insulate a provision from violating the subsection. Provisions that reduce the deficit may nonetheless violate the subparagraph. For example, the chair sustained a point of order under this subparagraph against provisions that would have imposed criminal penalties (thus raising revenues) under the Occupational Safety and Health Act.[79] And provisions that increase the deficit do not necessarily violate the subparagraph. Thus the parliamentarian advised in summer 1993 that provisions of that year's reconciliation bill that expanded the earned income tax credit, empowerment zones, and food stamps, each of which substantially increase the deficit, did not violate this test.[80]

Thus, this test can have its perverse effects. A senator can find it easy to defend as budgetary a provision that does nothing but spend a great deal of money. On the other hand, a provision that actually reduces the deficit but does so through the device of an extensive policy change will receive strict scrutiny. The language of the law dictates this result, however, as it does not address itself to how the provision affects the budget, merely to its so doing. Often, when Congress tries to react to a flaw in the budget process – here the dangers of omnibus reconciliation bills – Congress' proposed solution to the flaw leaves its own loopholes. And the proposed solution adds more coral to the reef of the budget process.

The fifth Byrd Rule test prohibits provisions that would worsen the deficit in years beyond those covered in the reconciliation bill, when taken together with the other provisions reported by the same committee. Congress added this test in 1987, during the period when Congress was trying to use the budget process

---

[78] See 143 Cong. Rec. S6177-80 (daily ed., June 24, 1997), *id.* at S6291, S6308 (daily ed., June 25, 1997).

[79] See 136 Cong. Rec. S15,771 (daily ed., Oct. 18, 1990); Frumin, *supra* note 41, at 625.

[80] See Omnibus Budget Reconciliation Act of 1993, §§ 13131, 13301-13303, 13901-13971, Pub. L. No. 103-66, 107 Stat. 312 (1993).

to balance the budget, and this test is one budget-process provision that has an explicit deficit-reducing policy goal. This test thus provides a constraint on Congress's desire to cut taxes by using reconciliation. As a consequence of this test, several reconciliation tax bills have made tax cuts sunset in the last year covered by the reconciliation instructions.[81] These sunsets have set up some significant decisions for Congress: Because of these sunsets, many of the Bush tax cuts are scheduled to expire by the end of 2010. By one accounting, making them permanent would cost more than $3 trillion over the next decade.[82] Recently, a reconciliation tax bill also has avoided violation of this test by providing offsetting revenue inflows in out-years.[83]

The sixth and final Byrd Rule test prohibits provisions that contain recommendations with respect to Social Security. This test parallels another Budget Act prohibition against reconciliation bills that contain recommendations with respect to Social Security. As a result of these parallel provisions, a senator may raise a point of order under the Byrd Rule that would result in excising only the offending provision, or raise a point of order under the other Budget Act section against the bill that would result in killing the entire bill.

VI. CONCLUSION

The United States controls its budget primarily through the congressional budget process. That process, more than any other, determines which government programs thrive and which decline. That process, more than any other, determines how large or small a deficit or surplus the government runs. That process, more than any other, determines the magnitude of the government's role in the economy.

From 1980 to 1996, that process had a bias toward deficit reduction. The process thus can take some of the credit for the government's finally balancing the budget in 1998. And from 1980 to 1996, that process impeded congressional pursuit of some social-policy goals, from providing health care to cutting taxes. Actors in the budget process found this frustrating. Since 1996, the process has been streamlined to allow a congressional majority to effectuate its fiscal policy

---

[81] Democratic Leader Daschle identified this consequence in an exchange with the presiding officer in 1996. *See* 142 Cong. Rec. S5418 (daily ed., May 21, 1996). For a discussion of this provision's effects forcing the majority to sunset tax provisions in the 2001 tax law, *see* Michael W. Evans, *The Budget Process and the "Sunset" Provisions of the 2001 Tax Law*, TAX NOTES, Apr. 21, 2003, at 405. Some have come to view these sunsets as budget gimmicks of the type described in Chapter 2, this volume.

[82] Center on Budget and Policy Priorities, TAX CUTS: MYTHS AND REALITIES (Sept. 27, 2006).

[83] *See* Tax Increase Prevention and Reconciliation Act of 2005, Pub. L. No. 109-222, 120 Stat. 345 (2006); Joint Committee on Taxation, ESTIMATED REVENUE EFFECTS OF THE CONFERENCE AGREEMENT FOR THE "TAX INCREASE PREVENTION AND RECONCILIATION ACT OF 2005" (May 9, 2006) (JCX-18-06).

goals. Congress has thus cut taxes, but we once again have deficits "as far as the eye can see."

The Baby Boom generation is beginning to retire, and increased government health care and Social Security costs are around the corner. Congress was right with the fiscal year 2008 budget resolution to return to a system that is once again biased toward fiscal balance. So the rules once again set forth a rigorous pay-as-you-go regime and limit reconciliation to deficit reduction. Choosing such a process means that Congress may have to forgo achieving some other policy goals. Some senators and representatives once again may find this frustrating. But our founders created a system naturally inclined to frustrate government action. They wanted it to be hard for the government to get things done, because then the government would have to organize a greater consensus before taking action. Congress would do well to return to that goal.

In the end, however, even a good budget process is no substitute for political will. As former CBO Director Rudy Penner once said, "The problem is not the process, the problem is the problem."[84] For most of the history of the congressional budget process, actors in that process believed in the value of fiscal responsibility. Restoring that belief might be the most fundamental budget-process reform.

---

[84] *The Problem Is the Problem*, Wash. Post, July 18, 1984, at A14 (editorial).

Questions for Chapter 1

1. As this chapter relates, the current budget process has grown up over time and through a series of statutes, from the 1974 Budget Act through Gramm-Rudman-Hollings in the 1980s through the 1990 Budget Enforcement Act through more recent enactments. What objectives does the congressional budget process serve? Have those objectives changed over the decades? What caused the changes that you identify? Possible reasons for lawmakers' adopting some sort of budget framework include the need to solve collective action problems in a multimember body; the hope that adopting a comprehensive budget process will saliently demonstrate to constituents legislative will in the budget arena; the desire to precommit to a difficult goal, such as deficit reduction, and to enforce that precommitment over time; or the expectation that it will change the balance of power between the executive and legislative branches so that the legislature can more effectively pursue its own agenda, rather than just react to presidential priorities. Which objective seems to predominate during the various eras of budgeting? Which are appropriate objectives for a budget framework? Are there other objectives?[85]

2. Most of the mechanisms to enforce the congressional budget process are internal rules. Each house of Congress has the constitutional power to determine its own rules of proceedings.[86] The main exception is the sequestration power that has been used to enforce spending caps and pay-as-you-go rules; that device has legislative force, and it is administered by the Office of Management and Budget in the executive branch, not a legislative agent. Congressional rules are a relatively weak form of enforcement because they can be waived – and even ignored – if lawmakers wish to evade them. Although the budget process

---

[85] For a discussion of some objectives of framework laws, in the context of congressional budgeting and other statutes, *see* Elizabeth Garrett, *The Purposes of Framework Legislation*, 14 J. Contemp. Legal Issues 717 (2005).

[86] U.S. Const. art. I, §5.

has been described as a precommitment device binding Congress, much as Ulysses bound himself to the mast to resist the Siren's temptations, unlike Ulysses, Congress has the power to free itself from its ropes.[87] Does the fact that they are merely congressional rules render internal enforcement mechanisms illusory or symbolic? Is there a difference between those two conditions; that is, can something be symbolic but also have real bite? What is their real force? Under what circumstances do congressional rules change legislator behavior, and when are they likely to be disregarded without upsetting voters? Does it matter that most of the congressional enforcement mechanisms are adopted as part of a statute, even though they are identified explicitly as changes to internal rules and amenable to change or repeal in the future through internal action and not necessarily subsequent legislation?[88]

3. Dauster believes that the congressional budget process had some influence in reducing the federal deficit in the 1990s. If budget procedures do have some real effect, why would members of Congress be willing to enact them? Presumably, many, if not most, election-minded lawmakers would prefer unfettered ability to send federal subsidies back to their states and districts so that voters are more likely to reelect them. What do you think motivates legislators to enact and then abide by budget rules that work to restrict spending and make it harder to pass tax expenditures? How would you test your hypothesis empirically to determine its accuracy? How has the congressional budget process altered the balance of power within Congress, and how would that affect the willingness of some lawmakers to retain the budget framework? Dauster argues at several points that the budget rules have empowered the majority party in Congress, relative to the minority, particularly in the Senate.[89] Who are the other winners and losers in the budget arena? Does your analysis help explain either the adoption of the rules in the first place or their persistence over time?

4. One major effect of the congressional budget process has been the increased use of omnibus reconciliation bills to enact sweeping legislative change. Why do lawmakers find reconciliation bills attractive vehicles for policy enactment? Even outside the budget context, Congress is doing increasing amounts of work

---

[87] For general discussions of precommitment, particularly through the adoption of constitutions *see* Jon Elster, Ulysses Unbound (2000); Jon Elster, *Don't Burn Your Bridge Before You Come to It: Some Ambiguities and Complexities of Precommitment*, 81 Tex. L. Rev. 1751 (2003); John Ferejohn and Lawrence Sager, *Commitment and Constitutionalism*, 81 Tex. L. Rev. 1929 (2003).

[88] *See* Aaron-Andrew P. Bruhl, *Using Statutes to Set Legislative Rules: Entrenchment, Separation of Powers, and the Rules of Proceedings Clause*, 19 J.L. & Pol. 345 (2003).

[89] For discussions of how rules alter the balance of power between the majority party and minority party, *see* Sarah A. Binder, Minority Rights, Majority Rule: Partisanship and the Development of Congress (1997); Douglas Dion, Turning the Legislative Thumbscrew: Minority Rights and Procedural Change in Legislative Politics (1997).

in omnibus legislation, which is "[l]egislation that addresses numerous and not necessarily related subjects, issues, and programs, and therefore is usually highly complex and long."[90] Some of the rules in the budget process are designed to rein in omnibus legislation, reducing the kinds of proposals that can be added to a reconciliation bill. Are these rules wise? Are they workable? Should other rules be adopted to discourage omnibus bills in the budget process, including omnibus appropriations bills as well as reconciliation vehicles, or to discourage them generally? What rules would you propose? How would you expect legislators to react to your new restrictions?

5. Drafters of budget laws have struggled to determine how rigid the framework should be. Some rigidity is necessary to achieve the objectives of the budget process that have proved to be difficult for lawmakers to achieve without a framework. Unexpected developments, however, may require flexibility in order to enact socially beneficial legislation. How rigid should budget rules be? Under what circumstances should Congress or other political actors be able to evade the rules? Through what process? For example, Congress built exceptions into Gramm-Rudman-Hollings for recessions and wars.[91] Would you include these exceptions? What other exceptions would you build into a federal budget framework? What are the challenges of defining exceptions in a framework that has to be applied in the future? If defining the universe of exceptions ex ante is challenging, requiring supermajority votes to waive budget rules under any circumstance may be another way to provide flexibility within a relatively rigid framework. Is a three-fifths majority vote an appropriate supermajority to waive budget rules? Can Congress constitutionally adopt supermajority voting requirements to enforce procedures, or does the Constitution require a majority voting rule except in certain cases listed in the Constitution?[92]

---

[90] Barbara Sinclair, Unorthodox Lawmaking: New Legislative Processes in the U.S. Congress 71 (2d. ed. 2000).

[91] For a discussion of the exceptions in Gramm-Rudman-Hollings, see Kate Stith, *Rewriting the Fiscal Constitution: The Case of Gramm-Rudman-Hollings*, 76 Cal. L. Rev. 593 (1988).

[92] See John O. McGinnis and Michael B. Rappaport, *The Constitutionality of Legislative Supermajority Requirements: A Defense*, 105 Yale L.J. 483 (1995); Jed Rubenfeld, *Rights of Passage: Majority Rule in Congress*, 46 Duke L.J. 73 (1996).

2 Budget Gimmicks

Cheryl D. Block

I. BUDGETARY CHALLENGES AND TEMPTATIONS

One pesky reality of budgeting is that it requires the use of numbers. Ideally, of course, federal budget information should offer an accurate picture of the nation's fiscal health. On the other hand, we should not have unreasonable expectations. Precise budget projections often require us to know the unknowable. Despite increasingly sophisticated modeling techniques, economists have no crystal ball to reveal future demographic, economic, and policy changes. This lack of complete information creates exponentially greater challenges as the time frame or "window" for budget projections extends into the future.[1] Lest they succumb to complete legislative paralysis, policymakers inevitably must use some estimate of the economic consequences of their actions. Despite sincere attempts to be fiscally responsible and without any deliberate attempt to manipulate or deceive, budget forecasters may simply get the numbers wrong. Many may fool themselves into thinking that they know the short- or long-term economic effects of their policy choices, suffering from what Michael Graetz has called "illusions of precision."[2] Such illusion or imprecision is not the primary focus of this chapter. Instead, my focus is on the deliberate manipulation of numbers or the use of other budget tricks in pursuit of a particular political agenda.

---

[1] A recent CBO report discusses the increasing uncertainty of budget projections and its efforts to establish a "confidence range" for such projections by studying how accurate their projections have been in the past. Congressional Budget Office, U.S. Cong., THE UNCERTAINTY OF BUDGET PROJECTIONS: A DISCUSSION OF DATA AND METHODS (Feb. 2003). *See also* Congressional Budget Office, U.S. Cong., HOW CBO FORECASTS INCOME (Aug. 2006).

[2] Michael J. Graetz, *Paint by Numbers Tax Lawmaking*, 95 COLUM. L. REV. 609, 613 (1995).

Cheryl D. Block recently joined the faculty at Washington University in St. Louis as a Professor of Law after many years on the faculty at the George Washington University Law School. The author wishes to thank the George Washington and the Washington University Law Schools for their research support for this project.

Taxpayers and the politicians who represent them often suffer from the same budget pathology. We want to have it all – increased spending for favored government programs, decreased tax burdens, and a budget surplus. Advocates for additional government spending or tax cuts have incentives to minimize apparent long-term costs, and advocates for spending cuts or tax increases have mirror incentives to maximize apparent long-term gains. This climate presents politicians with almost irresistible temptations to invent budget tricks designed to present legislative proposals in the best budgetary light.

My concern here is not just with the potential for irresponsible spending that may have a far greater impact on the deficit than the numbers would otherwise suggest. The more pernicious effect of budget gimmicks is that they can skew important policy choices. As legislators increase their emphasis on how legislative proposals are scored for budget purposes, they become distracted from genuine social and financial policy objectives. The result may be programs that are not structured in the most equitable or efficient fashion and that may have unintended behavioral consequences. In addition, a disproportionate focus on short-term budgetary impact may result in policy choices that impose lower costs now but significantly higher costs in the long run.

Although there is some overlap from one category to another, this chapter considers budget gimmicks as falling into three broad categories: (1) games with the numbers themselves, (2) timing games, and (3) procedural games. Many recent examples appear in the sections that follow. Since the Republicans have been in greater control of Congress over the past decade, the examples and criticisms may appear to be disproportionately biased against them. The Republican Party does not have a monopoly on budget games, however. Democrats too have been guilty of similar tricks when they have held control.

II. THE NUMBER GAME

A. Numbers Matter

In the game of budgetary politics, each side tries to portray its policies in the most favorable light. At the micro level, advocates of new spending programs seek projections that will portray them at the lowest possible cost. On the flip side, tax-cut proponents look for projections that minimize revenue loss. At the macro level, electoral campaigns often focus on the size of the deficit and the enormous debt we are passing on to future generations. Incumbents have an interest in keeping deficit concerns at bay; their opponents have an interest in painting a much darker picture. For one all too brief, luxurious moment in 2000, presidential candidates George W. Bush and Albert Gore actually had a rare opportunity to debate the size of a national surplus and how best to spend it. Sadly, we are confronted again today with deficits. The bottom line is that whether we find ourselves in periods of deficit or surplus, numbers are a very important part of political campaign rhetoric.

In addition to their rhetorical function, numbers have real consequences in the formal drafting of congressional budget resolutions and the enforcement of budget rules. Congressional budget resolutions establish specific allocations to spending committees, set overall caps on spending legislation, and direct revenue committees with regard to revenue to be raised. With varying degrees of success, Congress has attempted to impose fiscal discipline through budget enforcement rules, many of which are triggered by legislative action that would result in noncompliance with numerical limitations set by the congressional budget resolution.

Assessing the financial impact of any proposed legislative change requires two important pieces of economic information. The first is a base for purposes of comparison, referred to under current budgetary procedures as the "baseline." The baseline attempts to estimate future government revenues and expenses in the absence of any policy change. The second piece of information is an estimation of revenue that would be generated, or cost that would be incurred, as a result of proposed legislation, referred to as the legislative proposal's "score."

Baselines and scores became particularly important under the 1990 Budget Enforcement Act, which imposed two sets of strict statutory fiscal constraints. First, Congress was not to adopt spending legislation that would cause annual appropriations on discretionary spending to exceed caps established by the congressional budget resolution. Second, any new tax legislation or changes to entitlement programs were required to be revenue neutral. In other words, decreases in revenue or increases in spending had to be "paid for" through increases in revenue or decreases in spending elsewhere in the budget. Violations of these caps and "pay-as-you-go" restrictions were met with harsh consequences. In such cases, the Office of Management and Budget (OMB) was statutorily required to enforce across-the-board spending cuts, referred to as "sequesters," of all government programs or activities not explicitly exempted from the cuts. In this strict enforcement environment, numbers *really* mattered. If baselines could be made to appear higher, the costs of new programs would appear to be lower. A costly piece of proposed legislation might be saved if it received a low enough score.

Congress permitted its strict statutory spending caps and pay-as-you-go rules to expire at the end of 2002. Whether or not Congress reenacts statutory caps and pay-as-you-go restrictions, numbers still matter in the formal budget process for at least three reasons. First, even when they are not *statutorily* required, most budget resolutions themselves continue to include pay-as-you-go constraints and other limitations. Second, the congressional budget resolution makes specific allocations to each appropriations committee, which, in turn, makes second-order allocations to its subcommittees. Legislation that would cause totals to exceed these allocations is subject to a point of order that can only be waived by a three-fifths vote in the Senate. Third, the Senate increasingly has opted to use its streamlined, limited debate, reconciliation procedures in lieu of regular Senate rules to pass tax and spending legislation.

Under this reconciliation process, legislative proposals must stay within precise numerical limits set in reconciliation instructions. Failure to comply with reconciliation instructions is also subject to a point of order that can only be waived by supermajority vote. Although the "point of order" mechanisms used to enforce these budgetary constraints are weaker than the old sequester rules, budget games continue much as they did before.[3]

B. Picking Economic Assumptions and Estimation Methodologies

In a Congress that purports to be playing by its own rules, the success or failure of a particular legislative proposal can turn upon the proposal's score, which, in turn, depends upon a reasonably accurate baseline for purposes of comparison. In the imprecise world of budgetary mathematics, even seemingly small changes in estimation methodologies and economic or behavioral assumptions can lead to significantly different scores. Of course, legitimate differences of opinion over methodologies or assumptions are to be expected. The danger, however, is that policy advocates may be tempted to conveniently pick and choose those assumptions and methodologies that best suit a particular legislative agenda.

A case in point may be the ongoing debate over dynamic versus static scoring, described by some as the "Civil War of revenue estimating reform."[4] A truly static approach would project a proposal's revenue gain or loss without taking into account any "feedback effects" in the form of behavioral or macroeconomic response to the proposal's change in policy itself. In actual practice, official estimators already do consider some feedback effects, including, for example, the extent to which taxpayers would save more in response to reduced tax rates. Advocates for so-called dynamic analysis argue for broadening the range of macroeconomic effects taken into account in the scoring process. In other words, the scoring battle today is really over the degree of dynamism rather than the choice of one method over another. The real problem is that there is a wide variety of plausible dynamic-scoring models. This range of available models creates an environment ripe for maneuvering.

Perhaps the greatest danger is the inconsistent use of methodologies and assumptions in pursuit of a political agenda. As one witness at recent dynamic-scoring hearings observed, the focus should not be entirely on the dynamic versus static question, but on consistent and transparent approaches that permit useful comparisons of one set of numbers to another. One example of just such a problem is a recent suggestion that dynamic scoring be used for estimating tax but not spending proposals. The strategy here is used by tax-cut proponents who hope to use dynamic analysis to bolster the somewhat

---

[3] *See* William G. Dauster, "The Congressional Budget Process," which is Chapter 1 of this volume.

[4] Dan R. Mastromarco, *Improving the Revenue Estimating Process: Introduction to a Series*, 105 Tax Notes 1141 (2004).

counterintuitive argument that cuts will actually stimulate the economy, thus leading to long-term federal revenue increases rather than decreases. This same political group often lobbies for a substantially downsized federal government. Their reluctance to adopt similar dynamic-scoring approaches to government spending may be a fear that such analysis could be used to make a similarly counterintuitive argument that increased government spending might actually result in increased federal revenue.

Another possible scoring game takes advantage of fuzzy budget classification boundaries that distinguish tax from spending measures. In fact, the very classification of a budget item as a tax or expenditure is more manipulable than might first appear.[5] A slick maneuver is to convert what appears to be a tax increase into a spending cut. For example, both the Clinton and Reagan administrations at various points argued that increases in Social Security benefit taxes should be scored as spending cuts rather than tax increases, since the tax increases effectively reduced the total benefit received by individual taxpayers.

C. Shopping Revenue and Expenditure Estimates

i. Places to Shop

The availability of numbers from different official staffs – the OMB within the executive branch, and the Congressional Budget Office (CBO) and the Joint Committee on Taxation (JCT) within the legislative branch – offers ample opportunity for number shopping. Because of the potential for significant disagreement, these official budget scorekeeping staffs have established an informal "scorekeepers group," which meets annually to agree on common scorekeeping guidelines. Many of these then are published by the OMB.[6] Nevertheless, recent signs suggest that there may be some breakdown of this informal agreement. For example, the OMB recently made a unilateral decision to switch from a ten-year budget window back to five. In addition, disagreements have arisen over how to score expiring tax cuts that are likely to become permanent. The bottom line is that staffs of the different scoring entities will inevitably disagree. Thus, similar legislative proposals may be given different scores or start from different baselines.

Members on both sides of the aisle may take advantage of differing available cost estimates in the politically charged atmosphere of debate, particularly as the economic and political stakes of legislation increase. One recent case in point is President Bush's proposed prescription drug benefit plan, enacted in 2003. Members of Congress negotiated a deal in advance to limit costs

---

[5] *See* Daniel N. Shaviro, *Rethinking Tax Expenditures and Fiscal Language*, 57 Tax L. Rev. 187 (2004) for a good discussion of this manipulability of fiscal language.

[6] Exec. Office of the President, Office of Mgm't and Budget, Circular No. A-11, App. A (July 2004) (Scorekeeping Guidelines).

for a prescription drug benefit plan to no more than $400 billion over ten years. As it turns out, the CBO scored the proposed legislation's costs at $395 billion, an estimate that was critical to the legislation's passage. Through the course of the debate, however, some reports indicated that, using different assumptions, executive branch actuaries within the Centers for Medicare and Medicaid Services, which reports to the OMB, had estimated the costs at more than $500 billion. The administration allegedly refused congressional requests to officially release these numbers. Nevertheless, allegations were that some of the numbers were selectively released to opponents, who used them in the course of debate.

ii. Directed Scoring and Scorekeeping

One of the more dramatic budget games is the simple use of a magic budget eraser. Although the CBO is designated the official congressional scorekeeper, the Budget Committee ultimately is the final arbiter of the score for any piece of proposed legislation under the Congressional Budget Act.[7] As a practical matter, this generally means the Budget Committee chair. In a sense, the Budget Committee can be seen as "outsourcing" its scorekeeping authority to the CBO.

When the stakes are sufficiently high, however, the Budget Committee may use a practice known as "directed scoring" to direct the CBO *not* to use its own numbers but to adopt OMB figures instead. Thus, careful examination of the fine print behind various CBO estimation tables may uncover an entry somewhat euphemistically labeled "scoring adjustment."[8] In explaining one CBO estimate, Director Dan Crippen routinely gave this answer: "We include the effects of various scorekeeping directives and adjustments made by the budget committees, which would have the effect of reducing outlays attributed to appropriations bills. . . . In total, these adjustments come to about $17 billion for the House and $16 billion for the Senate."[9]

When it occurs, such "directed scoring" may be driven by majority-party efforts to manipulate numbers for political purposes or by Congress more generally to bypass budget enforcement rules that would otherwise be triggered. For fiscal year 2000, for example, the CBO reports that it was directed by Congress to use the OMB's estimates on defense spending.[10] House Armed Services

---

[7] 2 U.S.C. §601(f).

[8] Congressional Budget Office, U.S. Cong., COMPUTATION OF ON-BUDGET SURPLUS FOR FISCAL YEAR 2000. CBO Senior Analyst Susan Tanaka reported that, by definition, if the CBO labels something as a "scoring adjustment," it means that the CBO does not agree.

[9] Letter from Dan L. Crippen, Congressional Budget Office director, to Hon. John M. Spratt, Jr., ranking Dem. member, House Budget Comm. (Aug. 26, 1999), *reprinted in* TAX NOTES TODAY (Sept. 14, 1999).

[10] Congressional Budget Office, U.S. Cong., THE BUDGET AND ECONOMIC OUTLOOK: FISCAL YEARS 2001–2010, at 292 (Jan. 1, 2000).

Committee Chairman Floyd Spence was unapologetic. Forced to choose between directed scoring and spending reductions, he made it clear that he would continue to choose the former. As he noted, "[i]f it becomes necessary, I recommend a similar solution this year, and could not support any solution to an outlay-scoring problem that requires a reduction to the president's defense budget request."[11] This type of directed scoring might not be so troubling if it involved simply choosing between equally plausible sets of revenue projections. Given partisan disagreements over the appropriate size of the defense budget, however, it seems more likely that the majority party, which controlled both the legislative and executive branches, chose estimates from the executive branch OMB to satisfy the president's defense budget request.

Another controversial illustration of directed scoring involved the Railroad Retirement and Survivor's Improvement Act of 2001.[12] This act created a new National Railroad Retirement Investment Trust (RRIT) with rather broad investment authority. In a subtle form of directed scoring, the act explicitly provided that, for purposes of budget computations, transfers of specified assets to the trust were to be treated as a means of financing. Treating the transfers as "means of financing" rather than budget outlays meant scoring the legislation at a substantially lower cost. Although there was some dispute regarding the proper scoring approach, this directive was contrary to CBO estimates and the practice of the General Accountability Office (GAO), leading some to complain that the move was simply a "hocus pocus" ploy to avoid treating transfers of federal funds to the RRIT as a budget outlay.[13]

Perhaps surprisingly, the budget committees do not frequently turn overtly to the directed scoring game. An optimistic explanation is that the budget committees and their chairs take their fiscal responsibilities seriously and genuinely want to play by the rule book. Stated more broadly, legislators may have institutionalized social norms against the majority party's excessive use of its procedural control.[14] To the extent that voters pay attention to such budget gimmicks, those in a position of directed scoring power also may fear negative publicity regarding its overt partisan use. Also, principles of reciprocity suggest that the majority party may be concerned that persistent partisan use of its scoring authority would be met with similar use by the current minority if it should regain control.[15] Whatever the explanation, the good news is

[11] David Baumann, *Begin the Endgame*, 15 Nat'l J. 1126 (2000).

[12] Pub. L. No. 107–90, 115 Stat. 878, 887 (2001).

[13] 147 Cong. Rec. S12, 118 (daily ed., Nov. 29, 2001) (statement of Sen. Nickles).

[14] Robert Dahl suggests this as an alternative political theory of democracy, which he refers to as "polyarchal democracy." Robert A. Dahl, A Preface to Democratic Theory 63–89 (1956).

[15] Although there is substantial support in the political science literature for this reciprocity theory, some studies have questioned its explanatory power. *See, e.g.,* Douglas Dion, Turning the Legislative Thumbscrew: Minority Rights and Procedural Change in Legislative Politics 248 (1997).

that there seem to be at least some effective checks on excessive of directed scoring.

One situation in which the majority party may make more frequent use of its role as final scorer involves last-minute floor amendments or changes to legislation by the conference committee appointed to resolve differences between House and Senate bills. In such cases, the press of time makes it difficult or impossible to get a complete analysis from the CBO. This press of time, along with any uncertainties in underlying assumptions or methodologies, provides more latitude and perhaps a screen behind which party leaders can surreptitiously make the numbers come out right.

Although difficult to prove, a more subtle and hidden variation of directed scoring may be occurring with greater regularity. Budget observers on Capitol Hill report that the staffs of committees or members with an interest in particular legislation will scrutinize and question the CBO's estimates and sometimes apply pressure to revise the numbers. On the one hand, even the most rigorous analytic models cannot take all things fully into account, and some relevant data might be unavailable or unreliable. As a result, those participating in scoring meetings may be asking legitimate questions regarding underlying assumptions. In the prescription drug plan debate, for example, questions apparently were raised about the number of people who could be expected to take advantage of the new plans and the rate at which future health care costs could be expected to rise. On the other hand, there have been reports that the outcome of scoring meetings among CBO staff, congressional staff, and party leaders can sometimes be to simply change a 5 to a 4. Again, the climate of uncertainty offers opportunities for members, staffs, and lobbyists to pressure estimators to choose methods or assumptions that lead to the numbers they want.

D. Keeping it off the Record

i. Off-Budget Trust Funds and Other Earmarked Accounts

One major and long-standing budget trick is simply to keep numbers off the official budget entirely. Technically speaking, the term "off-budget" refers only to entities explicitly excluded from the budget by statute. These off-budget entities include only the Postal Service, and Social Security – and Medicare-related trust funds. In addition, significant government or government-related revenue or expenditure is kept *informally* off-budget through the use of trust funds or other specially earmarked accounts and government-sponsored enterprises (GSEs). Federal employee retirement funds are among the largest of these informally off-budget accounts.[16] Opportunities to pick and choose deficit or

---

[16] Howell Jackson's chapter, "Counting the Ways: The Structure of Federal Spending," which is Chapter 6 in this volume, discusses concerns with the federal budget's presentation of these retirement funds and similar programs that result in long-term government liabilities.

surplus numbers for political advantage arise then not only as a result of the different available baseline and scoring computations discussed earlier, but also from different ways of recording financial information relating to these special trust funds, and earmarked and other off-budget accounts. Thus, conversations about a federal deficit or surplus might alternatively be a reference to (1) "on-budget," meaning all financial information excluding the officially off-budget entities; (2) "off-budget," referring to budget totals from the officially off-budget entities only; (3) "unified," meaning all financial information including these entities; or (4) "federal funds," which excludes *all* trust funds from budget totals.[17]

The number games to be played here often take advantage of the fact that most trust and other earmarked accounts bring in more than they currently spend on a cash-flow basis, even if they have substantial liabilities over the long term. In other words, they operate on an annual surplus. With this in mind, one can understand the forces driving multiple bookkeeping for budget totals. On the one hand, Congress wants to appear to protect surpluses in accounts nominally earmarked to fund important Social Security and retirement programs by setting them aside. At the same time, the temptation to use surpluses from these accounts to "pay" for other programs and reduce the apparent size of the deficit can be almost irresistible, particularly in difficult economic times. Although formal budget rules now explicitly exclude Social Security outlays and revenues from budget totals, Congress and the president routinely ignore the restriction by reflecting off-budget surpluses from Social Security as an offset to on-budget deficits in many budget documents. Even though on-budget information is often also included in the same documents, the use of multiple budget totals can be confusing and misleading.

Another magic trick made possible through the use of various trust funds and earmarked account surpluses exacerbates the problem. The play here is analogous to simply transferring money from one pocket to another, using smoke and mirrors to make it appear that the overall amount in the combined pockets has grown. This device involves investing trust account surpluses in U.S. Treasury securities. The practical effect is a loan from the particular trust fund to the general federal fund. The sleight of hand here results from crediting the trust with interest income but *not* counting "interest" accrued on the intragovernmental debt as an expense.

ii. Emergency Supplemental Appropriations

One of the oldest and most basic gimmicks in the playbook is to fund government activities through emergency supplemental appropriations. Spending

---

[17] Yet another measure is the net operating-cost deficit. This calculation, which uses different accounting methods entirely, comes from the Treasury Department's annual *Financial Report of the United States Government. See* discussion *infra* section IIICi.

authorized through this process is effectively off-budget because budget rules do not count it as spending for purposes of allocation limits set in the budget resolution or as spending for purposes of restrictions in reconciliation instructions. The result is to free up funds that can be used for other spending programs.

A large part of the problem is the absence of an official definition. Despite OMB-proposed guidelines and numerous bills introduced in the House and Senate, Congress has yet to commit itself to an operational definition of the term "emergency." Perhaps the most extreme example of declaring an emergency that wasn't was the use of emergency supplemental appropriations in fiscal year 2000 to cover the cost of Census preparation – a regular government function required by the Constitution and a cost that surely was anticipated. Temptations to use supplemental appropriations are so strong that the Clinton administration proposed them even during years of federal government surplus.

The most glaring abuses of emergency appropriations budget rules seem to have diminished. Perhaps because negative publicity has pushed some of these gimmicks underground, a more subtle variation of the emergency card continues to be played. These more adroit moves use genuine emergencies as a screen behind which to divert funds to cover nonemergency expenditures. Some say that evidence of this kind of "backfilling" is growing. For example, over the past several years, Congress has been very receptive to authorizing sizable emergency appropriations for the war in Iraq and the 2005 hurricane disasters in the Gulf Coast. At the same time, pressure has been mounting for belt-tightening in discretionary spending funded through general annual appropriations. Thus, Congress in 2005 approved substantial emergency appropriations for the Iraq war but also voted for cuts in annual defense appropriations. One major concern with this is that military spending dollars can be difficult to trace. Agency officials may be able to find deft internal accounting procedures to use some portion of the generous emergency appropriation to make up for cuts in funding for regular operations. Although somewhat difficult to prove, many suspect that the Department of Defense quietly has agreed to tolerate cuts for the moment, assuming that they will be made up through subsequent emergency supplemental appropriations.

iii. Tax Expenditure Budget

It is now generally recognized that the federal government incurs some costs through direct tax-and-spend programs and others indirectly through "tax expenditures." The term "tax expenditure" refers to revenue loss attributable to special tax breaks designed as taxpayer subsidies to advance particular government policy objectives. For example, much of our modern welfare system is now delivered through an Earned Income Tax Credit (EITC) to employed low-income taxpayers. The EITC functions largely as a substitute for what otherwise might be direct welfare payments. Although budget rules now require enumeration of indirect spending in the form of foregone revenue, this information is not included in most budget documents for purposes of computing the federal deficit. At least in this respect, tax expenditures are effectively off-budget.

Another concern is the common misperception that tax breaks for particular activities do not have the same budgetary impact as direct spending. As a matter of political rhetoric, tax expenditures are sometimes sold to voters as a way of reducing the size of the government – taxpayers can keep more of their own money rather than have the government give direct spending handouts. Even though a direct spending program might be the better policy choice, a proposal packaged as a tax expenditure might be politically successful while the same idea pitched as direct spending would be attacked as fiscally irresponsible.

Perhaps even more important, unless they are scheduled to expire or are subsequently repealed, tax expenditures become a permanent fixture of the U.S. Tax Code. There is no built-in mechanism for regular assessment of their effectiveness and cost. Ongoing costs from such tax expenditures are built into the baseline and not scored as new spending in future budget years. All of this is not to suggest that tax expenditures are free from budget enforcement controls. For purposes of budget enforcement, tax expenditures are classified as mandatory spending as opposed to general appropriations. As such, they remain subject to such pay-as-you-go requirements as Congress may choose to include in the budget resolution or to similar limits included in Senate reconciliation instructions. Such budget restrictions generally apply only to *new* tax expenditures, however. *Existing* tax expenditures are thus advantaged in the annual competition for scarce budget resources.[18] In the end, the concern is that budget rules may contribute to temptations for proponents to structure their proposals as tax expenditures in order to hide some of their true budgetary impact.

III. TIMING GAMES

A. Basic Number and Timing Tricks Compared

Generally speaking, the budget gimmicks considered in the previous section involve manipulation of budget classifications and of the numbers themselves. Although they also involve manipulation of numbers, timing gimmicks

---

[18] Admittedly, existing tax expenditures remain potential victims of new tax-expenditure proponents who would like to "pay for" their favored programs through repeal or scale-back of existing ones. *See* Elizabeth Garrett, *Harnessing Politics: The Dynamics of Offset Requirements in the Tax Legislative Process*, 65 U. Chi. L. Rev. 501 (1998). At least according to some positive political theory models, however, interest groups are more likely to be successful in blocking new legislation than in upsetting the status quo. If so, those seeking to attack existing tax expenditures in order to pay for new ones face an uphill battle.

use different strategies to work their magic. These approaches emphasize the manipulation of the budget year in which particular items of revenue or expenditure are reported. Some of them involve simply accelerating receipts or delaying payments into alternate budget years or taking advantage of the fact that the federal budget operates under a fiscal year, which begins on October 1, while many government activities are based on a calendar year or some other time period. More sophisticated timing gimmicks manipulate numbers by using different or inconsistent methods of accounting.

B. Looking Through the Budget Window

To be of any value, budget information must be presented using a defined time frame. In past budgets, the presentation of information on a short, one-year basis provided an opportunity to engage in "myopic budgeting," a term sometimes used by budget observers to describe saving actual or apparent government spending in one budget year even though the overall costs over time are likely to be higher. In choosing the appropriate time period or "budget window," budget makers must resolve at least one difficult tension. On the one hand, short-term budgets, deliberately or inadvertently, may provide information that inaccurately reflects or distorts the long-term perspective so important to informed policy decisions. On the other hand, the necessarily more speculative nature of long-term projections can result in budget numbers that turn out to have been inaccurate with the benefit of hindsight. The 1990 Budget Enforcement Act attempted to resolve this tension by moving to a statutory five-year minimum budget window for purposes of the congressional budget resolution. Responding later to concerns that the five-year window was not sufficient to present accurate and useful longer-term budget information, Congress in 1997 began requesting ten-year budget information from the CBO. Consistent with the general informal agreement among legislative and executive branch scorekeepers to use similar scorekeeping methods, the executive branch simultaneously moved to ten-year budgeting.

Beginning with the president's proposed budget for fiscal year 2004, however, the OMB shortened its forecasting window from ten years back to five.[19] Also included in the president's 2004 budget was a major proposal to make permanent a number of tax cuts passed by Congress in 2001 and 2003. Use of a five- rather than ten-year budget window enabled the administration to present the tax proposal at a smaller projected revenue loss. Although the president's 2004 budget *summary* was based upon five-year projections, some budget information, most notably the costs of the president's proposed Medicare plan, was

---

[19] For a discussion of the OMB's change back to five-year budgeting, *see* Christopher J. Puckett, *Is the Experiment Over? The OMB's Decision to Change the Game Through a Shortening of the Forecast*, 11 GEO. J. POVERTY LAW & POL'Y 169 (2004).

projected over ten years. These modifications subjected the administration to charges that it was using selective changes in budget windows solely to promote the president's legislative agenda.

Whatever the political merits of the charge, several things are clear. First, changing the budget window from one year to the next or using budget windows inconsistently within the same budget year can be used as a device to manipulate budget numbers. Second, if the CBO uses one budget window and the OMB another, then useful comparisons between the president's annual budget proposal and the congressional budget resolution will be far more difficult. As it turns out, after a short period of using different windows, Congress subsequently followed the administration's lead back to a five-year budgeting. The congressional move to follow the administration should not be too surprising given that the same party controlled both the legislative and executive branches and presumably had a shared political agenda.

C. Accounting Gimmicks

i. Inconsistent Use of Cash and Accrual Accounting

Any accountant or economist preparing tax or budgetary data must use one of two major accounting alternatives – the cash-flow or the accrual method. Their key distinguishing feature is the accounting period or fiscal year used for reporting receipts and disbursements. To better understand many of the timing-related budget gimmicks discussed in the following sections, one must first appreciate the fundamental differences between cash-flow and accrual budget accounting.[20]

Cash-flow accounting simply records revenues in the fiscal year that they are received and expenses in the fiscal year that they are paid. In contrast, the accrual method records items of income and expense when the rights to receive and obligations to pay arise, even if no funds were received or paid at that time. In other words, accrual accounting is forward-looking. It takes into account *today* the present value of future receipts and subtracts *today* the present value of future liabilities. Accrual accounting is viewed in the accounting community as so far superior to cash-flow accounting as an accurate measure of financial health that public and private companies are required to use it under generally accepted accounting principles (GAAP) established by the Financial Accounting Standards Board (FASB). In fact, federal government departments and agencies also are required to use accrual accounting through a set of parallel rules that were established for government entities by the Financial Accounting

---

[20] For a more complete account of distortions and misleading budgetary information made possible by cash-flow budgetary accounting, *see* Cheryl D. Block, *Congress and Accounting Scandals: Is the Pot Calling the Kettle Black?* 82 Neb. L. Rev. 365, 393–421 (2003).

Standards Advisory Board (FASAB). Congress, on the other hand, does not hold itself to any formal, defined set of accounting standards and does not require accrual accounting for budget purposes.

Although Congress uses accrual accounting with respect to *some* items in the budget, cash-flow accounting is the general default rule used for recording most government revenues and expenditures on the budget. Perhaps more important, both the OMB's and the CBO's bottom-line assessments of the federal deficit are computed by using cash-flow methodology. In addition to these two sets of *budget* books kept by the CBO and the OMB, the executive branch keeps separate *financial* books with yet another measure of federal receipts and expenditures and the overall deficit. Among these is the annual *Financial Report of the United States Government*, prepared by the Treasury Department, which uses the accrual method. Differences between the cash-based federal budget and accrual-based financial accounts can be significant. The 2005 *Financial Report's* executive summary even includes an entire section entitled "Why the Accrual-Based Net Operating Cost Worsened While the Budget Deficit Improved."[21] The same report includes another section intended to "reconcile" its accrual-based information with "the more widely known budget deficit."[22]

Yet another report is prepared by the GAO to help readers understand the Treasury Department's *Financial Report*. The GAO report begins by pointing out that the federal government *generally* uses the accrual method and acknowledges that this method is the basis for generally accepted accounting principles used by private business enterprises. Federal government accrual accounting, it says, is "intended to provide a complete picture of the federal government's financial operations and financial position."[23] Yet, the report continues, cash-method accounting is used for the federal budget, "which is the federal government's primary fiscal planning and control tool. The budget helps establish national spending priorities and helps ensure that the federal government spends taxpayers' money in accordance with applicable appropriations laws."[24] Little more is offered to justify the difference. The Treasury Department's accrual-based *Financial Report* explains that the report is meant to "complement" the president's cash-based budget and should be "used with the budget as a planning and control tool not only for the current fiscal year but with a longer

---

[21] U.S. Dep't of Treas., FINANCIAL REPORT OF THE UNITED STATES GOVERNMENT 6 (2005) [hereinafter 2005 Treas. Rep.].

[22] *Id.* at 10. The report also includes an extremely complicated flow chart illustrating the relationship between its numbers and those in the unified budget. *Id.* at 5 (Chart A).

[23] U.S. Gen. Accounting Office, UNDERSTANDING THE PRIMARY COMPONENTS OF THE ANNUAL FINANCIAL REPORT OF THE UNITED STATES GOVERNMENT, GAO-05-958SP 5 (2005) [hereinafter 2005 GAO Rep.].

[24] *Id.*

term focus as well."[25] Here, too, not much more is offered by way of advice or explanation on how the two sets of books might be best used to complement one another.

One primary and explicit goal of the various financial and budget reports is "to make available to every American a comprehensive overview of the federal government's finances."[26] In the best of worlds, the multiplicity of federal government accounts of revenues and expenditures, several of which use different reporting methods, makes meeting that objective a major challenge. Even the most well-intentioned lawmakers may have trouble knowing how to respond to all of this information or use it constructively as a planning and control tool. Others less well intentioned may be tempted to use information or accounting methods selectively to advantage particular legislative proposals.

More alarming, however, is the potential collective misuse of the less economically accurate cash-flow approach to make what is, in fact, a zero-sum game appear to be more of a non-zero-sum game. Legislators interested in reelection want to provide constituents with everything – reductions in tax rates and increased spending on favored programs. In other words, legislators and constituents may share the same budget pathology. Using cash-flow budgetary accounting, Congress can authorize new or expanded government programs that will impose substantial long-term costs without reflecting those costs in the budget until the invoice arrives years into the future. Opportunities to minimize apparent costs through cash-method accounting and other timing gimmicks can free up funds for additional spending. In the meantime, pressures for tax cuts and increased spending for military and other government activities continue. How tempting it is to use budget tricks to play Scarlett O'Hara. After all, tomorrow is another day.

The failure to take the net present value of long-term government liabilities into account is especially acute with regard to large-scale social programs such as Social Security and Medicare. As a practical matter, these programs present the most challenging problems for estimators. The problems here are well known and many lawmakers and their constituents do seem to appreciate the magnitude of long-term liabilities and the extent to which budget figures may not accurately reflect government costs. Unfortunately, however, agreements on what to do about the problem are difficult to come by.

Albeit on a somewhat smaller scale, many other government programs raise similar concerns about proper budget accounting for long-term liabilities. These include retirement plans for government employees, programs to protect private pensions, financial institutions and their customers, loan and loan-guarantee programs, federal flood insurance, and the like. Howell Jackson's chapter in this book (Chapter 6) on the structure of federal spending

---

[25] 2005 Treas. Rep., *supra* note 21, at 4. [26] 2005 GAO Rep., *supra* note 23, at 1.

considers in depth the budget accounting issues raised by these programs. Consequently, my observations here will be brief.

It would be overstating the case to suggest that policymakers often use cash rather than accrual budgeting for major government retirement, social, and insurance programs as a budget gimmick. Not all budget observers even agree that moving to accrual budgeting for many of these programs would be a good idea. The problem with the current approach is inconsistent budget treatment of programs that appear to raise similar budget issues and to warrant similar budget treatment. For example, Congress has mandated accrual-based accounting for federal credit programs since 1990, but has not done so for federal insurance and government employee retirement plans. Inconsistent treatments of such programs may open possibilities for selective use of accrual-budget accounting practices to prefer one program over another. In such a climate, it is most important that legislators and budget observers carefully scrutinize budget numbers in full awareness of the discrepancies.

ii. Simple Delayed Payments or Accelerated Receipts

One extremely popular and basic budget gimmick uses cash-flow accounting to delay outflows until later years. One well-known example involved simply shifting defense expenditures into the subsequent year's budget by delaying military paychecks by one day. Employees may not have noticed much difference, but the maneuver moved billions of dollars from one budget year to another. Recent revenue and spending bills also provide flagrant examples. The 2005 revenue bill included a statutory provision requiring corporations to pay 105 percent of their estimated tax payment for the three-month period ending in September 2006. The bill further instructs these taxpayers to reduce the next required installment by 5 percent to compensate for previous overpayment.[27] Since the federal government's fiscal year begins on October 1, the provision was scored by the CBO as *increasing* revenue by $2.2 billion for fiscal year 2006 and *decreasing* revenue by the same $2.2 billion for fiscal year 2007. Equally glaring was a provision shifting $5.2 billion in outlays from 2006 to 2007 by temporarily halting payments to Medicare providers for the last six business days of the 2006 fiscal year.[28] Both the estimated tax and the Medicare payment provisions adopted by Congress in 2005 had no real substance. They were enacted for no reason other than to satisfy numerical budget reconciliation limitations on spending for each of the individual fiscal years and the aggregate budget window covered by the reconciliation instructions.

---

[27] Tax Increase Prevention and Reconciliation Act of 2005, Pub. L. No. 109–122, 109th Cong. §401 (2005).
[28] Deficit Reduction Act of 2005, Pub. L. No. 109–171, 109th Cong. §5004 (2005).

Another more systematic illustration of the same type of strategy is the advance appropriation. This move takes advantage of scoring rules that count appropriations as new budget authority for the fiscal year in which the funds become newly available and *not* when the appropriations are enacted – a basic cash-accounting-type technique. Congress can in effect accrue the obligation now without paying for it in the budget until later. This maneuver frees up funds that might otherwise be subject to current-year spending limitations. One problem here is that these strategies can become addictive. When you put off today's budget spending through advance appropriations, the "budget invoice" arrives tomorrow. To make good on the promise to score the budget expenditure against tomorrow's budget means to even further restrict tomorrow's spending.

The good news here is that Congress shows signs of breaking the habit. For the past several years, congressional budget resolutions have included a section entitled "Restrictions on Advance Appropriations" to place a cap on advance expenditures, which are to be identified in specific accounts by the joint statement of managers accompanying the budget resolution. Congress now seems to have settled into a reasonably steady annual diet of approximately $23 billion in advance appropriations. Assuming that Congress maintains this pattern, the budget numbers effectively even out from year to year. As a result, the advance appropriations game appears to be less problematic than it once was.

iii. Long-Term Timing Shifts

a) Variation on a Theme
Simple delayed payment dates or advance appropriations function generally as a device to shift short-run budget impact, most frequently moving a budget item forward from one budget year to the next. More complex variations on the theme are used to shift budget items over a longer period of time. These longer-run strategies focus more on budget windows rather than individual fiscal years. As budget expert Allen Schick notes, "the easiest way to remove a spending increase from the score is to schedule it to take effect beyond the period covered by the baseline."[29] Similarly, the easiest way to hide a revenue decrease is to schedule it to take effect outside of the budget window. To work their magic, these gimmicks also take advantage of cash-method budget accounting.

b) Phase-Ins
One way to reduce apparent revenue losses from tax cuts or increased expenditures is simply to phase them in over time, thus pushing costs into later budget years without need for any further legislative action that might otherwise be subject to later budget resolution restrictions. This strategy works because the

---

[29] Allen Schick, THE FEDERAL BUDGET: POLITICS, POLICY, PROCESS 68 (2000).

cash accounting perspective does not account for the net present value of liabilities accrued at the time of the legislation's passage but not actually "paid" until later. This phase-in device is especially useful as applied to costly increases in Medicare or similar types of entitlement spending.

The phase-in technique also is quite effective as applied to revenue decreases, particularly in the tax area. Congress recently has moved on a massive scale to phased-in tax cuts rather than cuts with a one-time effective date. The Economic Growth and Tax Relief Act of 2001 (EGTRA), for example, phased in major reductions in individual income tax rates through 2006. The 2001 act also achieved a gradual repeal of the estate tax through a combination of phased-in estate-tax rate reductions and a simultaneous phase-in of increases in generous estate-tax exemptions.[30] Although there is substantial skepticism over the claims, tax-cut proponents vigorously argue that such cuts will stimulate the economy, thus raising revenue and perhaps even paying for themselves. Whether the claim ultimately is vindicated or not, those who propose phased-in tax cuts as a stimulus can be accused of applying inconsistent logic. If the cuts really stimulate the economy, they arguably should be made effective immediately.

c) Sunsets

A reverse application of the same type of gimmick is to pass legislation with a fixed expiration date or "sunset." Two variations are possible here. First, during the era of tax increases in the 1990s, Congress took advantage of sunsets to enact a temporary new tax or tax increase despite expectations that the "temporary" provision would be extended beyond its nominal expiration date. The second variation is to enact tax cuts with set expiration dates despite intentions that the cut be made permanent.

Both variations of the sunset device take advantage of one important feature of CBO baseline projection methodology. That is, the CBO is instructed to prepare its baselines by using *current* law, without taking future statutory changes into account. Despite even a high probability that an expiring provision will be extended, budget rules direct the CBO to make its projections as if the provision died on its scheduled expiration date. Thus, a provision that increases revenue is viewed as eliminated on its stated expiration date. Revenues generated by its subsequent reenactment are not counted as part of the baseline. Instead, extension of the tax is scored from the baseline as generating new revenue, magically creating new resources that can be used to "pay for" additional spending. On the flip side, a provision that decreases federal receipts also is viewed as eliminated on its scheduled expiration date. Budget scores for the proposed decrease cannot take its likely extension into account, thus creating

---

[30] See William G. Gale and Peter R. Orszag, *An Economic Assessment of Tax Policy in the Bush Administration*, 2001–2004, 45 B.C. L. Rev. 1157 (2004).

an artificially rosier projection of the revenue reduction's long-term economic impact.

Historically, Congress limited itself to using sunsets for specific, narrowly defined tax deductions, credits, and rate cuts. For example, Congress enacted temporary deductions and credits for discrete types of activity, including the research and development (R & D) credit, the Work Opportunity Tax Credit (WOTC), and special bonus depreciation rules designed to encourage rebuilding in the aftermath of the 9/11 terrorist attacks and the devastating 2005 hurricane season in the Gulf Coast. Some of these deductions and credits, which came to be known as "extenders," were intended to provide only short-term economic stimulus for a new industry or short-term incentives to encourage particular investments. Other temporary provisions were genuinely intended as experimental pilot projects. The fixed expiration date was effectively a precommitment device forcing Congress to reassess the efficiency and effectiveness of the experiment.

Despite what may have been the best of intentions, temptations to turn some of these expiring tax provisions into "permanent extenders" have proven too great for many politicians to resist. As of 2003, for example, *Congressional Quarterly Weekly* reported that only one of more than 25 had been allowed to expire.[31] In some cases, special tax provisions have even been extended retroactively after the scheduled expiration date has passed. One cynical explanation for the "permanent extender" phenomenon is that politicians hope to keep campaign dollars flowing from special-interest groups who must continually lobby to retain beneficial tax breaks. In fact, the "extender" game has become a regular feature of annual budget negotiations, spawning a veritable cottage industry of specialized lobbyists. The other explanation is budget related. Unlike some of the more subtle tricks, this particular budget game is played quite openly. The Congressional Research Service explains that Congress turns to recurring extensions of technically "temporary" tax provisions because such extensions "have lower short run revenue costs than permanent law, although the ostensible lack of permanence often masks the long-term costs associated with the provisions."[32]

The so-called temporary R&D credit is among the most notorious examples of the extender game. First enacted in 1981 as a temporary credit scheduled to expire in 1985, the R&D credit since has been routinely extended, sometimes in five-year increments, but often for just one year at a time. This pattern continues despite overwhelming bipartisan support for the credit and numerous proposals that it be made permanent. Continued extension of the R&D credit is virtually a political given. The only question is the length of the extension.

---

[31] Jill Barshay, *"Temporary" Tax Breaks Usually a Permanent Reality*, Congressional Quarterly Weekly 2831 (Nov. 15, 2003).

[32] Cong. Res. Service, Report on Tax Extenders, RL32367, Doc. 2006–16512 (Aug. 4, 2006).

Whether the expiration date is set one year, 18 months, or five years out will depend almost entirely on budget numbers and the extent to which Congress either is required by budget rules or otherwise commits itself to find revenue raising "offsets" to pay for the costly extension.

The recent twist on sunsets has been to expand them beyond specially targeted tax deductions or credits, using them more broadly for general tax-rate cuts. The two most notable instances were EGTRA in 2001 and the Jobs and Growth Tax Relief Reconciliation Act of 2003 (JGTRRA). The 2001 act, for example, phased tax cuts *in* through 2006 only to have them expire after December 31, 2010. The Tax Code was to apply thereafter as if the statute had "never been enacted." Such maneuvers are worthy of the Mad Hatter in *Alice in Wonderland*. That the tax cuts were set to expire after ten, rather than some other number of years, was not arbitrary. Rather, it was purely an effort to bypass budget enforcement rules.[33] The dilemma for Republicans was that a permanent tax cut would be scored as a substantial long-term revenue loss. Democratic opponents threatened to use a Byrd Rule point-of-order challenge, arguing that the proposal was "extraneous" because it decreased revenues beyond the ten-year budget window.[34] The ten-year sunset clause was a rather slick end run. With rates technically set to revert to the higher pre-2001 rates at the end of 2010, the bill had to be scored as raising revenue beyond the ten-year window. Legislators at the time fully expected in subsequent legislation to make the tax cuts permanent, but revenue estimators' hands were tied by the rule requiring them to assume that current law did not change.

A subsequent scoring convention change proposed in the president's 2006 and 2007 budgets looks suspiciously like a "bait and switch" move now to use the ten-year sunset provision as an opportunity to advance the permanent tax-cut agenda. The president proposed that the official baseline for scoring tax bills be computed under the assumption that the 2001 and 2003 tax cuts are permanent. This would mark a distinct change from current practice, which computes the baseline under the assumption that current law remains unchanged. In other words, after enactment of the temporary tax provision, CBO baseline projections assumed that tax cuts expire as provided in the 2001 and 2003 statutory provisions. Thus, revenues are projected to increase in 2011 when tax rates revert to their higher pre-2001 levels. Under traditional baseline projection methods, proposed legislation to make the tax cuts permanent would eliminate this revenue increase and be scored as generating substantial revenue loss. The president's proposed scoring convention change, however, would score the cost of a bill to make tax cuts permanent against a baseline that already has assumed

[33] For an in-depth consideration of these sunsets and their implications, see William G. Gale and Peter R. Orszag, *Sunsets in the Tax Code*, 99 Tax Notes 1553 (2003); Rebecca M. Kysar, *The Sun Also Rises: The Political Economy of Sunset Provisions in the Tax Code*, 40 Ga. L. Rev. 335 (2006).

[34] William Dauster explains these procedural rules in Chapter 1 of this volume.

that they *were* permanent. In other words, the bill would be scored at *zero*. Such a midstream change in scoring methodology is yet another example of cherry-picking or inconsistent use of estimation assumptions and methodologies in pursuit of a political agenda.

d) Back-Loading Program Costs

A more subtle budget maneuver is to tinker with a proposal's programmatic details so that its revenue impact is "back loaded." Perhaps the best example involves special tax-preferred accounts designed as taxpayer incentives to save for retirement or to cover future medical, educational, or other expenses. The earliest version of such accounts, now referred to as "traditional" individual savings accounts (IRAs), was created in 1974. Taxpayer contributions to traditional IRA accounts are initially deductible and growth in earnings in the accounts is tax free. Taxpayers are required, however, to report amounts actually distributed upon retirement as taxable income. For budget purposes, this type of account is referred to as "front loaded" because the taxpayer has an immediate tax benefit from the up-front deduction, which results in a parallel up-front cost to the government in foregone revenue.

Since its inception in 1974, the IRA-type account has been an attractive tax vehicle, spawning a number of similar tax-prepaid savings or investment accounts. These recent iterations include the general Roth IRA in addition to other specifically focused accounts designed to encourage saving for medical and educational expenses. As with traditional IRAs, these newer tax-preferred accounts accrue income tax free over time. Although other details vary, the primary distinguishing feature of the more recent tax-preferred savings vehicles is that initial contributions are *not* deductible. Instead, later withdrawals of accumulated account balances are tax free. Roth IRAs and other similar accounts are referred to as back-loaded accounts. Since initial taxpayer contributions to back-loaded accounts are *not* deductible, there is no immediate foregone revenue to the government. Instead, the revenue impact occurs many years later as retirees make tax-free withdrawals. This program design is very attractive to high-bracket investors and also plays out rather nicely from the budget perspective. As with so many other budget gimmicks, the major culprit again is a cash-based budget perspective, which does not take into account the net present value of future lost revenue. Much of the long-term budget costs from these back-loaded accounts results from tax-free withdrawals so far into the future that the foregone revenue cost is not reflected within a ten-year, much less a five-year, budget window.

The tax-preferred account story also offers a classic illustration of ways in which short-term perspectives encouraged by the budget process can skew policy choices. Even though back-loaded accounts impose far greater *long-term* budget costs than traditional IRAs, Congress may be unable to resist temptations to choose them over traditional ones or to prefer such accounts over other programs that might make more policy sense. The budget gimmick here is even slicker than might first appear, though. The trick here is that legislation creating or expanding tax-favored, back-loaded investment accounts actually may be scored as *raising* revenues in the short run despite the substantial overall long-term cost.[35] These apparent revenue increases occur because long-term, tax-deferral advantages from back-loaded accounts are sufficiently attractive, particularly to high-income investors, that many of them will prefer the newer back-loaded accounts to traditional IRAs. The projected increased volume in nondeductible contributions to back-loaded accounts causes no immediate revenue loss to the budget. At the same time, starting from a baseline that assumes substantial budget costs from contributions to traditional accounts under current law, the expected reduced volume in deductible contributions to front-loaded accounts can be scored as a revenue increase. An even more significant revenue-increase mirage results from anticipated conversions of existing traditional accounts into back-loaded ones. This is because the long-term savings from the back-loaded accounts are so appealing that many high-income investors will elect to withdraw taxable income from traditional accounts for transfer into new accounts. Such conversions are even more likely if taxpayers are permitted to make rollover withdrawals from traditional IRAs without early-withdrawal penalties. The phantom revenue increase resulting from taxable withdrawals for conversion into the new accounts is transitional and short lived. Once the conversions have occurred, the revenue increases disappear.

e) Long-Term Leasing

Another popular gimmick that takes advantage of cash accounting is the long-term lease. Under cash-flow budgeting, outright government expenses for purchase or construction of necessary buildings or equipment are recorded immediately as such expenses are incurred. One way to shift costs to later budget years is to contract out capital-intensive tasks. So, for example, a government agency can enter into an agreement calling for a private contractor to construct and hold title to a building. Upon completion, the agency will occupy the space and pay rent for its long-term use. Even though the overall costs of such arrangements may be substantially higher in the long run, cash-method budget accounting creates incentives for federal managers to make economically inefficient choices. One CBO report noted that such ventures "are being structured to avoid the requirement for recognizing the costs of government

---

[35] For a thorough discussion of short- and long-term costs, *see* Jane G. Gravelle and Maxim Shvedov, *Proposed Savings Accounts: Economic and Budgetary Effects*, Rep. No. RL32228 *in* CONG. RES. SERVICE REPORT FOR CONGRESS 2–4 (June 30, 2006); Thomas L. Hungerford, *Savings Incentives: What May Work, What May Not*, Rep. No. RL33482 *in* CONG. RES. SERVICE REPORT FOR CONGRESS 9–12 (June 20, 2006). *See also* Karen C. Burke and Grayson M.P. McCouch, *Lipstick, Light Beer, and Back-Loaded Savings Accounts*, 25 VA. TAX REV. 1101 (2006).

investments up front" and that such treatment "could reduce the budget's ability to encourage cost-effective investment decisions."[36]

Despite new OMB scoring guidelines requiring that such federal government capital-lease or lease-purchase costs be scored at their net present value over the life of the contract, government misuse of the long-term lease maneuver to artificially improve the bottom line apparently continues. A recent example was a controversial Air Force leasing deal with the Boeing Corporation for aerial-refueling aircraft. The new scoring guidelines permit cash-type accounting only for leases classified as "operating leases." Although the CBO disagreed, the Air Force classified this as an "operating lease" for which it was not required to report the full up-front costs. The CBO estimated the long-run leasing costs as $1.3 billion to $2 billion more than an outright purchase.

IV. PROCEDURAL GAMES

The third major category of budget gimmicks involves games with rules. Many budget observers report that the most significant of these procedural games is manipulation of the Senate reconciliation process. Although the reconciliation process is optional, reconciliation bills have now become the procedure of choice for most spending, revenue, and debt-limit legislation. William Dauster's chapter (Chapter 1) on the budget process offers an excellent account of the history and operation of the optional budget reconciliation process. Given the useful illustrations of procedural budget games considered there, my observations here will be brief.

At least for now, the controversial procedural disputes over use of the reconciliation process have been resolved in favor of those advocating its legitimate use for tax-cut legislation even though the focus of the rules when they were originally enacted was deficit control. This resolution of the debate suggests that, whatever the original concerns that led to their creation, the statutory rules for reconciliation legislation offer a greater degree of latitude than one might have thought. As reconciliation increasingly becomes the procedure of choice, legislators have become more attuned to its potential as a political tool. The danger here is that reconciliation will become the breeding ground for a new generation of creative budget gimmicks.

One such recent development is the increasing use of multiple reconciliation bills, rather than the more traditional single bill. With this move, spending cuts and tax cuts are considered in separate spending and revenue bills. It is often politically expedient to take up the spending-cut bill first in order to appear fiscally responsible and only later to consider tax-cut legislation. Another way to make advantageous use of multiple bills is to split a proposed tax bill into

---

[36] Congressional Budget Office, U.S. Cong., The Budgetary Treatment of Leases and Public/Private Ventures 39 (Feb. 2003).

two, putting more popular and uncontroversial items in regular bills. This move removes the costs of popular provisions from the strictures of reconciliation limitations, leaving room for deeper tax cuts in the reconciliation bill. This device has even been used to place one part of the cut in a regular bill and the other in a reconciliation bill. The technique is especially useful when the minority and majority agree in principle about a tax cut, but disagree on how large it should be. The uncontroversial portion of the cut is included in regular legislation and the excess controversial cut desired by the majority is included in a reconciliation bill.

In the end, the reconciliation process is where the number game is now *really* played. Reconciliation instructions require appropriations and tax committees to stay within stated aggregate limits on spending and revenue, but they do not direct how to achieve that level of spending or revenue. Tremendous wrangling over details and creative moves to make the numbers come out right are inevitable. This reconciliation context also is the most likely place to uncover attempts to manipulate baseline estimates and proposed legislation scores. The manipulation of due dates for corporate estimated payments and the six-day delay in government payments to Medicare providers described earlier in this chapter are among the most flagrant examples. Members or their staffs often frantically tinker with statutory details to make the numbers work even in the final moments before the bill comes to a vote on the House or Senate floor.

V. CONCLUSION

The term "budget gimmicks" has a pejorative ring. Some understandably may take issue with characterizing several of the circumstances described in this chapter so negatively. There can be honest and reasonable differences of opinion, for example, on the best way to estimate baselines and score proposed legislation. In addition, not everyone agrees that a large-scale conversion from cash- to accrual-based budget accounting would improve the process or lessen opportunities to manipulate numbers. Whatever label one uses, the stories recounted in this chapter should move readers to think seriously about what might be done to minimize the deliberate manipulation of the budget process. To my mind, one of the most significant problems that cries out for reform is the reconciliation process. The continued expansive use of streamlined, limited-debate reconciliation procedures is a dangerous development. The need to comply with reconciliation instructions has inspired number games that appear every bit as substantial as or even worse than those played in earlier efforts to bypass pre-2003 statutory discretionary spending caps and pay-as-you-go rules. In addition, the process has inspired a new packaging game in which particular tax and spending proposals are shifted from one bill to another largely to take advantage of the reconciliation process.

Some improvements also can be made with respect to budget baselines and scoring. For one thing, budget makers need to give up the illusion of precision.

As suggested by some estimators, it might be more useful for Congress to work with "confidence ranges" rather than fixed estimates. Although scorekeepers have a reasonably good record of working together, recent developments suggest a slight movement away from the culture of coordinating scorekeeping guidelines. More formal efforts to coordinate and facilitate agreement on scorekeeping guidelines may be needed.

Differences among the several sets of federal budget and financial books also should be reduced. When some government books use cash and others accrual-based accounting, or when different books use different scoring conventions, the result can be a comparison of apples to oranges. If, as the Treasury Department's *Financial Report* suggests, legislators are truly to make use of accrual-based financial reports as a complement to cash-based budget information, there should be more systematic efforts and formal devices to assist legislators in the process. A related concern with the number of different available fiscal documents is the opportunity they present to manipulate. The greater the number of "official" places to look for financial and budgetary information, the greater the opportunity for politicians or program advocates to pick the numbers they like best.

Congress also should examine the way scores are prepared for last-minute changes from floor amendments or from conference committee negotiations. Perhaps authority as the final arbiter on such scores should not rest entirely with budget committee chairs. Although it is hard to know the extent to which lobbyists or congressional staff apply pressure on CBO staff to revise scores for proposed legislation, some formal rules might be useful to allow sufficient communication between staffs yet insulate CBO staff from at least some of this pressure. At a minimum, these might include open meeting rules to give public observers an opportunity to monitor scoring meetings.

Human nature is such that where there are rules, there will be attempts to find loopholes. Those who understand and can manipulate rules wield enormous power. As Representative John Dingell (D-Mich.) is reputed to have said about the legislative process, "If you let me write the procedure, and I let you write the substance, I'll [beat] you every time."[37] This observation is especially pertinent to budget accounting and procedural rules, which many say are so complex that they are truly understood only by a handful of budget insiders. Given the high stakes involved, it is unrealistic to imagine that temptation and opportunity to use budget gimmicks can be entirely eliminated. In the long run, Congress needs to consider a substantial overhaul of the budget process as it did in the Tax Reform Act of 1986 with respect to the Tax Code. In the meantime, modest improvements and clarifications with regard to bookkeeping, scoring, and the reconciliation process would go a long way toward limiting or eliminating some of the most deliberately manipulative budget gimmicks.

---

[37] Walter J. Oleszek, CONGRESSIONAL PROCEDURES AND THE POLICY PROCESS 12 (5th ed. 2001).

Questions for Chapter 2

1. This chapter demonstrates that political motives sometimes tempt legislators to play budget tricks to bypass procedural rules otherwise designed to impose congressional fiscal discipline. One reaction to this reality is to pass additional rules that work to restrain the evasive behavior. Legislators then react to the new rules, additional anti-circumvention rules are passed, and so on. Where does it end? Review Chapter 1, "The Congressional Budget Process," by William Dauster. Can you identify rules that are now part of the congressional budget process that were designed to discourage certain kinds of circumvention of the previous rules? How successful are the attempts to discourage budget games? What are the broader consequences for electoral accountability of increasingly complex and arcane rules governing the process of budgeting? For transparency of fiscal policy? For lobbying activity? Are well-funded interest groups seeking federal benefits in the same position as ordinary citizens when it comes to these issues?

2. Some budget rules lead those seeking federal benefits to prefer one programmatic structure for the desired relief over another for no reason other than to comply with (or evade) budget procedures. For example, if spending caps limit discretionary spending but budget rules do not effectively constrain the ability of Congress to pass tax expenditures, groups will turn their attention away from appropriators and toward the tax-writing committees. Is it necessarily a negative result that more subsidies may be enacted as tax expenditures than funded through discretionary spending?[38] What are the other consequences for fiscal policy and substantive policy of a budget framework that encourages

---

[38] For an interesting argument that it might be better for policies to go through the Senate Finance and House Ways and Means Committees as tax subsidies, and not as spending programs through the more specialized Appropriations Subcommittees, *see* Edward A. Zelinsky, *James Madison and Public Choice at Gucci Gulch: A Procedural Defense of Tax Expenditures and Tax Institutions*, 102 YALE L.J. 1165 (1993). *See also* Christopher Howard, *Testing the Tools Approach: Tax Expenditures Versus Direct Expenditures*, 55 PUB. ADMIN. REV. 439 (1995).

Congress to use tax subsidies and entitlement programs rather than traditional spending programs funded through annual appropriations?

3. Rules that apply only within certain budget windows may encourage particular kinds of behavior. For example, two different versions of a tax subsidy can provide the same present value to taxpayers but over very different time frames. Investment can be encouraged through expensing, which produces revenue loss in the first year of the investment expense, or through a back-loaded subsidy in the form of generous depreciation, which spreads the revenue loss over a longer time. If both forms of the subsidy are equivalent in present value terms, why do beneficiaries care about the form? Will they just use whichever format can survive the budget process more easily? Do taxpayers really believe they will receive all the benefit of a back-loaded subsidy? Do lawmakers believe they will get credit for such a provision, where the benefit has yet to be fully enjoyed by the next election? For another example, consider the Byrd Rule, arguably the only reason most major provisions of the tax bills passed during George W. Bush's presidency contained sunset clauses. What are the tax-policy consequences of these expiring provisions? Does uncertainty that the provisions will be reenacted undermine the ability of subsidies to produce the changes in taxpayer behavior they are designed to incentivize? Are expiring tax provisions subject to greater scrutiny when they are reenacted? What are the deadweight costs to society of the need to periodically renew expiring tax provisions? Some scholars have argued that lawmakers benefit from the Byrd Rule because it allows them to threaten interest groups that their tax subsidies will lapse unless they contribute campaign money and other valuable benefits to members of Congress.[39] In what other ways is the lobbying game changed by the budget rules?

4. One of the games that political actors play is to "pick and choose" among different revenue estimates. As Block points out, budget frameworks must rely on numbers of some sort, but projections of future revenues, expenditures, and economic trends are necessarily subject to some degree of uncertainty. How would you advise Congress to solve the problem of competing budget estimates? Can an effective budget framework use estimate ranges or take into consideration confidence factors? Should there be a "lookback" mechanism to force cuts in spending or increases in taxes if projections turn out to be wrong? If Congress moved to accrual accounting and away from cash-flow calculations, as Block recommends in some parts of the budget, what sort

[39] *See* Edward J. McCaffery and Linda R. Cohen, *Shakedown at Gucci Gulch: The New Logic of Collective Action*, 84 N.C. L. Rev. 1159 (2006) (analyzing the estate-tax provision in particular as an example of "rent extraction" by lawmakers); Fred S. McChesney, Money for Nothing: Politicians, Rent Extraction, and Political Extortion (1997) (making the rent extraction argument in the context of tax legislation in the 1980s and early 1990s).

of revenue-estimating games would then be possible? For example, accrual accounting makes the discount rate used to compute the present value of future benefits and liabilities tremendously important. Is it possible to find, or create, neutral expert entities to provide the numbers and do the accounting that then shapes the political process? Is that appropriate? Those in power sometimes use directed scoring to require that the CBO adopt OMB numbers rather than its own. OMB figures come from the executive branch and may not be entirely neutral. Are there ever circumstances in which directed scoring might be appropriate?

5. This chapter deals mainly with the numbers involved in estimating revenue loss and gain from budget decisions. Another set of numbers can have profound implications on budgeting, particularly on tax bills. Distributional tables provide information to lawmakers and others about the effect of changes in the tax laws on the tax burden shouldered by different income groups. These tables show the change in the current tax burden that would occur if a particular tax provision were enacted. For example, they may show that a tax increase falls mainly on upper-income Americans, or that a tax benefit will be enjoyed primarily by middle-income Americans. Alternatively, they might show that a tax reduction disproportionately benefits the very rich, without also reducing the tax burden on those with fewer economic resources. Not surprisingly, games are played with distributional tables, and the numbers used in them are subject to similar kinds of attacks as those deployed against revenue estimates.[40] No formal rules require that tax legislation be distributionally neutral or redistribute wealth from the upper quintiles to the lower quintiles. Nevertheless, distribution tables can be politically explosive. Are there any different concerns with respect to distributional analysis than with other kinds of revenue estimating? How should such tables be used in the tax context or in the larger budget context? What other kinds of numbers are likely to be important during the consideration of budget legislation, and what kinds of games can be played with those? Consider, for example, generational accounting.[41]

6. When faced with spending limits imposed by committee allocations or reconciliation instructions, legislators increasingly resort to funding activity through emergency, supplemental appropriations, which do not count for purposes of enforcing such limits. For several years, much of the expense for military operations in Iraq and Afghanistan has been funded through such emergency funding. Critics have complained that some of this spending for

---

[40] *See* Michael J. Graetz, *Distributional Tables, Tax Legislation, and the Illusion of Precision, in* Distributional Analysis of Tax Policy 15 (David F. Bradford ed., 1995).

[41] See Laurence J. Kotlikoff, Generational Accounting: Knowing Who Pays, and When, for What We Spend (1992).

ongoing military operations is not truly emergency spending and should be accounted for in the regular budget. How should the budget account for military operations that can be expected to continue for many years into the future? Some agencies, particularly the Department of Defense (DOD) can expect to receive substantial amounts from future supplemental appropriations. The DOD allegedly has been using some of these funds to backfill, or cover, earlier cuts in regular, annual defense spending. Under what circumstances might this type of backfilling be appropriate? Backfilling is possible because money is a fungible commodity. What tracing rules might be used to ensure that emergency appropriations are actually used to cover emergency, as opposed to nonemergency, activity? Is there a workable definition of "emergency" that would limit excessive use of supplemental appropriations?[42]

[42] *See* William G. Dauster, *Budget Emergencies*, 18 J. Legis. 249 (1992).

3 Transparency in the U.S. Budget Process

Elizabeth Garrett and Adrian Vermeule

The notion of "transparency" in government is very much in vogue both in the United States and worldwide, particularly in the arena of fiscal policy. The emphasis on openness is sensible because transparency serves crucial objectives in democracies. Transparency can promote public-spirited behavior by constraining bargaining based on self-interest and promoting principled deliberation instead. Even when self-interest is universal, providing information to principals about the actions of their agents – here, elected officials – reduces the costs of monitoring, thereby promising to improve governance in a representative democracy.

However, the word "transparency" often is used imprecisely to refer to a number of characteristics of an open system without much independent analysis of each aspect. Moreover, adherents of transparency are often insufficiently attentive to the costs of disclosure. Transparency can be in tension with other important democratic values and may even, in some cases, be self-defeating. The unconditional embrace of transparency lies in the power of the word itself – it connotes the opposite of secrecy and skullduggery, putting those who would argue for a tempering of openness in a difficult rhetorical position. This is unfortunate: It diminishes the willingness of

Elizabeth Garrett is the Sydney M. Irmas Professor of Public Interest Law, Legal Ethics, Political Science, and Policy, Planning, and Development at the University of Southern California, and Co-Director of the USC-Caltech Center for the Study of Law and Politics. Adrian Vermeule is Professor of Law at Harvard Law School. The authors appreciate helpful comments from Scott Altman, Jacob Gersen, Jeff Kupfer, Andrei Marmor, Mathew McCubbins, William Murphy, Jürgen von Hagen, David Weisbach, and participants at the conference on Fiscal Challenges at the University of Southern California Law School, and the excellent research assistance of Andrew Gloger (USC '07) and Meegan I. Maczek (USC '08). Some of the arguments made here flow from Professor Garrett's experience serving on the Bipartisan Tax Reform Panel, a federal advisory committee appointed by President Bush in 2005; these views are her own and not necessarily shared by any other panel members or staff.

many who study transparency to forthrightly consider the costs as well as the benefits.[1]

In this chapter, we propose to focus on one aspect of transparency in the federal budget process: requirements that deliberation and bargaining over budget policy occur publicly. There are several distinct arenas of budget policymaking; currently, each displays a slightly different mix of opacity and transparency. The arenas include decision making purely within the executive branch; policy recommendations by federal advisory committees; the legislative process, including committee consideration, floor deliberation, and conference committee decisions; and interbranch decision making in occasional budget summits. In each arena, there is a mixture of openness and secrecy; political players find private space for some deliberation, even in the face of aggressive open-meeting requirements, by taking advantage of gaps in any rules or statutes.

Is the current mix optimal, or at least the best that can be achieved given political constraints? Even without legal requirements for transparency, there would be a certain amount of openness in decision making because some publicity is in the agent-lawmakers' interest.[2] However, there is no reason to believe that the degree of transparency reached by political actors on their own would necessarily be optimal from society's point of view. Self-interested agents also have incentives to keep secret some aspects of budgeting that their principals would be eager to monitor – namely, the use of budgets to provide benefits to well-funded and well-organized special interests that will reward lawmakers with campaign funds.[3] It is hardly obvious that the status quo, where some deliberation occurs in secrecy notwithstanding open-meeting

---

[1] *See* James T. O'Reilly, *"Access to Records" Versus "Access to Evil": Should Disclosure Laws Consider Motives as a Barrier to Records Release?*, 12 KAN. J.L. & PUB. POL'Y 559, 559–560 (2003) (discussing emphasis on ever-increasing transparency in laws regulating government). For recent exceptions to this tendency, *see* Cary Coglianese, Richard Zeckhauser, and Edward Parson, *Seeking Truth for Power: Informational Strategy and Regulatory Policymaking*, 89 MINN. L. REV. 277 (2004) (assessing costs and benefits of disclosure in the federal regulatory context); Ellen E. Meade and David Stasavage, *Publicity of Debate and the Incentive to Dissent: Evidence from the U.S. Federal Reserve* (June 21, 2005) (unpublished paper), available at http://www.nyu.edu/gsas/dept/politics/faculty/stasavage/feddeliberation11.pdf (finding delayed disclosure, adopted in 1993, chilled dissent, and changed deliberations in the Federal Open Market Committee).

[2] *See* John Ferejohn, *Accountability and Authority: Toward a Theory of Political Accountability*, *in* DEMOCRACY, ACCOUNTABILITY AND REPRESENTATION 131 (Adam Przeworski, Susan C. Stokes, and Bernard Manin eds., 1999). Note, however, that the only test of this model reaches inconclusive results. *See* James E. Alt, *Three Simple Tests of Ferejohn's Model: Transparency and Accountability in U.S. States* (2005) (paper prepared for NYU Colloquium on Law, Economics, and Politics).

[3] *See* Alberto Alesina and Roberto Perotti, *Fiscal Discipline and the Budget Process*, 86 AM. ECON. REV. 401, 403 (1996) (noting that "politicians do not have an incentive to adopt the most transparent practices" because they want to maintain their informational advantage). Ferejohn's work suggesting that legislative agents have incentives toward some amount of

requirements, maximizes the benefits of transparency while minimizing its costs.

Our principal aim is to propose an optimal transparency scheme for the federal budget process; however, we also consider institutional and political constraints on attaining that scheme. Although focused on federal entities, our analysis can be applied to analogous state and local budget decision making as well. Section I provides a brief overview of transparency in the federal budget process, as it is currently structured. We then offer a two-stage analysis. In Section II, we address the optimal or first-best structure of transparency in the budget process, as though that structure could be imposed by an impartial designer of political institutions. We identify crucial trade-offs that determine the costs and benefits of transparency. One trade-off is that secrecy promotes good deliberation, while transparency deters self-interested bargaining. A second trade-off is that transparency ensures both accountability to voters, which is good, and also accountability to efficiency-reducing interest groups, which is bad. In light of these trade-offs, we sketch an optimal transparency structure for budgeting, a structure with two crucial features. First, the early stages of the budget process, including the formulation of a concurrent budget resolution by budget committees, will be secret or opaque, while the later stages will be transparent. Here the dual aim is to encourage good deliberation where that is possible and to hamper self-interested bargaining where that is likely. Second, even for later stages of the budget process, disclosure will be delayed, perhaps until well into the election cycle. Here the aims are, first, to deny interest groups immediate access to the details of ongoing decision making; and, second, to sort good from bad accountability by giving voters information when they need it while denying information to interest groups when they want it. In Section III, we consider institutional and political constraints that might rule out the optimal structure. We conclude that it is an open question whether the optimal structure is attainable, given reasonable assumptions about legislators' motivations and relevant constraints; there is no knockdown reason to think the structure we propose is unattainable or infeasible.

I. TRANSPARENCY IN THE FEDERAL BUDGET PROCESS

This section defines some terms and broadly describes the current mix of transparency and opacity in the federal budget process.

transparency to allow audit of their activities by principals does not suggest that these incentives will produce the optimal mix of transparency and opacity, but that "the agent has an interest in offsetting the effects of some of those [informational] asymmetries." Ferejohn, *supra* note 2, at 149.

A. Two Senses of "Transparency"

We focus on the transparency of the budget process, but this is only one sense of "transparency." The literature typically addresses both the transparency of the process, or of the inputs into the budget, and the transparency of the output itself, or of the budget documents produced by government officials. Although we will not directly assess transparency or intelligibility at the output stage, the two aspects of transparency are related. The more transparent the output, the more likely it is that outsiders can reason backwards to develop a sense of the inputs, without actually witnessing the process as it occurs.

In the fiscal arena, however, the process of using the output to discover the inputs can be challenging. Budgets are complex, so it can be difficult to separate all the strands and exceedingly difficult to trace decisions back to particular actors and particular motivations. Moreover, certain outputs can be the product of various inputs – some public-regarding, others the result of the influence of private-regarding behavior by interest groups. Even if the outcome is socially desirable, it may still be important in a democracy to understand whether it is the result of particular interest-group pressure brought to bear on key legislators. Finally, if the process is open, outsiders can more easily provide helpful information as deliberations occur and serve as "fire alarms"[4] to alert lawmakers and others to troubling provisions in a proposal that might be overlooked. Thus, we discuss the appropriate degree of transparency that should be accorded to budget deliberations in the context of a system where there is a substantial degree of transparency regarding the output, but where there are nonetheless reasons to be concerned about the openness of the decision-making process.

B. Transparency in the Budget Process: Current Rules

There are degrees of openness in the federal budget process, varying across different arenas of decision making. Generally, the process is an open one, particularly when it reaches Congress. In all stages of the process, however, players can find ways to bargain in private through informal interactions or negotiations with a subgroup of relevant decision makers that result in a deal later made public. This section will not present a comprehensive or detailed description of the rules and laws that shape federal budget transparency; we hope only to give a sense of the different mixes of opacity and transparency to provide a background for our subsequent analysis.

---

[4] *Cf.* Mathew D. McCubbins and Thomas Schwartz, *Congressional Oversight Overlooked: Police Patrol Versus Fire Alarms*, 28 Am. J. Pol. Sci. 165 (1984) (describing how interest groups can aid lawmakers in oversight of agencies by serving as fire alarms).

Some of the least transparent stages of the budget process are those that occur entirely within the executive branch. Most opaque are policy discussions that take place wholly within the executive branch among administrators, who are protected by the deliberative process component of executive privilege. Although this protection from disclosure is not absolute, the White House avidly guards the privacy of such policy deliberation. In 2001, for example, the deputy director of the Office of Management and Budget (OMB) reminded all agency and department heads of "the importance of continuing to preserve the confidentiality of the deliberations that led to the president's budget decisions."[5] This memorandum aims to protect from disclosure the documents developed before the president's budget has been formally presented to Congress, and it explicitly mentions keeping confidential the budget requests sent to an agency from its component parts, the agency's requests to the OMB, and the OMB's responses to the agency.

The protection of executive privilege becomes murky when the executive branch consults with people outside the administration for expertise and advice in formulating policy. When people other than executive branch officials play an important role in the formulation of policy, executive privilege may cease to apply and the interactions may become subject to the Federal Advisory Committee Act (FACA).[6] FACA is one of many "sunshine in government" acts passed in the 1970s and includes broad provisions requiring open meetings and public availability of documents.[7]

Once the budget reaches Congress, it is shaped by internal rules in the House and Senate, which generally require that committee hearings, including markups, and other meetings to transact legislative business be conducted in open session. Although the rules allow meetings to be closed, they limit executive sessions to circumstances where disclosure would "endanger national security, would compromise sensitive law enforcement information, [or] would tend to defame, degrade, or incriminate any person."[8] As with all internal rules, these are enforced internally; lawmakers can raise points of order and other objections if they believe a meeting has been closed contrary to the rules. All the relevant committees in the budget process – appropriations, budget, and tax-writing committees – operate under similar open-meeting requirements. Thus, meetings where testimony is taken or business is conducted can be closed only

---

[5] Office of Management and Budget, Memorandum M-01–17, Memorandum for Heads of Executive Departments and Agencies, Confidentiality of Pre-Decisional Budget Information (Apr. 25, 2001), *available at* http://www.whitehouse.gov/omb/memoranda/m01-17.html.

[6] 5 U.S.C. App. 2. (2006).

[7] *See* Jay S. Bybee, *Advising the President: Separation of Powers and the Federal Advisory Committee Act*, 104 YALE L.J. 51, 73–76 (1994) (describing legislative history, noting discussion focused on need to open proceedings to public).

[8] House Rule XI, cl. 2(g)(1). *See also* Senate Rule XXVI, para. 5(b) (providing similar reasons for executive session with some additional justifications such as relating "solely to matters of committee staff personnel or internal staff management").

in limited circumstances, such as committee meetings concerning the budget of intelligence agencies where discussions implicate national security. In particular, committee markups and votes on legislation relating to the budget must occur in public. In the post-reform Congress, more of the work of committees has been done in public, and committee hearings and markups are broadly publicized through television and other press coverage.

Notwithstanding open-meeting rules in Congress, a great deal of the bargaining related to the federal budget occurs in private. Congressional parties discuss broad policy issues in party caucuses that are not subject to open-meeting requirements. Increasingly, party leaders have used task forces made up of selected lawmakers – sometimes only from the majority party – to formulate legislative proposals, some of which may be incorporated into budget reconciliation bills.[9] Once the proposal goes to a committee or the full body, the meetings to debate and amend it are open to the public, but the preliminary work of the task force occurs largely in private and may crucially shape the ultimate product. Even during committee deliberations and conference committee negotiations, discussions occur between the committee leadership and individual members, among co-partisans on the committee, between staff of members and the committee, or in other groups of lawmakers and staff that are not considered official "meetings" or "hearings" subject to the transparency provisions of the internal rules. Although required by House and Senate rules to conduct their business in open meetings, conference committees routinely hold key gatherings behind closed doors, sometimes only among members of the majority party in both houses or, more frequently, just their leaders who negotiate deals in private before the overall bargain is presented to the whole committee in a pro forma public meeting.[10]

Budget deliberations on the floor of the House and Senate are public and televised. It is highly unusual for either house to go into a closed session, and consideration of the various budget vehicles – the concurrent budget resolution, appropriations bills, budget reconciliation acts, and the various conference reports – are not likely to trigger an executive session. Again, although the deliberations, amendments, and votes are public, and constitutionally required to be memorialized in a journal of proceedings,[11] many of the key deals are made

---

[9] For a discussion of the use of task forces, *see* Elizabeth Garrett, *Attention to Context in Statutory Interpretation: Applying the Lessons of Dynamic Statutory Interpretation to Omnibus Legislation,* *in* ISSUES IN LEGAL SCHOLARSHIP 9 (Robert Cooter, Daniel Farber, Philip Frickey, and James Gordley eds., 2002), *available at* http://www.bepress.com/ils/iss3/art1.

[10] *See, e.g.*, Lewis Deschler, DESCHLER'S PRECEDENTS OF THE UNITED STATES HOUSE OF REPRESENTATIVES, V. 16, H.R. Doc. No. 94–661, ch. 33 (1976). It was not until the 94th Congress that the House and Senate adopted rules requiring that conference committee meetings be held in open session. *Ibid.* at § 5.2. However, all that is required for a valid conference is a quorum on the signature sheet of the conference report and a public meeting of the conferees. *Id.* at § 5.8. The result is that a great deal of preliminary deliberations can be held behind closed doors.

[11] U.S. Const., art. I, § 5, cl. 3.

in the cloakrooms or members' Capitol hideaways and not made public except as they can be discerned from the provisions of the law ultimately enacted and any public claims of responsibility from the lawmakers involved.

Because the open-meeting requirements affecting congressional committees are contained in internal rules of the bodies or of the committees themselves, enforcement is a purely internal matter. As long as the members are content with the mix of transparency and opacity in the congressional budget process, no outside watchdog can challenge either the decision to hold some meetings behind closed doors or the validity of the legislation that emerges from the process on the basis that transparency rules were violated.

The force of the congressional rules is not clear for several reasons. First, legislative rules requiring transparency are often partially evaded by members who need to negotiate in private. They take advantage of gaps in the rules' coverage to discuss important issues informally behind closed doors. However, requiring transparency in formal rules is a signal to the public of lawmakers' commitment to openness and may increase the political cost of defecting from the rules if intermediaries like the press or challengers successfully make secret deliberations an issue for voters. Second, lawmakers might carry out a great deal of their work in public even without rules requiring them to do so. Ferejohn suggests that elected officials have an incentive to conduct a significant portion of their activities in public as a way to signal to their principals – the voters – that they are trustworthy. By adopting transparent practices, lawmakers offer voters better tools to monitor their responsiveness; voters are therefore more willing to trust officials with control over more resources.[12] However, empirical tests of this suggestion have not been conclusive, in either direction.[13]

One final stage in the budget process has an entirely different transparency profile. In some years, the legislative and executive branches clash over budget policy, and interbranch negotiations are required to pass the appropriations and reconciliation bills necessary to implement budget objectives and to keep the federal government operating. An informal device – the budget summit – has been used on several occasions when interbranch compromise was difficult but necessary. Because summits are not formal entities with rules governing their conduct and because the only people involved are elected officials from Congress and executive branch officials from the White House and departments, open-meeting rules do not apply. When a summit occurs, this final stage of deliberations concerning the federal budget is entirely opaque.

Given all this, the difficult question is whether the equilibrium with respect to openness that has been reached in the federal budget process – whether by explicit rule or by practice – is optimal. In the remainder of the chapter, we will

---

[12] *See* Ferejohn, *supra* note 2.   [13] *See supra* note 2.

assess two dimensions along which the degree of transparency can be evaluated. First, it can be measured according to what sort of discussion and deliberation it tends to encourage, namely, how transparency affects the mix of arguing and bargaining, and which type of deliberation is most suited to making decisions about the various aspects of budgeting. Second, we will assess how transparency may increase the power of interest groups to monitor and punish lawmakers, rather than empower voters to hold legislators accountable on Election Day, and whether different structures of disclosure could more effectively benefit voters without similarly benefiting organized special interests.

II. OPTIMAL TRANSPARENCY

We will first identify the key trade-offs that determine the costs and benefits of transparency across different arenas of the budget process. We then propose a framework of budget-process transparency that is plausibly optimal and might be imposed by a benevolent institutional designer. Later in Section III, we identify some institutional constraints and motivational problems that threaten to make this optimum unattainable.

A. Two Trade-offs

In any arena, the mix of transparency and opacity has two principal effects. One effect is that transparency can alter, at least marginally, the extent to which relevant actors engage in principled argumentation, on the one hand, or overt bargaining, on the other hand.[14] Both arguing and bargaining are indispensable processes for aggregating judgments or preferences into collective decisions, so optimal structures will combine both in some mix. Another effect is that transparency promotes accountability. The crucial question, however, is accountability to whom? Accountability can be good, when it runs from agents to principals, such as voters or constituents generally; it also can be bad, when it runs from agents to third parties, such as transfer-seeking groups. We take up these points in turn and then sketch an optimal transparency structure for federal budgeting.

As a preliminary note, in the following discussion we will bracket and ignore the distinction between two familiar accounts of what it means for legislators to offer public-spirited representation. On one account, legislators act as trustees to promote the general interest of the polity as a whole; on another, legislators act as delegates who are charged with promoting the interests only of their constituency, usually defined along geographic lines. The difference between

---

[14] This distinction is drawn from Jon Elster, *Arguing and Bargaining in Two Constituent Assemblies*, 2 U. PENN. J. CONSTL. LAW 345, 405–415 (2000).

these accounts, while important, is immaterial to our discussion. Instead we contrast both these accounts, on the one hand, with legislative capture by organized interest groups, on the other. By "capture" we mean systematic legislative behavior that exclusively promotes the interests of narrowly defined groups (much smaller than even the smallest constituency); such groups seek transfers that, while beneficial to themselves, inflict larger harms on disorganized constituents and society generally. That sort of representation is objectionable on either the trustee account of representation or the delegate account, so we need not engage the deeper issues here.

Our picture does assume that not all interest-group activity is good from the social point of view; to that extent, we reject the most optimistic versions of pluralist theory. Whatever the general case, this assumption should not be very controversial in the budget setting, where socially harmful transfers and wasteful competition to obtain such transfers are hardly unprecedented. Indeed, one reason for our focus on budgeting is our view that it is an arena particularly affected by interest-group activity that lowers the overall welfare of society in order to transfer benefits to an organized few. Of course, some interest-group activity is also socially beneficial, as when organized groups monitor each other, offset each other's influence, or supply voters and constituents with useful information. Nothing in these points is inconsistent with our proposals, as we subsequently discuss.

i. Arguing and Bargaining

Arguing, let us say, is deliberation (whether or not sincere in some subjective sense) that is pragmatically constrained to rest on impartial and internally consistent reasons.[15] The stuff of bargaining, by contrast, consists of credible threats and promises, usually, though not inevitably, in the service of the self-interest of the bargainers. Transparency dampens overtly self-interested bargaining and pushes officials in the direction of principled argumentation. In the glare of transparency, people tend to offer neutral principles related to the public good, not bargains based solely on private interests.

This marginal effect can either be good or bad, depending on the setting. Bargains may represent corrupt deals by which agents enrich themselves at principals' expense, but bargains also permit logrolls that may allow the legislative process to register the intensity of constituents' preferences,[16] and that

---

[15] See id. at 372–373.

[16] Logrolling may, of course, either permit socially beneficial trades or inflict socially harmful externalities on nontraders, depending on the details of the situation. "Today, no consensus exists in the normative public choice literature as to whether logrolling is on net welfare enhancing or welfare reducing, that is, whether logrolling constitutes a positive- or a negative-sum game." Thomas Stratmann, Logrolling, in PERSPECTIVES ON PUBLIC CHOICE: A HANDBOOK 322, 322 (Dennis C. Mueller ed., 1997).

help to appease policy losers by giving everyone something. Argument by reference to neutral principles, by contrast, often pushes policy toward the extremes, resulting in total victory or total defeat. Transparency also subjects public deliberation to reputational constraints: Officials will stick to initial positions, once announced, for fear of appearing to vacillate or capitulate, and this effect can make deliberation more polarized and more partisan. The framers closed the Philadelphia convention to outsiders precisely to prevent initial positions from hardening prematurely.[17] Finally, transparency may simply drive decision making underground, creating "deliberations" that are sham rituals while the real bargaining is conducted in less accessible and less formal venues, off the legislative floor.

   Although the relevant questions and answers relating to deliberative transparency vary from setting to setting, it is possible to offer a general guide to the relative costs and benefits of arguing and bargaining across contexts. The principal benefit of transparency is to dampen self-interested bargaining – including in this category bargaining by legislators who act as tightly constrained agents for self-interested private groups, a topic we take up shortly. The principal cost of transparency is that the glare of the public spotlight can produce bad deliberation that is not conducive to necessary compromise – deliberation infected by posturing and ideological polarization. This suggests a rule of thumb: *In general, the less information legislators have about how decisions will affect their interests, the less self-interested bargaining is possible in any event; the deliberative distortions produced by transparency are then all cost for no benefit.* On this logic, to the extent that legislators must necessarily act behind a partial "veil of uncertainty,"[18] opacity is better, all else equal, whereas transparency is better in settings where legislators have thick information about the effect of particular decisions on their interests.[19] As we will subsequently suggest, this suggests that earlier stages in the budget process should be more opaque than later stages, because earlier stages occur behind a partial veil of uncertainty.

ii. Accountability: Good and Bad

One of the primary rationales for increased transparency in government is to reduce the monitoring costs borne by the principals – voters – to ensure

[17] For details and references, *see* Adrian Vermeule, *The Constitutional Law of Congressional Procedure*, 71 U. Chi. L. Rev. 361, 372 n. 30 (2004).

[18] *See* Geoffrey Brennan and James M. Buchanan, The Reason of Rules 28–31 (1985); James M. Buchanan and Gordon Tullock, The Calculus of Consent 77–80 (1962). The source of the idea, although not of the phrase, is John C. Harsanyi, *Cardinal Utility in Welfare Economics and in the Theory of Risk Taking*, 61 J. Pol. Econ. 434, 434–435 (1953).

[19] *Cf.* Jon Elster, *Legislatures as Constituent Assemblies, in* The Least Examined Branch: The Role of Legislatures in the Constitutional State 189-191 (Richard W. Bauman and Tsvi Kahana eds., 2006).

that their agents – lawmakers – pursue their objectives. The principal–agent relationship does not fully describe the relationship between voters and elected officials, nor is it the only motive for transparency, but it captures a great deal of the interaction and provides a framework for analysis. We already have noted that the framework explains why, even in the absence of open-meeting requirements, one would expect to observe some level of transparency in democratic governments as lawmakers seek to increase voter confidence, thereby causing voters to allocate more resources to lawmakers' control.

Many who advocate strong transparency thus appeal to explicit or implicit principal–agent models. They argue that transparency will increase the ability of voters to hold elected officials accountable for their decisions because monitoring costs are reduced. Knowing that their behavior is observable, agents act differently, and principal–agent slack is reduced. Corrupt deals – meaning self-interested deals among agents, or between agents and third parties – will be deterred or chilled. All this assumes that legislators respond to electoral incentives, but even if one imagines legislators as good types or bad types in some fixed and exogenous sense, one might still defend transparency by reference to selection effects.[20] Putative candidates who value public office merely to further their self-interest might decide that a relatively transparent environment is not conducive to achieving their goals; thus, if transparency works as intended, only more trustworthy agents will seek elected office.

However, there is an intrinsic cost to transparency, even from an agency perspective, and even subject to the point that not all bargaining is bad. Transparency produces not only good accountability that promotes informed democratic participation and voting, but also bad accountability that promotes capture, in the sense already described. Once decision making is open to public view, it is not only voters in the lawmaker's district or state who observe the behavior; sophisticated and organized interest groups seeking inefficient transfers, and their lobbyists, can also monitor legislative behavior that occurs in transparent institutions.[21] Although some interest groups might prefer the secrecy of closed meetings, open sessions provide them a direct way of monitoring whether lawmakers keep their promises and how hard lawmakers work to deliver benefits or to protect the groups from harm.[22] Organized interests seeking transfers can weigh in while the legislation is being written. Indeed,

---

[20] *See generally* Timothy Besley, *Political Selection*, 19 J. Econ. Persp. 43 (2005); Adrian Vermeule, *Selection Effects in Constitutional Law*, 91 Va. L. Rev. 953 (2005).

[21] For other discussions of this cost to transparency, *see* Joseph E. Stiglitz, *On Liberty, the Right to Know, and Public Discourse: The Role of Transparency in Public Life*, Oxford Amnesty Lecture 22 (Jan. 27, 1999), *available at* http://www2.gsb.columbia.edu/faculty/jstiglitz/download/2001_On_Liberty_the_Right_to_Know_and_Public.pdf; Cass R. Sunstein, *Government Control of Information*, 74 Cal. L. Rev. 889, 896 (1986).

[22] For work suggesting that interest groups use their campaign contributions to obtain greater energy and attention on their issues from politicians, *see* David P. Baron, *Service-Induced Campaign Contributions and the Electoral Equilibrium*, 104 Q.J. Econ. 45 (1989); Richard L.

in a world of wireless, instant communication, lobbyists not only provide legislative language and expertise before markups, but they also e-mail input to staff via Blackberries while the meetings are occurring, ensuring that lawmakers hear their views at crucial moments and that they are aware that they are being watched closely. In a world of closed meetings, interest groups must rely on second-hand accounts and often cannot be sure what negotiations occurred. Furthermore, because most interest-group bargains in the budget context are not obviously corrupt, and many are low-salience bargains that voters will overlook even if they are made openly, the threat of disclosure may not appreciably reduce the level of private-regarding behavior. Thus, transparency may empower interest groups and lobbyists in one realm without substantially harming them in another.

Contrast this with the situation of the ordinary voter. Although she now can more easily monitor legislator behavior because of open-meeting requirements, she faces a significant collective action problem if she chooses to closely watch committee hearings. She bears all the costs of monitoring, yet there is little she can do on her own to punish a wayward representative. If she succeeds in changing legislative behavior through timely input or other intervention, all voters in her circumstances benefit without helping defray any of monitoring costs. The chance that she will succeed in changing legislative outcomes is low: She lacks the ability to provide the same level of input in real time that interest groups and lobbyists can. There are intermediaries like the press and challengers who can use transparency to monitor lawmakers on behalf of voters and bring egregious examples to their attention near Election Day. But lawmakers know it is not certain that voters will pay attention to press stories, and ordinary citizens are not organized to mount effective action even if they do notice the news. Certainly, lawmakers will be concerned that particular kinds of behavior will affect voters' decisions,[23] but most decisions made in a budgeting context are not sufficiently noteworthy to produce electoral consequences.

Our contrast between good and bad accountability, to voters and to interest groups, is deliberately overdrawn to clarify the issues. Of course, some interest groups are good, either because they supply pluralistic political competition that increases efficiency and overall accountability, or because they act as informational intermediaries. An example of the latter case involves good-government groups who use their access to supply voters with cues about the position of particular legislators, intelligible accounts of budgeting decisions, or other useful information. Other organized groups, protecting their own

---

Hall and Frank W. Wayman, *Buying Time: Moneyed Interests and the Mobilization of Bias in Congressional Committees*, 84 Am. Pol. Sci. Rev. 797 (1990).

[23] *See* R. Douglas Arnold, The Logic of Congressional Action 82–87 (1990). Empirical work suggests that voters do make electoral decisions based on budget policy. *See, e.g.,* Robert C. Lowry, James E. Alt, and Karen E. Ferree, *Fiscal Policy Outcomes and Electoral Accountability in American States*, 92 Am. Pol. Sci. Rev. 759 (1998).

interests, can serve as fire alarms to enhance monitoring during deliberations. But this is just one side of the coin.[24] By and large, the threat in the budget setting is that robust transparency will increase damaging special-interest transfers, by exposing decision makers to intensive scrutiny and threats of electoral retaliation. In the budget setting, the groups that benefit most from fishbowl transparency and immediate access to details of ongoing negotiations are tightly organized groups seeking transfers to particular economic interests, narrowly defined.

B. Two Proposals

In light of these trade-offs, we offer two proposals that would, if feasible and if implemented, improve the transparency framework of the federal budget process. Our guiding principles are (1) that opacity becomes more costly as the budget process proceeds and legislators gain more specific information about how decisions will affect their interests; and (2) that where disclosure does occur, it should be delayed if doing so will maximize the benefits of information to voters and constituents generally while minimizing information benefits to organized interest groups. Given these principles, we propose that decision making at the stage of overall budget allocation should be nonpublic, and that decision making at later stages should be made transparent, but only through delayed disclosure.

i. Closed Committee Sessions for Overall Allocation

Within Congress, the first basic stage of the budgetary process is the allocation of overall spending levels across budget categories or functions. The allocation is developed by the budget committees in both houses and then formalized through a concurrent budget resolution, which sets out a five-year budget plan. The concurrent budget resolution is the internal congressional vehicle that sets forth macro-budgetary objectives: It sets spending limits for discretionary programs; determines the amount of revenue that should be raised in taxes; reveals congressional priorities by dividing resources among various budget functions, which are the major categories of governmental activities; and provides for the debt limit. It does not require that any particular programmatic changes be made to achieve its broad goals, although the budget committees often include nonbinding recommendations for specific

---

[24] Party leaders seeking to enforce party discipline also might wish to monitor congressional committees. Our proposal does not eliminate the ability of congressional parties to learn of committee deliberations, even those we propose be kept entirely private, because they can place key party leaders on the committees with responsibility over the budget. Indeed, that is the practice now where powerful party leaders sit on tax-writing, budget, and appropriations committees.

changes or members add such suggestions on the floor. Filling in the details of the budget resolution is the province of the appropriations committees, the committees with jurisdiction over entitlement programs, and the tax-writing committees.

This concurrent resolution stage of the budget process is in some ways analogous to the process of constitution-making. It puts in place a framework within which bargaining can occur at subsequent stages; in effect, the resolution sets out constraints and then delegates authority to tax-writing committees, appropriations committees, and some other committees to make specific policy choices within those constraints, just as a constitutional convention sets out constraints within which later legislatures and agencies work. The constraints of the budget resolution are enforced through internal parliamentary devices such as points of order, some of which can be waived only with supermajority votes in the Senate.

The analogy is contestable; perhaps the real analogue to the constitution-making stage is the enactment of framework statutes such as the 1974 Budget Act.[25] The only point we need, however, is that the overall budget allocations are established behind a partial veil of uncertainty about how macro-level decisions will affect legislators' specific interests. At the stage of overall allocation, it is unclear what particular programs and appropriations will emerge from the later stages of the budget process, and hence unclear exactly how legislators' interests will be affected by large-scale choices. We do not mean to overstate the opacity of the veil; certainly, members think about the particular programs and tax provisions that will ultimately emerge from budget process when they make macro-budgetary decisions in the concurrent budget resolution.[26] However, the overall allocations are reminiscent of constitution-making because they make value choices at a relatively high level of abstraction, choosing overall priorities – more for guns or butter? – and then leave it to later periods to connect those priorities to particulars. Moreover, there is a separation of powers or responsibilities here: Large-scale allocative decisions and priority-setting are done by budget committees, whereas specific spending decisions at later stages are made by different committees with different memberships. This difference in control contributes to the uncertainty afflicting members at the earlier stage, thickening the veil.

At the overall allocation stage, then, legislators will be somewhat uncertain about how decisions affect their interests, which reduces the risk of self-interested bargaining. The remaining risk, however, is that transparency will induce bad deliberation, through posturing, premature hardening of positions,

---

[25] Pub. L. No. 93–344, 88 Stat. 297 (1974).

[26] *See* Elizabeth Garrett, *Rethinking the Structures of Decisionmaking in the Federal Budget Process*, 35 Harv. J. on Legis. 387, 409–415 (1998) (describing the interaction between allocations among budget functions and determinations of programmatic details).

and highly conflictual or principle-ridden debate. For the same reasons that closing off the federal constitutional convention was plausibly a successful decision – framers lacked sufficient information to pursue their own interests, while the lack of transparency produced better deliberation – so, too, it seems plausible that large-scale allocative choices might best be made behind closed doors. To be sure, the outputs of this opaque process eventually will be made public, when the concurrent resolution, accompanied by a report generally explaining its provisions, is enacted and the committees begin connecting allocations to particular programs, but the details of the deliberation and the actual votes in the budget committees producing the outputs need never be publicized, at least in principle. (Later we consider whether such a scheme is in fact feasible, given the incentives of relevant actors and the political and institutional constraints.)

Finally, at the allocation stage, there is a connection between the two senses of "transparency" identified in Section I. The budget resolution is a relatively intelligible document. It allocates money to general government functions, not to detailed programs or tax subsidies that are hard for outsiders to fully understand; a decision about how government trades off guns against butter is less detailed and less obscure than the decision about how to design the various programs to deliver the guns or butter. The relative intelligibility of the budget resolution strengthens the case for opacity during the committee deliberations that produce the resolution; any reduction in good accountability is less here than in other settings. Conversely, the budget resolution, because it proceeds at a high level of generality, tends to be the majority party's statement of its principles. This makes any public compromise particularly costly for the minority, which in turn encourages ideological posturing. Here opacity can lower the reputational and political stakes of disagreement, helping to avert bitter strife over principles and easing negotiations at later stages of the budget process.

At those later stages, the calculus changes. As legislators gain highly specific information about particular programs, as the veil of uncertainty shreds, there is increasing reason to fear that opacity will produce unchecked self-interested bargaining. Conversely, the principal cost of transparency – the poisoning of deliberation – diminishes in any event, just because there is less deliberation of any kind occurring. Bargaining over specifics comes to the fore, and transparency can help to chill or deter the most self-regarding bargains. The legislative work in the wake of the concurrent budget resolution is drafting appropriations bills to allocate money within the budget functions to various specific programs, writing revenue legislation with detailed tax subsidies, or constructing or revising actual entitlement programs. This is the prototypical arena of logrolling; the discussions in these committees tend to be less partisan and more pragmatic, at least for the vast majority of programs that are below most voters' radar screens. Organized interests seeking transfers are vitally concerned in all aspects of appropriation, entitlement, and revenue bills because they actually receive their benefits from this legislation. In contrast, the concurrent resolution merely defines the likely universe of resources available to fund the actual programs and tax subsidies.

How do these prescriptions match up with the current rules? Committee meetings considering appropriations bills, tax proposals, omnibus budget reconciliation acts, and entitlement programs are where much concrete bargaining takes place, and these hearings are generally subject to strong transparency requirements. This is as it should be given the logic we have set out. However, our logic suggests important changes in the framework shaping deliberation at other stages. First, committee deliberations at the macro-allocation stage culminating in a concurrent resolution should be opaque, contrary to current practice. Second, currently opaque budget summits, where the ultimate deals are struck when ordinary processes break down, should be subject to some transparency requirements, similar to those that we advocate for advisory committees but somewhat less far reaching than those we propose for congressional committees. Budget summits are entirely matters of logrolling and pragmatic compromise as the two branches, and sometimes the two parties, hammer out a bargain to keep the government running and avert a fiscal disaster. Quite obviously, political constraints may rule out either or both of these proposals, as we subsequently discuss.

Although we tentatively conclude that disclosure of certain stages of the budget process remains an important aspect of the budget framework and should be extended into realms currently closed, such as budget summits, we have not yet said anything about the timing of disclosure or what exactly should be disclosed. We turn next to that important aspect of transparency.

ii. Delayed Disclosure – in General

The trade-off between good and bad accountability arises from the existence of two audiences with frequently diverging objectives and with asymmetrical abilities to monitor lawmakers. Legislators know that the two audiences have vastly different capabilities to monitor and punish, so transparency operates to reduce principal–agent slack between organized interests and lawmakers more than it reduces slack between voters and their elected representatives. In principle, the solution would be to keep organized interests in the dark about legislative behavior while fully revealing it to voters. Although that solution is impossible – once information is provided to voters, it is provided to everyone – it may be possible, in some cases, to deprive transfer-seeking organized interests of the information while the deals are being struck and interest-group influence is most problematic, while at the same time ensuring that voters have access to information before they cast their ballots. Delayed disclosure is a tactic that may provide many, if not all, of the accountability benefits of transparency while mitigating its accountability costs.[27] A similar technique is used in some countries' open-records laws, which preserve confidentiality of some documents during official decision-making processes but allow broad dissemination at a later time to enable voters to learn about the inputs relevant to a decision once it has been announced.[28] It is also the technique used since 1993 by the Federal Open Market Committee (FOMC) of the Federal Reserve System. Minutes of FOMC meetings in which policy decisions are made are released three weeks after the meeting, and full transcripts from meetings held in one year are released after a delay of five years.[29]

The basic rationale for delayed disclosure here is to maximize the benefits of information to voters generally while minimizing the benefits of information to interest groups. This general aim in turn has two components. First, delayed disclosure prevents interest groups from bringing immediate pressure to bear on legislators and other policymakers while deliberations proceed. To be sure, legislators may anticipate punishment from interest groups who later learn that their demands have not been met. Under delayed disclosure, however, it is hard for interest groups to make effective real-time interventions. Delayed disclosure gives decision makers breathing space and room to maneuver.

Second, delayed disclosure can be structured to mitigate the ex ante threat of interest-group retaliation at election time. How can electorally relevant information be channeled to voters but not to interest groups? It is unclear whether this trick can in fact be accomplished, as we later emphasize; but it is possible that it can, because of the structure and timing of the modern political

---

[27] The idea of delayed disclosure – or, to put it differently, temporary secrecy – is not new. Others who write about fiscal transparency identify the timing of disclosure as a key variable in the success of open meetings in increasing accountability without disrupting deliberation that occurs best out of the public eye. See, e.g., David Heald, Fiscal Transparency: Concepts, Measurement and UK Practice, 81 Pub. Admin. 723, 746 (2003); Stiglitz, supra note 21, at 22. However, none has proposed a formal system of delayed transparency as a solution for the problem of dual audiences with divergent interests and different monitoring capabilities. In a related context, Coglianese, Zeckhauser, and Parson suggest keeping parts of agency rulemaking processes confidential for several years after the regulation is promulgated to encourage regulated entities to share information with government regulators. Coglianese, Zeckhauser, and Parson, supra note 1, at 339. This proposal responds to different concerns than those we identify here; the regulatory problem these authors identify is information asymmetry between the regulated and the regulators.

[28] See Maurice Frankel, Freedom of Information: Some International Characteristics 9 (2001) (paper from the Campaign for Freedom of Information) (discussing laws in Sweden, Portugal, and Finland); Andrea Prat, The Wrong Kind of Transparency, 95 Am. Econ. Rev. 862, 869–870 (2005) (discussing Sweden's open-records law and noting that more than 30 countries allow temporary secrecy for deliberations relevant to some decisions).

[29] See 12 C.F.R. § 281.1 (2006); Adoption of Procedure for Disclosing Policy Decisions by the Federal Open Market Committee, 81 Fed. Res. Bull. 265 n. 3 (Mar. 1995). See also Federal Open Market Committee v. Merrill, 443 U.S. 340 (1979) (holding FOMC was subject to FOIA); Merrill v. Federal Open Market Committee of the Federal Reserve, 516 F. Supp. 1028 (D.D.C.1981) (on remand, not requiring disclosure because it would harm government's monetary functions or commercial interests).

campaign. The key point is that *interest groups seeking to maximize their influence must act earlier in the election cycle than voters*, who can wait until Election Day to pass judgment on their agents. Interest groups must target campaign funds, advertising, and other resources at earlier stages of the electoral cycle; indeed, such resources are often most influential at the earliest stage, as parties are assessing the pool of potential candidates to decide which will become actual candidates, and as incumbents seek to discourage serious challengers. If interest groups must act before voters, then delayed disclosure can force interest groups to act in the dark while voters act with sufficient information.

To be sure, elections are a repeated game. Interest groups will be able to use the information disclosed before Election Day in one political cycle to allocate resources and enforce threats or promises in a later cycle. But the political discount rate – the rate at which politicians discount the future – will assure that an interest group's threat to punish the politician two elections hence will be less impressive than a threat tied to the next election. Delayed disclosure effectively lengthens the legislators' term of office, but only for groups enforcing bad accountability; such groups would plausibly prefer more frequent elections to maintain a tighter hold on legislators. For purposes of good accountability to voters, however, delayed disclosure does not effectively change the frequency of election; voters would still receive information in time to vote competently in the next succeeding election. Moreover, there is a positive rate of turnover even among federal legislators, for reasons unrelated to interest-group activity. The consequence is that in some fraction of cases, the legislator who angers the interest groups now will simply not be around to suffer punishment two elections hence. Legislators who know that they are in either their last or second-to-last term of office – and these tend to be highly senior and thus influential – cannot be affected by the threat. Overall, because elections are a repeated game, delayed disclosure cannot eliminate the ex ante threat of punishment by interest groups; but the political discount rate means that delayed disclosure can at least reduce the threat, thereby improving matters.

The devil is in the details, of course. The hard part is determining the right time to release the details of the budget negotiations. The delay should be long enough to reduce interest groups' ability to pressure lawmakers as they make decisions, but the information must be publicized early enough to influence electoral outcomes. This latter requirement means that the information must be available well before the actual elections because it will influence the decisions of other viable candidates, who must decide whether to challenge incumbents who participated in unsavory or questionable deals. The information, then, must be made public not only before the primary election, but also before the time candidates file to appear on the ballot. Disclosure also must occur early enough for challengers to begin to raise money necessary for successful campaigns. Such early disclosure also increases the power of interest groups because they can use the information to direct campaign resources to lawmakers who worked energetically on their behalf or to the opponents of those who reneged on deals. Disclosure after the period when interest groups' campaign contributions can make the most difference is the optimal time for publicity, but revealing information that late in the campaign also might reduce the ability of voters – and intermediaries like the press and challengers – to use the information appropriately. This is an optimization problem – the problem is to find the disclosure point that maximizes the difference between the benefits of information to voters and the benefits of information to efficiency-reducing interest groups.

The available information about costs and benefits is too crude to be sure where the exact optimum is located, but we suggest, as a reasonable guess, that disclosure should be delayed until a few weeks before the first primary elections for congressional seats. For many House seats, the primary is the only possible venue for competition, so continuing secrecy past this stage of the electoral cycle will deny voters a meaningful chance to act on the information. We emphasize that this date is only a guess – it may be too late in the electoral process to allow serious challengers to emerge, and it also may be too early, in that it would allow interest groups substantial influence in the campaign for the general election, although at least such groups will have reduced sway in the selection of the two major candidates.

Our proposal of delayed disclosure is speculative and offered to provoke creative thinking about how to structure transparency in government. We emphasize that our proposal might fail, for strictly factual reasons. It might turn out, in fact, that there just is no disclosure point that is both (1) sufficiently late so as to hamper the ability of interest groups to retaliate against legislators in the relevant election cycle, and also (2) sufficiently early as to give would-be challengers and informational intermediaries the material they need to inform voters. However, the current system, in which transfer-seeking interest groups get immediate information from budgeting committees, is an extreme or corner solution, one that is most unlikely to be the best possible arrangement, in light of all relevant costs and benefits. Quite plausibly some delay in disclosure would improve matters, both to give legislators breathing room and to hamper interest-group retaliation, although it is difficult to say in the abstract and with any precision how much delay would be best.

Finally, a clarifying point is in order. When we suggest that some deliberations be kept opaque and some be subject to delayed disclosure, we do not mean that the former will be kept secret permanently. In a long enough time frame, everything is disclosed, even presidential papers and highly classified documents. For our purposes, following the logic previously suggested, "delayed disclosure" just means disclosure that occurs after the deliberations, but sometime before the next election after the relevant budget is adopted; "opacity" means that the relevant deliberations are not disclosed in time for the next following election. The latter period of time might be very long indeed; when the FOMC adopted the five-year delay for disclosure meeting transcripts, some argued that the period was not long enough to ensure that deliberations were unaffected by the expectation of publicity, and that fear appears to be accurate. Meade and Stasavage find that FOMC deliberations after 1993 include fewer dissents and appear to consist more of "canned" statements, rather than the genuine discussion that occurred when participants believed their views would never be disclosed.[30]

iii. Delayed Disclosure – Congressional Committees

We now turn to problems of delayed disclosure in particular institutional arenas, within the larger budget process. A system of delayed disclosure might allow legislative bargaining in appropriations and tax-writing committees, within the framework of a concurrent budget resolution, to occur behind closed doors. Transcripts of deliberation would be kept, and any documents generated during the process would be retained for later release. If ongoing committee deliberations could be kept secret, then interest groups' ability to affect the details of spending and revenue decisions and to monitor lawmakers would be reduced. Permanent secrecy is not desirable, however, because it would insulate corrupt deals from publicity and eliminate the deterrent effect of disclosure. Thus transcripts, voting records, and other documents of committee deliberations would be fully disclosed after the budget was passed but before Election Day. Knowing that their discussions and deals will not be kept secret forever, lawmakers would have strong incentives to refrain from entering into bargains that could not withstand the sunlight of public disclosure. Moreover, because the output of the committee deliberations – the final mix of appropriations, entitlement spending, and taxes – would be public and floor deliberations would be open, obviously corrupt and questionable deals would likely be discovered and scrutinized as the budget was being developed. Thus, the fire-alarm monitoring provided as decision making occurs would not be eliminated, only somewhat reduced along with the less desirable aspects of interest-group involvement in budgeting.

If delayed disclosure were adopted in a budget framework law shaping committee deliberations, it should be accompanied by modifications in the Lobbying Disclosure Act (LDA)[31] to provide substantially better information about which representatives and senators are meeting with which lobbyists and on what topics. The concern is that temporary secrecy not only protects lawmakers from interest-group pressure that undermines the public interest, but it

---

[30] Meade and Stasavage, *supra* note 1, at 4–5. Although the FOMC did not disclose transcripts before 1993, it kept full transcripts beginning in 1976, so it is possible to measure the effect of delayed disclosure on deliberations.

[31] Pub. L. No. 104–65, 109 Stat. 691 (1995) [codified as amended in scattered sections of 2 U.S.C. (2000)].

also protects corruption. Efficiency-reducing bargains can be combated not only by the threat of ultimate disclosure of the details of deliberations but also by immediate disclosure of meetings that members of Congress hold with lobbyists. The public can reason from the fact of those meetings, and the amount of money spent to support them, about the likely influence exerted by an organized group on a key lawmaker at a pivotal time in the budget cycle. Currently, the LDA does not provide very specific information about which lawmaker a lobbyist meets with or about the precise subject matter of their discussions.[32] If the committee deliberations about budgeting that occur in the appropriations, tax-writing, and other committees are kept temporarily secret, as we suggest, then more aggressive disclosure of lobbying contacts would be required.

iv. Delayed Disclosure – Budget Summits

When they occur, budget summits typically involve a small group of people from the executive and legislative branches.[33] Deliberations that occur in summits are not open to the public, or even to other members of the legislature, although the ultimate deal is presented to Congress, typically in a conference report of an omnibus budget reconciliation act or an omnibus appropriations law, for an up or down vote. Thus, the output of this process is public, even if the inputs – from interest-group influence to political deals reached to provide a consensus document – are not. Often the product of a budget summit is not fully understood at the time it is presented to Congress because there is little time between the summit's proposal and the final vote, but the terms can be scrutinized by the press and opponents later to ensure accountability. Thus, delayed disclosure of some aspects of summit meetings promises to increase accountability relative to the status quo. We propose more limited disclosure of budget summit proceedings than of deliberations by congressional committees because the need to hammer out a compromise to solve a budget stalemate requires that participants be able to negotiate as freely as possible given the concerns of accountability. Thus, we propose an intermediate solution for budget summits that increases transparency relative to the status quo but not as far as we advocate for committees. The various drafts of the budget legislation as well as summaries of the meetings that identify the politicians behind particular changes but that do not include verbatim transcripts of the discussions would be disclosed, in the weeks following the summit, to provide better insight

---

[32] 2 U.S.C. § 1604(b)(2)(B). *See* Elizabeth Garrett, Ronald M. Levin, and Theodore Ruger, *Constitutional Issues Raised by the 1995 Lobbying Disclosure Act, in* THE LOBBYING MANUAL 143, 147 (William V. Luneberg and Thomas M. Susman eds., 3d ed. 2005).

[33] *See* Elizabeth Garrett, *The Congressional Budget Process: Strengthening the Party-in-Government*, 100 COLUM. L. REV. 702, 725 (2000).

into the deals reached while not unduly inhibiting the give-and-take process required to form a compromise.[34]

Furthermore, a system of delayed disclosure with respect to budget summits would prove superior to the more typical open-meeting rules that require immediate publicity of deliberations. One of the advantages of the current structure of budget summits is that political actors, working in private, can avoid fiscal train wrecks by reaching politically sensitive deals that may anger interest groups. When the deals are revealed, politicians can claim that they worked as hard as possible to further the objectives of groups affiliated with them, but they were forced to take the bitter with the sweet to craft a deal that is, all things considered, the best outcome. Because the product of summits is presented to Congress as a take-it-or-leave-it proposal, groups know that they have little ability to unravel the compromise once it emerges from the summit. In reality, participants in the summit often pragmatically retreat from extreme positions and work to craft a compromise that averts political and fiscal disaster. Although delayed disclosure may inhibit that dynamic somewhat – because politicians know they cannot escape accountability for their decisions after the drafts and meeting summaries are made public and their claims of working to protect certain interest groups' benefits may be undermined by the record of the discussions – temporary secrecy will still protect the interactions from immediate pressure and interference. Keeping the actual discussions secret also may allow politicians some cover from angry interest groups that will not be sure whether the politician compromised quickly or only after a hard-fought battle. As experience with the FOMC demonstrates, disclosure, whether simultaneous or delayed, inevitably affects the dynamics of negotiations. That is its purpose; the hard question is to get the balance of transparency and opacity right to allow compromise in an environment of accountability.

v. Delayed Disclosure – Advisory Committees

Another arena where rules of delayed disclosure should be adopted is decision making by federal advisory committees. These committees often consider

[34] This disclosure proposal has some similarity to the rules used by the European Central Bank (ECB), which holds a monthly press conference about its decisions but does not release detailed minutes or voting records of individual members. *See* Otmar Issing, *Communication, Transparency, Accountability: Monetary Policy in the Twenty-First Century*, FED. RES. BANK OF ST. LOUIS REV. 65, 72 (Mar./Apr. 2005); Manfred J.M. Neumann, *Transparency in Monetary Policy*, 4 ATLANTIC ECON. J. 353, 358 (2002) (contrasting FOMC and ECB practices). Similar rules of delayed disclosure should be considered for congressional task forces, particularly those that bring forward legislative proposals. These entities are different from budget summits, which are interbranch and often bipartisan, because they are often arms of the majority party and thus also may discuss party strategy that is appropriately kept confidential. But, to the extent that a task force is acting in the place of a congressional committee, then it should be subject to parallel rules of disclosure.

matters relevant to budgeting, from Social Security and entitlement reform to tax reform.[35] Federal advisory committees currently use techniques to allow them some opacity during decision making, notwithstanding provisions in the Federal Advisory Committee Act (FACA) that require relatively immediate disclosure of drafts and other documents to the public.[36] For example, President Bush's Advisory Panel on Federal Tax Reform that met during 2005 did not make public any drafts or other documents that were seen by four or fewer of the nine panel members, allowing five working groups of four members each to deliberate entirely behind closed doors. As long as these groups did not formally provide advice to the president, a federal officer, or an agency, they were not subject to FACA's transparency requirements. In reality, however, the real work of the panel occurred in private; the public meetings were used for taking testimony of witnesses selected by the panel and discussing reform themes that had been more fully debated and largely but not formally decided in the working groups.[37] It was not a coincidence that the tax panel's two reform options had virtually identical provisions affecting the individual tax code,[38] even though the two working groups responsible for the options had entirely different membership. By the time public deliberations occurred, key decisions had been at least informally reached and some of the most revealing disagreements had occurred in private.[39]

---

[35] Although our focus here is on advisory committees working in the budgeting arena, our recommendations apply to all federal advisory committees. In FY 2006, there were 927 active federal advisory committees. *See* Federal Advisory Committees Database at http://fido.gov/facadatabase/ (follow "Public Access" hyperlink; then select "Fiscal Year 2006"; then follow "Explore Data" hyperlink; then follow "GOV Totals" hyperlink).

[36] It seems clear that FACA was intended to subject all of an advisory committee's deliberations to public scrutiny as they occur. *See, e.g.,* H.R. Rep. No. 92–1017 (1972), *reprinted in* 1972 U.S.C.C.A.N. 3491, 3500 (stating that § 10(b) of the act, which requires that all records and files "which were made available to or prepared for or by each advisory committee" be made available to the public, "has the effect of assuring openness in the operations of advisory committees. This provision coupled with the requirement that complete and accurate minutes of committee meetings be kept serves to prevent the surreptitious use of advisory committees to further the interests of any special interest group. Along with the provisions for balanced representation . . . this requirement of openness is a strong safeguard of the public interest."). But the regulations interpreting the act have provided guidance to committees that seek to insulate some of their deliberations from public scrutiny. *See* 41 C.F.R. § 102–3.35(a); 41 C.F.R. § 102–3.160; 41 C.F.R. pt. 102–3, subpt. D, app. A; 66 Fed. Reg. 37728, 37729 (July 19, 2001).

[37] *See* Steven P. Croley and William F. Funk, *The Federal Advisory Committee Act and Good Government*, 14 YALE J. ON REG. 451, 488–490 (1997) (describing how subgroups generally evade disclosure requirements).

[38] President's Advisory Panel on Federal Tax Reform, SIMPLE, FAIR, AND PRO-GROWTH: PROPOSALS TO FIX AMERICA'S TAX SYSTEM 63–95 (2005).

[39] It is the case, however, that the working groups made no formal decisions about recommendations; rather, all such decisions were made by the full panel in open meetings or a public vote. *See* Letter (on file with authors) from Jeffrey Kupfer to Rob Wells, deputy bureau chief of Dow Jones Newswires (June 8, 2005) (noting that subgroups' work could be done in private because the panel would make all decisions about recommendations in open meetings).

This structure of private deliberations by subgroups and public deliberation by a full advisory committee is in some ways consistent with our recommendations for a mix of transparency and opacity. Confidential deliberations dampen posturing and partisanship and improve the quality of deliberations, because privacy allows advisory committees to consider reform alternatives and guidance that would elicit strongly negative interest-group reaction without interference from those groups. The problem with the current structure is that only subgroups of fewer than a majority of the full committee can discuss and deliberate in private, denying that environment to meetings of the full committee. This is an issue whether the advisory committee is made up of members working in their individual capacities to provide advice based on their independent judgment or whether they are appointed as representatives of a particular interest. In the latter case, immediate transparency of deliberations may make compromise even more difficult as representatives are unwilling to back away from their groups' positions in an environment that allows pressure to be applied as deliberations unfold. Again, we note that allowing some privacy for deliberations does not mean that disclosure never occurs; the option of delayed disclosure for advisory committees is one that could strike the right balance to elicit better advice and reduce the influence of organized special interests.

We therefore suggest several amendments to FACA to construct a formal system of delayed disclosure. First, the full panel should be allowed to deliberate in private, with the requirement that all these deliberations, as well as any by subgroups of the committee, be disclosed after the panel's report has been released. Votes and final decisions would have to occur in public or be revealed clearly in any report providing advice to the executive branch; the ultimate advice itself must be made public at the same time it is transmitted to the federal official or agency. Documents and working drafts generated by the full panel or subgroups should be automatically disclosed within some, relatively short time period after the release of the final report or, for committees that exist for several years, disclosure of documents should occur biennially.[40] Such a mandate for disclosure of drafts and other documents generated by subgroups would actually improve transparency because, as long as the subgroup does not directly advise the executive branch, those documents now never have to be made public.

Similarly, records of any private deliberations of working groups or the full panel should be maintained and disclosed after the advisory committee has been disbanded or regularly throughout the life of the committee. There is a cost to such delayed disclosure of the content of deliberations; although disclosure

---

[40] Federal advisory committees terminate after two years unless their duration is explicitly extended. In all cases, the committees must report publicly on their work every two years. *See* 41 C.F.R. § 102–3.75, subpt. B, app. A; 66 Fed. Reg. 37740 (July 19, 2001).

would provide better insight into the thought processes of panel members and the compromises reached, disclosure, albeit delayed, could inhibit robust discussion. We believe keeping a record of the discussion is warranted and would not chill deliberation severely; after all, off-the-record discussions are still possible in even less formal settings between individual members or with staff. Moreover, if panel members knew that disclosure would occur sometime in the future, they would be deterred from making arguments solely based on self-interest in the working group deliberations, and thus the overall discussions might be better suited to reach public-regarding outcomes. We do not believe that detailed transcripts of all meetings must be kept, so some spontaneous discussion would still occur, but summaries of the deliberations along the lines of those we envision for budget summits would be released after a period of time. Although members of federal advisory committees are not elected and therefore less accountable than many budget summiteers, they also do not determine the final policy but merely advise the government, which must then adopt the policy through congressional or agency action subject to extensive disclosure.

Second, all committee members, as well as staff, should disclose any contacts with lobbyists or interest groups so that the public has a sense of who has input into the process even if the substance of that input is not known during the advisory committee's deliberations. This disclosure should be relatively immediate, not delayed as would be the case for other disclosure. The LDA can serve as a model for this new requirement, but the recommendations just discussed with respect to Congress members to provide more specific information about lobbying contacts should be incorporated here as well. The LDA puts the burden of disclosure on lobbyists, not on committee members or staff, so the burden on people serving on federal advisory panels will not be substantial.

Third, we recommend that, with advisory committees, as well as with all the other budget institutions we have discussed, the rules concerning what must occur immediately in public and what can occur initially in private settings, with later disclosure, be clearly stated in a framework law. Each federal advisory committee no doubt reaches different kinds of accommodations concerning disclosure in relatively ad hoc ways, although specialized staff advise committees about the rules and precedents, and federal regulations adopted in 2001 set out some rules and examples concerning transparency. In our view, delayed disclosure is the optimal structure for decision making, but the decision to use temporary secrecy itself should be made openly,[41] and the rules should clearly provide the limits of secrecy and ensure that virtually all private deliberations of advisory committees be made public at some point.

---

[41] *See* Dennis F. Thompson, *Democratic Secrecy*, 114 Pol. Sci. Q. 181, 184–185 (1999) (arguing that any rules providing for temporary secrecy must be justified and the decision to allow such secrecy made through open and public decision making).

Adopting an explicit framework of delayed disclosure for much of the work of advisory committees, with final deliberations in public, is also justified because it will reduce the costs incurred currently as committees work to evade the current suboptimal rules. For example, the arrangements used by the Tax Reform Panel to circumvent FACA's open-meeting requirements hampered the panel's deliberations in tangible ways. Most significantly, private deliberation never occurred in a group of more than four of the nine members. Even with relatively balanced subgroups, that configuration denied the panel the input of all members on key issues until very late in the process, just weeks before release of the final report. It also enhances the power of staff relative to panel members because staff talk frequently with all members and attend all subgroup meetings. One panel member, who has been critical of FACA's disclosure provisions, suggests that the final report could have been more detailed had the full panel been able to deliberate privately;[42] certainly, more specific agreements on certain issues might have emerged had larger groups been able to interact. Let us underscore again that we are not recommending that advisory committees be allowed to keep their deliberations secret forever; only that more of their work should be closed to the public while it is occurring, with disclosure delayed only until after the release of the final report or other regular reporting.

III. SECOND-BEST PROBLEMS: MOTIVATIONS AND CONSTRAINTS

So far we have discussed the optimal framework for transparency in the budget process, on the deliberately counterfactual assumption that such a framework could be imposed and enforced by an impartial institutional designer. We now turn to a range of second-best problems. Such problems arise from two sources: institutional and political constraints on implementation, and the motivation of participants. In general, although such problems are real, it is unclear that the constraints are so tight as to rule out adoption of the optimal transparency framework.

A. The Supply of Optimal Rules

The first problem arises on what might be called the supply side. Even if the framework we have sketched is desirable, which actors, if any, will be motivated to adopt it? Our analysis presupposes that legislators are either self-interested

---

[42] *See* Heidi Glenn, *Frenzel Criticizes Sunshine Law Governing Tax Panel*, TAX NOTES 1126 (Nov. 28, 2005). Frenzel's remarks are not particularly consistent on this point: In this speech, he argued that more detail would have been possible with more secrecy, but he also contended that too much detail was included on the recommendations to revise the tax subsidy for interest on home mortgages. We do not agree with Frenzel's conclusion that the solution is to repeal the disclosure provisions. Chairman Connie Mack also has criticized FACA's open-meeting requirements. *See* Heidi Glenn, *Perspectives on Tax Reform From Connie Mack*, TAX NOTES 26 (Jan. 9, 2006).

or act, at least sometimes, as tightly constrained agents for interest groups and other self-interested actors. This is an instance of a general problem, called the "determinacy paradox" or "Bhagwati paradox."[43] Where the motives of relevant actors are endogenized as self-interested, and not assumed to be benevolent or public-spirited, there is little point in recommending reforms on public-regarding grounds. By hypothesis, public-spirited recommendations will fall on deaf ears.

Here two points are worth highlighting. First, it is valuable to identify (even approximately) the optimal structure of transparency rules. Absent that knowledge, reformers do not even know in which direction to push; in that case the question whether it is possible to attain ideal reforms does not even arise. Our primary aim here is to sketch desirable reforms, at the first-best level. Furthermore, our analysis should draw into serious question reformers' typical reaction to problems of accountability: increasingly aggressive disclosure rules aimed at immediate publicity. We suggest that a more nuanced approach is likely to yield better results, and that the option of delayed disclosure should at least be seriously considered.

Second, the supply-side problem is frequently overcome within Congress. Consider the range of framework statutes by which legislators act to dampen interest-group influence and to check their own (future) self-interested motivations. The Electoral Count Act of 1887[44] was intended to dampen partisanship and self-interest in the context of disputed presidential elections; the Base Realignment and Closure Acts,[45] first passed in 1988, reduced lawmakers' ability to protect military bases important to the economy of their district but not vital to the nation's defense; and aspects of the federal budget process make it more difficult for members of Congress to freely engage in distributive politics. One mechanism at work here is the veil of uncertainty. Legislators' uncertainty about how decisions will affect their interests not only helps to determine optimal transparency rules, as discussed in Section II, but also helps to ensure that the optimal transparency rules will be enacted. At any particular time, legislators can and do agree on framework statutes that improve future decision making for all concerned. In such cases agreement is possible because it is not clear, at the time of adoption, exactly whose interests will be benefited and whose hurt by the application of the framework rules in future periods.[46] There are important trade-offs, however; the uncertainty that produces impartiality can also reduce the proponents' short-run payoffs for creating the framework,

---

[43] *See* Brendan O'Flaherty and Jagdish Bhagwati, *Will Free Trade with Political Science Put Normative Economics Out of Work?*, 9 ECON. & POL. 207 (1996).

[44] 24 Stat. 373 (1887).

[45] For the first such act, *see* Defense Authorization Amendments and Base Closure and Realignment Act, Pub. L. No. 100–526, 102 Stat. 2623 (1988).

[46] *See* Elizabeth Garrett, *The Purposes of Framework Laws,* 14 J. CONTEMP. LEGAL ISS. 717, 736–741 (2005); Adrian Vermeule, *Veil of Ignorance Rules in Constitutional Law*, 111 YALE L.J. 399, 428–429 (2001).

and thus dilute the motivation to do so.[47] It is an open question whether these countervailing mechanisms might allow enactment of a framework statute implementing the transparency structure we propose.

This proposal – with opacity at some stages and delayed disclosure in others – might garner more sincere support from lawmakers than the current tendency toward immediate disclosure of all deliberation. It seems likely that at least some legislators have supported full disclosure only in response to constituent demands following scandals like Watergate, and they would be interested in our more nuanced proposal. Legislators might prefer to conduct some of their budget deliberations out of the public eye – or at least away from the immediate pressure of organized groups and their lobbyists. However, to the extent that our proposal will reduce the amount of campaign funds and other support provided to lawmakers from interest groups, they will prefer the status quo. Whether such a proposal could be sufficiently explained to constituents, given high current levels of distrust for elected representatives, is an open question.

B. Circumvention

Another problem is circumvention of transparency through informal arrangements. Sometimes transparency requirements seem futile, because all relevant actors desire to preserve opacity and can collude to keep real decision making out of the public eye, in a way that is difficult for external enforcers to monitor and prevent. Some even go so far as to claim that transparency rules are a sham, because they are systematically, or at least frequently, evaded.[48] The evasion phenomenon is real, but any conclusion that transparency requirements are ineffectual would be far too cavalier. Almost any institutional rules can be circumvented, but circumvention is costly; the higher the costs, the more effective the rule. Where transparency is imposed in order to chill self-interested bargains, the fact that self-interested bargains must be attempted through furtive whispers behind closed doors may be a sign that the transparency rules are working just as intended, rather than a symptom of failure. When self-interested actors must act by indirection, the costs of striking bargains will rise, and fewer of them will be struck.

C. Leaks

The circumvention problem is that actors can opt for secrecy in violation of rules prescribing transparency. The reverse problem is that of leaks, where

---

[47] *See* Adrian Vermeule, *Introduction: Political Constraints on Supreme Court Reform*, 90 Minn. L. Rev. 1154, 1166–1169 (2006).

[48] *See, e.g.,* Brian Fletcher, Case Comment, *Cheney v. United States District Court for the District of Columbia*, 28 Harv. Envtl. L. Rev. 605, 613 (2004) (arguing that one criticism of FACA is that "its requirements of balance and transparency are routinely ignored with impunity because the Act is largely unenforceable").

actors can opt for transparency in violation of rules prescribing secrecy. Perhaps uncoordinated leaks, difficult to deter (especially where the leaker is a legislator or staff member protected by the Constitution's Speech or Debate Clause), will undermine opacity, whatever the formal rules say. Recall in this connection Ferejohn's claim that legislators and other agents have individual-level incentives to supply transparency to constituents, even if doing so would be undesirable from the social point of view. Reporters and lobbyists will expend significant resources to ferret out the information before it is released, which could result in unproductive rent seeking as officials leak valuable information to favored members of the press or lobbyists with connections and clout.[49]

It is much too casual, however, to assume that leaks will inevitably undermine any regime of opacity. In both the executive branch and Congress, most secrets are kept, most of the time. Leaks make news because they occur against a less salient backdrop, that of a system in which national security intelligence, privileged and confidential documents and deliberations, and other information are routinely kept secret. The problem of leaks is real, but one must give specific and concrete reasons to think that opacity in one domain will be unsustainable, when opacity in other domains is in fact consistently sustained. Recall, as an important mechanism that reduces incentives to leak, that *noncredible leaks bring no benefit to the leaker.* Any legislator can come out of a closed session and report to interest groups that he advocated their pet projects, but the interest groups know that the legislator knows that the interest groups have no way to verify the claim; that common knowledge makes the claim noncredible.[50]

These remarks are general; let us focus concretely on the problem of leaks in various contexts where we have recommended delayed disclosure. The main challenge for delayed disclosure, and the main variable that differs across these contexts, is the size of the group that would have access to the confidential information at the time transparency could adversely affect deliberations. The fewer people involved in decision making, the easier it is to detect and prevent leaks. We will begin with those in which leaks are hardest to prevent and move to those where prevention is less costly. Because we do not advocate closing floor deliberations from the public at any time – even during deliberation on concurrent budget resolutions – we do not consider the effect of leaks in this context. Certainly, combating leaks would be more difficult with respect to

---

[49] *See* Stiglitz, *supra* note 21, at 11–12.

[50] For a different example of a proposal to reduce disclosure and eliminate the effects of leaks by rendering them noncredible, *see* Bruce Ackerman and Ian Ayres, Voting with Dollars: A New Paradigm for Campaign Finance (2002) (advocating secret donation booth in the campaign finance context to reduce the influence of special interests). Under their proposal, information could not be credibly provided about donations from interest groups because donors would have the ability to withdraw their donation for a period of time after it was made. Ackerman and Ayres also propose delayed disclosure, requiring disclosure of campaign contributions after a ten-year lag, but only to allow an audit of the government's actions, not to enhance accountability of elected officials.

floor debate because of the number of people involved – not just lawmakers themselves, but also their personal staffs and the staff of Congress.

i. Congressional Committees

Committees often have large memberships and substantial staffs, making it unclear whether delayed disclosure is a workable solution when applied to committee deliberations. Even if only the members of the committee and their staffs were privy to the details of deliberations, then several dozen, perhaps even more, people would have to maintain confidentiality in the face of temptations to disclose the information to interested parties. These parties can entice disclosure through implicit promises of campaign contributions and other help to lawmakers, and through hints of future employment to staff. Because records of the deliberations would be maintained for future release, people involved in the negotiations might be able to credibly provide confidential information to interested parties.

These considerations are hardly decisive, however. For one thing, there are legal penalties for showing nonpublic records to outside parties, such as interest groups or journalists, so the would-be leaker faces a dilemma between issuing a credible leak at the risk of prosecution, and avoiding the risk of prosecution by limiting himself to cheap talk. For another, we suggest complete opacity only at the stage of overall allocation by budget committees developing a budget resolution; at the stage of actual dickering, we propose that disclosure be delayed. At the former stage, the incentive to leak details to special interest groups is much reduced, because there are fewer details to leak and because it is less clear how particular interests will be affected by macro-level allocation. The very condition that makes opacity desirable – that actors work behind a partial veil of uncertainty – also reduces the benefits to be gained from leaks. At the latter stage, the incentive to leak is greater, but secrecy need only be temporarily enforced. More generally, many congressional committees do manage to maintain secrecy or opacity for many issues. Absent some further account suggesting special reason to fear leaks in the budget setting, there is no obvious reason that a regime of committee-level opacity in budget matters would be systematically infeasible, although occasional leaks would surely occur.

ii. Budget Summits and Advisory Committees

Here leaks can rather easily be monitored and deterred; the small number of participants makes it difficult for the leaker to hide in the crowd. Historically, budget summit participants usually have managed to keep their deliberations confidential against the threat of internal leaks. Although some contemporaneous news stories surrounding budget summits include unnamed sources floating trial balloons or strategically leaking information that harms their opponents, the political and fiscal conditions that lead to an interbranch summit are typically serious enough that participants understand secrecy is in their best interests. Details may become available some time after the summit as participants write memoirs or participate in interviews for analysis in books, magazine articles, or scholarly research. But leaks from these entities are unlikely to be prevalent because enforcement is much less challenging in the context of small groups.

Overall, the technique of delayed disclosure should be seriously considered as a way to achieve the goals of traditional disclosure while responding to the concern that interest groups and lobbyists are the true beneficiaries of open meetings. The strategy is least likely to work when the group that must keep the secret is so large that it is difficult to detect who leaks the information, and when the leaks can be accompanied by credible proof of the information's accuracy. Small groups such as budget summits and federal advisory committees should pose little problem; congressional committees are a larger challenge, but probably not an insuperable one.

IV. CONCLUSION

Our main emphasis, and the primary aim of the foregoing, has been to sketch an ideal or first-best framework for transparency in the federal budget process. The details of the framework are complex, but these are its outlines: Less transparency should obtain at earlier stages of the budget process, when participants are deliberating over broad goals; more transparency should obtain at later stages, when actors are dickering over specific programs. In the latter domain, delayed disclosure should be used where feasible to maximize the benefits of transparency for voters while minimizing its benefits for interest groups. This framework faces a range of institutional and political constraints and motivational problems, but these problems are not clearly insurmountable.

Questions for Chapter 3

1. Analyses like the one in this chapter depend crucially on assumptions about the motivations and behavior of political actors: legislators, executive branch officials, interest-group leaders, and voters. First consider legislators. What motivates them in deciding what legislation to support and how to allocate their time among various activities, such as lawmaking, casework, fund-raising, and press appearances? The trustee model of representation views the lawmaker as exercising independent judgment for the public interest, rather than merely following the wishes of a majority of her constituents. The delegate model of representation views the legislator as pursuing the interests of her constituents as their collective agent. These visions of the lawmaker may be more normative than descriptive, although frequently the two strands are intertwined and not carefully distinguished. In many cases, the two have identical normative implications; for example, both visions are transgressed by a legislator who takes bribes from a constituent.

Political scientists hoping to model legislator behavior and predict future actions have used various approaches; perhaps the most influential has been Mayhew's view of legislators as motivated by the desire to maximize their chances of reelection.[51] The reelection motivation is a methodological device to allow specific, testable predictions without determining the precise reasons a lawmaker wants to be reelected; no matter what her goal, she must remain in office to pursue it. In reality, lawmakers act for a variety of reasons, including self-interest, developing a reputation with colleagues in the legislative chamber, responding to constituents, and promoting their vision of the public interest. Fenno's classic study found that most legislators pursue several objectives at the same time, trading goals against each other and according no goal special

---

[51] *See* David R. Mayhew, Congress: The Electoral Connection (1974).

priority.[52] As you assess the studies in this book, be sure that you identify each author's assumptions about legislative behavior. Are those assumptions empirically proven? Are the authors relying on an ideal vision of a lawmaker, or a realistic one? Given the interests and motives that lawmakers will pursue, are certain provisions of framework laws apt to be successful in changing outcomes or behavior? Apply the same rigorous scrutiny to assumptions about the behavior and motivations of leaders of organized interest groups, of members of those groups, and of voters. The accuracy of the assumptions will influence the accuracy of the descriptions offered and, perhaps more importantly, the accuracy of any predictions about changes in future behavior likely to result from changes in institutional arrangements.

2. This chapter distinguishes between the formal rules and laws requiring transparency of deliberations about budgets and the informal practices that may allow some discussion to take place behind closed doors. One feature of modern lawmaking at the federal level has been the increasing power of party leaders, task forces, and budget summits to set policy, not only within the budget arena; these forums for decision making are not subject to open-meetings requirements.[53] Budget summits, which frequently are required before agreement can be reached on comprehensive budget frameworks or compromises can be struck to deal with fiscal crises, are conducted entirely behind closed doors. Gilmour has argued that compromise often requires some level of secrecy because politicians will have to back away from the extreme positions advocated by key constituencies. If they must bargain in public, they will not be willing to accept or make reasonable offers necessary to reach a middle ground.[54] How would the authors' proposal of delayed and limited disclosure affect the dynamics of budget summits? Would you expect that executive branch officials, typically political appointees, would respond differently than legislative branch officials, who are elected? How would you expect interest groups to use the new information? If budget summits are made a formal part of the reconciliation

---

[52] *See* Richard F. Fenno, Jr., Congressmen in Committees (1973); *see also* Richard F. Fenno, Jr., The Power of the Purse: Appropriations Politics in Congress (1966) (focusing on the appropriations committees before the adoption of the modern congressional budget process). For more recent assessments, *see* John W. Kingdon, Congressmen's Voting Decisions (3d ed., 1989); James B. Kau and Paul H. Rubin, *Economic and Ideological Factors in Congressional Voting: The 1980 Election*, 44 Pub. Choice 385 (1984); Ian Shapiro, *Enough of Deliberation: Politics is About Interests and Power, in* Deliberative Politics: Essays on Democracy and Disagreement 28 (Stephen Macedo ed., 1999).

[53] For a case study of the role of these entities in one pivotal reconciliation bill, *see* Anita S. Krishnakumar, *Reconciliation and the Fiscal Constitution: The Anatomy of the 1995-96 Budget "Train Wreck,"* 35 Harv. J. on Legis. 589 (1998).

[54] *See* John B. Gilmour, Strategic Disagreement: Stalemate in American Politics 132–152 (1995).

process, what transparency rules are likely to accompany that change in status? How would those rules affect the bargaining dynamics?

3. What other aspects of the budget process lead to opacity? Previous chapters have described the format of omnibus reconciliation bills and the complex, arcane budget rules that structure the congressional process. Some of those rules may increase transparency – for example, the point of order procedure that allows a member of Congress to bring attention to one part of a larger bill may focus attention on that provision and disaggregate it from the rest of the omnibus bill. But many of these rules seem to decrease transparency and make it difficult to determine responsibility for individual provisions and overall budget performance. Note, however, that the difficulty of unraveling deals is likely to be differentially felt, with voters and good-government groups at the greatest disadvantage in learning about the decisions and votes of their representatives, while organized interest groups with a concrete stake in the matter are most likely to figure out the story behind an omnibus bill. How would you reform the current budget process to improve transparency and accountability? Are there other facets of transparency in budgeting that this chapter does not consider that should be reassessed? What reforms would most increase the "good" accountability – that is, the accountability to voters?[55]

4. This chapter discusses federal advisory commissions, which are a pervasive feature of the federal government. Why do the executive branch and Congress set up advisory commissions? Given current budget challenges, what kinds of advisory commissions would be most useful in formulating fiscal policy? Who should serve on such commissions? Some policymakers have proposed advisory commissions to deal with politically sensitive issues such as reform of entitlement programs, particularly Social Security, comprehensive tax reform, or review of tax expenditures. In some cases, these reformers advocate adopting an internal congressional process that would require Congress to consider the package of reforms put forward by the commissions, perhaps without amendment or change.

The model for these recommendations is the base realignment and closure process, which has been used successfully several times since 1988 to scale back or close military bases. These laws delegate authority to determine which military bases to close or realign to a bipartisan independent commission of experts. The commission's recommendations, if accepted as a package by the president, are submitted to Congress. The base closure rules require that Congress

---

[55] For a political-science treatment of accountability, transparency, and the budget process, *see* Timothy Besley, PRINCIPLED AGENTS? THE POLITICAL ECONOMY OF GOOD GOVERNMENT 203–206 (2006).

affirmatively reject the recommendations, as a package, through a joint resolution in order to stop the recommendations from being enacted. The president has the ability to veto such a resolution, which is likely because he had to accept them before they can be sent to the legislature; thus, stopping the recommended closure likely needs support of two-thirds of both houses.[56] How could this sort of structure be used in the budget context? What specific issues lend themselves to consideration through this process of commission recommendations that are sent on a fast track through Congress? Does this reduce legislative accountability? Does it improve legislative decision making? Is it constitutional? In what circumstances are lawmakers likely to delegate this kind of authority to a commission?

[56] *See* Natalie Hanlon, *Military Base Closings: A Study of Government by Commission*, 62 U. Colo. L. Rev. 331 (1991).

4 European Experiences with Fiscal Rules and Institutions

Jürgen von Hagen

I. INTRODUCTION

The past two decades have seen a growing interest in fiscal rules. Fiscal rules specify numerical targets for key budgetary aggregates such as annual government deficits, debts, or spending.[1] Such rules have a long history at the subnational level,[2] and some countries, including Japan and Germany, have had less specific rules – such as the "Golden Rule," which limits government borrowing to investment spending – at the national level for a long time. What is new is the application of specific annual targets at the national level. It has been part of the reaction to the rapid rise in public debt levels and the emergence of unsustainable public-sector budget deficits starting in the 1970s. Thus, fiscal rules aim at improving fiscal discipline and reducing government deficits and debts.

The Fiscal Consolidation Agreement adopted in Japan in 1981 was an early example of a fiscal rule. It set annual targets for the increase in major spending aggregates. In 1996, the Japanese government adopted a new rule under the Fiscal Restructuring Targets, and in 1997 it passed the Fiscal Structural Reform Act, which set annual spending targets for several years. The U.S. Congress adopted a fiscal rule in the Balanced Budget and Emergency Deficit Control Act (Gramm-Rudman-Hollings Act I) of 1985, which established numerical targets for the

---

[1] For a discussion of general principles and the design of fiscal rules, *see* George Kopits and Steven A. Symansky, *Fiscal Policy Rules* [Int'l Monetary Fund (IMF) Occasional Paper No. 162, 1998]; Willem H. Buiter, *Ten Commandments for a Fiscal Rule in the E(M)U*, 19 Oxf. Rev. Econ. Pol'y 84, 84–99 (2003).

[2] *See, e.g.*, Jürgen von Hagen and Barry Eichengreen, *Fiscal Policy and Monetary Union: Federalism, Fiscal Restrictions, and the No-Bailout Rule* (Centre for Econ. Pol'y Res. Discussion Paper No. 1247, 1995).

Professor Jürgen von Hagen is a professor of economics at the University of Bonn. Professor von Hagen is also affiliated the Department of Business Economics and Public Policy at Indiana University.

federal budget deficit for every fiscal year through 1991. These targets later were revised and extended by the Balanced Budget and Emergency Deficit Control Reaffirmation Act of 1987 (Gramm-Rudman-Hollings Act II), which effectively postponed the goal of balancing the budget from 1991 to 1993. The Budget Enforcement Act of 1990 replaced the deficit targets by nominal ceilings on annual discretionary spending.[3] In Europe, the Maastricht Treaty introduced a fiscal rule for the member states of the European Union (EU) through the Excessive Deficit Procedure (EDP), which later was strengthened and complemented by the Stability and Growth Pact (SGP). The government of Canada enacted fiscal targets for the period from 1991–1992 to 1995–1996 through the Federal Spending Control Act.[4] These targets limited annual spending under all federal programs except those that are self-financing. In New Zealand, the Fiscal Responsibility Act of 1994 set out principles of prudent fiscal management promoting accountability and long-term fiscal planning. Although the act does not require this explicitly, New Zealand governments have defined specific numerical targets for public debt under the new fiscal regime. Similarly, the Australian government has operated under self-imposed targets for net public debt since 1998.[5] In Switzerland, a constitutional amendment was passed in 1998 requiring the federal government to balance the budget by 2001 and to set annual ceilings for federal government expenditures afterward.[6] The Convergence, Stability, Growth, and Solidarity Pact adopted by the member countries of the West African Economic and Monetary Union also contains numerical limits for certain fiscal aggregates.[7]

The effectiveness of fiscal rules to rein in excessive government spending and deficits remains an open question. There is now a large literature reviewing the experience with fiscal rules at the state level in the United States, showing that their effects on government deficits and debts are, at best, ambiguous, as governments can find ways to circumvent the restrictions placed on them.[8]

---

[3] Richard Peach, *The Evolution of the Federal Budget and Fiscal Rules*, 3 BANCA D'ITALIA WORKSHOP ON FISCAL RULES 217, 217–236 (2001).

[4] Suzanne Kennedy and Janine Robbins, *The Role of Fiscal Rules in Determining Fiscal Performance* (Dept. of Finance Working Paper No. 2001–16, 2001).

[5] *Id.*; Richard Hemming and Michael Kell, *Promoting Fiscal Responsibility – Transparency, Rules and Independent Fiscal Authorities*, 3 BANCA D'ITALIA WORKSHOP ON FISCAL RULES 433, 433-460 (2001).

[6] The United Kingdom adopted a much less specific fiscal rule in the late 1990s. *See, e.g.*, Kennedy and Robbins, *supra* note 4; Carl Emmerson, Chris Frayne, and Sarah Love, *The Government's Fiscal Rules* (The Inst. For Fiscal Stud. Briefing Note No. 16, 2001). *See also* Teresa Dabán Sánchez, Enrica Detragiache, C. Gabriel di Bella, Gian Maria Milesi-Ferretti, and Steven A. Symansky, *Rules-Based Fiscal Policy in France, Germany, Italy, and Spain* (IMF Occasional Paper No. 225, 2003) (provides a description of fiscal rules in a variety of countries).

[7] Ousmane Doré and Paul R. Masson, *Experience with Budgetary Convergence in the WAEMU* (IMF Working Paper No. 02/108, 2002).

[8] Fabio Canova and Paraskevi (Evi) Pappa, *The Elusive Costs and the Immaterial Gains of Fiscal Constraints* [Innocenzo Gasparini Inst. for Econ. Res. (IGIER), Bocconi Univ. Working Paper No. 295, 2004]. Canova and Pappa investigate the effectiveness of fiscal rules prevailing in most states of the United States and conclude that they contribute little to fiscal discipline.

The experience in Japan and the United States suggests that the fiscal rules did not lead to stronger fiscal discipline.[9] In this chapter, I review the experience with the Maastricht fiscal rule in Europe. In Section II, I explain the genesis and the substance of this rule in more detail. In Section III, I analyze the fiscal performance of the EU countries under the Maastricht fiscal rule. I show that its effect on government deficits and debt was weak on average in all EU countries, but strong in a number of countries. Furthermore, it had some impact on discretionary fiscal policy before the start of the European Monetary Union (EMU). In Section IV, I widen the scope of the analysis and consider the connection between fiscal rules and the institutional design of the budget process. Based on the European experience, I distinguish between weak and strong rules. Weak rules consist of a mere declaration of annual targets for key budgetary parameters. Strong rules add to this a design of the budget process that strengthens the government's ability to achieve these targets. I show that the Maastricht fiscal rule has contributed to improving budgeting institutions in those countries where the internal political environment is appropriate for a rules-based approach to fiscal discipline. However, this is not the case in all EU countries, and especially not in the large EMU economies. Section V concludes.

II. THE EUROPEAN FISCAL FRAMEWORK

A. The Excessive Deficit Procedure, and the Stability and Growth Pact

Numerical fiscal targets became relevant for all EU member states through the EDP, the cornerstone of the fiscal framework of the Treaty on European Union (TEU) signed in 1991.[10] The EDP combines the unconditional obligation on the part of the member states to avoid "excessive deficits" with a procedure providing for an annual assessment of their fiscal policies, and, if necessary, penalties for profligate behavior (Article 104 TEU). The TEU charges the European Commission with the task of monitoring budgetary developments and the stock of public-sector debt of the member states, checking in particular their compliance with two reference values, one for the ratio of the deficit to GDP and one for the ratio of public debt to GDP. These two reference values are set at 3 percent and 60 percent, respectively (TEU Protocol on the EDP). If a member state does not comply with these reference values, the European Commission is obliged to write a report to the European Council of Economics and Finance Ministers (ECOFIN) about the matter, unless the deficit and the debt are approaching their reference values in a way the European

---

[9] On Japan, *see* Jürgen von Hagen, *Fiscal Rules and Fiscal Performance in the European Union and Japan*, 24 MONETARY & ECON. STUD. 25, 25–60 (2006).

[10] Several member states of the European Union (EU), most notably Denmark, Ireland, and the Netherlands, embarked on fiscal consolidation programs based on numerical targets for the main budgetary aggregates already in the 1980s (Jürgen von Hagen, *Budgeting Procedures and Fiscal Performance in the European Union*, 42 EUR. COMM'N ECON. PAPERS, 1992).

Commission deems satisfactory, or the excess of the deficit over the reference value is exceptional and temporary. The European Commission's report must take into account whether the deficit exceeds public investment spending and "all other relevant factors, including the medium term economic and budgetary position" [art. 104(3)] of the country concerned.[11]

If the European Commission considers that an excessive deficit exists, it makes a recommendation to the ECOFIN to formally decide that this is indeed the case. ECOFIN represents the member states of the European Union. It votes on this recommendation by qualified majority after taking into account any observations the country concerned may make and the opinion of the Economic and Financial Committee (EFC). The EFC consists of representatives of the member states, the European Commission, and the European Central Bank. It advises the European Council in economic and financial matters (art. 114). Thus the decision whether or not an excessive deficit indeed exists is ultimately left to governments of the member states.

If ECOFIN rules that there is an excessive deficit, it makes confidential recommendations to the country concerned as to how to correct the situation within a given period of time. If the country does not take appropriate action and does not respond to ECOFIN's recommendations in a satisfactory way, the European Council may make its views and recommendations public, ask the government concerned to take specific corrective actions, and, ultimately, impose a financial fine on the country. In that case, the country would first be required to make a non-interest-bearing deposit with the European Community. The economic cost of this deposit is the interest foregone. If the excessive deficit still persists after two years, this deposit would be turned into a fine paid to the European Community.[12] ECOFIN can abrogate its decisions under the EDP at any stage of the process upon a recommendation from the European Commission. All European Council decisions in this context are made by qualified majority; once a country has been found to have an excessive deficit, its votes are not counted in these decisions.

An important aspect of the TEU was that countries had to stay below the two reference values defined by the EDP in order to qualify for EMU membership. While the reference value for public debt was soon neglected because too many countries had debt ratios larger than 60 percent in the mid-1990s, the political debate over the EMU stressed the absolute necessity of bringing deficits below 3 percent of GDP in order to be eligible for the EMU. This gave the deficit rules considerable power in the years before 1998, as the political and economic cost of disqualifying for the EMU was perceived to be very high by all European

---

[11] According to art. 104(3), the commission also may prepare a report if a member state complies with the criteria, but the commission sees the risk of an excessive deficit nevertheless.

[12] Note that neither the deposit nor its conversion into a fine affects the budget of the country in question, as both are financial transactions. Thus the payment of the fine cannot cause a country to have an excessive deficit.

governments. The decision on membership was made in the spring of 1998 and based on fiscal data for 1997. Once that decision had been made, the cost of running larger deficits was much lower.

B. The Stability and Growth Pact

The SGP was adopted by the European Council in 1997 to further develop the fiscal framework of the EMU.[13] It modifies the EDP in several ways. First, it sets up an early warning system strengthening the surveillance of the public finances of the member states. EMU member states submit annual Stability Programs to the European Commission and ECOFIN explaining their intended fiscal policies and, in particular, what they plan to do to keep the budget close to the new and stricter medium-term objective of "close to balance or in surplus." The Stability Programs strengthen the "preventive arm" of the fiscal rule, which aims at reducing the risk that countries will exceed the 3 percent deficit constraint. Implementation of these programs is subject to ECOFIN's scrutiny. Based on information and assessments by the European Commission and the EFC, ECOFIN can issue early warnings and recommendations to countries that risk significant deviations from the fiscal targets set out in their Stability Programs. These provisions were further developed in a set of ECOFIN decisions regarding the format and content of the Stability Programs.[14] In October 1998, ECOFIN endorsed a "code of conduct" specifying the criteria to be observed in the assessment of a country's medium-term budgetary position and data standards and requirements for the programs. In October 1999, ECOFIN recommended stricter compliance with and timelier updating of the programs. In July 2001, ECOFIN endorsed an appended code of conduct refining the format and the use of data in the Stability Programs, including the use of a common set of assumptions about economic developments outside the EMU. The European Commission has produced a detailed framework of interpretation of divergences from the targets set in the Stability Programs.[15]

---

[13] The idea of a Stability Pact originally was launched by Germany's Finance Minister Waigel in 1995 in an attempt to assure German voters critical of the EMU project that the stability of the European currency would not be endangered by profligate fiscal policies of the member states. For an account of the genesis of the SGP, *see* Antonio J. Cabral, *The Stability and Growth Pact: Main Aspects and Some Considerations on Its Implementation*, in THE EURO-ZONE: A NEW ECONOMIC ENTITY? 19 (Alexandre Lamfalussy, Luc D. Bernard, and Antonio J. Cabral eds., 1999); Jürgen Stark, *Genesis of a Pact*, in THE STABILITY AND GROWTH PACT: THE ARCHITECTURE OF FISCAL POLICY IN EMU 77–105 (Anne Brunila, Marco Buti, and Daniele Franco eds., 2001).

[14] *See* European Commission, *Specifications on the Implementation of the Stability and Growth Pact and Guidelines on the Format and Content of Stability and Convergence Programs* 23 (European Commission DG Economic and Financial Affairs, Mimeo, 2002).

[15] European Commission DG Economic and Financial Affairs, *1999–2000 Examination of the Stability and Convergence Programmes* (March, 27, 2007), *available at* http://ec.europa.eu/economy_finance/about/activities/sgp/year/year19992000_en.htm.

Second, the SGP gives more specific content to the vague notions of "exceptional" and "temporary" breaches of the 3 percent limit, and by defining the rules for financial penalties, and it speeds up the process by setting specific deadlines for the individual steps. Third, the SGP gives political guidance to the parties involved in the EDP, calling on them to implement the rules of the EDP in a more effective and timely way. It commits the European Commission in particular to using its right of initiative under the EDP "in a manner that facilitates the strict, timely, and effective functioning of the SGP."

The main impact of the SGP has been to reduce the weight of economic judgment and to raise the importance of numerical criteria and the surveillance of budgetary developments in the Maastricht fiscal framework. This has turned the framework from a rather loose one allowing for considerable judgment and discretion into a fairly rigid numerical rule focusing on annual budget deficits. In line with this increasing focus on the annual deficit, ECOFIN adopted a decision in 2003 that countries exceeding the 3 percent constraint should achieve annual reductions in their structural deficits by at least 0.5 percent of GDP annually. This requirement was reaffirmed in the SGP reform of March 2005.[16]

Somewhat ironically, Germany, the very country that had pushed for tighter fiscal rules in the EMU in the mid-1990s, was the second EMU member country and the first of the large member countries to violate the fiscal rules. Already in January 2002, the European Commission asked ECOFIN to issue an early warning to Germany, but, in view of the upcoming federal elections there, ECOFIN refrained from doing so. In January 2003, only four months after the elections, ECOFIN found that Germany had an excessive deficit. In the two years that followed, more countries were declared to have excessive deficits and a fierce debate broke out among economists and policymakers about the fiscal framework, which ultimately led to the reform of the SGP in March 2005. In this reform, the European Council adopted an explicit list of excuses for persistent government deficits and debts in excess of the thresholds set by the EDP. This decision further deprives the European Commission of its right to exert independent judgment on the fiscal performance of the EU member states; by giving excuses to governments for running large deficits as they wish, it may effectively mark the end of the fiscal rule in Europe.

III. FISCAL PERFORMANCE UNDER FISCAL RULES

A. Government Debt, Deficits, and Spending

Between 1992 and 1997, the average debt ratio of the EU member states increased by almost 16 percent, from about 60 percent to 75 percent (see Table 4.1). Between 1998 and 2003, it fell by 4.7 percent. Considering that the

---

[16] Council Regulation 1056/2005, 2005 (EC).

Table 4.1. Government debt since 1992

Period	Change in debt ratio (%)			
	All EU states	Large states	Intermediate states	Small states
1992–1997	15.8	18.8	4.1	3.3
1998–2003	−4.7	−4.9	−10.5	−7.1

Note: Large states are Germany, France, Italy, Spain, and the United Kingdom. Intermediate states are Belgium, the Netherlands, Austria, and Sweden. Small states are Denmark, Greece, Ireland, Luxembourg, Portugal, and Finland.
Source: European Economy Statistical Appendix, spring 2002, fall 2003.

latter period was one of strong economic growth, this is no big achievement. Judged from average performance, therefore, EU countries did not reduce their debt ratios over the past 13 years, despite the fiscal rule that was enacted with the Maastricht Treaty.

Behind this average performance, however, are very different patterns of individual country behavior. A few countries, such as Denmark, Ireland, Luxembourg, Portugal, Sweden, and the United Kingdom, already managed to reduce their debt ratios during the second half of the 1980s. As shown in Table 4.1, the large EU states experienced rising debt ratios between 1992 and 1997, while the intermediate and small EU states performed much better. This pattern continued after 1998, when the small and intermediate states experienced much more substantial declines in their debt ratios than the larger ones. In sum, the EU fiscal rule has done very little to stabilize the debt ratio on average, and its effectiveness varies strongly across countries.

Table 4.2 shows the deficit trends in the EU since the early 1980s. All EU countries except Greece and Austria already saw improvements in their budget balances in the second half of the 1980s, when economic growth had improved in Europe compared to the late 1970s and early 1980s. In contrast, comparing the average surplus ratios from 1992–1998 with those from 1986–1991 reveals that only five states – Belgium, Greece, Ireland, Italy, and the Netherlands – achieved improvements after the adoption of the Maastricht Treaty. The larger states – Germany, France, Spain, and the United Kingdom – all had increasing deficits during this period. Average deficits generally improved after 1998, but this may have been due to strong economic growth during the 1999–2000 period. As the European economies moved into a recession, surplus ratios began to fall again in most EU countries.

B. Discretionary Fiscal Policy

Fiscal outcomes such as deficit ratios are determined both by fiscal policy and endogenous economic developments. As Blöndal notes, annual economic growth rates are the most important determinants of fiscal performance in the

Table 4.2. Average budget balances (% of GDP)

Year	BE	DK	D	GR	ES	F	IE	I	L	NL	AT	P	SF	S	UK
81-85	−10.3	−5.3	−2.6	−7.6	−4.6	−2.2	−11.0	−11.0	1.1	−5.0	−2.6	−9.5	2.8	−4.5	−3.1
86-91	−6.1	−0.4	−1.9	−13.2	−3.8	−1.6	−2.6	−10.4	3.3	−4.2	−2.8	−4.1	3.5	2.9	−0.4
92-98	−4.9	−1.5	−2.8	−8.8	−4.7	−4.2	−1.1	−7.8	2.0	−2.6	−3.5	−5.7	−3.2	−4.7	−4.6
99-03	0.1	2.2	−2.6	−3.7	−0.5	−2.6	1.5	−2.3	3.6	−0.6	−1.2	−3.2	4.0	1.7	−0.7

Source: These are my own calculations based on European Economy Statistical Appendix, fall 2003.

short run.[17] It is, therefore, necessary to separate the effects of policy from the effects of economic growth to see how much of the observed developments can be attributed to government policy, as opposed to windfall gains and losses from strong economic growth and recessions. In this section, I use the growth-accounting approach proposed in Hughes-Hallett et al. for that purpose.[18] To separate the effects of growth and policy, I start from the observed primary surplus ratio, s, for a given year:

$$s_t = \frac{R_t - G_t}{Y_t} = (r_t - g_t), \tag{1}$$

where R denotes government revenues, G is noninterest government spending, Y is the GDP, $r = R/Y$, and $g = G/Y$. The annual change in this ratio is

$$\Delta s_t = \frac{\Delta R_t - \Delta G_t}{Y_{t-1}} - \frac{\Delta Y_t}{Y_{t-1}}(r_t - g_t) \tag{2}$$

I define a "neutral" fiscal policy as one that keeps the average tax rate and the volume of government spending unchanged over the previous year.[19] In other words, $r_t = r_{t-1}$ and $\Delta G_t = 0$. With this definition, the contribution of economic growth to the change in the surplus ratio is

$$\Delta s_t^g = \left(\frac{\Delta Y_t}{Y_{t-1}}\right) g_t. \tag{3}$$

Using this definition, I obtain the policy-induced change in the surplus ratio or the fiscal impulse as

$$\Delta s_t^P = \Delta s_t - \Delta s_t^g. \tag{4}$$

---

[17] Jón R. Blöndal, *Budget Reform in OECD Member Countries: Common Trends*, 2 OECDJ. BUD-GETING 7, 8 (2003).

[18] Andrew Hughes-Hallett, Jürgen von Hagen, and Rolf R. Strauch, *Budgetary Consolidation in EMU*, 148 EUR. COMM'N ECON. PAPERS (2001).

[19] The assumption of a constant tax ratio is in line with empirical estimates of macro-economic tax functions in OECD countries and does not contradict the fact that income taxes are progressive at the individual level.

Table 4.3. Fiscal impulses in the EU

Country	Standard deviation 1981–2003	Average 1981–1991	Average 1992–2003	p Value: A	Average 1999–2003	p Value: B
BE	1.440 .76(0.02)	−0.25	−0.67	0.41	−1.10	0.05
DK	2.131 .06(0.02)	−0.28	−1.22	0.12	−1.28	0.17
D	2.160 .61(0.00)	−1.28	−0.62	0.17	−0.98	0.08
GR	2.76	−0.37	−0.89	0.34	−2.28	0.00
E	0.98	−0.87	−0.75	0.38	−0.81	0.41
F	0.81	−1.12	−1.05	0.85	−1.48	0.10
IE	1.93	−0.20	−2.70	0.00	−3.17	0.20
I	1.32	−0.59	−0.38	0.36	−1.01	0.08
L	1.86	..	−2.00	..	−2.44	0.05
NL	1.42	−0.69	−1.34	0.14	−1.58	0.58
AT	1.23	−1.03	−0.98	0.46	−0.77	0.45
P	1.96	−0.24	−0.92	0.21	−0.71	0.36
SF	1.93	−1.51	−1.03	0.29	−1.54	0.19
S	2.21	−0.72	−1.39	0.24	−2.58	0.07
UK	1.40	−0.99	−1.18	0.38	−2.04	0.06

Note: For Belgium, Denmark, and Germany, I report sample standard deviations for 1981–1991 (upper entry), 1992–2003 (lower entry), and the p value of an F test for equal variances. For all other countries, the F test for equal variances did not reject the null hypothesis. The p value: A is the p value of a t test for equal means (one-sided test) between 1981–1991 and 1992–2003, accounting for unequal variances where necessary. The p value: B is the corresponding one-sided test for the mean of 1991–1998 being larger than the mean of 1999–2003.
Source: These are my own calculations.

This definition attributes any change in the average tax rate and all changes in government spending to discretionary fiscal policy.[20] I use this part as our indicator of discretionary fiscal policy, since it measures the active contribution of any policy actions to observed changes in the deficit ratio. Note that a positive value indicates a discretionary fiscal contraction, while a negative value indicates a discretionary fiscal expansion.

Table 4.3 reports the averages and standard deviations of the fiscal impulses for the EU countries from 1981 to 2003. The table bears a number of interesting observations. First, note that in three EU countries – Belgium, Denmark, and

---

[20] Alternatively, one might use the OECD's cyclically adjusted budget balances. These estimates, however, are based on past data and policies. If the introduction of fiscal rules induced changes in the comovements of cyclical output and budget balances, they could be quite misleading. Buti and van den Noord use a similar approach and come to similar conclusions regarding fiscal policy in the early years of EMU: Marco Buti and Paul van den Noord, *Discretionary Fiscal Policy and Elections: The Experience of the Early Years of EMU* (OECD Economics Department Working Paper No. 351, 2003); Marco Buti and Paul van den Noord, *Fiscal Policy in EMU: Rules, Discretion, and Political Incentives*, 206 EUR. COMM'N ECON. PAPERS (2004).

Germany – the volatility of fiscal impulses was smaller after 1991 than before. In these countries, the Maastricht fiscal rule seems to have induced a smoother course of fiscal policy over time. For the remaining countries, however, I could not reject the hypothesis of equal variances.

Second, I find that the average fiscal impulse was larger in six EU countries in 1992–2003 than in 1981–1991, and smaller in the other eight EU countries, indicating a less expansionary discretionary fiscal policy in the first group and a more expansionary policy in the second group. Only in Ireland, however, is the difference in means statistically significant, and, there, policy became more expansionary. This suggests that, to the extent that some EU countries achieved reductions in their deficit ratios in the 1990s, they benefited from the effects of economic growth rather than discretionary fiscal contractions.

Third, I find that the average fiscal impulse in 1999–2003 was more expansionary than the 1992–2003 average in all EU countries except Austria and Portugal. Thus, fiscal policy was more expansionary in these countries after the start of the EMU in 1999. The changes are significant in eight EU countries, that is, Belgium, Germany, Greece, France, Italy, Luxembourg, Sweden, and the United Kingdom. These governments apparently used the first chance for relaxing fiscal policy after the threat of not making it into EMU had disappeared.

To gain some further insights into the conduct of fiscal policy in the EU, I pool the fiscal impulses of all member states in a regression model. The data exclude Luxembourg, for which I do not have the fiscal data for all years of the 1980s. Table 4.4 reports the results for the period from 1981 to 1991. The baseline model projects the annual fiscal impulse on a constant, its own lag, the growth rate of GDP, and the lagged ratio of government debt to GDP. I also include a "crisis" dummy accounting for the fiscal effects of the Swedish and Finnish crises in 1991. Country fixed effects were not significant and were dropped from the model.

The table reveals some interesting properties of fiscal policy in the EU. First, the coefficient on the lagged fiscal impulse is negative, indicating that governments tend to reverse part of a given fiscal impulse in the following year. However, the coefficient is not statistically significant and I drop the lag from the model. Second, the coefficient on the lagged debt ratio is positive, indicating that discretionary policy reacts with a fiscal contraction to an increase in public debt relative to GDP. This can be regarded as a necessary condition for fiscal sustainability, as the debt ratio would be unbounded without such a reaction. The result also confirms the finding in Hughes-Hallett et al. that the likelihood of fiscal consolidations in EU and OECD member states during the period from 1960 to 1999 rises when the debt ratio increases.[21] Third, the coefficient on real GDP growth is significantly negative, indicating that discretionary fiscal policy

---

[21] Hughes-Hallett et al., *supra* note 18, (2001).

Table 4.4. Empirical models of fiscal impulses in the EU, 1981–1991

	Dependent variable: Fiscal impulse		
	Model 1	Model 2	Model 3
Constant	−0.72	−0.94	−0.70
p value	0.053	0.02	0.035
Lagged fiscal impulse	−0.28		
p value	0.73		
Crisis dummy	−6.31	−5.82	−5.17
p value	0.00	0.000	0.0005
Lagged debt ratio	0.013	0.013	0.014
p value	0.008	0.008	0.004
Real GDP growth rate	−0.27	−0.21	−0.21
p value	0.0004	0.003	0.003
Election dummy			−0.89
p value			0.002
R^2	0.21	0.17	0.22
F test (p value)	0.000	0.000	0.000
Number of observations	141	154	154

tightens when output slows down and eases when output growth rises. This procyclical pattern of discretionary fiscal policy in Europe is consistent with previous results.[22] It suggests that governments systematically counteract automatic stabilizers built into the tax system. Finally, I add a dummy "election" to the model, which has a value of one in election years and zero in all other years.[23] The result is reported as Model 3 in Table 4.4. The election dummy has a coefficient of –0.89, which is statistically highly significant. EU governments in the 1980s undertook discretionary fiscal expansions during election years.

[22] *See, e.g.*, Anne Brunila and Carlos Martinez-Mongay, *The Challenge for Fiscal Policy in the Early Years of EMU, in* EMU AND ECONOMIC POLICY IN EUROPE: THE CHALLENGE OF THE EARLY YEARS 150–169 (Marco Buti and Andre Sapir eds., 2002); Carlos José Fonseca Marinheiro, *Has the Stability and Growth Pact Stabilised? Evidence from a Panel of 12 European Countries and Some Implications for the Reform of the Pact* (CESifo Working Paper Series No. 1411, 2005). Buti and van den Noord (*supra*, note 20) find that their measure of the fiscal impulse is counter-cyclical, but they use output gaps rather than growth rates to measure cyclical effects. I also estimated fiscal impulses corrected for the trend in the ratio of government spending to GDP, approximating the trend by five-year moving averages. I did this to account for the fact that spending ratios generally trended downward in the 1980s and 1990s in many EU countries. The interpretation then is that the trend is not part of annual discretionary fiscal policy. The main difference in the results compared to those of Tables 4.4 and 4.5 is that the lagged debt ratio no longer appears with a positive coefficient. That is, the negative trend in the spending ratio reflects the governments' reaction to the positive trend in the debt ratios.

[23] The election dates from 1981 to 1991 are taken from Lijphardt's Elections Archive (www.dodgson.ucsd.edu/lij) and from the reports on "National Elections" in various issues of *Electoral Studies*. Post-1991 election dates are taken from the IFES Election Guide, www.cnn.com/world/election.watch (last visited September 28, 2006).

Table 4.5. Empirical model of fiscal impulses in the EU, 1992-2003

	Dependent variable: Fiscal impulse				
	Model 1	Model 2	Model 3	Model 4	Model 5
Constant	−1.24	−1.26	−0.83	−0.93	−1.13
p value	0.002	0.001	0.038	0.023	0.0035
Lagged fiscal impulse	0.016				
p value	0.85				
Lagged debt ratio	0.0097	0.0099	0.008	0.008	0.0088
p value	0.048	0.042	0.089	0.089	0.062
Real GDP growth rate	−0.19	−0.20	−0.19	−0.20	−0.21
p value	0.001	0.001	0.0009	0.0004	0.0002
EMU dummy			−0.73	−0.42	
			0.004	0.15	
Election dummy				0.54	0.71
				0.16	0.055
Election Dummy × EMU Dummy				−1.21	−1.64
				0.037	0.001
R^2	0.08	0.09	0.13	0.15	0.14
F test (p value)	0.02	0.0006	0.0004	0.00005	0.00005
Number of observations	168	168	168	168	168

Table 4.5 presents a similar analysis for the 1990s. Again, I start by regressing fiscal impulses on a lagged fiscal impulse, the lagged debt–GDP ratio, and the real GDP growth rate. As in the 1980s, fiscal impulses are not persistent over time. Thus, I drop the lagged fiscal impulse in Model 2. As before, the lagged debt ratio appears with a significant, positive coefficient; in other words, the sufficient condition for sustainability continues to hold. Note that the coefficients on the lagged debt ratio are very similar in the 1980s and 1990s and are not statistically different from each other. Thus, the fiscal rules of the 1990s did not affect the governments' adjustment to a buildup of government debt. Finally, the fiscal impulses remained procyclical in the 1990s.

Next, I add an "EMU" dummy to the model, which has a value of zero for all years from 1991 to 1998 and of one starting in 1999. Table 4.5 shows that this dummy has a coefficient of –0.73, which is statistically significant. This confirms that fiscal policy reverted to a more expansionary stance once the threat of not making it into the EMU because of excessive deficits had been relieved. Note that, given the procyclicality of discretionary fiscal policy observed before, this fiscal expansion cannot be explained by the weak economic performance of the EU economies after the year 2000. Note also that the intercept of Model 3 is smaller in absolute value than the intercept of Model 2 in Table 4.4. This suggests that discretionary fiscal policy was less expansionary during 1991–1998 than in the 1980s. Hence, the fiscal rules seem to have had some effect in the desired direction between 1991 and 1998, when the penalty for exceeding the deficit limits was large.[24]

Next, I include the election dummy in the model. Since the previous results indicate that the EU fiscal rules lost bite after 1998, I interact this dummy with the EMU dummy. Thus, the coefficient on the election dummy picks up any election-year effect on discretionary fiscal policy between 1992 and 1998, while the sum of the coefficients on the election dummy and the interactive dummy picks up the effect of elections on discretionary fiscal policy since the start of the EMU. Model 4 in Table 4.5 has the results. The coefficient on the election dummy has a positive sign, but it is not statistically significant. In contrast, the coefficient on the interactive dummy has a negative sign and is statistically significant. This suggests that, since the EMU started, governments have systematically run fiscal expansions during elections years. This result is consistent with similar findings in Buti and van den Noord.[25]

However, including the election dummy and the interactive dummy also results in the loss of statistical significance by the EMU dummy. In view of that, I drop the EMU dummy from this regression, retaining only the election dummy and the interactive dummy. The results are reported as Model 5 in Table 4.5. The election dummy now has a positive coefficient with a value of $p = 0.055$, and the interactive dummy has a negative coefficient with a value of $p < 0.01$. The model thus indicates that governments embarked on fiscal contractions during election years between 1992 and 1998. Since the start of the EMU, election years are characterized again by discretionary fiscal expansions. Since the EMU dummy was not significant in Model 4, this result suggests that the difference between the pre-EMU and the EMU periods is mainly in the electoral effects. The sum of the coefficients on the election dummy and the interactive EMU and election dummy is -0.93, which is very close to the coefficient on the election dummy in Model 3 of Table 4.4. Thus, the typical effect of elections on EU government budgets is the same in the period from 1999 to 2003 as it was during the 1980s.

The empirical results thus indicate that governments undertook discretionary fiscal contractions rather than expansions in election years between 1992 and 1998, and discretionary fiscal expansions in election years since the start of the EMU. This pattern is consistent with the career-concern model

---

[24] I also estimated a model interacting the EMU dummy with the lagged debt ratio and the real GDP growth rate. Neither interactive term had a significant coefficient. Nevertheless, the coefficient on the interacted lagged debt ratio was positive and the coefficient on the lagged debt ratio itself was 0.011, with a value of $p = 0.06$.

[25] Jürgen von Hagen, *Fiscal Discipline and Growth in Euroland: Experiences with the Stability and Growth Pact* (Center for European Integration Studies Working Paper No. B06–2003, 2003). Preliminary results using data up to 2001 suggested that the election effects are stronger in preelection years than in election years. Controlling for election-year effects, I do not find preelection year effects in our sample. This, too, is consistent with Buti and van den Noord (*supra*, note 20).

of the political business cycle, if one assumes that voters put a high priority on joining the EMU during the 1990s. As long as EMU membership was not secured, voters rewarded signals of fiscal discipline, as the latter would increase the chances of getting into the monetary union. Governments, therefore, had an incentive to undertake discretionary fiscal contractions in election years in order to look tough, and they did. Once EMU membership was secured, the old pattern of political budget-cycles reemerged.

This result indicates that the fiscal rules of the EMU framework affected government behavior as long as voters put a high priority on fiscal discipline. This suggests that the electoral process is critical in enforcing fiscal rules at the national level. For fiscal rules to be effective, voters must be aware of the rules and perceive that violating them would carry a significant cost. Thus, the framework setting up the rules must have sufficient visibility, and breaking the rules must have consequences voters care about. This seems not to be the case in the EU after the start of the monetary union.

IV. FISCAL RULES AND THE BUDGET PROCESS

A. Political Economy of the Budget Process

Political economy literature argues that the institutional framework of the government budget process is an important determinant of a government's fiscal performance.[26] Budgetary institutions encompass the formal and informal rules governing the drafting of the budget law, its passage through the legislature, and its implementation. These rules distribute strategic influence among the participants in the budget process and regulate the flow of information. In doing so, they have important effects on the outcomes of budgeting processes.

The theoretical argument starts from the *common pool externality* of public budgeting. This externality results from the fact that government spending is commonly targeted at specific groups in society while being financed from a general tax fund. This incongruence implies that those who benefit from specific public policies typically only pay a fraction of the taxes used to finance these policies. Policymakers representing constituencies that benefit from specific policies without paying their full cost demand more of these policies than they would if their constituencies had to cover their full costs. As a result, government spending and, ultimately, taxes grow excessively large. Putting the argument into a dynamic context, one can show that the common pool externality causes excessive deficits and debts, too.[27]

---

[26] *See* Jürgen von Hagen, *Fiscal Rules, Fiscal Institutions, and Fiscal Performance*, 33 Econ. & Social Rev. 263, 263–284 (2002); Jürgen von Hagen, *Political Economy of Fiscal Institutions, in* Oxford Handbook of Political Economy 464–478 (Barry R. Weingast and Donald Wittman eds., 2006) (for reviews of the literature).

[27] For a formal derivation, *see* Andrei Velasco, *Debts and Deficits with Fragmented Fiscal Policymaking, in* Fiscal Institutions and Fiscal Performance 37–58 (James M. Poterba and

The core of this argument is that public budgeting involves a coordination failure among the actors in the budget process.[28] Excessive spending and deficits can be avoided if these actors recognize the externality and take a comprehensive view of the costs and benefits of all public policies. This is where the importance of decision-making rules and institutions in the budget process comes in. Rules and institutions can induce the decision makers to internalize the budgeting externality.

Hallerberg and von Hagen identify two basic institutional approaches to achieve that – the *delegation approach* and the *contracts approach*.[29] The delegation approach vests significant strategic powers in a decision maker who is less bound to special interests than ministers heading spending departments. In the European context, this is typically the Minister of Finance. The delegation approach therefore builds on strong agenda-setting powers of the Finance Minister during the initial budget-planning stage. In the subsequent legislative-approval stage of the budget process, the executive's budget proposal must be sufficiently protected against legislative amendments to avoid major changes; in other words, the executive acts as a strong agenda-setter in parliament. In the final implementation stage, the Finance Minister has strong monitoring capacities regarding the actual budgetary developments and the power to correct and prevent any deviations from the budget plan.

The contracts approach focuses on a set of key budgetary targets negotiated at the start of the budget process. Participants in these negotiations often include the leaders of the parties forming the government together with the members of the executive branch. Once an agreement has been reached, the targets are considered binding for the rest of the budget process. Here, it is the process of negotiation that makes the participants realize the externalities created by the general tax fund. The Minister of Finance has the role of monitoring compliance with the targets and enforcing their implementation, but little discretionary power to set these targets. Under this approach, the legislature typically

---

Jürgen von Hagen eds., 1999); Jürgen von Hagen and Ian J. Harden, *Budget Processes and Commitment to Fiscal Discipline*, 39 Eur. Econ. Rev. 771, 771–779 (1995).

[28] One implication of this argument is that, the more *fragmented* the budget process is, that is, the more representatives of individual spending interests are allowed to make spending decisions in their own right, the larger the spending and deficit bias. Since the most important representatives of individual spending interests in European governments are the individual spending ministers, an implication of this proposition is that government spending and deficits grow with the number of spending departments and ministers in a country's government. Yianos Kontopoulos and Roberto Perotti, *Government Fragmentation and Fiscal Policy Outcomes: Evidence from OECD Countries, in* Fiscal Institutions and Fiscal Performance 81–102 (James M. Poterba and Jürgen von Hagen eds., 1999), and Bjorn Volkerink and Jakob de Haan, *Fragmented Government Effects on Fiscal Policy: New Evidence*, 109 Pub. Choice 221, 221–242 (2001), confirm this proposition empirically for OECD countries, although results vary across sample periods.

[29] Mark Hallerberg, and Jürgen von Hagen, *Electoral Institutions, Cabinet Negotiations, and Budget Deficits within the European Union, in* Fiscal Institutions and Fiscal Performance 209–232 (James M. Poterba and Jürgen von Hagen, eds., 1999).

has strong information rights vis-à-vis the executive, enabling it to check the executive's compliance with the targets. As under the delegation approach, the Finance Minister is strong in the implementation phase to correct and prevent deviations from the targets.

To evaluate the importance of budgeting institutions for fiscal performance and discipline, von Hagen in 1992, von Hagen and Harden in 1994 and 1996, and Hallerberg et al. in 2002 and 2004 and the literature following them construct indexes capturing the most important institutional features of the budget processes in EU countries.[30] The indexes are based on institutional data garnered from legal documents and questionnaires sent to finance ministry officials, central bank officials, members of parliament, and academics.

The index used here is composed of four subcategories focusing on different stages and aspects of the budget process. The first item, *budget negotiations*, captures important characteristics of the budget-planning stage in the executive branch of government. It is large when the budget process imposes a quantitative constraint on total spending, the deficit, or government debt early on, when the Finance Minister has strong agenda-setting powers relative to the other members of the executive branch, and when quantitative targets are set early and specifically for individual parts of the budget. The second item, the *parliamentary stage*, focuses on the role of parliament in the budget process. It is large when the executive has strong agenda-setting powers over the legislature, when the legislature votes on an overall constraint on the budget first, and when there is a vote on total spending. The third item, *informativeness*, captures several aspects of the transparency of the budget process. It is large if the budget is presented in one comprehensive document, if special funds are included in the budget, if a link is made to national account data, if loans of the government to non-government entities are reported in the budget, and if the respondents to the questionnaire judge the budget data as "transparent." Finally, the fourth item, *flexibility of execution*, captures the main rules of the implementation of the budget law. It is large if the budget law has strong binding power for the executive. This is the case if the Finance Minister has powerful instruments to prevent the spending ministers from overspending, if transfers of funds between parts of the budget and budgets of different fiscal years are limited, and if supplementary budgets are rare. The index is a weighted sum of the four

[30] Jürgen von Hagen, *Budgeting Procedures and Fiscal Performance in the European Communities.* 96, Commission of the European Communities, DG II ECON. PAPERS (1992); Jürgen von Hagen and Ian H. Harden, *National Budget Processes and Fiscal Performance*, 3 EUR. ECON.: REP. & STUD. 311, 311–418 (1994); Jürgen von Hagen and Ian J. Harden, "Budget Processes and Commitment to Fiscal Discipline," EUROPEAN ECONOMIC REVIEW 39, (1995), 771–79; Mark Hallerberg, Jürgen von Hagen, and Rolf R. Strauch, "Budgeting in Europe After Maastricht: Patterns of Reform and Their Effectiveness," HACIENDA PUBLICA ESPANOLA 167, 2004, 201–225; Mark Hallerberg, Jürgen von Hagen, and Rolf F. Strauch, *The Use and Effectiveness of Fiscal Norms in the European Union* (Dutch Ministry of Finance Working Paper, 2002).

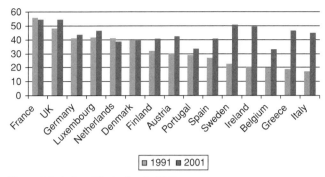

Figure 4.1. Index of Budgeting Institutions.

items, with weights of 1.0, 0.8, 0.8, and 0.67, respectively. The weights ensure that each item contributes the same maximum score to the index. Overall, a large value of the index indicates the existence of strong institutions reducing the common pool externality under the delegation or the contracts approach.

Figure 4.1 shows the index for all EU countries in 1991 and 2001. Italy, Greece, Ireland, and Sweden had very weak budgeting institutions in 1991. They also had the worst fiscal performance in the 1980s. Three of the large EU countries – Germany, France, and the United Kingdom – had the largest index values in 1991. As indicated in Figure 4.1, the EU countries with the weakest budgeting institutions in 1991 undertook institutional reforms during the 1990s, which are reflected in sizable increases in their index values.[31] Countries with relatively strong institutions in 1991, in contrast, did nothing or little to further improve their institutions. This different behavior is illustrated by the fact that the correlation between the index value in 1991 and the difference between the index in 2001 and 1991 is –0.83 and statistically significant. The data thus suggest that the pressure of the Maastricht fiscal rule has induced countries with weak budgeting institutions to improve the quality of their institutions.

Figure 4.2 shows the index values together with the average budget balances from Table 4.2. The first two averages are plotted against the institutional index of 1991; the last one is plotted against the index from 2001. The figure also indicates the correlation of each pair of series. These correlations are $r = 0.50$ for 1986–1991 and $r = 0.46$ for 1992–1998. Both are statistically significant. This very simple empirical analysis confirms the findings of earlier and econometrically more elaborate studies showing a significant effect of budgeting processes on fiscal performance.[32] For 1999–2003, the simple correlation vanishes as a

[31] For details of the reform, see Hallerberg, von Hagen, and Strauch, supra note 30, at 201, 201–225.

[32] See von Hagen, supra note 9; von Hagen and Harden, supra note 30; von Hagen, supra note 25; Mark Hallerberg, Rolf R. Strauch, and Jürgen von Hagen, The Use and Effectiveness of Budgetary Rules and Norms in EU Member States (Dutch Ministry of Finance Working Paper, 2001) (for EU countries); Ernesto Stein, Alejandro Grisanti, and Ernesto Talvi, Institutional Arrangements

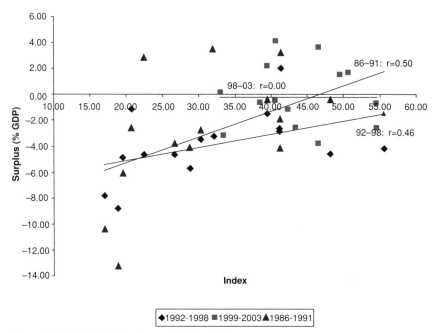

Figure 4.2. Budgeting Institutions and Budget Balances.

result of the improvements in budgeting institutions that the countries with weak institutions achieved during the 1990s. However, Hallerberg et al. show that, in a more sophisticated econometric evaluation, the index remains important for explaining differences in fiscal performance even after 1998.[33]

This evidence supports the conclusion that strengthening institutions that reduce the effects of the common pool externality on budget decisions and promote a comprehensive view of the costs and benefits of government activities leads to lower government deficits. Since a better institutional design of the budget process leads to a permanent improvement in fiscal performance, this analysis suggests that the Maastricht fiscal rule induced a lasting improvement in fiscal discipline in those EU states that reformed their budget processes. Note that this group includes mainly small countries with relatively weak fiscal performance in the 1980s, while the large EU states except Spain did not do

and Fiscal Performance: The Latin American Experience, in Fiscal Institutions and Fiscal Performance 103–134 (James M. Poterba and Jürgen von Hagen eds., 1999) (for Latin American countries); Kanokpan Lao-Arayo, *The Effect of Budget Structure on Fiscal Performance: A Study of Selected Asian Countries* (IMF Working Paper, 1997) (for Asian countries); Rolf R. Strauch, *Budget Processes and Fiscal Discipline: Evidence from the US States* (Zentrum für Europäische Integrationsforschung Bonn Working Paper, 1998) (for state governments in the United States).

[33] Mark Hallerberg, Jürgen von Hagen , and Rolf R. Strauch, *The Design of Fiscal Rules and Forms of Governance in European Union Countries*, Working Paper, ZEI (2006), forthcoming in the European Journal of Political Economy.

Table 4.6. Type of budget process

Country	Budget process in the 1990s
Austria	Delegation
Belgium	Contracts
Denmark	Contracts
Spain	Delegation
France	Delegation
Germany	Delegation
Greece	Delegation
Ireland	Contracts
Italy	Contracts (until 1995) Delegation (post 1995)
Luxembourg	Contracts
Netherlands	Contracts
Portugal	Contracts
Finland	Contracts
Sweden	Contracts
UK	Delegation

Source: Hallerberg et al. (2006).

much to improve their budgeting institutions. Thus, the results are consistent with the remarkably different performance of the small and the large states since 1991 that was already noted.

Hallerberg et al. explain that the choice between the delegation and the contracts approach depends on a country's political system and the incentive and enforcement mechanisms it generates for agreements on budgetary norms and guidelines.[34] Specifically, the delegation approach is based on hierarchical relations among the members of the executive branch. In democratic systems, such relations prevail within political parties. The delegation approach is, therefore, the appropriate one for one-party governments or coalition governments among closely aligned partners that typically run together in elections. In contrast, the contracts approach emphasizes agreement among more or less equal partners. It is appropriate for coalition governments among more competitive parties. The fiscal targets featured by the contracts approach are ineffective if the government can walk away from them with low political costs. Single-party governments can do that more easily than coalitions. Conversely, the delegation approach requires special powers for an individual member of the executive branch. This is feasible in one-party settings but awkward in multiparty coalitions, because delegation creates the potential for abusing the Finance Minister's privileged position to the benefit of his party. Based on an analysis of the electoral and party systems in the EU countries, these authors classify the EU countries as "delegation states" and "contract states" (see Table 4.6). Italy has two entries because of the constitutional reform in the mid-1990s. Note that the improvements in the budget processes during the 1990s occurred primarily in contracts states. Delegation states except Greece already had relatively strong budget processes at the beginning of the Maastricht process and did not do much to change them during that process.

B. Fiscal Rules and the Budget Process

The Maastricht fiscal rule, with its emphasis on numerical limits for the budget deficit and general government debt (EDP) and annual Stability Programs

[34] *Id.*

Table 4.7. Fiscal rules index, EU countries

Country	Horizon	Commit	Coalition	Stability program	Shock rules	MoF implementation	Fiscal rule index
Countries Following Contracts Approach							
B	4	4	4	2	4	1	15.0
DK	3	2	0	0	4	2	9.3
Ei	2	2	4	3	0	3	11.3
L	4	4	4	3	4	2	17.0
NL	3	4	4	3	4	1	15.3
P	2	4	0	0.5	4	2	10.5
SF	3	3	4	1	0	1	8.7
SW	2	4	2	1.5	0	0	6.8
Countries Following Delegation Approach							
A	2	3	0	1.5	0	4	8.8
D	3	3	0	1.5	0	2	7.5
E	3	2	0	1.5	0	3	7.8
F	2	3	0	1.5	0	4	8.8
Gr	2	2	0	0.5	0	4	7.2
I	3	2	0	1.5	0	3	7.8
UK	2	3	0	3.5	4	4	14.8

Note: Fiscal Rule Index = 2 × (Horizon + Commitment + Coalition)/3 + Stability Program + Shock Rules + MoF Execution.
Source: These are my own calculations

setting targets for deficits and governments spending (SGP), closely resembles the contracts approach to designing the budget process. Table 4.7 pursues this similarity in more detail, using the institutional data from 2001 collected in Hallerberg et al. The upper half of the table lists the countries for which the contracts approach is the appropriate one (see Table 4.6); the lower half of the table lists the countries for which the delegation approach is the more adequate one.[35]

Hallerberg et al. provide institutional data about the budgeting practices in the EU countries regarding specifically the governments' commitment to fiscal rules.[36] Here I look at the following aspects: The time horizon of a government's multiannual fiscal program, the degree of commitment to annual fiscal targets, the anchoring of the fiscal targets in the coalition agreement, the connection between the national budget and the national stability program, the existence of clear rules for dealing with shocks to expenditures or revenues during the fiscal year, and the strength of the Finance Minister to enforce the budget law during the implementation phase of the budget. I use the numerical coding of the institutional data to construct a "fiscal rules index." A large value on this

[35] Hallerberg et al., *supra* note 32.   [36] *Id.*

index indicates the following: a relatively long time horizon of the multiannual fiscal program, a strong political commitment to the annual fiscal targets, fiscal targets being written into the coalition agreement, a close connection between the fiscal targets embedded in the budget and those expressed in the Stability Program and between the annual budget process and the process of writing and updating the Stability Programs, the prevalence of rules for dealing with unexpected spending or revenue developments, and a relatively strong Finance Minister during the implementation phase. A low value on this index indicates a short time horizon or the nonexistence of a multiannual fiscal program, the interpretation of fiscal targets as being merely indicative, no mentioning of fiscal targets in the coalition agreement, a loose connection only between the fiscal targets spelled out in the budget and those of the Stability Program and between the annual budget process and the process of writing and updating the Stability Program, no rules for dealing with revenue or expenditure shocks, and a weak position of the Finance Minister in the implementation phase of the budget.

The last row of Table 4.7 reports the fiscal rule index. The table shows that Luxembourg has the strongest fiscal rule in the EU, followed by the Netherlands, Belgium, the United Kingdom, Ireland, Portugal, and Denmark. The median fiscal rule index among the EU countries is 8.8. I call fiscal rules with index values above the median *strong*, and rules with index values below the median *weak*. The table shows that countries following the contracts approach generally have strong fiscal rules, while the countries following the delegation approach generally have weak fiscal rules. Sweden and Finland are the only two contracts countries with a rules index below the median, while the United Kingdom is the only delegation country with an index strictly above the median. The difference between the two groups is statistically significant (a chi-square test has a value of $\chi^2 = 5.53, p = 0.019$). This shows that there is a significant, positive correlation strength of the fiscal rule and the design of the budget process in EU countries. Strong fiscal rules typically are embedded in budget processes designed according to the contracts approach. Conversely, countries following the delegation approach typically have adopted merely weak fiscal rules. The evidence thus suggests that countries adopting the contracts approach used the framework and pressure of the Maastricht process to develop strong fiscal rules. The delegation countries, excluding the United Kingdom, did not follow the same pattern.

Considering the individual items, Table 4.7 shows that the fiscal programs in contract states generally have longer time horizons than in delegation states, that the degree of commitment is stronger than in delegation states, and that the fiscal targets in all contract states but in no delegation state are anchored in coalition agreements. Furthermore, a majority of the contract states have explicit rules for dealing with revenue or expenditure shocks. The United Kingdom is the only delegation state where that is true.

C. Fiscal Rules, Budgeting Institutions, and Fiscal Performance

The correlation between the fiscal rule index and the budget surplus ratios across the EU states is not statistically different from zero. In view of the discussion in Section IV. B., this is not surprising: Countries with good budgeting institutions under the delegation approach achieved a high degree of fiscal discipline similar to states with strong fiscal rules and good institutions under the contracts approach. However, if I take the five states with a fiscal rules index above the EU average of 10.9, I see that a strong fiscal rule does make a difference. These states are Belgium, Ireland, Luxembourg, the Netherlands, and the United Kingdom. All five experienced a negative annual growth rate of the debt–GDP ratio since the start of the EMU. For the states with weak fiscal rules (i.e., an index below the mean), this is true for five out of ten. A chi-square test indicates that the difference in performance is statistically significant ($\chi^2 = 3.75$, $p = 0.052$). If I define the medium-term goal of "close to balance or in surplus" under the SGP as an average surplus ratio above −1.0 since the start of EMU, all five states with strong fiscal rules fulfill that condition, but only four out of six states with weak rules ($\chi^2 = 5.0$, $p = 0.025$) do so. Finally, since the start of the EMU, all five states with strong fiscal rules had an average expenditure ratio of at least 2 percent below the 1992–1998 average. For the states with weak rules, this is true only for six out of ten ($\chi^2 = 2.73$, $p = 0.098$). Thus states with strong fiscal rules have shown a better average fiscal performance since the start of the EMU – an example of Schick's verdict that "fiscal rules are effective only if they are supported by other changes in budgeting."[37]

Hallerberg et al. pursue this point in a more formal econometric analysis.[38] They develop a panel regression of the annual change in the government debt ratio on a number of control variables and institutional variables. The key variables of interest are an index measuring the strength of delegation in a country's budget process and an index measuring the strength of its fiscal rule. The results show that strengthening delegation in the budget process reduces the growth of public debt in delegation states, but not in contract states. Conversely, strengthening fiscal rules reduces debt growth in contract states, but not in delegation states. This confirms the suggestion that the effectiveness of fiscal rules and budgeting institutions depends critically on the political environment in which they are installed.

V. CONCLUSIONS

Formal fiscal rules limiting the annual government budget deficit are at the heart of the European fiscal framework for monetary union. The framework

---

[37] Alan Schick, *The Role of Fiscal Rules in Budgeting*, 3 OECD J ON BUDGETING, 8, 7–34 (2003).
[38] Hallerberg et al., *supra* note 33.

originally created by the Maastricht Treaty was further developed and refined by the Stability and Growth Pact. Fiscal performance under this pact has been different in different countries so far. Some countries, especially the smaller ones, have achieved substantial and lasting improvements in their budget balances and public debt ratios. Others, most notably Germany, Italy, and France, have not made much progress in that direction. Fiscal policy generally loosened in the EU once the threat of not making it into the EMU had disappeared in the late 1990s. After the start of the EMU, governments reverted to former patterns of political budget cycles, with significant fiscal expansions in election years.

In this chapter, I explore the link between the effectiveness of fiscal rules and the institutional design of the budget process. Excessive deficits and debts are the result of a common pool problem of public finances. The effects of this problem can be mitigated by budgeting institutions inducing the actors in the budget process to take a comprehensive view of the benefits and costs of all policies financed through the budget. Strong budgeting institutions – under the delegation or the contracts approach – have been found to result in lower deficits and debts in many parts of the world. I find that countries in Europe for which the contracts approach is the appropriate one have used the Maastricht process to strengthen their budgeting institutions. Several of them have adopted budgeting procedures at the national level that strengthen the implementation of the Maastricht fiscal rule. The empirical evidence suggests that the resulting strong fiscal rules have helped these countries maintain a high degree of fiscal discipline since the start of the EMU.

Other countries have kept the link between the Maastricht fiscal rule and their domestic budget processes rather frail, resulting in weak fiscal rules. Most of them are countries where the political system makes the contracts approach less adequate than the delegation approach. Strong budgeting institutions under this approach, however, are equally effective in strengthening and maintaining fiscal discipline.

A first conclusion from this analysis is that budgeting institutions matter more than fiscal rules. Fiscal rules seem attractive to rein in excessive deficits and debts because they are simple and easy to monitor. However, they are effective only in political environments where simplicity and easy monitoring are important for the enforcement of fiscal discipline. This is the case in countries where the solution to the common pool problem is based on agreements among equals – relatively competitive partners in coalition governments. But simplicity and easy monitoring contribute little to fiscal discipline in environments where the government can easily walk away from its own fiscal targets – the case of single-party governments or coalitions of closely aligned partners. In such environments, delegation is the appropriate mechanism to achieve fiscal discipline.

A second conclusion is that the European fiscal framework has failed to recognize that different political systems in the member states require different institutional mechanisms to achieve fiscal discipline. The current framework emphasizes the rules-based approach and has tried to refine the process of formulating and implementing a fiscal rule in much detail. Instead, it should have induced countries where the delegation approach is appropriate to strengthen their budgeting institutions in that direction. This, however, would require an explicit recognition of the differences among the EU countries' political systems and explicit recommendations on how to change specific institutions in individual countries. This is often deemed impossible at the EU level for fear that it would be perceived as an inappropriate intrusion of the EU into the internal affairs of its member states. If so, the EU should stress simply the importance of fiscal discipline and reprimand members with too lax policies, but leave the choice of the institutional design to achieve better discipline to the member states.

Questions for Chapter 4

1. As we have seen in several chapters, one of the challenges of any budget framework is enforcement. If politicians did not face temptations to defect from a policy of spending restraint, frameworks would be unnecessary. What enforcement mechanisms does von Hagen identify in his study of European Union budget policy? He discusses at least three: institutions within each country that are designed to facilitate coordinated budget policy and enforce certain budget objectives; enforcement steps that a centralized European entity, ECOFIN, can take to reduce "excessive" deficits; and, during the 1990s, the threat of denying a country membership into the European Monetary Union. The latter mechanism, the threat of refusing a country entry into the Monetary Union, seems to have provided voters with a concrete consequence of the failure to impose fiscal discipline. What are other ways to set up a framework so that it has sufficient visibility and so that breaking the rules has consequences voters care about? Has the United States tried to accomplish that goal of saliency with voters through its budget framework, and how successful have those attempts been? Is it easier to do in a federation of countries, like the EU, or in a single country, like the United States? Assess the strength of all the various enforcement mechanisms that this chapter discusses and compare them to the tools used in the United States during the various eras of budgeting. What lessons should the EU learn from the modern experience in the United States, and vice versa?

2. One significant difference between the countries in the European Union and the United States is that the former are parliamentary democracies. How does that change the dynamics of budgeting at the various key stages – creating a budget, trading off priorities, reaching certain macro-budgetary objectives, meeting deadlines for budgeting, and enforcing budgetary decisions? How do the two forms of government differ with respect to budget transparency at the various stages?[39]

---

[39] For a discussion of principles of transparency, *see* George Kopits, "Transparency in Government Operations" (May 2000) (paper presented at the Interamerican Development Bank

3. Where does the United States fall within the political economy analysis of fiscal institutions? Has it followed the delegation approach or the contracts approach? What can the United States learn from a close examination of European fiscal institutions as it thinks about future budget reform? What lessons cannot be transferred into the American constitutional experience? What other differences in governance institutions between European democracies and the United States will affect a budget framework? Consider, for example, differences in the number and structure of political parties, different versions of federalism within countries, ethnic makeup of the countries, frequency of elections, and systems of choosing representatives.

4. What is the right goal of a budget process designed to produce spending restraint or some sort of fiscal discipline? Through the Maastricht Treaty and the Stability and Growth Pact, the European Union has set bringing deficits below 3 percent of GDP as the goal for its member countries. In the United States, the rhetoric has long centered on achieving a balanced cash-flow deficit, and during the period of Gramm-Rudman-Hollings, the elimination of the deficit was the explicit goal of the congressional budget framework. For a discussion of the proposed constitutional balanced-budget amendment in the United States, see works by Daniel Shaviro and Theodore Seto.[40] What should be the goal of a budget framework? Should the goal vary over time, according to economic and other conditions in the country? How would any variance across years be determined? How is enforcement changed if the target is either a variable one or one that allows some amount of deficit? Is the EU method of linking the size of deficits to each country's GDP preferable to the U.S. fetish with a balanced cash-flow budget? Are there other ways to establish targets affecting the deficit, federal spending, or revenue collected that could provide the foundation for a framework law? In the end, does the budget framework itself matter? How often is the framework responsible for deficit reduction, or is it more likely that fiscal discipline is a result of economic factors that allow governments more easily to collect revenue to cover spending programs? In that case, what other objectives might a budget framework serve, if not to impose fiscal discipline?

5. This chapter provides an international comparison for the U.S. experience, analyzing fiscal policy and institutions in Western democracies in the European Union. Other international comparisons can be illuminating both to better

Conference on Transparency and Development in Latin America and the Caribbean), *available at* http://www.iadb.org/leg/Seminar/Documents/Transparency%20Kopitz%20Eng.pdf

[40] *See* Daniel Shaviro, Do Deficits Matter? (1997); Theodore P. Seto, *Drafting a Federal Balanced Budget Amendment that Does What it is Supposed to Do (and No More)*, 106 Yale L. J. 1449 (1997).

understand the U.S. circumstances and to consider optimal fiscal rules generally or for particular countries.[41]

---

[41] For other comparative work, *see* Hiromitsu Ishi, MAKING FISCAL POLICY IN JAPAN: ECONOMIC EFFECTS AND INSTITUTIONAL SETTINGS (2000); FISCAL INSTITUTIONS AND FISCAL PERFOR-MANCE (James M. Poterba and Jürgen von Hagen eds., 1999) (including chapters on OECD countries, Latin American countries, the EU, Canada, Australia, New Zealand, and Japan); Jürgen von Hagen, *supra* note 9.

Bibliography

ARTICLES

Alberto Alesina and Roberto Perotti, *Fiscal Discipline and the Budget Process*, 86 Am. Econ. Rev. 401 (1996).

James E. Alt, *Three Simple Tests of Ferejohn's Model: Transparency and Accountability in U.S. States* (2005) (paper prepared for NYU Colloquium on Law, Economics, and Politics).

David P. Baron, *Service-Induced Campaign Contributions and the Electoral Equilibrium*, 104 Q.J. Econ. 45 (1989).

Jill Barshay, *"Temporary" Tax Breaks Usually a Permanent Reality*, Congressional Quarterly Weekly 2831 (Nov. 15, 2003).

David Baumann, *Begin the Endgame*, 15 Nat'l J. 1126 (2000).

Timothy Besley, *Political Selection*, 19 J. Econ. Persp. 43 (2005).

Cheryl D. Block, *Congress and Accounting Scandals: Is the Pot Calling the Kettle Black?* 82 Neb. L. Rev. 365 (2003).

Jon R. Blöndal, *Budget Reform in OECD Member Countries: Common Trends*, 2 OECD J. Budgeting 7 (2003).

Willem H. Buiter, *Ten Commandments for a Fiscal Rule in the E(M)U*, 19 Oxf. Rev. Econ. Pol'y 84 (2003).

Karen C. Burke and Grayson M. P. McCouch, *Lipstick, Light Beer, and Back-Loaded Savings Accounts*, 25 Va. Tax Rev. 1101 (2006).

Marco Buti and Paul van den Noord, *Discretionary Fiscal Policy and Elections: The Experience of the Early Years of EMU* (OECD Economics Department Working Paper No. 351, 2003).

Marco Buti and Paul van den Noord, *Fiscal Policy in EMU: Rules, Discretion, and Political Incentives*, 206 Eur. Comm'n Econ. Papers (2004).

Jay S. Bybee, *Advising the President: Separation of Powers and the Federal Advisory Committee Act*, 104 Yale L.J. 51 (1994).

Fabio Canova and Paraskevi (Evi) Pappa, *The Elusive Costs and the Immaterial Gains of Fiscal Constraints* [Innocenzo Gasparini Inst. for Econ. Res. (IGIER), Bocconi Univ. Working Paper No. 295, 2004].

Cary Coglianese, Richard Zeckhauser, and Edward Parson, *Seeking Truth for Power: Informational Strategy and Regulatory Policymaking*, 89 Minn. L. Rev. 277 (2004).

Steven P. Croley and William F. Funk, *The Federal Advisory Committee Act and Good Government*, 14 Yale J. on Reg. 451 (1997).

Kenneth W. Dam, *The American Fiscal Constitution*, 44 U. Chi. L. Rev. 271 (1977).

William G. Dauster, *Budget Emergencies*, 18 J. Legis. 249 (spring 1992).

Bill Dauster, *The Day the Senate Died: Budget Measure Weakens Minority*, Roll Call, May 30, 1996, at 5.

Bill Dauster, *The Monster That Ate the United States Senate*, 18 Pub. Budgeting & Fin. 87 (summer 1998).

Helen Dewar, *Stockman Issues Blunt Warning; Budget Agreement Called Vital*, Wash. Post, Apr. 19, 1983, at A1.

Ousmane Doré and Paul R. Masson, *Experience with Budgetary Convergence in the WAEMU* [Int'l Monetary Fund (IMF) Working Paper No. 02/108, 2002].

Jon Elster, *Arguing and Bargaining in Two Constituent Assemblies*, 2 U. Penn. J. Constl. Law 345 (2000).

Carl Emmerson, Chris Frayne, and Sarah Love, *The Government's Fiscal Rules* (The Inst. For Fiscal Stud. Briefing Note No. 16, 2001).

Michael W. Evans, *The Budget Process and the "Sunset" Provisions of the 2001 Tax Law*, Tax Notes, Apr. 21, 2003.

Brian Fletcher, Case Comment, *Cheney v. United States District Court for the District of Columbia*, 28 Harv. Envtl. L. Rev. 605 (2004).

Alan Fram, *Washington Today: Whatever Happened to Gramm-Rudman?* Associated Press, Nov. 29, 1991.

Maurice Frankel, *Freedom of Information: Some International Characteristics* 9 (2001) (paper from the Campaign for Freedom of Information).

William G. Gale and Peter R. Orszag, *An Economic Assessment of Tax Policy in the Bush Administration*, 2001–2004, 45 B.C. L. Rev. 1157 (2004).

William G. Gale and Peter R. Orszag, *Sunsets in the Tax Code*, 99 Tax Notes 1553 (2003).

Elizabeth Garrett, *Harnessing Politics: The Dynamics of Offset Requirements in the Tax Legislative Process*, 65 U. Chi. L. Rev. 501 (1998).

Elizabeth Garrett, *Rethinking the Structures of Decisionmaking in the Federal Budget Process*, 35 Harv. J. on Legis. 387 (1998).

Elizabeth Garrett, *The Congressional Budget Process: Strengthening the Party-in-Government*, 100 Colum. L. Rev. 702 (2000).

Elizabeth Garrett, *Attention to Context in Statutory Interpretation: Applying the Lessons of Dynamic Statutory Interpretation to Omnibus Legislation, in* Issues in Legal Schol-arship 9 (Robert Cooter, Daniel Farber, Philip Frickey, and James Gordley eds., 2002), *available at* http://www.bepress.com/ils/iss3/art1.

Elizabeth Garrett, *The Purposes of Framework Legislation*, 14 J. Contemp. Legal Iss. 717 (2005).

Heidi Glenn, *Frenzel Criticizes Sunshine Law Governing Tax Panel*, Tax Notes 1126, Nov. 28, 2005.

Heidi Glenn, *Perspectives on Tax Reform From Connie Mack*, Tax Notes 26, Jan. 9, 2006.

Michael J. Graetz, *Paint by Numbers Tax Lawmaking*, 95 Colum. L. Rev. 609 (1995).

Richard L. Hall and Frank W. Wayman, *Buying Time: Moneyed Interests and the Mobilization of Bias in Congressional Committees*, 84 Am. Pol. Sci. Rev. 797 (1990).

Mark Hallerberg, Rolf R. Strauch, and Jürgen von Hagen, *The Use and Effectiveness of Budgetary Rules and Norms in EU Member States* (Dutch Ministry of Finance Working Paper, 2001).

Mark Hallerberg, Rolf R. Strauch, and Jürgen von Hagen, *Budgeting in Europe After Maastricht: Patterns of Reform and Their Effectiveness*, Hacienda Publica Espanola Monografia, 2004a, at 201.

Mark Hallerberg, Rolf R. Strauch, and Jürgen von Hagen, *The Design of Fiscal Rules and Forms of Governance in European Union Countries*, Eur. J. Pol. Econ. (forthcoming).

John C. Harsanyi, *Cardinal Utility in Welfare Economics and in the Theory of Risk Taking*, 61 J. Pol. Econ. 434 (1953).

David Heald, *Fiscal Transparency: Concepts, Measurement and UK Practice*, 81 Pub. Admin. 723 (2003).

Richard Hemming and Michael Kell, *Promoting Fiscal Responsibility – Transparency, Rules and Independent Fiscal Authorities*, 3 Banca D'Italia Workshop on Fiscal Rules 433 (2001).

Andrew Hughes-Hallett, Rolf R. Strauch, and Jürgen von Hagen, *Budgetary Consolidations in Europe*, 16 J. Japanese & Int'l Econ. 512 (2002).

Otmar Issing, *Communication, Transparency, Accountability: Monetary Policy in the Twenty-First Century*, Fed. Res. Bank of St. Louis Rev. 65 (Mar./Apr. 2005).

Andrew Jackson, pocket veto message (Dec. 4, 1833), *in* Sen. J. 20, 30 (Dec. 5, 1833).

Suzanne Kennedy and Janine Robbins, *The Role of Fiscal Rules in Determining Fiscal Performance* (Dept. of Finance Working Paper No. 2001–16, 2001).

George Kopits and Steven A. Symansky, *Fiscal Policy Rules* (IMF Occasional Paper No. 162, 1998).

Rebecca M. Kysar, *The Sun Also Rises: The Political Economy of Sunset Provisions in the Tax Code*, 40 Ga. L. Rev. 335 (2006).

Kanokpan Lao-Arayo, *The Effect of Budget Structure on Fiscal Performance: A Study of Selected Asian Countries* (IMF Working Paper, 1997).

Robert C. Lowry, James E. Alt, and Karen E. Ferree, *Fiscal Policy Outcomes and Electoral Accountability in American States*, 92 Am. Pol. Sci. Rev. 759 (1998).

Carlos José Fonseca Marinheiro, *Has the Stability and Growth Pact Stabilised? Evidence from a Panel of 12 European Countries and Some Implications for the Reform of the Pact* (CESifo Working Paper Series No. 1411, 2005).

Dan R. Mastromarco, *Improving the Revenue Estimating Process: Introduction to a Series*, 105 Tax Notes 1141 (2004).

Mathew D. McCubbins and Thomas Schwartz, *Congressional Oversight Overlooked: Police Patrol Versus Fire Alarms*, 28 Am. J. Pol. Sci. 165 (1984).

Ellen E. Meade and David Stasavage, *Publicity of Debate and the Incentive to Dissent: Evidence from the U.S. Federal Reserve* (June 21, 2005) (unpublished paper), *available at* http://www.nyu.edu/gsas/dept/politics/faculty/stasavage/feddeliberation11.pdf.

Manfred J. M. Neumann, *Transparency in Monetary Policy*, 4 Atlantic Econ. J. 353, 358 (2002).

Brendan O'Flaherty and Jagdish Bhagwati, *Will Free Trade with Political Science Put Normative Economics Out of Work?*, 9 Econ. & Pol. 207 (1996).

James T. O'Reilly, *"Access to Records" Versus "Access to Evil": Should Disclosure Laws Consider Motives as a Barrier to Records Release?*, 12 Kan. J.L. & Pub. Pol'y 559 (2003).

Richard Peach, *The Evolution of the Federal Budget and Fiscal Rules*, 3 Banca D'Italia Workshop on Fiscal Rules 217 (2001).

Christopher J. Puckett, *Is the Experiment Over? The OMB's Decision to Change the Game Through a Shortening of the Forecast*, 11 Geo. J. Poverty Law & Pol'y 169 (2004).

Andrea Prat, *The Wrong Kind of Transparency*, 95 Am. Econ. Rev. 862 (2005).

Teresa Dabán Sánchez, Enrica Detragiache, C. Gabriel di Bella, Gian Maria Milesi-Ferretti, and Steven A. Symansky, *Rules-Based Fiscal Policy in France, Germany, Italy, and Spain* (IMF Occasional Paper No. 225, 2003).

Alan Schick, *The Role of Fiscal Rules in Budgeting*, 3 OECD J. ON BUDGETING 8 (2003).

Daniel N. Shaviro, *Rethinking Tax Expenditures and Fiscal Language*, 57 TAX L. REV. 187 (2004).

Marsha Jean Simon, *The Real Rules of the Budget Game: Minority Fiscal Decision Making in the United States Senate* (June 2005) (unpublished Ph.D. dissertation, Massachusetts Institute of Technology).

Rolf R. Strauch, *Budget Processes and Fiscal Discipline: Evidence from the US States* (Zentrum für Europäische Integrationsforschung Bonn Working Paper, 1998).

Joseph E. Stiglitz, *On Liberty, the Right to Know, and Public Discourse: The Role of Transparency in Public Life*, OXFORD AMNESTY LECTURE 22 (Jan. 27, 1999), *available at* http://www2.gsb.columbia.edu/faculty/jstiglitz/download/2001_On_Liberty_the_Right_to_Know_and_Public.pdf.

Kate Stith, *Congress' Power of the Purse*, 97 YALE L.J. 1343 (1988).

Cass R. Sunstein, *Government Control of Information*, 74 CAL. L. REV. 889 (1986).

Dennis F. Thompson, *Democratic Secrecy*, 114 POL. SCI. Q. 181 (1999).

Adrian Vermeule, *The Constitutional Law of Congressional Procedure*, 71 U. CHI. L. REV. 361 (2004).

Adrian Vermeule, *Introduction: Political Constraints on Supreme Court Reform*, 90 MINN. L. REV. 1154 (2006).

Adrian Vermeule, *Selection Effects in Constitutional Law*, 91 VA. L. REV. 953 (2005).

Adrian Vermeule, *Veil of Ignorance Rules in Constitutional Law*, 111 YALE L.J. 399 (2001).

Bjorn Volkerink and Jakob de Haan, *Fragmented Government Effects on Fiscal Policy: New Evidence*, 109 PUB. CHOICE 221 (2001).

Jürgen von Hagen, *Fiscal Discipline and Growth in Euroland: Experiences with the Stability and Growth Pact* (Center for European Integration Studies Working Paper No. B06-2003, 2003).

Jürgen von Hagen, *Budgeting Procedures and Fiscal Performance in the European Communities* (Commission of the European Communities DG II Economic Papers 96, 1992).

Jürgen von Hagen, *Fiscal Rules, Fiscal Institutions, and Fiscal Performance*, 33 ECON. & SOCIAL REV. 263 (2002).

Jürgen von Hagen, *Fiscal Rules and Fiscal Performance in the European Union and Japan*, 24 MONETARY & ECON. STUD. 25 (2006).

Jürgen von Hagen and Barry Eichengreen, *Fiscal Policy and Monetary Union: Federalism, Fiscal Restrictions, and the No-Bailout Rule* (Centre for Econ. Pol'y Res. Discussion Paper No. 1247, 1995).

Jürgen von Hagen and Ian J. Harden, *Budget Processes and Commitment to Fiscal Discipline*, 39 EUR. ECON. REV. 771 (1995).

Jürgen von Hagen and Ian H. Harden, *National Budget Processes and Fiscal Performance*, 3 EUR. ECON.: REP. & STUD. 311 (1994).

Jürgen von Hagen, Andrew Hughes-Hallett, and Rolf R. Strauch, *Budgetary Consolidation in EMU*, 148 EUR. COMM'N ECON. PAPERS (2001).

The Final Word, CONGRESS DAILY, May 18, 1992.

The Problem Is the Problem, WASH. POST, July 18, 1984, at A14 (editorial).

Letter from Dan L. Crippen, Congressional Budget Office director, to Hon. John M. Spratt, Jr., ranking Dem. member, House Budget Comm. (Aug. 26, 1999), *reprinted in* TAX NOTES TODAY, Sept. 14, 1999.

European Commission, *Specifications on the Implementation of the Stability and Growth Pact and Guidelines on the Format and Content of Stability and Convergence Programs* 23 (European Commission DG Economic and Financial Affairs Mimeo, 2002).

European Commission DG Economic and Financial Affairs, *1999–2000* (March, 27, 2007), *available at* http://ec.europa.eu/economy_finance/about/activities/sgp/year/year19992000_en.htm.

BOOKS

Bruce Ackerman and Ian Ayres, VOTING WITH DOLLARS: A NEW PARADIGM FOR CAMPAIGN FINANCE (2002).

R. Douglas Arnold, THE LOGIC OF CONGRESSIONAL ACTION (1990).

Geoffrey Brennan and James M. Buchanan, THE REASON OF RULES (1985).

Richard Briffault, BALANCING ACTS: THE REALITY BEHIND STATE BALANCED BUDGET AMENDMENTS (1996).

Anne Brunila and Carlos Martinez-Mongay, *The Challenge for Fiscal Policy in the Early Years of EMU, in* EMU AND ECONOMIC POLICY IN EUROPE: THE CHALLENGE OF THE EARLY YEARS 150–169 (Marco Buti and Andre Sapir eds., 2002).

James M. Buchanan and Gordon Tullock, THE CALCULUS OF CONSENT: LOGICAL FOUNDATIONS OF CONSTITUTIONAL DEMOCRACY (1962).

Antonio J. Cabral, *The Stability and Growth Pact: Main Aspects and Some Considerations on Its Implementation, in* THE EURO-ZONE: A NEW ECONOMIC ENTITY? (1999).

Robert A. Dahl, A PREFACE TO DEMOCRATIC THEORY (1956).

William G. Dauster, BUDGET PROCESS LAW ANNOTATED (1993).

Douglas Dion, TURNING THE LEGISLATIVE THUMBSCREW: MINORITY RIGHTS AND PROCEDURAL CHANGE IN LEGISLATIVE POLITICS (1997).

Jon Elster, *Legislatures as Constituent Assemblies, in* THE LEAST EXAMINED BRANCH: THE ROLE OF LEGISLATURES IN THE CONSTITUTIONAL STATE 181 (Richard W. Bauman & Tsvi Kahana eds., 2006).

John Ferejohn, *Accountability and Authority: Toward a Theory of Political Accountability, in* DEMOCRACY, ACCOUNTABILITY AND REPRESENTATION 131 (Adam Przeworski, Susan C. Stokes, and Bernard Manin eds., 1999).

Alan S. Frumin, RIDDICK'S SENATE PROCEDURE (1992).

Elizabeth Garrett, Ronald M. Levin, and Theodore Ruger, *Constitutional Issues Raised by the 1995 Lobbying Disclosure Act, in* THE LOBBYING MANUAL 143 (W. V. Luneberg and T. M. Susman eds., 3d ed. 2005).

Mark Hallerberg, Rolf Strauch, and Jürgen von Hagen, THE USE AND EFFECTIVENESS OF FISCAL NORMS IN THE EUROPEAN UNION (2002).

Mark Hallerberg and Jürgen von Hagen, *Electoral Institutions, Cabinet Negotiations, and Budget Deficits in the EU, in* FISCAL INSTITUTIONS AND FISCAL PERFORMANCE (Jim Poterba and Jürgen von Hagen eds., 1999).

Yianos Kontopoulos and Roberto Perotti, *Government Fragmentation and Fiscal Policy Outcomes: Evidence from OECD Countries, in* FISCAL INSTITUTIONS AND FISCAL PERFORMANCE 81–102 (James M. Poterba and Jürgen von Hagen eds., 1999).

James Madison, THE FEDERALIST No. 58, (Clinton Rossiter ed., 1961).

Richard Munson, THE CARDINALS OF CAPITOL HILL; THE MEN AND WOMEN WHO CONTROL GOVERNMENT SPENDING (1993).

Walter J. Oleszek, CONGRESSIONAL PROCEDURES AND THE POLICY PROCESS (5th ed., 2001).

Allen Schick, THE FEDERAL BUDGET: POLITICS, POLICY, PROCESS (2000).

Jürgen Stark, *Genesis of a Pact, in* THE STABILITY AND GROWTH PACT: THE ARCHITECTURE OF FISCAL POLICY IN EMU 77–105 (Anne Brunila, Marco Buti, and Daniele Franco eds., 2001).

Ernesto Stein, Alejandro Grisanti, and Ernesto Talvi, *Institutional Arrangements and Fiscal Performance: The Latin American Experience, in* Fiscal Institutions and Fiscal Performance 103–134 (James M. Poterba and Jürgen von Hagen eds., 1999).

Thomas Stratmann, *Logrolling, in* Perspectives on Public Choice: A Handbook (Dennis C. Mueller ed., 1997).

Andrei Velasco, *Debts and Deficits with Fragmented Fiscal Policymaking, in* Fiscal Institutions and Fiscal Performance 37–58 (James M. Poterba and Jürgen von Hagen eds., 1999).

Jürgen von Hagen, *Political Economy of Fiscal Institutions, in* Oxford Handbook of Political Economy 464–478 (Barry R. Weingast and Donald Wittman eds., 2006).

Respectfully Quoted: A Dictionary of Quotations, no. 996 (1989).

Center on Budget and Policy Priorities, Tax Cuts: Myths and Realities (Sept. 27, 2006).

CASES

Bowsher v. Synar, 478 U.S. 714 (1986).

City of New Haven, Conn. v. United States, 809 F. 2d 900 (D.C. Cir. 1987).

Commonwealth of Pennsylvania v. Lynn, 501 F.2d 848 (D.C. Cir. 1974).

Federal Open Market Committee v. Merrill, 443 U.S. 340 (1979).

I.N.S. v. Chadha, 462 U.S. 919 (1983).

Merrill v. Federal Open Market Committee of the Federal Reserve, 516 F. Supp. 1028 (1981).

Train v. Campaign Clean Water, Inc., 420 U.S. 136 (1975).

Train v. City of New York, 420 U.S. 35 (1975).

State Highway Comm'n of Missouri v. Volpe, 479 F.2d 1099 (8th Cir. 1973).

CONGRESSIONAL RECORDS

The Balanced Budget Amendment: Hearings Before the House Comm. on the Budget, 2. 102d Cong., 2d Sess. 151–152 (1992) (serial no. 42).

128 Cong. Rec. S5506 (May 19, 1982).

127 Cong. Rec. 12,692 (June 17, 1981).

127 Cong. Rec. S6664 (daily ed. June 22, 1981).

131 Cong. Rec. S5863 (May 9, 1985).

131 Cong. Rec. S14,034 (daily ed., Oct. 24, 1985).

135 Cong. Rec. S12,589 (daily ed. Oct. 4, 1989).

136 Cong. Rec. S15,771 (daily ed., Oct. 18, 1990).

139 Cong. Rec. S7920 (daily ed., June 24, 1993).

139 Cong. Rec. S7921 (daily ed. June 24, 1993).

139 Cong. Rec. S10,675–78 (daily ed., Aug. 6, 1993).

141 Cong. Rec. S14,135 (daily ed., Sept. 22, 1995).

141 Cong. Rec. S16,016 (daily ed., Oct. 27, 1995).

142 Cong. Rec. S5415–20 (daily ed., May 21, 1996).

142 Cong. Rec. S5418 (daily ed., May 21, 1996).

142 Cong. Rec. S5516 (daily ed., May 23, 1996).

143 Cong. Rec. S6177–80 (daily ed., June 24, 1997).

143 Cong. Rec. S6291, S6308 (daily ed., June 25, 1997).

146 Cong. Rec. S4172–77 (daily ed., May 18, 2000) (remarks of Sens. Feingold and Wellstone).

147 Cong. Rec. S12, 118 (daily ed., Nov. 29, 2001).
149 Cong. Rec. S13,352–57 (daily ed., Oct. 28, 2003).
149 Cong. Rec. S13,435 (daily ed., Oct. 29, 2003).
151 Cong. Rec. S10,006 (daily ed., Sept. 14, 2005).
151 Cong. Rec. S10,072–73 (daily ed., Sept. 15, 2005).

CONGRESSIONAL REPORTS

Adoption of Procedure for Disclosing Policy Decisions by the Federal Open Market Committee, 81 FED. RES. BULL. 265 (Mar. 1995).
CONGRESSIONAL BUDGET OFFICE, U.S. CONG., THE BUDGET AND ECONOMIC OUTLOOK: FISCAL YEARS 2007 TO 2016 (2006).
CONGRESSIONAL BUDGET OFFICE, U.S. CONG., THE BUDGET AND ECONOMIC OUTLOOK: FISCAL YEARS 2001–2010 (Jan. 1, 2000).
CONGRESSIONAL BUDGET OFFICE, U.S. CONG., THE BUDGETARY TREATMENT OF LEASES AND PUBLIC/PRIVATE VENTURES (Feb. 2003).
CONGRESSIONAL BUDGET OFFICE, U.S. CONG., HOW CBO FORECASTS INCOME (Aug. 2006).
CONGRESSIONAL BUDGET OFFICE, U.S. CONG., COMPUTATION OF ON-BUDGET SURPLUS FOR FISCAL YEAR 2000 (2001).
CONGRESSIONAL BUDGET OFFICE, U.S. CONG., THE UNCERTAINTY OF BUDGET PROJECTIONS: A DISCUSSION OF DATA AND METHODS (Feb. 2003).
Cong. Res. Service, REPORT ON TAX EXTENDERS, RL32367, Doc. 2006–16512 (Aug. 4, 2006).
CRS Appropriations Team, EARMARKS IN APPROPRIATION ACTS: FY1994, FY1996, FY1998, FY2000, FY2002, FY2004, FY2005 (Jan. 26, 2006).
Lewis Deschler, 16 DESCHLER'S PRECEDENTS OF THE UNITED STATES HOUSE OF REPRESENTATIVES, H.R. Doc. No. 94–661 (1976).
DOCUMENTARY HISTORY OF THE FIRST FEDERAL CONGRESS OF THE UNITED STATES OF AMERICA (Charlene Bangs Bickford and Helen E. Veit eds., 1986).
OFFICE OF MGM'T AND BUDGET, CIRCULAR NO. A-11, APP. A (July 2004).
U.S. GEN. ACCOUNTING OFFICE, UNDERSTANDING THE PRIMARY COMPONENTS OF THE ANNUAL FINANCIAL REPORT OF THE UNITED STATES GOVERNMENT, GAO-05–958SP (2005).
Jane G. Gravelle and Maxim Shvedov, *Proposed Savings Accounts: Economic and Budgetary Effects*, Rep. No. RL32228 *in* CONG. RES. SERVICE REPORT FOR CONGRESS 2–4 (June 30, 2006).
Thomas L. Hungerford, *Savings Incentives: What May Work, What May Not*, Rep. No. RL33482 *in* CONG. RES. SERVICE REPORT FOR CONGRESS 9–12 (June 20, 2006).
Joint Committee on Taxation, ESTIMATED REVENUE EFFECTS OF THE CONFERENCE AGREEMENT FOR THE "TAX INCREASE PREVENTION AND RECONCILIATION ACT OF 2005" (May 9, 2006) (JCX-18–06).
Robert Keith, DEFICIT IMPACT OF RECONCILIATION LEGISLATION ENACTED IN 1990, 1993, AND 1997 (Sept. 21, 2005) (CRS rep. no. RS22098).
Robert Keith, SUBMISSION OF THE PRESIDENT'S BUDGET IN TRANSITION YEARS (July 31, 2001) (CRS rep. no. RS20752).
Robert Keith, OMNIBUS APPROPRIATIONS ACTS: OVERVIEW OF RECENT PRACTICES (Apr. 27, 2005) (CRS rep. no. RL32473).
Robert Keith and Bill Heniff Jr., THE BUDGET RECONCILIATION PROCESS: HOUSE AND SENATE PROCEDURES (2005) (CRS rep. no. RL33030).

Robert Keith and Allen Schick, INTRODUCTION TO THE FEDERAL BUDGET PROCESS (2004) (CRS rep. no. 98-721).

Donald R. Kennon and Rebecca M. Rogers, THE COMMITTEE ON WAYS AND MEANS: A BICENTENNIAL HISTORY: 1789–1989 (1989) (H. Doc. 244, 100th Cong., 2d Sess.).

Office of Management and Budget, ANALYTICAL PERSPECTIVES, BUDGET OF THE UNITED STATES GOVERNMENT, FISCAL YEAR 2007 (2006).

Office of Management and Budget, CIRCULAR A-11; PREPARATION, SUBMISSION, AND EXECUTION OF THE BUDGET, § 10 (2006).

Office of Management and Budget, Memorandum M-01–17, Memorandum for Heads of Executive Departments and Agencies, Confidentiality of Pre-Decisional Budget Information (Apr. 25, 2001), *available at* http://www.whitehouse.gov/omb/memoranda/m01–17.html.

President's Advisory Panel on Federal Tax Reform, SIMPLE, FAIR, AND PRO-GROWTH: PROPOSALS TO FIX AMERICA'S TAX SYSTEM (2005).

James V. Saturno, EMERGENCY SPENDING: STATUTORY AND CONGRESSIONAL RULES (May 11, 2005) (CRS rep. no. RS21035).

James V. Saturno, POINTS OF ORDER IN THE CONGRESSIONAL BUDGET PROCESS (May 19, 2005) (CRS rep. no. 97–865).

Allen Schick, LEGISLATION, APPROPRIATIONS, AND BUDGETS: THE DEVELOPMENT OF SPENDING DECISION-MAKING IN CONGRESS (May 1984) (CRS rep. no. 84–106).

Staff of S. Comm. on Appropriations, 109th Cong., UNITED STATES SENATE COMMITTEE ON APPROPRIATIONS; 138TH ANNIVERSARY; 1867–2005 (2005).

Staff of S. Comm. on the Budget, 105th Cong., THE CONGRESSIONAL BUDGET PROCESS; AN EXPLANATION (1998).

Staff of S. Comm. on the Budget, 108th Cong., BUDGET BULLETIN, Sept. 17, 2003.

Staff of S. Comm. on Finance, 97th Cong., HISTORY OF THE COMMITTEE ON FINANCE (1981).

The Treasury Department's annual FINANCIAL REPORT OF THE UNITED STATES GOVERNMENT.

U.S. DEP'T OF TREAS., FINANCIAL REPORT OF THE UNITED STATES GOVERNMENT (2005).

LEGISLATION

Balanced Budget and Emergency Deficit Control Act of 1985, Pub. L. No. 99–177, tit. II, 99 Stat. 1037, 1038 (1985).

Balanced Budget and Emergency Deficit Control Reaffirmation Act of 1987, Pub. L. No. 100–119, tit. I-II, 101 Stat. 754 (1987).

Balanced Budget Act of 1997, Pub. L. No. 105-33, 111 Stat. 251 (1997).

Budget Enforcement Act of 1990, Pub. L. No. 101-508, tit. XIII, 104 Stat. 1388, 1388-573–1388-630 (1990).

12 C.F.R. § 281.1 (2006) 31. Pub. L. No. 104-65, 109 Stat. 691 (1995).

C.F.R. § 102-3.35(a).

C.F.R. § 102-3.160.

41 C.F.R. pt. 102-3, subpt. D, app. A.

41 C.F.R. § 102-3.75, subpt. B, app. A.

Congressional Budget Act § 301(b)(4), 2 U.S.C. § 632(b)(4).

Congressional Budget Act § 310(a), 2 U.S.C. § 641(a).

Congressional Budget Act § 313, 2 U.S.C. § 644.

Defense Authorization Amendments and Base Closure and Realignment Act, Pub. L. No. 100-526, 102 Stat. 2623 (1988).

Deficit Reduction Act of 2005, Pub. L. No. 109-171, 120 Stat. 4 (2006).

Economic Growth and Tax Relief Reconciliation Act of 2001, Pub. L. No. 107-16, 115 Stat. 38 (2001).

66 Fed. Reg. 37728, 37729, 37740 (July 19, 2001).

Fiscal Responsibility for a Sound Future Act, S. 851, 109th Cong. (introduced Apr. 19, 2005).

H.R. Con. Res. 32, 1st Cong., 1st Sess. (1789).

H.R. Con. Res. 67, 104th Cong., 1st Sess., § 202 (1995).

H.R. Con. Res. 95, 108th Cong., 1st Sess., § 505 (1999).

H.R. Con. Res. 218, 103d Cong., 2d Sess., § 23 (1994).

H.R. Rep. No. 92-1017 (1972), *reprinted in* 1972 U.S.C.C.A.N. 3491, 3500.

House Rule XI, cl. 2(g)(1).

Jobs and Growth Tax Relief Reconciliation Act of 2003, Pub. L. No. 108-27, 117 Stat. 752 (2003).

Medicare Prescription Drug, Improvement, and Modernization Act of 2003, Pub. L. No. 108-173, 117 Stat. 2066 (2003).

Omnibus Budget Reconciliation Act of 1993, §§ 13131, 13301–13303, 13901–13971, Pub. L. No. 103-66, 107 Stat. 312 (1993).

Personal Responsibility and Work Opportunity Reconciliation Act of 1996, Pub. L. No. 104-193, 110 Stat. 2105 (1996).

Pub. L. No. 67-13, 42 Stat. 20 (codified as amended in scattered sections of 31 U.S.C.).

Pub. L. No. 93-344, 88 Stat. 297 (1974) (codified as amended at 2 U.S.C. §§ 601–688).

Pub. L. No. 101-508, tit. XIII, 104 Stat. 1388, 1388-573–1388-630 (1990) (codified as amended in scattered sections of 2 U.S.C., 15 U.S.C. § 1022, 31 U.S.C §§ 1105, 1341, 1342).

Pub. L. No. 107-90, 115 Stat. 878, 887 (2001).

Senate Standing Rule XVI(4).

Senate Standing Rule XXII(2)

Senate Standing Rule XXVI, ¶ 5(b).

Senate Standing Rule XXX (Dec. 19, 1850).

Taxpayer Relief Act of 1997, Pub. L. No. 105-34, 111 Stat. 788 (1997).

Tax Increase Prevention and Reconciliation Act of 2005, Pub. L. No. 109-222 (2006).

U.S. Const. art. II, § 1, cl. 1.

U.S. Const., art. I, § 5, cl. 3.

2 U.S.C. §601(f).

2 U.S.C. § 1604(b)(2)(B).

5 U.S.C. App. 2. (2006).

31 U.S.C. § 1105(a).

Working Families Tax Relief Act of 2004, Pub. L. No. 108-311, 118 Stat. 1166 (2004).

24 Stat. 373 (1887).

PART TWO

UNDERSTANDING FEDERAL DEFICITS AND PUBLIC DEBT

F or the general public, the federal deficits and public debt are the most visible and commonly encountered manifestations of budget policy. Newspapers faithfully track the rise and fall of the federal deficits, politicians routinely decry the state of the government's fiscal affairs, and New York's Times Square even features an electronic billboard that tracks the total outstanding federal debt in real time. Notwithstanding the ubiquity of the terms *federal deficit* and *public debt* in our national discourse, the meaning and importance of these terms is often obscure. To begin with, the numbers at issue are often astronomical. Annual federal deficits run in the hundreds of billions of dollars; the national debt reaches into the trillions of dollars. And, increasingly, experts have begun to speak in terms of unfunded obligations for entitlement programs that surge into the tens of trillions of dollars. But beyond the difficulty of comprehending the significance of number of this magnitude, there are also complexities in understanding what the federal deficit and public debt actually represent and what levels of deficit and debt would be appropriate for a country such as our own. As we will see, there are many ways to measure federal deficits and debt, and different measurements may be more appropriate in different contexts. The calculation of deficits and debt also has political implications, and so politicians are keenly interested in how these numbers are assembled and reported to the general public.

We begin our consideration of debts and deficits with an economist's perspective, written by Professor Michael Boskin, who once served as chairman of the President's Council of Economic Advisers and thus has had first-hand experience dealing with the subject. His analysis explores the many different ways in which deficits and debts could be measured and then discusses the complex and multifaceted mechanisms whereby fiscal policy interacts with the real economy, both today and in the future. As his chapter suggests, public finance theory provides important, though not necessarily determinate, insights into appropriate levels of deficits and public debt. Professor Boskin also introduces a number of new measures used to monitor the federal government's fiscal balance over the long term, when federal entitlement programs such as Social Security and Medicare are projected to make increasingly large demands on federal resources.

In Chapter 6, Professor Howell Jackson unpacks the most common measures of federal deficits and public debt used in popular discussions of federal fiscal policy today and explains their significance for both politicians and the general public. He then explains the numerous ways in which these traditional measures offer an incomplete picture of the financial obligations that the federal government has undertaken, and he discusses how substantial commitments of other sorts escape capture under these common budgetary aggregates. In part these omissions are by-products of our budget procedures, which focus on cash inflows and outlays, as opposed to more comprehensive measures of assets and liabilities. Professor Jackson then introduces the Financial Statements of the U.S. Government – an alternative presentation of federal finances based on principles of accrual accounting – and explores how these statements present a more complete picture of federal finances. Finally, Professor Jackson discusses how the Financial Statements might be augmented to reflect the mounting unfunded obligations of federal social insurance programs such as Social Security and Medicare to give a truly comprehensive picture of federal fiscal policy. The chapter concludes with a brief discussion of how these more expansive presentations might facilitate entitlement reform.

Finally, in Chapter 7, Professors Jonathan Baron and Edward McCaffery, leading figures in the emerging discipline of behavioral public finance, introduce the political psychology of federal deficits. Their chapter begins with a review of how the insights of behavioral economics might bear on matters of fiscal policy. Then, through an innovative set of experiments, they explore the extent to which political leaders might be able to exploit inconsistencies in public perceptions of fiscal matters – particularly deficits and spending cuts – to alter the direction of our fiscal policies. The particular focus of attention is a political strategy known as "starve the beast," whereby politicians first seek to gain public support for lower taxes and then use resulting deficits to promote spending cuts that would otherwise not have been possible. The question Professors Baron and McCaffery consider is whether the general public is susceptible to political machinations of this sort. Their experiments suggest that the public may not respond in exactly the manner envisioned by proponents of the starve-the-beast strategy.

5 Economic Perspectives on Federal Deficits and Debt

Michael J. Boskin

I. INTRODUCTION

Are large deficits good, bad, or irrelevant? In fact, they can be each, depending upon circumstances. Large deficits potentially cause two separate but related problems: shifting the bill for financing the current generation's consumption to future generations and crowding out private investment. Thus, deficits are more problematic well into a solid economic expansion; when their impact is primarily on domestic investment[1] and hence future income, rather than private saving[2] or foreign capital imports; when the level of the national debt, the accumulation of all previous deficits, is high or rapidly rising toward high levels; when they finance consumption, not productive public investment; when they do not constrain future spending; or if they lead to inflationary monetary policy. So the net effect of the budget position in any given year likely reflects a balancing of these considerations. Despite all the rhetoric, serious deficit-induced economic problems are unlikely over the next decade, although longer-term budget problems are potentially far more serious.

Further, the usual nominal dollar measures of the deficit and debt can be extremely misleading.[3] The deficit and debt must be compared to the size of the

---

[1] Thus, deficits might be more problematic in an economy with a chronically low rate of saving and investment.

[2] Some economists argue that it is irrelevant whether taxes or debt are used to finance a given level of spending. The argument is that debt implies an equivalent present value of future taxes and that forward-looking consumers will anticipate these higher future taxes and adjust their saving a corresponding amount, so there will be no net wealth effect of government bonds. While most economists, myself included, do not fully accept this view, it probably has partial validity and thus is another reason crowding out is less than dollar for dollar, as discussed further in the notes that follow.

[3] *See* Michael J. Boskin, *Federal Government Deficits: Some Myths and Realities*, 72 Am. Econ. Rev. 296–303 (1982).

Michael J. Boskin is the T. M. Friedman Professor of Economics and Hoover Institution Senior Fellow at Stanford University.

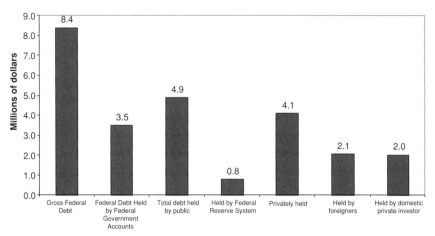

Figure 5.1. Holding of the national debt as of March 30, 2006 (*source*: U.S. Department of the Treasury, Treasury Bulletin).

economy, a rough measure of its ability to service the debt. Thus, debt burdens often are proxied by the debt–GDP ratio. The deficit is affected heavily by the business cycle. Inflation erodes the value of the previously issued national debt; in other words, the real debt declines with inflation (and conversely increases with deflation). Much of the debt is held in government accounts or by the Federal Reserve System (see Figure 5.1). The government has many assets as well as debts. The deficit measures how much the government borrows but does not distinguish whether the borrowing finances consumption or investment. Unlike private business accounting, the federal government has neither traditionally maintained a capital budget nor made much use of accrual accounting. In short, deficit figures reveal nothing about why and for what the added debt is incurred. Finally, the deficit is the difference between spending and taxes, the level, composition, structure, and growth of which are the far more fundamental fiscal indicators. For example, a balanced budget says nothing about whether the spending is efficient, effective, or necessary. In terms of overall macroeconomic indicators – the level and growth rate of GDP per capita – the current U.S.-size government and a modest deficit are likely to outperform a European-size government and a balanced budget.[4] The budget balance – surplus or deficit – is the outcome of a complex interaction of the entire current and expected future fiscal program (tax rates, spending, deficits, and debt) and the economy, and perhaps also the polity.

[4] It is worth noting that the large European economies not only have much higher ratios of taxes and government spending to GDP than the United States, but their government debt–GDP ratios are worse as well. This simplified historical international comparison seems to suggest that large tax increases may just lead to more spending, not to significantly improved fiscal balances. The much larger European tax and spending ratios to GDP primarily finance extensive social welfare spending, providing a relatively higher income support level to a larger fraction of the population, perhaps reflecting less tolerance for income inequality even if the higher taxes and spending potentially impose large costs on the average level of income.

It is appropriate, but not necessary, to finance (some) long-lived investments by government borrowing, since the benefits will accrue for many years and future taxpayers might equitably bear part of the burden. The economic harm caused by taxes rises with the square of tax rates.[5] Keeping tax rates stable over time and debt financing (or absorbing) temporary large swings in government spending such as defense buildups (drawdowns) may therefore produce efficiency gains.[6] In every year of World War II, for example, U.S. federal government borrowing exceeded tax revenues.

These and other problems have led some who focus on the current nominal dollar deficit to serious misinterpretations of fiscal history as well as current events. It is necessary to dig below the headline deficit numbers to see what is really going on in the budget in the short, medium, and long run.

To make sense of these issues, economists employ several related measures in addition to the traditional unified nominal cash budget balance, often called the headline deficit (see Box 5.1). The cyclically adjusted budget surplus or deficit adjusts the unified budget for business-cycle effects on revenue and outlays. The "standardized surplus or deficit" removes some transitory items, such as deposit insurance outlays and receipts from allies for Desert Storm during the Gulf War of 1991 and the inflation component of interest outlays, as well as the cyclical factor. The primary deficit nets out interest, the cost of servicing the previous debt. The primary balance determines the evolution of the national debt (the present value of future primary surpluses must equal the national debt, net of assets). A balanced primary budget means current noninterest outlays are paid by current revenues, and the present value of the inherited debt burden is neither rising nor falling. I have long argued for a capital budget, which separates out public capital investment, from computers to planes, net of depreciation (of course, not all public investment is productive), from operating expenses (including depreciation of capital), but the government has been slow to produce one.[7] Finally, we might usefully expand the operating budget to net out an estimate of our most important investment: any systematic national security buildup or drawdown relative to normal requirements.

Rough balance of a standardized primary operating budget implies that, on average over the cycle, additions to the debt burden are only for investment purposes, not to finance current consumption at the expense of future taxpayers, a much more precise measure than the headline nominal budget deficit of the extent to which borrowing is paying for current expenses or, to quote the late Sen. Pat Moynihan, "throwing a party." A balanced headline budget thus only means "balance" in the sense of paying for our own consumption, if there is no

---

[5] Thus, doubling tax rates quadruples the "deadweight loss" caused by taxes distorting economic decisions.

[6] Except perhaps their real interest carrying cost. In what follows, for simplicity I sometimes do not deduct the current year real interest carrying costs.

[7] It should be noted that incentives to redefine current outlays as capital expenditures would have to be resisted.

Box 5.1. Alternative budget surplus–deficit concepts

---

1. *Unified* nominal surplus–deficit = nominal revenues − nominal outlays; "headline" numbers.
2. *Operating* surplus–deficit = unified deficit − net investment (i.e., public capital investment − depreciation of public capital).
3. *Primary* surplus–deficit = unified deficit − interest outlays on inherited debt.
4. *Cyclically adjusted* surplus–deficit: deficit adjusted to "standard employment" (i.e., removes effect, positive and negative, of cycle on revenues and outlays; i.e., removes effect of "automatic stabilizers").
5. *Standardized* surplus–deficit: adjusts for cycle and some other transitory items (e.g., the inflation component of interest, receipts from allies for Desert Storm, deposit insurance outlays for failed S&Ls), that are unlikely to affect real income.
6. *Standardized primary operating* surplus–deficit: adjusts for cycle, transitory items, interest outlays on inherited debt and net investment; best measure of whether current taxes are sufficient to finance current federal government consumption outlays.
7. *Actuarial* deficits: projects spending and revenue for Social Security and Medicare spending over 75-year horizon.
8. Fiscal gap–generational account/fiscal imbalance: estimates gap between projected spending and projected revenues over very long-run time frame (often far beyond the 75-year time frame of the actuarial projections) under alternative assumptions; percentage of GDP and percentage changes in taxes and spending, immediately or over time, needed to close the gap.

---

inflation, no preexisting debt or capital investment, and so on. Put the other way around, a balanced headline budget in this sense is usually really a "surplus." Finally, several measures are designed to highlight the serious long-run imbalances in Social Security and Medicare: actuarial balances, generational accounts, fiscal gaps, and fiscal imbalances, which are subsequently discussed.

II. RECENT BUDGET POLICY

Deficits (or, more accurately, *increases* in deficits) are not only natural but also desirable in recessions and early in recoveries. In a downturn, receipts collapse and spending automatically increases; these so-called automatic stabilizers help cushion the decline in after-tax incomes and mitigate swings in economic activity. The impact of the economy on the budget balance is swifter, surer, and larger than the impact of the budget balance on the economy. In the severe recession of 1982, for example, automatic stabilizers accounted for more than half of the then-record deficit. Virtually all economists agree such automatic stabilizers should be allowed to operate and that additional short-run discretionary fiscal stimulus is most desirable when confronting a potentially severe long-lived downturn, especially once the Federal Reserve has about exhausted traditional monetary policy responses. Thus, between 2001 and 2003, when the Federal Reserve reduced the fed funds rate to 1 percent in a downturn with even a small risk of becoming a Japanese-style deflation and lost decade, additional fiscal policy insurance was desirable. The standard measure of short-run fiscal stimulus, the change in the cyclically adjusted budget deficit, went from a surplus of 1.2 percent of GDP in 2001 to a deficit of 3.1 percent of GDP in 2003. The 2003 tax rate reductions and dividend and capital-gains relief provided important long-run benefits of improved incentives and likely were more potent in the short run than the 2001 temporary rebates. This would appear to have been one of the largest and best-timed uses of countercyclical fiscal policy in history, helping to prevent a much worse downturn, but it would have been better still if the rate cuts had been implemented immediately in 2001 and if policies also had been enacted to control the budget well into the economic expansion.[8]

Returning to the "throwing a party" argument, for the fiscal year FY06, Table 5.1 projects the headline deficit at $260 billion, or 2.0 percent of GDP.[9] Note that this is low enough to prevent the debt burden from rising. The inflation component of interest at $90 billion exceeds some factors working in the other direction to reduce the standardized deficit to 1.8 percent of GDP. There is roughly $44 billion of nonmilitary investment outlays net of depreciation. The Bush military and homeland security buildups, excluding Iraq and Afghanistan, amount to about $120 billion, $30 billion of which is net investment and some of which is temporary. Iraq and Afghanistan add another $100 billion, almost all of which is temporary (if the total cost winds up at $500 billion, the annual carrying charge would be $25 billion at 5 percent interest). So netting these effects easily gets us to a (real continuing current) surplus. Thus, taxes pay for just about everything but real net interest, net tangible investment, and the security buildup. The borrowing finances investment, increased security spending, and real interest on the inherited debt. Of course, some argue that their dollar cost greatly exaggerates the value the investments are leaving future generations along with any debt, but that is the basis on which the argument ought to occur. Future generations will have both a modestly larger debt, a larger public capital stock and, hopefully on balance, a safer world, although that won't be known for a long time. While in the long run the economy might be better served with low taxes and less spending, the deficits of the past few years were a reasonable response to war and recession. Prosperous peacetime is when the debt burden ought to be declining.

---

[8] Opponents of the tax cuts offered two criticisms: the worsening of the budget balance and the distributional consequences of the tax cut. I deal here with the macroeconomics, which were very favorable in the short run. The long-run consequences are still to be determined by the future evolution of taxes, spending, and debt. Distributional issues are discussed in the following notes.

[9] The actual numbers came in slightly lower at year-end, $248 billion and 1.9 percent GDP. Projections of future deficits will rise and fall but are likely to maintain the same qualitative properties as those discussed herein.

Table 5.1. Alternative budget measures billions of current dollars (% of GDP)

Year	(1) Surplus/deficit (−)	(2) Standardized Surplus–deficit (−)	(3) Standardized primary surplus–deficit (−)	(4) Standardized primary operating surplus–deficit (−)	(5) Standardized primary operating surplus–deficit (−) net of security investment
2006	−260	−228	−109	−30	+60/+135
	(−2.0)	(−1.8)	(−0.8)	(−0.2)	(0.5)/(1.1)
1999	126	12	187	209	141
	(1.5)	(0.1)	(2.0)	(2.2)	(1.6)
1992	−290	−186	−45	−19	−38
	(−4.5)	(−2.9)	(−0.5)	(−0.3)	(−0.6)
1984	−185	−143	−76	−42	−8
	(−4.7)	(−3.6)	(−1.9)	(−1.1)	(−0.2)

Note: Under standardized primary operating surplus–deficit (−) net of security investment, +60 shows the net military and homeland security buildup, excluding cost of Iraq and Afghanistan, and +135 shows the replacement of an estimated $100 billion annual cost of Iraq and Afghanistan with an estimated $25 billion interest cost on an estimated $500 billion total cost.

Source: Author's calculations are from the following sources: CBO, The Cyclically Adjusted and Standardized Budgets Measures: Updated Estimates, March 2006; CBO, The Budget and Economic Outlook: An Update, August 2006; OMB, The Budget of the United States, FY 2007, Historical Tables; OMB, The Budget of the United States, FY 2007: Analytical Perspectives. FY 2006 author's calculations are based on the two CBO reports.

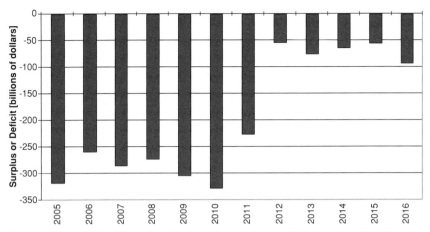

Figure 5.2. Projected position of the U.S. federal budget (*source*: CBO, August 2006; 2005 actual data).

It is likewise instructive to probe deeper into the oversimplified budget myths surrounding previous administrations (again, Table 5.1). For example, in 1999, the seventh year of the Clinton administration, the nominal budget was in surplus to the tune of $126 billion, or 1.5 percent of GDP, but the Congressional Budget Office (CBO) estimates that the cyclical and temporary items virtually eliminate the surplus. The headline surplus was just an artifact of the bubble. But the substantial primary surplus indicates serious progress was being made in reducing the debt–GDP ratio, although mostly as a result of large military spending cuts (38 percent relative to GDP). In 1992, the last year of the George H. W. Bush administration, the (until recently) record nominal budget deficit was $290 billion or 4.5 percent of GDP but, net of cyclical and temporary items like deposit insurance outlays to finally clean up the S&Ls,[10] the primary budget was roughly balanced. Finally, in 1984, the fourth year of the Reagan administration, the nominal deficit was $185 billion, about 4.7 percent of GDP, but netting cyclical factors, temporary items, the inflation component of interest, net investment, and the military buildup, the deficit was $8 billion, or 0.2 percent of GDP. The borrowing financed net investment, the military buildup that many authorities credit with helping to win the Cold War, and interest on the inherited debt, not current consumption expenditures, not a "party." These examples illustrate the potential importance of digging behind the headline deficit.

A. The Medium Run

The CBO projects continuing deficits over the next decade (see Figure 5.2). The debt–GDP ratio peaks at 38 percent and then declines (Figure 5.3). For

---

[10] The original obligation for this accrued primarily in the 1970s and compounded in the 1980s.

Table 5.2. Projected deficits in CBO's estimate of the president's budget

| | | | | | Actual | | | | | | | | Total | |
	2005	2006	2007	2008	2009	2010	2011	2012	2013	2014	2015	2016	2007–2011	2007–2016
						Deficit								
In billions of dollars														
Outlays	2,472	2,675	2,766	2,820	2,906	3,017	3,167	3,270	3,463	3,631	3,812	4,044	14,676	32,895
Revenues	2,154	2,304	2,431	2,585	2,712	2,852	2,964	3,111	3,268	3,434	3,608	3,794	13,453	30,758
Deficit	−318	−371	−335	−236	−194	−165	−204	−158	−195	−197	−204	−205	−1,133	−2,137
As a percentage of GDP														
Outlays	20.1	20.4	20.1	19.4	19.0	18.8	18.9	18.7	18.9	19.0	19.1	19.4	19.2	19.1
Revenues	17.5	17.6	17.6	17.8	17.8	17.8	17.7	17.8	17.8	18.0	18.1	18.2	17.7	17.9
Deficit	−2.6	−2.8	−2.4	−1.6	−1.3	−1.0	−1.2	−0.9	−1.1	−1.0	−1.0	−1.2	−1.5	−1.2
Debt held by the public	37.4	38.0	38.5	38.3	37.8	37.1	36.7	36.1	35.7	35.2	34.8	34.5	n.a.	n.a.

Source: CBO, An Analysis of the President's Budgetary Proposals for Fiscal Year 2007, March 2006 (subsequent CBO revisions of their baseline budget forecast sharply reduce the first few years' deficit projections, but increase the later years' deficit projections).

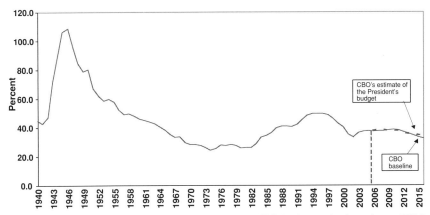

Figure 5.3. National debt as percentage of GDP (*source*: CBO, budget projections, August 2006; CBO, Preliminary Analysis of the President's Budget Request for 2006, March 2006).

the president's budget, the CBO projects more than $2.1 trillion in cumulative additional debt over the next decade (see Table 5.2). This reflects a debt–GDP ratio that rises slightly to peak at nearly 39 percent in two or three years, below the post-World War II historical average and far below Euroland and Japan (Figures 5.3 and 5.4). It then declines for the rest of the decade through 2016 even if the tax cuts are made permanent and if the post-1998 splurge in spending is slowed substantially, both of which are proposed by the president. With interest outlays projected at about 2 percent of GDP, the president's end-of-decade deficit of 1.2 percent of GDP would be a primary *surplus* reducing the debt burden. This is hardly a debt spiraling out of control, leading to inflation fears fueling capital flight, a financial crisis, and economic calamity. The resulting net deficit will cause a small increase in interest rates. Evidence here is weak, but the best estimate is 25 basis points (bp) or slightly more per

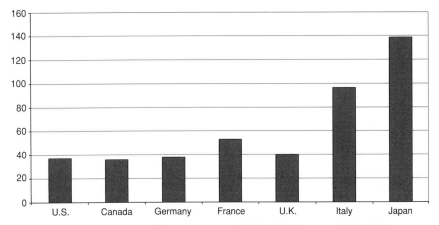

Figure 5.4. Central government debt as percentage of GDP, 2004 (*source*: OECD, CBO).

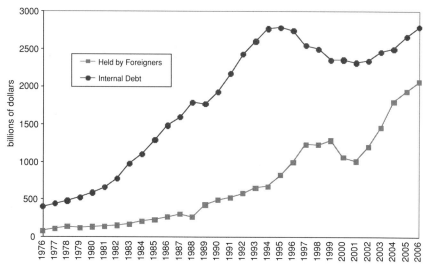

Figure 5.5. National debt: internal versus external (as of March 30, 2006) (*source:* U.S. Department of the Treasury, Treasury Bulletin).

1 percent of GDP (here no more than 40 bp) – less, once any additional feedback effects of rate cuts on revenue and deficits on future spending are included.[11] This, in turn, will reduce domestic investment, but less than dollar for dollar, as the deficit partly will be financed from abroad (Figure 5.5).[12] The effect is important, but it is hardly a cause for hysteria.[13]

These relatively benign projections mask several policy assumptions that, if inaccurate, would cause the deficit and debt to grow substantially. First, the Congressional Budget Office assumes current law expiration of the Bush tax cuts and some other temporary tax cuts; no additional appropriations for Iraq, Afghanistan, or Katrina-related reconstruction of the Gulf Coast; and that

---

[11] Deficits eventually exert some restraint on the course of subsequent government spending – empirically, perhaps 20 cents on the dollar. The gross historical experience in the late 1990s–2001 at the federal level and in California suggests that running a surplus leads to great pressure for legislatures to spend. Hence, it is unclear that a systematic policy of running budget surpluses, e.g., in anticipation of future fiscal pressures, is even feasible.

[12] External debt does not cause a substitution of government bonds for tangible capital in domestic portfolios and hence does not crowd out private investment, although the future returns to the capital accrue to foreigners. There is a concern that foreign holdings of U.S. government securities may be more mobile than domestic holdings and thus pose more risk of an abrupt dislocation, as subsequently discussed.

[13] The deficits causing serious inflation or a financial and economic collapse scenario theoretically would occur when bondholders reach, or anticipate reaching, an upper limit to the share of their wealth they are willing to hold in government bonds, as would likely be the case with the debt ratios projected several decades hence in Table 5.3. There then would be intense pressure on the central bank to monetize the deficit by buying up the bonds. The anticipation of inflation (alternatively, strong depreciation of the currency) then could lead to a rise in interest rates, reduced capital formation, slower growth, and even recession if abrupt enough.

Table 5.3. Long-run budget projections of 2007 budget policy (% of GDP)

Item	1980	1990	2000	2010	2020	2030	2040	2060	2080
Receipts	19.0	18.0	20.9	17.9	18.9	19.4	20.0	21.3	22.4
Outlays									
Discretionary	10.1	8.7	6.3	6.1	5.6	5.6	5.6	5.6	5.6
Mandatory									
Social Security	4.3	4.3	4.2	4.2	4.9	5.8	5.9	6.1	6.4
Medicare	1.1	1.7	2.0	2.8	3.7	5.0	6.1	7.9	10.4
Medicaid	0.5	0.7	1.2	1.5	1.9	2.1	2.3	2.8	3.3
Other	3.7	3.2	2.4	2.3	1.9	1.6	1.4	1.1	0.9
Subtotal mandatory	9.6	9.9	9.8	10.8	12.4	14.4	15.7	17.8	21.0
Net interest	1.9	3.2	2.3	1.9	1.4	1.5	2.3	4.7	9.4
Total outlays	21.7	21.8	18.4	18.9	19.4	21.6	23.6	28.2	36.1
Surplus or deficit (−)	−2.7	−3.9	2.4	−1.0	−0.6	−2.2	−3.6	−6.9	−13.7
Primary surplus or deficit (−)	−0.8	−0.6	4.7	0.9	0.9	−0.6	−1.3	−2.1	−4.2
Federal debt held by the public	26.1	42.0	35.1	37.5	26.2	28.8	43.3	89.6	177.4

Source: OMB, Analytical Perspectives, FY 2007.

discretionary spending will grow no more than inflation. The CBO estimate of the president's FY06 budget, of course, makes the Bush tax cuts permanent. The other major issue is the alternative minimum tax (AMT). Congress has been passing piecemeal one-year fixes. Neither the CBO baseline nor the president's budget contains a permanent AMT fix. Indeed, the AMT and real bracket creep are the primary reasons revenues are projected to rise from their current 18 percent of GDP, equaling the historical 18 percent average, to just under 20 percent in the ten-year budget window and almost 24 percent thereafter. If these assumptions prove to be fallacious, either the deficit will grow, taxes will rise, or the growth in spending will need to be restrained further.[14]

B. The Long Run

In the long run – that is, looking out several decades and more – the budgetary posture of the federal government is projected to deteriorate, as expenditures for Social Security, and especially Medicare and Medicaid, are scheduled to claim increasing shares of GDP (see Table 5.3). The interpretation of these long-range projections is, however, problematic. As is subsequently discussed, the projections reflect a continuation of current policies and depend on a number of

---

[14] A rough estimate is that if all assumptions prove fallacious – the AMT is "fixed"; defense rises 5 percent above inflation and the remainder of discretionary spending 4 percent; CBO's estimates for a gradual phasedown in Iraq, Afghanistan, and Katrina are too optimistic – the result is a deficit of 3.0 percent of GDP that would grow, not shrink, thereafter. Whether these adjustments are good public policy is another matter, but implementing them moves forward the time when the deficit does become a much more serious issue.

Box 5.2. Effects of deficits under different conditions

1. Good, desirable, acceptable:
   - For countercyclical device, automatic stabilizers in recession, early recovery; additional discretionary policy desirable in extreme cases after Federal Reserve moves aggressively;
   - For financing investment (that passes stringent cost–benefit analysis); and
   - For tax smoothing of large, temporary spending swings (e.g., wars).
2. Bad, harmful:
   - Crowds out private investment (rather than increasing private saving or crowding in foreign capital);
   - Causes central bank to monetize the deficit and leads to inflation;
   - High debt–GDP ratio leads to expectations of inflation, depreciation of currency, capital flight, financial panic;
   - Especially in low-private-saving context.
3. Irrelevant:
   - Ricardian equivalence idea of private saving offsetting public borrowing; for given level of spending and assuming the deficit doesn't affect future spending or the structure of taxes.

---

assumptions about medical costs, economic growth, and demographic changes that may not come to pass.

III. THE ECONOMICS OF DEFICITS AND DEBT

As mentioned in the introduction, deficits can be economically helpful, harmful, or irrelevant under different conditions. Because so much of the discussion ignores these factors – focusing on the headline (nominal unified) budget balance – it is useful to dwell on this point. Box 5.2 summarizes the main categories of conditions. Three cases illustrate the point that the economics of deficits depends on a lot more than the size of the deficit. First, government borrowing from abroad to finance productive public investment might be highly desirable and intergenerationally a net plus for future generations.

Second, there is a strong case for smoothing tax rates. Because the excess burden of taxation goes up with the square of tax rates, we should not just tax finance unusually large swings in government spending. This would imply high tax rates when spending is high, and low tax rates when spending is low. It is better to smooth tax rates so the tax share of GDP is sufficient to fund the "average level" of spending. This implies equalizing tax rates, borrowing when spending is high, and retiring debt when spending is low. The impact of raising taxes for budget balance could be severe; for example, in World War II, raising taxes to fund the entire war effort would have meant federal taxes would have gone from 9.8 percent of GDP in 1940 to (at least) 43.6 percent in 1944. That undoubtedly would have devastated even the wartime economy. In fact, we only raised taxes to 21 percent of GDP, financing the majority of World War II spending with debt, which then was reduced (relative to GDP) postwar. If presidents were rated primarily on the change in the national debt (held outside the government), FDR would be rated among our worst presidents; sized to today's economy, the national debt rose almost $10 trillion, two and one-half times the current debt. The debt financing of World War II has correctly not been regarded as a mistake by historians or economists.

Third, a highly indebted government running large deficits that would cause the debt–GDP ratio to explode might drive interest rates up so much as to cause a severe downturn or, with a compliant central bank, initiate hyperinflation. There is an upper limit to the amount of public debt the public will hold in order to maintain some diversification. So if the government keeps issuing more and more bonds, the central bank eventually buys them and expands the money supply; the result is inflation, even hyperinflation as in Weimar Germany and Eastern Europe after World War II.

The expectation of higher interest and inflation rates produces real effects now, such as decreased investment. Especially in developing countries, this also can lead to capital flight. At other times, this process actually can be beneficial. If the economy is stuck in a low-level liquidity trap with outright deflation, would issuing massive amounts of government bonds or money help? Enough monetary expansion implies expectations of inflation. Enough expansion of government debt implies eventually enough money, because the obligations of the central bank are part of the consolidated obligations of the government and the public eventually will stop holding more debt.[15] These issues were central to Japan in the past decade, the United States in the Great Depression, and the FED's concern over outright deflation early in this decade.

A. The Incidence of the National Debt

The national debt is the accumulation of all previous deficits.[16] The debt must be retired or refinanced as it matures. If it is retired, tax revenues must be used to pay it off; if it is refinanced, interest must be paid, which implies tax revenues to pay the interest. Does this imply there is a burden of the debt? One view is that we just "owe it to ourselves." This is "true," as far as it goes, for internal debt. External debt, which has been increasingly important to the contemporary United States, is owed to foreigners to whom the interest will

---

[15] *See* Lars E.O. Svensson, *How Should Monetary Policy Be Conducted in an Era of Price Stability?* (Nat'l Bureau of Econ. Research Working Paper No. 7516, 2000), *available at* http://www.nber.org/papers/w7516.

[16] Measuring deficits and debt is not easy. As discussed herein, substantial assets, inflation erosion of previous debt, and contingent and implicit future obligations, for example, are important to keep in mind.

accrue and in whose portfolios any substitution of the debt for capital occurs.[17] Further, we need to look more closely at "ourselves." Future taxpayers will be paying future bondholders. Does this imply future generations pay the debt? To see, we have to look at how the debt may affect the economy.

B. How Do Taxes and Spending Affect the Economy?

Taxes, spending, deficits, and debt have several potential effects. First are the direct effects on short-run aggregate demand from changes in government outlays, taxes and transfer payments on consumption, and changes in business taxes on investment. These cash-flow effects generally are measured as the change in the cyclically adjusted or standardized deficit or surplus. They can turn into longer-run effects because of differential productivity of public and private spending.

Second are the incentive effects on aggregate supply from changes in productive government investment or the effective real marginal tax rates on private investment and saving, labor supply, and human capital formation.

These important effects in principle depend not just on the amount of deficit and debt, but also current and expected future tax rates, spending levels and composition, and expected future debt. *But spending, taxes, deficits, and debt and their evolution are linked by the government's intertemporal budget constraint and perhaps also by political dynamics.* Thus, for example, tax or spending changes causing shifts in deficits can have very different effects depending on whether they are (expected to be) temporary or permanent, and on whether the tax changes affect saving and investment. We will explore this issue of the effects of deficits and associated future tax and spending changes further in the paragraphs that follow.

For the debt to affect private behavior, the financing activity must cause or enable (at least some) private households or firms to do something different from what they already were doing. There are several candidates: (1) There is the traditional wealth effect,[18] in which households are or feel wealthier because of the government bonds they hold. Thus, current consumption increases. This, however, only works if households are myopic,[19] because the debt and the present value of future taxes to pay the interest just cancel, or (2) the debt allows better risk bearing, such as across generations or types of assets,[20] or (3) it allows households to achieve greater liquidity. The key is that *different*

---

[17] *See* Peter A. Diamond, *National Debt in a Neoclassical Growth Model*, 55 Am. Econ. Rev. 1126–1150 (1965).

[18] *See* Franco Modigliani, *Long Run Implications of Alternative Fiscal Policies and the Burden of the National Debt*, 71 Econ. J. 730–755 (1961).

[19] *See* Robert A. Mundell, *Money, Debt and the Rate of Interest*, *in* Monetary Theory: Inflation, Interest, and Growth in the World Economy 1–13 (Robert A. Mundell ed., 1971).

[20] *See* James Tobin, *The Burden of the Public Debt: A Review Article*, 20 J. Fin. 679–682 (1965).

households, people, and generations can be affected differently by the debt and the future taxes. Before we explore this in more detail, it is useful to set up a simple two-period example of a typical household.

C. Deficits and Future Taxes

Assume there are two periods, where

T_i = taxes (net of transfers) in i, assumed to be "lump sum,"
G_i = government purchases in i,
d_i = deficit in i,
D = debt at start of Period 2 = deficit from Period 1 = d_1.

Assume there is no preexisting debt. Then, in Period 1,

$$d_1 = G_1 - T_1,$$

which the government finances by selling bonds.

In Period 2, the government must collect taxes to repay debt (perpetual rollover has the same present value), including interest, as well as purchases.

$$T_2 = (1 + r)D + G_2.$$

Substituting, we get

$$T_2 = (1 + r)(G_1 - T_1) + G_2.$$

Rearranging, we have

$$T_1 + T_2/(1 + r) = G_1 + G_2/(1 + r).$$

This latter equation is the government's budget constraint. It is fundamental to all analyses of deficits and debt.

Now suppose the government cuts taxes in Period 1 by ΔT but leaves spending the same. In Period 2, it must raise taxes by $(1 + r)\,\Delta T$. So from a household point of view, there is no change in its intertemporal budget constraint (shown graphically in Figure 5.6 by the straight line; recall the taxes are assumed to be lump sum, so there is no effect on the after-tax rate of return, r, at which households borrow and save).

This line details how the household can trade its present income (Y_1) and future income (Y_2) by borrowing or saving at the rate of interest, r, in order to consume more or less than its income in Period 1, and conversely in Period 2. The household decides its optimal intertemporal consumption (saving) by reaching the highest possible indifference curve, i, with consumption C_1 in Period 1 and C_2 in Period 2. Note the household saves in Period 1, that is, consumes less than its income, to augment its Period 2 consumption beyond

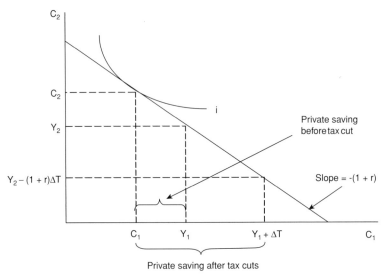

Figure 5.6. Effect of a deficit on consumption.

that period's income. The tax cut just results in an *equal* increase in private saving.

So in this case, the tax cut does *not* affect consumption. The decrease in public saving is offset by an exactly equal increase in private saving. This is the famous "Ricardian equivalence" result; debt is "neutral" given the level of government spending. It doesn't matter whether this spending is financed by debt or taxes because debt is just future taxes with an identical present value.

There are conditions under which deficits do matter and affect private spending.[21] These include the following. First, there is myopia concerning the future taxes to pay the interest;[22] thus, the household incorrectly perceives its wealth as rising from the tax cut today because it fails to fully value its future taxes. Second, there are borrowing constraints – studies conclude about a quarter of the population is liquidity constrained;[23] a household may want to consume more today and less in the future (relative to income), but because it cannot freely borrow at the prevailing interest rate, it is prevented from doing so. A tax cut raises its current income and allows it to consume more today (moving from point A to point B in Figure 5.7 and increasing consumption from C_1 to C_1^* and decreasing C_2 to C_2^*). Third, there are distortionary taxes (especially on capital). Fourth, there is risk, if the public debt enables a reduction of risk

---

[21] *See, e.g.,* B. Douglas Bernheim, *Ricardian Equivalence: An Evaluation of Theory and Evidence* (Nat'l Bureau of Econ. Research Working Paper No. 2330, 1987), *available at* http://www.nber.org/papers/w2330.

[22] *See* Tobin, *supra* note 20.

[23] Robert E. Hall and Frederic S. Mishkin, *The Sensitivity of Consumption to Transitory Income: Estimates from Panel Data on Households,* 50 ECONOMETRICA 461–481 (1982).

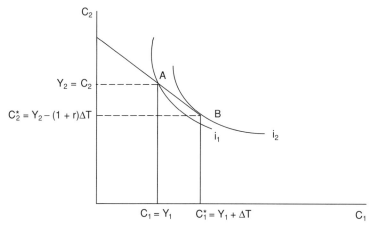

Figure 5.7. Effect of a deficit on liquidity-constrained consumers.

in private portfolios.[24] Fifth, there is precautionary saving.[25] How important are these factors? How large are the likely deviations from "neutrality"? First let us turn to the various types of effects a deficit can have on the economy. To do that, we must first review some national income accounting.

D. The Budget Position in National Income Accounting

First, some notation. Let

Y = national income,
C = private consumption,
S = private saving, and
T = taxes – transfers (net taxes).

The fundamental accounting identity for the economy is that national income = national output = national spending.

$$Y = C + I + G + NX. \tag{1}$$

Here,

I = domestic investment,
G = government goods/services purchases, and
NX = net exports of goods and services.

Households spend or save their disposable (after-tax) income.

$$Y - T = C + S \quad \text{or} \quad Y = C + S + T. \tag{2}$$

---

[24] *See* Tobin, *supra* note 20.
[25] *See* R. Glenn Hubbard, Jonathan Skinner, and Stephen P. Zeldes, *Precautionary Saving and Social Insurance*, 103 J. Pol. Econ. 360–399 (1995) (discussing the effects of asset-based, means-tested welfare programs on precautionary saving of the low-income population).

Thus,

$$S + (T - G) = I + \text{NX}.$$

In other words, private + public saving = investment + net exports.
   Further,

$$\text{NX} = \text{NFI},$$

net foreign investment (investment by Americans abroad less domestic U.S. investment by foreign residents).
   Thus, finally,

$$S + (T - G) = I + \text{NFI}. \qquad (3)$$

Private plus government saving = national saving = investment at home and abroad, or stated simply, the nation's investment must be financed by the nation's saving.

   Now we can see from Equation 3 the possible effects of deficits. For example, holding G constant, reducing T, implies an increased deficit or decreased surplus and, thus, national saving declines. Thus, Equation 3 can be satisfied by any combination of increased private S, decreased domestic I, and decreased NFI. This potential effect of the deficit on national saving is the initial driver of the effects of deficits on the economy, but we also must include any direct effects of the tax reduction (e.g., by changed rates) on saving, investment, human investment, and labor supply, and any effect of the deficit on future spending to get the net impact of this fiscal policy. It is important to understand that more than just accounting is included; S and I depend on tax rates; future G depends on current and expected future deficits, for example. The whole set of changes to G and T may affect expectations about future G, T, marginal tax rates, d and D, and, hence, S and I.

   If private saving increases less than $1 for $1, this implies that investment at home and abroad must decline. Lower domestic investment implies a smaller capital stock, which means lower future income, higher returns to capital, and lower wages than otherwise would have occurred in the future. Lower NFI implies domestic residents own less foreign capital (or foreign residents own more domestic capital), which implies the capital income of domestic residents falls (or foreigners receive more capital income from U.S. assets); it also implies lower NX and usually implies appreciation of the currency.

   The lower domestic investment usually is deemed to occur because of a deficit causing a rise in interest rates. This process, called "crowding out," is illustrated in Figure 5.8: The lower national saving drives up interest rates from r_0 to r_1 and reduces investment from I_0 to I_1. The degree of crowding out depends on the interest elasticity of investment. The most commonly used estimates are in

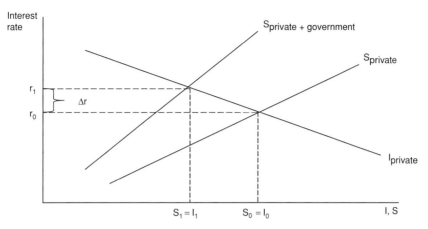

Figure 5.8. Crowding out of private investment, closed economy: $I_0 - I_1$ = private investment "crowded out" by government borrowing.

the −0.7 range.[26] Note that if saving is at all interest elastic, private saving also will rise; a 10 percent increase (say, from 4 to 4.4 percent) likely would raise saving by 1 percent to 5 percent.[27] In any event, investment demand appears to be more interest-elastic than private saving.

In an open economy with a global capital market, investment also can be financed by inflows of foreign capital (a decline in NFI). In the extreme case, diagrammed in Figure 5.9, government borrowing increases the inflow of foreign capital from $I_1 - S_1$ to $I_1 - S_2$, that is, by $S_1 - S_2$, and there is no effect on interest rates or domestic investment.

Certainly, the United States is at the epicenter of the global capital market. Our public debt is traded globally. But it is likely that dollar-denominated assets, Treasury securities in particular, are not what economists call perfect substitutes for either the debt of other governments or other fixed-income securities (mortgages, state and local bonds, agencies) or other global financial instruments. Thus, we might expect the supply of capital from the rest of the world (ROW) to be highly, but not perfectly, elastic and eventually to become progressively more inelastic as foreigners reach an upper bound to the share of their wealth they are willing to hold in Treasuries.

For these and other reasons, the effect of deficits or debt on interest rates is both difficult to measure and controversial. A deficit in Period 1 from cutting income taxes combined with a subsequent tax increase could, in the extreme,

---

[26] There is a long history of contentious academic debate on the size of the interest elasticities of saving and investment. All studies suffer from one or more difficulties of methodology, measurement, or interpretation. These estimates are my best judgment, based on numerous econometric studies and their critiques.

[27] See Michael J. Boskin, *The Effects of Taxes on Saving and Economic Growth* (March 2005) (testimony to the President's Commission on Tax Reform).

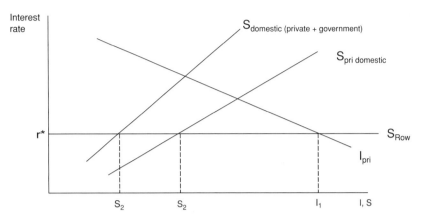

Figure 5.9. Crowding out of private investment, open economy–global capital market: Government borrowing increases inflow of foreign capital from $I_1 - S_1$ to $I_1 - S_2$ (i.e., by $S_1 - S_2$).

reduce consumption and interest rates, and increase investment and income in the short run,[28] in contrast to the usual assumption. Thus, it is an empirical matter to try to establish the net effects of the debt operation. The evidence is not overwhelming, but the best estimate is roughly a 25- or 30-bp increase in interest rates per each 1 percent of GDP deficit.[29] As detailed in the previous paragraphs, the CBO medium-term forecast would suggest about a 40-bp marginal effect of the president's budget relative to a balanced medium-term budget – assuming no effect on future spending through the political process and no positive supply-side impact from tax-rate reductions. Many other factors influence interest rates – such as monetary policy, inflation, inflation expectations, and the output gap between GDP and potential GDP, – some of which are likely to have a larger or swifter potential impact on interest rates than do deficits. Forty basis points may seem small, but it is economically consequential in the long run. A simplified standard assumption might be 50 percent decreased I, 30 percent decreased NFI, and 20 percent increased S for a change in the deficit, which of course would be highly dependent on the tax and spending specifics generating the initial deficit.

Thus, the 1.3 percent of GDP deficit reduces national saving by perhaps 1 percent of GDP relative to a balanced budget, crowding out about 0.7 percent

[28] *See* Kenneth L. Judd, *Debt and Distortionary Taxation in a Simple Perfect Foresight Model*, 20 J. MONETARY ECON. 51–72 (1987).

[29] For more recent results and discussion of earlier literature, *see* Eric M. Engen and R. Glenn Hubbard, *Federal Government Debt and Interest Rates, in* NBER MACROECONOMIC ANNUAL 2004, 83–138 (Mark Gertler and Kenneth Rogoff eds., 2005); William G. Gale and Peter R. Orszag, *Economic Effects of Sustained Budget Deficits*, 56 NAT'L TAX J. 463–485 (2003); Thomas Laubach, NEW EVIDENCE ON THE INTEREST RATE EFFECTS OF BUDGET DEFICITS AND DEBT, BOARD OF GOVERNORS OF THE FED. RES. SYS. (2003), *available at* http://www.federalreserve.gov/pubs/feds/2003/200312/200312pap.pdf.

of GDP in domestic investment. In a steady state, the capital stock and national income rise more slowly than in the absence of the deficit, other things (e.g., tax rates) being constant.[30] Alternatively, in the thought experiment carried out by Mankiw and Elmendorf,[31] retiring the entire national debt would increase output by about 3 percent. They assume, as do most economists, that the economy is dynamically efficient, with the (risk-adjusted) return to capital above the growth rate, and thus that more capital formation is desirable.

E. Other Economic Effects of Deficits and Debt

Deficits and debt have a variety of other (potential) effects. First, an increase in debt may drive up interest rates, and the Federal Reserve may or may not respond. In the long run, because there is an upper limit to government debt holdings by the private sector, attempts to issue more bonds eventually may cause inflation, which ultimately may be a fiscal (rather than purely monetary) phenomenon.[32] Indeed, it is widely believed such a process started the great postwar U.S. inflation in the late 1960s. Monetization of the debt, as occurred in Weimar Germany, leading to hyperinflation, is currently not significant in most advanced countries.

Second, deficits can shift the timing or affect the nature of the deadweight losses caused by taxes distorting economic behavior. Debt service on internal debt is just a transfer. As lump-sum taxes are unavailable, distortionary taxes will be used. Thus, a budget deficit implies smaller deadweight losses now, larger deadweight losses later. The composition of taxes, even the expected composition of taxes, can matter. The combination of capital-income taxes and long-horizon saving behavior can be particularly damning to the debt-neutrality hypothesis.[33]

Third, inflation acts as a tax on money balances. The inflation tax, called "seignorage" from the practice of the sovereign clipping coins in Medieval times, is the inflation rate times money balances. At the levels of money balances and inflation in modern advanced economies, seignorage is not substantial, but

---

[30] *See* Engen and Hubbard, *supra* note 29; Matthew D. Shapiro, *Comment on E. Engen and R. G. Hubbard, "Federal Government Debt and Interest Rates,"* in NBER MACROECONOMIC ANNUAL 2004, 148–156 (Mark Gertler and Kenneth Rogoff eds., 2005); Gale and Orszag, *supra* note 29.

[31] *See* Douglas W. Elmendorf and Gregory Mankiw, *Government Debt,* in HANDBOOK OF MACROECONOMICS, VOLUME 1C (John B. Taylor and Michael Woodford eds., 1999).

[32] Michael Woodford, *Fiscal Requirements for Price Stability,* 33 J. MONEY, CREDIT & BANK-ING 669–728 (2001); Michael Woodford, *Control of the Public Debt: A Requirement for Price Stability?,* in THE DEBT BURDEN AND MONETARY POLICY (Guillermo A. Calvo and Mervyn King eds., 1997); Michael Woodford, *Price Level Determinacy Without Control of a Monetary Aggregate,* 43 CARNEGIE-ROCHESTER CONFERENCE SERIES 1–46 (1995); Thomas J. Sargent and Neil Wallace, *Some Unpleasant Monetarist Arithmetic,* 5 FED. RES. BANK OF MINNEAPOLIS Q. REV. 1–17 (1981).

[33] Elmendorf and Mankiw, *supra* note 31; Judd, *supra* note 28.

in some episodes in developing countries and certainly historically, it has been an important revenue source.

Fourth, inflation also affects the real value of the national debt. If the preexisting debt $= D_0$ and Inflation $= \Pi$, this implies a decline in the real value of debt $= \Pi D_0$. So to get the "real" deficit, we must subtract the decline in the real value of preexisting debt. For the United States, with $4 trillion of debt held outside the government, a 2.5 percent inflation rate implies a $100 billion decline in the real value of debt if it was all long-term and not indexed. Adjusting for these factors suggests the first $75 billion or more of the deficit is not a real deficit at all. The real or inflation-adjusted deficit is the nominal deficit deflated by the price level minus the decline in the real value of the previously issued debt.

Fifth, deficits also can affect future spending: If future taxpayers are not adequately represented in current decisions, or if deficits present an illusory "something for nothing" choice, or if a deficit constrains future policymakers because higher D may mean it is harder to raise D more (which ultimately may affect future government spending), the current deficit may, through political dynamics, partly self-correct (as subsequently discussed).

F. The Overlapping-Generations Model

Let us return to how the deficit affects private behavior in a model that extends beyond the single household, two-period model, to a model that incorporates overlapping generations (Table 5.4). Each generation works W years, then retires for R years. The following example assumes, for simplicity, that work years (W) $=$ retired years (R) and there are no prework years; there is no economic or population growth, no interest, and no inflation. All amounts are per person (note: $5K per capita in U.S. $=$ $1.5 trillion). Those living initially get tax cuts of $5,000 each. Those paying the higher taxes later include some who did not get the initial benefit because they were not yet born. So the fiscal operation *transfers income from the future working generation to today's retirees.* This is the fundamental nature of government debt. If those groups respond differently to the debt and future taxes, the intergenerational transfer of resources can have important economic effects, on which more follows in the paragraphs to come. Note that if the debt had financed productive public investment, such as transportation infrastructure or scientific research and development, that raised future incomes, the younger generation might well be better off.[34] So the economic effects of deficits are not automatically to help current citizens at the expense of future taxpayers, but that is the basic case

---

[34] The short-run economic effects of deficits on aggregate demand also may be considerably different if they finance public capital investment. *See* D. A. Aschauer, *Fiscal Policy and Aggregate Demand*, 75 Am. Econ. Rev. 117–127 (1985).

Table 5.4. The effect of debt on overlapping generations

Government	Private households		
	Gen 3 (unborn)	Gen 2 (W)	Gen 1 (R)
Year 1: government issues debt ($5K/person) to finance tax cuts			
−5,000		+5,000	+5,000
	Gen 3 (W)	Gen 2 (R)	Gen 1 (deceased)
Year 30: government raises C taxes to pay off the debt			
5,000	−5,000	−5,000	
Total 0	−5,000	0	5,000

most people have in mind when they discuss the intergenerational inequity of deficits.

Robert Barro famously expanded the debt-neutrality hypothesis to the overlapping-generations model.[35] It is not just any individual household for which debt is neutral, but all households, all present and future overlapping generations, he argued. Suppose the utility of households in each generation depends on their own consumption and the utility of their children. Since their children's utility depends on their own consumption and their children's utility, each generation's utility depends on its own consumption and the utility of all (infinite) future generations. It turns out this will imply the equivalence of debt and taxes (debt neutrality), given government spending, under certain assumptions.[36]

Why? Since the present value of taxes is unchanged by debt, future taxes just offset the current decrease in taxes: An altruistic intergenerationally linked family has the same intertemporal budget constraint with tax or debt finance. If there is an operative bequest motive, private intergenerational intrafamily transfers just restore the status quo ante, netting the debt and future taxes. If the present generation leaves future generations more debt, its private saving will rise and higher private bequests will just offset the higher public debt. No generation experiences a wealth change, and hence no change in spending occurs.[37] Of course, the issues that caused debt not to be neutral for a single family as just described (myopia, risk, precautionary saving, distortionary

---

[35] Robert J. Barro, *Are Government Bonds Net Wealth?*, 82 J. Pol. Econ. 1095–1117 (1975).

[36] The time horizon may not be as extreme as it seems. *See* James Poterba and Lawrence H. Summers, *Finite Lifetimes and the Effects of Budget Deficits on National Savings*, 20 J. Monetary Econ. 369–391 (1987) (showing that a tax cut serviced at 5 percent interest forever implies 77 percent of the current value will be paid off in 30 years).

[37] *See* B. Douglas Bernheim and Kyle Bagwell, *Is Everything Neutral?*, 96 J. Pol. Econ. 308–338 (1988) (highlighting the extreme nature of Ricardian equivalence by noting we are all descendents of Adam and Eve, all intergenerationally linked, and therefore "everything is neutral").

taxes, liquidity constraints) also come into play here, as do finite lives and the possibility of nonaltruistic operative bequest motives.[38] One important implication of Ricardian equivalence is that the age (or generation) distribution of resources within a family is irrelevant; only the family's aggregate resources matter, a proposition Larry Kotlikoff and I rejected econometrically.[39] Thus, most economists, including me, believe Ricardian equivalence breaks down, at least as a full explanation, in the real world.[40] Deficits and debt are likely to have real effects, including effects on generational equity.

It is important to have a broader perspective on generational equity. There are three ways for government policy to transfer resources across generations and hence affect generational equity: (1) pay-as-you-go social insurance (tax the young, transfer to the old); (2) capital-income taxes (tax savers, who are middle age, reducing private capital and, hence, income for future generations); and (3) public debt (borrow to finance current spending; higher taxes on future taxpayers to pay interest or pay off debt). Hence, the government has several policy instruments to affect the capital stock, future income, and generational equity. The potential effects on future living standards from the crowding out of private investment by federal budget deficits could be offset by curtailment of the growth of Social Security and Medicare transfers on the one hand, or by replacement of the corporate and personal income taxes with something resembling a flat-rate consumed-income tax on the other, as subsequently discussed.

Finally, it is important to place the discussion of intergenerational equity in the broader context of the causes and consequences of economic well being, that is, of economic growth. First, historically, at least for recent centuries in the developed world, each generation is much wealthier than the generation that preceded it. Real GDP per capita in the United States in 2005 was about $39,000 in 2000 dollars, about double the level 30 years before. That occurred because of private saving and investment and technology from public and private research and development of new potential products and processes. Further, there is much tax-financed spending (in addition to large amounts of family spending) on children, such as for education. So looking just at public debt can miss important aspects of generational equity.

Thus, any discussion of deficits and debt must be placed in the broader perspective of the entire fiscal program, whether one is concerned with potential short-run effects on aggregate demand, long-run supply-side effects, or intergenerational equity. To understand this in more detail, it is worth digressing and focusing just on taxes and spending, ignoring deficits for a moment.

---

[38] See Olivier J. Blanchard, *Debt, Deficits, and Finite Horizons*, 93 J. POL. ECON. 223–247 (1985).
[39] See Michael J. Boskin and Laurence J. Kotlikoff, *Public Debt and U.S. Saving: A New Test of the Neutrality Hypothesis*, 23 CARNEGIE-ROCHESTER CONFERENCE SERIES 55–86 (1985).
[40] See, e.g., Bernheim, *supra* note 21.

The evolution of taxes and spending is a primary determinant of the level and growth of real GDP and, hence, over a long span of time, affects the ability of the economy to provide rising living standards, low unemployment, and upward economic mobility rather than relative economic stagnation and socioeconomic ossification.

Under current law, the federal government tax burden is projected to rise by more than one-third as a share of GDP in coming decades, because of the combined effects of the alternative minimum tax, real bracket creep, and other factors.[41] Several decades ago there was great concern about potential "fiscal drag" on the economy from taxes rising as a share of GDP. There still should be.

The economies of Western Europe set their taxes and government spending at about half of GDP. In the United States, the figure is just under one-third (including state and local government). From the history of the last quarter-century, the current level of government in the United States economy appears consistent with economic growth and standards of living rising solidly. A substantially higher tax and spending burden does not appear consistent with such performance. To see why, consider Figure 5.10, which portrays the negative correlation between economic growth rates and government tax and spending burdens in the OECD countries. Many other factors influence growth rate and per-capita income differentials, which is why, of course, all countries don't lie exactly on the line. But moving from U.S. tax levels to Western European levels might cut the growth rate by up to a full percentage point. Over a generation, that cumulates to huge differences in standards of living.[42] Indeed, France, Germany, Italy, and the United Kingdom have standards of living 30 percent lower than the United States.

By far the most important aspect of economic performance is the rate of economic growth, because that growth determines future living standards. The most important way the tax system affects living standards is through the rate of saving, investment, work effort, entrepreneurship, and human capital investment. Modern scholarship in public economics demonstrates that immense harm is done by high marginal tax rates, especially on capital income. Income taxes double tax saving – first when income is saved, and again when the saving earns a return on interest, dividends, or capital gains. This tax distortion, or wedge, between the before-tax return to investment by firms and the after-tax return to saving is potentially very damaging. While the size of the tax wedge is modest for short periods, say a year, it grows exponentially larger with longer horizons;[43] for example, saving for a child's education or one's own retirement could span several decades. This is a major reason virtually all prominent

---

[41] *See* Congressional Budget Office, U.S. Cong., The Long-Term Budget Outlook (Dec. 2005).
[42] *See* Edward C. Prescott, *Prosperity and Depression*, 92 Am. Econ. Rev. 1–15 (2002).
[43] *See* Boskin, *supra* note 27.

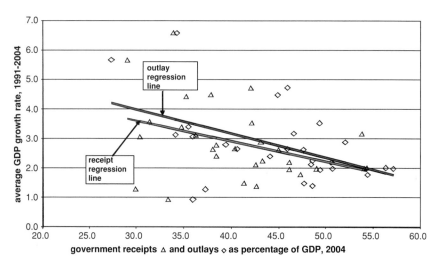

Figure 5.10. Relation between economic growth and tax burden (OECD countries).

academic economists who have studied the issue recommend taxing consumption or that part of income that is consumed. Such a tax is neutral with respect to saving and investment (intertemporal neutrality), and also among types of investment (atemporal neutrality). Think of intertemporal neutrality as a level playing field goalpost to goalpost, and atemporal neutrality as level sideline to sideline. Even a perfect income tax (which would require measuring true economic depreciation and inflation adjustment of many items, among other difficulties) only would achieve atemporal neutrality, not the far more important intertemporal neutrality. A pure consumption tax, however levied, would guarantee both. Note that the consumption–saving neutrality is independent of the structure of marginal rates. A progressive consumed-income tax can be neutral for traditional saving and investment. It is, however, important to note several practical issues in comparing real-world, as opposed to textbook, income and consumption taxes. First, intangible investment such as research and development accounts for a sizeable portion of investment and is accorded "consumption tax" treatment by expensing in the income tax. Second, both income and consumption taxes tax above-normal returns to saving. Third, an impure consumption tax, such as one that allowed deductibility of both saving and interest, could wind up subsidizing investment. Most current "tax systems" are really hybrids of pure income and pure consumption taxes or, even more precisely, range from subsidy to single, double, triple, or quadruple taxation of saving.

In modern economies and in the economic development process, human capital, the investment in knowledge and skills of the labor force primarily through education and on-the-job training, is vitally important to growth. And the consumption-tax neutrality argument for human investment only holds for a flat rate. As I first demonstrated 30 years ago,[44] it is the progressive rate structure that deters human capital investment. Most on-the-job training and much of higher education costs are financed by foregone earnings, which are not taxed. To take a simple example, suppose an early career worker earns $60,000, but one-third of his or her time is spent acquiring skills. Thus, the $60,000 is pay for the two-thirds time; the other one-third time is compensated by the skill acquisition. To economists, the worker is earning $90,000, paying $30,000 for the skills and netting $60,000. But the structure of the job (not to mention personal tax savings) makes it convenient to suppress the $30,000 "transaction" between the worker and the firm. It is as if the foregone earnings were included in taxable income, but then immediately expensed. A flat tax rate does not affect the net returns to such human investment decisions, but a progressive rate structure would reduce the returns and impede investment because the higher earnings generated by the investment would be taxed at a higher rate than that at which the investment was expensed. Thus, there is a serious trade-off between the goals of equity and efficiency in the tax system. Low-rate(s) consumed-income taxes combined with efficient and targeted transfers would appear to be the best combination in many circumstances.[45]

There are several political economy reasons to favor low flat-rate taxes. If everybody pays at a common rate, it will be harder to expand government and raise the rate, because a larger fraction of potential voters will have a stake in limiting the spending to that with perceived net benefits. The more progressive the tax system becomes and the more taxes become concentrated among the few, the easier it is to expand government spending that fails cost–benefit tests at the expense of a minority paying the bulk of costs. This was Milton Friedman's most important insight when he first proposed a flat tax in *Capitalism and Freedom.* This aspect of the case for a flat tax unfortunately has been almost lost in recent decades, as attention has focused on the important goal of simplicity, as in the postcard filing in the Hall–Rabushka flat tax.[46]

Highly progressive rates also create an unhealthy dynamic in which revenues surge disproportionately in booms, the legislature spends it all (or more), and, in the next downturn, it is "impossible" to "cut" spending, leaving a growing fiscal gap and pressure to raise taxes to allow spending to ratchet up in the next boom. This is precisely what happened in California in 1999–2001 when revenues from capital gains, stock options, and the very progressive income tax surged far more than rapidly rising income during the tech bubble, and state spending went up faster still. The inevitable correction led to a crisis, with the state's credit rating below Puerto Rico's and the governor recalled.

[44] Michael J. Boskin, *Notes on the Tax Treatment of Human Capital* (Nat'l Bureau of Econ. Research Working Paper No. 116, 1975), *available at* http://www.nber.org/papers/w0116.

[45] *See* Michael J. Boskin, *A Broader Perspective on the Tax Reform Debate*, 110 TAX NOTES 393 (Jan. 23, 2006).

[46] Robert Hall and Alvin Rabushka, THE FLAT TAX (1983).

At present, there is a much higher ratio of people who are net income recipients to people who are taxpayers than in any time in recent U.S. history, reflecting not only traditional transfers but also the rapid growth of the earned-income tax credit and other features of the income tax itself. Does it make sense to continue an income-tax system in which almost half the population pays virtually no taxes? If the median voter has no "skin in the game," not even a tiny pro rata share of the financing of general government, the constituency for limiting government spending will be weak, and the economy, which ultimately will have to finance the growing government spending by either current or future taxes, eventually may be severely damaged.

As the Baby Boom generation approaches retirement, the fraction of the population in any given year who are receiving more than they are paying will grow. This might be dealt with both on the tax side (smaller underground economy, decreased proportion of population off the income-tax rolls) and, especially, on the transfer payment side (slower benefit growth for the well-off in entitlements programs) and soon, or there is a growing risk of sliding into a spiral of higher benefits, higher tax rates, a weaker economy, and ever-greater political conflict between taxpayers and transfer recipients.[47]

There is a rapidly closing window within which to have a national strategic debate about the role of government in the economy, about the level and structure of spending and taxes. In a few years, the demographics may drive an unstable political economy with an ever-larger fraction of voters demanding higher spending financed by higher taxes on a dwindling fraction of the population. Witness how difficult it is for the Europeans – with their larger ratios of benefit recipients to taxpayers – to make reforms that would be considered trivial in the United States, even from much higher levels of spending and taxes.

The collective interest is in keeping the hand of government in the economy relatively light; in keeping tax rates as low as possible; and in preventing spending and tax decisions from gradually turning the economy into the economic equivalent of France or Germany, for that would surely portend serious economic problems. Replacing the corporate and personal income taxes with something closer to a pure flat-rate consumption tax that prevented the tax share in GDP from rising much would be an important step in doing so.

What is more important – preventing tax rates from rising, reforming the tax code, or deficit reduction? The economic effects of lower rates and especially the reforms outlined herein go in the same direction as deficit reduction – higher capital formation and future income. Hence, *all* these things are desirable: controlling the growth of transfer payments to balance the budget (at least as defined more carefully) *and* "reducing" taxes, which amounts to preventing the tax share of GDP from rising much, *and* tax reform. Further, the economic

---

[47] *See* Laurence Kotlikoff and Christain Hagist, *Who's Going Broke? Comparing Health Care Costs in Ten OECD Countries* (Nat'l Bureau of Econ. Research Working Paper No. 11833, 2005), *available at* http://www.nber.org/papers/w11833.

effects of deficits can be very different, depending upon whether the deficits are replacing income taxes or financing spending.[48]

The natural desire to focus on just one number to describe a complex process is certainly understandable. And, in some cases, the level or change in the deficit (or surplus), for all its flaws, does convey the big picture. But this tendency does come with a cost. In some cases as just described, it can be very misleading. In virtually all cases, it is insufficient to describe the full set of economic effects and may not even get the net result right. For that, we usually also need to specify what has happened to taxes, not just the levels, but real effective marginal tax rates on labor, capital (new and old), consumption, and the like. As to spending, we need to specify not just the level but also the composition among purchases and transfers, and within purchases, for consumption and capital investment. In addition, we must add what is going on in the economy, in the level and growth of GDP, inflation, and so on. Finally, we must specify long-run contingent and potential debt, as well as its sources and interactions with the economy, not just to "alert us" to possible problems but also because they can have real economic effects now, before they actually occur or are, to paraphrase the late Herb Stein, "stopped." In short, a complete, careful analysis specifies not only the current deficit and debt but also imbeds it in the full fiscal program of current and expected future taxes, spending, and evolution of the debt. In particular, it is unfortunate at best, deeply misleading at worst, that focus on the deficit conveys the impression that it is a matter of indifference, or at least second-order importance, how any imbalance is rectified – that it doesn't much matter whether and which taxes are raised or spending reduced (growth slowed). That is simply wrong.

IV. MEASURING THE LONG-RUN POSITION OF THE BUDGET: LOOKING BEHIND THE HEADLINE DEFICIT

The deficit is a flow of income in a period of time, usually a year. The debt – the accumulation of all previous deficits – is a stock at a point in time. Correspondingly, numerous other stocks and flows must be considered in evaluating the government's current and projected future financial position. Let's start with a current balance sheet. What would it include?

A. Government Balance Sheet

The federal (and state and local) government owns many assets, from planes and computers to land and mineral rights. The federal government also finances

---

[48] The persistence of deficits appears to depend on whether tax reduction or military or nonmilitary spending "shocks" generated the initial deficit. *See* Benjamin M. Friedman, *Deficits and Debt in the Short and Long Run* (Nat'l Bureau of Econ. Research Working Paper No. 11630, 2005), *available at* http://www.nber.org/papers/w11630.

a large fraction of state and local government capital, from highways to sewer systems. Measuring capital, investment, and depreciation is not easy,[49] but the Bureau of Economic Analysis[50] and the Office of Management and Budget[51] do so.

Likewise, the federal government finances substantial research and development. If one purpose in analyzing the national debt is to assess the degree to which burdens are being left to the future, it makes sense to account for net public investment in tangible capital and research and development, and for the public assets being left to and for the future.

Similarly, the federal government – as do state governments – owns vast amounts of land and mineral rights, a modest portion of which it leases for rent and royalties. Clearly, the value of the land and mineral rights rises over time to reflect the scarcity value (it also fluctuates with perturbations in land and energy prices). While some of this will never and should never be monetized (e.g., Yosemite National Park), some of it will and should be in future decades. To get a measure of national wealth, it would seem necessary to value at least the portion of these assets that might be monetized and net it against explicit debt. Further, the opportunity cost of not monetizing these assets would be more transparent and should be used in sensible cost–benefit analysis in deciding which assets to monetize and when. If the recent run-up in oil and natural gas prices proves to be, even in part, durable, the mineral rights figure will soar, both because of the higher yields from the royalties and the likelihood that more will be found and produced.

The federal government also has financial assets, such as receivables and deferred taxes that have already accrued in tax-deferred saving vehicles such as IRAs and 401(k)s. The tangible capital, land, and mineral rights amount to about $3 trillion; the accrued value of taxes on the more than $13 trillion in the tax-deferred saving is another $2.5 trillion to $3 trillion.

Finally, the federal government has financed substantial education and R&D;[52] rough estimates of the value of that capital (although much of it is not monetizable *by the government*) is $2.5 trillion.

The federal (and state and local) government has explicit debt. The national debt amounted to $8.4 trillion gross in the middle of fiscal year 2006 (see Figure 5.1), but much of that is held by the government and the FED. The

[49] *See* Michael J. Boskin, Marc S. Robinson, and Alan M. Huber, *Government Saving, Capital Formation, and Wealth in the United States, 1947–1985, in* THE MEASUREMENT OF SAVING, INVESTMENT, AND WEALTH 287–356 (Robert E. Lipsey and Helen Stone Tice eds., 1989).

[50] *See* U.S. Bureau of Econ. Analysis, CHANGES IN NET STOCK OF PRODUCED ASSETS (FIXED ASSETS AND INVENTORIES), NATIONAL INCOME AND PRODUCT ACCOUNTS TABLES (2006).

[51] *See* Exec. Office of the President, Office of Mgm't and Budget,*Net Stock of Federally Financed Physical Capital*, THE BUDGET OF THE UNITED STATES, FY2007, ANALYTICAL PERSPECTIVES, Table 6–4 (2006).

[52] *See* Robert Eisner, HOW REAL IS THE FEDERAL DEFICIT? (1986).

Table 5.5. Estimates of fiscal imbalance–actuarial deficit ($ trillion present value)

	Gokhale and Smetters	Trustees
Total ($)	68.6	79.2
Social Security ($)	8.7	12.8
Medicare ($)	65.9	68.4

Source: J. Gokhale & K. Smetters, *Fiscal and Generational Imbalances: An Update,* Cato Inst. Paper No 0501, 2005 (the present value of real GDP is estimated as $772 trillion so the gap amounts to about 8 percent of GDP).

debt held outside the government was $4.1 trillion. The unfunded federal employee pensions and health benefits are another $4.0 trillion, although these are obviously potential future obligations, subject to forecast error and political risk.

To these totals, one must add the expected value of any contingent debt, such as for deposit insurance, loan guarantees, the Pension Benefit Guaranty Corporation, possibly losses by Fannie Mae and Freddie Mac, and the potential (massive) unfunded future liabilities of social insurance programs, especially Social Security and Medicare (see Figures 5.11 and Table 5.5), on which more follows in the subsequent paragraphs.

A government balance sheet quickly would show the *explicit current* national debt to be quite manageable relative to the size of the economy, and even just relative to explicit assets. But the immense size of the potential unfunded liabilities – if they ultimately are to be funded – dwarfs the traditional national debt.

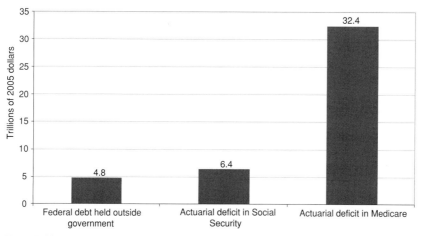

Figure 5.11. Federal debt and potential unfunded Social Security and Medicare liabilities: 75-year trustees' horizon (*source*: SSA Trustee's Report, 2006).

B. The Long-Run Debt

The debt evolves in a manner that is not intuitive. Recall from the government's budget constraint that the net present value of future *primary* surpluses must cover the current debt net of at least monetizable assets,

$$D_0 \leq \sum_t^\infty \frac{T_t - G_t}{(1 + r)^t} + A_0,$$

where

D_0 = government debt,
A_0 = government assets,
G = outlays other than interest, and
T = revenues.

Currently, as noted here, D_0 is 38 percent of GDP.

Note that a balanced budget is not required to reduce the debt–GDP ratio. With the debt at just under 40 percent of GDP, nominal growth of 5.0 percent (3.0 percent real, 2.0 percent inflation) implies that a deficit under 2.0 percent of GDP would reduce the debt burden. More formally, a deficit–GDP ratio smaller than the (nominal) growth rate of the economy times the debt–GDP ratio will reduce the debt burden. Finally, since the headline deficit includes interest payments, the national debt could be paid off without ever running a surplus! When the deficit is less than the government's interest payments, what we already defined as a primary surplus, progress is being made in reducing the (present value of the debt) burden. In fact, a string of primary surpluses could pay off the debt.

C. Generational Accounts and Fiscal Gaps

The fundamental long-term relationship is the government's intertemporal budget constraint, which requires that subsequent net tax payments of current and future generations be sufficient in present value (PV in the following equation) to cover the present value of future government consumption as well as pay off the government's current net indebtedness (net of initial government assets). Failure to satisfy the constraint implies the government defaults on its explicit and implicit liabilities, thereby satisfying the constraint by "taxing" creditors (bondholders) and potential creditors (future Social Security recipients to the extent we have properly modeled their expected benefits). Thus, the budget constraint can be manipulated in various ways to highlight the gap between projected revenues and outlays and the projected transfers of resources between generations through a system of generational accounts (GA). For example,

PV of remaining net tax payments of existing generations (TE)		PV of net tax payments of future generations (TF)		PV of all future government noninterest outlays + net (of assets) debt (G) + (D)
	+		=	
	+		=	

Rewriting, we label the difference,

$$G - (TE + TF - D) = FG,$$

as the fiscal gap (FG).[53] A positive FG implies the government's fiscal program is not sustainable; D, G, and/or T eventually must change, unless the projections prove to have been too pessimistic.

To estimate such a long-run fiscal gap, we need projections of population, taxes, transfers, government purchases, initial government net debt, and a discount rate. Because the entitlement-program (Social Security and Medicare) outlays are projected to exceed projected dedicated revenue, and because this gap, particularly for Medicare, is projected to get progressively worse, these fiscal gaps, fiscal imbalances, and generational account measures usefully highlight the effects beyond the 75-year horizon used in the Social Security and Medicare Trustees actuarial projections. It is worth noting that it is very unlikely that those people not already retired or near retirement expect to receive anything close to the mechanical benefit projections from the current benefit formulas. Indeed, younger workers routinely say they expect to receive nothing, for example, from Social Security. The Social Security Administration routinely informs the population in an annual statement that there will only be sufficient revenue in a few decades to pay roughly three-fourths of the benefits. Finally, most of the FG occurs in the far-distant future, and thus will be paid by those not yet born. It is a stretch to call changes in such benefits "cuts," "broken promises," or "defaulting on obligations." Further, the vast majority of the transfers that give rise to the FG involve the projected increase in real benefits per beneficiary to middle-class and well-off retirees.

While the details of the estimates are very sensitive to assumptions such as those for growth and discount rates, excess (of GDP) medical cost growth, and the like, the big picture is the same from all these types of forecasts: These programs (indeed the entire fiscal program) are unsustainable. To be sure, as

---

[53] *See* Alan J. Auerbach, William G. Gale, and Peter R. Orszag, *Sources of the Long-Term Fiscal Gap*, 103 TAX NOTES 1049 (May 14, 2004); Alan J. Auerbach, Jagadeesh Gokhale, and Laurence J. Kotlikoff, *Generational Accounting: A Meaningful Way to Evaluate Fiscal Policy*, 8 J. ECON. PERSP. 73–94 (1994); Jagadeesh Gokhale and Kent Smetters, *Fiscal and Generational Imbalances: An Update, in* TAX POLICY AND THE ECONOMY, VOLUME 20, 193–223 (James M. Poterba ed., 2006).

the late Herb Stein remarked, "something that cannot go on forever will stop." But how and when it stops could be quite consequential.

These are formulas, not legal commitments. In fact, Social Security payments come out of "trust funds," so if sufficient revenues are not available, benefits must adjust. In this sense, it is not clear whether projecting the unfunded benefit formula or the taxes should be regarded as current law. But there is an implicit contract, a powerful political commitment to the program. Certainly those already retired or soon to retire have incorporated features of the current program into their retirement planning. So it would be unreasonable to alter the program for them. Those in middle age have partially adjusted and have, as noted above, much warning about the future solvency issues. And young workers, or those not yet working or not yet born, have not based decisions on the current program. Indeed, young workers probably overstate the likely changes they will face. This suggests that reforms that, after a grace period, slowly compound to significance over several decades make the most sense. However, in the past, adjustments have been made: For decades, benefits were adjusted up periodically (1940 through 1972); more recently, they were curtailed – in 1983 and the 1990s – by taxing benefits and raising the retirement age. Currently, we are adding benefits, such as prescription drugs to Medicare. The problem is not just demographics. As explored in Box 5.3, the entire long-run Social Security deficit could be eliminated by slowing the growth of real benefits per recipient and making other relatively minor adjustments in benefit design. Current Social Security tax rates are sufficient for rising real benefits or a doubling of the recipient population, but not both. For Medicare, the majority of the problem is excess (of GDP) cost growth; demographics account for a minority of the problem.[54]

Despite the strong assumptions and great uncertainty, these measures usefully point out long-run imbalances and unsustainability; they also highlight potential effects on future generations who are not fully represented in the political process. Thus they are a valuable supplement to the usual annual budget projections. But as with traditional budget numbers, the FG's focus on a single number achieves simplicity by sacrificing fuller information, and unfortunately it conveys a sense of neutrality with respect to how these large gaps are closed. In fact, significant differences are likely in the economic effects of closing any gaps on the spending and tax sides of the budget. As with the traditional deficit measures, two fiscal programs with an identical FG can have vastly different effects on the economy.

Returning to intergenerational equity, GA measures usefully highlight potential resource transfers across generations, indicating, for example, large increases in taxes (a doubling of future payroll taxes, for example) on future generations to finance projected vast increases in real benefits amid more

---

[54] *See* Kotlikoff and Hagist, *supra* note 47.

Box 5.3. Would Social Security reform cut benefits?

Given much misunderstanding of long-run projected deficits in the entitlement programs, it is worth taking a look at what could be done about them. Critics of Social Security reform often claim that reform proposals entail massive cuts in guaranteed benefits. In reality, nobody's benefits need to be cut and nobody's taxes need to be raised. Current tax rates, given projected economic growth, are sufficient to maintain real retirement benefits at current levels. The system's problems derive from the current benefit formula, which implicitly schedules real Social Security benefits per recipient to double in the next few decades. This occurs because of the following:

1. The formula used to calculate the initial level for a retiree's Social Security benefits is indexed to wages rather than prices. From 1960 to 2004, the average wage index rose 1.1 percent per year faster than consumer prices, as measured by the Consumer Price Index (CPI).

2. People will be living longer, which increases the present value of total lifetime Social Security benefits.

3. The change in the CPI, which indexes Social Security benefits postretirement, over-states inflation by about 80 bp/year despite some valuable improvements made by the Bureau of Labor Statistics.[55] Although perhaps part of this would not apply to seniors.

The claims that guaranteed benefits will be cut and promises broken are relative to projecting the current benefit formula forward indefinitely. However, the Social Security Administration sends future beneficiaries an annual statement that clearly states that the current system cannot pay such benefits; in a few decades, under current law, there will be only 74 cents in taxes coming into the Trust Fund, from which benefits must be paid, for every dollar of projected benefits. Further, Congress often has changed benefits in the past, most recently by taxing them, and is certain to do so in the future. The Supreme Court has ruled there is no "right" to the benefits. There is nothing "guaranteed" about the benefits; they involve substantial economic, demographic, and political risk.

A set of commonsensical reforms would strengthen and modernize Social Security, improve incentives, and eliminate the drag that uncertainty over future funding causes for families and the economy. First, we could move from wage indexing to price indexing, but raise benefits more rapidly for people below the poverty level. This would eliminate most of the long-term insolvency, and do so in a manner that leads to rapidly rising real benefits for people with low incomes, and more slowly rising real benefits for people with higher incomes. Next, we could prospectively increase the retirement age in several decades slightly beyond that in current law, while maintaining a strong early-retirement option. Combined with a somewhat more accurate CPI (the BLS' chained CPI), these reforms would deal with the long-run solvency issues. And they would fully deliver what

(continued)

[55] Alan J. Auerbach, William G. Gale, and Peter R. Orszag, *The Budget: Plus Ça Change, Plus C'est La Même Chose*, TAX NOTES, April 17, 2006, at 349.

Box 5.3. *(continued)*

is Social Security's most important mission, as stated at its inception by President Franklin D. Roosevelt, of providing "the average citizen protection against poverty-ridden old age."

A favorite question posed by critics of reforming Social Security is this: Why act now, when there is no problem, let alone crisis? The first Baby Boomers will begin to receive Social Security in 2008. The fraction of voters receiving benefits will increase 50 percent in 20 years and double in 50 years, relative to the fraction of voters paying taxes, making reform ever more difficult. And, once delayed, reform is ever more likely to lead to vastly higher taxes without slower benefit growth.

With reform now, by the time the demographics really bite in two or three decades, the solvency problem will be solved, and families and the economy will have time to adjust gradually without severe disruption. If we wait and make changes abruptly, with large tax increases or benefit cuts or some combination all at once, wrenching adjustments would be required for beneficiaries, taxpayers, and the economy. Thus, reform really is urgent. Enacting these sensible reforms now would strengthen the economy, spare future retirees and taxpayers disruption in their personal finances, and ensure that Social Security plays an important and appropriate role in future retirement income security.

fiscally difficult demography. But it is useful to remember that such transfers fail to highlight valuable contributions of the generally poorer older generations. To see this, compare the year 1900 to the year 2000. Real per-capita income rose about tenfold, from $4,000 to $38,000. The large transfers to the "start-up" generations in Social Security and Medicare went to those who also financed the Baby Boomers' education, fought World War II, and survived the Great Depression. While the Baby Boomer generation would be even richer if the transfers had not been made to their parents' and grandparents' generations, it is not clear what the *net* resource transfer really was. Again, the intergenerational equity argument must be understood in the context of generally rising standards of living and the full fiscal program.

Finally, the FG measure could be gamed in the political process in the same way traditional short-run annual deficit projections and restrictions are gamed. It is all too easy to envision a large increase in Medicare benefits in the short run "paid for" by a "freeze" on Medicare payments 50 years in the future that nobody believes would ever actually occur.

In several decades, Social Security and Medicare deficits are expected to be vastly larger than the unified deficits projected for the next decade (Table 5.5, Figure 5.11). The long-run deficit projections run in the several tens of trillion dollars in net present value. These valuations typically are made over a 75-year horizon (Figure 5.11) or an infinite horizon basis (Table 5.5). Such projections are misleading in their assumptions of quite modest long-run annual growth, increases in health care outlays well in excess of GDP growth (although not as much as recently) for the better part of a century (that will only happen if the health benefits are sufficient to induce such spending), large real-benefit increases in Social Security, and continuous tax cuts to offset real bracket creep, the AMT, and other factors that, left unattended, would raise taxes relative to GDP by one-third (see Figure 5.12). On the other hand, they project (only) modest gains in life expectancy and an ever-worsening budgetary political dynamic. Even with less stark projections, however, large deficits and looming tax increases still would need to be addressed, by restraining the growth of spending and by future tax reduction and reform, to avoid substantial negative fiscal effects on future incomes.

Some economists argue we should systematically run surpluses in preparation for the looming problems associated with the retirement of the Baby Boom generation. Theoretically, that could raise national saving, "crowd in" investment, and increase future income. But sizeable budget surpluses historically have been unsustainable, resulting instead in large increases in spending, tax cuts, or both (e.g., the Social Security surpluses financing the rest of government and the federal and California budgets in the late 1990s bubble). Hence, it may not even be feasible to run systematic budget surpluses.

Thus, while it is important to control spending and stabilize or reduce the debt–GDP ratio over the coming decade, far more important are commonsense Social Security and Medicare reforms that gradually and cumulatively would address looming liabilities. For example, price indexing of Social Security would eliminate the astronomical deficit without anybody's benefits being cut or anybody's taxes raised. Such reforms would have little impact on the budget in the next decade, although they might positively affect saving, the capital stock, and income.[56] Every year, potential unfunded accrued liabilities grow and the fraction of voters receiving benefits rises relative to those paying taxes, thus making it increasingly difficult to enact the necessary reforms.

V. SUMMARY AND CONCLUSION

We may summarize our tour through economic theory, econometric evidence, and actual and projected data on deficits and debt in a series of lessons.

Deficits can be economically helpful, harmful, or irrelevant, depending upon circumstances such as the state of the business cycle, the need for temporary government spending swings, public capital investment, the reaction of the central bank, foreign capital flows, and private saving.

---

[56] On the change in the CPI overstating inflation, *see* David E. Lebow and Jeremy B. Rudd, *Measurement Error in the Consumer Price Index: Where Do We Stand?*, 41 J. ECON. LIT. 159–201 (2003); Michael J. Boskin, *Causes and Consequences of Bias in the Consumer Price Index as a Measure of the Cost-of-Living*, 33 ATLANTIC ECON. J. 1–13 (2005). Thirty basis points or so of this bias would be eliminated if and when the BLS moves to its far more accurate chained CPI as the official measure of consumer inflation.

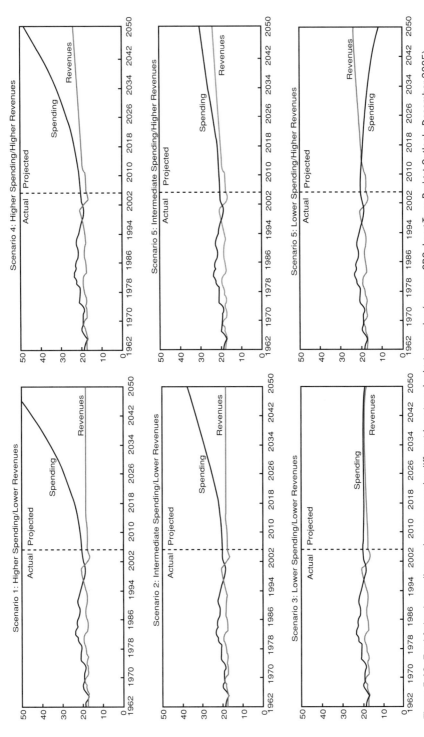

Figure 5.12. Total federal spending and revenues under different long-term budget scenarios (*source:* CBO, Long-Term Budget Outlook, December 2005).

The usual measures of the deficit and debt can be – and at times have been – quite misleading as a guide to the effects of the budget on short-run aggregate demand, long-run supply-side growth, or intergenerational equity. Cyclical conditions affecting revenues (and, to a lesser extent, spending), inflation eroding the real value of preexisting debt, government assets, and capital investment belying the lack of separate capital and operating budgets, numerous arbitrary aspects of deficit measures, and the lack of forward-looking information on serious long-term imbalances in entitlement programs all render the headline nominal unified budget deficit a very incomplete snapshot of the full fiscal program – of the level, composition, structure, and growth of spending and taxes that are the far more fundamental fiscal measures.

To deal with these issues, economists use a variety of additional budget concepts. A real standardized primary operating budget nets out cyclical, temporary, and inflation effects, interest on the inherited debt and net (of depreciation) capital investment, and is the best measure of whether the current cash flows of the budget are covering current consumption outlays. Such a measure does not, however, capture the longer-run potential effects of policy. For that, a FG measure, despite significant limitations, can be quite helpful.

Substantially higher taxes and spending appear to be inconsistent with strong economic growth, as witnessed by the large economies of Europe falling 30 percent behind U.S. living standards largely as a result of their much higher tax and spending ratios to GDP (roughly one-half compared to one-third). Further, those higher taxes have not resulted in smaller deficits and debt; quite the contrary, they have resulted in much higher spending on welfare programs and even larger deficits and debt.

Taxes are projected to rise from their 18 percent historical average to about 20 percent over the next decade – a level reached only temporarily in high inflation and bubble periods in recent decades[57] – and to 24 percent thereafter. That large step toward European-level taxation is due primarily to growth of the alternative minimum tax (or AMT) and real-bracket creep. Preventing it will require strong control of spending growth and continuous tax cuts (to prevent the increase in taxes relative to GDP) and tax reform.

Sizeable budget surpluses historically have been unsustainable, resulting instead in large increases in spending and, to a lesser extent, tax cuts. Hence, it may not even be feasible to run systematic budget surpluses.

The Ricardian equivalence notion that (given spending) deficit, and tax finance are equivalent, is an important benchmark to calibrate the effects of deficits, but it does not appear to be an accurate representation of reality. Several theoretical reasons plus the weight of econometric evidence suggest that deficits do crowd out some private investment.

---

[57] Martin Feldstein, *Social Security and Saving: New Time Series Evidence*, 49 Nat'l Tax J. 151–164 (1996).

The amount of crowding out depends on a number of factors. A benchmark case might be that every dollar of U.S. federal government deficit is matched by 50 cents less domestic investment, 20 cents increased private saving, and 30 cents decreased net foreign investment.

Deficits and debt are themselves only part of the picture. The level and structure of taxes, especially marginal tax rates on capital, labor, and consumption, and the extent of any productive public investment matter as well. Thus, one needs to specify the entire fiscal program – current and expected future deficits, debt, tax rates, and spending – to evaluate the effect on short-run aggregate demand, long-run growth, and intergenerational equity of deficits and debt.

It would appear that recent deficits were roughly consistent with textbook economic responses to war and recession. The current and medium-term projected deficits are consistent with a stable debt–GDP ratio; indeed, President Bush's budget results in an end of the decade primary surplus if the much stronger spending control is executed. Numerous pressures could severely affect that possibility. Raising tax rates on capital income, as some have proposed, would be a particularly counterproductive response to deficits, partly negating the long-run benefits of deficit reduction.

Quantitatively, the current and ten-year projected deficits and debt are quite manageable. The net-of-assets current debt held outside the government is a modest fraction of GDP; the debt–GDP ratio is slightly below historical averages and far below Euroland and Japan. Even at current levels, however, they do moderately reduce national saving, capital formation, and future income.

The projected longer-term fiscal imbalances amount to several tens of trillions of dollars in discounted present value. The vast bulk of these consist of projected rising real transfers per beneficiary to the middle class and well-off. Demographics play an important, but minority, role.

Focusing on just one measure, a single or series of annual deficits or a long-run fiscal gap, can convey the impression that it is economically irrelevant how the gap is closed, that higher taxes are no more harmful than restrained spending growth. That is potentially an economically dangerous notion, as substantial evidence demonstrates that, at levels well short of the 50 percent or so common in Western Europe, larger ratios of taxes and government spending to GDP retard economic growth and damage living standards, both as a result of traditional tax distortions and of the closely related welfare state disincentives and regulatory apparatus.

The fiscal gap or imbalance measures refer to very long-run projected potential, not actual explicit, liabilities, and they are quite "backloaded." Over half occur beyond the 75-year horizon of the Social Security and Medicare trustees' actuarial projections. That leads some to be quite complacent, invoking (Herb) Stein's law that something that cannot go on forever will stop. But it matters how and when it stops. Dealing with these potential problems sooner rather than later enables policy responses that are gradual and cumulative, minimizing abrupt changes that can be wrenching economically for individuals and the economy.

Finally, economic policy should focus on the denominator as well as the numerator of the debt–GDP ratio. Maximizing noninflationary growth requires generally supportive economic policy, not just closing a fiscal gap, including (1) the lowest possible tax rates and tax reform as discussed herein; (2) spending control (with serious cost–benefit tests); (3) sensible Social Security and Medicare reform along the lines previously discussed; (4) regulatory and litigation reform; (5) strengthening the global trading system; and (6) sound monetary policy.

Properly implemented, such a set of policies would produce a stable-to-falling debt–GDP ratio, except in economic downturns or periods of temporarily large military spending or other public investment. The nominal dollar headline unified budget still might run a deficit, but the true "burden of the debt" would be declining.

Questions for Chapter 5

1. To what extent can economic analysis help us answer the question of how large the federal deficit or public debt should be? Professor Boskin's analysis highlights the importance of considering the purposes for which deficits are employed: Do they contribute to the well-being of the future generations that will shoulder the burden of additional public debt? But one also must factor in the extent to which private saving adjusts for deficits, the availability of foreign sources of financing, and the impact on economic growth of higher or lower levels of taxation. How might the sophisticated framework presented in the chapter be factored into a political process that also must be attuned to a variety of equitable considerations and attentive to the interests of current constituents upon whose goodwill politicians depend for today's votes?

2. When politicians and lay observers discuss fiscal policy, they often assume that the federal budget should be balanced and the goal of federal budget policy should be a balanced budget. Indeed, constitutional amendments often are proposed to impose balanced-budget requirements. As Professor Boskin's chapter explains, balanced budgets are not always the best policy from an economic perspective, and our typical measure of deficits – the "headline" deficit – can be quite misleading and incomplete. Does it therefore follow that our political leaders and pundits should change the way they discuss deficits and debt levels? Would it be practical to draft a constitutional provision that requires an economically appropriate level of deficit spending? Do state constitutions that require only that state operating budgets be in balance (and allow deficit financing for capital projects) guarantee an economically preferable fiscal balance? If a standard of optimal deficits cannot practically be written in law, should experts at least try to educate the public about how to distinguish appropriate from excessive deficits and public debt levels? Or, are there advantages in having public discourse on federal fiscal policy center on measures of deficit and public debt that the experts, such as Professor Boskin, consider to be materially flawed?

3. While the calculation of past deficits is fairly straightforward, much debate over fiscal policy concerns projected deficits in the future, and these projections are extremely difficult to estimate with accuracy. To begin with, economic activity has substantial impact on fiscal policies. A booming economy will increase revenue, while a recession will increase certain kinds of spending and reduce revenue. Projecting fiscal policy further into the future is complicated by the fact that many spending programs need new appropriations each year, and some important tax measures, including many of President Bush's tax cuts enacted earlier this decade, are scheduled to expire over the next few years. Sometimes, the most recent year's budget includes extraordinary items – such as emergency relief of unusually destructive national disasters typically funded through supplemental appropriations – that are not expected to recur in the future. Depending on how one deals with these and similar issues, projections can suggest very different budgetary "baseline" projections for future deficits or surplus. Oftentimes, the Congressional Budget Office and the Office of Management and Budget will make quite different projections based on different assumptions about future fiscal policy.[58] In terms of framing public debate over budget policy, is it preferable to use assumptions that project lower levels of future deficits or higher levels of deficits? Is the answer different for projections based on federal legislation scheduled to expire, as opposed to projections about economic assumptions?

4. The largest fiscal challenge facing the United States is the expected rise in entitlement spending for Social Security and Medicare as the Baby Boomer generation enters retirement over the next two decades. As traditional budgetary projections look out only five or ten years, most of this increase in spending obligations appears beyond our standard budgetary windows. For this reason, economists have begun to develop new budgetary measures, described in Professor Boskin's chapter, that estimate the present value of future benefit payments and tax revenue associated with Social Security and Medicare. Sometimes these projections extend out for 75 years; other times they attempt to capture current policies over an infinite horizon. While these estimates depend on a large number of assumptions about economic growth and demographic trends, they attempt to quantify the fiscal burden of entitlement programs in a way that facilitates comparisons between the fiscal burden imposed by these programs and the explicit debt of the federal government. Critics of these new measures object to estimates that emphasize the cost of future spending on benefits for the elderly population as opposed to other forms of future government spending, such as expenditures for education or the military. Is

---

[58] Extreme care should be taken in interpreting changes in tax burdens from either temporarily inflated levels, as in the high inflation year of 1980 or the tech stock bubble year of 2000, or temporarily depressed levels, as in the recession troughs of 1982, 1991, and 2001.

entitlement spending for retirees different than other forms of federal spending? Is it relevant that workers must contribute payroll taxes in order to be eligible for most Social Security and Medicare benefits?

5. In Box 5.3, Professor Boskin offers a perspective on how the Social Security system could be reformed to regain solvency. Critical to his discussion is the question of whether his proposed reforms would constitute a "cut" in benefits. He argues that no cuts are necessary because his reforms would simply restrain the rate at which inflation-adjusted benefits are increased (or indexed) over time. In particular, while he supports the current formula for the near term, he argues it should not be used as the baseline in the distant future, e.g. for those not yet born. Other experts resist this argument on the grounds that the benefit schedules written into current law were designed to guarantee Social Security participants a specific level of retirement income (measured as a fraction of earnings at retirement) and that any reduction in these promised benefits constitutes a benefit cut. Which side of this debate has the better argument? Or, put differently, what is the appropriate budgetary baseline to use for the discussion of entitlement reforms?

6 Counting the Ways

The Structure of Federal Spending

Howell E. Jackson

In the realm of budget policy, numbers are important. The size of the deficit, the level of public debt, and a handful of commonly cited ratios all have great political salience in budgeting decisions. When the Congressional Budget Office (CBO) issues a report or the president unveils his annual budget proposal, these actions immediately are evaluated by reference to key budgetary measures. These measures are based on particular accounting principles, most of which were developed decades ago with minor adjustments over time.[1] Accounting principles are not, however, immutable. Other principles apply in other jurisdictions and indeed different principles are applied in assembling the Financial Reports of the United States Government, to which neither the general public nor budget experts pay much attention.[2] The question I explore in this chapter

---

[1] The foundation of modern budgetary aggregates is the REPORT OF THE PRESIDENT'S COMMISSION ON BUDGET CONCEPTS (Oct. 1967). To a large degree, this chapter calls for a reconsideration of the principles articulated in that report.

[2] The figures discussed in this article are drawn largely from the FISCAL YEAR 2005 FINANCIAL REPORT OF THE UNITED STATES GOVERNMENT (Dec. 2005), *available at* http://www.gao.gov/financial/fy2005financialreport.html. The report was reproduced in a printed version with a foreword by Representative Jim Cooper (D-Tn.) in the summer of 2006. *See* FINANCIAL REPORT OF THE UNITED STATES GOVERNMENT (2006). For a useful comparison of the FINANCIAL REPORT OF THE UNITED STATEMENTS GOVERNMENT and traditional budgetary measures, *see* Congressional Budget Office, COMPARING BUDGET AND ACCOUNTING MEASURES OF THE FEDERAL GOVERNMENT'S FISCAL CONDITION (Dec. 2006) (hereinafter "CBO Comparison").

Howell Jackson is the James S. Reid, Jr., Professor of Law at Harvard Law School. This chapter benefited from the work of students in the author's Federal Budget Policy Seminar at Harvard Law School and conversations with Alan Auerbach, Jim Cooper, Richard Fallon, Beth Garrett, Daryl Levinson, Deborah Lucas, Dan Meltzer, Daniel Shaviro, and Matthew Stephenson, as well as comments and suggestions from participants at the February 2006 Conference on Fiscal Challenges: An Interdisciplinary Approach to Budget Policy held at USC Law School and at a session of the NYU Tax Colloquium in March 2006. The author also is grateful for generous financial support from the John M. Olin Center for Law, Economics, and Business at Harvard Law School. An earlier version of this chapter formed the basis of the author's inaugural lecture for the James S. Reid, Jr., Chair at Harvard Law School.

is whether we should move toward different methods of accounting – methods more similar to the rules of accrual accounting applied in other sectors of the economy – to inform public debate over federal budget policy.

The structure of my analysis is straightforward. First, I review the key measures of fiscal performance that currently frame federal budget policy, examining both the content of these measures themselves and the principal reasons why these measures are thought to be relevant to public understanding of fiscal matters. I then identify several important aspects of our federal government's fiscal affairs that are not captured in these standard measures. Most of the areas I discuss are currently reported in the Financial Reports of the United States Government, though some appear only as supplementary materials and not in the principal statements of financial condition. In many cases, the information omitted from our traditional budgetary aggregates is material, and these omissions compromise the integrity of public debate over fiscal decisions. I conclude with some preliminary thoughts about the implications of my critique of traditional budgetary measures and then suggest a general framework that should inform the rules of accounting for federal budget policy. Throughout the chapter, I report budget aggregates through fiscal year 2005, the most recent year for which complete financial information (including Social Security and Medicare) was available when this volume went to press.

I. PUBLIC DEBATE OVER FEDERAL BUDGET POLICY: MEASURES AND MEANING

What are the key measures of fiscal performance that policy experts distill from the mountains of budgeting minutiae to help the general public understand how the federal government is managing its financial affairs? And why do policy experts center on these particular measures of fiscal performance as focal points for public debate?

A. Three Key Measures of Fiscal Performance

The most common measure of our national government's fiscal performance is the federal budget's total deficit or surplus. Typically, this measure is calculated on an annual basis, as it was when the CBO reported the FY2005 total deficit at $318 billion and projected, albeit in a somewhat stylized manner, a FY2006 deficit of $337 billion.[3] (Table 6.1 presents summary information from the CBO's January 2006 Budget and Economic Outlook.) These two annual deficit estimates – the recent fiscal year's and the next – were widely reported

---

[3] *See* Congressional Budget Office, THE BUDGET AND ECONOMIC OUTLOOK: FISCAL YEARS 2007–2016 (Jan. 2006) (hereinafter "CBO January 2006").

Table 6.1. Selected elements of historical and projected federal budgets: 2001 through 2010 (billions of dollars)

	Actual						Projected			
	2001	**2002**	**2003**	**2004**	**2005**	**2006**	**2007**	**2008**	**2009**	**2010**
Total revenues outlays	$1,991	$1,853	$1,783	$1,880	$2,154	$2,312	$2,461	$2,598	$2,743	$2,883
Discretionary spending	$649	$734	$825	$895	$968	$999	$1,000	$1,022	$1,040	$1,060
Mandatory spending	$1,008	$1,106	$1,182	$1,238	$1,320	$1,432	$1,488	$1,572	$1,667	$1,755
Net interest	$206	$171	$153	$160	$184	$217	$244	$263	$277	$289
Total outlays	$1,863	$2,011	$2,160	$2,293	$2,472	$2,648	$2,732	$2,857	$2,984	$3,105
Total deficit	$128	–$158	–$378	–$413	–$318	–$337	–$270	–$259	–$241	–$222
Public debt held by public (Year-end)	$3,320	$3,540	$3,913	$4,296	$4,592	$4,925	$5,204	$5,477	$5,732	$5,967
Total deficit as percent of GDP	1.3%	–1.5%	–3.5%	–3.6%	–2.6%	–2.6%	–2.0%	–1.8%	–1.6%	–1.4%
Public debt at year-end as percent of GDP	33.0%	34.1%	36.1%	37.2%	37.4%	37.6%	37.8%	37.8%	37.6%	37.2%

Source: CBO, The Budget and Economic Outlook: Fiscal Years 2007 to 2016 (Jan. 2006).

in the popular press the day after CBO released its report,[4] and they are the most frequently cited measures of federal budget results. Occasionally, public attention also is directed to a multiyear aggregation of these annual measures of fiscal performance, as was the case back in January 2001 when the CBO projected $5.0 trillion of cumulative surpluses for FY2001 through FY2010.[5] By way of comparison, the January 2006 CBO report projected aggregate *deficits* over this same ten-year horizon of nearly $2.5 trillion, more than $1.1 trillion of actual accumulated deficits for the past five fiscal years, and more than $1.3 trillion projected for the next five. If one were to look for a single statistic to explain the recent resurgence of public and political interest in federal budget policy, it would be this precipitous $7.5 trillion swing from a $5 trillion ten-year projected surplus in 2001 to a $2.5 trillion ten-year deficit for the same projection period five years later.

A closely related measure of fiscal balance is the amount of federal debt held by the public. Several years ago, public-debt levels gained political salience because of concerns that mounting federal surpluses might force the federal government to redeem substantially all federal debt, thereby eliminating an important financial instrument and perhaps forcing the federal government to invest its excess cash reserves in private capital markets.[6] More recently, concerns have focused on increases in public debt outstanding. Mounting annual deficits mean that the amount of public debt outstanding is on the rise again, a potentially deleterious side effect of fiscal imbalance.

Although, as I subsequently explain, there is not a perfect match between total budget deficits and annual increases in public debt outstanding, the relationship is quite strong. So, for example, the CBO's January 2006 projections indicated that the federal public debt would increase from $4.6 trillion at year-end FY2005 to nearly $6.0 trillion at year-end FY2010; that increase of $1.4 trillion is comparable for the five-year annual deficits projected during that period for the federal government's total budget. In other words, measures of public debt outstanding can be thought of as a cumulative measure of the federal government's total annual deficits and surpluses. For that reason, public debt and changes in public debt are convenient summary measures of fiscal performance, often used in public debate over federal budget policy.

A somewhat more refined measure of federal budget policy deals with the composition of federal spending. As illustrated in Table 6.1, budget experts often distinguish between various categories of federal spending, most

---

[4] *See, e.g.,* Jackie Calmes, *CBO See Wider Deficit this Year and in 2016 if Tax Cuts Don't End,* WALL ST. J., Jan. 27, 2006, *at* A4 (reporting a $318 billion deficit for FY05 and projected deficit of $360 billion in FY06, which includes the $336 billion deficit reported herein, plus estimated additional costs for supplemental spending on military activities and flood relief).

[5] *See* Congressional Budget Office, THE BUDGET AND ECONOMIC OUTLOOK: FISCAL YEARS 2002–2011 (Jan. 2001).

[6] Howell E. Jackson, *Could We Invest the Surplus?,* TAX NOTES 1245 (Feb. 26, 2001).

typically discretionary spending, mandatory spending, and net-interest payments. These divisions sometimes confuse members of the general public, as they do not track more familiar programmatic lines (such as defense spending or public-works projects) but instead relate to the manner in which Congress authorizes federal outlays and, hence, have a high degree of salience to budget experts. As illustrated in Table 6.2, experts often highlight the declining share of discretionary spending in the federal budget (going from 39.15 percent of total outlays in FY2005 to a projected 34.14 percent in FY2010) as compared with the rising share of mandatory spending (going from a 53.41 percent share in FY2005 to a projected 56.52 percent in FY2010). While this long-term trend was interrupted in the first half of this decade as costs associated with Defense Department spending and other Bush administration priorities expanded discretionary spending, the rise in relative importance of mandatory spending is projected to dominate long-term budget projections, as was emphasized in another recent CBO report.[7] Also occasionally mentioned in discussions of the changing composition of federal spending is the growing significance of net-interest payments, projected in the CBO's January 2006 report to rise from 7.44 percent of total outlays in FY2005 to 9.31 percent in FY2010.

So, to recap, the public implicitly is being asked to keep track of three basic issues in thinking about the federal budget. The first two are aggregate measures of fiscal balance: the annual total deficit or surplus – measured annually or over some multiyear time horizon – and the amount of public debt outstanding. The third measure concerns the distribution of total federal outlays, principally the division between discretionary and mandatory spending but also sometimes including net-interest payments.

B. Why Do We Care About These Measures of Fiscal Performance?

Suppose, by way of illustration, some well-intentioned member of the general public was confronted with the three measures of fiscal performance just mentioned – essentially the information presented in Tables 6.1 and 6.2 – and then asked why policymakers care so much about these particular numbers. This perfectly reasonable question could be answered in a number of different ways, but I think most experts in the field would stress the measures' values in assessing the past performance of the federal government in fiscal affairs, in predicting a likely result of future performance over the next few years, and finally in identifying the relative ease with which Congress and the president will be able to make fiscal adjustments (at least with respect to spending decisions) in the near term. In the following subsections, I will expand upon each of these considerations and also say a few words about several complicated and unresolved normative issues that the considerations raise.

---

[7] *See* Congressional Budget Office, THE LONG-TERM BUDGET OUTLOOK (Dec. 2005).

Table 6.2. Composition of total federal outlays historical and projected: 2001 through 2010 (percentage of total outlays)

| | Actual | | | | | | | Projected | | |
	2001	2002	2003	2004	2005	2006	2007	2008	2009	2010
Discretionary spending share	34.85%	36.51%	38.21%	39.04%	39.15%	37.73%	36.60%	35.77%	34.85%	34.14%
Mandatory spending share	54.08%	54.99%	54.70%	53.97%	53.41%	54.08%	54.47%	55.02%	55.86%	56.52%
Net-interest share	11.07%	8.50%	7.09%	6.99%	7.44%	8.19%	8.93%	9.21%	9.28%	9.31%

Source: CBO, The Budget and Economic Outlook: Fiscal Years 2007 to 2016 (Jan. 2006).

i. Retrospective Assessment of Past Fiscal Performance

There are a host of reasons why we might care about the relationship between government revenues and outlays as reflected in both total budgetary aggregates (that is, total deficits and surpluses) and changes in public-debt levels. Within the budgetary context, the most prominent concern is that the costs of excessive deficits and unbridled growth in public debt will have to be borne by taxpayers and other national stakeholders in future years. Experts use deficits and changes in the level of public debt as scorecards for determining how fiscally responsible our political leadership has been on this dimension. A separate justification for focusing on these measures is the impact of deficits and public debt on private capital formation: If the government is borrowing excessively to finance increases in public debt, private borrowers may be crowded out of the market. Again, measures of recent deficits and changes in debt levels are one useful measure of the federal government's appetite for capital.

Of course, simply noting that deficits and debt levels are useful for identifying excessive burdens on future taxpayers and excessive crowding out of private capital markets does not provide particularly useful guidance as to the normative question of how large deficits or debt levels should be. And within budget policy circles, there is a good deal of confusion and disagreement about this normative issue. Proponents of balanced-budget amendments and the targets written into the original Gramm-Rudman-Hollings Act implicitly aimed for a deficit target of zero. While one cannot deny the elegance of a balanced-budget goal, there are many reasons to suspect that it is a poor policy guidepost in many contexts. In an inflationary environment, a balanced budget implies a declining real level of debt. It is not entirely clear why the government should always want to reduce the real level of public debt. One might just as easily postulate a constant real level of debt as a reasonable policy goal, in which case the optimal deficit would be a function of the size of the debt relative to government spending and the rate of inflation. Or one might target a constant level of public debt as a percentage of the GDP, in which case one also would have to include real GDP growth in calculating optimal deficits for any given year.[8]

A further complication in setting normative criteria for budgetary aggregates or public debt is the manner in which federal resources are deployed and the incidence of their benefits. High deficits and rising federal debt during World War II often are cited to illustrate this point. Because the benefits of these wartime expenditures accrued to future generations in the form of a (relatively) peaceful world, the ordinary rules of fiscal balance were thought not to apply in the first half of the 1940s. While this illustration is compelling, it is less clear

---

[8] For a more formal treatment of these considerations, *see* Michael J. Boskin, "Economic Perspectives on Federal Deficits and Debt," Chapter 5, this volume.

what other kinds of federal expenditures have a similar impact on optimal debt and deficit levels, and when the merits of governmental expenditures might counsel for more crowding out of private investment than is usually desirable. Many kinds of government spending might be characterized as investments to benefit future generations – for example, infrastructure projects or expenditures on public education – and there is disagreement over which projects provide legitimate justification for deficit financing. Finally, macro-economic considerations, in the Keynesian sense, also suggest that the overall condition of the national economy may have an influence on optimal deficit and debt levels. In brief, deficits and debt levels are important, but experts are hard pressed to tell us in what precise way they are important or exactly how to determine when they are out of synch with fully theorized criteria.

In the absence of a fully developed theory of deficits and debt, we proceed in a world of common wisdom and rules of thumb. Back in the first Reagan administration, OMB Director David Stockman worried over $200 billion a year deficits as far as the eye could see, and there was general consensus among experts that deficits at this level (roughly 6 percent of GDP, or $738 billion if based on the 2005 GDP) were excessive. Today, some policy experts assert that the $1.1 trillion in cumulative deficits during FY2001 through FY2005 also exceeded reasonable upper bounds, but others defend the deficits as not substantially higher than the average annual deficit that the United States has run since the mid-1960s (2.3 percent of GDP).[9] A further defense of recent deficits stresses the fact that recent expenditures for national security justify some degree of fiscal imbalance, much as World War II expenditures justified fiscal imbalance six decades ago.

With respect to public debt, there is also a tendency to survey historical trends and reverse engineer normative guidelines. So, for example, the OMB often presents charts illustrating that public-debt levels have ranged between a low of 23.9 percent of the GDP in 1974 to a high of 49.4 percent in 1993, and emphasizing that levels at year-end 2005 were 37.4 percent of GDP, very close to the midpoint of the range over the past 45 years.[10] Again, there is not a fully formed theory on the matter, but there seems to be some rough consensus among policy experts that public-debt levels between 30 percent and 40 percent of GDP constitute a tolerable burden for future generations and presumably an acceptable degree of crowding out for the capital markets. Not only is this the range within which the United States government has operated for more than a half a century without untoward economic consequences, it is consistent

---

[9] *See* CBO January 2006, *supra* note 3, at xiii ("At 2.6 percent of gross domestic product (GDP), this year's [FY2006's] deficit would be slightly larger than the 2.3 percent average recorded since 1965.").

[10] *See, e.g.,* Office of Management and Budget, THE NATION's FISCAL OUTLOOK (Feb. 2006), *available at* http://www.whitehouse.gov/omb/budget/fy2007/outlook.html.

with the fiscal guidelines that the European Union has established for member states in the Euro zone.[11]

To conclude, there is general agreement among budget experts that deficits and changes in public-debt levels are important measures of past fiscal performance. While there is no similar consensus as to what levels of those measures to maintain, the common practice is to evaluate deficit and debt measures as a percentage of current GDP and to benchmark recent performance against historical ranges.

ii. The Value of Prospective Measures: Trends and Benchmarks

Unlike past budgetary aggregates, which are largely objective reflections of past events, prospective measures depend upon a series of assumptions about what might happen over the next year or more. One could make these projections in a variety of ways, and there is actually a fair amount of controversy among budgetary experts about how these projections should be done.[12] The CBO estimates used in this chapter were based on statutory standards, which require the use of current laws and, on the spending side, project current-year spending into the future.[13] In brief, the CBO "baseline" projection rules work as follows: Discretionary spending is projected to increase with inflation, and mandatory spending is projected to increase with a more liberal formula that takes into account changes in the projected number of beneficiaries. Revenues are projected to track current laws, and where certain provisions are scheduled to expire – like the Bush administration tax cuts of recent years – those sunsets are assumed to go into effect, regardless of the likelihood of intervening changes in law.

While one can quibble about the specific assumptions underlying these baseline projections, budget policy experts focus on them because these projections convey the consequences of our current fiscal commitments as extrapolated into the future – akin to the vision the Ghost of Christmas Future conveyed to Ebenezer Scrooge. And, just as we care how well government officials have

---

[11] See Jürgen von Hagen, "European Experiences with Fiscal Rules and Institutions," Chapter 4, this volume. Although, in my experience, analysts typically do not extrapolate optimal deficit guidelines from these bands of acceptable public debt, one can easily derive implicit deficit levels with a formula that includes current public-debt levels, targeted public-debt levels, and expected rates of nominal increase in the GDP. This approach assumes that, once public debt reaches the targeted level – say, 30 percent of GDP – a country can incur deficits at a level that will sustain the public debt as a constant percentage of GDP. As long as there is real economic growth, the real levels of public debt will be increasing.

[12] See Alan J. Auerbach et al., *New Estimates of the Budget Outlook New Estimates of the Budget Outlook: Plus Ça Change, Plus C'est la Même Chose*, TAX NOTES, April 17, 2006, at 349; Jared Shirck and Francis Shen, The Role of Estimation in Budget Procedures: Baselines (May 4, 2005), *available at* http://lawweb.usc.edu/cslp/conferences/fiscal%20challenges/documents/4-Baselines.pdf.

[13] See 12 U.S.C.A. § 907 (West 2006) (definition of baseline).

managed fiscal affairs in the immediate past, we are concerned about how our fiscal fate will unfold in the immediate future. If we persist in current policies, how closely will revenue and spending align in future years? To what degree will future spending exceed revenues, thereby deferring additional costs to future years and crowding out private investment through the issuance of public debt? As before, the underlying normative questions of how large projected deficits and public-debt level can grow before they become problematic remain obscure, but the notion that the public should be attuned to these projections is universally accepted. And, in the extremes, the appropriate course of action may be clear. In the early 1980s, deficits of $200 billion as far as the eye could see prompted a variety of congressional reforms, including the creation of much of our current federal budgetary process. Projections of ten-year surpluses in excess of $5.0 trillion in 2001 prompted a political consensus for fiscal adjustments in the opposite direction. But in both instances, actions were precipitated by projections of future trends in fiscal balance or imbalance.

A related, but distinct, role of future projections is to set a benchmark against which policy changes can be scored. These baseline projections are supposed to represent fiscal results if the federal government leaves its fiscal policies on automatic pilot. The fiscal implications of future governmental actions – that is, deviations from the status quo – thus are evaluated against projections, both in the terms of the direction of a potential change and the magnitude of its effect. In times of budgetary stringency, political leaders often are assessed according to how well they perform in reducing projected deficits. So, for example, congressional leaders might take credit for reconciliation bills that cut Medicaid spending as compared with levels included in CBO baseline projections made at the start of the budgeting process.[14] Or, taking a multiyear perspective, critics of the Bush administration might buttress charges of fiscal mismanagement by comparing the administration's fiscal performance over the past five years against the fiscal surpluses projected at the end of President Clinton's presidency. Budgetary projections also can be used to set prospective reform agendas. For example, several years ago, President Bush set his own fiscal target by proposing to halve the FY2009 deficit from the projected FY2004 deficit made in February 2004.[15] Congressional budget resolutions commonly set similar targets for annual improvements against baseline projections, and congressional budget procedures often set longer-term schedules for spending reductions against baseline levels. Thus, projected budgetary aggregates and public deficit levels become public benchmarks against which politicians score fiscal points or incur fiscal penalties. While ultimate fiscal results matter in the

[14] *See, e.g.*, Deborah Solomon, *Wrestling with Medicaid Cuts*, WALL ST. J., Feb. 16, 2006, at A4. *See also* Allen Schick, THE FEDERAL BUDGET PROCESS 58–20 (2000) (explaining how current service baselines allow Congress to impose annual cuts but still permit annual increases in program expenditures).
[15] *See, e.g.*, Office of Management and Budget, *supra* note 10.

long run, results as compared with expectations have a high degree of political salience in the short term.

The dual functions of budgetary projections explain why the conventions underlying baseline methodologies have become so controversial. On the one hand, to the extent that these projections present the likely fiscal consequences of continuing current policies, incumbent politicians have an incentive to make these projections look as favorable as possible. So, for example, the Bush administration's budgetary policies will appear on a more balanced path if, as is the case with the CBO projections used in this chapter, projections fail to extrapolate future spending for supplemental appropriations in FY2005 or assume the expiration of major tax cuts after FY2010. To project fiscal responsibility, politicians have an incentive to low-ball future deficits. Since budgetary projections also serve as a benchmark to assess future legislative reforms, however, countervailing incentives work in the opposite direction. High projected spending levels make it easier for politicians to find politically advantageous spending cuts, and projections that assume the extension of expiring tax cuts make it easier to extend those cuts.[16] Assessing the relative merits of different methodologies for budgetary baselines is beyond the scope of this chapter. But the fact is that these methodologies have become controversial, and this controversy supports my claim that these projections have assumed a high degree of political salience.

iii. The Capacity to Adjust Spending Decisions and the Risk of Fiscal Ossification

Although budgetary aggregates – whether deficits or surpluses – usually capture the headlines, a persistent subplot in many stories about the federal budget is the changing composition of federal expenditures, most significantly the relentless rise in annual expenditures on entitlement programs such as Social Security, Medicare, and Medicaid. At one level, concern over growth in these items is puzzling, as one might have thought that it was a good thing for a society to allocate a greater share of public resources dedicated to the elderly, the infirm, and the impoverished. But, in budgetary circles, these trend lines are identified as problematic because they are growing faster than the overall economy and also often faster than the growth in federal revenues. Moreover, the manner in which Congress approves spending for these mandatory programs is quite different than traditional appropriations for other governmental activities. Whereas the traditional process requires both authorizing substantive

---

[16] So, for example, critics of the recent Tax Reform Panel have complained that the panel's recommendations were biased in favor of lower taxes by working off of a baseline that included, among other things, extensions of President Bush's tax cuts. *See, e.g.*, Leonard E. Burman and William G. Gale, *A Preliminary Evaluation of the Tax Reform Panel's Report*, Tax Notes, Dec. 5, 2005, at 1349.

legislation and annual appropriations, mandatory spending often (though not always) is locked in through permanent appropriations. Rather than requiring annual enactments for continued funding, mandatory programs often persist in the absence of legislative intervention.[17] So, while the baseline projections of spending over multiyear horizons represent a best guess as to trends in current fiscal commitments, some of those commitments are more difficult to adjust than others.

So, referring back to Table 6.2, consider projections for FY2010. The CBO's January 2006 projections indicated that 9.31 percent of projected spending will take the form of net-interest payments, probably the most binding of all federal outlays inasmuch as reductions in net-interest payments imply a default of public debt. Mandatory spending, the vast majority of which is based on social-insurance programs, was projected to constitute another 56.52 percent of outlays in FY2010. Only 34.14 percent of projected outlays are for discretionary programs, including the Defense Department and almost all general government functions. By highlighting the changing composition of federal outlays, budget experts are calling attention to the fact that nearly two-thirds of the federal budget will be on some form of automatic pilot by the end of this decade. Since the net-interest portion of this growth only can be addressed through reductions in prior-year deficits, the strong implication is that we need to do something to reduce entitlement spending and that our commitments to these programs have become too large for us to afford.

Once again, this framing of our budget choices raises some nice normative questions. Is there a good reason to distinguish so sharply in the legislative procedures – really the default rules – for spending on mandatory programs as opposed to discretionary items? Is there something about the constituencies for mandatory programs that warrants procedural safeguards against spending cuts? Do the beneficiaries of these programs have such strong reliance interests that changes in program terms should be made only under extraordinary circumstances and outside of annual appropriation reviews? Or should we perhaps be concerned by the antimajoritarian implications of putting spending programs on automatic pilot and therefore act to resist the special interests that have inserted these spending rules into the federal budget process? Looking over a list of mandatory programs – which include a wide range of social services, retirement, and disability benefits for federal workers and military personnel – is it possible to imagine a coherent theory that justifies the budgetary preference

---

[17] Thus, mandatory programs over time can take on a distinctly countermajoritarian flavor. Their persistence need not reflect majority support, but rather the blocking power of minority interests. Take, for example, the Social Security program, which initially was launched and most recently amended at times in which both houses of Congress had Democratic majorities (the New Deal and 1983). Even if subsequent majorities of both houses and the president favored Social Security reform, there was no guarantee that reform would occur, as minority interests, particularly in the Senate, have considerable power to obstruct reform proposals.

for this group of expenditures as opposed to the many other ways in which the federal government allocates its financial resources?

These are large and difficult questions, which I have no intention (or hope) of answering here. My point is simply that an important element of our public debate over budgetary projections is the increasing extent to which net-interest payments and mandatory programs threaten to ossify our fiscal future. In the immediate term, this raises the question of whether we should make some substantial downward adjustments in these commitments. Over the longer term, we need to consider whether to reduce the number of programs permitted to operate under fiscal automatic pilot procedures, thereby reducing what may have become excessively sticky fiscal commitments and resulting reliance interests.

II. A CRITIQUE OF EXISTING MEASURES OF FISCAL PERFORMANCE

Having identified both the principal measures we currently employ to evaluate federal fiscal policy and the functions these measures are supposed to serve, I now consider whether there are important elements of our fiscal life that these measures fail to capture or substantially misrepresent. To a large degree, I proceed here by argument through a laundry list. Ordered loosely by the magnitude of their significance, I subsequently describe four aspects of fiscal policy that are not fully reflected in the budgetary measures we typically employ.[18] Each omitted area bears directly on at least one of the purported functions of our current budgetary measures. Accordingly, their omission potentially compromises the integrity of public debate over federal fiscal policy. For the most part, these omitted areas can be quantified, and, to the extent practical, I include estimates of their significance and growth over the first half of this

[18] I might well have added, as a fifth aspect, the magnitude of future appropriations specified in authorizing statutes. Authority to appropriate is not the same as an appropriation, and executive branches and agencies cannot obligate funds based solely on authorizing statutes. Authorizing statutes do, however, have some bearing on future spending levels. At a minimum, they set benchmarks for "full funding," about which constituents can complain if the president recommends or Congress appropriates at levels less than those authorized, as for example has happened in public debate over the No Child Left Behind Act. Accordingly, authorizing bills might be understood to set soft baselines for certain programs that may be a good deal higher than those included in most CBO and OMB projections. I do not include authorization levels in my analysis here because the degree of commitment they represent has become relatively limited over time and because a substantial share of discretionary spending is now made without authorizing statutes, notwithstanding the continued existence of House and Senate rules that formally impose procedural limitations on such appropriations. *See* Congressional Budget Office, Unauthorized Appropriations and Expiring Authorizations (Jan. 2006). *See also* Mark Champoux and Dan Sullivan, Authorizations and Appropriations: A Distinction Without Difference? (May 10, 2006), *available at* http://www.law.harvard.edu/faculty/hjackson/auth_appro_15.pdf. Accordingly, it seems implausible that any reform in budgetary measures would be based on estimates derived from authorized levels of appropriations as opposed to actual spending.

decade. I conclude with a presentation of the aggregate effects of these omitted areas on fiscal performance over the past half decade.

While the selection of areas presented in this analysis may seem a touch random, there is a common theme. Consider for a moment a lobbyist in Washington, D.C., whose task is to gain access to federal resources for a client. Assume further that the budgetary measures discussed in the preceding section are binding in the sense that these measures make it difficult for politicians to satisfy the lobbyist's needs with the immediate outlays of cash, which would increase the reported deficit and levels of public debt. How might a lobbyist advance his or her client's interests under these conditions? What follows, in essence, is a list of suggestions. Each arguably can benefit the lobbyist's client and none is captured fully by the budgetary measures upon which we traditionally rely. But gains for the lobbyist's client also constitute burdens for the federal government and future generations. So budgetary measures that fail to reflect obligations arising out of these strategies may understate the growth of fiscal burdens – both historically and prospectively – and also may disguise the extent of fiscal ossification. The exclusion of these strategies from budgetary aggregates also means that they do not factor into the baseline for budgetary reform.

A. Trends in Unexpended Budgetary Authority

It often is remarked that the federal budgetary process is based on obligation authority.[19] Under pain of criminal sanction, executive officers and agency officials are not permitted to obligate federal resources (much less pay out cash) in the absence of explicit budget authority.[20] So an important component of all spending bills is the inclusion of budget authority, which may come in the form of annual budget authority or multiyear budget authority. None of the budget measures discussed so far in this chapter concerns budget authority. Rather, they depend (for the most part) on "outlays," that is, the amount of cash payments made from the U.S. Treasury during the course of the fiscal year. For programs that depend on annual budget authority, outlays are apt to approximate budget authority. But for programs with multiyear budget authority, this equivalence will not hold true.[21] And, herein, lies potential mischief.

---

[19] See Government Accountability Office, The Methods for Tracking Funds in the Federal Government, in A Glossary of Terms Used in the Federal Budget Process App. III (Sept. 2005) (GAO-05–734 SP) (distinguishing obligational accounting from proprietary accounting). See also Cheryl D. Block, *Congress and Accounting Scandals: Is the Pot Calling the Kettle Black?*, 82 Neb. L. Rev. 365, 404 (2003).

[20] See Antideficiency Act, 31 U.S.C.A. § 1341 (2006). This criminal sanction is distinct from, but serves to safeguard, the requirements of U.S. Const., art. I, § 9, cl. 7, that funds not be withdrawn from the Treasury without appropriation by Congress.

[21] For an illuminating discussion as to how differences in outlays and budget authority affected the Gramm-Rudman-Hollings Act sequestration rules, see Kate Stith, *Rewriting the Fiscal Constitution: The Case of Gramm-Rudman-Hollings*, 76 Cal. L. Rev. 593, 640–641 (1988).

Table 6.3. Budget authority outstanding: 2001 through 2005 (billions of dollars; year-end)

	2001	**2002**	**2003**	**2004**	**2005**
Unobligated budget authority	$341	$343	$383	$407	$541
Obligated but unliquidated budget authority	$693	$741	$790	$864	$928
Total budget authority outstanding	$1,034	$1,084	$1,173	$1,271	$1,469
Total budget authority outstanding as % of total outlays	55.5%	53.9%	54.3%	55.4%	59.4%
Total budget authority outstanding as % of GDP	10.3%	10.4%	10.8%	11.0%	11.9%

Source: Financial Reports of the United States Government: FY2001, FY2002, FY2003, FY2004, FY2005.

Without having any impact on current-year deficits, a lobbyist can lock in future spending for clients by obtaining multiyear budget authority. In recent years, outstanding budget authority at year-end has been increasing, both in terms of unobligated budget authority and in terms of obligated but unliquidated authority (see Table 6.3). Not only has this outstanding authority been increasing in absolute terms, but it also has become larger as a percentage of current-year outlays – growing from 55.5 percent of outlays at year-end FY2001 to 59.4 percent of outlays at year-end FY2005. So, it would appear, lobbyists have been relatively more successful in obtaining long-term budgetary authority over the past half decade, quite plausibly as a result of increases in defense spending where long-term budget authority – for example, for weapons systems – is more common. Some of this increase also may be due to growth in Medicaid, where annual budget authority typically covers state funding into one quarter of the next fiscal year.

The growth in outstanding budget authority has implications for the budgetary aggregates reviewed earlier in this chapter. When one considers projections with respect to discretionary spending in FY2007 and beyond, appropriation committees do not have quite as much budgetary flexibility as the numbers superficially suggest.[22] Compared to the past, an increasing percentage of outlays already have been authorized. While Congress can rescind unobligated budgetary authority, and even has some capacity to back out of obligated authority (potentially subject to contractual damage awards), the presence of large and growing outstanding budgetary authority balances at fiscal year-ends indicates that our fiscal hands are even more bound than traditional

---

[22] Certain recisions, however, may give rise to liability for damages authorized under the Tucker Act. *See* Stacy Anderson and Blake Roberts, Capacity to Commit in the Absence of Legislation: Takings, Winstar, FTCA, & the Court of Claims (May 4, 2005), *available at* http://lawweb.usc.edu/cslp/conferences/fiscal%20challenges/documents/12-CapacitytoCommitt.pdf. *See also* Robert Porter, Contract Claims Against the Federal Government: Sovereign Immunity and Contractual Remedies (May 2, 2006), *available at* http://www.law.harvard.edu/faculty/hjackson/ContractClaims_22.pdf.

Table 6.4. Subsidy cost of federal loan and guarantee programs (billions of dollars)

	2001	2002	2003	2004	2005
Annual loan and guarantee subsidy costs	$1	$5	$12	$7	$14
Loan guarantee liabilities (year-end)	$28	$28	$35	$43	$48
Loan guarantee liabilities as % of GDP	0.3%	0.3%	0.3%	0.4%	0.4%

Source: Financial Reports of the United States Government: FY2001, FY2002, FY2003, FY2004, FY2005.

presentations suggest. Moreover, this ossification extends to discretionary spending, not just mandatory spending.

B. Loans and Guarantees

Another important area in which past congressional action has committed the government to future expenditures is in the area of loans and guarantees. Here, however, the commitments partially are reflected in the budgetary aggregates. As a result of the Federal Credit Reform Act of 1990, the federal budget accounts for the subsidy cost of direct loans and loan guarantees in the year in which the loan is made or the guarantee extended.[23] Table 6.4, drawn from the Financial Reports of the United States Government, presents an estimate of the annual level of these subsidies for the past five years, with the most recent year – FY2005 – showing a subsidy cost of $14 billion. The Federal Credit Reform Act represents an unusual bit of accrual accounting appended onto federal budgeting aggregates, which otherwise are limited to comparing revenues and outlays. This accounting convention means that when the federal government makes a direct loan or extends a loan guarantee, the projected "subsidy" cost of that transaction must be reflected in the federal budget that year. So, the $14 billion of subsidy costs for FY2005 reported in Table 6.4 factored into the year's $318 billion total deficit. This aspect of these financial arrangements is reflected in total budget deficits and surpluses.

But the liabilities associated with federal guarantees are not fully incorporated into all of our budgetary aggregates. Although the cost of subsidies is reflected in annual deficit totals, the liabilities that these deficits generate are not considered part of the public debt of the United States. At least as far as commonly cited cumulative budgetary aggregates are concerned, these loan

---

[23] For an introduction to the Federal Credit Reform Act, *see* Neill Perry and Puja Seams, Accrual Accounting for Federal Credit Programs: The Federal Credit Reform Act of 1990 (Apr. 20, 2005), *available at* http://lawweb.usc.edu/cslp/conferences/fiscal%20challenges/documents/6-AccrualAccounting.pdf. While the Federal Credit Reform Act forces the budget process to recognize some of the costs associated with lending and guarantee programs, academic observers increasingly are concerned that the act's recognition rules understate the cost of the programs by ignoring market risks. For an introduction to this issue, *see* Deborah Lucas and Marvin Phaup, The Cost of Risk to the Government and Its Implications for Federal Budgeting (Feb. 2007) (unpublished manuscript on file with author).

liabilities are effectively off-balance-sheet liabilities. Thus, the $48 billion of loan guarantees outstanding at year-end FY2005 (see Table 6.4) do not figure into the public-debt numbers reported in Table 6.1 and prominently factored into public debates about public-debt burdens as a percentage of GDP.[24]

To be sure, the magnitude of our loan guarantee liabilities is quite small in comparison to our public-debt levels ($48 billion versus $4.5 trillion at year-end FY2005), and so one might well dismiss this omission as nonmaterial. But the general point that the federal government might be incurring financial liabilities that are functionally similar to explicit public debt but not included in public debates over fiscal policies is important. And, as we will see shortly, the magnitude of other omissions is often highly material. Moreover, in most other contexts, the recognition of the liability does not factor into annual deficit totals at the time the commitment is made. Rather, the liabilities factor into budgetary aggregates only when they are liquidated, well after there is any realistic opportunity to reduce their magnitude and without ever having been subject to the kind of public scrutiny and consent associated with traditional annual appropriations.

C. Other Accrual Measures Not Reflected in Current Budgetary Aggregates

Many kinds of federal financial activities share the same basic structure as loan guarantees: the commitment of financial obligations now – often associated with the receipt of a premium-like payment or service – with the expectation, often contractual, that the government will liquidate the obligation at some point in the future. In this section, I will review two important illustrations – the operations of the Pension Benefit Guaranty Corporation (PBGC) and various benefits for federal workers and military personnel. I use these examples both because of their financial importance and because estimates of their magnitude can be derived from the Financial Statements of the U.S. Government and other publicly available reports. I conclude this section with a review of the aggregate financial performance of the U.S. government, as reported in its financial reports, in comparison to the budgetary aggregates that commonly inform public discussion of the subject.

i. Pension Benefit Guaranty Corporation

As can be gleaned from any number of recent press accounts, the financial condition of the PBGC has been deteriorating over the past few years. Table 6.5

---

[24] It also may be the case that annual implicit interest costs of subsidized direct loans and direct guarantees are not reported in budgetary aggregates. These subsidies are recognized in the federal budget on a discounted basis, which means that they grow in size until recognized. This implicit interest should, in theory, be recognized on an annual basis, but it may not be under current practices.

Table 6.5. Annual losses and insurance program liabilities of the PBGC (billions of dollars)

	2001	2002	2003	2004	2005
PBGC Annual Report					
Net income (loss) for year	−$2	−$11	−$8	−$12	$0
Net position at year-end	$8	−$3	−$11	−$24	−$23
Financial Reports of the United States Government					
PBGC insurance program liabilities (year-end)	$14	$29	$45	$61	$70
PBGC liabilities as % of GDP	0.1%	0.3%	0.4%	0.5%	0.6%

Source: Financial Reports of the United States Government: FY2001, FY2002, FY2003, FY2004, FY2005. Annual Reports of the PBGC: FY2001, FY2002, FY2003, FY2004, FY2005.

extracts selected statistics from the corporation's annual reports, which show that the PBGC has incurred net losses (on an accrual basis) for four out of the past five years. Its net position – basically its net worth on a book-value basis – has shifted from a positive $8 billion to a negative $23 billion in the past five years. The liabilities of the PBGC, like those of other federal insurance programs, are reflected in the Financial Reports of the United States Government, which has increased its estimate of the corporation's recognized liabilities from $14 billion to $70 billion since FY2001. Indeed, if one digs into the footnotes of these reports, one finds even larger levels of possible losses (from companies such as General Motors that may attempt to terminate underfunded pension plans in the next few years and pass on substantial additional losses to the PBGC). Most experts agree that the PBGC will incur substantial additional losses over the next few years, with long-term losses likely to push the corporation's net position in the range of negative $50 billion to $100 billion over the next five years.

In contrast to the grim economic reality of the PBGC's financial condition, federal budgetary aggregates factor in only the PBGC's current revenues and outlays. In an Orwellian reversal, this difference means that the financial operations of PBGC actually have made a positive contribution to the reported federal budget (reducing recorded deficits) over the past five years, because cash inflows from PBGC premiums and other sources actually have exceeded its outlays. Moreover, in the president's FY2007 budget proposal (as well as recently enacted reconciliation legislation), increased PBGC premiums are projected to generate more budgetary savings over the next few years, even though it is almost certain that the corporation's financial condition will deteriorate further in that period.

Return now to the traditional budgetary aggregates discussed earlier. Missing from the aggregate deficits reported for the past four years is the decline in financial prospects of the PBGC. Indeed, rather than showing five-year losses of about $31 billion suggested from the corporation's own accrual-based financial statements, the federal budget scored PBGC activities as a net fiscal contribution during these years. Absent also from the public-debt measure is any recognition of the financial obligations of the PBGC, estimated in the Financial Reports of the United States Government as a $70 billion liability at year-end FY2005 or as a $23 million negative net position reported in the PBGC's annual report for the same period. While there are undoubtedly differences between the PBGC's liabilities and explicit federal debt – among other things, the PBGC is not formally backed by the full faith and credit of the United States – one wonders whether our public-debt measure is well designed to summarize the country's accumulated financial obligations at the end of each fiscal year if it omits entirely these PBGC obligations.[25]

ii. Military Personnel, Civil Government Employee, and Veteran Benefits

An even more substantial set of federal obligations relates to benefits owed to military employees, veterans, and civilian employees.[26] Some of these costs are reflected in the federal budget as outlays, but a substantial amount of accruals (including implicit interest on past accruals) is not included in federal budgetary aggregates. Table 6.6 summarizes the level of benefit accruals that have *not* been included in traditional budgetary aggregates for the past five years. These amounts are on the order of hundreds of billions of dollars a year, with the aggregate levels of benefits payable in the range of trillions of dollars. (Note that these liabilities are gross figures and not offset for corresponding balances that are reported separately as assets on the Financial Statements of the U.S. Government.) Neither the existence of these figures nor their annual increase is reflected in our traditional budgetary aggregates discussed earlier.

iii. Net Position of the United States

With time and effort, one could work through every element of the Financial Statements of the U.S. Government and consider the extent to which the component elements are omitted from traditional budgetary aggregates. In highlighting the financial results of the PBGC and various federal benefit programs, I have chosen areas that strike me as particularly problematic omissions from

---

[25] Analogous to the PBGC, but slightly more removed from direct federal control, are the many government-sponsored enterprises (GSEs), such as Fannie Mae and Freddie Mac. Though owned by the government, these firms arguably do expose the federal government to possible liability, and hence their financial performance arguable bears on the government's overall financial position. For further discussion of GSEs, *see* Block, *supra* note 19, at 435. *See also* Richard S. Carnell, *Handling the Failure of a Government Sponsored Enterprise*, 80 WASH. L. REV. 565 (2005).

[26] For additional discussion of this topic, *see* Hiroyuki Kohyama and Allison Quick, Accrual Accounting in Federal Budgeting: Retirement Benefits for Government Workers (May 1, 2006), *available at* http://www.law.harvard.edu/faculty/hjackson/RetirementBenefits_25.pdf.

Table 6.6. Accrued benefit costs not reflected in the federal deficit (billions of dollars)

	2001	2002	2003	2004	2005
Accrued costs from military employee benefits	$407	$32	$101	$143	$170
Accrued costs from veterans benefits	$139	$157	$106	−$30	$198
Accrued costs from civilian employee benefits	$39	$39	$80	$69	$62
Total accrued costs of benefits not reflected	$585	$229	$287	$182	$430
Total accrued costs as % of GDP	5.8%	2.2%	2.6%	1.6%	3.5%
Total benefits payable at year-end	$3,361	$3,589	$3,880	$4,062	$4,492
Benefits payable as % of GDP	33.4%	34.6%	35.8%	35.2%	36.5%

Source: Financial Reports of the United States Government: FY2001, FY2002, FY2003, FY2004, FY2005.

federal budgetary aggregates. Each area is functionally similar to the loan guarantees. Each year the government receives a benefit (analogous to a loan guarantee premium and the gratitude of a constituent who received credit support) in exchange for an obligation to expend resources in the future. In the case of the PBGC, actual premiums are taken in today in exchange for a financial commitment to support failed private pension programs in the future. With benefit programs, the government receives today the services of employees and military personnel who accept reduced current wages, and in exchange it commits to benefit payments in the future. Total deficit measures that omit these obligations while recognizing the benefits of PBGC premium receipts and lower wages misrepresent the burdens imposed on future taxpayers from current governmental activities. Similarly, public-debt measures that omit the implicit liabilities of these programs understate the cumulative burden of past governmental operations.

I leave to another day the question of whether other aspects of the accrual accounting system reflected in the Financial Statements of the United States Government also should be incorporated into our budgetary aggregates.[27] For readers who are interested in the areas of difference, I would commend Table 6.7, in which I have reproduced a quite informative reconciliation statement, which illustrates the factors generated for the United States net operating losses of

---

[27] For additional background on the FINANCIAL REPORTS OF THE UNITED STATES GOVERNMENT, and the Financial Accounting Statement Advisory Board (FASAB) that promulgated the rules under which these reports are prepared, *see* David Burd and Takeshi Fujitama, FASAB & the Financial Statements of the United States: Comparing Budgetary Aggregates to Financial Statements (May 3, 2005), *available at* http://lawweb.usc.edu/cslp/conferences/fiscal%20challenges/documents/13-FASAB.pdf.

Table 6.7. United States government reconciliations of net operating cost and unified budget deficit for the years ended September 30, 2005, and September 30, 2004 (billions of dollars)

	2005	2004
Net operating cost	(760.0)	(615.6)
Components of Net Operating Cost Not Part of the Budget Deficit:		
Increase in Liability for Military Employee Benefits:		
Increase in military pension liabilities	57.7	98.7
Increase in military health liabilities	108.6	42.3
Increase in other military benefits	3.3	2.4
Increase in liability for military employee benefits	169.6	143.4
Increase/(Decrease) in Liability for Veterans Compensation (Note 11):		
Increase/(decrease) in liabilities for veterans	150.1	(39.7)
Increase in liabilities for survivors	47.2	9.6
Increase in liabilities for burial benefits	0.5	0.1
Increase/(decrease) in liability for veteran's compensation	197.8	(30.0)
Increase in Liabilities for Civilian Employee Benefits:		
Increase in civilian pension liabilities	43.6	39.8
Increase in civilian health liabilities	24.6	21.7
(Decrease)/increase in other civilian benefits	(5.9)	7.2
Increase in liabilities for civilian employee benefits	62.3	68.7
Increase/(Decrease) in Environmental Liabilities:		
Increase/(decrease) in Energy's environmental liabilities	8.1	(1.7)
Increase in all others' environmental liabilities	2.5	1.0
Increase/(decrease) in environmental liabilities	10.6	(0.7)
Depreciation expense	79.7	89.9
Property, plant, and equipment disposals and revaluations	47.8	0.2
Increase in benefits due and payable	14.1	2.9
Increase in insurance programs	31.0	37.0
Increase/(decrease) in other liabilities	15.1	(4.7)
Seigniorage and sale of gold	(0.8)	(0.7)
Increase/(decrease) in accounts payable	7.8	(2.1)
(Increase)/decrease in accounts and taxes receivable	(9.7)	0.3
Components of the Budget Deficit Not Part of Net Operating Cost:		
Capitalized Fixed Assets:		
Department of Defense	(110.2)	(83.2)
Civilian agencies	(36.4)	(28.9)
Total capitalized fixed assets	(146.6)	(112.1)
Increase in inventory	(10.5)	(8.8)
Increase in securities and investments	(18.2)	–
Increase in other assets	(5.0)	(11.7)
Principal repayments of precredit reform loans	9.7	(8.5)
Net amount of all other differences	(13.2)	23.2
Unified budget deficit	(318.5)	(412.3)

Source: Financial Report of the United States Government: FY2005.

Table 6.8. Key results from financial reports of the United States (billions of dollars)

	2001	2002	2003	2004	2005
Statement of Conditions					
Net operating costs	−$515	−$365	−$665	−$616	−$760
Net operating costs as % of GDP	−5.1%	−3.5%	−6.1%	−5.3%	−6.2%
Balance Sheet					
Total assets	$926	$997	$1,394	$1,397	$1,456
Federal debt securities held by public	$3,359	$3,573	$3,945	$4,329	$4,624
Other liabilities	$4,026	$4,244	$4,554	$4,778	$5,291
Total liabilities	$7,385	$7,817	$8,499	$9,107	$9,915
Net position	−$6,459	−$6,820	−$7,105	−$7,710	−$8,459
Net position as % of GDP	−64.2%	−65.6%	−65.5%	−66.7%	−68.8%

Source: Financial Reports of the United States Government: FY2001, FY2002, FY2003, FY2004, FY2005.

$615.6 billion and $760.0 billion on an accrual basis in FY2004 and FY2005 but "only" $412.3 billion and $318.5 billion in budgetary deficits for the same two years. For current purposes, I would point readers to Table 6.8, which summarizes the key statistics from the accrual-based Financial Reports of the United States Government for the past five years. Emphasized here are net operating losses (analogous to, but much larger than, our total budget deficits) and the net position of the United States (similarly in spirit to, but broader and larger than, our public debt). The quite substantial differences between these two reporting approaches raise, in my view, some fundamental questions about the accuracy and completeness of our current budgetary measures.

D. Social-Insurance Commitments

A final area of federal financial activity to consider includes social-insurance programs such as Social Security and Medicare, our most important forms of mandatory spending. As I and others have explored elsewhere,[28] these programs have functional similarities to other forms of federal guarantees and employee benefits. In exchange for payroll taxes paid during their working lives, participating workers become eligible for future pensions, retiree heath, and various other ancillary benefits. So current revenue streams, principally from payroll taxes, are associated with the accrual of future statutory liabilities. Our current budgetary principles recognize current revenues but ignore the

---

[28] *See* Howell E. Jackson, *Accounting for Social Security and Its Reform*, 41 HARV. J. LEGIS. 59 (Winter 2004). *See also* Jagadeesh Gokhale and Kent Smetters, FISCAL AND GENERATIONAL IMBALANCES (2003).

accrual of liabilities for future payments. Instead, current revenues are offset with current outlays to liquidate liabilities that the federal government incurred in the past. Whereas both of these social-insurance programs would report substantial and increasing losses if their financial statements were prepared in a manner that recognized the current accumulation of future obligations and the implicit interest cost of previously incurred obligations, the total budgetary aggregates we commonly employ (the $318 billion deficit of FY2005) actually count Social Security as a positive contribution in the amount of the program's $173 billion cash-flow surplus that year. Our common measures of public debt entirely omit statutory obligations under these social-insurance programs.

In prior writings, I have developed methodologies for converting the annual accrual of liabilities for social-insurance programs into measures analogous to more common budgetary aggregates.[29] In Table 6.9, I report a summary of this presentation format for both Social Security and Medicare for the most recent five years for which data are available. The measure featured here is the "closed-group liability" for each program.[30] This measure reflects the present value of benefits due to all current participants less the present value of all future tax contributions that current participants are expected to pay into the program. The measure reflects the financial burden or liability being passed on to future generations.[31]

The magnitude of the figures reported in Table 6.9 is striking. The closed-group liability of the Social Security system alone is more than three times the public debt, and has been growing by more than $500 billion a year since the beginning of the decade, with most of the growth coming from increases in commitments to working-age Americans between 15 and 61 years old. Annual

---

[29] At least partially in response to prior academic writing on the subject, the Federal Accounting Standards Advisory Board recently published a "preliminary views" document in which a majority of the board recommended that the federal government start recognizing the government's social-insurance obligations on an accrual accounting basis. *See* Federal Accounting Standards Advisory Board, Preliminary Views – Accounting for Social Insurance, Revised (Oct. 23, 2006), *available at* http://www.fasab.gov/pdffiles/socialinsurance_pv.pdf. The approach to accrual accounting proposed by the majority of the FASAB board differs in certain technical respects from the approach utilized in this chapter, but the underlying premises are similar. For a brief discussion of the political hurdles that the FASAB proposal still has to surmount, *see* Howell E. Jackson, *Big Liability: Social Security, Medicare, and Accounting,* THE NEW REPUBLIC ONLINE (July 12, 2006), *available at* http://www.tnr.com/docprint.mhtml?i=w060710&s=jackson071206.

[30] Gokhale and Smetters refer to this measure as the program's generational imbalance. *See* Gokhale and Smetters, *supra* note 28, at 10–15.

[31] In this presentation, following FASAB guidelines, no offset is included for trust fund balances. The measures of closed-group liability included in Social Security Administration documents typically do include such offsets, because their focus is the trust funds as separate entities. As this chapter – and FASAB requirements more generally – present a consolidated government perspective, trust fund offsets are inappropriate.

Table 6.9. Closed group obligations of Social Security and Medicare programs (billions of dollars; calendar years)

	2001	2002	2003	2004	2005
Social Security Program					
Increase in closed-group liability for participants 62+	$108	$249	$219	$409	$402
Increase in closed-group liability for participants 15-61	$567	$277	$591	$622	$991
Total increase for year	$675	$526	$810	$1,031	$1,393
Closed-group liability at year-end	$11,216	$11,742	$12,552	$13,583	$14,976
Total increase for year as % of GDP	6.7%	5.1%	7.5%	8.9%	11.3%
Closed-group liability as percentage of GDP	111.5%	113.0%	115.8%	117.6%	121.8%
Medicare Program					
Increase in closed-group liability for participants 62+	$21	$290	$968	$211	$217
Increase in closed-group liability for participants 15-61	$392	$1,821	$8,640	$1,513	$2,484
Increase in closed-group liability	$413	$2,111	$9,608	$1,724	$2,701
Offset for projected increase (decrease) In general revenues	($131)	$1,203	$7,383	$1,152	$1,149
Increase in adjusted closed-group liability	$544	$908	$2,225	$572	$1,552
Adjusted closed-group liability at year-end	$6,298	$7,206	$9,431	$10,003	$11,555
Adjusted increase for year as % of GDP	4.1%	20.3%	88.6%	14.9%	22.0%
Adjusted closed-group liability as % of GDP	62.6%	69.4%	87.0%	86.6%	94.0%

Source: Financial Reports of the United States Government: FY2005 and 2006 Trustees Reports for Social Security and Medicare.

increases of "legacy debt" of Social Security therefore have been a good deal larger than annual increases in public debt. Yet, the accrual of liabilities in the Social Security system is wholly absent from our traditional federal budgetary aggregates.

The annual growth in unfunded liabilities of Medicare over the past five years also has been substantial. It is, however, more difficult to estimate the growth in Medicare liabilities because the program only partially is funded through dedicated revenues and thus some amount of future general revenues probably should be allocated to the program in order to produce a fair estimate of the fiscal gap associated with this program. Following a methodology proposed by Auerbach, Gale, and Orszag, I have adjusted the annual increase in reported closed-group obligations of Medicare to reflect projected increases in the amount of general revenues available for the program.[32] Table 6.9 indicates that the degree of Medicare underfunding has increased substantially since the beginning of the decade. The massive spike in liabilities in FY2003 from the enactment of the Medicare Part D Prescription Drug Benefit is a major factor here, but so too is the implicit interest charges associated with preexisting Medicare liabilities. Again, our principal budgetary aggregates – total deficits and public debt – omit the fiscal impact of mounting Medicare liabilities.

E. An Alternative Perspective on Budgetary Aggregates and Trends

As a final exercise, I present in Table 6.10 an alternative presentation of the fiscal policies of the United States over the past five years.[33] The table starts with our traditional budgetary aggregates – total reported deficits or surpluses as well as explicit public-debt levels – and then adds net losses and changes in net position from the Financial Reports of the United States Government as well as changes in the closed-group liabilities of Social Security and changes in adjusted closed-group obligations of Medicare. Not factored into this analysis is the impact of increased levels of outstanding budgetary authority, because I lack an obvious means of quantifying the financial impact of these increases.

While one could quibble about the manner in which I have converted these obligations into annual increases in fiscal burden and accumulated measures of financial burdens, the basic lesson of the table is hard to resist. In a variety of ways, financial claims against the United States have grown much faster in the past five years than is suggested by our traditional budgetary aggregates. Compared to GDP, the annual increase in these claims has exceeded 17 percent in all years and reached 34.1 percent in 2003,[34] the year in which Congress enacted a new prescription drug benefit. Similarly, the level of accumulated financial burden – the analog to public debt – has jumped by more than 10 trillion dollars between 2001 and 2005, rising from 238.3 percent of GDP to 284.6 percent.

Not only does this alternative presentation call into question the validity of our traditional measures of annual deficits and public debt, but it also suggests that the ossification in our spending latitude is even greater than currently

---

[32] To make these projections, I assumed that Medicare would continue to receive the same ratio of general revenues to dedicated payroll-tax contributions for Part B and D in the future as it did in the most current fiscal year. This methodology generates a substantially smaller adjusted closed-group liability for Medicare than does the projection method favored by Gokhale and Smetters, who assume no general-revenue contributions for future Medicare benefits.

[33] A prior and less complete attempt at a similar consolidation appeared in Howell E. Jackson, *Mind the Gap*, Tax Notes, Dec. 20, 2004, at 4.

[34] The annual data in this table represent a blend of calendar-year information of Social Security and Medicare and fiscal-year information for all other data.

Table 6.10. Alternative presentations of overall fiscal policies (billions of dollars; calendar years for social security and medicare)

	2001	2002	2003	2004	2005
Annual impact of fiscal policies					
Total budget deficit or (surplus) as reported	−$128	$158	$378	$413	$318
Change in other net U.S. operating costs	$643	$207	$287	$203	$442
Change in Social Security closed-group liability	$675	$526	$810	$1,031	$1,393
Change in Medicare adjusted closed-group liability	$544	$908	$2,225	$572	$1,552
Total annual impact	$1,734	$1,799	$3,700	$2,218	$3,705
Total annual impact	17.2%	17.3%	34.1%	19.2%	30.1%
Accumulated burdens from past fiscal policies					
Public debt outstanding	$3,320	$3,540	$3,913	$4,296	$4,592
Net U.S. position minus public debt Outstanding	$3,139	$3,280	$3,191	$3,414	$3,867
Closed-group liability of Social Security	$11,216	$11,742	$12,552	$13,583	$14,976
Adjusted closed-group liability of Medicare	$6,298	$7,206	$9,431	$10,003	$11,555
Total accumulated burden	$23,973	$25,768	$29,088	$31,295	$34,989
Total accumulated burden as % of GDP	238.3%	248.0%	268.3%	270.9%	284.6%

appreciated. Once one recognizes the extent of our overall financial obligations, the implicit interest payments on these obligations also become clear. The obligations presented in Table 6.10 largely are based on present-value estimates of future payments. Thus, with each passing year these obligations increase, reflecting an implicit interest charge on these obligations. While traditional budgetary projections of the sort reflected in Table 6.2 show annual net-interest payments for the last years of this decade running in the range of $200 billion to $300 billion, the total interest costs for the federal government (explicit and implicit) must be on the order of ten times higher – that is, more than a $1 trillion a year. This hidden interest charge is the critical fact of our country's fiscal condition, but it is wholly absent from our public debate over fiscal matters.

Finally, this alternative presentation raises questions as to whether our traditional budgetary aggregates present a true measure of the impact of federal fiscal policies on capital markets. The off-balance-sheet liabilities that I have included in my alternative presentation do not, for the most part, draw funds directly out of private capital markets and, in that sense, do not crowd out other private borrowers, but these liabilities may have a similar indirect effect. Many of these liabilities represent assets for private individuals – for example Social Security retirement payments, Medicare commitments, benefits for government employees, and even solvency protection for private pension plans. The existence and growth of these claims likely reduce private savings of other kinds, thereby reducing the supply of capital to some degree. The extent of this effect is contested,[35] but given the magnitude of the government's off-balance-sheet liabilities today – and their continuing growth – the impact of the effect is most likely substantial. Budgetary aggregates that focus solely on public debt or current deficit totals thus understate the impact of federal fiscal policy on private capital raising.

III. IMPLICATIONS, EXTENSIONS, AND FURTHER LINES OF RESEARCH

In the main, the foregoing analysis has been limited to an extended critique of a current approach to budgetary aggregates as inadequate to fulfill the purposes for which they are designed: providing meaningful summary information about past financial performance and future trends in the nation's fiscal matters. My argument is that there is a host of ways in which financial claims are perfected against the United States – that is, fiscal burdens *imposed* on the federal government. Many important liabilities are wholly or largely absent from traditional measures of fiscal performance, as evidenced by standard CBO and OMB presentations. These omissions call into question the usefulness of traditional measures, either as report cards or predictions of our fiscal future. Moreover, to the extent that politicians and the general public rely on macroeconomic rules of thumb to guide their scrutiny of fiscal matters – believing that public debt in the range of 40 percent to 60 percent of GDP is acceptable, or deficits in the range of 2 percent to 3 percent of GDP are fine – one wonders whether the guidelines are appropriately specified for the modern context.

The analysis raises many interesting and difficult questions about the political economy of the federal budget process. If, as my analysis assumes, current budgetary aggregates impose some degree of discipline on traditional spending through current outlays, but impose less stringent constraints on the accrual of other kinds of obligations, then a number of implications follow. First, we would expect to see claimants who could satisfy their needs through less constrained forms of spending to be more successful than those who must work through traditional annual outlays. Arguably, the spike in Medicare obligations in 2003 – largely undetected through traditional budgetary aggregates – would be consistent with this hypothesis. We might further predict that, at the margin, politicians would attempt to meet constituent demands by providing support with spending that is less well monitored and regulated than traditional

---

[35] *See* Jackson, *supra* note 28, at 97–98.

appropriations. So, rather than providing current job training to workers in declining manufacturing sectors, Congress might countenance increased guarantees of unfunded pension obligations through the PBGC. Or rather than increase the current wages of federal employees, the legislature might enrich their benefits, the cost of which need not be recognized until future years. In many contexts, there will be plausible off-balance-sheet substitutes for direct spending.[36] This latter point suggests that a further cost of different levels of budgetary discipline is that there may be efficiency losses in forcing claimants (like workers in declining industries) to accept a less preferred form of federal support (e.g., PBGC guarantees) because of budgetary rules. Finally, underlying these positive claims is a complex normative issue: Is there some reason – possible flaws in our political culture and needs of particular constituencies – that some claimants should be subject to different degrees of budgetary discipline than others? If so, do these normative considerations justify the current contours of budgetary aggregates or some other structure?[37]

My analysis also poses some challenging questions on the boundaries of law and accounting, particularly if one is motivated to expand upon our traditional budgetary aggregates and propose a new and more comprehensive system of budgetary accounting. To what extent should we expect the law to tell us which commitments are "legally binding" and therefore appropriate for inclusion in budgetary aggregates? At first blush, this may seem a plausible and bright line for establishing financial obligations. I am, however, skeptical that the law can fully solve this problem. It is certainly the case that the current structure of budgetary aggregates does not turn on the presence or absence of legal duties, commonly understood. Many of the liabilities reported on the balance sheet of the Financial Reports of the United States Government, but not captured

---

[36] A major reason why the Federal Credit Reform Act of 1990 was enacted was to prevent Congress from substituting what appear to be costless guarantees for what appeared to be excessively expensive loans. So my hypothesis regarding spending substitution has some historical basis. *See also* CBO Comparison, *supra* note 2, at 8 (noting advantages of accrual accounting over traditional budget measures in managing federal programs). Other predictions included in the text are speculative, but might be subject to empirical validation or disproof.

[37] The federal process is replete with other illustrations of privileged spending and constrained competition for budgetary resources. As discussed earlier, important procedural differences advantage most forms of mandatory spending as compared with discretionary spending. When Congress sets separate multiyear discretionary caps for defense programs and nondefense programs, constituents funded in one area do not have to compete with those funded in other areas. Section 302(b) allocations to appropriations subcommittees have a similar effect. *See* David Burd and Brad Shron, Analysis & Critique of Specialized Rules: Discretionary Caps, Spending Targets, and Committee Allocations (May 4, 2005), *available at* http://lawweb.usc.edu/cslp/conferences/fiscal%20challenges/documents/1-SpecializedRules.pdf. The PAYGO rules themselves forced a form of competition in which tax cuts and mandatory spending were forced to compete against each other in order to survive procedural points of orders. *See* Ellen Bradford and Matthew Scogin, PAYGO Rules and Sequestration Procedures (May 4, 2005), *available at* http://lawweb.usc.edu/cslp/conferences/fiscal%20challenges/documents/2-PAYGO.pdf. All of these channeling mechanisms raise difficult normative questions, worthy of further study.

in traditional budgetary aggregates, are legal obligations of governmental entities – for example, loan guarantees or employee and military benefits. Even
the PBGC program represents a statutory commitment, albeit one from an
entity that is not explicitly supported by the full faith and credit of the federal
government. Strictly speaking, even Social Security and Medicare involve legal
obligations defined by federal statute, albeit ones for which there are not currently full appropriations for when the Social Security trust funds are depleted
in several decades. So current budgetary rules do not come close to accounting
for all federal obligations that represent legal duties.

Another legalistic way of approaching financial obligations is to distinguish
between those obligations that Congress could rescind by legislative action
from other obligations. This distinction usually is made with respect to Social
Security, where the statute specifies and the Supreme Court has confirmed that
Congress is free to change benefit formulas at any time. Some argue that, at least
with respect to social-insurance programs, the fact that Congress could amend
benefits provides a complete justification for not recognizing the liabilities that
current statutory obligations represent. From a law professor's perspective,
this distinction is not as sharp as it initially might appear to others. Under
the doctrine of sovereign immunity, the U.S. government constitutionally is
empowered to avoid any legal obligations, even, in theory, explicit public debt,
but also guarantees, contracts, and most other financial obligations. Private
parties can proceed against the federal government on these and other claims
only because Congress affirmatively has waived sovereign immunity in a variety of contexts. But the government could withdraw that waiver.[38] Of course
the government doesn't – at least, the United States government hasn't for the
past 200 years – but that is because the political and economic costs of waiver
are thought to be prohibitive. But, similar reasons explain why Congress does
not lightly exercise its power to alter Social Security benefits. Social Security
obligations, like public debt and like all other governmental obligations, are
binding not for purely legal reasons, but for political ones. In all cases, the government has the "legal" option of adjusting statutory entitlements or exerting
sovereign immunity, but it just does not choose to do so.[39]

[38] A possible limitation to this proposition exists when government action constitutes an unconstitutional taking of property or a violation of the Contract Clause. Arguably, such an action
gives rise to legal liability for the federal government, but uncertainty remains over whether
government might avoid payment on even these claims by failing to appropriate funds. For
an introduction to some of the difficult issues these questions raise, *see* John Harrison, "New
Property, Entrenchment, and the Fiscal Constitution," Chapter 13, this volume.

[39] Among public law scholars, there is apparently some debate over the meaning of sovereign
immunity: whether the doctrine authorizes the government to escape legal liability or whether
the doctrine merely permits the government to evade enforcement of private legal rights.
For my purposes, these disagreements are metaphysical niceties, which do not bear on my
functional claim that the government has wide latitude to avoid financial obligations when
the political will exists.

So if legal rules are not determinative, how should we decide which financial commitments should be incorporated into our basic financial aggregates? An alternative approach is to look to the accounting discipline and seek to identify those obligations (1) that arise out of past transactions and (2) that give rise to probable future economic sacrifice – in other words, a functional, probabilistic approach that considers both the likelihood of future expenditures and the context in which those obligations arose. Working quickly through some of the areas canvassed in this chapter, this approach would point in the following directions.

Outstanding Budgetary Authority at Fiscal Year-End

Though outstanding budgetary authority does give rise to future economic sacrifice, in most cases, past transactions will not yet have occurred, even with obligated resources, so perhaps this authority should not be recognized unless (and until) some substantial amount of service has been provided or goods delivered. However, prominent disclosure – akin to footnotes in corporate financial statements – would be appropriate for these latent liabilities and it might make sense to specify in budgetary projections what share of projected discretionary spending already is "locked in" by advanced appropriations.

Loan Guarantees

These obligations satisfy the accounting definition of liabilities, entailing both past transactions and future economic sacrifice, and should be included in measures of cumulative financial burdens as well as annual changes in those burdens.

PBGC Financial Obligations

Like loan guarantees, past transactions have occurred in the receipt of premium payments and the extension of insurance coverage. The probable future economic sacrifice dimension is contested because of the absence of full faith and credit support for the PBGC. Some evaluation of probability is called for in such contexts, and one could look both to past precedent – like the savings and loan bailout – and current expectations to draw a conclusion here. The FASAB requirements underlying the Financial Reports of the United States Government call for consolidation of corporations such as the PBGC, and that strikes me as the most sensible conclusion in this context, though conceivably one could imagine other similarly structured entities with different budgetary accounting treatment. Privately owned GSEs, such as Fannie Mae, are not consolidated into the Financial Reports of the United States Government, but a treatment similar to the one utilized for the PBGC may well be appropriate in expanded budgetary aggregates.[40]

---

[40] See *supra* note 25. Even if one accepts that these GSEs are supported by an implicit federal guarantee, the task of recognizing such liabilities in accounting terms is complex because

Military, Civilian, and Veteran Benefits

To the extent that these benefits arise out of past employment or military service, their value should be recognized as part of the government's cumulative financial burden, and the accrual of new benefits and implicit interest on previously accrued benefits should be added into a comprehensive measure of changes in financial burdens.

Mandatory Spending

Here, I think, the application of accounting definitions is complex and probably varies from context to context. The case for recognition is strongest with respect to the Social Security program: Benefits are based on years of labor-force participation and fixed by statutory formula. Political support for the current structure of Social Security benefits is substantial, partially as a result of well-situated interest groups but also because participant reliance interests in these benefits are quite strong, fueled by annual personalized disclosure statements reporting projected benefit levels.[41] In some respects, the Medicare program is similar in that the receipt of benefits is tied to labor-force participation and payroll taxes, albeit much more loosely than is the case with Social Security. The benefit levels are, however, not as well specified as Social Security and have been changed on numerous occasions in the past. While the scale of Medicare commitments is staggering, quantifying their probable economic impact is more difficult.[42] Finally, there are a host of other mandatory spending programs. The range of programs is so broad that it is difficult to make categorical statements, but, for the most part, eligibility for other benefits depends not on past service or the payment of earmarked fees; rather, eligibility depends on current status when the benefits are received. Thus, the future economic sacrifice associated with these programs does not generally arise out of past work experience in the same way Social Security and Medicare benefits do. One could quite easily imagine a system of budgetary aggregates that quantifies the future costs of Social Security and Medicare but not the costs of most other mandatory spending items.

Discretionary Spending

Finally, one might ask whether budgetary aggregates should quantify future economic sacrifices projected for various forms of discretionary spending. This point typically is made in the form of a rhetorical challenge: "Why not

the scope of the potential liability is large but the probability of payment being required is low. Accounting for other low-probability, high-impact events – such as nuclear accidents or extreme natural disasters – present similar difficulties.

[41] *See* Howell E. Jackson, "Accounting for Social Security Benefits," *in* BEHAVIORAL PUBLIC FINANCE (Edward J. McCaffery and Joel Slemrod eds., 2006).

[42] In its recent preliminary draft on social insurance, a majority of FASAB members have voted in favor of recognizing Medicare obligations once participants have satisfied statutory requirements of working for 40 quarters. *See supra* note 29.

calculate the cost of future federal spending on education or transportation if you are going to make those calculations for Social Security?" The answer here is, I think, twofold. First, like some forms of mandatory spending, most discretionary spending does not arise out of past transactions. Rather, future discretionary spending is based on future status and transactions. A second justification for distinguishing between discretionary spending and some social-insurance programs is the fact that our levels of discretionary spending fluctuate a good deal more over time than do our levels of annual outlays for major social-insurance programs such as Social Security and Medicare. Thus, the future economic sacrifice for discretionary programs is not nearly as probable as that of social-insurance programs. If one plots federal spending as a percentage of GDP over long periods of time, there is considerably more variation in categories of spending that are subject to annual discretionary allocations as compared to those that are funded through more permanent mandatory spending. Education spending, dependent as it is on annual appropriations and continuous political support, varies considerably over time. The growth in Medicare spending as a percentage of GDP, in contrast, has been consistent and persistent. More generally, if one compares annual fluctuations in all major areas of government expenditures, the two major social-insurance programs – Social Security and Medicare – stand apart from all other functions in claiming either stable or increasing shares of federal spending over multiple decades.

Finally, let me conclude with a word about potential connections between accounting reform and substantive reform of underlying social-insurance programs. Among budget policymakers, much has been written about long-term fiscal imbalance, focusing particularly on entitlement spending. Most experts agree – and I certainly do not dispute – that any sensible solution to our long-term fiscal problems depends on addressing (read *reducing*) entitlements to some degree. Against this background, one might plausibly object to any accounting reform that would recognize social-insurance spending as an existing obligation of the federal government. This objection to the expansion of budgetary aggregates proceeds not on theoretical grounds but simply out of a pragmatic fear that recognizing these liabilities will make it more difficult to adjust them downward.[43] While I am not entirely unsympathetic to this line of argument, I also think there are two important countervailing considerations. First, the current recognition of unfunded social-insurance costs is apt to focus political attention on the present magnitude of these obligations in a way that long-term projections focusing on budgetary imbalances – of two, three, or even four decades in the future – cannot. Second, by including the continuing accretion in these obligations over the next five- or ten-year horizon, my proposed approach would give Congress and the president a short-term target

---

[43] *See, e.g.,* Peter Diamond and Peter Orszag, *Accrual Accounting for Social Security*, 41 Harv. J. Legis. 173, 175 (2004).

against which they can measure success.[44] So, for example, political leaders might aspire to cut the ratio of financial burden to GDP from 281 percent at year-end 2005 to 200 percent by year-end 2010.[45] It is conceivable that this target could be met with only modest reductions in outlays for social insurance over the next five years. For a combination of these and related reasons, I think that it is plausible that the recognition of certain off-balance-sheet obligations that are not currently reflected in current budgetary aggregates (or even in the current Financial Reports of the United States Government) actually might improve the prospects for meaningful entitlement reform in the next few years, rather than having the opposite effect.

IV. CONCLUSION

The measures of federal fiscal performance that dominate public debate over budgetary policy are substantially incomplete and omit the financial impact of many governmental activities. Broader measures of financial performance are, however, available and could be used as a basis for more complete presentations of the financial postures of the federal government. Were these new measures to become the basis of public discourse of federal fiscal policy, the benefits could be substantial, both in terms of improving federal spending decisions and clarifying the fiscal challenges that this country faces.

---

[44] For a sketch of how such goals might be set in the context of Social Security, *see* Howell E. Jackson, *The True Cost of Privatizing Social Security*, TAX NOTES, Jan. 3, 2005, at 109. *See also* Jackson, *supra* note 28, at 134–136.

[45] Several years ago, Senator Lieberman proposed legislation that would have created a point of order with respect to legislation that increased the country's fiscal gap above certain percentages. The logic of this point of order is similar to the point I make here. But rather than depending on congressional rules, my approach would rely on public debate and political processes to monitor broader budgetary aggregates. For an overview of the Lieberman proposal and related issues, *see* Trenton Hamilton and Matthew Scogin, Broader Budget Aggregates: Proposed Reform Legislation (May 4, 2005), *available at* http://lawweb.usc.edu/cslp/conferences/fiscal%20challenges/documents/14-BroaderBudgetAggregates.pdf.

Questions for Chapter 6

1. Is accounting irrelevant? A potential objection to Professor Jackson's criticism of current government accounting practices is that accounting treatments do not matter, as long as the underlying facts are publicly available. As all of the information presented in Professor Jackson's analysis is drawn from government documents, one might therefore argue that members of the public (as well as policy experts) are already aware of this information. So any change in budgetary aggregates would have no impact on either political outcomes or economic guidance. Do you agree? There is some empirical evidence that accounting treatments do affect political outcomes, at least in the context of off-budget treatment of social-insurance programs.[46] Moreover, in the context of state budgeting, it appears that recent reforms requiring the current recognition of accrued cost for health care benefits is having an impact on the willingness of state legislatures to continue offering these benefits at the same level as in the past.[47] Still, one must acknowledge that this is a point of uncertainty. If accounting measures do not matter, then the force of Professor Jackson's argument is much diminished.

2. Many of the federal government's commitments that Professor Jackson identifies as omitted from traditional budgetary aggregates reflect political accommodations enacted into law over time. Programs that obtain multiyear appropriations are one illustration of this phenomenon, but so too are innovations in budgetary procedures in the 1960s and 1970s that were designed to remove certain spending programs (like entitlements) from the annual appropriation process.[48] Is it realistic to ask politicians to adopt accounting conventions that

---

[46] Sita Nataraj and John B. Shoven, *Has the Unified Budget Undermined the Government Trust Funds?* (Nat'l Bureau of Econ. Research Working Paper No. W10953, Dec. 2004).

[47] *See* Stanley C. Wisniewski, *Potential State Government Practices Impact of the New GASB Accounting Standard for Retiree Health Benefits*, 25 PUBLIC BUDGETING & FIN. 104 (Mar. 2005).

[48] *See* William Dauster, "The Congressional Budget Process," which is Chapter 1 of this volume.

incorporate long-term spending commitments into current budgetary aggregates when the political process has already privileged those programs by moving them outside of the ordinary annual cycle of appropriations? Should we perhaps just accept different levels of fiscal commitment as a by-product of raw political power – not necessarily a good thing, but one that is inherent in our democratic system of government? Aside from reforming our measures of accounting, are there ways in which our budgetary procedures might be reformed to make it more difficult for interest groups to make long-term commitments to favored constituent groups, or are these kinds of long-term commitments sometimes appropriate?

3. What is the relationship between the modified system of accrual accounting that Professor Jackson advocates for the federal government and the economic measures of the deficit that Professor Boskin described in Chapter 5? See particularly Box 5.2 and Professor Boskin's discussion of generational accounts and fiscal gaps.

4. Though little known outside of official Washington, the Financial Report of the United States Government does offer an alternative perspective on federal finances based on principles of accrual accounting, and proposals currently are pending before the Federal Accounting Standards Advisory Board to enhance those statements along the lines Professor Jackson proposes. The relationship between these financial reports and the congressional budget process is evolving and unsettled. While some countries employ accrual accounting in their legislative procedures, most countries with accrual accounting financial statements do not.[49] To what degree can the Financial Reports of the United States Government influence public policy if it is not incorporated into congressional processes?

5. One of the most contentious debates in government accounting circles is whether the federal government's commitments to social-insurance programs like Social Security and Medicare should be recognized as liabilities at the time workers accrue benefits under statutory formula or whether that recognition should be delayed until the payments are due and payable. Critics of early recognition emphasize that the federal government has legal latitude to change benefit programs at any time and that adjustments almost certainly will have to be made to the benefits currently promised to the Baby Boomer and future generations. The early recognition of these liabilities, in essence, equates them to the public debt of the federal government. How problematic is it to report the government's implicit and explicit debts together, in the manner Professor

[49] Jón Blöndal, *Issues in Accrual Budgeting*, 4 OECD J. ON BUDGETING 103 (2004).

Jackson proposes? Should a corporation be permitted to reduce the amount of its debts if there is a high probability that the company will be unable to pay those debts when they become due? Are accounting conventions for private corporations a useful analogy for the analysis of government accounting rules?

7 Starving the Beast

The Political Psychology of Budget Deficits

Jonathan Baron and Edward J. McCaffery

I. INTRODUCTION: BUDGET DEFICITS, POLITICS, AND BEHAVIORAL ECONOMICS

Budget deficits arise in part because voters support the policies that lead to them. This is so despite the fact that many voters want to avoid deficits. They favor policies that undercut their own goals, and politicians – who often have the same preferences as those who elect them – respond. Politicians (and economists) still differ on the appropriate size of the budget. When those who favor smaller government gain power, they sometimes adopt a strategy of "starving the beast," which involves cutting taxes today with the expectation that spending cuts will follow tomorrow. The assumption is that tax cuts are easier to swallow than spending cuts, but then aversion to deficits will kick in and permit spending cuts as well.

We present experimental evidence that many people actually do not desire tax cuts without spending cuts. Although people choose to reduce a deficit with spending cuts when they are asked in the abstract what to do, the budget cuts are not so palatable when people are asked about cuts in particular categories. When people are forced by a question to balance the budget, they still show this aversion to specific spending cuts, although they are willing to cut specific spending somewhat to close a deficit. Dedicated taxes also may help people accept both taxes and spending when these are warranted.

Jonathan Baron is Professor of Psychology at the University of Pennsylvania, where he teaches Judgments and Decisions, and Behavioral Law and Economics.

Edward J. McCaffery is Professor of Law, Political Science and Economics at the University of Southern California, and Visiting Professor of Law and Economics at the California Institute of Technology.

This work was supported by NSF grant SES 02–13409. The authors thank Judith Baron for some of the ideas. Earlier versions of this chapter were presented at workshops at the University of Toronto Law and Economics departments, Stanford Law School, and the University of Southern California. The authors thank workshop participants for their helpful comments, especially John Matsusaka and Howell Jackson.

Budget deficits, the subject of this volume, almost invariably have a psychological dimension. This occurs because of the confluences of two realities. First, the *facts* of the government's fiscal affairs exist independently from the *descriptions* of the facts. This distinction is illustrated nicely in the preceding chapters, by Jackson and Boskin respectively, which explore a number of different ways to measure the gap between public revenues and expenditures, and which also discuss whether or not any particular way of describing that gap is accurate.[1] These are matters of descriptions, not facts (although the distinction is confounded by the social fact that government budgetary rules often treat different descriptions of the same underlying facts differently, so that it matters, for example, whether a given expenditure is described as on or off budget). Second, human beings, contrary to the stark axioms of rational choice theory, do indeed react differently to different descriptions of the same underlying states of the world; this is the canonical finding of the heuristics and biases literature, most famously associated with the work of Kahneman and Tversky.[2] Citizens who like their glasses half full get angry when they hear that they are half empty; words matter.

Much of our joint work for some time now has concerned the relevance of inconsistent human judgment and decision making – broadly speaking, behavioral economics – for public finance.[3] People, limited in their time, resources, and abilities, simply cannot and do not form consistent judgments on a wide array of matters affecting them. In private markets, the impersonal forces of competition and the market help to counteract these biases: We all can benefit from the virtues of marginal cost pricing, for example, even if few of us could calculate the fair price of a loaf of bread or a box of cereal. In public settings, in contrast, the very absence of a market means that rationality (or consistency) need not obtain: Indeed, the best politicians may be the best framers of public decisions, not the optimal welfare maximizers. In this chapter, we use our standard experimental method – questioning subjects via the Internet – to test whether or not politicians successfully might manipulate the public political agenda to get ordinary citizens, averse to both budget deficits and spending cuts, to reverse their preferences and accept spending cuts based on the "optics" of public finance. This is, in short, a take on the question lurking in Boskin's prior chapter, and the eponymous question in Shaviro's book: Do deficits matter?[4]

---

[1] *See* Howell Jackson, "Counting the Ways: The Structure of Federal Spending," Chapter 6 of this volume; Michael Boskin, "Economic Perspectives on Federal Deficits and Debt," Chapter 5 of this volume.

[2] *See* Daniel Kahneman and Amos Tversky, *Prospect Theory: An Analysis of Decision Under Risk*, 47 ECONOMETRICA 263–291 (1979); *see also* Jonathan Baron, THINKING AND DECIDING (3rd ed. 2000).

[3] *See generally* Edward J. McCaffery and Jonathan Baron, *Thinking About Tax*, 12 PSYCHOLOGY, PUB. POL'Y, & LAW 106–135 (2006).

[4] *See* Boskin, *supra* note 1; *see also* Daniel Shaviro, DO DEFICITS MATTER? (1999).

We find, perhaps ironically, that they may not, or at least not in all the ways that some commentators think that they do.

II. POLITICS

Politicians, social scientists, and citizens disagree sharply about the appropriate size of government. The issue captures a major political division in modern democracies, between those favoring a larger or smaller government. Both sides have difficulty arguing against the apparently revealed preferences of the citizenry for the status quo. Thus small-government advocates argue that big government is bad, on citizens' own lights, but that the people have been led to support it because they do not think about long-term issues and thus desire overly generous present programs.[5] Big-government advocates argue in contrast that government is if anything too small, because of pressure for low taxes, which appeal to citizens on the basis of narrow and myopic self-interests, in contrast to a more enlightened self-interest or an altruistic concern for those at the bottom of the heap.

This way of putting matters underscores a surprisingly common element between the two extremes. Both sides assume some degree of irrationality or inconsistency on the part of the people, specifically a disconnect between the present and the future, a failure to integrate beliefs and actions over time. Both Boskin and Jackson, for example, describe the inconsistency between present tax policies and projections for spending on Medicare and Social Security in the United States.[6] Small-government partisans fear that citizens will want such programs now, neglecting their long-term costs, and then will be reluctant to cut these programs later. Big-government partisans – who assume that such programs are desirable, that government support of medical care should be extended to more (or all) of the population, and/or that other public goods and services will require additional spending – fear that citizens will support tax cuts now, ignoring the long-term effects of any resulting deficit (or diminished surplus) on the ability of the government to do its job in the future.

Note that all of these posited sets of attitudes stand in contrast to a "rational choice" or "rational expectations" model of politics, where citizens properly integrate their actions over time and deficits do not even matter.[7] A stark rational model would lead to the time invariance of fiscal political preferences, meaning that citizens would not change their underlying preferences based on the timing of the imposition of fiscal policies.

---

[5] James M. Buchanan and Gordon Tullock, THE CALCULUS OF CONSENT: LOGICAL FOUNDATIONS OF CONSTITUTIONAL DEMOCRACY (1962).

[6] *See* Jackson, *supra* note 1; Boskin *supra* note 1.

[7] *See* Robert J. Barro, *Are Government Bonds Net Wealth?*, 82 J. POLITICAL ECON. 1095–1117 (1974); but cf. Boskin, *supra* note 1 (describing but rejecting such a view).

III. BEHAVIORAL ECONOMICS

A tradition of scholarship known as "behavioral economics" or "behavioral decision making" (as if economics and decision making did not otherwise involve behavior has uncovered consistent evidence of human irrationality in judgments and decisions. Irrationality is not just a matter of error – which is random and can occur in both directions – but of systematic biases leading to particular deviations from the predictions of economic models or other related normative models such as statistics, probability theory, expected utility theory, and so on.

Examples of such biases that are relevant to public finance include the following:[8]

- The status quo (endowment) effect: People are reluctant to change the status quo, overvaluing their existing endowments and undervaluing what they lack. This applies to simple goods and to public policies. For example, people who otherwise might prefer universal health care provided by the government will oppose it because it will involve a tax increase, even though their health insurance costs may decrease even more.
- Default (omission) bias: When choices are available, people are inclined to accept the default, the result of omission as opposed to action. Note that the default bias is not the same as the status quo bias; for example, when new employees choose pension or insurance plans, they tend to choose the default option.
- Anchoring and underadjustment: Similar to the last two effects is a tendency, when one is making a quantitative judgment such as choosing an appropriate tax rate, to anchor on a salient reference point, such as the current tax rate, when adjusting for necessary changes, such as those needed to pay for increased spending. Thus, the adjustment is typically too small.
- Isolation effects: People tend to focus on what is immediately before them, ignoring secondary effects that they could easily imagine. For example, they may favor business taxes and other hidden taxes because they do not spontaneously think about the incidence of such taxes.[9] This effect may lead people to support shortsighted public policies such as subsidies, price controls, or trade restrictions.
- Identified-victim effect: A related result is that when people are identified, even with just a name (which everyone must have), sympathy for them increases. Concern about people's fate is less when they are considered as anonymous parts of a mass.[10] As Stalin noted, "a single death is a tragedy;

---

[8] *See* generally Baron THINKING AND DECIDING 6, *supra* note 2.

[9] Edward J. McCaffery and Jonathan Baron, *Isolation Effects and the Neglect of Indirect Effects of Fiscal Policies*, 19 J. BEHAVIORAL DECISION MAKING 289–302 (2006).

[10] *See* Karen E. Jenni and George Loewenstein, *Explaining the Identifiable Victim Effect*, J. RISK & UNCERTAINTY 235–257 (1997). *See also* Deborah A. Small and George Loewenstein, *Helping the*

a million deaths is a statistic." This bias also can apply to victims of cuts in government programs.

- Framing: As a result of isolation and other biases, people give conflicting answers, depending on what they are asked. For example, when the question concerns fairness in the application of a graduated income tax to spouses, they may favor *marriage neutrality* when asked if marriage should affect the total tax of a couple, and they may favor *couples neutrality* when asked if couples who earn the same should be taxed at the same rate. The combination is impossible given progressive marginal tax rates.[11]

- Inconsistent discounting: Although economic theory implies that, other things being equal, we should discount the future at a constant rate, humans (including politicians) behave as if they had a higher discount rate for events in the near future than for those in the distant future. This effect may give the impression of myopia, except the effect applies only for the near future. Hence, people borrow on credit cards for frivolous consumption, and governments pass short-term fixes for immediate problems without thinking about future implications.

Behavioral economics generally sides with the common political suspicion that citizens are not fully consistent in their preferences over time. Once a government program is in place, it will become part of the status quo and thus can be hard to cut. The thumb is on the side of continued government growth. On the other hand, citizens are averse to taxes: People are unwilling to trade a loss, an increase of taxes from the status quo T1 to some new level T2, in exchange for a gain in goods or services from G1 to G2, even though they would chose G2 and T2 over G1 and T1 if neither were the status quo.

IV. THE POLITICAL PSYCHOLOGY OF DEFICITS

We consider in this chapter whether politicians sensibly might put the prior insights together and exploit inconsistencies in citizens' views on levels of spending and taxation. In particular, we examine a potentially psychologically savvy political strategy used by small-government advocates that has come to be called "starving the beast," (STB) a term usually attributed to David Stockman, the budget director in U.S. President Ronald Reagan's first administration.[12]

Victim or Helping a Victim: Altruism and Identifiability, 26 RISK & UNCERTAINTY 5–16 (2003); Tehila Kogut and Ilana Ritov, *The "Identified Victim" Effect: An Identified Group, or Just a Single Individual?*, 18 RISK & UNCERTAINTY 157–167 (2005); George Loewenstein, Deborah Small, and James Strnad, *Statistical, Identifiable and Iconic Victims and Perpetrators*, in BEHAVIORAL PUBLIC FINANCE (Edward J. McCaffery and Joel Slemrod eds., 2006).

[11] Edward J. McCaffery and Jonathan Baron, *Framing and Taxation: Evaluation of Tax Policies Involving Household Composition*, 25 J. ECON. PSYCHOLOGY 679–705 (2004).

[12] Actually, the phrase seems to emanate from the late Senator Daniel Moynihan's incorrect remembrance of Stockman's book; *see* John Maggs, *Feeding the Beast*, NAT'L J., March 2005, at

The idea is to cut taxes before cutting spending – taxes being the lifeblood of the government qua beast – and then to use the resulting deficit as a political argument to reduce spending, or to reject new spending. The technique is intended as a way out of the inertial force of the status quo, where endowment effects preclude government constriction. Most commentators agree that this strategy has been used by both Reagan and the current U.S. President, George W. Bush. In both cases, large deficits resulted from fiscal policies.[13] The extent to which tax cuts reduced future spending is not clear, but at least government may have grown less than it would have without the tax cuts, because the emergence of substantial deficits changed the baseline for future judgments. As commonly understood, the STB strategy is based on an assumed initial condition, two propositions, and an assumed final condition as follows.

Initial condition: Notwithstanding the appeal of lower taxes, the general public will not initially support proposals for smaller government that entail specific, identifiable, spending cuts from current levels, at least partially because of preferences for the status quo and identified-victim effects associated with specific spending cuts.

Proposition 1: Notwithstanding the initial condition, STB adherents can gain support for immediate tax cuts that are imposed without identifying specific spending cuts but with a vague commitment to general spending cuts in the future. The public accepts such a proposal, overcoming status quo biases, because the public values gains from immediate tax cuts viewed in isolation.

Proposition 2: Once deficits emerge at a future date, the fiscal frame is altered and deficit aversion forces the public to overcome its dislike of specific spending cuts, partially anchoring their spending preferences with the tax rates that have been reduced, perhaps aided through the adoption of balanced-budget constraints.

Final condition: The STB strategy thereby effects a preference shift, causing the general public to accept smaller government as a final condition when citizens were not willing to do so initially.

V. SOME EXPERIMENTS

We carried out several experiments to explore the logic of the STB strategy and to understand whether it is likely that the strategy is based on accurate assumptions about the behavior of the general public, and, if not, where the

689, 689. Nonetheless, there seems to be no doubt that the phrase originated as a description of Ronald Reagan's fiscal policies.

[13] The chapters by Jackson and Boskin in this volume, *supra* note 1, do not dispute this general conclusion, but instead note that the "real" deficit to worry about is the (seldom discussed) long-term deficit in entitlements, which could be mitigated by higher taxes or by modest cuts in commitments, such as an increase in the retirement age.

strategy might go off track. In general, we found limited evidence that the STB strategy would work. While there is some support for Proposition 1 – that the public can be persuaded to accept tax cuts matched with unspecified spending reductions, but not with specific spending cuts – other aspects of the STB strategy seem to be based on an incorrect theory of the biases in citizens' judgments about public finance.

Our results come from experiments carried out on the World Wide Web.[14] The subjects were drawn from a panel of about 1,500 people who have done other experiments for pay. A typical experiment takes 10 to 20 minutes, for which we pay each subject $3 or $4. Typically, the subjects see 20 to 30 web pages presented in a random order chosen for each subject, each page showing a hypothetical case and asking a few questions about it. About 80 subjects do each study. The subjects are not a random sample of any particular population, although they turn out to be typical of the U.S. adult population in age, income, and education,[15] but not in gender, since most are women. Our main questions concerned within-subject effects and comparisons of different experimental conditions, and typically obtain strong statistical significance. Our results concerning overall attitudes seem generally close to those of opinion polls that have sampled the U.S. population systematically, lending ecological validity to our experiments.

VI. WHY MIGHT PEOPLE SUPPORT THE INITIAL TAX CUT IN THE STB STRATEGY?

Our first set of questions concerns whether and why the public might be willing to accept initial tax cuts in the first stage of the STB strategy. In our experiments, we presented people with information about current levels of taxation and spending, and we asked them to adjust both levels to what they would prefer. We tested three general hypotheses about why citizens might support tax cuts in the absence of specific spending cuts.

One, people might not be bothered by deficits. The public might prefer lower taxes and higher spending. They may think that it makes sense to borrow for projects that help the future, that debt is not bad because it transfers money from taxpayers to bondholders, or even that they might die before the ultimate tab comes due. In any of these conditions, support for STB would be rational, or logically consistent over time, and so we term these "rational preference" explanations. If such explanations are correct, then people, when asked to adjust

---

[14] Jonathan Baron and Edward J. McCaffery, Starving the Beast: The Psychology of Budget Deficits (December 27, 2005) (unpublished manuscript, on file with University of Pennsylvania Institute for Law and Economics), *available at* http://ssrn.com/abstract=589283.

[15] *See* Linda Babcock et al., *Gender Differences in the Propensity to Initiate Negotiations, in* Social Psychology and Economics 239–262 (David De Cramer, et al. eds., 2006).

rates of taxation and spending, will tend to choose lower levels of taxation and higher levels of spending. Note that this hypothesis does not depend on the existence of any cognitive biases.

Two, people might simply be *myopic* and think excessively or even exclusively about the short term. They might neglect the fact that deficits must be covered in the future, and so ignore the inchoate future tax increases or spending increases. Or they may engage in a kind of *optimism bias*,[16] believing that matters will work out in the end. We call these the "myopia–optimism bias" explanations. In either case, people would favor budget deficits in the short term and respond differently when asked about the future than when asked about the present.

Three, people might support the first stage of STB because, when presented with a public-policy question about tax cuts, they think only or primarily about tax cuts. That is, they suffer from an *isolation effect*, deciding matters as if with blinders on, and focusing only or primarily on what is before them. When thinking about tax cuts, a natural aversion to losses – tax aversion – leads people to support the cuts. Note that this effect is distinct from the myopia explanation already noted: The isolation effect is not so much a matter of stronger or different preferences over the near term (a kind of present bias) as it is about a decisional process or heuristic that has subjects think about only narrowly framed issues, one at a time.

In one experiment designed to explore these hypotheses, we presented people with hypothetical government budgets in which taxes and spending varied independently, leading to deficits, surpluses, or balanced budgets. We asked people for their preferences about taxes and spending, in the long term and short term. We compared their preferred levels to the starting levels that they were given. We also explored whether they adjust completely so as to maintain a constant balance and size of government, or, conversely, whether they under-adjust, in which case they would fail to correct existing surpluses and deficits. The results reveal that subjects prefer levels of taxing and spending that fail to fully correct existing deficits or surpluses.

The experiment began with an introductory page, describing the experiment and some information about debt and deficits, as seen in Table 7.1. After this initial page, the subjects a series of pages in which they were asked for their input, as subsequently explained. A typical screen contained a statement of the baseline condition, questions, and options (with variables shown in brackets), as seen in Table 7.2.

The three levels of taxing and spending were combined to produce nine combinations. Each of these was presented in a short-term condition (as shown

---

[16] *See* generally Daniel Kahneman and Dan Lovallo, *Timid Choices and Bold Forecasts: A Cognitive Perspective on Risk Taking*, 39 MANAGEMENT SCIENCE 17–31 (1993) (discussing optimism bias); Colin F. Camerer and Dan Lovallo, *Overconfidence and Excess Entry: An Experimental Analysis*, 89 AM. ECON. REV. 306–318 (1999) (providing additional background).

Table 7.1. Experiment description

This is about taxes and spending by the U.S. government. At any given time, taxes can be higher than spending, a surplus, or spending can be higher than taxes, a deficit.

When there is a surplus, the government can cut taxes, increase spending, or reduce the debt. (The U.S. debt is about three times the size of the annual federal budget, so there is plenty of room to reduce it.) Reducing the debt saves money in the future, which can be used either for future tax cuts or spending increases.

When there is a deficit, the government can raise taxes, reduce spending, or borrow more. An increase in the debt means higher taxes or lower spending in the future.

In all of these cases, assume that the economy is performing normally. It does not need special stimulation or dampening.

Right now, a typical American household pays about 20 percent of income in federal taxes combined (including payroll taxes). The rich pay somewhat more because the income tax is graduated (higher percent for higher income), but payroll taxes are actually lower for the rich, as a percent of income.

Some questions here ask you about where budget changes should be made. Increases or decreases in spending can occur in the following categories:

- Health care and public health;
- Social Security (pensions);
- Aid specifically for the poor;
- Armed forces (including foreign military aid);
- Foreign aid for health programs, including AIDS treatment and prevention; and
- Scientific research, including health research.

There are other categories, such as interest on the national debt.

Table 7.2. Baseline condition, questions, and options

The current level of government spending per household comes to 15 percent [20 percent, 25 percent] of the typical household's income.

The current level of total taxes (all levels) comes to 15 percent [20 percent, 25 percent] of the typical household's income.

What would you do about government spending in next year's budget? (Pick the closest.)
　　Cut government spending from 15 percent of income to 5 percent
　　Cut government spending from 15 percent of income to 10 percent
　　Leave government spending unchanged at 15 percent of income
　　Increase government spending from 15 percent of income to 20 percent
　　Increase government spending from 15 percent of income to 25 percent

What would you do about total taxes in next year's budget? (Pick the closest.)
　　Cut total taxes from 25 percent of income to 15 percent
　　Cut total taxes from 25 percent of income to 20 percent
　　Leave total taxes unchanged at 25 percent of income
　　Increase total taxes from 25 percent of income to 30 percent
　　Increase total taxes from 25 percent of income to 35 percent

The choices you have made so far imply that the government will have a
balanced budget　　　　　surplus of . . .　　　　　　　　　　　　　　　deficit of . . .

[Toggling between these options occurs by clicking a different button.]

in Table 7.2) or in a long-term condition, where the question was, "what should the government aim for over the long term?" The resulting 18 cases were presented in a random order chosen for each subject. (We also asked additional questions that we do not report here.)

The results provided no support for rational preference or myopia-optimism bias as hypotheses about why people might support tax cuts in the absence of spending cuts. Indeed, the general result was that subjects on the average preferred a slight surplus, and they also preferred a smaller government than the 20 percent figure we gave them. (We cannot conclude, however, that they prefer smaller government in general: They may think that the 20 percent figure is higher than the present size of government.) Moreover, subjects responded the same way to questions about the long term as to questions about the immediate future.

Subjects also demonstrated a marked anchoring and underadjustment effect, being influenced by the posited starting levels of tax and spending. Thus, when the budget began in deficit, it tended to stay that way, even though, on the average, subjects wanted to reduce the deficit.

These findings, taken together, seem to count heavily against the rational-preference explanation, as subjects do not want deficits, as a general matter, and also against the myopia–optimism bias accounts, as again subjects do not choose deficits in the short term or near term. Subjects are generally tax averse but are *also* deficit averse. Given free rein, they generally support cutting taxes but aim to balance the budget by cutting general levels of spending. They are not naively optimistic. But they are influenced by initial conditions, however thinly framed or presented.

VII. DOES IT MAKE A DIFFERENCE IF *SPECIFIC* CUTS ARE REQUIRED?

The results we have described so far suggest that a government like that of the United States could reduce its size without serious political repercussions, suggesting that the manipulations associated with the STB strategy are unnecessary. People want lower taxes and lower spending, at least if they are led to believe that current taxes and spending are as high as 20 percent of household income. Further, if a deficit already exists because of prior decisions to cut taxes or increase spending, people seem willing to cut spending so as to reduce the deficit.

One problem with this conclusion is that, in the experiment just described, subjects might have thought only about spending cuts *in the abstract*. When spending is presented as a single total category, people will prefer spending cuts to match tax cuts. When *specific* spending cuts must be made, however, people may oppose these cuts in particular programs. Deficits result. This is the identified-victim effect for spending.

Table 7.3. Second experiment: Introductory page

Some questions here ask you about where budget changes should be made. Increases or decreases in spending can occur in the following categories (with very rough estimates of current spending in percent):

Spending category	Current spending (%)
Health care and public health	25
Social security (pensions)	20
Aid specifically for the poor	15
Armed forces (including foreign military aid)	25
Foreign aid for health programs, including AIDS treatment and prevention	2
Scientific research, including health research	5

Other categories, such as interest on the national debt, cannot be changed. Thus, any spending changes must be in the categories listed.

It is also an example of an isolation effect. When people are asked about cuts in general, they focus on this question and fail to ask themselves where the cuts might fall. If they are forced to look at specific categories, they might change their attitude toward spending cuts, thereby suggesting the use of an STB strategy by proponents of small government.

In a second experiment, we told subjects, somewhat realistically, that only certain categories of the budget could be cut, and we asked how they would change the levels of spending in each category. The design and instructions were very much like those in the first experiment, except that we removed the short-term condition, because we found no short-term–long-term divergence, and we added a new condition in which subjects made particular judgments about category spending. We attempted to approximate the major categories of spending in the U.S. federal budget. (Subjects could comment, and no subject commented that the numbers seemed unrealistic.) In this way, we began to test the identified-victim explanation, which is that people oppose particular budget cuts, although they are happy with spending reductions in the abstract.

The introductory page read much like that of the first experiment, with the following significant change, as seen in Table 7.3.

The items for 9 of the 18 trials were like those in the first experiment, with current government spending levels of 16 percent, 20 percent, or 24 percent of income crossed with the same three levels of taxation (leading to surpluses or deficits of up to 8 percent). On the other 9 of the 18 trials, we replaced the spending question with specific questions about spending in each of the six categories. As in the health care example subsequently given here, in Table 7.4, each category was listed in terms of its overall proportion of government spending and its proportion of average household income.

Table 7.4. Second experiment: Question of health-care spending

What would you do to the spending levels in each of the following categories in this case? Remember, these are the only categories that allow changes in spending. (Pick the closest to what you think.)

Health care and public health (25% of government spending, 6% of income)
Cut spending from 6% of income to 0%.
Cut spending from 6% of income to 3%.
Leave spending unchanged.
Increase spending from 6% of income to 9%.
Increase spending from 6% of income to 12%.

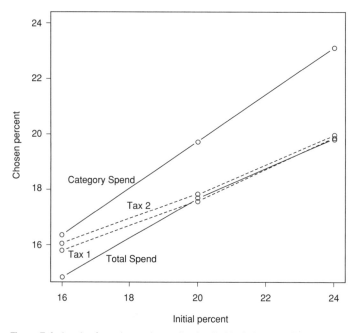

Figure 7.1. Levels of taxation and spending implied by judgments. Taxation levels are dashed lines; spending levels are solid lines.

When cuts were described in the abstract, the results were essentially the same as those of the first experiment: Subjects favored smaller government and balanced budgets (or small surpluses). In the condition with specific cuts, however, subjects were unwilling to cut spending at all. They were thus inconsistent between the two kinds of spending judgments. They failed to internalize their own resistance to specified cuts when they made judgments of overall cuts. They did not generally understand that they are susceptible to an identified-victim bias.

Figure 7.1 shows the mean judgments for the four conditions. Tax 1 and Total Spend are from the trials with the questions about general spending levels as well as taxation. Tax 2 is the level of taxation from the trials with category-spending

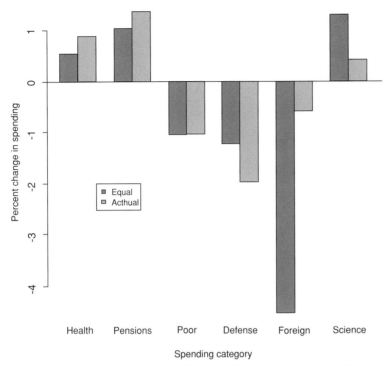

Figure 7.2. Category-spending changes, in percent of spending, calculated as if all categories were equal parts of the budget, or the actual percents given to the subjects.

questions, and Category Spend is the level of spending inferred from the answers to the category-spending questions. What Figure 7.1 demonstrates is that respondents chose substantially higher levels of spending – indeed often increased spending – when asked to make spending cuts based on specific categories. Adjustments to the level of taxation were minimal in the trials with specific categories, and not nearly large enough to offset higher spending.

Figure 7.2 shows spending changes as a function of category, both for the actual changes, calculated on the assumptions given to the subjects, and changes under an "equal" condition in which each of the six categories was assumed to be one-sixth of listed spending (the listed categories comprise 92 percent of all government spending). Though subjects were willing to cut some spending, their favorite target for cuts was foreign aid, which comprises only a small proportion of the budget. However, even with the strong desire to cut foreign aid, when we analyze the data as if all categories were equal in spending (as shown in Figure 7.2), it does not change the main result: deficits occur. It appears that one primary source of the reluctance to cut particular categories is the identification of the categories.

A third experiment included conditions in which initial spending in each category was not specified. We asked about spending changes as a proportion

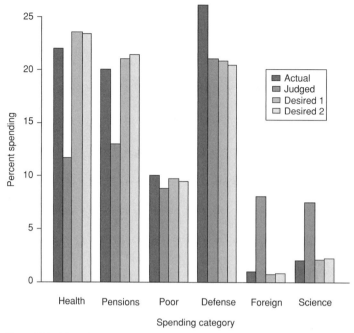

Figure 7.3. Allocations.

of current spending in each category rather than as a proportion of income. We also asked additional questions about current spending in each category.[17] By asking about spending changes with and without information about current allocation, we could test, in a preliminary way, whether people wanted to cut allocations as a result of misjudging their current size. For example, the cuts to foreign aid observed in Figure 7.2 seem to be an artifact of the perceived inflated size of that category. Such cuts may be supported only because subjects exaggerate the share of foreign aid in the budget. In this case, the difference in spending change between conditions where the allocation was provided and conditions where the allocation not provided should correlate with the difference between allocation judgments (in the not-provided condition) and actual allocations (in the allocation-provided condition).

This experiment replicated the principal results of the prior one. Once again, subjects were much more willing to cut spending in general than to cut spending when they were asked to do it category by category. This was true whether we used our estimates or the subjects' own judgments of present spending in each category.

Figure 7.3 shows the actual allocations that we provided, the judged allo-cations, and the desired spending levels, where Desired 1 is in the condition where the allocation information was not provided to subjects and Desired 2

---

[17] The current spending questions could be answered from memory if subjects remembered and believed what we told them, but we attempted to ask these questions as early as possible, without giving up the randomization of condition order.

is the condition where such information was provided. Notice that foreign aid and science are overestimated substantially. Subjects also tended to underestimate the actual allocation to categories that they presumably support, based on self-interest, such as health and pensions, while overestimating the allocation to categories that are not in their direct self-interest, particularly foreign aid and science. Only in the case of defense – in fact, the highest allocation – did subjects both underestimate the actual magnitude and seek to make significant cuts. The important result, however, is that the identified-victim effect did not change overall when subjects made their own estimates.

VIII. DEUS EX MACHINA: FORCING A BALANCED BUDGET

Suppose that the government succeeds in reducing taxes, thereby creating a deficit. Could the deficit then be used to force the public to accept spending cuts in particular programs, as well as in the abstract? A fourth experiment added in a condition that subjects had to present a balanced budget to see if such a constraint might complete the STB strategy.

We hypothesized that, given the right frame, it may indeed be possible to get spending cuts in the later period that could not have been obtained initially. People may be more reluctant to raise taxes than to cut spending once a deficit exists. We examined this issue by asking people to adjust both taxes and spending, and we manipulated the status quo. We hypothesized that when the status quo includes a deficit, people will resist tax increases, so they will be inclined to cut spending. The sum of taxes and spending thus will decline as we move from surplus to deficit. If this prediction holds, a deficit, once created, will tend to lead to spending reductions, as desired by the advocates of the STB strategy. But this process may take some time. Responses to the adjustment questions may be influenced by the starting point of both spending and tax levels. Do people have an ideal government size in mind, as would befit a rational, consistent set of preferences? Or are they influenced by the status quo? If people do not adjust to obtain the same ideal level, then once deficits (or surpluses) are in place, people will not be inclined to remove them immediately. We looked for such anchor and underadjustment effects.

The experiment was similar to previous experiments except that, in half the pages, subjects were required to balance the budget. In these pages, the computer program balanced the budgets automatically by matching taxes to spending each time that subjects changed either. In the category condition, adjustments in spending that resulted from tax changes were made in both the overall spending – which was displayed although it was not directly controllable – and in the categories, which were changed so that they summed to 81 percent of the total spending level (since the listed categories always accounted for 81 percent of total spending). We also used a new method of presentation in which the taxation and spending levels were shown both as numbers and as horizontal red bars.

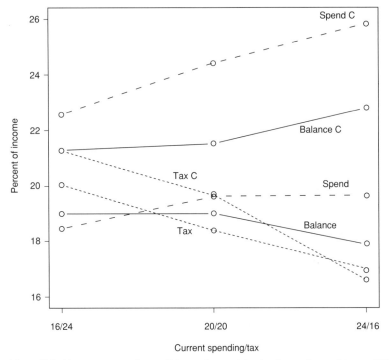

Figure 7.4. Mean responses by condition and current levels of spending and taxes. "C" indicates that spending was allocated by category. "Balance" (solid lines) indicates that the program forced taxes and spending to be equal. Short dashes are taxes; long dashes are spending. The horizontal axis shows the spending–tax conditions (e.g., 24/16 means 24 percent spending and 16 percent taxes).

Figure 7.4 shows the results, with dashed lines for spending, dotted lines for taxes, and solid lines for "balanced," where, by design, taxes equaled spending. For each, there is both an overall line and a line indicating that choices were broken down by categories. Consistent with the prior experiments, subjects tended to favor spending cuts relative to the status quo when they set spending in general, but they favored spending increases when they allocated spending by category.

As found before, subjects favored tax cuts when they could control taxes directly, both in general (Tax) and when they set spending by category (Tax C). Although subjects apparently made some attempt to raise taxes to cover their higher spending in the category condition, the deficit was once again higher in that condition, here by 5.9 percent. When the program forced a balanced budget, however, subjects still favored a larger budget when they set categories (mean 21.9 percent) than when they set spending in general (mean 18.6 percent). However, mean category budget size did not significantly exceed the mean status quo budget size (20 percent), although general budget size was below it. Importantly, the category effect on spending was smaller when balance was forced (3.2 percent) than when it was not, comparing Spend C to Balance C. Thus, forcing a balanced budget mitigated the effect of spending even in categories.

A final experiment replicated the one just described, except that it separated out the decisions about overall spending level and category-specific spending, giving the subjects control over one or both. (When subjects controlled both, each was adjusted in response to a change in the other, so that the overall level and the individual categories were always consistent.) In part this final experiment ruled out an explanation of the prior findings, namely that the category-spending decisions led to a higher total government spending than overall spending decisions precisely because the subjects lacked control over allocations in the latter cases. The category effect on spending levels might result from subjects' being happier with spending when they could control its allocation.[18] In the prior experiments, when subjects set overall levels of spending, they did not control the allocation of spending by categories, so that their lower overall responses might have reflected a rational, consistent distrust of government decision makers setting allocations. By allowing subjects to control the distribution of spending when they set overall levels, we removed this reason for spending reduction.

The results were very clear. Control of spending categories had essentially no effect when subjects set overall spending. The deficit in these cases was still relatively small, and spending was low. Only when subjects set category spending without also setting overall spending was there a large deficit.

This result suggests that some support for reduced spending could be obtained by getting the public to focus on the level of overall spending in the abstract.

IX. WHAT DOES THIS ALL MEAN? A DISCUSSION

Our results provide little support for any simple strategy of cutting the size of government by cutting taxes first. Importantly, this is not because the citizens are fully rational decision makers; they are not. The various heuristics and biases that people show tend to cancel each other out, however, and in the end the endowment effect – reflected in the success of the strategy of identifying the victim as a way to prevent spending cuts – wins out. This means that a strategy of cutting taxes now and then cutting spending later is unlikely to succeed, although citizens will go along with the tax cuts in the first instance.

More specifically, we found that the public does not support deficits, even temporary ones. Cutting taxes will put money in people's pockets, and perhaps they will be grateful, but they also will view the government as irresponsible unless there are also cuts in spending. Yet the status quo effect will make it

---

[18] We thank Richard Craswell for bringing this possibility to our attention.

difficult to restore balance by raising taxes once a deficit is created, as the necessary tax increases will get coded as a loss, to be resisted if at all possible.

Moreover, and most interestingly, although people may support spending cuts in the abstract, they resist cuts in specific programs. This renders the STB strategy unlikely to succeed to any significant degree, at least absent some binding constraint that could force cuts across programs, such as a balanced-budget amendment. Historical evidence also suggests the ineffectiveness of STB.[19] The U.S. government did not shrink much, if at all, under Reagan, and it has expanded under George W. Bush.

In sum there is inconsistency in public judgments, but it is not the commonly assumed optimism or myopia bias. Rather, it is a failure to properly anticipate the depth of the difficulty in making *specific* cuts when people (citizens or legislators) endorse general cuts. People seem to think that government spends too much in general but that spending on each program, on the average, is about right.

If people are forced or otherwise led to close a deficit, our results, especially in the experiment with forced balancing, do suggest that people may be willing both to raise taxes and to cut spending as a way to balance the budget: They will split the difference, so to speak, and so do what they are otherwise reluctant to do, namely, cut specific spending. Hence a roadmap for the ultimate success of STB emerges: Cut taxes today, and force citizen input on overall spending tomorrow . . . but only if the beast-starver can somehow get the citizens not to notice that cuts in overall spending require cuts in specific programs. Given the salience of identifiable victims and the political pressures to identify them, this seems unlikely.

Our conceptualization does suggest two broad ways for governments to avoid deficits. One is to keep everything abstract: to pass laws, as in the form of constitutional restrictions, about balanced budgets. In the abstract, sub-jects support fiscal balance. Many state governments in the United States are indeed required to have balanced budgets each year, and the U.S. government occasionally has tried to bind itself in advance by various budgetary rules.

An alternative takes the opposite tack: to make everything concrete and specific. We could break taxes down into categories dedicated to particular services, as in the case of the various wage taxes in the United States: In this case, the aversion to deficits, which we have found repeatedly, would manifest itself within each specific tax–spend category. (In the last main experiment,

---

[19] *See* Daniel Shaviro, *Can Tax Cuts Increase the Size of Government?* 18 CANADIAN J. LAW & JURIS. 135–152 (2005). Shaviro argues that tax cuts today, in part because of their need to be offset by spending cuts or tax increases tomorrow, and in part because of their collateral effects on the economy, can lead to larger government. He also argues that the size of the government, to the extent it is a meaningful variable at all, cannot be measured from simple income and expenditure statements. Insofar as our experimental work casts doubt on the likelihood that STB tax cuts will lead to later spending cuts, we support Shaviro's analysis and skepticism.

we also found that setting spending by categories led to higher spending even when balance was forced; presumably, subjects were satisfying their desires for spending in each category even when they saw what it cost in terms of its effect on the overall budget.) If citizens come to think of each tax as linked with a particular service, they may be less willing to cut taxes;[20] indeed, this could explain why the Social Security and Medicare tax in the United States, now the largest tax for *most* American taxpayers, is also the one major federal tax that has *never* been cut.[21] This alternative may lead to a larger, more active government than the first method, which would be binding only in the abstract.

It also may be possible simply to confront people with the conflict in their opinions, as a device of argumentation. Advocates of larger government often are tempted to answer their opponents, who want to cut both taxes and spending, by asking what exactly they want to cut. The usual answer, some variation on "government waste," may stop working if proponents of cuts also are confronted with the conflicts in their demands and are pressed to be specific. But then that would be rational, as politics seldom is.

Our conclusions may seem pessimistic for those who want to rein in government. Unless some other mechanism can be found, they would support the conclusion of Buchanan and Tullock that constitutional limits are the best approach.[22] On the other hand, it may be the case that government is not too large, at least in terms of what it spends. The true size of government might be best assessed – in the spirit of the chapters by Jackson and Boskin,[23] as well as the paper by Shaviro[24] – not just in terms of taxing and spending, but through the government's influence on behavior. We ought, perhaps, to count government omissions as well as actions.

The true cost of government may be much higher now than is apparent from taxes and spending alone. It may include losses resulting from a failure to reduce illness and environmental degradation, or to replace declining, nonrenewable resources. It also should include unfunded mandates of all sorts, including the cost of restrictions on individual liberty, as well as regulation. It may well be that higher taxes and higher spending can reduce these other costs, thus reducing the total (often hidden) cost of government. This sort of transparency, however, may have to wait until people can at least see through a failed strategy like starving the beast.

---

[20] *See* Elizabeth Garrett, *Harnessing Politics: The Dynamics of Offset Requirements in the Tax Legislative Process*, 65 U. CHI. L. REV. 501–569 (1998).

[21] *See* Edward J. McCaffery and Jonathan Baron, *The Humpty Dumpty Blues: Disaggregation Bias in the Evaluation of Tax Systems*, 91 ORGANIZATIONAL BEHAVIOR & HUMAN DECISION PROCESSES 230–242 (2003).

[22] *See* Buchanan and Tullock, *supra* note 5.   [23] Jackson, *supra* note 1; Boskin, *Supra* note 1.

[24] Shaviro, *supra* note 19, at 135–152.

Questions for Chapter 7

1. In recent years, a good deal of academic work has been done on the subject of behavioral economics – identifying and quantifying the extent to which individuals can make inconsistent or irrational choices in a variety of contexts, including investment decisions and routine commercial transactions. Professors Baron and McCaffery have been prominent in pushing this mode of analysis into the political arena, inquiring as to whether cognitive biases of similar sorts may affect political decisions, particularly with respect to fiscal policy. How well do you think the insights of behavioral economics translate into this new context? For example, does it matter that political decisions are based on the actions of a large number of citizens, as political decisions are not made individually but rather in most contexts by the median voter? Does the presence of multiple information intermediaries – that is, the press and pundits – suggest that our political processes will suffer from fewer cognitive biases than decisions of individual citizens in other contexts?

2. As Professors Baron and McCaffery note in their opening paragraphs, the two previous chapters devoted considerable attention to different ways in which one could define deficits and debt, and to arguing for the advantages of some definitions over others. Should we therefore infer that Professors Boskin and Jackson are also devotees of behavioral public finance?

3. An interesting finding of the Baron and McCaffery experiments is the extent to which their respondents changed their views on their preferred level of spending cuts once they were informed of the actual current levels (see Figure 7.3). Most prominent is the change in preferred cuts in foreign aid, where the general public tends to overestimate current expenditures by a good deal. Also of interest – and potentially problematic for entitlement reform – is the fact that respondents favor even greater spending increases once they are informed of the actual level of federal spending going to these problems. If you were trying to devise a reform proposal for Social Security or Medicare, or trying to increase

support for aid for relief to Sub-Saharan Africa, how would you make use of this information?

4. In interpreting their experimental results, Professors Baron and McCaffery suggest that the "starve the beast" strategy is unlikely to be effective in the absence of a binding budgetary constraint to force the public to accept spending cuts. Consistent with this insight is the fact that Congress had to adopt the Gramm-Rudman-Hollings Act in the mid-1980s in order to deal with the skyrocketing deficits after the substantial tax cuts of President Reagan's first term. While the act's deficit targets were not fully realized – indeed, they were routinely exceeded and occasionally relaxed – they did impose some degree of spending discipline. As explored in some detail in subsequent chapters, a number of state constitutions include balanced-budget constraints. In reviewing discussion of these provisions, consider whether experience at the state level is consistent with the findings of Professors Baron and McCaffery.

5. To the extent that cognitive biases of the general public would permit politicians to pursue STB strategies and manipulate voters into adopting fiscal programs (first lower taxes and then specific spending cuts) that voters otherwise would not endorse, is it inappropriate for politicians to pursue such strategies? If experts could demonstrate that cognitive biases prevented some segments of the population from noticing the imposition of new taxes, would it be appropriate for politicians to target those citizens for new taxes? More generally, should we be concerned that politicians might exploit the study of behavioral public finance to manipulate public preferences?

Bibliography

ARTICLES

Stacy Anderson and Blake Roberts, *Capacity to Commit in the Absence of Legislation: Takings, Winstar, FTCA,* & *the Court of Claims* (May 4, 2005) (available at http://lawweb. usc.edu/cslp/conferences/fiscal%20challenges/documents/12-CapacitytoCommitt. pdf).

D. A. Aschauer, *Fiscal Policy and Aggregate Demand,* 75 Am. Econ. Rev. 117 (1985).

Alan J. Auerbach, William G. Gale, and Peter R. Orszag, *New Estimates of the Budget Outlook New Estimates of the Budget Outlook: Plus Ça Change, Plus C'est la Même Chose,* Tax Notes, April 17, 2006, at 349.

Alan J. Auerbach, William G. Gale, and Peter R. Orszag, *Sources of the Long-Term Fiscal Gap,* Tax Notes, May 14, 2004, at 1049.

Alan J. Auerbach, Jagadeesh Gokhale, and Laurence J. Kotlikoff, *Generational Accounting: A Meaningful Way to Evaluate Fiscal Policy,* 8 J. Econ. Persp. 73 (1994).

Jonathan Baron and Edward J. McCaffery, *Starving the Beast: The Psychology of Budget Deficits* (December 27, 2005) (unpublished manuscript, on file with University of Pennsylvania Institute for Law and Economics).

Robert J. Barro, *Are Government Bonds Net Wealth?,* 82 J. Political Econ. 1095 (1974).

B. Douglas Bernheim and Kyle Bagwell, *Is Everything Neutral?,* 96 J. Pol. Econ. 308 (1988).

Douglas Bernheim, *Ricardian Equivalence: An Evaluation of Theory and Evidence* (Nat'l Bureau of Econ. Research, Working Paper No. 2330, 1987), available at http://www. nber.org/papers/w2330.

Olivier J. Blanchard, *Debt, Deficits, and Finite Horizons,* 93 J. Pol. Econ. 223 (1985).

Cheryl D. Block, *Congress and Accounting Scandals: Is the Pot Calling the Kettle Black?* 82 Neb. L. Rev. 365 (2003).

Jón Blöndal, *Issues in Accrual Budgeting,* 4 OECD J. On Budgeting 103 (2004).

Daniel Kahneman and Dan Lovallo, *Timid Choices and Bold Forecasts: A Cognitive Perspective on Risk Taking,* 39 Management Science (1993).

Daniel Kahneman and Amos Tversky, *Prospect Theory: An Analysis of Decision under Risk,* 47 Econmetrica 63 (1979).

Michael J. Boskin, *Notes on the Tax Treatment of Human Capital* (Nat'l Bureau of Econ. Research, Working Paper No. 116, 1975), available at http://www.nber.org/ papers/w0116.

Michael J. Boskin, *Federal Government Deficits: Some Myths and Realities*, 72 AM. ECON. REV. 296 (1982).

Michael J. Boskin and Laurence J. Kotlikoff, *Public Debt and U.S. Saving: A New Test of the Neutrality Hypothesis*, 23 Carnegie-Rochester Conference Series 55 (1985).

Michael J. Boskin, *Causes and Consequences of Bias in the Consumer Price Index as a Measure of the Cost-of-Living*, 33 ATLANTIC ECON. J. 1 (2005).

Michael J. Boskin, T*he Effects of Taxes on Saving and Economic Growth* (March 2005) (testimony to the President's Commission on Tax Reform).

Michael J. Boskin, *A Broader Perspective on the Tax Reform Debate*, Tax Notes, Jan. 23, 2006, at 393.

Ellen Bradford and Matthew Scogin, *PAYGO Rules and Sequestration Procedures* (May 4, 2005) (available at http://lawweb.usc.edu/cslp/conferences/fiscal%20challenges/documents/2-PAYGO.pdf).

David Burd and Takeshi Fujitama, *FASAB & the Financial Statements of the United States: Comparing Budgetary Aggregates to Financial Statements*, (May 3, 2005) (available at http://lawweb.usc.edu/cslp/conferences/fiscal%20challenges/documents/13-FASAB.pdf).

David Burd and Brad Shron, *Analysis & Critique of Specialized Rules: Discretionary Caps, Spending Targets, and Committee Allocations* (May 4, 2005) (available at http://lawweb.usc.edu/cslp/conferences/fiscal%20challenges/documents/1-SpecializedRules.pdf).

Leonard E. Burman and William G. Gale, *A Preliminary Evaluation of the Tax Reform Panel's Report*, TAX NOTES, Dec. 5, 2005, at 1349.

Jackie Calmes, *CBO See Wider Deficit this Year and in 2016 if Tax Cuts Don't End*, WALL ST. J., Jan. 27, 2006, at A4.

Colin F. Camerer and Dan Lovallo, *Overconfidence and Excess Entry: An Experimental Analysis*, 89 AM. ECON. REV., 306 (1999).

Richard S. Carnell, *Handling the Failure of a Government Sponsored Enterprise*, 80 WASH L. REV. 565 (2005).

Mark Champoux and Dan Sullivan, *Authorizations and Appropriations: A Distinction Without Difference?* (May 10, 2006) (available at http://www.law.harvard.edu/faculty/hjackson/auth_appro_15.pdf).

Peter A. Diamond, *National Debt in a Neoclassical Growth Model*, 55 AM. ECON. REV. 1126 (1965).

Peter Diamond and Peter Orszag, *Accrual Accounting for Social Security*, 41 HARV. J. LEGIS. 173, 175 (2004).

Federal Accounting Standards Advisory Board, Preliminary Views – Accounting for Social Insurance, Revised (Oct. 23, 2006) (available at http://www.fasab.gov/pdffiles/socialinsurance_pv.pdf).

Martin Feldstein, *Social Security and Saving: New Time Series Evidence*, 49 NAT'L TAX J. 151 (1996).

Benjamin M. Friedman, *Deficits and Debt in the Short and Long Run* (Nat'l Bureau of Econ. Research, Working Paper No. 11630, 2005), available at http://www.nber.org/papers/w11630.

William G. Gale and Peter R. Orszag, *Economic Effects of Sustained Budget Deficits*, 56 NAT'L TAX J. 463 (2003).

Elizabeth Garrett, *Harnessing Politics: The Dynamics of Offset Requirements in the Tax Legislative Process*, 65 U. CHI. L. REV. 501 (1998).

J. Gokhale & K. Smetters, *Fiscal and Generational Imbalances: An Update* (Cato Inst. Paper No 0501, 2005).

Robert E. Hall and Frederic S. Mishkin, *The Sensitivity of Consumption to Transitory Income: Estimates from Panel Data on Households*, 50 ECONOMETRICA 461 (1982).

Trenton Hamilton and Matthew Scogin, *Broader Budget Aggregates: Proposed Reform Legislation* (May 4, 2005) (available at http://lawweb.usc.edu/cslp/conferences/fiscal%20challenges/documents/14-BroaderBudgetAggregates.pdf).

R. Glenn Hubbard, Jonathan Skinner, and Stephen P. Zeldes, *Precautionary Saving and Social Insurance*, 103 J. POL. ECON. 360 (1995).

Howell E. Jackson, *Could We Invest the Surplus?*, TAX NOTES, Feb. 26, 2001, at 1245.

Howell E. Jackson, *Accounting for Social Security and Its Reform*, 41 HARV. J. LEGIS 59 (Winter 2004).

Howell E. Jackson, *Mind the Gap*, TAX NOTES, Dec. 20, 2004, at 4.

Howell E. Jackson, *The True Cost of Privatizing Social Security*, Tax Notes, Jan. 3, 2005, at 109.

Howell E. Jackson, *Big Liability: Social Security, Medicare, and Accounting*, THE NEW REPUBLIC ONLINE (July 12, 2006) (available at http://www.tnr.com/docprint.mhtml?i = w060710&s = jackson071206).

Karen E. Jenni and George Loewenstein, *Explaining the Identifiable Victim Effect*, J. RISK & UNCERTAINTY 235 (1997).

Kenneth L. Judd, *Debt and Distortionary Taxation in a Simple Perfect Foresight Model*, 20 J. MONETARY ECON. 51 (1987).

Daniel Kahneman and Dan Lovallo, *Timid Choices and Bold Forecasts: A Cognitive Perspective on Risk Taking*, 39 MANAGEMENT SCIENCE 17 (1993).

Hiroyuki Kohyama and Allison Quick, *Accrual Accounting in Federal Budgeting: Retirement Benefits for Government Workers* (May 1, 2006) (available at http://www.law.harvard.edu/faculty/hjackson/RetirementBenefits_25.pdf).

Tehila Kogut and Ilana Ritov, *The "Identified Victim" Effect: An Identified Group, or Just a Single Individual?*, 18 RISK & UNCERTAINTY 157 (2005).

Laurence Kotlikoff and Christain Hagist, *Who's Going Broke? Comparing Health Care Costs in Ten OECD Countries* (Nat'l Bureau of Econ. Research, Working Paper No. 11833, 2005) (available at http://www.nber.org/papers/w11833).

David E. Lebow and Jeremy B. Rudd, *Measurement Error in the Consumer Price Index: Where Do We Stand?*, 41 J. ECON. LIT. 159 (2003).

Deborah Lucas and Marvin Phaup, *The Cost of Risk to the Government and Its Implications for Federal Budgeting* (Feb. 2007) (unpublished manuscript on file with author).

John Maggs, *Feeding the Beast*, NAT'L J., March 2005, at 689.

Edward J. McCaffery and Jonathan Baron, *The Humpty Dumpty Blues: Disaggregation Bias in the Evaluation of Tax Systems*, 91 ORGANIZATIONAL BEHAVIOR & HUMAN DECISION PROCESSES 230 (2003).

Edward J. McCaffery and Jonathan Baron, *Framing and Taxation: Evaluation of Tax Policies Involving Household Composition*, 25 J. ECON. PSYCHOLOGY 679 (2004).

Edward J. McCaffery and Jonathan Baron, I*solation Effects and the Neglect of Indirect Effects of Fiscal Policies*, 19 J. BEHAVIORAL DECISION MAKING 289 (2006).

Edward J. McCaffery and Jonathan Baron, *Thinking about Tax*, 12 PSYCHOLOGY, PUB. POL'Y, & LAW 106 (2006).

Franco Modigliani, *Long Run Implications of Alternative Fiscal Policies and the Burden of the National Debt*, 71 ECON. J. 730 (1961).

Sita Nataraj and John B. Shoven, *Has the Unified Budget Undermined the Government Trust Funds?* (NBER Working Paper W10953, Dec. 2004).

Neill Perry and Puja Seams, *Accrual Accounting for Federal Credit Programs: The Federal Credit Reform Act of 1990* (Apr. 20, 2005) (available at http://lawweb.usc.edu/cslp/conferences/fiscal%20challenges/documents/6-AccrualAccounting.pdf).

Robert Porter, *Contract Claims Against the Federal Government: Sovereign Immunity and Contractual Remedies* (May 2, 2006) (available at http://www.law.harvard.edu/faculty/hjackson/ContractClaims_22.pdf).

James Poterba and Lawrence H. Summers, *Finite Lifetimes and the Effects of Budget Deficits on National Savings*, 20 J. Monetary Econ. 369 (1987).

Edward C. Prescott, *Prosperity and Depression*, 92 Am. Econ. Rev. 1 (2002).

Thomas J. Sargent and Neil Wallace, *Some Unpleasant Monetarist Arithmetic*, 5 Fed. Res. Bank of Minneapolis Q. Rev. 1 (1981).

Matthew D. Shapiro, *Comment on E. Engen and R. G. Hubbard, "Federal Government Debt and Interest Rates,"* in NBER Macroeconomic Annual 2004, 148 (Mark Gertler and Kenneth Rogoff eds. 2005).

Daniel Shaviro, *Can Tax Cuts Increase the Size of Government?* 18 Canadian J. Law & Juris. 135 (2005).

Jared Shirck and Francis Shen, *The Role of Estimation in Budget Procedures: Baselines* (May 4, 2005) (available at http://lawweb.usc.edu/cslp/conferences/fiscal%20challenges/documents/4-Baselines.pdf).

Deborah A. Small and George Loewenstein, *Helping the Victim or Helping a Victim: Altruism and Identifiability*, 26 Risk & Uncertainty 5 (2003).

Deborah Solomon, *Wrestling with Medicaid Cuts*, Wall St. J., Feb. 16, 2006, at A4.

Kate Stith, Rewriting the Fiscal Constitution: The Case of Gramm-Rudman-Hollings, 76 Cal. L. Rev. 593 (1988).

Lars E.O. Svensson, *How Should Monetary Policy Be Conducted in an Era of Price Stability?* (Nat'l Bureau of Econ. Research, Working Paper No. 7516, 2000), available at http://www.nber.org/papers/w7516.

James Tobin, *The Burden of the Public Debt: A Review Article*, 20 J. Fin. 679 (1965).

Stanley C.Wisniewski, *Potential State Government Practices Impact of the New GASB Accounting Standard for Retiree Health Benefits*, 25 Public Budgeting & Fin. 104 (Mar. 2005).

Michael Woodford, *Price Level Determinacy without Control of a Monetary Aggregate*, 43 Carnegie-Rochester Conference Series 1 (1995).

Michael Woodford, *Fiscal Requirements for Price Stability*, 33 J. Money, Credit & Banking 669 (2001).

BOOKS

Linda Babcock et al., *Gender Differences in the Propensity to Initiate Negotiations*, in Social Psychology and Economics (David De Cramer et al. eds., 2006).

Jonathan Baron, Thinking and Deciding (3rd ed. 2000).

Michael J. Boskin, Marc S. Robinson, and Alan M. Huber, *Government Saving, Capital Formation, and Wealth in the United States*, in The Measurement of Saving, Investment and Wealth (Robert E. Lipsey, Helen Stone Tice eds., 1989).

James M. Buchanan and Gordon Tullock, The Calculus of Constraint: Logical Foundations of Constitutional Democracy (1962).

Robert Eisner, How Real is the Federal Deficit? (1986).

Douglas W. Elmendorf and Gregory Mankiw, *Government Debt*, in Handbook of Macroeconomics, (John B. Taylor and Michael Woodford eds., Volume 1C 1999).

Eric M. Engen and R. Glenn Hubbard, *Federal Government Debt and Interest Rates*, in NBER Macroeconomic Annual (Mark Gertler and Kenneth Rogoff eds., 2005).

Jagadesh Gokhale and Kent Smetters, *Fiscal and Generational Imbalances: An Update*, in Tax Policy and the Economy (James M. Poterba eds., Volume 20 2006).

Jagadeesh Gokhale and Kent Smetters, Fiscal and Generational Imbalances (2003).

Robert Hall and Alvin Rabushka, The Flat Tax (1983).

Howell E. Jackson, *Accounting for Social Security Benefits*, in Behavioral Public Finance (Edward J. McCaffery and Joel Slemrod eds., 2006).

Thomas Laubach, New Evidence on the Interest Rate Effects of Budget Deficits and Debt, Board of Governors of the Fed. Res. Sys. (2003).

George Loewenstein, Deborah Small and James Strnad, *Statistical, Identifiable and Iconic Victims and Perpetrators*, in Behavioral Public Finance (Edward J. McCaffery and Joel Slemrod eds., 2006).

Robert A. Mundell, *Money, Debt and the Rate of Interest*, in Monetary Theory: Inflation, Interest, and Growth in the World Economy (Robert A. Mundell ed., 1971).

Allen Schick, The Federal Budget Process (2000).

Daniel Shaviro, Do Deficits Matter? (1999).

Michael Woodford, *Control of the Public Debt: A Requirement for Price Stability?*, in The Debt Burden and Monetary Policy (Guillermo A. Calvo and Mervyn King eds., 1997).

GOVERNMENT REPORTS

Congressional Budget Office, U.S. Cong., The Budget and Economic Outlook: Fiscal Years 2002–2011 (Jan. 2001).

Congressional Budget Office, U.S. Cong., The Long-Term Budget Outlook (Dec. 2005).

Congressional Budget Office, U.S. Cong., The Budget and Economic Outlook: Fiscal Years 2007–2016 (Jan. 2006).

Congressional Budget Office, U.S. Cong., Unauthorized Appropriations and Expiring Authorizations (Jan. 2006).

Congressional Budget Office, U.S. Cong., An Analysis of the President's Budgetary Proposals for Fiscal Year 2007 (March 2006).

Congressional Budget Office, U.S. Cong., The Cyclically Adjusted and Standardized Budgets Measures: Updated Estimates (March 2006).

Congressional Budget Office, U.S. Cong., Preliminary Analysis of the President's Budget Request for 2006 (March 2006).

Congressional Budget Office, U.S. Cong., The Budget and Economic Outlook: an Update (August 2006).

Congressional Budget Office, U.S. Cong., Comparing Budget and Accounting Measures of the Federal Government's Fiscal Condition (Dec. 2006).

Office of Management and Budget, *Net Stock of Federally Financed Physical Capital* in The Budget of the United States, FY 2007, Analytical Perspectives, (2006).

Office of Management and Budget, Analytical Perspectives (2007)/.

Office of Management and Budget, The Nation's Fiscal Outlook (2006).

Report of the President's Commission on Budget Concepts (Oct. 1967).

U. S. Bureau of Econ. Analysis, Changes in Net Stock Produced, Assets (Fixed Assets and Inventories), National Income and Product Accounts Tables (2006).

U.S. Government Accountability Office, *The Methods for Tracking Funds in the Federal Government*, in A Glossary of Terms Used in the Federal Budget Process App. III, GAO-05-734 SP (2005).

U.S. Gen. Accounting Office, Fiscal Year 2005 Financial Report of the United States Government (Dec. 2005).

U.S. Department of the Treasury, Treasury Bulletin.

SSA Trustee's Report, 2006.

LEGISLATION

12 U.S.C.A. § 907 (West 2006).

Antideficiency Act, 31 U.S.C.A. § 1341 (2006).

PART THREE

BUDGETING AND FISCAL CONSTRAINTS AT THE STATE LEVEL

T his section explores the impact of different institutional arrangements and budgetary practices on state fiscal behavior. How do
constitutional and legislative budgetary processes affect state fiscal decision making, and what insights are provided to our understanding of
these processes more generally? Because states in the United States regularly
change their budgetary processes, yet share many social, economic, and cultural
characteristics, they offer a potentially rich environment in which to explore
the consequences of changes in the arrangements that govern fiscal decision
making.

The three chapters that make up this section combine empirical and theoretical analyses of these questions and continue this book's multidisciplinary
perspective. The authors in this section, who include political scientists and
economists, all bring a policy analytic perspective to our understanding of fiscal
behavior – focusing on the impacts of changing processes on fiscal outcomes.

In Chapter 8, Juliet Ann Musso, Elizabeth A. Graddy, and Jennifer Bravo
Grizard provide an overview of state budgetary practices and review the insights
that empirical research has provided about their likely impacts on fiscal performance. They document considerable variation across states in eleven of the
budgetary practices that most commonly enter the debate about budgetary
reforms. Their analysis of recent empirical work, however, finds little indica-
tion that most changes in budgetary practices will improve fiscal performance.
Only "hard" balanced-budget requirements show promise, and that assumes
an effective enforcement mechanism either by the legislature or the courts.

In Chapter 9, Tracy M. Gordon considers the impact of institutions designed
to limit the size or growth of government. These efforts, which include tax and
expenditure limits, balanced-budget requirements, and executive-veto provisions, were popular during the 1990s, but their impacts are unclear. This chapter
puts these institutional changes into the broader political economy literature,
and in so doing raises important questions about the underlying behavioral

assumptions and our ability to generalize the experiences of the states with these arrangements.

In Chapter 10, Thad Kousser, Mathew D. McCubbins, and Kaj Rozga provide a detailed look at a specific fiscal intervention – tax and expenditure limits (TELs) – on a broad set of fiscal outcomes in four Western states. Their analysis considers both the nature of the provisions and the political context of the states in which they were implemented. They find that TELs generally fail to constrain growth in the size of government.

Together these chapters raise questions about the extent to which states can serve as the oft-cited laboratory for understanding institutional arrangements, and about the effectiveness of popular interventions. Future research must resolve conceptual and methodological limitations on our ability to establish the causal impacts of specific institutions and procedures. These authors offer, however, suggestions for how future empirical efforts can be improved and provide insights that national and subnational jurisdictions can use as we seek ways to ensure more effective fiscal behavior.

8 Budgetary Arrangements in the 50 States

In Search of Model Practices

Juliet Ann Musso, Elizabeth A. Graddy,
and Jennifer Bravo Grizard

Recent interest in state fiscal institutions has produced a burgeoning theoretical and empirical literature that addresses the fiscal, economic, and political impacts of these institutional arrangements. Scholars and policymakers look to the states to understand the effect of specific reforms on budgetary outcomes, and to gain general insight into the capacity of institutional reforms to improve performance of state as well as federal budget processes. Indeed, the states offer rich potential for our efforts to understand and predict the consequences of fiscal policy.

The states and their constituent local governments collect a substantial share of public receipts in the United States, approximately 40 percent in 2004.[1] Therefore, their fiscal policies have important impacts on their citizens and on the economic performance of the country. More importantly, considerable variation exists among the states with respect to fiscal policy and not infrequent changes in these policies. It is this variability that offers the potential for a better understanding of the consequences of specific fiscal practices.

Here, we consider the most important budgetary practices used across the 50 states and review the insights that empirical research has provided about their likely impacts on fiscal performance. We begin by describing the incidence of the state budgeting arrangements we review, followed by a discussion of the conceptual and methodological challenges that confront efforts to evaluate budgetary policies at the state level. Next we review the empirical literature and analyze our current state of understanding of the effectiveness of these budgetary arrangements. We conclude with suggestions for future research.

---

[1] U.S. Census Bureau, THE 2006 STATISTICAL ABSTRACT (2006), *available at* http://www.census.gov/compendia/statab/.

Juliet Musso is an associate professor of public policy; Elizabeth Graddy is a professor of public policy; and Jennifer Bravo Grizard is an MPP graduate of the University of Southern California. The authors greatly appreciate the support of the James Irvine Foundation, which partially funded this research.

Table 8.1. Gubernatorial budget powers, by region and population groups (in percentages)

Region or quintile	Executive initiates budget	Line-Item veto	Item reduction	Rescission powers unrestricted	Limited
Region					
West	38	92	15	31	38
North-Central	58	92	33	33	42
South	36	86	21	0	57
Northeast	64	64	27	9	18
Population quintiles (in millions)					
1.8.2–33.9	40	100	40	20	0
2.5.1–8.0	70	60	50	20	60
3.2.9–4.9	40	100	0	10	70
4.1.3–2.8	40	80	20	0	40
5.0.4–1.2	50	80	10	40	30
All states	48	84	24	18	40

Source: Analysis based on data from the National Conference of State Legislatures, *Book of the States* (2005).

I. VARIATION IN STATE BUDGETARY PRACTICES

We focus here on a broad set of the most common budgetary processes across U.S. states. Specifically, we consider supermajority vote requirements, balanced-budget and reserve requirements, changes in budget cycles, tax and expenditure limitations, and a set of arrangements that defines the balance of legislative and executive power over the budget (arrangements for initiation of the budget, the line-item veto, item reduction, and rescission powers). The processes considered here are those that have most frequently entered the debate about budgetary reforms.

Tables 8.1 and 8.2 summarize the incidence of these practices among U.S. states, by region and by population grouping.[2] Table 8.1 presents the arrangements that define the balance of power between the executive and the legislature. Table 8.2 presents the other arrangements.

According to the 2006 National Conference of State Legislatures,[3] all but three states work primarily from a budget developed by the executive branch; in Arizona, Colorado, and Texas, a strong legislative tradition prevails and the gubernatorial budget often is disregarded. Legislatures in all but three states – Maryland, Nebraska, and Virginia – have virtually unchecked powers to modify the proposed budget as they choose. Table 8.1 summarizes information from

[2] Table 8.5 provides the assignment of states to region and population quintiles.
[3] National Conference of State Legislatures, Legislative Budget Procedures: A Guide to Appropriations and Budget Processes in the States, Commonwealths and Territories (2006), *available at* http://www.ncsl.org/programs/fiscal/lbptabls/index.htm#dveloprb.

Table 8.2. Incidence of budgetary arrangements among states, by region and population groups (in percentages)

Region or quintile	Supermajority to enact budget	Rainy-Day fund	Balanced-Budget requirement	No deficit carry-over	Biennial budget	TELs
Region						
West	15	77	77	92	54	85
North-Central	17	92	83	75	67	42
South	14	93	86	93	36	57
Northeast	27	100	64	36	27	50
Population quintiles (in millions)						
1.8.2–33.9	20	90	80	40	20	50
2.5.1–8.0	0	100	60	60	70	80
3.2.9–4.9	20	90	100	90	40	70
4.1.3–2.8	30	90	90	100	50	50
5.0.4–1.2	20	80	60	90	50	50
All states	18	90	78	76	46	60

Source: Analysis based on data from the National Conference of State Legislatures, *Book of the States* (2005).

the National Conference of State Legislatures on the power of the executive branch to execute a gubernatorial veto and to reduce the budget following its enactment.

There is a regional pattern to the gubernatorial role in budget initiation. The executive branch is more likely to have the power to initiate budgets in Northeastern and North-Central states, relative to Western and Southern states. This regional pattern of gubernatorial power, however, does not hold across all the indicators. The most common gubernatorial power is the *line-item veto*, which allows a governor to remove specific items from the budget. This power is held by governors in 42 states (84 percent of states). It is notably less likely in Northeastern states, where only 64 percent of governors hold this power.

Far less common is the power of *item reduction*, which allows governors to cut spending levels for individual programs. Governors in only 12 states (24 percent of states) have this power. These are most likely to be governors of large states. States in the two largest population quintiles are much more likely to allow their governors this power than smaller states.

The ability of the executive branch to undertake rescissions, that is, to cancel budgetary authority after enactment, tilts the balance of political power toward the executive branch. But, it also provides flexibility, giving administrators greater ability to respond to fluctuating fiscal conditions. Only nine states have no restrictions on the executive power to reduce the budget following enactment. These states are most likely to be small (lowest population quintile) and located in either the Western or North-Central regions. The remaining states have a wide array of provisions regulating executive powers to reduce budgetary authority. Ten states permit only an across-the-board percentage reduction; 7 states cap the amount by which budget items can be reduced; 13 require consultation with the legislature; and 29 states have some other form of arrangement that is not simple to characterize.

States also vary in the extent to which they have procedures in place for enacting supplemental appropriations when the legislature is out of session. Twenty-five states permit supplemental appropriations only during the legislative session, whereas the remaining states have an array of different rules regarding the processing of such requests outside of the legislative session. The state arrangements for midcycle supplemental appropriations are so complex that it is difficult to typify or categorize them in any straightforward manner, and hence we do not provide a tabulation of this arrangement.

Consider now the broader set of budgetary processes summarized in Table 8.2, which include budget periodicity provisions, tax and expenditure limitations, balanced-budget and reserve requirements, and supermajority vote requirements. The most common requirement is for a "rainy-day" reserve fund, a rule shared by 90 percent of states. Also relatively common are rules that attempt to enforce balance and periodicity in budgeting – the requirement for a balanced budget (78 percent of states) and restrictions on carrying forward an operating deficit (76 percent of states). In contrast, requirements for supermajority votes to enact budgets are the least common. Only 18 percent of the states impose such restrictions.[4] They are most popular in the Northeast.

Much more variation occurs with respect to the budgetary period (46 percent of states have a biennial budget) and the presence of tax or expenditure limits (60 percent of states). As will be discussed later, the latter two also have been more variable over time. Many states have shifted back and forth between annual and biennial budgeting. Tax and expenditure limits, however, are largely a late 20th century innovation, and also much more common in Western states than in the rest of the country.

II. CHALLENGES TO EVALUATION

Two types of challenges complicate our efforts to understand the effects of state fiscal institutions. The first are conceptual – the lack of clarity regarding the appropriate theoretical framework to use in evaluating budgetary institutions, and the lack of consensus on how to measure fiscal success. The second are methodological – there may be too few cases (states) to support differentiation in the impacts of specific budgetary arrangements, especially if they interact,

---

[4] Note these requirements are distinct from supermajority requirements to impose taxes. While not strictly budgetary processes, these requirements are likely to have an important influence on a state's fiscal processes.

and there are concerns about endogeneity in the choice of fiscal arrangements with state characteristics.

As to conceptual frameworks, somewhat competing traditions of thought exist with respect to fiscal policy. The first primarily emphasizes the complexity of the process and the extent to which information failures and bounded rationality limit "optimization" in the budgetary process. This is exemplified by Wildavsky's classic work in which he argues that there is no true theory of budgeting that establishes processes that support optimal resource allocation and that tie programmatic activities to outcomes.[5] Rather, it is common for budgetary processes to be incremental in character, wherein slight changes are made each year to the baseline budget by various departments or agencies based on the needs of specific projects, with very little, if any, attention paid to long-term policy objectives.

Wildavsky's description of the incremental nature of budgeting is primarily positive, but it contains an implicit normative critique that traditional budget procedures tend to shortsightedness, a lack of long-term planning toward specific goals or objectives, and overspending because the future effects of the current budget are not explicitly considered. Incremental budgeting, some believe, makes it difficult to achieve changes in resource allocation, and decentralized decision making at the agency or department level emphasizes isolated programs rather than comprehensive packages of programs across agencies designed to achieve specific goals.

The incremental approach to budgeting observed by Wildavsky also can be considered a form of bounded rationality in response to the political conflict and information constraints associated with resource allocation. The constraints that Wildavsky identifies as impeding federal budgetary control also apply to state budgetary processes: entitlements that are beyond the reach of annual budgeting, partisanship, and revenue volatility. Many states experience even more extreme constraints than the federal government in that they are squeezed between "top down" federal mandates on the one hand, and the "bottom up" pressures of direct democracy on the other, as in California, where fiscal policies are increasingly established through the initiative process.[6] While this view of boundedly rational budgeting does not promote particular institutional reforms, it suggests that budgetary arrangements make a difference to the extent that they diffuse or exacerbate the factors that lead to incrementalism, such as complexity and information failures.

While the classic political science literature on budgeting focused on incrementalism in response to bounded rationality and value conflict, early economic perspectives on fiscal policy considered how fiscal arrangements

[5] Aaron B. Wildavsky, THE POLITICS OF THE BUDGETARY PROCESS (2nd ed., 1974).
[6] Juliet Musso, Elizabeth Graddy, and Jennifer Grizard, *State Budgetary Processes and Reforms: The California Story*, 26 PUB. BUDGETING & FIN. 1 (2006).

might promote optimal fiscal policy. Oates[7] and Wallis and Weingast[8] characterize this line of work as "first generation fiscal federalism." The first-generation fiscal federalism literature suggests that jurisdictional fragmentation can promote fiscal efficiency inasmuch as variations in fiscal outcomes within lower-level jurisdictions (states, localities) may correspond to differences in constituent preferences.[9]

More recent work on budgeting produced by rational-choice economists and political scientists places less emphasis on complexity and bounded rationality, and more on information asymmetry, bargaining, and principal–agent dilemmas. This work falls largely within the public-choice tradition ("second generation fiscal federalism" according to Oates and Wallis and Weingast.)[10] The political economy tradition typically views fiscal policy from a government-failure perspective, assuming that goal-seeking behavior among bureaucrats and politicians results in government processes that are unresponsive and inefficient. The classic study in this tradition is Niskanen's *Bureaucracy and Representative Government*, which theorizes that monopolistic bureaus take advantage of information asymmetries to produce services for which costs exceed benefits on the margin.[11] Like monopoly firms, bureaus do not face incentives to be efficient in production and arguably will generate large surplus payments to factors of production (for example, government professionals). The public-choice tradition in budgeting typically emphasizes the relationship between the legislature and the executive, and, in particular, the agenda-setting power of the legislative branch relative to the veto powers of the executive.[12] In addition to institutional factors, partisan control of the executive and legislative branches is theorized to influence budgetary outcomes, as are such factors as electoral transitions, and partisan ability to override a gubernatorial veto.

The incrementalist–pluralist and public-choice traditions might be thought to support somewhat different proposals for institutional reform. To the extent that budgetary problems arise as a result of complexity, information failures, and bounded rationality, one would seek reforms aiming to increase the

---

[7] Wallace E. Oates, Fiscal Federalism (1972).

[8] *See* John Joseph Wallis and Barry R. Weingast, "Dysfunctional or Optimal Institutions? State Debt Limitations, the Structure of State and Local Governments, and the Finance of American Infrastructure," Chapter 11 of this volume.

[9] Oates, *supra* note 7; Charles M. Tiebout, *A Pure Theory of Local Expenditures*, 64 J. Pol. Econ. 416 (1956).

[10] Wallis and Weingast, *supra* note 8.

[11] William A. Niskanen, Bureaucracy and Representative Government (1971).

[12] James E. Alt and Robert C. Lowry, *Divided Government, Fiscal Institutions, and Budget Deficits: Evidence from the States*, 88 Am. Political Sci. Rev. 811 (1994); James E. Alt and Robert C. Lowry, *A Dynamic Model of State Budget Outcomes under Divided Partisan Government*, 62 J. Politics 1035 (2000); Thomas Romer and Howard Rosenthal, *Political Resource Allocation, Controlled Agendas, and the Status Quo*, 33 Pub. Choice 27 (1978).

transparency and coherence of the process. If, however, one considers that political self-interest or partisanship leads to suboptimal outcomes, the prescription might emphasize institutional reforms designed to diffuse partisanship or to check the pursuit of political interest. These might include, for example, something akin to federal pay-as-you-go (PAYGO) rules or, as suggested by Garrett and Vermeule[13] institutional rules that shield lawmakers from ideological or partisan attack when making tough fiscal decisions.

A second conceptual complication that makes it difficult to sort out "model practices" is the wide variety of outcome measures used by researchers, most of which relate imperfectly to norms of allocative efficiency. Many of the earlier public finance studies used measures such as tax and expenditure levels or rates of growth. These are somewhat noisy proxy measures for efficiency, at the least because they do not acknowledge the possibility that budgetary arrangements might influence the *mix* as well as the *level* of spending and revenues. Nor is it evident what level or growth rate in expenditures is optimal from an economic standpoint. More recent studies have attempted to incorporate better measures of the fiscal strength of a state, such as bond ratings or borrowing costs.[14]

From a methodological perspective, the key challenge is that a large number of factors likely influence fiscal outcomes, and there are not sufficient cases (states) to control for all of them. For example, the size of states and differences in the historical context in which states adopted their governing frameworks make it difficult to generalize regarding the effects of budgetary institutions. Large states may require substantially different processes than their smaller counterparts in that they have more urbanized and diverse populations, a likelihood of greater political conflict, and greater environmental uncertainty. Moreover, regional variations may be important to consider as states within a particular region are more likely to share a common historical heritage and general political culture.[15]

A related methodological problem is that budgetary arrangements may interact with each other. For example, it may be difficult to isolate the effects of an expenditure limit in a state that also has a rainy-day prudent reserve requirement. Similarly, Knight[16] argues that an interaction between balanced-budget rules and supermajority voting requirements is likely.

[13] *See* Elizabeth Garrett and Adrian Vermeule, "Transparency in the U.S. Budget Process," Chapter 3 of this volume.

[14] Craig L. Johnson and Kenneth A. Kriz, *Fiscal Institutions, Credit Ratings, and Borrowing Costs,* 25 Pub. Budgeting & Fin. 84 (2005); James M. Poterba and Kim S. Reuben, Pub. Policy Inst. of Cal., Fiscal Rules and Bond Yields: Do Tax Limits Raise the State's Borrowing Costs? (1999).

[15] Daniel Elazar, American Federalism: A View from the States (2nd ed. 1972); Paula S. Kearns, *The Determinants of State Budget Periodicity: An Empirical Analysis,* 13 Pub. Budgeting & Fin. 40 (1993).

[16] Brian G. Knight, *Supermajority Voting Requirements for Tax Increases: Evidence from the States,* 76 J. Pub. Econ. 41 (2000).

Finally, it also is acknowledged widely that state fiscal arrangements cannot be treated as exogenous.[17] Fiscal arrangements may reflect state political preferences, or they may be reactions to recent financial events, requiring control for endogeneity through the use of instrumental variables or other modeling approaches. These approaches require the identification of factors that explain the choice of fiscal arrangements but are not correlated with broader state political preferences. With only 50 states, it is difficult to develop modeling procedures that simultaneously can control for the effects of endogeneity and the likelihood of interaction effects amongst budgetary arrangements.[18]

III. ANALYSIS OF STATE BUDGETING INSTITUTIONS

With the conceptual and methodological difficulties just reviewed in mind, we turn now turn to a review of recent empirical work on state budgeting institutions and the impact of these institutions on budgetary outcomes. We focus on work addressing supermajority vote requirements; balanced-budget and reserve requirements; budget cycle changes; tax and expenditure limits; and the balance of legislative and executive powers.

A. Supermajority Vote Requirements

Only three states, California, Arkansas, and Rhode Island, require a two-thirds vote to enact the state budget. Six additional states require a supermajority vote under particular circumstances, either when an expenditure ceiling is exceeded or in the event of late passage of the budget. Some critics have argued that supermajority provisions act against rationalism in budgeting because they are likely to result in political logrolling in order to attain sufficient support to pass the budget.[19] Little empirical evidence is available to judge such claims, as few states employ supermajority requirements on the budget.

Perhaps the more important supermajority requirements are those that require a supermajority vote of elected officials or the electorate to raise taxes. While these are not strictly budgetary institutions, they are fiscal arrangements that are likely to influence the ability of lawmakers to enact companion

---

[17] See Tracy M. Gordon, "The Calculus of Constraint: A Critical Review of State Fiscal Institutions," Chapter 9 of this volume; Brian Knight and Arik Levinson, *Rainy Day Funds and State Government Savings*, 52 Nat'l Tax J. 459 (1999); Knight, *supra* note 16; *see* Thad Kousser, Mathew D. McCubbins, and Kaj Rozga, "When Does the Ballot Box Limit the Budget? Politics and Spending Limits in California, Colorado, Utah, and Washington," Chapter 10 of this volume.

[18] Knight, *supra* note 16.

[19] John W. Ellwood and Mary Sprague, *Options for Reforming the State Budget Process, in* Constitutional Reform in California: Making State Government More Effective and Responsive 329 (Roger G. Noll and Bruce E. Cain eds., 1995).

bills to assist in balancing a budget through revenue augmentation. As Knight describes, 13 states have enacted supermajority requirements for revenue increases; all but three of these were enacted as part of or following the "tax revolt" of the late 1970s.[20] These supermajority revenue requirements are found in Southern or Western states, and, with the exception of California and Florida, in small states.

Little empirical research is available on the impact of supermajority voting requirements, presumably because of the difficulty of controlling for the joint effects of endogeneity and interaction with other fiscal institutions described above. Using two-stage least squares to control for endogeneity, and comparing strong and weak balanced-budget states, Knight does find that supermajority requirements are associated with both lower tax rates and lower spending rates, with a greater impact on spending rates in states that have strong balanced-budget requirements.

B. Balanced-Budget and Reserve Requirements

Requirements for enactment of a balanced-budget requirement and of a budget reserve are relatively common, particularly among Western and large states. These requirements in practice apply to operating expenditures and do not prohibit debt financing of capital investment.[21] In addition, deficit financing restrictions are common in Western states and smaller states. Restrictions on deficit financing taken with the requirement for a balanced budget together aim to promote the norms of periodicity (ensuring that the budget expenditures and revenues are counted within an established accounting period, in this case one year). The extent to which they are likely to promote political–fiscal discipline in budgeting, however, depends critically on enforcement. As Poterba argues, most states employ "soft" balanced-budget requirements that do not include any enforcement mechanism. Poterba further states that "the General Accounting Office[22] reports that there have never been lawsuits to challenge state budgeting outcomes, even though there have been instances when budgets failed to balance. The GAO's 1985 survey suggested that state policymakers view tradition, or a history of balanced budgets, as the primary factor encouraging them to maintain budget balance."[23]

A more recent Harvard Law School briefing paper similarly concludes, "despite some arguments that the courts *could* in fact handle the complexities of budget policy if they wanted to, the evidence from the states suggests

---

[20] Knight, *supra* note 16.
[21] National Conference of State Legislatures, STATE BALANCED BUDGET REQUIREMENTS (1999), *available at* http://www.ncsl.org/programs/fiscal/balreqs.htm.
[22] The General Accounting Office is currently known as the Government Accountability Office.
[23] James M. Poterba, *Balanced Budget Rules and Fiscal Policy: Evidence from the States*, 48 NAT'L TAX J. 329 (1995).

that courts are (explicitly) reticent to get their hands dirtied with balanced budgeting matters."[24]

It is possible that deficit financing restrictions might have greater effect than the mere requirement for enactment of a balanced budget in that they limit the long-term carry-forward of a budgetary imbalance. Poterba argues that it is extremely difficult to forecast the outcomes of such budgetary institutions because they are endogenous with other state characteristics such as political culture, preferences, and political economy.[25] Nonetheless some evidence shows that stricter balanced-budget rules (e.g., those restricting end-of-year budget deficits or prohibiting deficit financing) do appear to reduce spending. For example, Poterba finds, in an analysis of 27 states with annual budgets, that states with stricter balanced-budget requirements reduce spending more under deficit conditions.[26] Similarly, Bohn and Inman show that spending tends to be lower over time in states with more rigorous antideficit laws.[27] In a study of the relationship between partisan control and spending, Alt and Lowry find that "faced with an unexpected recession or inheriting a deficit, unified party governments not subject to deficit carryover laws might allow it to grow (if they remained in office) while those subject to such laws eliminate deficits more quickly."[28] The evidence further suggests that antideficit rules tended to achieve budget balance through spending reductions as opposed to increased taxes.

C. The Budget Cycle: Annual Versus Biennial Appropriations

The rationale for a biennial budget would appear to be more closely related to concerns about bounded rationality and information failure, inasmuch as biennial budgeting aims to reduce political transaction costs and support long-term planning in budgetary processes. As Table 8.3 indicates, 21 states employ biennial budget cycles, somewhat more typically Western and North-Central states. Interestingly, there has been a fair amount of experimentation at the state level with the length of the budgetary cycle.[29] According to legislative surveys undertaken by the National Conference of State Legislatures, 24 states have

---

[24] Laurel Brown and Blake Roberts, *Alternative Procedures: Line Item Vetoes and Balanced Budget Amendments* 11 (Harvard Law School Federal Budget Policy Seminar Briefing Paper No. 3, 2005), *available at* http://www.law.harvard.edu/faculty/hjackson/AlternativeProcedures_3.pdf.

[25] Poterba, *supra* note 23.

[26] James M. Poterba, *State Responses to Fiscal Crises: The Effects of Budgetary Institutions and Politics*, 102 J. POL. ECON. 799 (1994).

[27] Henning Bohn and Robert P. Inman, *Balanced Budget Rules and Public Deficits: Evidence from the U.S. States* (Nat'l Bureau of Econ. Research Working Paper No. W5533, 1996).

[28] James E. Alt and Robert C. Lowry, *Divided Government, Fiscal Institutions, and Budget Deficits: Evidence from the States*, 88 AM. POL. SCI. REV. 811, 823 (1994).

[29] Ronald K. Snell, *Annual and Biennial Budgeting: The Experience of State Governments* (National Conference of State Legislatures, 2004), *available at* http://www.ncsl.org/programs/fiscal/annlbien.htm#t1.

Table 8.3. Annual and biennial budgeting states

Annual session: Annual budget (29 states)	Annual session: Biennial budget (15 states)	Biennial session: Biennial budget (6 states)
Alabama	Arizona[†]	Arkansas
Alaska	Connecticut	Montana
California	Hawaii	Nevada
Colorado	Indiana	North Dakota*
Delaware	Kentucky	Oregon*
Florida	Maine	**Texas**
Georgia	Minnesota	
Idaho	Nebraska	
Illinois	New	
Iowa	Hampshire	
Kansas	North Carolina	
Louisiana	**Ohio**	
Maryland	Virginia	
Massachusetts	Washington	
Michigan	Wisconsin	
Mississippi	Wyoming*	
Missouri		
New Jersey		
New Mexico		
New York		
Oklahoma		
Pennsylvania		
Rhode Island		
South Carolina		
South Dakota		
Tennessee		
Utah		
Vermont		
West Virginia		

Note: Boldface indicates the ten most populous states.
*These are biennial-budget states that enact a consolidated two-year budget. Other biennial budgets enact two annual budgets at one time.
[†]In Arizona, biennial budgeting is limited to smaller state agencies.
Population estimates are for 2000.
Source: Ronald K. Snell, Annual and Biennial Budgeting: The Experience of State Governments, National Conference of State Legislatures (October 2004), available at http://www.ncsl.org/ programs/fiscal/annlbien.htm#t1.

changed their budgetary cycle since 1968. Of these, 12 have shifted from biennial to annual appropriations, and only 3 from annual to biennial budgeting. Five states have shifted from biennial to annual budgeting, followed by a second shift back to biennial budgeting, and Iowa has changed its budgetary cycle three times: from biennial to annual in 1975, back to biennial in 1979, and to an annual cycle in 1983. According to Snell, only three states enact a "true" biennial budget in which all spending is consolidated over a two-year period.

Most of the remaining states enact two separate annual budgets and may revisit the budget annually.

Scant empirical evidence exists on the determinants and effects of budgetary cycles. One of the few systematic studies of the choice of budget cycle found that states were more likely to utilize annual budgeting under conditions where there was volatility in revenue sources, and in regions with dominant political cultures that were considered, according to Elazar's trichotomy of political culture, to be "individualistic."[30] Kearns argues that biennial budgeting is more likely to fit with a "moralistic" political culture such as that found in the South or Midwest, cultures that would tend to rely on "participation in search for the common good."[31] In contrast, individualistic political cultures, as would apply in California, are those that tend more to view government from the perspective of the marketplace. Kearns hypothesizes that "Individualistic political cultures might be more likely to adopt annual budgets, depending on the revealed preferences of the voter/taxpayers and their elected representatives"[32] and also finds that higher state expenditures tend to be associated with use of annual budgeting, although this finding is hard to interpret because of the potential for endogeneity of the explanatory variable. She suggests that the apparent trend for higher expenditures in annual-budget states may relate in part to increased opportunity for political manipulation over the biennial period, and further speculates, "Biennial budgeting gives assurance to lobbyists and their interest groups that the political favors obtained in biennial budget states are . . . durable."[33]

In order for biennial budgeting to support greater rationality in the budgeting process, one would expect it to be accompanied by improved budgetary or managerial practices, such as requirements for long-term planning or forecasting or financial performance review. Snell reports that the differences in executive control and managerial practices across states do not seem to covary with the choice of budgetary cycle. Moreover, Snell reports that two early evaluations of the shift from biennial to annual budgeting did not appear to find that the change in cycle was accompanied by significant shifts in practices. The state of Connecticut, for example, which shifted to a biennial cycle in 1991, justified this change as supporting long-term planning and program evaluation, but it is not clear that these improvements have attended the change in cycle. Snell gives this report:

> A Connecticut legislative committee reviewed the biennial process along with other legislative budget processes in 2003. It reported that the process had not met expectations. "Beginning with the first biennium," it observed, "the governor

---

[30] Kearns, *supra* note 15.   [31] *Id.* at 48.
[32] Paula S. Kearns, *State Budget Periodicity: An Analysis of the Determinants and the Effect on State Spending*, 13 J. Pol'y Analysis & Mgmt. 331 (1994); Kearns, *supra* note 15.
[33] Kearns, *supra* note 32, at 344.

and legislature have proposed new and expanded programs along with significant policy changes in each year of the cycle. As a result, second-year adjustments and revisions are often extensive. There is also no evidence that legislators or state agencies give greater attention to program outcomes and performance measures in the second year of the cycle."[34]

In sum, there is little empirical evidence to suggest that biennial budgeting promotes programmatic review and an insufficient assessment of the effect of cycle arrangements on budgetary outcomes. After reviewing state evidence, Young and McClelland conclude: "All in all, the anecdotal and survey evidence shows that neither an annual nor a biennial budget will be the deus ex machina of budgetary efficiency. Rather, legislators' dedication to realizing a sound budget is more important."[35]

D. Tax and Expenditure Limits

As Table 8.2 and Map 8.1 illustrate, in 2005, 30 states limited taxes, expenditures, or both. Tax and expenditure limits vary considerably across the states, making it difficult to generalize about their structure. Often these limitations are tied to an index such as growth in personal income, inflation, or population with a requirement that excess revenues must be returned to the taxpayers.[36] In some cases, appropriations are established as a set percentage of projected revenues, which in effect builds in a rainy-day reserve.[37] It is particularly common to find such tax and expenditure limitations (TELs) in the Western states, where the preponderance of these restrictions were enacted through the citizen initiative process. They are particularly common in the second and third population quintiles, states between 2.9 and 5.1 million in population. It is more common to find restrictions on expenditures than revenues; only three states, and, most famously, Colorado, impose limitations on both taxes and expenditures. Mullins and Wallin find little evidence that the movement toward adoption of TELs was motivated by a sense that government was "too big," but rather a desire to increase efficiency and reduce taxes. They argue, "Support may have been motivated by a combination of 'wishful' thinking and a self-interested attempt to shift the burden of government finance."[38]

The paradox of TELs is that while they are apparently designed to reduce the public-choice problems of budgeting already discussed by better aligning the interests of principals with the wishes of the agent, they in turn are subject

---

[34] Snell, *supra* note 29.

[35] Stuart Young and Drew McClelland, *Implementing Biennial Budgeting for the U.S. Congress* (Harvard Law School Federal Budget Policy Seminar Briefing Paper No. 20, 2006), at 16, *available at* http://www.law.harvard.edu/faculty/hjackson/BiennialBudget_20.pdf.

[36] National Conference of State Legislatures, STATE TAX AND EXPENDITURE LIMITS – 2005 (2005), *available at* http://www.ncsl.org/programs/fiscal/tels2005.htm.

[37] *Id.*   [38] *Id.* at 15.

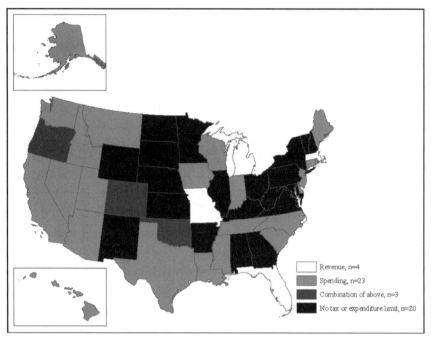

Map 8.1. State tax and expenditure limits, 2005 (*source:* National Conference of State Legislatures, State Tax and Expenditure Limits – 2005, downloaded January 25 from http://www.ncsl.org/programs/fiscal/tels2005.htm).

to a principal–agent problem in implementation and enforcement. As Kousser et al. discuss, the agent (legislatures, subsequent voters) may not adhere to policies established by the principal (previous legislatures, previous voters).[39] Another apparent paradox is that the instrument for passage that would appear most likely to lead to effectiveness – an initiative process that takes the limit out of the hands of legislatures – itself imposes limitations on success. Gerber et al. show that the initiative process more often is used for "extreme" measures that differ substantially from legislative preferences because the costs of the process are high – only when public sentiment is substantially at odds with prevailing norms will such initiatives prevail.[40] Because these initiatives impose restrictions that are divergent from the preference of most legislators, they argue, legislative compliance tends to be low. They theorize, "our effort produces an ironic result: the kinds of policy changes that are most likely to prevail as initiatives . . . are less likely to be implemented and enforced, all else constant."[41]

[39] *See* Kousser et al., *supra* note 17.
[40] Elisabeth Gerber, Arthur Lupia, and Mathew D. McCubbins, *When Does Government Limit the Impact of Voter Initiatives? The Politics of Implementation and Enforcement,* 66 J. POL. 43 (2004).
[41] *Id.* at 45.

Research regarding the effects of TELs on state spending has not been conclusive. Kousser et al. examine the political and institutional factors that influence the "bite" of TELs in four Western states, and conclude, "TELs failed to constrain the size of government in three of the four states that we examined, and in the fourth state there is anecdotal evidence that politicians are finding their way around the limits."[42] Clingermayer and Wood find somewhat higher reliance on debt financing in states with fiscal caps, suggesting that debt financing functions as an end run around TELs.[43] Conversely, in an interrupted-time-series analysis of the effects of limits in three early adopters – South Carolina, Michigan, and Tennessee – King-Meadows and Lowery find weak evidence that fiscal caps restricted the growth of government, while finding "no support that caps have been evaded via end-runs associated with fiscal decentralization, reduced reliance on non-tax revenue, and increased reliance on state debt."[44]

Some evidence also shows that voters relax TELs when they begin to seriously constrain spending. California provides a good example of this observation, as the appropriations limit enacted in 1979, through the initiative process, was exceeded by the State in only one year, 1986–1987, in which there was a taxpayer rebate amounting to $1.1 billion.[45] Subsequently, state appropriations have not exceeded the limit, in no small part because the measure was relaxed through the initiative process in 1990.[46] Recently, what was arguably the most restrictive spending limit, Colorado's TABOR (Taxpayer's Bill of Rights, enacted by initiative in 1992) was suspended for five years in November 2006, again through the initiative process.

The specifics of tax and expenditure limitations vary considerably, and there is a strong likelihood that they interact with other state fiscal policies, such as supermajority requirements for tax increases and limitations on deficit financing. In a 1999 Public Policy Institute of California study, Poterba and Reuben found evidence to suggest that expenditure limits reduced borrowing costs at the state level, while strict revenue limits were associated with higher borrowing costs, suggesting that strict revenue limits increase lenders' perceptions of risk.[47] This finding also is supported by Johnson and Kriz, who found expenditure

---

[42] *See* Kousser et al., *supra* note 17.

[43] James C. Clingermayer and B. Dan Wood, *Disentangling Patterns of State Debt Financing*, 89 Am. Pol. Sci. Rev. 108 (1995).

[44] Tyson King-Meadows and David Lowery, *The Impact of the Tax Revolt Era State Fiscal Caps: A Research Update*, 16 Pub. Budgeting & Fin. 102 (1996).

[45] Legislative Analyst's Office, The State Appropriations Limit (2000), *available at* http://www. lao.ca.gov/2000/041300_gann/041300_gann.html.

[46] Prior to the passage of Proposition 111, the growth factor was based on population growth and the inflation rate. Proposition 111 based the population growth factor on a weighted average of population and K–14 school enrollment growth, and changed the cost-of-living adjustment from the rate of inflation to the rate of personal income growth. These changes were retroactive and had the effect of increasing the limit by an amount of approximately $6 billion in 2000 (*id.*).

[47] Poterba et al., *supra* note 14.

limits to be associated with higher state bond ratings, whereas debt limits were associated with lower state bond ratings and higher borrowing costs.[48] One must be cautious, however, about generalizing these results given the limited number of states with tax limitations and the possibility of endogeneity with respect to the choice of instrument.

As Kousser et al. argue, it is difficult to assess the effects of TELs because the comprehensive fiscal data required to conduct a rigorous interrupted-time-series analysis are not available prior to the 1970s, when many states adopted TELs.[49] Moreover, from a standpoint of best practices, it is difficult to evaluate cases such as California and Colorado, in which the electorate subsequently relaxed or suspended revenue or expenditure limits. Whether such an action should be interpreted as a lamentable failure of the principal–agent relationship or as a commendable adaptation to new conditions or better information depends critically on the ideological orientation and goals of the evaluator.

E. Balance of Legislative and Executive Powers

Given the recurrent debate about the appropriate balance of powers in budgeting at the federal level, there has been surprisingly little empirical attention to the effects of variance in executive power in state budgeting. Douglas and Hoffman assess the effects of gubernatorial "impoundment" or rescission of appropriations, which as already noted is present in some form in more than half the states.[50] Based on a survey of state budget officers, they conclude that gubernatorial rescission most frequently is used to achieve budgetary balance or to ensure fiscal prudence, for example to prevent agency expenditures of unanticipated savings, to control spending, or to prevent unnecessary expenditures. State budget officers did not commonly report that rescission powers were used for political aims, such as "to eliminate pork barrel projects, eliminate programs inconsistent with the governor's policy agenda, or punish or reward legislators."[51] Given that these conclusions are based on a single survey of budget officials, many of whom may be employed within the executive branch, they must be viewed as suggestive at best.

There is a somewhat larger literature regarding the effects of gubernatorial veto powers in the budgeting process.[52] As Lauth describes, the logic behind

---

[48] Johnson and Kriz, *supra* note 14.   [49] *See* Kousser et al., *supra* note 17.

[50] James W. Douglas and Kim U. Hoffman, *Impoundment at the State Level: Executive Power and Budget Impact*, 34 Am. Rev. Pub. Admin. 252 (2004).

[51] *Id.* at 255.

[52] Glenn Abney and Thomas P. Lauth, *The Line-Item Veto in the States: An Instrument for Fiscal Restraint or an Instrument for Partisanship?* 45 Pub. Admin. Rev. 372 (1985); Glenn Abney and Thomas P. Lauth, *The End of Executive Dominance in State Appropriations*, 58 Pub. Admin. Rev. 388 (1998); Burton A. Abrams and William R. Dougan, *The Effects of Constitutional Restraints on Governmental Spending*, 49 Pub. Choice 101 (1986); Douglas Holtz-Eakin, *The Line-Item Veto and Public Sector Budgets: Evidence from the States*, 36 J. Pub. Econ. 269 (1988);

gubernatorial veto powers is that the executive will tend to be more fiscally conservative, all else equal, than legislatures, because "individual legislators find it difficult to ignore constituency expectations and the electoral advantages associated with bringing home the bacon. . . . Governors, the argument continues, with a more diverse, state-wide constituency, may be better able to balance competing spending claims at a lower overall level of state spending."[53] It has been argued that executive veto powers may unduly increase the power of the governor to impose particular policy preferences, or reduce fiscal discipline on the part of the legislature. Legislatures moreover can deflect the line-item veto by bundling items into broad categories that are politically unpopular to line out. Hence Lauth argues that the power to reduce appropriations, found in only 12 states, is much more important than line-item powers, which are present in almost all states.

Abney and Lauth argue that increasing professionalism in state legislatures has severely reduced gubernatorial dominance in the budgeting process.[54] They suggest that the shift in authority toward state legislatures has increased their fiscal discipline, and argue "rational decision making in the state appropriations process is most likely where both branches are institutionally strong."[55] It should be noted that this assumption is in direct conflict with the justification for TELs and balanced-budget powers, which assume that legislative power leads to abuse and unchecked growth in government. Abney and Lauth's work is empirically limited inasmuch as it relies primarily on cross-sectional surveys of state budget officials. As they acknowledge, a need persists for better longitudinal analysis to document and evaluate shifts in the balance of powers.[56]

Nice examines the effect of variation in line-item veto powers on state spending and finds no evidence that states with stronger gubernatorial veto powers have reduced spending.[57] Holtz-Eakin, in a longitudinal analysis, finds that the line-item veto has short-term effects when the governor is in the minority (regardless of party), but that it has no apparent long-term effect on spending.[58] These results conflict with the official perceptions surveyed by Abney and Lauth. It should be noted that the limited empirical work done on the effect of veto powers has not typically examined their potential interactions with other institutional factors, such as the presence of supermajority vote requirements, balanced-budget requirements, or TELs.[59] There is a need for more fine-grained longitudinal analysis, a task that is made difficult by the complexity of

---

Thomas P. Lauth, *The Line-Item Veto in Government Budgeting*, 16 PUB. BUDGETING & FIN. 97 (1996); David C. Nice, *The Item Veto and Expenditure Restraint*, 50 J. POL. 487 (1988).
[53] Lauth, *supra* note 52, at 100.   [54] Abney and Lauth (1998), *supra* note 52.
[55] Abney and Lauth (1985), *supra* note 52.
[56] Abney and Lauth (1985, 1998), *supra* note 52.
[57] Nice, *supra* note 52.   [58] Holtz-Eakin, *supra* note 52.
[59] Abney and Lauth (1985, 1998), *supra* note 52.

Table 8.4. Assignment of states to region and population quintiles

State	Number	State	Number
Population Quintile 1			
California	33,871,648	Pennsylvania	12,281,054
Texas	20,851,820	Ohio	11,353,140
New York	18,976,457	Michigan	9,938,444
Florida	15,982,378	New Jersey	8,414,350
Illinois	12,419,293	Georgia	8,186,453
Population Quintile 2			
North Carolina	8,049,313	Tennessee	5,689,283
Virginia	7,078,515	Missouri	5,595,211
Massachusetts	6,349,097	Wisconsin	5,363,675
Indiana	6,080,485	Maryland	5,296,486
Washington	5,894,121	Arizona	5,130,632
Population Quintile 3			
Minnesota	4,919,479	South Carolina	4,012,012
Louisiana	4,468,976	Oklahoma	3,450,654
Alabama	4,447,100	Oregon	3,421,399
Colorado	4,301,261	Connecticut	3,405,565
Kentucky	4,041,769	Iowa	2,926,324
Population Quintile 4			
Mississippi	2,844,658	New Mexico	1,819,046
Kansas	2,688,418	West Virginia	1,808,344
Arkansas	2,673,400	Nebraska	1,711,263
Utah	2,233,169	Idaho	1,293,953
Nevada	1,998,257	Maine	1,274,923
Population Quintile 5			
New Hampshire	1,235,786	South Dakota	754,844
Hawaii	1,211,537	North Dakota	642,200
Rhode Island	1,048,319	Alaska	626,932
Montana	902,195	Vermont	608,827
Delaware	783,600	Wyoming	493,782

Notes: Definitions of regions are as follows. West: Alaska, Arizona, California, Colorado, Hawaii, Idaho, Montana, Nevada, New Mexico, Oregon, Utah, Washington, and Wyoming (13 states); North-Central: Illinois, Indiana, Iowa, Kansas, Michigan, Minnesota, Missouri, Nebraska, North Dakota, Ohio, South Dakota, and Wisconsin (12 states); South: Alabama, Arkansas, Florida, Georgia, Kentucky, Louisiana, Mississippi, North Carolina, Oklahoma, South Carolina, Tennessee, Texas, Virginia, and West Virginia (14 states); Northeast: Connecticut, Delaware, Maine, Maryland, Massachusetts, New Hampshire, New Jersey, New York, Pennsylvania, Rhode Island, and Vermont (11 states).

institutional and political factors that likely interact with executive powers, and the limited size of a 50-state sample.

IV. CONCLUSION

Among the variety of arrangements thought to improve fiscal rationality and prudence, the only measure that appears demonstrably successful is a "hard" rather than "soft" balanced-budget requirement. The empirical literature supports the favorable effects of deficit restrictions on such measures as a state's cost of borrowing, suggesting that this is one of the more promising budgetary reforms, with the caveat that it must be both possible to define budgetary balance and legislatures must be willing to respect (or courts to enforce) balanced-budget requirements.

There is much less evidence that other arrangements make much of a difference. A number of states have experimented with variants in periodicity, but apparently without enacting the budgetary practices that would support greater rationality in fiscal policymaking. The effects of TELs are still subject to debate, in part because of technical issues related to data availability and endogeneity, in part because the strong or "extreme" measures that would be more likely to reduce spending typically have been superseded by subsequent initiatives, as in California and Colorado. And, while public-administration scholars and budget officials argue that gubernatorial veto powers (and particularly the power to reduce rather than simply eliminate line items) can act in the interests of fiscal responsibility, the few studies of veto powers do not empirically support this claim. There is clearly a need for continued attention to the interaction effects among the variety of fiscal institutions at the state level, and particularly to the manner in which gubernatorial veto and rescission powers may interact with other fiscal arrangements.

Questions for Chapter 8

1. This chapter documents considerable variation in the adoption of budgetary practices across states in different regions and population groupings. The patterns may offer insight into factors that affect the choice of particular budgetary practices, in addition to those raised elsewhere in this section, such as political ideology and previous fiscal behavior. How important might demographic factors, like size and ethnic diversity, be? Does the importance of region suggest spatial patterns of reform dissemination, or does it act as a proxy for historical differences in the development of political institutions? If in fact social, demographic, political, and cultural factors are important in the choice of fiscal institutions, what does this suggest about our ability to draw general inferences about the effectiveness of specific budgetary practices from the states?

2. Musso, Graddy, and Grizard argue that balanced-budget requirements are the most promising budgetary practice for improving fiscal rationality and prudence, but only if the requirements are enforced. Richard Briffault (in Chapter 14 of this volume) provides several examples of how the courts have chosen to enforce state budgetary restrictions. What insights do Briffault's findings have for our expectations of the capacity of the courts to perform this enforcement role? Jürgen Von Hagen (in Chapter 4 of this volume) also considers enforcement strategies in his study of European Union budgetary policy. What insights does that study of national governments in Europe offer for states in the United States?

9 The Calculus of Constraint

A Critical Review of State Fiscal Institutions

Tracy M. Gordon

Recent state fiscal crises have renewed academic and policy interest in institutions designed to limit the size or growth of government. Examples include tax and expenditure limits, balanced-budget rules, the executive line-item veto, and debt restrictions. This chapter provides a critical review of these fiscal institutions and their effectiveness, drawing on recent empirical research and highlighting unresolved questions in the literature. In particular, the chapter explores how fiscal institutions fit within dominant models of political economy, including the median-voter model and Leviathan view of government. The chapter concludes by offering an alternative contracting perspective and drawing testable propositions for future work.

I. INTRODUCTION

Recent years have been tumultuous for state government finances. A mild national recession in the early 1990s was felt strongly in certain states, prompting substantial tax hikes, spending cuts, and a depletion of fund balances. State revenues rebounded dramatically in the late 1990s, buoyed by income from the realization of capital gains and the exercise of stock options. These revenues fueled additional spending on politically popular areas such as education, health care, and tax relief.

This fiscal boom, however, was short-lived. Stock market declines in 2001 together with worsening economic conditions and a reluctance to take

Tracy M. Gordon is an Assistant Professor in the School of Public Policy at the University of Maryland and an adjunct fellow at the Public Policy Institute of California. The author acknowledges James M. Buchanan and Gordon Tullock, whose *The Calculus of Consent* (1962) inspired this chapter's title, and thanks Jaime Calleja Alderete, Elizabeth Graddy, Jon Sonstelie, Lynette Ubois, and participants in the Fiscal Challenges: An Interdisciplinary Approach to Budget Policy conference for their many helpful comments. David Haskel provided excellent research assistance. All remaining errors are the author's alone.

corrective actions generated widening gaps between projected revenues and expenditures. At the start of fiscal year 2004, states faced a combined gap of more than $78 billion. In 37 states, projected budget shortfalls were equivalent to at least 5 percent of total spending. In 19 states, they represented more than 10 percent of overall expenditures.[1]

More recently, state finances again have improved with the economy. States ended fiscal year 2006 with budget surpluses of more than $57 billion, or 10 percent of total expenditures.[2] Nevertheless, several analysts have warned that states will continue to face structural budgeting challenges in the years ahead because of rapidly escalating Medicaid costs, volatile or deteriorating tax bases, and looming retiree pension and health care obligations.

These events have stimulated policy interest in budget rules designed to control the size and growth of government. For example, in 2005, legislatures in 23 states considered spending limits modeled after Colorado's Taxpayers' Bill of Rights (TABOR), a constitutional amendment that caps state revenues at population growth plus inflation.[3] Proponents claim that these rules would have curtailed state spending growth during the 1990s and prevented the massive budget shortfalls that followed. Critics argue that TABOR limits are overly restrictive, compelling severe reductions in education, health care, and social services when these services are most needed and when countercyclical state spending can aid national economic recovery.

TABOR amendments are only one example of a tax and expenditure limit (TEL) that restricts annual revenue or expenditure increases to a fixed numerical target. These limits belong to a larger class of state fiscal institutions that includes balanced-budget requirements, enhanced executive powers over the budget such as the line-item veto, and limits on the amounts or types of debt states may issue. Although TELs emerged during the "tax revolt" of the 1970s and surged again in popularity during the 1990s, others fiscal institutions have a longer history. Many balanced-budget rules and executive-veto provisions, for example, date to states' founding constitutions, while debt restrictions emerged after several governments defaulted on their borrowing in the 1840s.[4]

Academic researchers have long been drawn to the study of state fiscal institutions. These studies often aim to shed light on national and international policy debates, such as whether the United States should adopt a constitutional balanced-budget amendment or how to ensure fiscal discipline in the European

---

[1] National Conference of State Legislatures, STATE BUDGET AND TAX ACTIONS 2003 PRELIMINARY REPORT (2003).

[2] National Conference of State Legislatures, STATE BUDGET AND TAX ACTIONS 2006 PRELIMINARY REPORT (2006).

[3] Center for Budget and Policy Priorities, STATE TABOR PROPOSALS – 2005 LEGISLATIVE SESSION (2005). Chapter 10 by Kousser et al. includes a detailed discussion of state experiences with TABOR amendments.

[4] See Chapter 11 by John Wallis and Barry Weingast, this volume, for a history of debt limits.

Union.[5] Focusing on the U.S. states enables researchers to take advantage of the rich institutional variation that exists at this level of government while avoiding the large unobserved differences that can hinder cross-country comparisons.

Efforts to draw policy lessons often are complicated, however, by weak or conflicting empirical results. The mixed empirical record for fiscal institutions may be due to their endogeneity. That is, fiscal institutions may simply represent the "congealed preferences" of the voters or legislators who enacted them.[6] To the extent that these preferences are overlooked, observed relationships between institutions and outcomes will be biased. This bias may be positive or negative. For example, if a shift in tastes leads to both the adoption of a fiscal limit and an alternate path for government spending, estimated effects of the limit will be biased upward. Conversely, if states with a history of overspending are more likely to adopt a restrictive fiscal rule, these rules may appear ineffective in a cross-sectional comparison. Understanding the origins of fiscal institutions is thus critical to evaluating their effectiveness.

This chapter reviews the existing literature on fiscal institutions from an interdisciplinary perspective rooted in economics, political science, public policy, and law. Following a brief overview of the history and prevalence of these institutions, it summarizes key empirical results and highlights technical issues that complicate identifying a causal relationship between fiscal institutions and policy outcomes. The chapter then explores how fiscal institutions may or may not fit within dominant models of political economy, including the median-voter model and Leviathan views of government. It also proposes an alternative contracting perspective based on strategic considerations as well as problems of credible commitment and dynamic inconsistency. The chapter concludes by offering directions for future work.

II. OVERVIEW OF FISCAL INSTITUTIONS

Several types of rules govern budgeting in the U.S. states. At one level, states follow certain procedures in the production, adoption, and implementation of a budget. For example, states may rely on annual or biennial budget cycles, single or multiple budget committees, and incremental-, performance- or zero-based budgeting. These practices may influence fiscal outcomes by governing transactions among policymakers and the availability of information at different stages of the process and to different policy actors. They are the focus of the chapter by Graddy et al.[7]

---

[5] *See, e.g.,* Jürgen von Hagen, *A Note on the Empirical Effectiveness of Formal Fiscal Restraints,* 44 J. Pub. Econ. 199 (1991); James Poterba, *Do Budget Rules Work?, in* Fiscal Policy: Lessons From Empirical Research 53 (A. Auerbach ed., 1997).

[6] William Riker, *Implications for the Disequilibrium of Majority Rule for the Study of Institutions,* 74 Am. Pol. Sci. Rev. 432 (1980).

[7] Juliet Ann Musso, Elizabeth A. Graddy, and Jennifer Bravo Grizard, "Budgetary Arrangements in the 50 states: In search of Model Practices," Chapter 8 of this volume.

In contrast, this chapter focuses on institutions that set the background for fiscal decision making, analogous to the "fundamental political, social, and legal ground rules" that structure economic and political activity.[8] It also focuses on institutions with explicitly fiscal objectives and not political institutions, such as the voter initiative or term limits, that may affect fiscal outcomes by altering the distribution of voter preferences or the incentives facing potential candidates for public office.[9]

Specifically, this chapter considers the following:

- TELs that link revenue or expenditure increases to a numerical target;
- Legislative supermajority or popular-majority-vote requirements for new taxes;
- Balanced-budget rules that apply *ex ante* to a governor's proposed budget or *ex post* to a legislature's enacted budget, sometimes also prohibiting carrying a deficit forward into the next fiscal year;
- Enhancements of executive budget authority to make midyear spending reductions or veto specific line items; and
- Limits on the types or amount of borrowing or debt held by the public.

The remainder of this section describes each of these institutions in detail.

A. TELs and Vote Requirements

TELs emerged during the so-called tax revolt of the late 1970s and early 1980s. Although several notable measures from this era affect local property taxes,[10] more often TELs restrict state revenues, expenditures, or both.

As of 2005, 30 states had TELs and some states had multiple limits. Twenty-three limits applied to expenditures, four applied to revenues, and three applied to both expenditures and revenues. In addition, some states had limits linking appropriations to estimated state revenues. These appropriations limits generally are considered merely advisory. Roughly half of all TELs were constitutional and half were statutory.[11]

Although many prominent limits were adopted by citizen initiative, the most common source of a TEL was the state legislature. Legislatures proposed and passed 14 TELs in place as of 2005 and proposed ten limits that voters approved as legislative referendums. Voters enacted eight TELs through the initiative process and the two remaining limits emerged from constitutional conventions.

---

[8] L. Davis and D.C. North, Institutional Change and American Economic Growth 6 (1971).

[9] Timothy Besley and Anne C. Case, *Political Institutions and Policy Choices: Evidence from the United States*, J. Econ. Literature, 2003, at 7.

[10] *See, e.g.,* California Proposition 13, Massachusetts Proposition 2½, *Supra* note 8.

[11] Mandy Rafool, State Tax and Expenditure Limits – 2005 (2005).

TELs are considered "binding" if they are difficult to override, for example if they are constitutional and amendments require a supermajority vote from both houses of the state legislature plus voter ratification. Statutory TELs also may be binding if they require a legislative supermajority or popular-majority vote to override or amend. By this definition, 18 TELs in place as of 2005 were binding.

The stringency of a TEL depends on its revenue or expenditure target. Measures like TABOR that are tied to population growth plus inflation are more restrictive than those tied to personal-income growth, which tends to increase more rapidly. As of 2005, only six TELs were linked to population and inflation whereas 19 depended on personal income.

TELs also may be more stringent if they require rebates of surplus revenues to taxpayers. Ten limits required such rebates as of 2005. Some TELs further prohibited unfunded mandates or transfers of program responsibility so that states could not evade the limit by shifting expenditures to local governments.

Related to TELs are legislative supermajority and voter-approval requirements for new taxes. Sixteen states had such requirements in place as of 2005. Thresholds for a legislative supermajority ranged from three-fifths to three-fourths. Supermajority or voter-approval requirements may pertain to all taxes or specific taxes, such as corporate or sales taxes only. The constraining effect of such rules generally depends on party control of the state legislature.

B. Balanced-Budget Rules

Federal budget debates frequently invoke the fact that all states except Vermont have some type of balanced-budget requirement (BBR). These requirements, however, vary considerably from state to state. Some rules are constitutional, some are statutory, and some are not codified but based on judicial interpretations of constitutional provisions on indebtedness.

There are three primary types of BBRs. The most lenient type requires governors to submit a balanced budget (44 states). More stringent BBRs require that legislatures enact or that governors sign a balanced budget (40 and 34 states, respectively).[12] These rules are all prospective in nature. The most severe type of BBR requires that actual revenues and expenditures are in balance and prevents a state from carrying a deficit forward into the next fiscal year. These rules existed in 37 states as of 1999, the last year for which comprehensive data are available.[13]

---

[12] National Association of State Budget Officers, BUDGET PROCESSES IN THE STATES (2002).

[13] National Conference of State Legislatures, LEGISLATIVE BUDGET PROCEDURES: A GUIDE TO APPROPRIATIONS AND BUDGET PROCESSES IN THE STATES, COMMONWEALTHS, AND TERRITORIES (1999).

Balanced-budget rules also vary in their scope. They typically apply to current but not capital expenditures and to state general funds but not funds earmarked for specific purposes, such as highway trust funds, federal funds, or public-sector enterprises. In a 1992 survey, most states reported that their BBRs covered at least 75 percent of total budgets. Nine states, however, indicated that their rules applied to 50 percent to 75 percent of the budget and three said that their rules covered less than half of the budget.[14]

C. Line-Item Veto

Governors have wide-ranging authority over state budgets, including the ability to reorganize departments or to spend unallocated funds without legislative approval. In 36 states, they have at least conditional authority to make midyear spending reductions in response to unforeseen events or fiscal emergencies. Conditions include requirements that cuts be uniform across agencies or limited to a fixed amount. In some states, governors also must consult with an independent state agency or the state legislature before making spending cuts.[15]

A more powerful gubernatorial tool is the ability to selectively reject provisions of the legislative budget. Forty-two states allow their governors to reject specific lines from the budget and 40 states allow them to alter particular items – including paragraphs, sentences, and, in some cases, individual letters – as long as these changes do not alter the "original meaning" of the budget legislation.[16]

D. Debt Limits

States vary in their ability to issue debt for long-lived capital projects. Eleven states prohibit the issuance of guaranteed long-term debt that pledges the full faith and credit of the state or whatever taxes are necessary to meet principal and interest payments. These states may still issue bonds secured by specific sources of income (i.e., revenue bonds).

Of the 39 states that allow general obligation bonds, all but nine states have rules limiting debt outstanding as a percentage of state budgets or at a specific dollar amount.[17] Some states have procedural requirements, such as approval from a legislative supermajority (12 states) or popular majority (20 states), to issue general obligation bonds above a minimal amount. In some cases, these provisions may be overridden by a voter referendum or a declaration of fiscal emergency by the governor. In addition, as Kiewiet and Szakalay[18] point out,

---

[14] National Association of State Budget Officers, STATE BALANCED BUDGET REQUIREMENTS: PROVISIONS AND PRACTICE (1992).

[15] *Supra* note 12.   [16] *Supra* note 11.

[17] *Id.*

[18] Rod Kiewiet and Kristin Szakalay, *Constitutional Limits on Borrowing: An Analysis of State Bonded Indebtedness*, 12 J. L., ECON. & ORG. 62 (1996).

even states with prohibitions on guaranteed debt may borrow to cover "casual" deficits or to address extraordinary circumstances.

III. DO FISCAL INSTITUTIONS WORK?

An emerging consensus in the political economy literature indicates that "institutions matter."[19] However, this consensus is often challenged by empirical findings of small, weak, or counterintuitive effects. One issue is that fiscal institutions are a diverse set of tools with a variety of aims including the containment of revenues, spending, deficits, or debt. Mixed findings may be due to different choices of outcome variables as well as differences among institutions in the proportion of budgets covered or in their susceptibility to evasion through superficial accounting changes.[20]

More fundamentally, as noted earlier, institutions may be endogenous, or merely proxies for political preferences and other omitted variables. Many studies take state institutional variation to be exogenous and, after accounting for contemporaneous political, economic, and demographic effects, attribute any remaining fiscal differences to the presence of an institution. Following this approach, Abrams and Dougan,[21] for example, find no effect of the line-item veto, TELs, or strict BBRs on state spending.

The exogeneity assumption is appealing because state institutions often have a long history and thus are considered predetermined. This identification strategy will be flawed, however, if unmeasured state characteristics drive both the adoption of institutions and fiscal outcomes and these unobserved features are correlated over time. For example, states with strong progressive political traditions may have been more likely to enact fiscal institutions in the early 20th century, and they also may continue to attract residents who are more politically engaged. A particularly difficult case is where lagged values of the fiscal outcome (e.g., higher spending) lead to the adoption or enforcement of an institution.

A second group of studies exploits the panel nature of data on state fiscal institutions. These models permit the inclusion of state and year indicator variables or fixed effects, thereby potentially absorbing the effects of state history or political culture as well as economic conditions or events affecting all states in a given year. Holtz-Eakin,[22] for instance, presents cross-sectional estimates of the effects of the line-item veto that are similar to those found in previous studies. However, his panel estimates that also control for both divided government and party control of legislature show that the line-item veto can be effective

---

[19] *See, e.g.,* Besley and Case, *supra* note 9.   [20] *See* Poterba, *supra* note 5.

[21] Burton A. Abrams and William R. Dougan, *The Effects of Constitutional Restraints on Governmental Spending,* 49 PUB. CHOICE 101 (1986).

[22] Douglas Holtz-Eakin, *The Line Item Veto and Public Sector Budgets: Evidence from the States,* 36 J. PUB. ECON. 269 (1988).

in lowering spending and raising taxes, thereby reducing deficits. Similarly, Bohn and Inman[23] find that strict balanced-budget rules reduce spending after controlling for state fixed effects.

As we have seen, however, some institutions such as balanced-budget rules and debt limits do not vary much over time. In this case, state fixed effects are perfectly correlated with the presence of an institution and may not enter separately into the model. Many studies that pool multiple observations per state thus rely on cross-sectional variation for identification.

One way to circumvent this problem is to focus on a time-varying relationship that theory suggests should be mediated by the presence of a restrictive fiscal institution.[24] For example, Poterba[25] examines the interaction of fiscal rules and deficit shocks. He finds that states with strict balanced-budget rules and TELs are quicker to reduce spending in response to a shock, particularly when there is unified party control of the executive and legislative branches of government.

Another identification strategy is to rely on an instrumental variable that affects the adoption of an institution but not the policy variable of interest. The instrument is essentially substituted for the institution in either a two-stage or single-equation model. For example, Rueben[26] uses the availability of the citizen initiative and recall procedures as instruments for the likelihood of a strict TEL. She finds that taxes constitute a lower proportion of personal income in states with these rules. State expenditures are also lower, but these differences are offset by higher government spending at the local level. Similarly, Knight[27] uses the availability of direct legislation as well as the ease of amending the state constitution as instruments and finds that supermajority requirements reduce taxes. Because these instruments do not vary over time, however, these models do not include state indicator variables to absorb the effects of political history or culture. More generally, a question arises with time-invariant instruments as to why they affect the adoption of a fiscal institution in any given year.

In sum, establishing a causal relationship between fiscal institutions and outcomes is complicated. Ignoring factors that may drive both the enactment of a fiscal institution and government finances can bias empirical results. Including state and year fixed effects can account for long-term differences in state political culture or contemporaneous conditions that affect government finances.

[23] Henning Bohn and Robert P. Inman, *Balanced Budget Rules and Public Deficits: Evidence from the U.S. States* (Nat'l Bureau of Econ. Research Working Paper No. W5533, 1996).

[24] Besley and Case, *supra* note 9.

[25] James M. Poterba, *State Responses to Fiscal Crises: The Effects of Budgetary Institutions and Politics*, 102 J. Pol. Econ. 799 (1994).

[26] Kim S. Rueben, *Tax Limitations and Government Growth: The Effect of State Tax and Expenditure Limits on State and Local Government* (Public Policy Institute of California Working Paper, 1996).

[27] Brian J. Knight, *Supermajority Voting Requirements for Tax Increases: Evidence from the States*, 76 J. Pub. Econ. 41 (2000).

However, fixed effects cannot account for state-specific temporal changes, such as changes in unobserved attitudes. Fixed effects also may not be feasible where institutions do not change over the period of observation. This situation may require an instrumental variable that is correlated with the passage of a fiscal limit but not the outcome of interest. Evaluating a potential instrument requires understanding why institutions are adopted, or enforced after years of latency, and how even a fixed instrument can help precipitate this change.

IV. WHY DO FISCAL INSTITUTIONS COME ABOUT?

In light of the importance of understanding the causes that drive the adoption of fiscal institutions to appropriately model their consequences, it is unfortunate that traditional models of political economy leave many questions on fiscal institutions unanswered. This section reviews these models and their applicability to fiscal institutions with an emphasis on empirically testable hypotheses.

A. Median-Voter Model

The median-voter model holds that, under certain conditions, the favored outcome of the voter at the median of the preference distribution in a series of repeated binary comparisons will be a stable majority-voting equilibrium. A related insight is that candidates in a two-party election should gravitate toward the median of the preference distribution as long as they are able to commit to this position.[28] Conditions for this equilibrium typically include restrictions on individual preferences, in particular single-peakedness or symmetry around an ideal point, as well as a single-dimensional policy space.[29]

The ubiquity of the median-voter model in political economy research is due in part to its direct translation into an empirically testable relationship between government expenditures and voter characteristics. For example,

$$G_i = \alpha P_i + \beta Y_i + \eta_i, \tag{1}$$

where G_i is the level of public spending in community i, P_i is the tax price of a public good, Y_i is the income of the median voter, and η_i is an error term. If these variables are expressed in logarithms, their coefficients have the interpretation of elasticities of demand with respect to price and income, respectively. Empirical tests of the median-voter model have confirmed a positive relationship between public spending levels and the economic characteristics of voters.[30]

[28] Anthony Downs, An Economic Theory of Democracy (1957).

[29] Duncan Black, The Theory of Committees and Elections (1958); H. R. Bowen, *The Interpretation of Voting in the Allocation of Economic Resources*, 58 Q.J. Econ. 27 (1943).

[30] Thomas E. Borchering and Robert T. Deacon, *The Demand for Services of Non-Federal Governments*, Am. Econ. Rev. 891 (1972); Theodore C. Bergstrom and Robert P. Goodman, *Private Demands for Public Goods*, 63 Am. Econ. Rev. 280 (1973).

However, the prevalence of fiscal institutions poses a challenge to the median-voter model: if the median voter prefers a smaller public sector and his or her preferences are decisive, why should additional constraints on elected representatives be necessary?

One explanation is that, although stable, the majority-voting equilibrium is not necessarily efficient. The reason is that this outcome does not account for the intensities of voter preferences. If voters who prefer lower expenditures have more inelastic demand for public spending with respect to income, and all voters face a constant tax price, the welfare difference between preferred and actual spending levels for the low-demand group may exceed this difference for the high-demand group.

In this context, fiscal limits that reduce expenditures below the amount desired by the median voter achieve net welfare gains. The realization of these gains, however, depends on the availability of mechanisms for "winners" to compensate "losers" under the fiscal limit. In practice, it is unclear how such compensation would occur. For example, citizen-initiated TELs do not typically include provisions to compensate those who would prefer higher public spending.

Another possibility is that fiscal limits arise because the median voter's preferences have changed, perhaps in response to an exogenous shock. For example, Fischel[31] attributes the passage of California's Proposition 13 to a state Supreme Court decision mandating the equalization of school finances across districts, thereby severing the relationship between local property taxes and school resources. Dougan[32] suggests that in this context voters may rely on fiscal limits as a signal of a preference shift that is less costly than replacing incumbent representatives. Similarly, legislators may support fiscal limits under these circumstances to signal that they recognize a change has occurred despite inevitable lags in adjustment.

Other explanations for fiscal institutions in a median-voter framework involve violations of assumptions underlying the model. In particular, preferences may be multipeaked. A well-known example occurs when there are private alternatives to public-service provision yet all voters are liable for the tax cost of public services, as in the case of K–12 education.[33] Under these circumstances, a voting equilibrium may not exist or it may not correspond to the preferences of the median voter. In particular, a coalition of low- and high-demand consumers can ensure a level of public-service delivery that is lower than desired by the median voter.[34]

[31] William A. Fischel, *Did Serrano Cause Proposition 13?*, 43 NAT'L TAX J. 465 (1989).
[32] William R. Dougan, *The Effects of Tax and Expenditure Limits on State Governments* (George G. Stigler Center for Study of Economy and State Paper No. 54, 1988).
[33] A. Atkinson and J. Stiglitz, LECTURES ON PUBLIC ECONOMICS 303–304 (1980).
[34] Dennis Epple and Robert Romano, *Ends Against the Middle: Determining Public Service Provision When There are Private Alternatives*, 62 J. PUB. ECON. 297 (1996).

Similarly, the policy space may include more than one dimension, such as the level of public spending and regulation, ideology, or even personality. If this is the case, a stable majority-voting equilibrium can still exist under strong symmetry conditions on preferences.[35] In practice, these conditions are so restrictive that majority cycling should be the norm in the absence of a voting agenda.[36]

If we allow for multipeaked preferences or a multidimensional policy space, fiscal institutions may be viewed as the result of cycling majorities. However, if this were the case, we would expect substantial volatility in this area, as shifting coalitions of voters or legislators proposed and rescinded fiscal rules. Although voters do occasionally suspend or modify existing limits (e.g., Colorado's TABOR in November 2005), in practice we do not observe the policy "chaos" predicted from theory.

In sum, the prevalence and stability of fiscal institutions is puzzling in light of the median-voter model unless there has been a permanent shift in underlying voter preferences and institutions are a cost-effective signal of this change. The median-voter model has been criticized on a number of grounds, however, including the restrictiveness of its assumptions. More fundamentally, the model ignores the supply side of politics and the potentially nonwelfare-enhancing objectives of government actors. To understand these objectives requires another perspective, as discussed in the next section.

B. Leviathan View

Traditional public economics views budget deficits as the result of a benevolent social planner's tax-smoothing problem.[37] The public-choice school challenges this normative view by portraying governments as revenue- or budget-maximizing Leviathans. In this framework, constitutional rules are needed to secure the benefits of government in terms of property-rights enforcement and public-goods provision while minimizing the threat of excessive taxation and spending.[38]

An immediate question provoked by this framework is how exploitative governments can persist in spite of electoral competition. The primary answer

---

[35] Charles Plott, *A Notion of Equilibrium and its Possibility Under Majority Rule*, 57 Am. Econ. Rev. 787 (1967).

[36] Richard D. McKelvey, *Intransitivities in Multidimensional Voting Models and Some Implications for Agenda Control*, 2 J. Econ. Theory 472 (1976); Kenneth A. Shepsle, *Institutional Arrangements and Equilibrium in Multidimensional Voting Models*, 23 Am. J. Pol. Sci. 27 (1979).

[37] Robert J. Barro, *On the Determination of the Public Debt*, 87 J. Pol. Econ. 940 (1979); Robert Lucas and Edith Stokey, *Optimal Fiscal and Monetary Policy in an Economy Without Capital*, 12 J. Monetary Econ. 55 (1983).

[38] Geoffrey F. Brennan and James M. Buchanan, The Power to Tax: Analytical Foundations of a Fiscal Constitution (1980); Geoffrey F. Brennan and James M. Buchanan, *The Logic of Tax Limits: Alternative Constitutional Constraints on the Power to Tax*, 32 Nat'l Tax J. 11 (1979); Geoffrey Brennan and James M. Buchanan, *Towards a Tax Constitution for Leviathan*, 8 J. Pub. Econ. 255 (1977).

is information asymmetries between voters and their elected representatives. In particular, government outputs are difficult to measure, particularly when there are no competitors, leaving voters to monitor inputs or activities instead. A related principal–agent problem can exist between legislators and executive agencies charged with carrying out government programs.[39]

Another potential source of government exploitation is agenda control. In particular, legislators or bureaucrats may use their monopoly over the budget to propose a "take-it-or-leave it" reversion level of spending below that which would be preferred by the median voter. This reversion offer defines a range of alternatives up to a point that is equivalently above the median voter's ideal level of spending. The median voter is indifferent between these two outcomes if his or her preferences are symmetric around an ideal point. Thus, public spending may not be at the median voter's preferred level but some positive multiple of that quantity.[40]

In addition, groups outside of government will attempt to skew the policy agenda, expending resources up to the value of potential gains or rents to do so.[41] In response, policymakers will not necessarily maximize consumer welfare but some combination of this quantity plus interest-group benefits. Interest groups will be more sensitive to changes in proposed policies because they bear more concentrated benefits or costs compared to voters.[42] As a result, policymakers may forego increases in electoral support from informed voters in exchange for campaign contributions from interest groups that can be used to win over uninformed voters.[43]

If governments do not act as benevolent social planners, fiscal institutions may be a necessary corrective. Indeed, Brennan and Buchanan[44] viewed the adoption of a strong fiscal constitution in a pregovernmental setting as the only effective means of protection against Leviathan.

A question arises, however, as to why such limits do not exist universally, or at least in all states where voters can enact legislation directly through the initiative process. A solution to this apparent difficulty is that in states with

---

[39] William A. Niskanen, *Bureaucrats and Politicians*, 18 J.L. & ECON. 617 (1975); William A. Niskanen, BUREAUCRACY AND REPRESENTATIVE GOVERNMENT (1971); William A. Niskanen, *Non-Market Decision Making: The Peculiar Economics of Bureaucracy*, AM. ECON. REV. 293 (1968).

[40] Thomas Romer and Howard Rosenthal, *The Elusive Median Voter*, 12 J. PUB. ECON.143 (1979); Thomas Romer and Howard Rosenthal, *Bureaucrats Versus Voters: On the Political Economy of Resource Allocation by Direct Democracy*, Q.J. ECON., Nov. 1979, at 563.

[41] Gordon Tullock, *The Welfare Costs of Tariffs, Subsidies, and Theft*, 5 W. ECON. J. 224 (1967).

[42] George J. Stigler, *The Theory of Economic Regulation*, 3 BELL J. ECON. & MGMT. SCI. 33 (1971); Sam Peltzman, *Toward a More General Theory of Regulation*, 19 J.L. & ECON. 211–40 (1976).

[43] David P. Baron, *Electoral Competition with Informed and Uniformed Voters*, 88 AM. POL. SCI. REV. 33–47 (1994); Gene M. Grossman and Elhanan Helpman, *Electoral Competition and Special Interest Politics*, 63 REV. ECON. STUD. 265 (1996).

[44] Geoffrey F. Brennan and James M. Buchanan (1980), *supra* note 38.

the initiative, the threat alone of a fiscal limit may be sufficient to prevent government exploitation. For example, Gerber[45] and Matsusaka[46] find social and fiscal policies closer to the ideal points of voters in states where direct legislation is permitted.

However, a more vexing problem for the Leviathan model is that fiscal institutions often are adopted by legislatures themselves. For example, 14 of 34 TELs in place as of 2005 were enacted by legislatures as statutes while another ten were enacted by voters after being referred to an election by the state legislature. Moreover, half of these legislatively originated TELs existed in states where the citizen initiative was unavailable. Explaining these limits requires a different kind of model.

C. Contracting Perspective

The hallmark of fiscal institutions is that they remove discretion over the budget. This feature raises the question of why legislators would ever limit their own future choices, assuming that fiscal constraints are binding. One answer comes from new institutional economics literature applied to the organization of Congress. Namely, legislators may be willing to sacrifice power to obtain costly information or enforce durable bargains.[47] In particular, legislators may be willing to cede power to solve a collective-action problem.[48]

A type of collective-action problem occurs whenever the benefits of spending are localized yet costs are borne by all. The result is overspending, particularly when there is also a legislative norm of universalism or reciprocity.[49] Institutional fixes to this common-resource problem include delegations of authority to party leaders for decisions on committee assignments, the sequence of voting, and amendment rules (e.g., closed versus open voting rules).

Legislatures similarly may be willing to adopt institutions that limit the size or growth of government to address the fiscal commons problem. Restrictive fiscal institutions thus should be more common in states with larger legislatures, where the "law of $1/n$" suggests there will also be higher public spending. Empirical tests of this proposition are complicated by a potential reverse causality problem – higher spending may generate demand for more legislators. In studies of this question, researchers thus have relied on instruments for

---

[45] Elisabeth R. Gerber, *Legislative Response to the Threat of Popular Initiatives*, 40 Am. J. Pol. Sci. 99 (1996).

[46] John G. Matsusaka, For the Many or the Few: How the Initiative Process Changes American Government (2004).

[47] Barry R. Weingast and William J. Marshall, *The Industrial Organization of Congress; or, Why Legislatures, Like Firms, are not Organized as Markets*, 96 J. Pol. Econ. 132 (1988).

[48] Gary W. Cox and Mathew D. McCubbins, Legislative Leviathan (1993).

[49] Barry R. Weingast, Kenneth A. Shepsle, and Christopher Johnsen, *The Political Economy of Benefits and Costs: A Neoclassical Approach to Distributive Politics*, 89 J. Pol. Econ. 642 (1981).

legislative size, including the lagged-values of this variable and topographical variation such as rivers and streams.[50]

Apart from efficiency, legislators may enact restrictive fiscal institutions for strategic reasons. For example, Knight[51] provides a theoretical justification for the apparent anomaly that the bulk of supermajority-vote requirements are enacted by Democratic state legislatures. He shows that the median legislator in these states may be willing to sacrifice having a pivotal vote on taxes to prevent the median legislator from within his or her own party from exercising agenda-setting power to propose reversion offers resulting in higher tax rates.[52]

The durable nature of fiscal constraints suggests that legislators also may use these rules to "insulate" policy preferences over time.[53] More formally, the current government acts as a principal to the subsequent government agent. Although it cannot observe the efforts of its successor, it can design an incentive schedule that induces the desired behavior by manipulating state variables in the future government's decision problem.

In support of this notion, Persson and Svensson[54] demonstrate that a fiscally conservative government strongly attached to its ideal level of public spending will issue excessive debt to constrain future spending choices. Similarly, Alesina and Tabellini[55] show that a government can use borrowing strategically to impose its own priorities on the composition of future spending. In addition, Glazer[56] shows how a desire to influence future policy can bias current spending toward capital projects.

An implication of these models is that dynamic, strategic behavior should be more common when electoral prospects of the party in control of the legislature are weak. De Figueiredo[57] finds this to be the case in the adoption of the line-item veto. Namely, fiscal conservatives with a history of being in the minority or a greater prospective likelihood of being voted out of office are more likely to enact this restrictive institution. Another testable implication of this argument is that fiscal institutions should be adopted when there is greater ideological division between the two major parties.

In addition to controlling their successors, legislatures may adopt restrictive fiscal institutions to bind themselves. Governments often face *ex post* incentives

---

[50] Reza Baqir, *Districting and Government Overspending*, J. POL. ECON., Dec. 2002, at 110.

[51] Knight, supra note 27.

[52] *See, e.g.*, Romer and Rosenthal, *supra* note 40.

[53] Terry M. Moe, *The Politics of Bureaucratic Structure*, in CAN THE GOVERNMENT GOVERN? (John E. Chubb and P. E. Petersen eds., 1989).

[54] Torsten Persson and Lars O. Svensson, *Why a Stubborn Conservative Would Run a Deficit: Policy with Time-Inconsistent Preferences*, Q.J. ECON., May 1989, at 325.

[55] Alberto Alesina and Guido Tabellini, *A Positive Theory of Fiscal Deficits and Government Debt*, 57 REV. ECON. STU. 403–414 (1990).

[56] Amihai Glazer, *Politics and the Choice of Durability*, 79 AM. ECON. REV. 1207 (1989).

[57] Rui J. P. de Figueiredo, Jr., *Endogenous Budget Institutions and Political Insulation: Why States Adopt the Item Veto*, 8 J. PUB. ECON. 2677 (2003).

to deviate from *ex ante* optimal policies. In the macroeconomics literature this is known as a dynamic inconsistency problem.[58] The paradigmatic case involves a government announcing an inflation target and then reneging once firms have responded with their own wage contracts, allowing slightly more inflation to yield output gains. As a result, forward-looking rational agents will not believe a proposal unless it is credible, self-enforcing, or optimal for a government to carry out in the future. Future incentive compatibility thus imposes a constraint on the current decision problem, with potential welfare costs including failures to undertake Pareto-improving investments.[59]

Dynamic inconsistency problems can arise in fiscal as well as monetary policy. For example, political candidates may announce spending platforms that reflect preferences of the median voter, but these candidates may implement their own ideologies once in office.[60] Because they cannot credibly commit to another position, candidates will choose platforms that at least partially diverge from the median voter's ideal point in two-party elections rather than the full-convergence result predicted by the median-voter model.[61]

More directly analogous to the inflation example, incentives to deviate from an announced fiscal policy may arise as a result of the announcement itself. For example, setting a lower target for overall public spending may induce more vigorous lobbying on the part of interest groups as they compete for a larger proportion of a smaller whole. Fiscal institutions can alleviate this pressure by raising the costs of government responsiveness to future conditions.[62] For example, Lowry et al. show that voters react more negatively to deficits and adverse changes in bond ratings when strict balanced-budget rules are in place. In this sense, fiscal institutions heighten attention to budgeting and delegate monitoring and enforcement of fiscal discipline to interested third parties.[63]

Based on this reasoning, we would expect legislatures to enact fiscal limits when they are ideologically inclined toward smaller government yet face difficulties in credibly committing to this policy. Commitment problems may be more severe when there are larger state legislatures, stronger interest groups,

---

[58] Finn E. Kydland and Edward C. Prescott, *Rules Rather Than Discretion: The Inconsistency of Optimal Plans*, 85 J. Pol. Econ. 473 (1977); Robert J. Barro and David B. Gordon, *A Positive Theory of Monetary Policy in a Natural Rate Model*, 91 J. Pol. Econ. 589 (1983); Finn E. Kydland and Edward C. Prescott, *Rules Rather Than Discretion: The Inconsistency of Optimal Plans*, 85 J. Pol. Econ. 473 (1977).

[59] Timothy Besley and Stephen Coate, *Sources of Inefficiency in a Representative Democracy: A Dynamic Analysis*, 88 Am. Econ. Rev. 139 (1998).

[60] *See, e.g.*, Joseph P. Kalt and Mark A. Zupan, *Capture and Ideology in the Economic Theory of Politics*, 74 Am. Econ. Rev. 279 (1984).

[61] Alberto, Alesina, *Credibility and Policy Convergence in a Two-Party System with Rational Voters*, 78 Am. Econ. Rev. 796 (1988).

[62] D. Rodrik and R. Zeckhauser, *The Dilemma of Government Responsiveness*, 7 J. Pol'y Analysis and Mgmt. 605 (1988).

[63] Mathew McCubbins and Thomas Schwartz, *Congressional Oversight Overlooked: Police Patrols Versus Fire Alarms*, 28 Am. J. Pol. Sci. 165 (1984).

and weaker electoral accountability from other sources such as term limits and the citizen initiative. The latter implication distinguishes the credible commitment explanation from the strategic use of fiscal institutions. For example, legislators with longer terms in office should have less need to bind their successors.[64] However, they will face greater incentives during their own terms to deviate from announced policies. Aware of this problem, legislators may adopt restrictive fiscal institutions, analogous to other examples of individuals exercising self-control.[65]

V. CONCLUSIONS

This chapter has provided a critical review of state fiscal institutions. Although recent state fiscal crises have heightened attention in this area, these rules have deep historical roots. They have long been a source of academic study because of their parallels to national and international structures as well as their centrality to the intersection of politics and economics.

The chapter shows that fiscal institutions are prevalent throughout the United States. They also exhibit considerable variation. Studies that ignore this heterogeneity may overlook the effectiveness of certain types of institutions. More troubling, many studies of fiscal institutions fail to account for the causes of institutions and the extent to which these factors also may determine fiscal outcomes.

To shed light on the causes of fiscal institutions, this chapter reviews the dominant median-voter and Leviathan models of political economy. Though illuminating budget politics more generally, these approaches provide little insight into the timing of an institutional change. The median-voter model can accommodate fiscal institutions as signals of a lasting shift in voter preferences, but it does not suggest sources of this change other than an exogenous shock. The Leviathan framework implies that fiscal institutions are needed to restrain the opportunistic behavior of policy actors, yet it does not explain how these institutions emerge outside of a stylized constitutional setting or from legislators themselves.

This omission is unfortunate because the dynamics of institutional choice are at the crux of the identification issue. In particular, the choice of an appropriate instrumental variable depends on a theoretical understanding of institutional change. To this end, the chapter has proposed an alternative contracting perspective. In a static context, this approach suggests that fiscal institutions may be Coasian solutions to a fiscal commons problem or a conflict over agenda control

---

[64] W. Mark Crain and R. D. Tollison, *Time Inconsistency and Fiscal Policy: Empirical Analysis of U.S. States, 1969–89*, 51 J. Pub. Econ. 153 (1993).

[65] Richard H. Thaler and H. M. Shefrin, *An Economic Theory of Self Control*, 89 J. Pol. Econ. 392 (1981).

within a party. However, the dynamic nature of fiscal institutions allows for strategic interactions between successive legislatures and commitment devices within a given legislature over time. Distinguishing between the latter two explanations may be possible based on the presence or absence of other political institutions that promote electoral accountability or self-control. This is a promising direction for future work.

Questions for Chapter 9

1. Several authors in this volume raise the issue of the consequences of endogeneity in the choice of fiscal institutions. Endogeneity here refers to the possibility that an apparent relationship between fiscal institutions and fiscal performance could reflect the influence of a variable not included in the analysis. Past fiscal performance in the jurisdiction or voter preferences about fiscal behavior, for example, could affect both the choice of fiscal institutions and fiscal performance.[66] The danger is that we believe a relationship exists when in fact one does not (i.e., estimates of the relationship are biased). For example, a newly fiscally conservative state may adopt a tax or expenditure limitation (TEL) and, at the same time, choose to reduce expenditures. This could make the TEL appear more effective than it is, as the outcome reflects a change in preferences, not the effectiveness of the policy intervention. Gordon offers the most complete description of the nature of this problem and explores its implications for drawing empirical inferences. What are the implications of her analysis for our ability to draw on the experiences of U.S. states for insights into the effectiveness of fiscal institutions more generally? How are the implications different for the federal government than for the component nations of the European Union? How might the broad trends toward smaller government throughout much of the world over the past two decades affect these concerns?

2. After developing the importance of understanding the origins of fiscal institutions, Gordon analyzes how the choice of fiscal institutions fits within the current dominant political economy models. She finds both the median-voter and the Leviathan models wanting, and argues that a contracting perspective in which legislators are willing to cede some power to solve a collective-action problem offers a more compelling theoretical framework for understanding the

---

[66] For a broader discussion, *see* Alberto F. Alesina and Roberto Perotti, *Budget Deficits and Budget Institutions* (Nat'l Bureau of Econ. Research Working Paper No. 5556, 1995); James M. Poterba, *Budget Institutions and Fiscal Policy in the U.S. States*, 86 Am. Econ. Rev. 2 (1996).

choice of fiscal institutions. Which collective problems are the most problematic for our understanding of the implications of changes in fiscal institutions? What are the implications of this framework for understanding reforms that derive from the initiative process? Importantly, she argues that this framework can explain the timing of institutional changes. How does the contracting framework inform the dynamics of institutional choice, and how will this understanding enhance our ability to draw meaningful conclusions about the effectiveness of specific institutional reforms?

10 When Does the Ballot Box Limit the Budget?

Politics and Spending Limits in California, Colorado, Utah, and Washington

Thad Kousser, Mathew D. McCubbins, and Kaj Rozga

The debate over whether to enact a tax and expenditure limit (TEL) in California has been one of the key policy battles of Arnold Schwarzenegger's governorship. During the recall campaign, Schwarzenegger voiced his support for a limit as a cold turkey cure for the legislature's "addiction" to spending.[1] Soon after his election, he threatened to propose an initiative capping total expenditures, though he eventually compromised and worked with Democrats to enact a tighter balanced-budget requirement.[2] Two years later, he followed through on his threat and put a spending limit on the ballot, only to see it lose badly when voters blanched at the school funding cuts that it might deliver. Rarely mentioned in this debate over whether California needs a TEL, however, is the fact that it already has one.

Proposition 4, the "Gann limit," was passed in 1979 as part of the state's famed tax revolt and established a formula limiting the growth of expenditures of tax dollars. Although its formula has been modified, the Gann limit is still in effect, and Poterba and Rueben's cross-state analysis of TELs still categorizes it as "binding."[3] Yet California's fiscal history – along with the current debate over a spending limit – suggests that the Gann limit has not constrained the growth of state government. Since its passage, total spending in the state has continued to exceed the national average by about the same margin. In only one year did the limit force the state to give its taxpayers a rebate, and the

---

[1] John Simerman, *Schwarzenegger's Advisors Work on Plan to Cap California Spending*, CONTRA COSTA TIMES, Oct. 22, 2003.
[2] Dion Nissenbaum, *The First 100 Days: Schwarzenegger Exploits Intellect, Gift for Connecting with People*, SAN JOSE MERCURY NEWS, Feb. 22, 2004; Harrison Sheppard, *What's Been Done? What's Still to Do?*, L.A. DAILY NEWS, Feb. 21, 2004.
[3] James M. Poterba and Kim S. Rueben, *Fiscal News, State Budget Rules, and Tax-Exempt Bond Yields*, 50 J. URBAN ECON. 537 (2001).

Mathew D. McCubbins is the Chancellor's Associates Chair and Distinguished Professor of Political Science; Thad Kousser is an associate professor of political science; Kaj Rozga is a graduate; all of the University of California, San Diego.

"wiggle room" measured by the difference between state funds subject to the limit and the cap itself has averaged $4.8 billion annually since Proposition 4's passage.[4] Some of this leniency likely was anticipated by the sponsors of the initiative, and some may be due to the way that 1978's Proposition 13 made it harder to raise taxes in the state. Still, the moral of the Gann limit's story is that California's existing TEL has done little to curb state spending.

This is not terribly surprising. Tax and expenditure limits belong to a general class of political phenomena that attempt a tough trick: locking in the preferences of a set of political principals by constraining the future actions of potentially hostile agents. Either voters are trying to limit state lawmakers, or legislators in one era are attempting to slow the growth of government under future lawmakers.[5] Regardless, the proponents of these limits face the common principal–agent delegation problem, made especially challenging by the fact that they are trying to constrain behavior long into the future, when they are likely not to be around to monitor it.[6] This is similar to the dilemma faced by legislators attempting to control the executive branch,[7] legislators on the floor delegating power to committees,[8] members of Congress trying to discipline the budgetary decisions of future Congresses,[9] and voters giving over power to elected officials.[10]

Tax and expenditure limits seem to fall into this category, because lawmakers charged with implementing a limit may be hostile to the goals of its backers. If

[4] California Department of Finance, GOVERNOR'S BUDGET 2005 – BACKGROUND INFORMATION, CHART L: HISTORICAL DATA, STATE APPROPRIATIONS LIMIT, *available at* http://www.dof.ca.gov/HTML/BUD_DOCS/backinfo.htm (last visited Feb. 2005).

[5] Fifteen of the 53 tax or spending limits enacted in the American states (some states have enacted both types of limits, and some multiple limits of each type) were adopted through the initiative process. Daniel R. Mullins and Bruce A. Wallin, *Tax and Expenditure Limitations: Introduction and Overview*, 24 PUB. BUDGETING & FIN. 2, 13 (Dec. 2004). Legislators played a role in the adoption of the others, either in an attempt to constrain future spending or to act collectively to restrain themselves from their individual incentives to spend.

[6] In fact, Proposition 4 author Paul Gann has passed away, though the "People's Advocate" antitax group that he founded lives on.

[7] David Epstein and Sharyn O'Halloran, DELEGATING POWERS: A TRANSACTION COST POLITICS APPROACH TO POLICY MAKING UNDER SEPARATE POWERS (1999); John D. Huber and Charles R. Shipan, DELIBERATE DISCRETION? THE INSTITUTIONAL FOUNDATIONS OF BUREAUCRATIC AUTONOMY (2002); D. Roderick Kiewiet and Mathew D. McCubbins, THE LOGIC OF DELEGATION: CONGRESSIONAL PARTIES AND THE APPROPRIATIONS PROCESS (1991); Arthur Lupia and Mathew D. McCubbins, THE DEMOCRATIC DILEMMA: CAN CITIZENS LEARN WHAT THEY NEED TO KNOW?(1998).

[8] Gary M. Cox and Mathew McCubbins, LEGISLATIVE LEVIATHAN: PARTY GOVERNMENT IN THE HOUSE (1993); Richard F. Fenno, CONGRESSMEN IN COMMITTEES (1973); Keith Krehbiel, INFORMATION AND LEGISLATIVE ORGANIZATION (1991); David Rohde, PARTIES AND LEADERS IN THE POSTREFORM HOUSE(1991).

[9] Allen Schick, THE FEDERAL BUDGET: POLITICS, POLICY, PROCESS (1995).

[10] Elisabeth R. Gerber and Arthur Lupia, *Campaign Competition and Policy Responsiveness in Direct Legislation Elections*, 17 POL. BEHAV. 287 (1995); Arthur Lupia, *Busy Voters, Agenda Control, and the Power of Information*, 86 AM. POL. SCI. REV. 390 (1992).

lawmakers were fiscally conservative, why would anyone need to constrain them in the first place? We expect that the lawmakers subject to a spending or revenue limit are canny operators with demanding constituencies who often want to see government grow at a faster rate than the limit prescribes. Because it can be difficult to monitor state fiscal actions, lawmakers may have the ability to circumvent limits in ways that are buried deep in the details of thousand-page budget documents. From this viewpoint, it makes sense that the first studies of TELs "found limitations to be less effective than their sponsors may have desired."[11] But the framers of limits are also strategic political actors who can anticipate end runs around their limits and attempt to stop them or at least dictate their form. Especially in the most recent wave of TELs, their proponents may have figured out how to be effective principals. Whether they can be successful, to what extent, and what shape the evasions of constraints take are all important not only for assessing the effectiveness of TELs as a mechanism for controlling budgets but also for learning about principal–agent relations in general.

To answer these questions, we consider how political incentives might determine the effectiveness of fiscal limits, and then explore our hypotheses using a new approach. Our main conjecture is that principal–agent problems will prevent most tax and spending limits from having their intended effect of reducing the size of state government. But some may work better than others, and we begin by reviewing previous research that focuses on the letter of TEL laws to explain their effectiveness. We agree that this is important, but what have been ignored by the public economics literature are the political incentives of the agents charged with implementing these laws. The impact also should be governed by the ideological preferences of future lawmakers, the ease of amending state constitutions, and the need for the limits in the first place. Beginning with a detailed look at California's TEL experience, we demonstrate how politics often can dampen the impact of fiscal institutions.

We then explore our hypotheses more systematically in Colorado, Utah, and Washington by using a research design that departs from the approach of much of the existing literature[12] in two ways. First, we conduct time-series analyses within states that change their fiscal institutions, rather than cross-sectional analyses across states with different rules. This allows us to isolate the effect of

---

[11] Mullins and Wallins, *supra* note 5, at 15.

[12] James Cox and David Lowery, *The Impact of Tax Revolt Era State Fiscal Caps*, 3 Soc. Sci. Qu. 492 (1990); Marcia Howard, *Tax and Expenditure Limitations: There Is No Story*, 9 Pub. Budgeting & Fin. 83 (1989); Craig Johnson and Kenneth Kriz, *Fiscal Institutions, Credit Ratings, and Borrowing Costs*, 25 Pub. Budgeting & Fin. 84 (2005); Michael J. New, *Limiting Government through Direct Democracy: The Case of State Tax and Expenditure Limitations*, Cato Policy Analysis No. 420 (2001); James M. Poterba and Kim S. Rueben, Fiscal Rules and State Borrowing Costs: Evidence from California and Other States, Public Policy Institute of California (1999); Kim S. Rueben, Tax Limitations and Government Growth: The Effect of State Tax and Expenditure Limits on State and Local Government (mimeograph), Massachusetts Institute of Technology (1995); Dean Stansel, *Taming Leviathan: Are Tax and Spending Limits the Answer?*, Cato Policy Analysis No. 213 (1994).

a TEL while holding other state characteristics constant, instead of attributing all of the differences in fiscal patterns across states to the presence or absence of TELs. Second, we look at a number of indicators of state fiscal behavior at the same time, rather than exploring patterns in measures such as spending or credit ratings separately. By viewing the full picture of a state's actions, we can better determine whether its leaders are circumventing a TEL.[13]

I. EXPECTATIONS ABOUT THE EFFECTS OF TELs

Much of the literature that analyzes TELs focuses on the letter of the law to see how they shape state fiscal behavior[14] or to advise antitax activists about how to design the most constraining laws.[15] The contention is that specific provisions of TELs matter. Poterba and Rueben classify expenditure limits as either binding or nonbinding.[16] Stansel and New explore various provisions of TELs one by one, asking what makes a TEL more or less binding on the actors of a government.[17]

Stansel, for example, hypothesizes that a TEL that covers all types of spending, rather than only the expenditure of tax revenues, will be more effective.[18] Further, Stansel and New argue that when the limit counts devolution of responsibilities to local government against the overall limit or applies to both state and local governments, a TEL will be more effective.[19] The National Council of State Legislatures claims that a TEL indexed to inflation will be more effective than one that is based on growth of personal income.[20] Stansel also argues that when voter approval or a large legislative supermajority is required for the state to declare a fiscal emergency to suspend its TEL, the TEL will be more effective.[21]

Holding all these legal provisions constant, the political and fiscal conditions in a state should also help to explain a TELs effectiveness. A given TEL is more likely to be effective if the lawmakers who set the level of future spending are more fiscally conservative. This means that, ironically, TELs work when you least need them. This is especially likely when a legislature imposes a limit on itself freely, or when a tax revolt leads not only to a TEL initiative but also to a rightward shift in the composition of the legislature. Regardless of the reason,

---

[13] We are employing a nonequivalent dependent variable or pattern-matching design. In abstract terms, we have a treatment, X, that we expect to affect a set of dependent variables, Y_1, Y_2, $Y3$, etc. We look to see if X has the pattern of outcomes in the year that we expect. We are implementing this design in multiple cases, as each state adopts a TEL.

[14] Cox and Lowery, *supra* note 12; Howard, *supra* note 12; Johnson and Kriz, *supra* note 12; Mullins and Wallin, *supra* note 5; Poterba and Rueben, *supra* note 12; Rueben, *supra* note 12.

[15] New, *supra* note 12; Stansel, *supra* note 12.   [16] Poterbra and Rueben, *supra* note 12.

[17] New, *supra* note 12; Stansel, *supra* note 12.   [18] Stansel, *supra* note 12.

[19] New, *supra* note 12; Stansel, *supra* note 12.

[20] E-mail from National Conference of State Legislatures to the authors, *State Tax and Spending Limits 2004* and *Appendix* (Mar. 2005) (on file with the authors).

[21] Stansel, *supra* note 12.

fiscal conservatives have preferences that are most closely in line with those of the agents who imposed the limit. We therefore expect that a conservative state government will be more likely to hold to the spirit of a TEL law than a more liberal one, holding its provisions constant.

To test this hypothesis, we must measure the ideology of lawmakers. Research shows that Democrats in one state may be more conservative than Democrats in another,[22] therefore we look at both how liberal or conservative that party is compared to other state parties and which party controls a state. We focus more on legislators than governors, because study after study has found no link between party control of the governor's office and the size of state revenues or spending.[23]

Second, we predict that in a state where it is easier to amend the constitution, a TEL is less likely to be effective. In contrast to the federal government's founding document, most state constitutions are long, frequently amended, and concerned with many narrow policy questions. This is especially true where it is easier to amend a state's constitution.[24] The ability to change the highest law in the land opens up an opportunity for state lawmakers or interest groups to avoid the strictures of a TEL without actually altering the limit itself. Even when the TEL is enshrined in the state's constitution,[25] lawmakers or initiative backers can write an exemption into the constitution that is, *ipso facto*, a constitutionally permissible violation of the TEL. As our case study will relate, California has done this several times by passing tax increases for cigarettes (Propositions 10 and 99) and gasoline (as part of Proposition 111) that generated revenues that were specifically exempted from Proposition 4's spending limits. This is a common way that states can avoid constitutional strictures. As Kiewiet and Szakaly show, several states have constitutional provisions that prohibit borrowing large sums of money but do so nonetheless by passing bonds that are written as constitutional amendments.[26]

---

[22] Robert Erikson, Gerald Wright, and John McIver, STATEHOUSE DEMOCRACY: PUBLIC OPINION AND POLICY IN THE AMERICAN STATES(1993).

[23] For a review and new evidence of executive branch influence, *see* Thad Kousser and Justin Phillips, *Who Sets the Size of State Government? Comparing Models of Interbranch Conflict* (prepared for presentation at the 2005 Meeting of the Western Political Science Association, 2005).

[24] States that allow direct citizen provisions provide perhaps the easiest route to constitutional amendment, but Bowler and Donovan show that even initiative states vary considerably in the obstacles that voters must surpass to pass initiatives. Shaun Bowler and Todd Donovan, *Measuring the Effect of Direct Democracy on State Policy: Not All Initiatives are Created Equal*, 4 ST. POL. & POL'Y Q. 345 (2004).

[25] New hypothesizes that "constitutional TELs should be more effective than statutory TELs because they are more difficult to change." Again, this is a theory about changing the provisions of a TEL, and again New does not find any evidence in favor of this proposition. *See* New, *supra* note 12, at 6.

[26] D. Roderick Kiewiet and Kristin Szakaly, *Constitutional Limitations on Borrowing: An Analysis of State Bonded Indebtedness*, 12 J.L. & ECON. 62 (1996).

Third, we posit that in a low-spending state without a fiscal crisis, the lack of need for a TEL will make it less likely to be effective in reducing spending. If it "ain't broke," TELs won't fix it. The approach of our empirical analysis can be thought of in medical terms: We will look at how the treatment of a TEL, given in different dosage levels, affects a state's fiscal health. But what if the patient is not ill to begin with? We expect that when a TEL is passed in a state that already spends less than the rest of the nation and is not experiencing any sudden rise in expenditures, it will not produce any effects.

It is worth discussing one final variation in the political context of TELs passed through initiatives that could influence their effectiveness: the nature of the group proposing it. As Smith demonstrates, the groups that backed antitax initiatives in the mid-1990s differed greatly in their levels of professionalism, organizational history, grassroots reach, and campaign spending.[27] "Once stripped of their populist rhetoric," Smith finds, "it becomes clear that the organizations backing the 1996 initiatives were for the most part not grassroots operations."[28] How should variation in the nature of these groups influence the effectiveness of their efforts? We expect that it alters the provisions of their proposals and their success at the ballot box, but not the TEL's effectiveness afterward. Holding constant the characteristics of the fiscal limit that they backed, the goals and resources of an initiative's authors should have no independent influence on how binding it is in action. We agree that the first part of this causal path deserves further exploration, but assume that the path ends once the letter of the law and its success are determined.

II. MEASURING THE FULL IMPACT OF FISCAL INSTITUTIONS

These hypotheses detail our expectations about how our treatment, the passage of a TEL, its provisions, and the context of its implementation affect our dependent variable, the fiscal outcomes for a state. What is the strongest research design to test these claims? In this section, we lay out the strategy of our investigation and show how it differs from the approaches of most existing work. Our research design relies on time-series analyses of states that change their fiscal rules and looks at multiple measures of their fiscal behavior in order to render a more complete verdict on a TEL's effectiveness.

Many previous studies explore the effects of state fiscal institutions by making cross-state comparisons, often supplemented by multiple observations of each state over time. They typically regress some measure of fiscal behavior upon a dichotomous variable indicating the presence in each state of their institution of interest (a treatment) as well as a set of control factors that are meant to make

---

[27] Daniel A. Smith, *Peeling Away the Populist Rhetoric: Toward a Taxonomy of Anti-Tax Ballot Initiatives*, 24 Pub. Budgeting & Fin. 88 (2004).
[28] *Id.* at 109.

the states in the cross-state comparison actually comparable. They interpret the coefficient on their treatment variable as the estimated effect of the institution. This inferential strategy relies explicitly upon the assumption that their set of control variables captures all of the other relevant differences between states and that these variables establish a proxy pretest, or baseline, against which each state's posttest behavior (its behavior after the TEL) can be judged. We find reasons to doubt this assumption, and we suspect that the types of states that adopt TELs differ from non-TEL states in unmeasured ways and that these differences may also influence their fiscal behavior. In short, fiscal rules (the treatment) may be endogenous, caused by state-to-state differences that also affect a state's finances (the dependent variable).

We are not alone in our suspicions. Knight contends that supermajority tax-increase requirements are endogenous,[29] and Rueben proposes that state spending limits are endogenous.[30] Both take the same approach of using instrumental variables to purge the estimated effects of the treatment, fiscal rules, of their bias, contamination from the fiscal outcomes. Both find that this approach significantly alters their findings. While these works are clear improvements on analyses that do not take endogeneity seriously, the utility of their approach for our purposes is limited. Most importantly, it does not allow us to compare the effectiveness of different kinds of TELs. The instruments that they use, primarily the ability of citizens to propose initiatives, can help to predict the presence of TELs, but not their characteristics.

A design that allows us to compare the effects of different types of limits while recognizing that they are not randomly assigned to states is the classic "interrupted time-series" study.[31] Our treatment group is composed of states that enacted a TEL during the period of our study. We conduct a pretest by observing their fiscal behavior prior to the enactment and a posttest by taking observations in the years after the treatment was applied. Because other changes may be occurring in these states over time, we guard against history and maturation threats by comparing the history of TEL states to a control group of states that never enacted a TEL.[32] We can estimate the effect of a TEL by comparing the differences between treatment and control states before its passage to the differences afterward.

---

[29] Brian G. Knight, *Supermajority Voting Requirements for Tax Increases: Evidence from the States*, J. Pub. Econ. 41 (2000).

[30] Rueben, *supra* note 12.

[31] Donald Campbell and H. Laurence Ross, *The Connecticut Crackdown on Speeding: Time Series Data in Quasi-Experimental Analysis*, 3 Law & Soc'y Rev. 33 (1968).

[32] Stansel provides a strong research design that approximates this approach. Stansel, *supra* note 12. However, rather than comparing TEL states to a set of control cases, he compares states with a particular type of TEL to the national averages in the five years before and after they enacted their limits. This national average is calculated from some states with other types of TELs and some states without any TELs, so the observed differences probably understate the effects of a particular sort of TEL.

In order to see which types of TELs are most effective, and under what political circumstances, we use a block design that draws its statistical power from grouping together states with similar types of TELs and political conditions. Blocking designs reduce the amount of noise in the observed relationship between the pretest and posttest observation. We then can compare the estimated effect of one block of TELs with the estimated effect of another block. This requires us to look at the enactment of many fiscal rule changes. At this stage of our research, we focus on the wave of TEL enactments in the West about a decade ago, which provides us with four cases. When we look at other regions and expand our data collection to cover the years leading up to the tax revolt and its aftermath (1970–1990), we will add another 20 cases. Table 10.1 reports the presence and timing of TEL enactments, as well as two key provisions of the laws.

We also depart from most previous works by looking at a range of state fiscal behaviors at the same time. The effects of TELs on some of these measures have been studied before. Many authors study spending and revenue levels; New (2001) looks at local as well as state spending,[33] and Poterba and Rueben and Johnson and Kriz examine the effects of TELs on state borrowing costs or credit ratings.[34] We have not come across investigations of the effects of TELs on other aspects of state behavior, such as total debt levels and the use of charges and fees. But what most clearly is missing from the literature is an examination of the impact of TELs on the entirety of a state's fiscal situation.

This is crucially important, since a major theme in the literature is that states can travel a variety of circuitous routes to circumvent the impact of TELs. They may shift spending to local governments, raise money through direct charges and fees that are not covered by some limits, or finance more capital projects through bonds. If these paths are blocked, they may engage in budget gimmickry that avoids public scrutiny. Nonetheless, these effects are in fact noticed by bond houses that give states credit ratings. In order to capture all of these maneuvers, our empirical sections look at four indicators of state fiscal behavior.[35]

A. Total Expenditures by State and Local Government, per Capita

Reported in appropriate editions of the U.S. Census Bureau's annual *State and Local Government Finance* publication, this measure captures the totality of spending within a state. If a state is able to circumvent a TEL by shifting government responsibilities to cities and counties, state-only spending may go

---

[33] New, *supra* note 12.
[34] Johnson and Kriz, *supra* note 12; Poterbra and Rueben, *supra* note 12.
[35] The data and coding used for the analysis in this chapter are available upon request from us or can be downloaded at http://mccubbins.ucsd.edu/. We are grateful to the research assistance of Geoffrey Peppler in assembling this data set.

Table 10.1. State fiscal institutions

State	Year passed Spending limit	Revenue limit	Constitutional or statutory?	Income or inflation?
Alabama				
Alaska	1982		constitutional	Inflation
Arizona	1978		constitutional	Income
Arkansas				
California	1979		constitutional	Income
Colorado	1992	1992	constitutional	Inflation
Connecticut	1991		statutory	greater of two
Delaware				
Florida		1994	constitutional	Income
Georgia				
Hawaii	1978		constitutional	Income
Idaho	1980		statutory	Income
Illinois				
Indiana				
Iowa				
Kansas				
Kentucky				
Louisiana	1993	1991	constitutional	Income
Maine				
Maryland				
Massachusetts		1996	statutory	state wages
Michigan		1978	constitutional	Income
Minnesota				
Mississippi				
Missouri	1980	1996	constitutional	state revenues
Montana	1981		statutory	Income
Nebraska				
Nevada	1979		statutory	Inflation
New Hampshire				
New Jersey	1990		statutory	Income
New Mexico				
New York				
North Carolina	1991		statutory	Income
North Dakota				
Ohio				
Oklahoma	1985		constitutional	Inflation
Oregon	1979, 2001	2000	statutory constitutional	income state revenues
Pennsylvania				
Rhode Island	1992		constitutional	state revenues
South Carolina	1980		constitutional	greater of two
South Dakota				
Tennessee	1978		constitutional	Income
Texas	1978		constitutional	Income
Utah	1989		statutory	Both

| State | Year passed | | Constitutional or statutory? | Income or inflation? |
	Spending limit	Revenue limit		
Vermont				
Virginia				
Washington	1993	1979	statutory	Inflation
West Virginia				
Wisconsin				
Wyoming				

Note: Colorado passed a statutory spending limit in 1991 and then a constitutional limit in 1992. Nevada's 1979 limit is classified as nonbinding in Poterba and Rueben (1999).

Source: Data on the presence and timing of TELs are taken from Poterba and Rueben (1999), and details of their constitutional status and indexing mechanism are from the National Conference of State Legislatures (2005).

down but this measure will remain unchanged. We collected this time series from fiscal year 1969 to 2000.

B. Revenues Raised Through Charges and Fees, per Capita

Again recorded in *State and Local Government Finance,* this measure serves as a check on whether states move through a loophole that many TELs leave open. In California, for instance, the spending limit only applies to revenues raised through taxation, allowing lawmakers to spend as much as they would like from funds obtained through college tuition, license fees, state parks admissions, and other such charges. We collected this time series from fiscal year 1969 to 2000.[36]

C. State Debt, per Capita

We collected aggregate debt figures from the U.S. Census Bureau's annual *State Government Finance* publication, and used population figures from *State and Local Government Finance* to convert them into per capita measures. When states are prevented from raising taxes or from spending tax revenues, they increasingly may rely on borrowing to finance capital improvement projects. We collected this time series from fiscal year 1988 to 2002.[37]

---

[36] For both total state and local spending and revenues from charges and fees, we gathered data fiscal years 1997–2000 from the Census Bureau's website, http://www.census.gov/govs/www/estimate.html, accessed in March 2005. The data from fiscal years 1969–1996 were recorded from hard copies of the census publication by Rod Kiewiet, who generously has shared it with us. Unfortunately, the Census Bureau does not report state-by-state detailed spending and revenue figures from fiscal year 2001, ending our time series.

[37] Debt data from fiscal years 1992 to 2002 are available on the Census Bureau's Web site, http://www.census.gov/govs/www/state.html, accessed in January 2005, and data from 1988–1991 were provided to us by the Census Bureau's Ben Shelak, to whom we are grateful.

D. State Bond Ratings, According to Moody's Investor Service

We gathered these ratings from the U.S. Census Bureau's *Statistical Abstract of the United States*, for 1995 to 2002, and from January issues of *Moody's Bond Record* for calendar years 1988 to 1994.[38] Bond raters and their clients have an immense financial stake in closely monitoring state fiscal behavior, and Johnson and Kriz show that ratings closely predict state borrowing costs.[39] Looking at this measure allows us to see how lenders view TELs and to identify whether these constraints are combated through budget chicanery.

Our research design allows us to report our spending, revenue, and debt figures in current rather than constant dollars. Rather than directly comparing one state's figures in the period before a TEL enactment to the period after enactment, we will be looking at how states match up against a control group in both eras. When inflation spikes or nationwide changes in the responsibilities of state governments shift, these changes will affect the baseline group as well as the TEL states. Our control group is made up of the 26 states that never enacted tax or expenditure limits, through fiscal 2000. Figure 10.1 reports our measures for these states, giving a sense of the absolute levels for each figure and how they change over time. In our analysis of four TEL states in Section III and IV, we will report the ratios of each state's fiscal numbers to the non-TEL average. If enactment of a limit significantly alters this ratio, that will provide evidence of a change in behavior.

III. CALIFORNIA'S SPENDING LIMIT

A. Introduction

California's spending limit, Proposition 4, passed with 74.3 percent of the vote in a November 1979 special election. The fact that the Gann limit won such a large share of the vote demonstrates that voters at the time agreed

---

[38] We take the state's overall bond rating in January of a year as our measure of its average rating over that fiscal year. Although ratings from the two other major credit agencies, S&P and Fitch, are available in the Statistical Abstract beginning in 1995, we only had access to Moody's ratings for 1988–1994. Moody's Investor Service, *Moody's Bond Record* (Jan. eds. 1988–1994). However, our confidence in relying on only one rating service is bolstered by the observation that, during the 1995–2002 period, ratings from the three agencies correspond quite closely. To construct average bond ratings, we assume that ratings are interval variables for which the distance between any two points next to each other on the scale is the same as the distance between any two other adjacent points. A state with an AAA rating is scored a ten, and one point is deducted with each drop of a rating level. Because many states are not typically rated by Moody's, we exclude these cases from our analysis and only have 18 states in the control group of cases that never enacted a TEL.

[39] Johnson and Kriz, *supra* note 12.

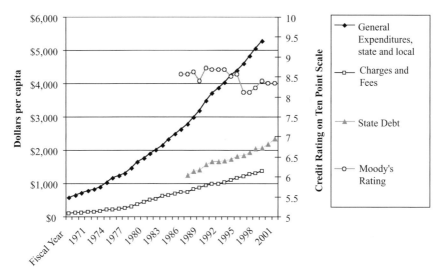

Figure 10.1. Fiscal patterns in states that never enact TELs (26 states).

with proponents of the tax revolt about the need for structural limitations on state government spending. Furthermore, the mandate seemed to indicate that California voters had a vested interest in monitoring the implementation of the expenditure limit in order to ensure its effectiveness at restraining government spending, and to make necessary changes and improvements if it lacked effectiveness. Yet little research has attempted to measure the impact of the Gann limit on California's fiscal policy. In a study for the Cato Institute, New looked at the language of expenditure limits and found that Proposition 4 was ultimately ineffective because, among other reasons, it did not cap total spending and was diluted by subsequent initiatives such as Proposition 111.[40]

Our study expands on the analysis of these structural factors while undertaking a new approach that looks beyond the letter of California's law and focuses on political and institutional contexts that weakened the Gann limit's ability to constrain state spending. We agree that California's appropriations limit did little to curb spending. This becomes especially clear when we compare the state to a control group: states that have not enacted a tax limit or an expenditure limit. From its inception, the Gann limit was a mostly superficial constraint on the fiscal management of California, and it was practically gutted when the passage of Proposition 111 fueled growth in the cap to practically unreachable levels in the 1990s. Based on an in-depth look at California's experiment with the Gann limit, focusing not only on its language but also on its political and institutional environment, we elucidate the hypotheses listed earlier.

[40] New, *supra* note 12.

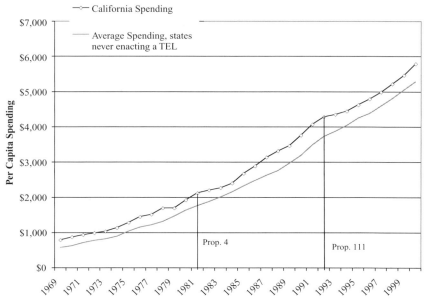

Figure 10.2. California's state and local spending and the Gann limit.
(Note: Vertical lines denote fiscal 1981, the first budget written under the constraints of the Gann limit; and fiscal 1992, the first budget constructed under the new Proposition 111 formula. Source: U.S. Census Bureau's *State and Local Government Finance.*)

B. Did the Gann Limit Work?

Proposition 4 had little impact on the trend in California's overall state spending. To judge its growth in expenditures to a baseline, we compare California's levels of spending to the average spending of the 26 states that never enacted a tax or expenditure limit. This comparison allows us to control for any national trends in inflation, the devolution of federal programs to states, and other widespread fiscal shifts (i.e., to exclude most history threats). Figure 10.2 shows that California's spending continued to grow at a pre-Gann-limit pace throughout the 1980s and 1990s, always exceeding the comparison group's average.

California clearly outspent the average non-TEL state both before and after Proposition 4's implementation, with the gap growing in the late 1980s. Figure 10.2 seems to refute even New's notion that the Gann limit managed to constrain spending in its early years and only became ineffective when it was amended by Proposition 111.[41] It is of course important to note that Proposition 13, passed in 1978, kept revenues down over this period by limiting local property taxes and requiring a legislative supermajority to raise state taxes. Even in the context of the larger tax revolt, though, California's total expenditures

[41] *Id.*

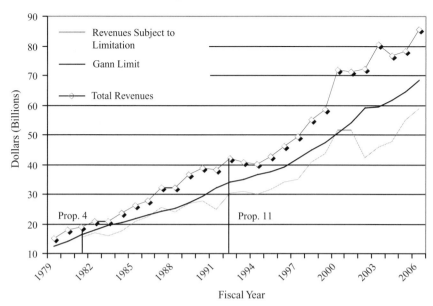

Figure 10.3. California's spending cap and revenue levels.
(Note: See caption to Figure 10.2 for explanation of vertical lines. Source: Chart A-1 and Chart L of California Department of Finance, 2005.)

continued to rise. If the success of the Gann limit is to be judged by how California's spending evolved in relation to states without tax or expenditure limits, then our findings show that it failed to constrain the growth of California government in the 1980s and 1990s.

To show why the Gann limit did not lead to a drop in spending growth, we compare the rise of the limit itself to the trend in the revenues that were subject to it and to total revenues overall. We find that because Proposition 4 applies only to a portion of the total revenue stream coming into state government, California lawmakers have been able to boost total spending by raising more and more money from alternate sources (which we will later detail). The Gann limit sets a cap on the expenditure of revenues from taxation, which increases over time based on a population-plus-inflation index.[42] Figure 10.3 displays the growing gap between revenues subject to limitation and total revenues. It also shows that the Gann limit rarely constrained state spending in California directly; the limit has been reached only twice since the passage of Proposition 4 in 1979. This occurred in fiscal 1987 and fiscal 2000, and only in the first case did the limit trigger a tax rebate.

It is also possible that Proposition 4 indirectly constrained the state's policymakers. They may have wished to increase taxes but realized that the Gann

---

[42] Proposition 4 calls for the use of the lower of the following two: CPI or per capita personal income. Every year before Proposition 111, the former was lower than the latter.

limit would prevent them from spending all of the money that the tax hike raised. But if this were the case, we would expect these savvy policymakers to raise revenues to just under the amount that the Gann limit allowed them to spend. Instead, there is often a wide gap between revenues subject to the limit and the ceiling itself. Graphically, the distance between the "Gann limit" line and the "revenues subject to limitation" line is one measure of how constraining the limit has been. When this gap is large, lawmakers retain great flexibility in their opportunities to raise taxes and spend the proceeds, without violating Proposition 4.

Figure 10.3 shows that this gap is often wide, leaving lawmakers with considerable wiggle room under the Gann limit even when their total spending on state government far exceeds the cap. Furthermore, 1990's Proposition 111 changed the calculation of the spending cap from one based on inflation to one based on personal income, accelerating the limit's growth rate. Opponents to the proposition warned that the initiative "guts the Gann limit on government spending – under the formula being proposed, government would never reach a spending limit."[43] Indeed, Figure 10.3 supports this notion, as the gap between the Gann limit and revenues subject to limitation reached unprecedented levels after 1991.

Circumstances surrounding the two instances in which the Gann limit was reached put into question the effectiveness of Proposition 4 in limiting California's spending. The more celebrated of the two occurrences was in fiscal year 1987, when revenues subject to limitation under Proposition 4 exceeded the appropriations limits by $1,183,000,000.[44] Proponents of Proposition 4 hailed the subsequent $1.1 billion tax refund as proof of the effectiveness of a successfully implemented expenditure limit. New cites this as evidence that "the Gann Limit proved to be relatively effective at keeping spending in check."[45] The large excess in revenues subject to limitation in 1987, however, was due not to careless spending in Sacramento, but rather to federal tax reform that provoked massive sell-off in capital gains.[46] Therefore, the one instance in which the Gann limit seemed to effectively constrain the spending of the state was

[43] March Fong Eu, State of California, secretary of state, *California's Ballot Pamphlet, Primary Election, June 5, 1990* at 20 (1990).

[44] California Department of Finance, CHART L, *supra* note 4.

[45] Michael New, *The Gann Limit Turns 25*, BUS. DAILY, Oct. 28, 2004.

[46] The link between the federal tax reform and California's finances was explained to us by Fred Silva, former California State Senate budget advisor, in a phone interview conducted by us on February 17, 2005. According to Moore and Silvia, "The 1986 Tax Reform Act constituted the largest capital gains tax hike in more than 50 years, raising the top marginal tax rate on long-term capital gains (assets held for more than one year) from 20 percent to 28 percent – a 40 percent increase." Stephen Moore and John Silvia, *The ABCs of the Capital Gains Tax*, CATO INSTITUTE POLICY ANALYSIS No. 242 (1995). California residents realized many capital gains in sales conducted just before this tax increase took effect, bringing a large one-time boost to the state coffers.

due to an exogenous shock of no bearing on the fiscal motivations of state lawmakers before or after 1987.

Proposition 111's amendment of the limit, which requires two consecutive years of excess revenues before a refund must be given, made it even less likely that taxpayers would get a refund. The second instance in which tax revenues exceeded the Gann limit was in fiscal 2000, when an excess of $975,000,000 was collected by the state.[47] However, revenues subject to the limit were $2,425,000,000 below it the next year, more than wiping out the surplus from the previous year and leaving lawmakers free to spend all of these funds. The unambiguous lesson from the recent history of state spending in California is that Gann limit did not bring a major shift in the fiscal policy choices of California's lawmakers.

C. Why Did the Gann Limit Fail to Slow State Spending Growth?

It is clear, therefore, that Proposition 4 failed to meet the demands of voters who supported the initiative. Instead, the Gann limit faded into obscurity and, other than a tax rebate in 1987, became seemingly a nonissue in the state's fiscal planning. How and why did California's lawmakers manage to cope with Proposition 4 to the point where it had no lasting, discernable impact on state spending? The remainder of our analysis will focus on explaining some of the main reasons for the ineffectiveness of the Gann limit. First, we analyze how the language of Proposition 4 intentionally allowed lawmakers to continue spending at relatively high levels by relying more on nontax revenues like debt and user charges and fees. We then observe how changes to the language of the limit itself, particularly those enacted by Proposition 111, have further restricted its effectiveness. Second, we explore why the enactment of the Gann limit as an initiative, and the political and institutional context in which it was created and has existed ever since, made California's expenditure limit ultimately a dead letter.

D. The Letter of the Law

A fundamental analysis of the effectiveness of an expenditure limit begins with a full understanding of its actual language and structure. No two expenditure limits are alike, as they can vary across numerous legal and political dimensions. Mullins and Wallin note that state government TELs take the form of revenue limits, expenditure limits, a combination of both, or restrictions on "growth in general fund expenditures or appropriations," and that they can be "tied to growth in population, income, prices, the economy, or wages."[48] Poterba and

---

[47] California Department of Finance, CHART L, *supra* note 4.
[48] Mullins and Wallin, *supra* note 5, at 9.

Rueben argue that they can be binding or not.[49] The provisions of California's particular brand of spending limit help to explain its impact. We show that the Gann limit's exclusion of nontax revenues from the limit and the formula that Proposition 111 used to calculate the cap left California's spending limit incapable of taming total state spending.

The state's expenditure limit is a ceiling based on annual appropriations for the prior fiscal year. In practice, Proposition 4's formula adjusted this limit according to changes in population and inflation. Revenues that are subject to the limit and that exceed it must be returned to taxpayers, either by a rebate or tax rate change.[50] The key detail that hindered the Gann limit's impact on state spending, however, was that it limited only expenditures of revenues from taxation. The circumscribed reach of Proposition 4 fit with the intent of its authors, according to one of them. Craig Stubblebine, now an emeritus economics professor at Claremont McKenna College, was a member of the committee that drafted the Gann initiative. It exempted nontax revenues from its limits, he reports, "Because if the state provides the services and people want to buy it, and they have other suppliers to chose from, then why limit that?"[51] When asked if the exemption was a political compromise, Stubblebine replied, "Oh, heavens no, it was a way to make sure that the limit didn't stop people who wanted to buy five copies of a marriage license from doing so."[52]

The exclusion of nontax revenues in the calculation of the Gann limit left many avenues open for the state to raise money that it could spend freely. Figure 10.4 traces out one of these avenues, "charges and fees." Funds raised from university tuitions, state parks and recreation admissions, state solid-waste management and utility revenues, license fees, and other nontax revenue streams are not subject to California's spending limit. Historically, California has been a state that relied less on charges and fees as a percentage of revenue than the comparison group. But in fiscal year 1979 and years following, California witnessed a sharp increase in the portion of its revenues that it raised from charges and fees. In fiscal year 1969, fees and charges made up 18.1 percent of

---

[49] Poterba and Rueben, *supra* note 12.

[50] According to the ballot-issue summary available at http://traynor.uchastings.edu/library/ Research%20Databases/research_databases_main.htm in February 2005, proceeds from taxes include tax revenues, proceeds from the investment of tax revenues, and service charges and fees determined to be in excess of the costs of providing them. Revenues not subject to state limitation include "State financial assistance to local governments . . . , payments to beneficiaries from retirement, disability insurance, and unemployment insurance funds, payments for interest and redemption shares on state debt . . . , appropriations needed to pay for state's cost of complying with mandates imposed by federal laws and regulations or courts order." Since our study focuses on the effects of expenditure limits on state governments, we do not go into detail about the provisions of Proposition 4 that limit local appropriations, though they are similar to those of the state

[51] Telephone interview by Thad Kousser with Craig Stubblebine, professor emeritus, Claremont McKenna College (Mar. 25, 2005).

[52] *Id.*

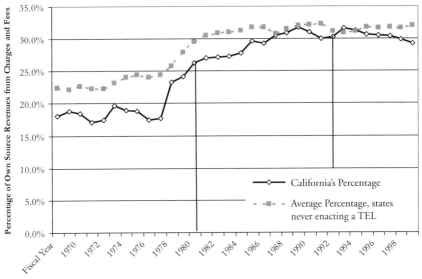

Figure 10.4. California's growing reliance on revenue from charges and fees. (Note: See caption to Figure 10.2 for explanation of vertical lines. Source: U.S. Census Bureau's *State and Local Government Finance*.)

the state's revenue (compared to 22.4 percent in the average non-TEL state); by 1979, the state's figure increased to 23.3 percent (compared to 25.8 percent in the comparison group). By 1994, California's proportion, 31.6 percent, exceeded the control-group average of 30.9 percent. Many studies attest that Proposition 13, which drastically lowered a major revenue source in property tax and required a two-thirds majority to pass new taxes, is the most likely cause of California's increased reliance on user fees and charges.[53] One year later, the passage of Proposition 4 further promoted the use of charges and fees as they were categorized with nontax revenues and therefore not subject to limitation.

Borrowing more money through bonds became another means by which lawmakers could continue to spend at pre-Proposition 4 levels well into the 1980s and 1990s. As Figure 10.5 shows, growth in California's real debt accelerated in the mid-1980s and early 1990s. We believe that the delay between the enactment of Proposition 4 and the actual increase in debt is due to the time it takes to put a bond authorization on the ballot, have it pass, and then issue all of the bonds associated with it. Regardless, California began to borrow much more after the passage of its spending limit, especially during the 1990s. None of these revenues counted against the spending cap. New issues of bonds

[53] David W. Lyon, *From Home Rule to Fiscal Rule: Taking Measure of Local Government Finance in California*, PUBLIC POLICY INSTITUTE OF CALIFORNIA (2000); Michael Shires, *Patterns in California Government Revenues Since Prop. 13*, PUBLIC POLICY INSTITUTE OF CALIFORNIA (1999).

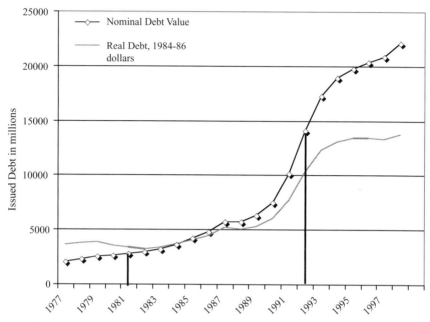

Figure 10.5. California's rising debt. (Note: See caption to Figure 10.2 for explanation of vertical lines. Source: U.S. Census Bureau's *State Government Finance*.)

became another means by which lawmakers could, through the use of nontax revenues, dampen the effects of the tax revolt.

Yet it is important to note again that policymakers, and the drafters of Proposition 4, were in fact fully aware that the exclusion of nontax revenues would allow increases in spending to continue by shifting reliance to these alternate revenue sources. Fred Silva, former Senate budget staffer, explains that "The reason I am sensitive to saying that the governor or the legislature made an end run around the initiative was that the way it was structured was narrow in its limitation from the beginning."[54] Even Proposition 4's ballot summary clearly stated that "The impact of this measure will depend upon future actions of state and local governments with regard to appropriations that are not subject to the limitation of this measure."[55] From its conception, therefore, the Gann limit's fate as an effective expenditure limit rested on what the letter of its law did not do, rather than in what it did.

By turning to alternate sources of revenue, such as debt and user charges, lawmakers are able to undermine the spirit of the tax-revolt era and spend freely.

---

[54] Telephone interview with Fred Silva, senior advisor, Public Policy Institute of California (Feb. 17, 2005).

[55] *Id.* The ballot issue summary was accessed at http://traynor.uchastings.edu/library/ Research%20Databases/research_databases_main.htm in Feb. 2005.

Following the trail of money as it enters in the form of revenues until its exit as expenditures is a tenuous and difficult task. One way to uncover the presence of "budget games," that is, if legislators are employing budget gimmicks that shift funds around to avoid the Gann limit, is to look at a state's credit rating. Bond agency ratings may punish states for engaging in such tricks, or they may simply change a state's rating as a mark of approval or disapproval of a TEL's passage and the fiscal implications that it brings.

Several studies have shown that credit agencies closely monitor the fiscal institutions and management of a state to judge its default risk, particularly its ability to make interest payments in the face of adverse events.[56] Johnson and Kriz lay out the groundwork for why "a state's credit rating and its fiscal institutions are highly correlated."[57] While Poterba and Rueben find that "expenditure limits such as Proposition 4 lower borrowing costs because they make it easier for the state to service its debt,"[58] we already have noted our concerns about their cross-sectional research design. In fact, the history of bond ratings in California tells a different story: Lenders penalized the state for passing the Gann limit.

In 1980, following the passage of Proposition 4, Moody's Investor Service lowered California's bond rating from Aaa to Aa, and Standard and Poor's Corporation (S&P) lowered it from Aaa to Aa+.[59] The state's own report on its bond history cited as the primary reason for the downgrades the "uncertainty over impact of Proposition 13 and the Gann spending limit."[60] In 1980 and 1994, credit agencies attributed downgrades in California's credit rating to the state's increasing debt burden, which we categorize as one type of budget avenue lawmakers have pursued to avoid the Gann limit.

One final way in which the letter of the Gann limit is self-defeating results from how its expenditure cap is formulated to increase over time. For a TEL

---

[56] Johnson and Kriz, *supra* note 12; Poterba and Rueben, *supra* note 12.

[57] Johnson and Kriz, *supra* note 12, at 88. "The financial and debt factors rating agencies consider, such as the government's operating financial condition, tax rate levels, spending levels, and debt burden, are directly related to the factors that fiscal institutions exert influences over." *Ibid.*

[58] Poterba and Rueben, *supra* note 12, at Part IV.

[59] Bond ratings are for general obligation bonds. Summary reports appear in CALIFORNIA DEPARTMENT OF FINANCE, GOVERNOR'S BUDGET 2005 – BACKGROUND INFORMATION, CHART K-1 – CHART K-6, *available at* http://www.dof.ca.gov/HTML/BUD_DOCS/backinfo.htm (last visited Feb. 2005). S&P and Fitch's run on an index with the following ranking, highest to poorest: AAA, AA, A, BBB, with + (higher rating) and – (poorer rating) used to denote levels in between (AA+ is better than AA–). Moody's index has the following rank ordering, from best to worst: AAA, AA, A, BAA, with numbers 1–3 denoting levels in between (AA1 is a better rating than AA2, which is better than AA3). Moody's Investor Service, *supra* note 38.

[60] California Department of Finance, GOVERNOR'S BUDGET 2005 – BACKGROUND INFORMATION, CHART K-6: HISTORY OF CALIFORNIA GENERAL OBLIGATION BOND RATINGS, *available at* http://www.dof.ca.gov/HTML/BUD_DOCS/backinfo.htm (last visited Feb. 2005).

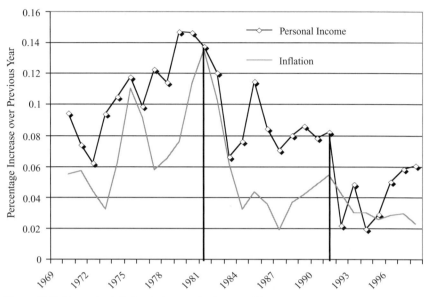

Figure 10.6. Comparing inflation to the growth of personal income. (Note: See caption to Figure 10.2 for explanation of vertical lines. Source: U.S. Census Bureau's *State Government Finance.*)

to be a binding constraint on state spending, the rate of growth of the limit must closely resemble the growth in resources available to a state. Proposition 4 indexed the limit to increases in population and, because it turned out to be lower than growth in personal income, to inflation. Though Stansel and New have pointed out that an "inflation plus population growth" index for an expenditure limit is most effective at limiting spending,[61] we find that in California's case it is still an imperfect tool for gauging the optimal rate of increase for state spending. The infrequency of Gann-limit breaches since 1979 seems to support the notion that California's calculation of its appropriation's limit was set too high for constraining state expenditures. Studies have found that many early-stage revenue and expenditure limitations during the tax-revolt era failed to limit spending as a result of overinflated growth in the limit itself.[62]

Proposition 111, which switched the cap to an index of the growth in personal income and attendance in public schools, pushed the limit to grow even faster. Figure 10.6 shows that the high growth rate in the Gann limit following Proposition 111 is due to a historical trend in which growth in personal income has exceeded inflation (as measured by the CPI) in every year between 1969 and 1992. This trend helps to explain the increasing gap after 1991 between the appropriations limit and revenues subject to limitation, seen in Figure 10.3.

[61] New, *supra* note 12; Stansel, *supra* note 12.   [62] Kiewiet and Szakaly, *supra* note 26.

Proposition 111, therefore, made an already weak Gann limit obsolete as its levels exceeded any reasonable increase in revenues.

E. Political Reactions to a TEL: The Case of the Gann Initiative

For the remainder of this case study, we look at the strategies of circumvention in California. Following our simple principal–agent analogy, we would expect better implementation of an expenditure limit in states without an initiative process, and therefore in places where they were enacted by a willing legislature. This would follow the typical path of public policy, in which the principal delegates the decision-making process to a willing agent, resulting in the enactment and subsequent enforcement of an effective expenditure limit. The prediction is the opposite for states where an expenditure limit is passed through an initiative process. We expect that in these instances, legislatures will circumvent the provisions of the TEL, if at all possible, as the TEL seeks to force the agent (the legislature) to implement a law at odds with its other incentives (to win reelection, to keep power, and so on). In California, the legislature failed to pass a bill proposed by state legislator Robert Boatwright that would have created a spending limit, and the state's residents responded by forcing upon its representatives in the capital the duties of enforcing an expenditure limit that they had actively opposed.

And indeed, the California legislature did not look like a likely place where expenditure limits would be implemented. The ideology of the state's legislators and governors can provide an accurate prediction of the willingness of California lawmakers to implement any kind of expenditure limit, and especially one forced upon them through the initiative process. We would expect compliance with an expenditure limit to be an increasing function of the conservatism of a state's legislatures and governors. Based on Erikson, Wright, and McIver's finding that more conservative states tend to spend less money,[63] fiscal conservatism should promote an expenditure limit and help ensure its implementation. According to an index of party-elite ideology measured around the time of the passage of Proposition 4, California's Democratic political elites were the most liberal in the country, while its Republican elites were closer to the middle of the pack.[64] Unfortunately for the backers of the Gann initiative,

---

[63] Erikson, Wright, and McIver, *supra* note 22.

[64] *Id.* at 102–103. Using a composite of ideology studies from the 1970s and 1980s, Erikson, Wright, and McIver generate an index of scores that compares the following: "State scores for the activist (county chairs plus convention delegates) and electoral (congressional candidates plus state legislators) components as well as for the overall samples of party elites." Erikson, Wright, and McIver, *supra* note 22. Moving away from zero into positive numbers indicates increasingly liberal ideologies, while moving toward negative numbers indicates increasingly conservative ideologies. The Democratic elite overall score of 7.47 decomposes as follows: 3.44 for activists and 4.03 for electoral elites. The Republican elite overall score of –3.44 decomposes as follows: –2.12 for activists and –1.28 for electoral elites. *Id.*

Democrats have controlled both houses of the legislature in every year but one since its passage. It is not surprising, then, that they took many actions to maintain high governmental spending.[65]

The ease of amending California's constitution provides an institutional reason to doubt that the Gann limit would be binding. In fact, the limit constantly faces the threat of being sidestepped by constitutional amendments. The clearest example comes in the recent history of cigarette, tobacco, and gas taxes in California. In 1988, Proposition 99 created an additional tax on cigarette and tobacco distributors. Proposition 111 raised the California gas tax and truck weight fees in 1990. In 1998, Proposition 10 further increased the cigarette tax, this time by $.50 per pack.[66] All these propositions exempted the tax revenues that they raised from the spending limit, showing how easily a constitutional amendment can be overridden by subsequent constitutional changes.[67]

One of the Gann limit's authors, Craig Stubblebine, explains the problem faced by TEL supporters in language similar to our hypothesis about the ease of amending state constitutions. "If people find the limits too constraining, they will find a way out of them. That means voters, legislators, interest groups. Here's the dilemma, in my judgment. Take a state like California that has a very well developed initiative process. That's a godsend for passing the Gann limit, but it also provides an avenue for anyone who wants to get around [it]. The easier it is to do an initiative, the less effect a limit will have over time."[68]

F. Lessons from California

Our case study of California shows that both legal and political factors can prevent an expenditure limit from effectively constraining state spending. We expect our findings to extend to other states. Our analysis of trends in California's total spending levels, use of charges and fees, debt, bond ratings, and cost

---

[65] One of Proposition 4's authors, Craig Stubblebine, notes that just as political realities dictated the effectiveness of the Gann limit, the extent to which politicians circumvented the initiative may have dictated their political fates: "If you had applied the original Gann limit, the state wouldn't have gotten into the problem that it got into in the early 2000s. It would have smoothed out the spending increase in the late 1990s that came from the dotcom boom, and Gray Davis would still be governor." Telephone interview by Thad Kousser, *supra* note 51.

[66] Details of all three propositions can be found at the Hastings Law Library's California Ballot Measures Database, *available at* http://holmes.uchastings.edu/library/Research%20Databases/CA%20Ballot%20Measures/ca_ballot_measures_main.htm.

[67] This only includes those instances when a proposition passed. There were also attempts to levy taxes on alcohol (Alcohol Surtax Fund, 1990 General Election) and gas (Public Transportation Trust Funds, 1994 General Election).

[68] Telephone interview by Thad Kousser, *supra* note 51.

of living indexes leads us to conclude that Proposition 4 was and is incapable of constraining state spending. We will use similar measurements for determining the effectiveness of other types of expenditure limits in our multiple-state analysis.

In addition to the letter of the law, we argue that the effectiveness of TELs also depends on the political and institutional context in which they exist. In California, the expenditure limit was enacted through the initiative process and targeted at an unreceptive legislature. The liberal ideology of the policymakers undermined implementation and constitutional amendments were employed to make the Gann limit a nonbinding constraint on state spending. In our multiple-state analysis, we expect to find a pattern of results similar to what we found in California. Limits passed by initiative, those enacted in states where it is easier to amend the constitution, and those that depend upon liberal lawmakers for implementation all should be less effective.

IV. OTHER TAX AND EXPENDITURE LIMITS

This section explores whether the ineffectiveness of the Gann limit is a phenomenon unique to California, or whether a similar story holds in other states. The scope of our multiple-state investigation is limited by data availability. Many states passed their TELs in the first wave of the tax revolt, but our comprehensive fiscal measures only start in the mid-1980s. Because we do not yet have the full picture of the policies chosen by Arizona, Idaho, Montana, Nevada, and Oregon in the 1970s, we cannot analyze the effects of their circa-1979 TEL enactments at this time. We focus instead on Colorado, Utah, and Washington, the states that passed revenue and spending limits more recently.

We look at each state individually, comparing its fiscal patterns to the averages in our group of control states (those that never enacted a TEL). Our tables track four facets of fiscal behavior over time, reporting the ratio of a Western state's levels to the control group's average. To measure a TEL's overall effectiveness, we look at whether it changes total state and local spending levels. If it does not reduce the size of government, relative to the control-group average, then we look at other measures to see how lawmakers may have circumvented their limit. Did they begin to raise more money from fees, or sell more bonds? How did credit agencies respond to the new fiscal rules? Our four time series allow us to answer these questions. Finally, we compare the effectiveness of limits in these three states. Paying attention to the letter of each TEL law and the political conditions under which it went into effect allows a tentative exploration of our hypotheses.

Colorado's Taxpayer's Bill of Rights (TABOR) initiative, passed in 1992, has many of the characteristics that prior research would suggest are necessary to ensure its success.[69] This constitutional amendment limits all taxes and revenues at the state and local level, and requires voter approval for any tax increases or to change TABOR itself. The caps on expenditures and revenues are indexed to inflation, rather than personal income.[70] The amendment's drafters appear to have learned from the mistakes of past TELs. Political conditions in Colorado also generally bode well for the initiative's effectiveness. Colorado had a Republican-controlled legislature throughout the period of our study, but TABOR came into effect just when gubernatorial party control was beginning to shift. The state was moving from the era of moderate Democratic governors Dick Lamm (1974–1986) and Roy Romer (1986–1998) into conservative Republican Bill Owens' tenure. Presumably, a unified Republican government would be unlikely to attempt to circumvent the spirit of a TEL. Even though it was imposed externally by a citizen initiative, TABOR set limits that subsequent state lawmakers, especially after 1998, would want to follow.

Figure 10.7 shows that Colorado's strict spending and revenue limits appear, at first, to constrain the size of government. Prior to TABOR's passage, total spending in Colorado hovered a bit above the control-group average, and spiked in fiscal 1993 on the eve of its implementation. But state and local expenditures have declined since then, moving below the control-case average in fiscal 1996 and staying below it. Total spending dropped from a mean of 4 percent above the control-state average from fiscal 1984–1993 to just at the national average over the 1994–2000 period. Nontax fees and long-term borrowing declined slightly as well, consistent with the limit's overall effectiveness. Credit agencies do not typically rate Colorado, so we cannot use their informed judgments here. Still, the clear story, at least until fiscal 2000, is that TABOR brought a moderate decline in the size of Colorado government, relative to states without TELs.[71]

The acid test of its effectiveness came after the 2004 elections, however, when Democrats gained control of both houses of the state's legislature. Since then, the Colorado legislature passed a higher education voucher plan that awards money to students who then take the money to a state university or one of a few private universities participating in the plan. Prior to the higher education

[69] The Colorado General Assembly did pass a spending limit in 1991, e-mail from National Conference of State Legislatures, *supra* note 20, but since TABOR came in the next year, it is not possible to measure the impact of this TEL.

[70] *Id.*

[71] Colorado is a prime example of a phenomenon we have discussed in a previous paper (Kousser and McCubbins 2005) about the difficulty voters have in making trade-offs during the initiative process. Thad Kousser and Mathew D. McCubbins, *Social Choice, Crypto-Initiatives and Policy Making by Direct Democracy* (prepared for delivery at Conference on Direct Democracy at UC Irvine, California, Jan. 14–15, 2005). Colorado state expenditures are restricted by TABOR but another initiative (Amendment 23 approved by voters in 2000) requires annual increases in K–12 education. *See* http://www.coloradobudget.com/amend23_101.cfm for a brief discussion of how TABOR and Amendment 23 interact.

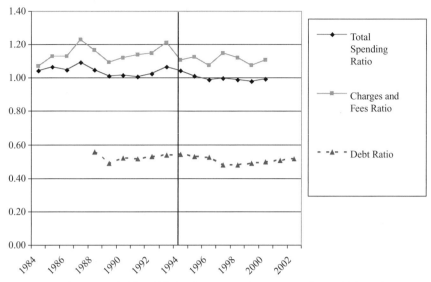

Figure 10.7. Colorado's 1992 TABOR TEL. (Note: Vertical line denotes fiscal 1994, the first budget written under the constraints of TABOR.)

voucher plan, state money was given directly to the universities and tuition was subject to TABOR revenue limits; however, with money now flowing directly to students, college tuition no longer is capped by TABOR and state universities can raise tuition as they see fit.[72] The design of this voucher plan is a classic example of how political agents attempt to work around the limits imposed by their principals, and suggests that even if TABOR appears successful on its face we have to be aware of how the state has increased tuition or fees in other areas that used to be funded by the state.

Finally, the epilogue to the TABOR story illustrates one of our hypotheses by showing that spending limits can be most easily undone in the states where it is easiest to amend the constitution. By 2005, anticipated cuts under TABOR were so severe that Colorado's Republican Governor Bill Owens, a fiscal conservative, backed a drive to call a five-year "Timeout for TABOR."[73] Because Colorado has the initiative process, Owens was able to work with legislative leaders and the state's political establishment to place this temporary suspension of the state's spending cap on the November 1, 2005 ballot as Proposition C. In an election that featured only half as much turnout as the contest in which TABOR first passed, Proposition C won with 52 percent of the vote while its companion Proposition D – which would have earmarked how state officials could spend their new money – failed.[74] At least for the next five years, Colorado lawmakers

[72] Chris Frates, *Fiscal Folly?*, 31 St. Legislatures 20 (Jan. 2005).
[73] Evan Halper, *Would State Budget Cap Pinch Like Colorado's?*, L.A.Times, Oct. 23, 2005.
[74] Fred Brown, *Election's Winners and Losers*, Denver Post, Nov. 6, 2005, at E-06.

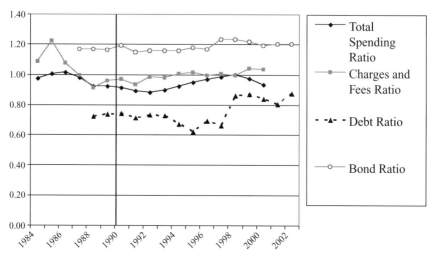

Figure 10.8. Utah's 1989 legislative spending limit. (Note: Vertical line denotes fiscal 1990, the first budget written under the constraints of Utah's spending limit.)

will be able to spend what they can raise in any way they choose, thanks to their ability to amend the state's constitution.

Utah's legislature imposed a spending limit upon itself in 1989, an important political consideration auguring for its potential success. But note that the legislature's action may not have reflected a sincere inclination to cut spending, because the presence of the initiative process in the state means that lawmakers may have been attempting to avoid a more stringent citizen spending cap. Their motivations also are puzzling given that Utah traditionally has had a frugal state budget, in keeping with its political culture. This may be a case in which there was no illness that required the treatment of a TEL. Regardless, the preferences of future lawmakers are promising for the implementation of the law. Utah Republicans, firmly in control of the state government, traditionally have ranked among the most conservative elected officials in the nation, and even the state's Democrats lean toward the right side of the spectrum.[75] Many of the political conditions in the state set its limit up for success, as does the letter of its law. The limit is indexed to inflation, requires a supermajority to override, and automatically adjusts if programs are transferred from state to local governments.[76]

Yet Figure 10.8 shows that the limit has failed to restrain spending growth. Utah's total state and local spending was $230 per capita below the control-group average the year the limit passed, but it grew during the 1990s and caught up with the baseline in fiscal 1998. Looking at other fiscal indicators hints at how this has happened. Utah has increasingly turned to nontax charges and

[75] Erikson, Wright, and McIver, *supra* note 22, at 103.
[76] E-mail from National Conference of State Legislatures, *supra* note 20.

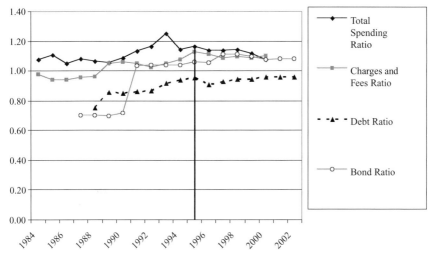

Figure 10.9. Washington's 1993 spending limit initiative. (Note: Vertical line denotes fiscal 1995, the first budget written under the constraints of Washington's spending limit.)

fees, and began taking out more debt in the late 1990s (though its credit rating remained perfect throughout the entire time series). The overall story from this traditionally conservative state is that its lawmakers were good fiscal stewards prior to the treatment and are good fiscal stewards afterward. The constraint was never needed, which seems to explain why it has not affected spending.

Voters in our final Western state, Washington, passed a direct initiative to limit spending in November 1993. They did so presumably to stop the spending growth that began in the late 1980s and peaked in fiscal 1993 under Democratic control of both legislative houses. The following year, voters gave Republicans overwhelming control of the lower house of the state legislature. But Democrats made gains in both houses, gaining full control of Washington government by the end of the decade through the election of Governor Gary Locke.[77] These political conditions – an externally imposed initiative seeking to limit the actions of a government increasingly sympathetic to spending growth – do not set it up for success. Neither did the letter of the law. Washington's limit is statutory rather than constitutional and, even though it is tied to inflation, it works on a three-year average.[78]

Figure 10.9 shows that it has not constrained the growth of government in Washington. Total spending already had dropped from its peak in the fiscal 1994 budget written just before the initiative passed. In the 11 fiscal years of our study before the limit went into effect, Washington spent on average 11 percent more than the control-group states. In the six years after the limit was passed,

---

[77] National Conference of State Legislatures, *Elections Data Tables, electronic forma* (2002).
[78] E-mail from National Conference of State Legislatures, *supra* note 20.

Table 10.2. Characteristics and effectiveness of TELs in case-study states

State	TEL provisions	Political context	Need for a TEL?	Effectiveness
California	weak	unfavorable	yes	Ineffective
Colorado	strong	favorable	yes	Effective
Utah	strong	favorable	no	Ineffective
Washington	weak	unfavorable	yes	Ineffective

total state and local spending in Washington averaged 13 percent higher than states without TELs. The other indicators show that Washington's government also has begun to charge more fees and to borrow more, relative to other states, since its voters imposed a limit. Just as in Utah and in California, Washington's spending limit has not brought any discernible drop in its expenditures. Table 10.2 summarizes our findings in this section, reporting the factors likely to influence a TEL's success in each state and its ultimate level of effectiveness.

V. CONCLUSIONS

Our close analysis of fiscal behavior before and after the enactment of spending limits in four Western states does not provide enough cases to reach a final verdict on our hypotheses about when ballot-box measures will be most likely to limit state budgets. It does, however, present clear evidence in favor of our central conjecture. Based upon the logic of principal–agent relationships, we doubted that those who enact tax and spending limits would be able to constrain the future actions of lawmakers possessed of different goals and direct control of state purse strings. Our data confirmed our doubts. Records of spending patterns show that TELs failed to constrain the size of government at all in three of the four states that we examined, and in the fourth state there is anecdotal evidence that politicians are now finding their way around the limit. Looking at other measures of fiscal behavior also suggests the ways in which lawmakers have been able to circumvent limits. These findings are consistent with the general failure of attempts to limit the federal budget. There may be some short-term effect while attention is directed at the political agents, but once attention is diverted, the change in process appears to have little effect.

Johnson and Kriz declare that "taxpayers use fiscal institutions as a vehicle to reduce their basic principal–agent problem that government officials may use taxpayers' resources in ways that are not in the taxpayers' best interest."[79] We agree that TELs represent attempts at this difficult task. However,

---

[79] Johnson and Kriz, *supra* note 12, at 85.

the additional principal-agent problem posed by entrusting these same officials with impending TELs compounds the taxpayers' dilemma. Our preliminary comparisons show that those who wanted to keep taxes low in California, Utah, and Washington did not make themselves any better off than taxpayers in states without spending limits.

Questions for Chapter 10

1. Kousser, McCubbins, and Rozga argue that the effectiveness of tax and expenditure limits (TELs) will vary with both the nature of their provisions and the political context in which they are implemented. The latter argues for within-state longitudinal analyses of their impact. A longitudinal or time-series analysis tracks the outcome variable over time within the jurisdiction, for example, explaining a particular state's annual expenditures per capita. Why is longitudinal analysis likely to be more effective than cross-state analysis (e.g., explaining differences in per capita expenditure levels across states in a given year) in determining the effectiveness of these interventions? The authors also argue for multiple indicators of fiscal outcomes. How do each of these estimation strategies affect concerns about endogeneity in the adoption of TELs? What are the implications for our ability to generalize their findings to other jurisdictions?

2. Kousser, McCubbins, and Rozga emphasize the principal–agent challenges associated with efforts by current political actors to constrain their own behavior and the future actions of their successors. Based on their case study of California's experience with the Gann initiative, the authors argue this TEL was ineffective because of the relative ease with which it could be circumvented to raise revenues, and because the limit was enacted via the initiative process and imposed on an unreceptive liberal legislature. Does this case suggest that we should have different expectations about the impacts of TELs passed via an initiative process versus those passed by legislatures? What model of voter behavior would explain both support for a fiscally conservative TEL initiative and the election of liberal legislators? How might a dynamic model of contractual behavior such as that suggested by Gordon provide insight to this question?

3. The four states explored by these authors are in the Western United States. The authors compare their fiscal outcomes with those of a control group of

states that did not adopt TELs. Musso, Graddy, and Grizard found regional differences across states in their use of a broad set of budgetary practices. What does this suggest about possible regional differences in fiscal preferences, institutions, and behavior within the United States? What implications might such differences have for how we analyze fiscal outcomes? How might a diffusion model of innovation[80] inform our understanding of the spread of fiscal reforms, and thus affect our understanding of the adoption and consequences of these processes?

[80] *See, e.g.*, Frances Stokes Berry and William D. Berry, "Innovation and Diffusion Models in Policy Research," Chapter 7 in THEORIES OF THE POLICY PROCESS 169–200 (P. Sabatier ed., 1999).

Bibliography

ARTICLES

Glenn Abney and Thomas P. Lauth, *The Line-Item Veto in the States: An Instrument for Fiscal Restraint or an Instrument for Partisanship?*, 45 PUB. ADMIN. REV. 372 (1985).

Glenn Abney and Thomas P. Lauth, *The End of Executive Dominance in State Appropriations*, 58 PUB. ADMIN. REV. 388 (1998).

Burton A. Abrams and William R. Dougan, *The Effects of Constitutional Restraints on Governmental Spending*, 49 PUB. CHOICE 101 (1986).

Alberto Alesina, *Credibility and Policy Convergence in a Two-Party System with Rational Voters*, 78 AM. ECON. REV. 796 (1988).

Alberto F. Alesina and Roberto Perotti, *Budget Deficits and Budget Institutions* (Nat'l Bureau of Econ. Research Working Paper No. 5556, 1995).

James E. Alt and Robert C. Lowry, *Divided Government, Fiscal Institutions, and Budget Deficits: Evidence from the States*, 88 AM. POLITICAL SCI. REV. 811 (1994).

James E. Alt and Robert C. Lowry, *A Dynamic Model of State Budget Outcomes Under Divided Partisan Government*, 62 J. POLITICS 1035 (2000).

Robert J. Barro and David B. Gordon, *A Positive Theory of Monetary Policy in a Natural Rate Model*, 91 J. POL. ECON. 589 (1983).

Reza Baqir, *Districting and Government Overspending* (Int'l Monetary Fund Working Paper No. 01/96, 2001).

Reza Baqir, *Districting and Government Overspending*, J. POL. ECON., Dec. 2002.

David P. Baron, *Electoral Competition with Informed and Uniformed Voters*, 88 AM. POL. SCI. REV. 33 (1994).

Robert J. Barro, *On the Determination of the Public Debt*, 87 J. POL. ECON. 940 (1979).

Theodore C. Bergstrom and Robert P. Goodman, *Private Demands for Public Goods*, 63 AM. ECON. REV. 280 (1973).

Timothy Besley and Anne C. Case, *Political Institutions and Policy Choices: Evidence from the United States*, 4 J. ECON. LITERATURE 7 (2003).

Timothy Besley and Stephen Coate, *Sources of Inefficiency in a Representative Democracy: A Dynamic Analysis*, 88 AM. ECON. REV. 139 (1998).

Henning Bohn and Robert P. Inman, *Balanced Budget Rules and Public Deficits: Evidence from the U.S. States* (Nat'l Bureau of Econ. Research Working Paper No. W5533, 1996).

Thomas E. Borchering and Robert T. Deacon, *The Demand for Services of Non-Federal Governments*, AM. ECON. REV. 891 (1972).

322

H. R. Bowen, *The Interpretation of Voting in the Allocation of Economic Resources*, 58 Q.J. Econ. 27 (1943).

Shaun Bowler and Todd Donovan, *Measuring the Effect of Direct Democracy on State Policy: Not All Initiatives are Created Equal*, 4 St. Pol. & Pol'y Q. 345 (2004).

Geoffrey F. Brennan and James M. Buchanan, *The Logic of Tax Limits: Alternative Constitutional Constraints on the Power to Tax*, 32 Nat'l Tax J. 11 (1979).

Geoffrey Brennan and James M. Buchanan, *Towards a Tax Constitution for Leviathan*, 8 J. Pub. Econ. 255 (1977).

Fred Brown, *Election's Winners and Losers*, Denver Post, Nov. 6, 2005, at E-06.

Laurel Brown and Blake Roberts, *Alternative Procedures: Line Item Vetoes and Balanced Budget Amendments* 11 (Harvard Law School Federal Budget Policy Seminar Briefing Paper No. 3, 2005), *available at* http://www.law.harvard.edu/faculty/hjackson/AlternativeProcedures_3.pdf.

Donald Campbell and H. Laurence Ross, *The Connecticut Crackdown on Speeding: Time Series Data in Quasi-Experimental Analysis*, 3 Law & Soc'y Rev. 33 (1968).

James C. Clingermayer and B. Dan Wood, *Disentangling Patterns of State Debt Financing*, 89 Am. Pol. Sci. Rev. 108 (1995).

James Cox and David Lowery, *The Impact of Tax Revolt Era State Fiscal Caps*, 3 Soc. Sci. Qu. 492 (1990).

W. Mark Crain and R. D. Tollison, *Time Inconsistency and Fiscal Policy: Empirical Analysis of U.S. States, 1969–89*, 51 J. Pub. Econ. 153 (1993).

Rui J. P. de Figueiredo, Jr., *Endogenous Budget Institutions and Political Insulation: Why States Adopt the Item Veto*, 8 J. Pub. Econ. 2677 (2003).

William R. Dougan, *The Effects of Tax and Expenditure Limits on State Governments* (George G. Stigler Center for Study of Economy and State Paper No. 54, 1988).

James W. Douglas and Kim U. Hoffman, *Impoundment at the State Level: Executive Power and Budget Impact*, 34 Am. Rev. Pub. Admin. 252 (2004).

Dennis Epple and Robert Romano, *Ends Against the Middle: Determining Public Service Provision When There Are Private Alternatives*, 62 J. Pub. Econ. 297 (1996).

William A. Fischel, *Did Serrano Cause Proposition 13?*, 43 Nat'l Tax J. 465 (1989).

Chris Frates, *Fiscal Folly?*, 31 St. Legislatures 20 (Jan. 2005).

Elisabeth R. Gerber, *Legislative Response to the Threat of Popular Initiatives*, 40 Am. J. Pol. Sci. 99 (1996).

Elisabeth R. Gerber and Arthur Lupia, *Campaign Competition and Policy Responsiveness in Direct Legislation Elections*, 17 Pol. Behav. 287 (1995).

Elisabeth Gerber, Arthur Lupia, and Mathew D. McCubbins, *When Does Government Limit the Impact of Voter Initiatives? The Politics of Implementation and Enforcement*, 66 J. Pol. 43 (2004).

Amihai Glazer, *Politics and the Choice of Durability*, 79 Am. Econ. Rev. 1207 (1989).

Gene M. Grossman and Elhanan Helpman, *Electoral Competition and Special Interest Politics*, 63 Rev. Econ. Stud. 265 (1996).

Evan Halper, *Would State Budget Cap Pinch Like Colorado's?*, L.A. Times, Oct. 23, 2005.

Douglas Holtz-Eakin, *The Line-Item Veto and Public Sector Budgets: Evidence from the States*, 36 J. Pub. Econ. 269 (1988).

Marcia Howard, *Tax and Expenditure Limitations: There Is No Story*, 9 Pub. Budgeting & Fin. 83 (1989).

Craig L. Johnson and Kenneth A. Kriz, *Fiscal Institutions, Credit Ratings, and Borrowing Costs*, 25 Pub. Budgeting & Fin. 84 (2005).

Joseph P. Kalt and Mark A. Zupan, *Capture and Ideology in the Economic Theory of Politics*, 74 Am. Econ. Rev. 279 (1984).

Paula S. Kearns, *The Determinants of State Budget Periodicity: An Empirical Analysis*, 13 PUB. BUDGETING & FIN. 40 (1993).

Paula S. Kearns, *State Budget Periodicity: An Analysis of the Determinants and the Effect on State Spending*, 13 J. POL'Y ANALYSIS & MGMT. 331 (1994).

D. Roderick Kiewiet and Kristin Szakaly, *Constitutional Limitations on Borrowing: An Analysis of State Bonded Indebtedness*, 12 J.L. & ECON. 62 (1996).

Tyson King-Meadows and David Lowery, *The Impact of the Tax Revolt Era State Fiscal Caps: A Research Update*, 16 PUB. BUDGETING & FIN. 102 (1996).

Brian G. Knight, *Supermajority Voting Requirements for Tax Increases: Evidence from the States*, 76 J. PUB. ECON. 41 (2000).

Brian Knight and Arik Levinson, *Rainy Day Funds and State Government Savings*, 52 NAT'L TAX J. 459 (1999).

Thad Kousser and Mathew D. McCubbins, *Social Choice, Crypto-Initiatives and Policy Making by Direct Democracy*, 78 S. CAL L. REV. 949 (2005).

Thad Kousser and Justin Phillips, *Who Sets the Size of State Government? Comparing Models of Interbranch Conflict* (prepared for presentation at the 2005 Meeting of the Western Political Science Association, 2005).

Finn E. Kydland and Edward C. Prescott, *Rules Rather than Discretion: The Inconsistency of Optimal Plans*, 85 J. POL. ECON. 473 (1977).

Thomas P. Lauth, *The Line-Item Veto in Government Budgeting*, 16 PUB. BUDGETING & FIN. 97 (1996).

Robert Lucas and Edith Stokey, *Optimal Fiscal and Monetary Policy in an Economy Without Capital*, 12 J. MONETARY ECON. 55 (1983).

Arthur Lupia, *Busy Voters, Agenda Control, and the Power of Information*, 86 AM. POL. SCI. REV. 390 (1992).

David W. Lyon, *From Home Rule to Fiscal Rule: Taking Measure of Local Government Finance in California* (Public Policy Institute of California Paper, 2000).

Mathew McCubbins and Thomas Schwartz, *Congressional Oversight Overlooked: Police Patrols Versus Fire Alarms*, 28 AM. J. POL. SCI. 165 (1984).

Richard D. McKelvey, *Intransitivities in Multidimensional Voting Models and Some Implications for Agenda Control*, 2 J. ECON. THEORY 472 (1976).

Moody's Investor Service, *Moody's Bond Record* (Jan. eds. 1988–1994).

Stephen Moore and John Silvia, *The ABCs of the Capital Gains Tax*, CATO INSTITUTE POLICY ANALYSIS NO. 242 (1995).

Daniel R. Mullins and Bruce A. Wallin, *Tax and Expenditure Limitations: Introduction and Overview*, 24 PUB. BUDGETING & FIN. 2 (2004).

Juliet Musso, Elizabeth Graddy, and Jennifer Grizard, *State Budgetary Processes and Reforms: The California Story*, 26 PUB. BUDGETING & FIN. 1 (2006).

Michael J. New, *Limiting Government Through Direct Democracy: The Case of State Tax and Expenditure Limitations*, CATO INSTITUTE POLICY ANALYSIS NO. 420 (2001).

Michael J. New, *The Gann Limit Turns 25*, Bus. Daily, Oct. 28, 2004.

David C. Nice, *The Item Veto and Expenditure Restraint*, 50 J. POL. 487 (1988).

William A. Niskanen, *Non-Market Decision Making: The Peculiar Economics of Bureaucracy*, AM. ECON. REV. 293 (1968).

William A. Niskanen, *Bureaucrats and Politicians*, 18 J.L. & ECON. 617 (1975).

Dion Nissenbaum, *The First 100 Days: Schwarzenegger Exploits Intellect, Gift for Connecting with People*, SAN JOSE MERCURY NEWS, Feb. 22, 2004.

Sam Peltzman, *Toward a More General Theory of Regulation*, 19 J.L. & ECON. 211 (1976).

Torsten Persson and Lars O. Svensson, *Why a Stubborn Conservative Would Run a Deficit: Policy with Time-Inconsistent Preferences*, Q.J. Econ., May 1989, at 325.

Charles Plott, *A Notion of Equilibrium and its Possibility Under Majority Rule*, 57 Am. Econ. Rev. 787 (1967).

James M. Poterba, *Balanced Budget Rules and Fiscal Policy: Evidence from the States*, 48 Nat'l Tax J. 329 (1995).

James M. Poterba, *Budget Institutions and Fiscal Policy in the U.S. States*, 86 Am. Econ. Rev. 2 (1996).

James M. Poterba, *State Responses to Fiscal Crises: The Effects of Budgetary Institutions and Politics*, 102 J. Pol. Econ. 799 (1994).

James M. Poterba and Kim S. Rueben, *Fiscal News, State Budget Rules, and Tax-Exempt Bond Yields*, 50 J. Urban Econ. 537 (2001).

William Riker, *Implications for the Disequilibrium of Majority Rule for the Study of Institutions*, 74 Am. Pol. Sci. Rev. 432 (1980).

D. Rodrik and R. Zeckhauser, *The Dilemma of Government Responsiveness*, 7 J. Pol'y Analysis and Mgmt. 605 (1988).

Thomas Romer and Howard Rosenthal, *Bureaucrats Versus Voters: On the Political Economy of Resource Allocation by Direct Democracy*, Q.J. Econ., Nov. 1979, at 563.

Thomas Romer and Howard Rosenthal, *The Elusive Median Voter*, 12 J. Pub. Econ. 143 (1979).

Thomas Romer and Howard Rosenthal, *Political Resource Allocation, Controlled Agendas, and the Status Quo*, 33 Pub. Choice 27 (1978).

Kim S. Rueben, *Tax Limitations and Government Growth: The Effect of State Tax and Expenditure Limits on State and Local Government* (Public Policy Institute of California Working Paper, 1996).

Harrison Sheppard, *What's Been Done? What's Still to Do?*, L.A. Daily News, Feb. 21, 2004.

Kenneth A. Shepsle, *Institutional Arrangements and Equilibrium in Multidimensional Voting Models*, 23 Am. J. Pol. Sci. 27 (1979).

Michael Shires, *Patterns in California Government Revenues Since Prop. 13* (Public Policy Institute of California Paper, 1999).

John Simerman, *Schwarzenegger's Advisors Work on Plan to Cap California Spending*, Contra Costa Times, Oct. 22, 2003.

Daniel A. Smith, *Peeling Away the Populist Rhetoric: Toward a Taxonomy of Anti-Tax Ballot Initiatives*, 24 Pub. Budgeting & Fin. 88 (2004).

Dean Stansel, *Taming Leviathan: Are Tax and Spending Limits the Answer?*, Cato Institute Policy Analysis No. 213 (1994).

George J. Stigler, *The Theory of Economic Regulation*, 3 Bell J. Econ. & Mgmt. Sci. 33 (1971).

Richard H. Thaler and H. M. Shefrin, *An Economic Theory of Self Control*, 89 J. Pol. Econ. 392 (1981).

Charles M. Tiebout, *A Pure Theory of Local Expenditures*, 64 J. Pol. Econ. 416 (1956).

Gordon Tullock, *The Welfare Costs of Tariffs, Subsidies, and Theft*, 5 W. Econ. J. 224 (1967).

Jürgen von Hagen, *A Note on the Empirical Effectiveness of Formal Fiscal Restraints*, 44 J. Pub. Econ. 199 (1991).

Barry R. Weingast and William J. Marshall, *The Industrial Organization of Congress; or, Why Legislatures, Like Firms, are not Organized as Markets*, 96 J. Pol. Econ. 132 (1988).

Barry R. Weingast, Kenneth A. Shepsle, and Christopher Johnsen, *The Political Economy of Benefits and Costs: A Neoclassical Approach to Distributive Politics*, 89 J. POL. ECON. 642 (1981).

Stuart Young and Drew McClelland, *Implementing Biennial Budgeting for the U.S. Congress* 16 (Harvard Law School Federal Budget Policy Seminar Briefing Paper No. 20, 2006), *available at* http://www.law.harvard.edu/faculty/hjackson/BiennialBudget_20.pdf.

BOOKS

A. Atkinson and J. Stiglitz, LECTURES ON PUBLIC ECONOMICS (1980).

Frances Stokes Berry and William D. Berry, *Innovation and Diffusion Models in Policy Research*, Chapter 7 in THEORIES OF THE POLICY PROCESS 169–200 (P. Sabatier ed., 1999).

Duncan Black, THE THEORY OF COMMITTEES AND ELECTIONS (1958).

Geoffrey F. Brennan and James M. Buchanan, THE POWER TO TAX: ANALYTICAL FOUNDATIONS OF A FISCAL CONSTITUTION (1980).

Gary M. Cox and Mathew McCubbins, LEGISLATIVE LEVIATHAN: PARTY GOVERNMENT IN THE HOUSE (1993).

L. Davis and D. C. North, INSTITUTIONAL CHANGE AND AMERICAN ECONOMIC GROWTH (1971).

A. T. Denzau, R. J. Mackay, and C. L. Weaver, *On the Initiative-Referendum Option and the Control of Monopoly Government*, in TAX AND EXPENDITURE LIMITATIONS 191 (H. F. Ladd and T. N. Tideman eds., 1981).

Anthony Downs, AN ECONOMIC THEORY OF DEMOCRACY (1957).

Daniel Elazar, AMERICAN FEDERALISM: A VIEW FROM THE STATES (2nd ed., 1972).

John W. Ellwood and Mary Sprague, *Options for Reforming the State Budget Process*, in CONSTITUTIONAL REFORM IN CALIFORNIA: MAKING STATE GOVERNMENT MORE EFFECTIVE AND RESPONSIVE 329 (Roger G. Noll and Bruce E. Cain eds., 1995).

David Epstein and Sharyn O'Halloran, DELEGATING POWERS: A TRANSACTION COST POLITICS APPROACH TO POLICY MAKING UNDER SEPARATE POWERS (1999).

Robert Erikson, Gerald Wright, and John McIver, STATEHOUSE DEMOCRACY: PUBLIC OPINION AND POLICY IN THE AMERICAN STATES (1993).

Richard F. Fenno, CONGRESSMEN IN COMMITTEES (1973).

Keith Krehbiel, INFORMATION AND LEGISLATIVE ORGANIZATION (1991).

John D. Huber and Charles R. Shipan, DELIBERATE DISCRETION? THE INSTITUTIONAL FOUNDATIONS OF BUREAUCRATIC AUTONOMY (2002).

D. Roderick Kiewiet and Mathew D. McCubbins, THE LOGIC OF DELEGATION: CONGRESSIONAL PARTIES AND THE APPROPRIATIONS PROCESS (1991).

Arthur Lupia and Mathew D. McCubbins, THE DEMOCRATIC DILEMMA: CAN CITIZENS LEARN WHAT THEY NEED TO KNOW?(1998).

John G. Matsusaka, FOR THE MANY OR THE FEW: HOW THE INITIATIVE PROCESS CHANGES AMERICAN GOVERNMENT (2004).

Terry M. Moe, *The Politics of Bureaucratic Structure, in* CAN THE GOVERNMENT GOVERN? (John E. Chubb and P. E. Petersen eds., 1989).

William A. Niskanen, BUREAUCRACY AND REPRESENTATIVE GOVERNMENT (1971).

Wallace E. Oates, FISCAL FEDERALISM (1972).

James Poterba, *Do Budget Rules Work?, in* FISCAL POLICY: LESSONS FROM EMPIRICAL RESEARCH 53 (A. Auerbach ed., 1997).

James M. Poterba and Kim S. Rueben, FISCAL RULES AND STATE BORROWING COSTS: EVIDENCE FROM CALIFORNIA AND OTHER STATES (1999).

James M. Poterba and Kim S. Reuben, FISCAL RULES AND BOND YIELDS: DO TAX LIMITS RAISE THE STATE'S BORROWING COSTS? (1999).

David Rohde, PARTIES AND LEADERS IN THE POSTREFORM HOUSE (1991).

Kim S. Rueben, TAX LIMITATIONS AND GOVERNMENT GROWTH: THE EFFECT OF STATE TAX AND EXPENDITURE LIMITS ON STATE AND LOCAL GOVERNMENT (mimeograph) (1995).

Allen Schick, THE FEDERAL BUDGET: POLITICS, POLICY, PROCESS (1995).

Aaron B. Wildavsky, THE POLITICS OF THE BUDGETARY PROCESS (2nd ed., 1974).

CONGRESSIONAL REPORTS

CALIFORNIA DEPARTMENT OF FINANCE, GOVERNOR'S BUDGET 2005 – BACKGROUND INFORMATION, CHART K-1 – K-6: HISTORY OF CALIFORNIA GENERAL OBLIGATION BOND RATINGS, *available at* http://www.dof.ca.gov/HTML/BUD_DOCS/backinfo.htm (last visited Feb. 2005).

CALIFORNIA DEPARTMENT OF FINANCE, GOVERNOR'S BUDGET 2005 – BACKGROUND INFORMATION, CHART L: HISTORICAL DATA, STATE APPROPRIATIONS LIMIT, *available at* http://www.dof.ca.gov/HTML/BUD_DOCS/backinfo.htm (last visited Feb. 2005).

CENTER FOR BUDGET AND POLICY PRIORITIES, *State TABOR Proposals – 2005* March 4. Fong Eu, State of California, secretary of state, *California's Ballot Pamphlet, Primary Election, June 5, 1990* (1990).

LEGISLATIVE SESSION, WASHINGTON, D.C.: CBPP (2005).

LEGISLATIVE ANALYST'S OFFICE, THE STATE APPROPRIATIONS LIMIT (2000), *available at* http://www.lao.ca.gov/2000/041300_gann/041300_gann.html.

NAT'L ASSOCIATION OF STATE BUDGET OFFICERS, STATE BALANCED BUDGET REQUIREMENTS: PROVISIONS AND PRACTICE, WASHINGTON, D.C.: NASBO (1992).

NAT'L CONFERENCE OF STATE LEGISLATURES, LEGISLATIVE BUDGET PROCEDURES: A GUIDE TO APPROPRIATIONS AND BUDGET PROCESSES IN THE STATES, COMMONWEALTHS, AND TERRITORIES, DENVER, NCSL (1999).

NAT'L CONFERENCE OF STATE LEGISLATURES, STATE BALANCED BUDGET REQUIREMENTS (1999), *available at* http://www.ncsl.org/programs/fiscal/balreqs.htm.

NAT'L ASSOCIATION OF STATE BUDGET OFFICERS, BUDGET PROCESSES IN THE STATES, WASHINGTON, D.C.: NASBO (2002).

NAT'L CONFERENCE OF STATE LEGISLATURES, STATE BUDGET AND TAX ACTIONS 2003 PRELIMINARY REPORT, DENVER: NCSL (2003).

NAT'L CONFERENCE OF STATE LEGISLATURES, BOOK OF THE STATES (2005).

NAT'L CONFERENCE OF STATE LEGISLATURES, STATE TAX AND EXPENDITURE LIMITS – 2005 (2005), *available at* http://www.ncsl.org/programs/fiscal/tels2005.htm.

NAT'L CONFERENCE OF STATE LEGISLATURES, LEGISLATIVE BUDGET PROCEDURES: A GUIDE TO APPROPRIATIONS AND BUDGET PROCESSES IN THE STATES, COMMONWEALTHS AND TERRITORIES (2006), *available at* http://www.ncsl.org/programs/fiscal/lbptabls/index.htm#dveloprb.

NAT'L CONFERENCE OF STATE LEGISLATURES, STATE BUDGET AND TAX ACTIONS 2006 PRELIMINARY REPORT, DENVER: NCSL (2006).

MANDY RAFOOL, STATE TAX AND EXPENDITURE LIMITS – 2005, WASHINGTON, D.C. NCSL (2005).

Ronald K. Snell, *Annual and Biennial Budgeting: The Experience of State Governments,* Nat'l Conference of State Legislatures, (October 2004) *available at* http://www.ncsl.org/programs/fiscal/annlbien.htm#t1.

U.S. Census Bureau, The 2006 Statistical Abstract (2006) *available at* http://www.census.gov/compendia/statab/.

U.S. Census Bureau, State and Local Government Finance.

U.S. Census Bureau, website, http://www.census.gov/govs/www/estimate.html, accessed in March 2005. The data from fiscal years 1969–1996, 1992–2002 and from 1988–1991.

PART FOUR

INTERGOVERNMENTAL ASPECTS OF BUDGET POLICY

This book is designed to enable readers to perceive and understand connections that they might have overlooked: connections among different disciplines; connections among budgetary institutions in the legislative and executive branches of federal and state governments; connections between U.S. budgetary policy and fiscal policy in other countries; connections between the perceptions of voters and policymakers and actual budget policy. In this section, we examine more closely intergovernmental connections that influence fiscal outcomes.

John Joseph Wallis and Barry Weingast's examination of state constitutional debt limitations and their effect on the choice of financing methods for infrastructure differs from previous chapters in two crucial ways. First, they provide the first sustained analysis of local governments and their role in fiscal policy as they issue bonds to build roads, schools, sports stadiums, and other public goods. Any complete assessment of local government must take account of state constitutional and statutory provisions because local governments are created by the state and their powers are dramatically affected by state decisions. Second, Wallis and Weingast provide a different sort of comparative analysis than we have seen before: their analysis is historical, comparing infrastructure financing in the United States at three different periods over a 150-year time span. Although other chapters may have provided some historical context for contemporary budget institutions, this chapter is the most sustained empirical comparison of budget institutions and their consequences across a substantial period of time.

The authors' historical analysis explains aspects of the current constitutional structure that governs state and local government debt, a structure that developed over time as public officials reacted to financial crises brought about by previous policies. The result is a complex and fragmented local government system, consisting of many institutions focused on particular purposes, such as school, water, and sewer districts, alongside more traditional institutions, such as cities and counties. These special governments often have different boundaries than county and city governments and have independent power to issue debt. Wallis and Weingast conclude that the flexibility that now character-izes the structure of local government has been largely beneficial, allowing the creation of units that match an infrastructure project's beneficiaries to those who must finance it. Because of this matching of benefit and cost, it is likely that infrastructure decisions in the United States will be welfare enhancing.

In contrast, Chapter 12 does not provide such a rosy view of the results of intergovernmental interactions. David Super focuses on the connection between federal fiscal policy and state fiscal policy. Issues related to fiscal fed-eralism have received increasing attention in the courts and Congress. A series of Supreme Court cases have dealt with the constitutional issues relevant to conditional spending and federal mandates applied to state officials.[1] Outcry from state policy makers about "unfunded mandates" levied by the federal government led to passage of the Unfunded Mandates Reform Act of 1995.[2] Super's analysis of this crucial intergovernmental relationship goes beyond the rhetoric of unfunded mandates and provides a comprehensive set of issues that affect state and national fiscal policy. One problem that this chapter clearly illuminates is that state fiscal policy is much more vulnerable than federal bud-get decision making to business cycles, a reality that federal lawmakers often ignore when reacting to economic downturns, thereby exacerbating the states' precarious fiscal condition.

This chapter is not only descriptive, but it also provides procedural and substantive recommendations for federal and state budget policy in light of the intergovernmental interactions Super carefully sets forth. For example, he argues that the differences between state and federal governments lead to the conclusion that much of the aid to low-income Americans is better provided by the federal government, rather than the state and local governments that increasingly bear the financial burden of such programs. In contrast, aid to the elderly and persons with disabilities is better assumed by states because it is not as dependent on economic volatility. The complexities of budgeting in a federal system are numerous – not only are there vertical interactions between state and federal levels, but there are also horizontal interactions because one state's budget decisions may affect the economic environment of other states.

In the end, these chapters underscore the need for sensitivity to complexity and nuance as budget policy decisions are made. Policymakers need to under-stand how budget rules have developed over time to respond to crises in the past; and they need to be aware that a decision at one level of government may influence the options of policymakers at other levels who face different political and economic constraints.

---

[1] *See, e.g., South Dakota v. Dole*, 483 U.S. 203 (1987) (providing clear statement requirement for federal conditions applied to state assistance); *Printz v. United States*, 521 U.S. 898 (1997) (finding provisions of the Brady Act to be unconstitutional commandeering of state officials).
[2] Pub. L. No. 104–4, 109 Stat. 48 (codified in scattered sections of 2 U.S.C.).

11 Dysfunctional or Optimal Institutions?

State Debt Limitations, the Structure of State and Local Governments, and the Finance of American Infrastructure

John Joseph Wallis and Barry R. Weingast

I. INTRODUCTION

American state and local governmental fiscal institutions present a contrast. Many scholars regard these institutions as dysfunctional: balanced-budget provisions do not produce balanced budgets; debt restrictions do not restrict debt issue; tax and expenditure limitations limit neither taxes nor expenditures; and budget stabilization funds fail to provide budget stabilization. Richard Briffault, for example, concludes "state constitutional debt restrictions have been circumvented by new and creative financing devices that tend to drive up the cost of borrowing, encourage the fragmentation of state governments, and facilitate the evasion of balanced budget requirements."[1]

In contrast, American state and local governments are quite responsible by any reasonable measure of fiscal probity. They borrow large amounts of funds and rarely fail to service or repay their debts. The vast majority of state and local debt is issued to finance infrastructure investments, and American infrastructure is in many respects the best in the world. The decentralized structure of American government, while far from perfect, often is held up as a system of how to constrain the powers of government through the institutional mechanism of federalism.

---

[1] Richard Briffault, BALANCING ACTS: THE REALITY BEHIND STATE BALANCED BUDGET REQUIREMENTS 51 (1996). Chapter 5 of Briffault has a comprehensive survey of the literature on the effectiveness of fiscal rules. *Id.* at 55–62. "In other words, legal balanced budget requirements per se do not compel balance." *Id.* at 59. There is also an extensive economics literature on the effectiveness of fiscal rules, particularly debt limitations and balanced-budget restrictions. For a review of this literature, see James Poterba, *Balanced Budget Rules and Fiscal Policy: Evidence from the States*, 48 NAT'L TAX J. 329 (1995).

John Joseph Wallis is a professor of economics, University of Maryland and research associate, NBER, and was a Visiting Scholar, Hoover Institution, Stanford University while this paper was written. Barry R. Weingast is a senior fellow, Hoover Institution, and the Ward C. Krebs Family Professor, Department of Political Science, Stanford University.

We resolve the apparent contradiction of these two views by looking deeper into the effect of fiscal rules on the structure of American governments. The structure of American state and local governments has changed frequently, if episodically, since 1776. We argue that scholars have failed to appreciate the degree to which fiscal issues have shaped the structure of American state and local government.

Our main hypothesis is that the current structure of state and local governments and their proven ability to provide infrastructure result from two centuries of evolution of constitutional rules, primarily fiscal rules about government borrowing. The structure works well at constraining state and local governments to make investments in public infrastructure and services that generate positive social returns. Canals, roads, improvements to rivers and harbors, railroads, and banks all helped transform a large portion of Americans from self-sufficient farmers into market specialists for national and international markets. Roads, water, sewer, gas, electric, solid-waste disposal, schools, and fire services all fostered the growth of cities necessary for American industrialization.

Paradoxically, the effect of fiscal restrictions over time has been to produce more borrowing and larger governments. Fiscal restrictions allow borrowing and constrain governments to issue debt for socially useful positive purposes and, ultimately, repay it. The system works, and citizens are willing to pay higher taxes and service a larger government debt because they receive infrastructure projects of greater value.

Our approach is both historical and conceptual. We address three historical questions. First, how do we explain the dramatic changes in the structure of state and local governments over the course of the 19th and early 20th centuries? Second, how do we explain the dramatic change in the structure of state and local debt? In 1841, state debt was nine times local debt; in 1902, local debt was eight times state debt. Third, how do we interpret the evolving constitutional rules regulating state and local debt? Our focus is on the years from 1840 to 1933, the time when state and local governments adopted many of the rules that govern their internal fiscal structure.

Public finance often takes the nature of government policies as given. "Second-generation fiscal federalism" (SGFF) alters this perspective by assuming that different policies have incentive effects on the behavior of the politicians and, further, that policy rules will change over time in response to these incentives.[2] As a result, some budget rules are more likely to create problems with

---

[2] Oates and Weingast explore the distinction between first- and second-generation models and provide surveys of second-generation models. *See* Wallace Oates, *Toward a Second-Generation Theory of Fiscal Federalism*, 12 INT'L TAX & PUB. FIN. 349 (2005); Barry R. Weingast, *Second Generation Fiscal Federalism: Implications for Decentralized Democratic Governance and*

debt finance than others. An important normative question of SGFF is how to design fiscal institutions so that the incentives of political officials align with the citizens they represent. We focus primarily on the structure of governments – the distribution of government functions and revenue source between levels of government – and the rules about how governments authorize new borrowing.

Early Americans learned about fiscal organization through trial and error. As a result, the evolutionary history of state and local governments exhibits a recurring cycle of behavior. Governments pursued policies under their existing rules, which then caused problems, including fiscal crises. The crises were followed by adjustments in the rules. The new rules produced a new set of policies, often followed by another set of crises and another round of rule changes.

Three major cycles occurred from the birth of the republic through the mid-20th century. In the first cycle, from 1790 to 1850, states invested heavily in financial and transportation infrastructure. States reacted to the financial crisis, culminating in the state defaults of the 1840s, with a series of constitutional amendments that created procedural restrictions on state debts that made it more costly for states to finance infrastructure through debt issue. In the second cycle, from 1840 to 1870s, infrastructure investment shifted decisively to local governments. The shift to local borrowing produced local default crises in the 1870s. States again responded constitutionally, extending procedural restrictions and specific limitations on the issue of local government debt in the 1870s. In the third cycle, from the 1880s to the 1930s, the effect of restrictions on local general governments created incentives for the development of "special governments": school districts, sewer and water districts, and utility districts whose boundaries may extend across local governments or exist completely within existing local governments. After the turn of the 20th century, states began limiting the liability that state and general-purpose governments assume for special-district debts.

Changes in government structure fall into two categories. The first involves the location of government functions. The *substitution hypothesis* maintains that greater restrictions on *state* borrowing fostered the growth of *local* governments as government functions and borrowing moved to smaller government units. The second involves the type of governments that existed. The *government jurisdiction hypothesis* holds that Americans reacted to the recurring cycles of debt problems by designing a flexible set of new local

Economic Development (Hoover Institution Stanford University Working Paper, 2006). Wallis, Sylla, and Legler provide a SGFF model that explains the evolution of the early American banking system into a competitive industry. *See* John Joseph Wallis, Richard Sylla, and John Legler, *The Interaction of Taxation and Regulation in Nineteenth Century Banking, in* THE REGULATED ECONOMY: A HISTORICAL APPROACH TO POLITICAL ECONOMY 121 (Claudia Goldin and Gary D. Libecap eds., 1994).

governments, special governments, that more closely matched beneficiaries and taxpayers.

In general, changes in the structure and jurisdiction of American governments over time have produced more and smaller governments. These smaller governments better match the citizens who benefit from the project being built, with the taxpayers responsible for servicing bonded debts. More closely matching taxpayers and beneficiaries has the effect of ensuring better decisions about which projects are built. The development of smaller jurisdictions required the articulation of liability rules. In many cases, special district governments are solely liable for their bonded debts. Lenders who cannot depend on the deep pockets of general governments to bail out special districts will pay much closer attention to fiscal viability of proposed projects, thereby mobilizing the private market to police public borrowing.

This institutional structure is not perfect, but nonetheless, on balance, it is quite positive. America has some of the finest infrastructure in the world. State and local governments issue huge amounts of debt each year, and yet very few fail to make good on their bonds.

This chapter proceeds as follows. Section II presents a brief overview of the history of governmental structure and infrastructure provision. Section III discusses our political approach to governmental policymaking with respect to infrastructure projects. Section IV provides evidence of state governmental behavior in the first cycle, including the emerging state debt crisis after 1841. Section V discusses the first round of constitutional revisions in reaction to the debt crisis. Section VI examines the effects of procedural debt restrictions on state borrowing between 1841 and 1860. Section VII turns to the shift in infrastructure provision from state to local governments in the second cycle. Section VIII raises some of the complications involved in home rule. Section IX treats the growing importance of special governments in the second and third cycles. Section X returns to local governments, including limited liability for special government debt. Our conclusions follow.

II. GOVERNMENT STRUCTURE AND INFRASTRUCTURE: A BRIEF HISTORY

Table 11.1 gives the number of governments by type from 1942 to 2002, for the Census of Government years. Two features of this data are striking: the large number of governments – especially given that there are only 50 states and 3,000 counties – and the significant decline in the number of governments over the 20th century. Nearly all of the action is in two types of governments. The number of school districts declined from 108,579 in 1942 to 15,014 in 2002, while the number of special districts rose from 8,299 to 35,052. The number of counties, municipalities, townships, and villages has been relatively constant.[3]

---

[3] There were 18,189 counties, municipalities, towns, and townships in 1942, and 18,976 in 2002.

Table 11.1. Number of governments, by level and type, 1942 to 2002

Year	Total	National	State	Local Total	County	Municipal	Township and town	School districts	Special districts
1942	155,116	1	48	155,067	3,050	16,220	18,919	108,579	8,299
1952	116,807	1	50	116,756	3,052	16,807	17,202	67,355	12,340
1957	102,392	1	50	102,341	3,050	17,215	17,198	50,454	14,424
1962	91,237	1	50	91,186	3,043	18,000	17,142	34,678	18,323
1967	81,299	1	50	81,248	3,049	18,048	17,105	21,782	21,264
1972	78,269	1	50	78,218	3,044	18,517	16,991	15,781	23,885
1977	79,913	1	50	79,862	3,042	18,862	16,822	15,174	25,962
1982	81,831	1	50	81,780	3,041	19,076	16,734	14,851	28,078
1987	83,237	1	50	83,186	3,042	19,200	16,691	14,721	29,532
1992	86,743	1	50	86,692	3,043	19,296	16,666	14,556	33,131
1997	87,504	1	50	87,453	3,043	19,372	16,629	13,726	34,683
2002	87,576	1	50	87,525	3,043	19,429	16,504	13,506	35,052

Table 11.2. Government debt by level of government: levels and shares 1838 to 2002

Year	Debt ($ millions)			Share (%)			State share of S&L debt
	State	Local	National	State	Local	National	
1838	172	25	3	86.0	12.5	1.5	87
1841	190	25	5	86.4	11.4	2.3	88
1870	352	516	2,436	10.7	15.6	73.7	41
1880	297	826	2,090	9.2	25.7	65.0	26
1890	228	905	1,122	10.1	40.1	49.8	20
1902	230	1,877	1,178	7.0	57.1	35.9	11
1913	379	4,035	1,193	6.8	72.0	21.3	9
1922	1,131	8,978	22,963	3.4	27.1	69.4	11
1932	2,832	16,373	19,487	7.3	42.3	50.4	15
1942	3,257	16,080	67,753	3.7	18.5	77.8	17
1952	6,874	23,226	214,758	2.8	9.5	87.7	23
1962	22,023	58,779	248,010	6.7	17.9	75.4	27
1972	59,375	129,110	322,377	11.6	25.3	63.1	32
1982	147,470	257,109	924,600	11.1	19.3	69.6	36
1992	369,370	584,774	2,999,700	9.3	14.8	75.9	39
1997	456,657	764,844	3,772,300	9.1	15.3	75.5	37
2002	642,202	1,042,904	3,540,400	12.3	20.0	67.8	38

The changing number and type of governments is evidence of flexibility in American government structure. In contrast to the 35,000-plus special districts in 2002, in 1880, there were probably no more than a handful of special districts. Twenty-two percent of these districts provide infrastructure and services in natural resources (soil conservation, flood control, and water supply); 20 percent provide utilities, sewerage, solid-waste disposal, and water supply; 16 percent provide fire-protection services; 10 percent provide housing; and the remaining 32 percent are spread over a wide variety of functions. The structure and administrative form of these governments is fitted to the services they provide or investments they make. Special districts usually are fingered as major culprits in state government attempts to circumvent or subvert debt limitations by creating special governments' taxing and borrowing authority and through creative intergovernmental financial accounting.[4]

Table 11.2 gives the overall picture on government debt by level of government. The table begins with two estimates for 1838 and 1841, and then presents Census numbers from 1870 to the present. A striking feature of the table is the large variation in the debt of state governments as a share of total government debt. The three historical cycles are clear in the table. In 1841, at the end of the 1830s internal improvement boom (the first cycle), state debt was

---

[4] *See* Briffault, *supra* note 1. The numbers on special districts by function are taken from U.S. Census Bureau, GC02(1)-1, *Government Organization*, 1 2002 CENSUS OF GOVERNMENTS No. 1, 13–14 (2002).

86 percent of all government debt. By 1922, state debt had fallen to 3 percent of all government debt. Over the course of the 20th century, state debt rose again, comprising between 10 percent and 12 percent of all government debt since the 1970s, even with the enormous increase in national government borrowing since the 1980s.[5]

Relative to local government borrowing, the state decline and recovery is even more marked. In 1913, local debt was 72 percent of all government debt and more than triple national government debt. In 1932, local debt had grown to almost equal national government debt again (national debt had risen during World War I and gradually declined thereafter). The Great Depression and World War II brought national government borrowing to a prominence that it has yet to relinquish.

Although the national government borrows primarily to finance wars and budget shortfalls, state and local governments borrow primarily to fund infrastructure investments in education, transportation, and utilities. In 2002, state and local governments owed a total of $1.7 trillion. Debt for education was 20 percent of all state and local debt, and debt for utilities was 13.3 percent. The totals, however, are somewhat opaque about function, since most of the debt outstanding was issued as "public debt for private purposes" (25.3 percent) or "other" (41.3 percent).[6] A large portion of bonds issued in any year are to refinance existing debt; those debt issues end up in the "other" category, rather than in the function for which the bonds originally were issued.

We get a better idea of how much state and local governments spend on infrastructure by looking at capital outlays. Table 11.3 gives state and local expenditures for capital outlay by function in 2002, which totaled $257 billion. The last two lines of the table give the total amount of new debt issued in fiscal 2002, $262 billion, and the amount of debt retired, $162 billion. The bulk of capital outlay went for education, 27.8 percent, and highways, 25.7 percent, with a substantial amount going to utilities, 11.8 percent. Not all capital outlays were financed by borrowing, of course, but a large percentage of them were. The large majority of state and local borrowing has always gone to finance infrastructure.

In contrast, the national government spends very little on infrastructure, at least directly. In 1996, total capital outlays by all governments – national, state, and local – were $225 billion. Of that total, only $21 billion were national government outlays, and, of that, $15 billion went to national defense. Beyond infrastructure spending, the nature of national government spending differs considerably from state and local spending in that it is far less geographically

---

[5] Prior to World War II, the national government borrowed primarily to finance wars, but since 1945 the national government has borrowed primarily to fund budget deficiencies.

[6] U.S. Census Bureau, GC02(4)-5, *Compendium of Government Finances: 2002*, 4 2002 CENSUS OF GOVERNMENTS No. 5 (2002).

Table 11.3. State and local government capital outlay, fiscal 2002,
by function (millions of dollars)

Outlay	Amount	Percent of total
All capital outlay	257,214	
Education	71,582	27.8
Social service	7,177	2.8
Transportation		
Highways	66,170	25.7
Air	8,551	3.3
Parking	329	0.1
Water	1,691	0.7
Public safety	8,726	3.4
Natural resources	4,247	1.7
Parks and recreation	9,093	3.5
Housing and comm. dev.	6,939	2.7
Sewerage	11,574	4.5
Solid waste	1,607	0.6
Govt. administration	8,156	3.2
Other	20,139	7.8
Utilities	30,228	11.8
Water	11,198	4.4
Electric	6,538	2.5
Gas	358	0.1
Transit	11,514	4.5
Exhibit:		
Long-term debt issued	262,339	
Long-Term debt retired	162,463	

Source: U.S. Census Bureau, GC02(4)-5, Compendium of Government
Finances: 2002, 4 2002 Census of Governments No. 5 (2005).

specific and far more diffuse. In the 2002 fiscal year, the national government outlays were $2,011 billion.[7] Of the total, $348.9 billion was for defense,
$853.3 billion for Social Security, Medicare, and Medicaid, and $171 billion
for net interest. A whopping $1,373.2 billion, or 68 percent of all national
government expenditures, was for programs whose incidence is not geographically specific or is spread throughout the country by formulaic allocations.[8]
The national government therefore tends to provide "geographically dispersed
public goods." When the national government spends money in one place or
state, it tends to spend money in every state and in all places. We will see the
reasons for the national spending patterns in the next section.

---

[7] Congressional Budget Office, Historical Budget Data, Table 5 (Jan. 26, 2006), *available at*
http://ftp.cbo.gov/budget/historical.pdf.
[8] This is not to imply that defense spending is not geographically specific, e.g., military bases,
but that military defense as a general public good is not geographically specific.

III. A POLITICAL MODEL OF GOVERNMENT SPENDING

In this section we introduce a model of how a democratic polity makes decisions about financing an infrastructure investment. We have cast the model in formal terms in other publications; here we simply give the intuition.[9]

Financing infrastructure investment in a democracy is complicated by uneven geographic distribution of benefits and costs. Investments often yield very large benefits for a small portion of citizens while imposing costs in the form of taxes for all the rest. Some districts, counties, or states benefit more because of proximity to the canal, railroad, bank, highway, sewage system, water system, electrical system, school buildings, or parks. As a result, the net benefits of government spending for each infrastructure project are negative for most voters. Under a majority-rule democracy, if a majority of the voting population receives negative benefits, no infrastructure measures will pass.

How were states able to undertake significant infrastructure investments in transportation and finance in the early 19th century? The basic intuition is simple. There are four types of government financing options for infrastructure.

A. Normal Taxation

Normal taxation relies on the use of existing taxes spread throughout the population. Under normal conditions, a democracy is politically incapable of financing geographically concentrated infrastructure by using normal taxation. A majority of voters pay taxes and receive no benefits and thus refuse to support the project.

B. Universalism, or Something for Everyone

The something-for-everyone approach covers two different means of allocating government expenditures among all of the districts, counties, or states (or individuals). The first is that expenditures are governed by an explicit formula that allocates funds to states or districts. For example, the current formula allocates national highway funds among the states based on population, land area, and miles of rural post roads. Similarly, the legislation authorizing spending under homeland security guarantees each state a minimum of 0.75 percent of the total expenditures, regardless of risk and other factors. As a result, every state is guaranteed a positive share of these funds.

---

[9] For formal models *see* John Joseph Wallis, *Constitutions, Corporations, and Corruption*, 65 J. ECON. HIST. 211 (2005). *See also* John Joseph Wallis and Barry R. Weingast, *Equilibrium Federal Impotence: Why the States and Not the American National Government Financed Economic Development in the Antebellum Era* (Hoover Institution Stanford University Working Paper, 2005).

The second mechanism is universalism. The idea is that, although allocation to districts may be discretionary, most districts expect to receive some funds.[10] Coalition politics, demographics, and programmatic need also may play a role in allocation. Something-for-everyone policies are the easiest policies to implement politically.

The problem with something-for-everyone policies is twofold. First, standard models of a higher jurisdiction providing local projects face a standard common-pool problem, sometimes called the "law of $1/n$": In the presence of n local jurisdictions represented in the legislature, each representative comes from a district that gains the full value of the project, but pays on the order of only $1/n$ of the total costs.[11] Therefore, local voters and their representatives demand far larger local public-goods projects. The result is significant economic inefficiency. Second, this method of finance faces significant difficulties in providing large-scale, lumpy, geographically specific infrastructure investments.[12] In particular, something-for-everyone policies could not be used to finance the public infrastructure investment with the highest returns for states in the early 19th century, namely canals. It was simply too expensive to build enough canals to command a majority of votes, let alone a canal to every county in the state. In contrast, something-for-everyone could be used to finance highway construction in the 20th century, since it is feasible to build roads to every county.

C. Benefit Taxation

Benefit taxation allocates the taxes used to finance a project according to the benefits received by individuals. Let the total benefits of a project be B, which is greater than total costs. The benefits going to individual i are B_i. Then benefit taxation sets an individual's tax share as

$$t_i = B_i / B. \qquad (1)$$

Under benefit-taxation schemes, every individual is (weakly) better off from provision of the project, since individuals who receive no benefits pay no taxes.

The genius of benefit taxation is twofold. First, a scheme of financing infrastructure investments with user fees closely approximates a benefit tax. Second,

[10] Barry Weingast, *A Rational Choice Perspective on Congressional Norms*, 24 Am. J. Pol. Sci. 245–262 (1979).

[11] Barry Weingast, Kenneth A. Shepsle, and Christopher Johnsen, *The Political Economy of Benefits and Costs: A Neoclassical Approach to Distributive Politics*, 89 J. Pol. Econ. 642–664 (August 1981). (*See also* Robert P. Inman, *Federal Assistance and Local Services in the United States: The Evolution of a New Federalist Fiscal Order, in* Fiscal Federalism: Quantitative Studies. (Harvey S. Rosen ed., 1988); Brian Knight, *Legislative Representation, Bargaining Power, and the Distribution of Federal Fund Evidence from the U.S. Senate*, presented at the conference Fiscal Challenges: An Interdisciplinary Approach to Budget Policy (Feb. 10, 2006).

[12] Interstate highways are lumpy and geographically specific, but they possess the unique feature of existing in every state – thus, something for everyone.

if property taxes capture the benefits of public services through capitalization in land values, then the property taxes serve as a form of benefit taxation.[13] The property tax has played a central role in state and local provision of infrastructure, as we subsequently discuss.

D. Taxless Finance

The final option to finance investment avoids raising new taxes to provide infrastructure altogether, and a good portion of infrastructure is provided without levying any taxes.[14] This sounds too good to be true, and often it is. A better term might be "contingent taxless finance," since these schemes implicitly require that taxpayers assume a contingent liability. The idea underlying taxless finance is to fund the current construction of a project through private sources who provide funds in exchange for certain privileges or a return on the revenue from the project itself. As this mechanism is the least well understood of the four, we provide greater detail about its operation.

For centuries, governments have used the private, joint-stock corporation as a vehicle of taxless finance. In the early 19th century, governments often provided some infrastructure or a service by chartering a private corporation to provide the infrastructure or service. The terms of the charter gave the corporation particular advantages, perhaps even a monopoly. The first business corporation in England was the Russia Company in 1553, given a monopoly on the trade with Russia. The Virginia Colony was started with the charter of the Virginia Company in 1606. This type of taxless finance was financially safe – no bonds were issued at all – but politically costly, as it involved giving special privileges to a distinct group of citizens.

Other taxless finance schemes involved state borrowing. In early-19th-century America, capital was scarce, and state governments often provided a significant amount of the capital of a private firm chartered to build a canal or a turnpike by issuing state bonds.[15] The critical piece that made these projects attractive to voters – and that made them potentially taxless – is that they held the promise that tolls or dividends from the project would service the bonds issued for construction. In reality these were contingent taxless finance projects: If the project failed to service the bonds, then citizens assumed that liability.

In some cases, as with the Erie Canal, taxpayers never had to pay any taxes *ex post* because the canal worked as promised. It generated sufficient tolls to

---

[13] For an accessible introduction to this literature, *see* the papers *in* Wallace Oates, LOCAL GOVERNMENT AND THE PROPERTY TAX (2001).

[14] The issue of taxation is at the heart of the legal dispute over public authority and special district finance. If special local governments levy taxes, then their debts should count against state and/or local debt limitations. If their revenues are fees, then their debts should not count.

[15] In the 20th century, the national government created and invested in a number of private corporations for similar reasons, including Fannie Mae and Sallie Mae.

service the canal bonds. In other cases, such as the Pennsylvania Mainline Canal begun in 1826, taxpayers were left holding the bag when the venture failed and the state went bankrupt in 1842. Taxless finance schemes also were used at the national level to finance the First and Second Bank of the United States in 1791 and 1816 (successfully) and to finance the Central Pacific and Union Pacific railroads in the 1860s (with less salutary results).

The central problem with taxless finance is that it can be politically manipulated. How can voters tell if the promoters' promises are reliable? Voters in Pennsylvania in 1828, Indiana in 1836, and Missouri in 1854 were encouraged to support bond issues under the impression that they would never have to service the bonds. In each of these cases the expectations were not fulfilled, and voters eventually had to pay higher taxes to service state debts. Because those making the investment do not bear the full consequences of their decisions, they have less incentive to ensure that the project generates a net surplus. This mechanism requires that voters have some belief in the project's likely success. Yet voters' expectations are not likely to be accurate, particularly voters who are far removed from the project's locality. No market mechanism coordinates these beliefs or provides evidence for false ones. Moreover, because of the contingent liability, bond markets provide a weak constraint in this case: Bondholders know that if the project fails, the general taxpayers will be asked to cover the bonds.

E. Implications

This approach yields the following predictions. First, normal taxation rarely will be used to finance infrastructure. Second, something-for-everyone is politically sustainable, but not practical for large specific projects. It may be used for dispersed projects and is thus more likely to be used by the national government (such as for lighthouses). We should observe both benefit taxation and taxless finance used to fund infrastructure. However, the Constitution prohibits the national government from using benefit taxation. The states therefore should be observed to use this method, while the federal government should not. Taken together, these implications suggest that states, and not the national government, should finance the very largest infrastructure projects in the early 19th century.

IV. EVIDENCE FROM THE FIRST CYCLE: STATE AND NATIONAL BORROWING AND SPENDING, 1790 TO 1860

Tables 11.4 and 11.5 present evidence in support of our predictions. Table 11.4 studies the $60 million that the national government spent on transportation improvements between 1790 and 1860 (plus an item about the Union

Table 11.4. Model predictions and national spending patterns, 1790 to 1865

Method	Prediction	Amount ($)	Cases
Normal taxation	No	1,917,000	Chesapeake and Delaware Chesapeake and Ohio
Something for everyone	Yes, small projects	41,435,000	Unspecified navigation Rivers Harbors Aids to navigation Internal navigation Miscellaneous roads
Benefit taxation	No	0	
Taxless finance	Yes, big projects	4,750,000 6,800,000 5,250,000	Public land funds Cumberland Road Land grant equivalents (4,000,000 acres)
Total		60,152,000	
Other taxless finance			
		2,000,000 7,000,000 30,000,000	First Bank of the United States Second Bank of the United States Union Pacific Railroad

Source: John Joseph Wallis and Barry R. Weingast, *Equilibrium Federal Impotence: Why the States and Not the American National Government Financed Economic Development in the Antebellum Era* (Hoover Institution Stanford University Working Paper, 2005).

Pacific Railroad). It organizes these expenditures by method of finance: $2 million for projects financed by normal taxation; $41 million for something-for-everyone projects; nothing financed by benefit taxation; and $17 million for taxless finance projects. Table 11.5 presents information on the $186 million of

Table 11.5. Model predictions and state spending patterns, 1790 to 1840, from state debt outstanding in 1841

Method	Prediction	Amount ($)	Cases
Normal taxation	No	0	

Something for everyone	Yes, but unlikely
	    projects are too small
		0	Some education and
			    roads

Benefit taxation	Yes	53,000,000	Canals and RR, in NY, OH, IN, IL
Taxless finance	Yes	53,000,000 80,000,000	Banks in the South Transportation in the North
Total		186,000,000	

Source: John Joseph Wallis and Barry R. Weingast, *Equilibrium Federal Impotence: Why the States and Not the American National Government Financed Economic Development in the Antebellum Era* (Hoover Institution Stanford University Working Paper, 2005).

the state debt outstanding in 1841 that can be allocated to one of the four forms of financing.[16] As predicted, none of the state projects used normal taxation or something-for-everyone projects, but $53 million was borrowed for projects financed by benefit taxation and $133 million was borrowed for taxless finance projects.

The national government relied extensively on something-for-everyone projects. Typically, national transportation projects were financed through omnibus "rivers and harbor" legislation, including funding for dozens of individual projects spread throughout the country. Most of these projects were small and localized. Throughout the nation's history, when the national government participated in infrastructure investment, it tended to use something-for-everyone policies. Even today, national government expenditures are concentrated in geographically dispersed functions. State governments, on the other hand, initially used a mix of benefit taxation and taxless finance. It was in reaction to the dangers of taxless finance that the first budget rules were adopted in the 1840s.

V. THE FIRST RULES AND THEIR EFFECT ON STATES: THE FIRST CYCLE OF CONSTITUTIONAL CHANGES

Between 1790 and 1841, state governments borrowed more than $200 million to invest in canals, railroads, and banks.[17] In 1841 and 1842, eight states and the Territory of Florida defaulted on their sovereign debts. Florida and Mississippi repudiated all of their debts. Louisiana, Arkansas, and Michigan repudiated part of their debts.

The defaults created a political crisis. In response, 12 states wrote new constitutions between 1842 and 1852. Eleven of those constitutions mandated procedural restrictions on the way state and local governments borrowed money (Indiana banned state borrowing altogether). These constitutions contained the first constitutional provisions with respect to borrowing. To be clear, we use the phrase *debt restrictions* to mean procedural restrictions on the issue of debt, and the phrase *debt limitation* to mean absolute limits on the amount of debt a state or local government can issue. Absolute limits may be stated in dollars or as fractions or percentages of assessed value or personal income.

Significantly, the constitutional provisions were not intended to eliminate state and local borrowing. Eliminating taxless finance was the goal, and doing

---

[16] Over the entire period 1790 to 1860, state and local governments spent an estimated $450 million on transportation investments, seven times the national expenditures. Carter Goodrich, GOVERNMENT PROMOTION OF CANALS AND RAILROADS, 1800–1890 (1960).

[17] Reginald C. McGrane, FOREIGN BONDHOLDERS AND AMERICAN STATE DEBTS (1935); B. U. Ratchford, AMERICAN STATE DEBTS (1941); Wallis, *supra* note 10; John Joseph Wallis, Richard Sylla, and Arthur Grinath, *Sovereign Default and Repudiation* (Nat'l Bureau of Econ. Research Working Paper No.W-10753, 2004).

that involved three related constitutional changes. First, states had to prohibit themselves from investing in private corporations or giving individual corporations special deals to provide public services. The result was the widespread adoption of general incorporation acts and prohibitions on public investment in private corporations. Second, states had to prohibit themselves from giving tax breaks to corporations and other interests to provide public services. The result was the general property tax imposed at the same rate on all property. Third, states had to require that taxes be raised before money was borrowed. This required voters to approve tax increases (and legislatures to implement tax increases).[18]

It is critical to understand that states sought to eliminate taxless finance in the 1840s, not to prevent government borrowing.[19] With the exception of Indiana, every state allowed borrowing, in general or for specific purposes, subject to these procedural requirements: (1) the purpose and amount of debt issued be identified; (2) taxes sufficient to service and redeem the debt be levied; and (3) voters approve the new taxes in a referendum.[20]

Delegates expressed their convictions at the constitutional conventions in the 1840s. For example, Judge Kilgore of Indiana used the following words in favor of procedural restrictions and against the absolute ban on state debt in the Indiana constitutional debate:

> If, with the light of the past to guide them, with the heavy burthens [*sic*] of the present to remind them of past errors, the people coolly and deliberately decide

---

[18] The text of the New Jersey Constitution of 1844, Article 4, Section 6, Part 4 is typical of the 1840s procedural debt restrictions:

> The legislature shall not, in any manner, create any debt or debts, liability or liabilities, of the State which shall, singly or in the aggregate with any previous debts or liabilities, at any time exceed one hundred thousand dollars, except for purposes of war, or to repel invasion, or to suppress insurrection, unless the same shall be authorized by a law for some single object or work, to be distinctly specified therein; which law shall provide the ways and means, exclusive of loans, to pay the interest of such debt or liability as it falls due, and also to pay and discharge the principal of such debt or liability within thirty five years from the time of the contracting thereof, and shall be irrepealable until such debt or liability, and the interest thereon, are fully paid and discharged; and no such law shall take effect until it shall, at a general election, have been submitted to the people, and have received the sanction of a majority of all the votes cast for and against it, at such election; and all money to be raised by the authority of such law shall be applied only to the specific object stated therein, and to the payment of the debt thereby created. This section shall not be construed to refer to any money, that has been, or may be, deposited with this State by the government of the United States.

See The NBER/Maryland State Constitution Project, *available at* http://www.stateconstitutions. umd.edu.

[19] The evidence and argument is detailed in Wallis, *supra* note 9. The major conclusion of Goodrich's article *The Revulsion Against Internal Improvements* is that states were not trying to prevent state and local investments in infrastructure, but to modify the process through which projects were selected and funded. *See* Carter Goodrich, *The Revulsion Against Internal Improvements*, 10 J. Econ. Hist. 145 (1950).

[20] The constitutional changes are described in detail in Wallis, *supra* note 9.

at the ballot-boxes to again borrow money, I shall aid to place no Constitutional barriers in their way to prohibit them from carrying out their will; *provided*, sir, that at the time they give the Legislature authority to contract a debt they provide by direct taxation for the payment of the interest, and the canceling of the principal, within twenty-five years. Right here, sir, and nowhere's else, was the great error committed by the people and their representatives in 1836 [leading to Indiana's debt crisis]. Gentlemen may confine themselves to the simple assertion that the people of that day were mad; I shall not deny it; they were mad, and very mad; but, Mr. President, had a provision been made before the public debt was created that a direct tax must be levied, high enough to pay the interest and to wipe out the whole debt in eighteen or twenty-five years, all would have been comparatively well. A provision of this kind, sir, would have brought the people to their right senses, and my word for it, before State Bonds to the amount of four millions of dollars had been sold, they would have risen and denounced the whole system as projected.[21]

Judge Kilgore castigated the perils of taxless finance and called for benefit taxation in the form of a direct tax, which in 1850 meant *ad valorem* property taxation, before any future debt could be issued.[22]

States changed their constitutions to require that taxes be raised before bonds were issued and so eliminated taxless finance. Since everyone's taxes went up immediately, such tax increases were normal taxation. Nonetheless, because of the way property taxes were administered in the 19th century, these tax increases had an element of benefit taxation. States did not set a permanent tax rate and then collect whatever taxes came in. Typically the state or local government established an amount to be raised by the property tax, divided by total assessed valuation, to determine that year's tax rate, and then allocated the taxes amongst taxpayers according to their share in the assessed value of all the property in the state. This means that, holding constant the total amount raised by the property tax, if property values rise in areas that benefit from the project, so too will property taxes, implying that property taxes fall in areas where property values do not rise.

In terms of the model we presented earlier, a bond referendum eliminates taxless finance while creating a higher bar for benefit taxation. Since all voters are voting to have their current taxes raised immediately, even voters who receive no benefits from the project still pay higher taxes. Now a majority of voters must receive positive net benefits before they will vote yes on the bond proposal.

---

[21] 1 Report of the Debates and Proceedings of the Convention for the Revision of the Constitution of the State of Indiana 1850 676, Indiana Constitutional Convention (1850–1851).

[22] Events in Indiana are considered in detail in John Joseph Wallis, *The Property Tax as a Coordinating Device: Financing Indiana's Mammoth System of Internal Improvements, 1835 to 1842*, 40 Explorations in Econ. Hist. 223 (2003). The general movement to rewrite constitutions and eliminate taxless finance is the subject of Wallis, *supra* note 9.

We expect three results. In general, it will be easier to obtain majorities in smaller jurisdictions where infrastructure provision more closely matches the voters. First, debt restrictions should reduce the borrowing of state governments. Second, debt restrictions may increase local borrowing.[23] Third, debt restrictions create pressure to form new governments whose boundaries closely match the beneficiaries of the infrastructure investment. These special districts provide better matches of taxpayers and beneficiaries of public services. Because a greater portion of voters experience a rise in property values, voters are more likely to approve surplus-generating projects.

VI. THE QUANTITATIVE EFFECTS ON STATE DEBT, 1841 TO 1860

Table 11.6 provides information on state debt in 1841, 1853, and 1860, and state and local debt in 1870, 1880, 1890, and 1902. We take these numbers from the Census, which did not collect information on local government until 1870.[24] The first panel of the table gives average debt by level of government in the nation at each date, as well as the number of states in existence at that date and the aggregate level of all debt. The second panel of the table reports similar averages for states without any type of state-level debt restrictions. The third panel reports averages for states with debt restrictions. The first state debt restrictions were adopted after 1842, so none of the states in 1841 had debt restrictions.

Table 11.7 compares 1841 and 1860 by using a difference-in-difference estimate. Average state debt, in levels and per capita, are given in the first rows of the table for states with and without debt restrictions. The difference in the level and per capita debt is given in the last column of the table. For example, between 1841 and 1860, total debt rose in states without restrictions from $3,185,239 to $7,733,462, a difference of $4,548,224. In contrast, total state debt in states with restrictions fell from $11,827,651 to $8,314,827, a difference of $3,512,825.[25] The difference in the two differences provides an estimate of the effect of state debt restrictions in reducing state borrowing. States without debt restrictions increased their debts by $8,061,048 more than states with debt restrictions. The effect of debt restrictions was equally large if measured in per capita terms. In 1840, nominal per capita income was $91 and in 1860 it was

---

[23] There are two qualifications. First, if state and local projects are not substitutes, then reducing state borrowing should have no effect on local borrowing. It appears that state and local spending were good substitutes for one another. Second, state debt restrictions also may apply to local as well as state governments. This occurred later in the 19th century.

[24] Hillhouse suggests that local government debt was quite small in 1840, only about $25 million. While it grew before the Civil War, there are no acceptable aggregate estimates of local debt, although there are series for individual cities. Albert Miller Hillhouse, MUNICIPAL BONDS: A CENTURY OF EXPERIENCE (1936).

[25] There is a slight rounding error in the calculation. The exact difference is $3,512,824.77.

Table 11.6. State, local, and total (state and local) debt, 1841 to 1902

Year	State debt ($) Average	State debt ($) Average per capita	Local debt ($) Average	Local debt ($) Average per capita	All debt ($) Average	All debt ($) Average per capita	N	Level of all debt($)
All states 1841	7,026,311	14.76					27	189,710,399
1853	6,210,578	8.86					31	192,527,913
1860	8,042,312	8.83					32	257,353,990
1870	9,536,936	11.87	13,835,629	12.45	23,372,567	24.32	37	864,784,971
1880	6,844,233	5.62	24,089,003	15.70	30,933,237	21.32	38	1,175,463,010
1890	4,717,936	3.93	20,484,164	14.16	25,202,100	18.09	44	1,108,892,382
1902	5,120,332	4.85	35,651,168	21.11	40,771,500	25.97	45	1,834,717,513
No restrictions								
1841	7,026,311	14.76					27	189,710,399
1853	5,385,091	7.08					16	86,161,459
1860	7,733,462	12.71					15	116,001,937
1870	13,486,446	19.72	9,363,183	10.97	22,849,633	30.69	15	342,744,489
1880	7,915,780	8.18	20,696,995	21.41	28,612,775	29.59	6	171,676,647
1890	3,901,057	4.80	17,921,466	16.56	21,822,522	21.36	6	130,935,133
1902	11,918,256	5.73	32,523,594	21.95	44,441,850	27.67	6	266,651,102
Restrictions								
1841*	—						0	
1853	7,091,097	10.76					15	106,366,454
1860	8,314,827	5.41					17	141,352,053
1870	6,844,089	6.51	16,885,024	13.45	23,729,113	19.97	22	522,040,482
1880	6,643,318	5.14	24,725,005	14.62	31,368,324	19.77	32	1,003,786,363
1890	4,846,917	3.79	20,888,800	13.79	25,735,717	17.58	38	977,957,249
1902	4,074,498	4.72	36,132,333	20.99	40,206,831	25.70	39	1,568,066,411

*In 1841, no states had debt restrictions.

Sources: 1841: William Cost Johnson, Report of William Cost Johnson, No. 296, 27th Cong., 3d Sess. (1843). 1853: B. U. Ratchford, American State Debts 127, Table 9 (Duke University Press, 1941). (Ratchford constructed his estimates for 1853 based on Census Office, Department of the Interior, History of States Debts, in Report on Valuation, Taxation, and Public Indebtedness, The Tenth Census, 1884.) 1860–1902: Census Office, Department of the Interior, The Eighth Census (1860); Census Office, Department of the Interior, The Ninth Census (1870); Census Office, Department of the Interior, The Tenth Census (1880); Census Office, Department of the Interior, The Eleventh Census (1890); U.S. Census Bureau, 1902 Census of Governments (1902).

Table 11.7. Difference-in-difference estimates of the effect of state debt restrictions, 1841 to 1860

Average state debt		1841 ($) (1)	1860 ($) (2)	Difference ($) (2)–(1)
Levels of debt				
No restriction	(3)	3,185,239	7,733,462	4,548,224
Restriction	(4)	11,827,651	8,314,827	(3,512,825)
Difference-in-difference	(3)-(4)			8,061,048
Per capita debt	(5)			
No restriction	(6)	12.11	12.71	0.60
Restriction	(5)-(6)	18.07	5.41	(12.66)
Difference-in-difference				13.26

$137.[26] States with debt restrictions had $13.26 less per capita debt than states without restrictions. The debt restrictions therefore had large and immediate impacts on state borrowing before the Civil War.

The table provides a nice example of endogeneity. The states that ultimately adopted debt restrictions had much higher total and per capita debts in 1841 than did states without debt restrictions. The debt restrictions were the result, not the cause, of high debts in 1841.[27] Total state debt per state stayed roughly constant between 1841 and 1860, but state debt per capita fell steadily over those years (see Table 11.9, subsequently cited near Section VIII).

State debts rose dramatically during the Civil War, as evidenced by the increase in state debt from 1860 and 1870. So there is a prewar, during the war, and postwar story to be told. Debt restrictions mattered during the war. Between 1860 and 1870, total debt rose from $8 million to $13 million in states without restrictions (from $12.71 to $19.72 per capita), and fell from $8 million to $7 million in states with restrictions ($6.51 to $5.14 per capita).

VII. PLAYING AGAINST THE RULE: LOCAL GOVERNMENTS IN THE SECOND CYCLE, 1870 TO 1902

During the 1870s states adopted new or made substantial changes to their existing debt provisions that affected both the state and local levels. State debt restrictions really mattered for state borrowing between 1841 and 1870. What about local borrowing?

---

[26] Louis D. Johnston and Samuel H. Williamson, *The Annual Real and Nominal GDP for the United States, 1790 – Present*, Econ. Hist. Serv., Apr. 1, 2006, *available at* http://eh.net/hmit/gdp/.

[27] This is not the case in every state. New Jersey and Rhode Island had no state debts and were the first two states to adopt procedural restrictions in the 1840s.

The Census did not begin collecting systematic information on local governments until 1870 and did not conduct a complete census of all local governments until 1902. We therefore have only scattered information about local government borrowing, taxing, and spending before the Civil War. We expect that procedural restrictions on state borrowing will increase local borrowing, even if local governments face the same procedural restrictions. Thus it may appear that governments are subverting the intent of the constitutional rule by shifting borrowing to the local level. When local governments increase their borrowing, they appear to be "playing against the rule": a creative reaction by which political officials and citizens create new ways to borrow within the rules.

Did this happen after 1870? We know from Table 11.2 that state debts were roughly nine times local debts in 1841, and that by 1902, local debts were roughly eight times state debts. Did debt restrictions and limitations have anything to do with the shift?

During the 1870s, states significantly tightened their constitutional restrictions on debt. As already discussed, states in the North and South borrowed heavily during the Civil War and came out of the war with substantial debts. As new states entered, some adopted procedural debt restrictions and others adopted more stringent debt limitations. Table 11.8 provides a brief summary of state constitutional provisions with respect to state and local borrowing.

Columns 1 and 2 of the table present state debt restrictions before 1860 and between 1865 and 1890. States with a "0" had no restrictions on debt; states with a "1" had some type of procedural restrictions; states with a "2" had provisions that limited the absolute amount of debt issued in some way.[28] States also began limiting the borrowing of local governments by absolute prohibitions on debt issue, debt limitations tied to property valuations, limits on the purpose of debt issue, and several cases of tax or expenditure limitations. Column 3 notes whether local governments were, in any substantial way, affected by state rules.

Between 1865 and 1875, Southern states underwent Reconstruction. In the 1870s, Southern states rewrote their constitutions and several formally repudiated their Reconstruction debts. By 1880, all of the former Confederate states except Arkansas had adopted some form of debt restriction; Georgia, Louisiana, and Virginia adopted absolute limits, and most imposed a variety of restrictions on local governments.

Between 1870 and 1902, the growth of the economy, industrialization, and immigration all fostered rapid increases in the size of cities, particularly the large

---

[28] Whether a state is a "1" or a "2" is a matter of interpretation. Some states appear to have absolute limits, but they state them in a way that gives the states a considerable amount of leeway in the amount of debt they issue, and thus are classified as restricted states, "1," rather than limited states, "2." Ohio and Alabama are examples of such states.

Table 11.8. State constitutional debt and borrowing provisions, 1841 to 1890

State	State debt measure Pre-1860 (1)	State debt measure Post-1860 (2)	Local provisions (3)	Debt measure (4)	Local provisions (5)
Alabama	0	2	1	1875	1875
Arkansas	0	0	1		1874
California	1	1	1	1849, 1879	1879
Colorado		2	1	1876	1876
Connecticut	0	0	1		1877
Delaware	0	0			
Florida	0	1	1	1868, 1875	1868, 1875
Georgia	0	2	1	1877	1877
Idaho		1	1	1889	1889
Illinois	1	1	1	1848, 1870	1870
Indiana*	2	2	1	1851	1851, 1881
Iowa	1	1		1857	
Kansas	1	1		1859	
Kentucky	1	1		1850	
Louisiana**	1	2	1	1845, 1879	1879
Maine*	2	2	1		1868, 1878
Maryland	1	1	1	1851, 1867	1867
Massachusetts	0	0			
Michigan	1	1	1	1850	1850
Minnesota	1	1	1	1857	1879
Mississippi	0	1	1	1875	1875
Missouri	0	2	1	1875	1875
Montana	1	1	1	1889	1889
Nebraska		2	1	1866, 1875	1875
Nevada		2	1	1864	1864
New Hampshire	0	0	1		1877
New Jersey	1	1		1844	
New York	1	1	1	1846	1846, 1874, 1884
North Carolina	0	1	1	1876	1876
North Dakota		2		1889	1889
Ohio	1	1	1	1851	1851
Oregon	2	2	1	1857	1857
Pennsylvania	1	1	1	1858, 1873	1873
Rhode Island	1	1			
South Carolina	0	1	1	1868, 1873, 1884	1868, 1884
South Dakota		2		1889	1889
Tennessee	0	1	1	1870	1870
Texas	2	2		1845, 1876	1876
Utah		2			
Vermont	0	0			
Virginia	0	2		1870	
Washington		1		1889	1889

(continued)

Table 11.8 (*continued*)

State	State debt measure Pre-1860 (1)	Post-1860 (2)	Local provisions (3)	Debt measure (4)	Local provisions (5)
West Virginia		2	1	1872	1872
Wisconsin	1	1	1	1848	1848, 1874
Wyoming		1	1	1889	1889

Note: The provision in the table is taken from the Census reports from 1880 and 1890, supplemented by the constitutional texts on the NBER/Maryland Constitution project (see subsequent source note). In the first and second columns, states are blank if they are not yet states (with the exception of Florida in 1841); have a "0" if they have no restrictions on state debt; have a "1" if they have a restriction that limits the procedures by which states can issue debts, typically a referendum; and have a "2" if the have absolute dollar limits on debt. States with local provisions, the fourth column, are states with some type of restriction or regulation on the issue of debt by local governments. These range from procedural restrictions, e.g., referendums, to absolute dollar limits and percentage valuation limits.

The dates in Column 4 refer to the first year a state adopted a debt restriction or limitation, and subsequent years where significant changes occurred. The dates are not absolutely accurate, in the sense that they do not consider the Confederate or Reconstruction constitutions in Southern states. Several Reconstruction constitutions had debt limits that were ignored, and interpreting those limits is problematic. The dates in Column 5 refer, with the same caveat, to local provisions.

*Indiana and Maine had absolute limit provisions in their constitutions before the Civil War.

**Louisiana wrote constitutions in 1845, 1852, 1861, 1864, 1868, and 1879, as well as in 1898 and 1913. The table only refers to the original 1845 provisions and the modifications made in 1875.

Source: Census Office, Department of the Interior, The Tenth Census (1880); Census Office, Department of the Interior, The Eleventh Census (1890); The NBER/Maryland State Constitution Project, http://www.stateconstitutions.umd.edu.

urban commercial and industrial centers. Urbanization should have increased local government borrowing even in the absence of changes in constitutional borrowing rules.

The question we want to ask, therefore, is whether local governments in states with state debt restrictions had higher or lower debts over the entire period from 1870 to 1902. The results are presented in Table 11.9. These regressions take advantage of the changing debt requirements over time, the rise and fall of state and local debts at the state level, and changes in urbanization and population; they also add dummy variables for individual years. State-level debt restrictions lower state borrowing, as shown in Panel A of the table. In the local regressions, Panel B, states with state-level debt restrictions *increase* local debt, while local debt restrictions reduce local debt.[29] More urban states have much more local

---

[29] The coefficients on state and local debt restrictions in the local regressions are not statistically significant, and there are issues of interpretation here. Since this is the entire universe of states, the coefficients represent the true effect of the debt restrictions on local debt. But the high standard errors indicate that the effect varies widely across states. The coefficients on state debt restrictions in the state equation are both economically and statistically significant.

Table 11.9. Regression estimates of state and local debt, 1870 to 1902

Panel A: State

Dependent	Level of state debt		Per capita state debt		Level of state debt		Per capita state debt	
Independent variable	Coefficient	st error	Coefficient	st error	Coefficient	st error	Coefficient	st error
Intercept	9,292,359	2,029,667	13.77	2.74	10,161,444	2,165,667	16.53	2.97
State Restriction	(4,905,118)	1,901,064	−7.46	2.56	(4,614,832)	1,964,779	−5.21	2.69
Urban Percent	4,034,493	3,906,331	−4.92	5.27	2,744,200	4,107,100	−0.51	5.63
1880 Dummy					(2,142,993)	2,283,895	−4.77	3.13
1890 Dummy					(4,617,386)	2,231,702	−6.35	3.06
1902 Dummy					(4,674,494)	2,262,138	−5.07	3.10
Population					1,657	631	−0.00	0.00
R2	0.05		0.06		0.12		0.09	
Adj-R2	0.04		0.04		0.08		0.06	

Panel B: Local

Dependent	Level of local debt		Per capita local debt		Level of local debt		Per capita local debt	
Independent variable	Coefficient	st error	Coefficient	st error	Coefficient	st error	Coefficient	st error
Intercept	(18,410,000)	7,760,798	4.58	1.83	(26,320,000)	6,323,013	3.39	2.16
Local Restriction	11,064,605	7,098,332	−1.83	1.67	229,460	5,713,277	−2.65	1.95
State Restriction					(3,041,143)	5,884,710	2.09	2.01
Urban Percent	124,420,000	16,214,434	46.20	3.82	73,658,320	11,959,404	47.55	4.08
1880 Dummy					1,829,106	6,822,660	2.55	2.33
1890 Dummy					(8,113,325)	6,798,510	−1.39	2.32
1902 Dummy					(1,665,995)	6,883,020	4.37	2.35
Population					25,005	1,819	−0.00	0.00
R2	0.27		0.49		0.68		0.53	
Adj-R2	0.27		0.48		0.67		0.51	

(continued)

Table 11.9 (continued)

Panel C: Total

Dependent	Level of total debt		Per capita total debt		Level of total debt		Per capita total debt	
Independent variable	Coefficient	st error	Coefficient	st error	Coefficient	st error	Coefficient	st error
Intercept	(10,980,000)	9,762,210	19.54	4.22	(15,550,000)	6,960,270	20.68	4.39
Local Restriction	2,506,339	9,354,929	−3.22	4.05	(6,825,340)	6,477,793	−2.09	4.08
State Restriction	5,726,548	8,436,828	−7.82	3.65	(2,470,045)	6,289,083	−6.03	3.96
Urban Percent	127,800,000	17,633,198	40.41	7.63	75,323,769	13,164,718	45.69	8.30
1880 Dummy					623,064	7,510,274	−1.04	4.73
1890 Dummy					(11,620,000)	7,483,689	−6.36	4.72
1902 Dummy					(5,225,603)	7,576,717	0.70	4.78
Pop					26,773	2,002	−0.00	0.00
R2	0.25		0.20		0.66		0.23	
Adj-R2	0.24		0.18		0.65		0.19	

debt, but the effect of debt restrictions on local borrowing remains even when urbanization is controlled for. The effect of state debt restrictions was to raise local borrowing.

VIII. COMPLICATIONS AND HOME RULE IN THE SECOND CYCLE, 1875 TO 1900

The empirical results demonstrate that states with debt restrictions and limitations had smaller state debts and larger local debts, controlling for population size and urbanization. The results do not, however, establish a causal relationship between state fiscal institutions and the changes in the structure of state and local government. Many other factors also changed at the end of the 19th century, and identifying causal relationships would require far more detailed empirical tests than we undertake in this chapter. Rather than giving up in the face of complexity, however, it seems that we can grasp one of the thorniest problems and turn it to our advantage.

"Home rule" is the historical term associated with the movement that began in the late 19th century to give local governments, initially municipalities and counties, more control over their internal structure, elected officials, and policies. Home rule presents a serious statistical problem, since changes in local government borrowing may have been a result of changes in the fiscal rules under which local governments operated. While debt restrictions can be characterized by a small set of quantitative variables, home-rule provisions are enormously complicated and cannot be easily incorporated into an empirical analysis. Moreover, the late 19th century was not just a period of home rule, but it was also a period of state rule. Many more state governments tightened their control over local governments (Table 11.8) than loosened control through home rule. States also began imposing administrative control over local specific public functions, such as water supply and sewers.[30] A close look at the changing relationship between state and local governments after 1870 reveals that no simple empirical analysis will allow us to delineate the lines of causation and interaction between fiscal and political institutions and fiscal outcomes.

On the positive side, however, it seems clear that the regulation of state debt issue quickly led to the involvement of states in local debt issue. New York provides a good example. Article 8, Section 9 of the New York Constitution of 1846 (which enacted the state procedural debt restriction) read as follows: "It shall be the duty of the Legislature to provide for the organization of cities and incorporated villages, and to restrict their power of taxation, assessment, borrowing money, contracting debts and loaning their credit." In 1875, the Constitution was amended (Article 9, Section 11) to make explicit the way in

---

[30] *See* Jon C. Teaford, THE UNHERALDED TRIUMPH: CITY GOVERNMENT IN AMERICA, 1870–1900 104 (1984).

which the state regulated local debt issue: "No county, city, town or village shall hereafter give any money or property, or loan its money or credit to or in aid of any individual, association or corporation, or become directly or indirectly the owner of stock in, or bonds of, any association or corporation; nor shall any such county, city, town or village be allowed to incur any indebtedness except for county, city, town or village purposes."

The section was amended again in 1884 to include additional provisions that did the following:

1) They allowed local governments to borrow without limit for "aid or support of its poor."
2) They limited borrowing by counties or cities with more than 100,000 inhabitants from becoming indebted for more than 10 percent of the assessed value of real estate.
3) They allowed counties and cities to issue "certificates of indebtedness or revenue bonds issued in anticipation of the collection of taxes."
4) They allowed for the issue of "bonds to provide for the supply of water," but mandated a maximum term of 20 years and the establishment of a sinking fund.
5) They imposed a tax limit in counties and cities with more than 100,000 inhabitants of 2 percent of the assessed valuation of real and personal property.

The specific nature of the 1884 amendments is revealing. New York allowed more freedom for local governments to borrow to finance relief expenditures or water systems. But it clamped down on the ability of large cities to issue bonds, both with a restriction on the amount of debt that could be issued and the amount of taxes that could be raised to service debt. At the same time it opened a loophole for debt secured by future revenues. It is difficult to determine whether, on balance, the specifics of the amendment made it harder or easier for local governments in New York to borrow.

New York's regulation of local borrowing was not unique in timing or complexity. States began asserting a formal constitutional right to limit the debt of local governments and public corporations in the 1840s (Table 11.8). By 1890, 36 states had imposed, or asserted the right to impose, regulations on local borrowing. In 22 states, constitutional provisions limited the amount of debt local governments could issue; 16 states had specific limits, and 12 of those states specified maximum debts as a percentage of assessed property value.

Without a great deal more empirical work, it impossible to say whether debt restrictions caused a change in state or local borrowing, or the reverse. But they do support a major element in our history of the second cycle. States deliberately responded to the increase in local borrowing by changing the constitutional structure of the state and local system. Moving government activity to the local level was not something that just happened. State and local governments consciously decided to have local governments assume more of the burden of infrastructure investment and public-service provision.

IX. THE RISE OF SPECIAL-PURPOSE GOVERNMENTS IN THE SECOND AND THIRD CYCLES, 1850 TO 1933

The reaction of both state and local governments to the constitutional changes of the 1840s opened up new possibilities and challenges, many unanticipated. In 1851, five years after enshrining a procedural debt limitation in the constitution of 1846, the New York legislature "enacted a law directing the Comptroller to issue $9,000,000 of 'canal revenue certificates' for the purpose of enlarging the Erie Canal and completing the Genesee Valley and Black River Canals."[31] The bonds were issued without a tax increase or a bond referendum. The bonds were to be paid out of a special fund established with future surplus canal revenues. The bond issue was upheld in *People v. Newell*,[32] but overturned as unconstitutional in *Rodman v. Munson*.[33]

The decision overturning the law induced some consternation, ultimately leading to a bond referendum and tax increase to fund the debt. The argument proposed in favor of the law "that the constitution did not intend to prohibit debts 'which would certainly and eventually pay for themselves'" was refuted decisively by Judge Strong:[34]

> Indeed, the most extravagant works in the state, and some of them were very extravagant, had been urgently supported, and finally adopted, upon that supposition. The convention [in 1846] had the sagacity to see that the practice of granting away the public money upon the annual productiveness of such works was a dangerous one, and that in fact no human foresight could enable the legislature to determine with certainty that any projected improvements "would certainly and inevitable [*sic*] pay for itself." Indeed, there had been sad mistakes on that subject, for which the state had severely suffered. The convention knew that the legislature had too readily listened to sanguine, loose and interested calculations, and no doubt designed to avert the danger of incurring heavy debts under such pretenses.[35]

Judge Strong understood that the purpose of the constitutional debt restriction was precisely to eliminate taxless finance, to make it impossible for promoters to fund projects that would "certainly and eventually pay for themselves"

---

[31] William J. Quirk and Lawrence E. Wein, *A Short Constitutional History of Entities Commonly Known as Authorities*, 56 Cornell L. Rev. 521, 538 (1971).

[32] *People v. Newell*, 13 Barb. 86 (N.Y. Sup. Ct.), *rev'd*, 7 N.Y. 9 (1852), *cited in* Quirk and Wein, *supra* note 32, at 539.

[33] *Rodman v. Munson*, 13 Barb. 63 (N.Y. Sup. Ct.), *aff'd*, 13 Barb. 188 (N.Y. Sup. Ct.), *aff'd sub nom. Newell v. People*, 7 N.Y. 9 (1852), *cited in* Quirk and Wein, *supra* note 32, at 539.

[34] Quirk and Wein, *supra* note 32, at 539, citing *Rodman v. Munson*, 13. Barb. 188, 204 (N.Y. Sup. Ct), *aff'd sub nom. Newell v. People*, 7 N.Y. 9 (1852).

[35] *Id.*

without raising current taxes. Judge Strong spoke against taxless finance as clearly as Judge Kilgore had in Indiana.

But the underlying issue was more complicated. What was the problem with a state's issuing bonds whose security was surplus canal funds, for which creditors could not make claims on the state in the absence of a canal fund surplus? The impossibility of clearly defining a canal fund surplus doomed the cause of this particular issue of New York bonds. But surely there were cases where a distinct fiscal source could be identified, the burden of which fell primarily on individuals who benefited from the service provided by the government and where it was possible to insulate the state and its taxpayers for liability in case the revenues did not materialize. Equally, there were cases where a majority (or more) of taxpayers could be induced to acquiesce to a rate increase to fund bonds for the provision of a valuable public service. Sometimes the taxpayers were located within the boundaries of an existing government, but sometimes it was necessary to create such a government, a special district or public authority (e.g., the New York Port Authority), whose boundaries overlapped several existing jurisdictions or whose boundaries were smaller than an existing jurisdiction (e.g., school districts).

Whether these special districts were financed by user fees or by property taxes, it was possible to create governments financed by benefit taxation. Good economic and political reasons existed for creating more local governments. Indeed, if we press the logic of social welfare maximization embodied in our conceptual model, a society with flexible governmental forms can craft governments to provide infrastructure and market-enhancing public goods in ways that a society with inflexible government forms (e.g., boundaries) cannot. Better outcomes can be reached by allowing fragmentation of government into flexible, potentially overlapping government units – what might be called "Tieboutizing" local governments. But these benefits come with serious downside risk.

First, it was absolutely necessary to prevent local governments from investing in private corporations. One of the most common forms of taxless finance was for governments to issue bonds, turn the bonds over to the private company to purchase stock, and require the private company to service the bonds, thus eliminating the need to raise current taxes. This type of arrangement had been used by the national government to finance the First and Second Banks of the United States and the Union Pacific Railroad. It had been used by Florida, Mississippi, Louisiana, and Arkansas to finance banks. A procedural debt restriction would not, by itself, prevent voters from approving a bond issue to invest in a private corporation that would service these bonds! It was well understood by the 1870s that such taxless finance arrangements were an invitation to trouble.

Not surprisingly, state constitutions began stipulating that no local governments could invest in private corporations. Almost all of the states with "local provisions" in Table 11.8 prohibited local governments from investing in private corporations.[36] Constitutions also began making it clear that state and local governments were not responsible for the debts of special governments, special districts, or public authorities.[37] This was the second round of constitutional prohibition of taxless finance. The constraints on local government borrowing and investment produced a growing number of special local governments. The Tieboutization of local government was well underway.

X. BACK TO LOCAL GOVERNMENTS: LIMITING LIABILITY FOR SPECIAL-DISTRICT DEBT IN THE THIRD CYCLE

Anyone who has attended a school board meeting to establish boundaries or a county council meeting to site a road learns that no local governments are so small that they contain a homogenous population within their jurisdictions. Nonetheless, relative to larger governments, local governments tend to be small enough, homogenous enough, or flexible enough in creating their boundaries that they are able to finance a considerable amount of infrastructure even when required to gain majority approval for bond referenda. Local governments also have been endowed by the various debt rules that govern them with a credible ability to raise funds through private capital markets. It may seem backward, but stringent debt restrictions – particularly debt restrictions that prohibit special-purpose governments from gaining access to general government revenues – improve governments' ability to promote infrastructure investment and raise money in capital markets. To get to those issues, we first need to address the circumstances under which fragmented government is a good thing.

Suppose that a good infrastructure project (one that yields more in benefits than it costs) brings positive net benefits to 20 percent of the citizens in a state. Further suppose that location of the benefited citizens is not coincident with a local government – that the benefits are spread across existing local jurisdictions. Further suppose that there are no externalities from the project. The state cannot build the project because of the majority-rule provisions: The project only benefits 20 percent of the voters. No local jurisdiction covers the citizens who benefit. So a government structure with fixed states and local governments cannot build this project. If, however, a group of citizens can form a special district, then they can create a jurisdiction with majority support to

---

[36] The census of 1880 section on "constitutional provisions relating to state and local debts" opens with a table of state restrictions on "the power of state and minor political divisions to lend their credit to or in aid of corporations, etc., or to become stockholders in any corporations." *See* Census Office, *supra* note 6, at 649.

[37] Quirk and Wein have a great discussion of how this debate played out in the New York Constitutional convention of 1938, where the protagonist wanting to prevent the constitution from prohibiting state or local governments from assuming the debts of public authorities was Robert Moses. *See* Quirk and Wein, *supra* note 31.

generate the taxes and financing necessary to build the project. Put simply, the system of flexible, special districts helps provide a greater variety of public goods and services.

Several problems arise with implementing a scheme of infrastructure investment carried out by special districts. First, who gets to be a government? Second, who gets to draw the boundaries? Third, how does the state ensure that the taxes will be levied, the project will be built, and the debt will be repaid? All these problems fall under the general rubric of "transparency," that is, knowing what the government is doing, and clearly there are lots of transaction costs in implementing such a scheme.

The initial restrictions placed on local governments in the 1870s were intended to eliminate taxless finance. In addition to forbidding local governments from investing in private corporations, state constitutions required bond referenda and higher taxes for any new debt issue. Some states also instituted debt limits for local governments. Local governments, however, were able to maneuver within these restrictions. Because local governments were not bound by state requirements to levy general property taxes, they could levy special assessments on improvements approved by micro-electorates.[38] From special assessments, it was a small step to special taxing districts. By 1884, New York allowed cities to issue bonds in anticipation of revenues without violating their local debt ceilings. By the 1890s, public authorities were beginning to appear, special-purpose governments with the power to issue debt payable out of special revenues, such as port fees or bridge tolls.

Taxless finance arose in this environment in a new guise. Remember that taxless finance usually involved the taxpayers assuming a contingent liability if the project failed. If a public purpose, pursued by a public authority, financed by bonds to be repaid from user fees or special assessments, who was ultimately responsible for the debt? Were state or local governments expected to assume either a direct or a moral obligation to repay debt if the public authority they created went bankrupt? Where was the contingent obligation? Were special districts just another version of the taxless, but contingent, finance of the 1830s?

What appears to have happened in most states is the creation of constitutional bright lines about debt liabilities. In the 1938 New York constitutional convention, a debate arose over this issue. The public authorities, led by the legendary Robert Moses of the Triborough Bridge Authority, battled with reformers at the convention who wished to make it constitutionally clear that neither the state nor any local government was liable for the debts of a public authority.[39] The result of the constitutional convention, adopted by the voters, made it very

---

[38] *See* Robin Einhorn, PROPERTY RULES (1991) for a detailed history of how Chicago financed street and sewer improvements by using special assessments street by street. Water supply, however, required a citywide program, and so faced a much higher bar.

[39] Quirk and Wein, *supra* note 31, at 552–579. The debate concerned the amendments proposed by Abbot Law Moffat and Philip Halpern. *Id.*

clear that public authorities were solely liable for their bonds. In other words, special-purpose governments in New York could not create liabilities for either the state or local governments. In order to have a hope of receiving an adequate return, prospective bondholders had substantial incentives to make sure that the public authority was a sound investment on its own terms.

These provisions added a constitutional twist, since they did not prohibit taxless finance. The state and local governments of New York already had shown too much ingenuity in evading the attempts of previous constitution writers to believe that taxless finance could be completely banned. Instead, the provisions adopted by New York in 1938 provided credible and effective attempts to ensure that taxless finance indeed would be taxless for the state. By eliminating the contingent obligation of the general taxpayers to stand liable for special-purpose government debts, these new provisions greatly reduced the common-pool problems associated with financing projects. Making taxpayers of the special jurisdiction solely liable for the project provided taxpayers, political officials, and bondholders with stronger incentives to evaluate proposed projects. No doubt these provisions could be abused, and they certainly have been, but the provisions marked another stage in the long battle in reducing the perils of taxless finance.

The new set of institutions helped align the interests of political officials with those of their citizens. In many respects, the mature system, arrived at the end of three cycles of action, problems, and new constitutional rules, comes close to being optimal. The formation of special governments combines with the insistence that these governments alone are responsible for their debt to produce good incentives for political officials, citizens, and the bondholders. In particular, limits on the responsibility of debt eliminate a series of incentive and common-pool problems.

XI. CONCLUSIONS

The United States has some of the best infrastructure in the world, much of it provided by state and local governments, most of it financed by government borrowing, and a long history of fiscal probity. Despite those facts, American voters and scholars still worry that state and local governments fail to play by the rules they themselves establish. We have outlined a history illuminating the dynamic relationship among debt finance of infrastructure, the constitutional rules governing borrowing at the state and local level, and the structure of state and local governments.

During America's first 150 years, state and local governments went through three cycles of financing projects, debt problems, and new constitutional rules: 1790 to 1850, 1850 to 1880, and 1880 to 1933. States were the primary builders of infrastructure from 1790 to 1850. After states ran into financial distress during the debt crisis of 1841, they enacted new constitutional rules that made it more difficult for states to finance new infrastructure, particularly infrastructure that was geographically specific. The requirement for statewide majority approval effectively prohibited state financing of a wide range of valuable projects whose effects were local.

Per our substitution hypothesis, a major response to these state-level procedural restrictions was to move government borrowing for infrastructure to the local level. A second cycle of defaults in the 1870s, this time at the local level, led to stricter restrictions on local borrowing. In the third cycle, per our governmental jurisdiction hypothesis, those restrictions led to creative responses in the form of special districts and public authorities in the early 20th century. The development of those special purpose governments led to more strict enforcement of taxless finance.

We have drawn on SGFF models to study aspects of the demand, supply, and finance of infrastructure projects. Our main result is the importance of aligning the set of taxpayers and beneficiaries of the projects. By the mid-20th century, state, local, and special governments served an important and powerful role in providing infrastructure. The flexibility of this form of government allowed special districts to align the project's beneficiaries and the taxpayers who must finance it. A pivotal institutional feature of these governments is that they alone, and not a general government, are responsible for their debts.

Special district responsibility for debt has two related incentive effects. First, when a general government is liable, taxpayers will agree to finance projects that benefit themselves but which do not create a new social surplus. The reason is that taxpayers are not fully liable for the costs of the project, some of which will be borne by the taxpayers of the general government. Second, when the general government backs this debt, bondholders are much less concerned about the project's success – as long as they believe the general government is sound, they don't have to worry. Strict liability for special-district debt, therefore, forces both taxpayers and bond markets to scrutinize projects more carefully and to choose only positive surplus projects – only these have a hope of attaining financing.[40] Briffault emphasizes the second source of incentives: One result of the mature system governing state and local borrowing is that "The real discipline for the state thus comes from capital markets."[41] But it is not these incentives alone that matter. The bond market induces important effects on those who design special districts and the associated projects.

Our approach suggests that the fiscal institutions governing debt and infrastructure provision in mid-20th-century America were good ones in the sense that they limit the ability of citizens from undertaking projects that fail to create

---

[40] Not all special districts are solely liable for their debts, but many are, particularly those providing infrastructure. For an overview of special districts, *see* Nancy Burns, THE FORMATION OF AMERICAN LOCAL GOVERNMENTS: PRIVATE VALUES IN PUBLIC INSTITUTIONS (1994).

[41] Briffault, *supra* note 1, at 61.

a positive social surplus. Infrastructure finance around the world has trouble doing exactly this, as the American financial problems in the 19th century and the more recent problems in Argentina and Brazil reveal.

The evolution of constitutional rules produced a very fragmented form of government in the United States. Fragmentation, of course, has both good and bad features. Since 1942, the vast majority of government units created in the United States have been special districts (Table 11.1). Moreover, America has some of the best infrastructure in the world. Not all public infrastructure is provided by special purpose governments by any means; traditional local governments still provide most of it. But the system seems to work well in several dimensions; this chapter has tried to explain why.

Questions for Chapter 11

1. In this chapter, Wallis and Weingast reveal an interesting connection between the choice of infrastructure financing strategy and governmental form. It is a connection that is not likely to be on the minds of either voters or administrators when such decisions are made. One consequence is a proliferation of special districts. These governmental forms have, by design, a single service and geographically based focus. What are the implications of an increase in special district governments for effective state fiscal policy? The authors highlight the benefit of better alignment of service benefits and funding, but significant disadvantages are associated with this trend. How should we address the implications of spillover effects in certain types of infrastructure projects? What about coordination costs across governments? Finally, is it more difficult to stop providing services that have been funded via special districts?[42] Although the nature of the trade-off between the benefits and costs of special districts will vary by the service or projects being financed, what are the implications of these concerns for the overall efficiency and effectiveness of state fiscal decision making and policy implementation?

2. Wallis and Weingast analyze the popularity of the increased role of the private sector in infrastructure financing decisions. Although often touted as a consequence of the new public-management movement of the past two decades, these authors reveal a long history within the United States of private financing of public infrastructure projects. What they call "taxless finance" offers considerable appeal to voters, who may not fully understand their contingent liability for these projects. Their discussion raises concerns about the potential inefficiencies associated with this public finance strategy, including the deficiencies in its risk structure. However, as state and local governments continue to face

---

[42] *See* Elizabeth Graddy and Ke Ye, *When do we "Just Say No"? Policy Termination Decisions in Local Hospital Services* (USC School of Policy, Planning, and Development Working Paper, 2007).

cycles of fiscal instability (*see* Chapter 12 by David Super), we can expect the use of this financing strategy to increase. How can we structure these strategies to reduce the likelihood of inefficiency? Better information available to voters, transparency in project development, and development of risk-sharing structures across both public and private parties to these arrangements may be worth further exploration.

3. The chapter, and indeed the essays in the book as a whole, focuses on the United States. Would international comparisons, both with developed and developing countries, give us a better handle on how well American institutions function? Have similar rules and institutions regarding debt finance developed elsewhere? What were their consequences in other countries?

4. In the 20th century, a wide array of fiscal devices developed to constrain the way governments behave: balanced-budget rules, line-item vetoes, tax limitations, and rainy-day funds, for example. How do these other fiscal institutions interact with debt provisions? Are states with looser procedural debt restrictions more or less likely to adopt other fiscal constraints? Are states with higher debt levels more, or less, likely to adopt other fiscal mechanisms to limit taxes and expenditures?

12 Federal–State Budgetary Interactions

David A. Super

I. INTRODUCTION

The foregoing chapters on federal fiscal policy never stray far from the fundamental goal of balance. Some may focus on near-term balance; others may be more concerned with long-term actuarial balance in major social insurance programs' financing mechanisms; still others may address the intergenerational equity of the unified federal budget. A simple-minded attempt to translate these concerns to the state level would suggest that states have no significant structural budgetary problems: All but one state is required to balance its budget annually, and all regularly do so. Sometimes balance comes easily; sometimes it comes amidst pitched political battles with temporary government shutdowns. In the end, however, all states have budgets that, at least to a first approximation, are balanced. The question of balance, per se, therefore is not particularly central to debates about state fiscal policy.

That does not mean, however, that state fiscal policy is fundamentally unproblematic. Indeed, by some measures the public may be even less satisfied with state fiscal policy than with federal. Budgetary problems probably end proportionately more political careers at the state level. A steady stream of ballot initiatives addresses both the grand structure of state budgets and removes particular decisions from annual budgetary debates.

This chapter explores the similarities and differences between federal and state fiscal policies. It examines the causes of popular dissatisfaction with states' fiscal performance, suggesting that serious problems exist, but in areas and at times that have heretofore escaped broad notice. It suggests both internal modifications to state fiscal rules and changes in the relationships between federal and state governments that can address these problems and improve states' ability to play their roles in the federal system.

David A. Super is a professor of law at the University of Maryland School of Law.

A. Crucial Differences Between Federal and State Budgets

Federal fiscal policy is far more prominent than that of the states, and thus provides a natural jumping-off point for the study of state finances. The analogy has its value, but must be taken with caution. This section identifies seven important structural differences between the federal and state budgets that must be kept in mind when attempting to transfer insights from the study of one level to the other.

First, states always balance their budgets. Most state constitutions require annual balance; where they do not, politically untouchable statutes or long-standing traditions impose the same mandate. To be sure, the accounting procedures states rely upon to reach balance are hardly immaculate. Some costs and revenues are excluded from these calculations, some estimates reflect wishful thinking, and state budget negotiators occasionally turn to bookkeeping gimmicks to close a final gap. The cumulative effect of these imperfections, however, is trivial when compared with either the aggregate size of state budgets or the acknowledged and unacknowledged deficits at the federal level. State budget policy is, therefore, fundamentally far less a question of enforcing rules than of determining what those rules should be.

Second, states have no assigned role in regulating the national economy. Mainstream economists largely accept countercyclical correction, along with financing infrastructure and smoothing temporary spending surges (such as wars) as legitimate justifications for deficits at the federal level. State fiscal constitutions typically make at least modest provision for multiyear financing of infrastructure, and some include small "rainy-day" funds providing token relief against financial crises. State fiscal policy, however, has no analogue to the notion that federal deficits and surpluses at different points in the business cycle can help achieve macro-economic stability.

This is not inevitable. State budget deficits could stimulate a slack economy as well as, or better than, a federal deficit. States running surpluses could ease excess demand that risks stimulating price spirals. Indeed, given the regional component of many slowdowns and booms, state fiscal policy might prove more effective than many federal measures. Our federal system, however, has not devised a workable way of enlisting states in correcting economic swings. Doing so seems to risk allowing federal officials to intrude unacceptably upon state sovereignty or having state politicians hide their fiscal indulgences beneath the veneer of stimulating the economy. Nonetheless, the lack of a formal state role in making macro-economic policy should not blind us to the important impact state policies have on the national economy or, conversely, to the business cycle's dramatic effect on state budgets.

Third, states are price-takers to a far greater degree than the federal government. Transportation and communications advances have rendered applicable to states many of the characteristics Charles Tiebout identified a half-century ago in local governments.[1] Each offers an increasingly mobile population a package of services and costs (taxes) much as private firms compete for customers. A state whose package includes too few services that mobile citizens and businesses desire relative to the price it is charging will fear losing people and economic activity to its peers. Scholars have suggested that the economically rational locality will tailor this package to maximize appeal to more affluent individuals, who will pay more in taxes than they consume in services; this may be particularly true because the most affluent people are among the most mobile.[2] A corollary is that states may be tempted to minimize their safety-net programs and maintain relatively regressive tax structures to dissuade net service users from locating there. Thus, economic competition supplements political debate as an engine shaping fiscal policy far more at the state level than it does federally.

This sort of argument can easily be taken too far. Some could find comparable employment elsewhere in the country, but the information and moving costs of obtaining those jobs are high enough that only large differences in the perceived value of the state's services-and-taxes package could motivate a move. Still, enough relatively rootless people – for example, those finishing school or losing jobs in declining regions, immigrants, returning emigrants – choose homes each year that states may fear that a persistently unappealing package will have long-term costs.

Moreover, businesses each year must decide where to locate, whether to expand existing facilities or establish new ones, or where to jettison excess capacity. Accordingly, the "business climate" plays a far more consistent role in state fiscal policy debates than it does at the federal level. A favorable business climate commonly is equated with low taxes. The increasing business mobilization against tax and expenditure limits modeled on Colorado's Taxpayers' Bill of Rights (TABOR) demonstrates that this oversimplifies.[3] Businesses will oppose taxes whose proceeds are wasted, but in purchasing government, like other inputs, most focus on the relationship between cost and value rather than cost alone. Nonetheless, a state that allows its fiscal situation to deteriorate with excessive borrowing or deferred expenditures has far less leeway than the federal government to make up the lost ground with a sharp shift in fiscal policy.

---

[1] Charles Tiebout, *A Pure Theory of Local Expenditures*, 64 J. Pol. Econ. 416, 418–420 (1956).

[2] Mark Schneider, The Competitive City: The Political Economy of Suburbia (1989); Paul Peterson, City Limits (1981); James M. Buchanan, *Principles of Urban Fiscal Strategy*, 11 Pub. Choice 1 (1971).

[3] *See, e.g.*, Will Shanley, *Letter Warns States to Fight Initiatives*, Denver Post, Aug. 3, 2006, at C1; Kell Kelly, *TABOR is Unpatriotic*, Daily Oklahoman, Oct. 6, 2006, at 17A. The state chambers of commerce in Arizona, Michigan, Montana, and Oklahoma, as well as numerous local and industry-specific business groups, helped defeat TABOR spin-offs proposed in 2006.

Fourth, the nature of state spending and taxes differs from that at the federal level in ways that significantly affect fiscal management. The federal government's largest intergenerational transfers – Social Security, Medicare, and the aged component of Medicaid – favor the elderly, have their costs and benefits rigorously, and relatively transparently, accounted for, and are politically strong. States' major intergenerational transfers are mixed: The aged component of Medicaid shifts resources to the older generation, but the children's component and public education favor youth. The benefits of Medicaid long-term care, at least superficially, are relatively transparent: They fund a certain number of days of care. The benefits of any particular package of children's Medicaid services or education expenditures are subject to extensive debate. As a result, while the existence of these programs is not controversial, their funding level often is and can fluctuate considerably.

On the revenue side, states are vulnerable to external interference in their revenue-raising abilities to a far greater extent than Congress. In part as a result, the revenue sources available to states show both structural and cyclical deterioration. The Supreme Court has strictly limited states to taxing transactions occurring, and income earned, within their borders. Congress, in turn, has limited states' ability to tax Internet transactions. It has considered further limitations on states' ability to tax businesses. More generally, because members of Congress need not fill gaps they create in state budgets, they can reap the political rewards of cutting state taxes without assuming any of the costs. As increasing amounts of commerce take place across state lines or over the Web, the fraction subject to state taxation will decline steadily. Moreover, Congress has compelled states to choose between further revenue losses and increasing the cost and complexity of tax administration by cutting or eliminating federal taxes whose administration had been linked to state taxes. Because states may have political and administrative difficulties enacting legislation promptly to correct for new restrictions when they appear, the consequences of this dynamic federal interference are greater than one might expect from the terms of the restrictions alone.

Substantive differences in states' taxing authority can make it difficult for them to prevent their revenues from deteriorating when they are needed most: during economic slumps. A large portion of their revenues come from sales and business-activity taxes that rise and fall sharply with the business cycle. These taxes both exacerbate fiscal crises and feed revenue gluts. State personal and corporate income taxes are only modestly less volatile. On their face, property taxes are the least cyclically sensitive: They may reflect long-term economic declines in an area, but state and local governments rarely reassess property values merely because of cyclical swings. Precisely because property taxes continue to extract similar amounts even after a recession has reduced many owners' ability to pay, they have taken the brunt of taxpayers' revolts. As a result, property taxes supply a declining share of state revenues.[4] This decline is sharpest during economic downturns, thus defeating with policy interventions the natural advantage property taxes have over most other revenue streams in recessions.

Fifth, states typically have less sophisticated fiscal analysis capabilities than does the federal government. Congress has its own expert budget office; many state legislatures, by contrast, must depend on the governor's budget office, whose estimates may be skewed to favor the governor's agenda. The Congressional Budget Act and Senate rules often have required budget forecasts to cover ten years (and occasionally more); states typically consider only balance for the coming year or biennium. States also lack the sophisticated means the federal system has for differentiating between moneys Congress has allowed an agency to spend ("budget authority"), moneys the agency has bound itself to pay outsiders ("obligations"), and moneys the agency actually has spent ("outlays"). Collectively, this leaves state budgetary rules vulnerable to manipulation and evasion through artificial timing shifts.

Sixth, state budget processes are subject to much more extensive procedural regulation. Rules prohibiting substantive legislation on budget bills are in place at both the federal and state levels, but only at the state level are they judicially enforceable. State constitutional rules prohibiting laws from embracing more than one subject or any subject not reflected in their titles limit opportunities for logrolling; the far more limited federal rules with similar ends are enforceable only on the Senate floor.[5] Item vetoes give governors more leverage in budget negotiations, with both the power to delete spending items and the ability to demand money for their preferred projects on pain of eliminating those of key legislators.

Finally, direct democracy, unknown at the federal level, has had a profound effect on the budget processes of states that have it. Voters can and do alter their states' fiscal constitutions frequently. Moreover, while the need to compromise often moderates swings in legislative fiscal policy, initiative and referendum operates on a binary basis. Partisans, often extremists, write an initiative largely to maximize the achievement of their goals should it pass; they need show moderation only on the handful of issues straightforward enough that the electorate could understand and reject an extreme position. This threat is asymmetrical: Only certain kinds of budgetary policies generate strong enough feeling to

---

[4] Between 1970 and 1980, property taxes fell from almost 40 percent of state and local tax revenues to barely 30 percent. National Conference of State Legislatures and National Governors' Association, FINANCING STATE GOVERNMENT IN THE 1990s 57–62 (Ronald K. Snell ed., 1993).

[5] The paramount federal antilogrolling provision is the Byrd Rule, which prohibits nongermane provisions in the Senate's budget reconciliation bills. It explicitly limits only what the Senate can consider, not what a final statute can do. Senate and House rules also bar nongermane amendments to appropriations bills, but the House Rules Committee overrides that and other rules at will.

produce a successful voters' uprising. Tax cutting, education funding, transportation, and some health and environmental causes can; aid to low-income people, the upkeep of most infrastructure, and most unglamorous services cannot. This gives leverage to legislators supporting these favored programs well in excess of their numbers. Conversely, it requires other participants in the regular budget process to estimate where the tipping point is beyond which taxes or reductions in educational spending will generate sufficient anger to pass a ballot initiative.

Not only might such a ballot initiative radically change those legislators' budgetary priorities, but it also is likely to change which voters will appear at the polls. Thus, for example, legislators unsympathetic to education funding might believe they could survive voting for unpopular cuts in a normal election but may fear that triggering a schools ballot initiative might bring out proeducation voters who might not be sufficiently motivated by legislative elections alone. These considerations are likely to weigh heavily in states whose constitutions require voter ratification of tax or spending increases: Even if approval is likely, marginal legislators may fear bringing more antagonistic voters to the polls.

B. Goals of State Fiscal Policy

A meaningful discussion of the relationship between federal and state fiscal policy requires some sense of the goals state policy ought to achieve. Advocates of federal budget reform typically focus on intergenerational equity, sound macroeconomic management, or particular substantive priorities such as keeping taxes low or broadening public health care coverage. State requirements for annual balance mute concerns about intergenerational equity, and states have no assigned role in managing the national economy. Many of those active in state budget debates have narrow substantive agendas: tax limitation, funding for education, aid to local governments, and the like. The lack of broad consensus around substantive priorities, however, makes such goals an unsuitable foundation on which to build lasting structures.

This section suggests three broad principles against which state fiscal policy should be tested.

i. Integration into State Political System

State budgets are just one component of state public policy, albeit an important one. State budgets will be most effective if they are coordinated with the government's regulatory and proprietary policies. It seems unlikely that the electorate has one set of preferences for budgetary purposes and another for regulatory policy. In addition, because money is fungible, all aspects of budgetary policy necessarily interrelate with one another. This all-encompassing nature of budgetary policy makes it far more important that it reflect popular will than, say, some isolated body of regulations or the operation of some minor business the state owns. Unfortunately, the complexities of budgetary policy, and of the external factors that shape state budgets, make this a formidable task.

Six criteria seem fundamental to identifying budget processes that complement rather than compromise the rest of the state's political system.[6] First, sound procedures will produce budgets faithful to the long-term public will. The requirement of annual balance, when juxtaposed against cyclical changes in revenues and spending demands, produces a predictable pattern of booms and busts. A sound budget process will give reserve-building policies the realistic opportunity to defeat more profligate responses to revenue gluts so that cuts during subsequent recessions may be moderated. Put another way, the budget process will avoid undervaluing public revenues that happen to arrive during times of fiscal strength.

Second, a sound state budgetary system will avoid distorting the state's political process. A policymaking process that systematically deviates from the electorate's preferences represents a political market failure. This deviation could derive from a lack of transparency that allows narrow interests to co-opt the process. It also could come from provisions that exempt certain interests from having to justify themselves in budgetary debates or that allow those interests to frame decisions in ways that help preordain the results.

More broadly, an obscure budgetary process could mislead the public about which officials have performed well or badly. Elections in this country adjudicate both values and competence. From time to time, when voters feel compelled to discipline inept or venal politicians with views they basically share, we temporarily get a government out of step with the values of the majority of the electorate. A confusing budgetary process may induce voters to turn out officials still matching their policy preferences on the basis of bad results that no one could have prevented; conversely, it also may allow officials to take credit for fiscal successes they did little to produce and so win reelection despite otherwise unsatisfactory performance.

Third, sound budget procedures should be conducive to meaningful priority setting. Even sophisticated experts cannot simultaneously compare all items in a complex budget, but they can and should aggregate functions into coherent groups for comparison. Revenues should be compared with spending; within the spending category, education should be contrasted with corrections, health, transportation, and other major functions of government; within education,

---

[6] These structural norms occupy an intermediate position between the purely procedural norms that Musso, Graddy, and Grizard analyze in Chapter 8 of this volume, and norms prescribing specific substantive outcomes. The former focus on the legitimacy and efficiency of the states' budgeting processes specifically; these seek to enhance the legitimacy and efficiency of the state political systems of which budgetary rules are a part.

higher education should be juxtaposed with K-12, and so on. A process devoid of functional groupings or one that bundles disparate programs in ways that make it impossible to make systematic choices among aggregates is likely to produce a budget less satisfactory to the public than others that could be designed.

Fourth, state budget processes should facilitate coordination with other state policies. A system that, for example, produces a new regulatory system but fails to meet its funding needs is likely to mislead voters about the extent of protection they enjoy. Either the decision to regulate or the decision to underfund is likely to result from a political distortion, presumably either insufficient barriers to creating new programs or excessive ones to funding them. In either case, operational inefficiencies and public misinformation are likely to result.

Fifth, an optimal state budgetary process will avoid generating unnecessary complexity in the state's substantive policies. Such complexity might result from subtle distinctions between permissible and forbidden legislation. For example, federal budget rules compelled housing assistance programs to abandon their established practice of signing long-term contracts with owners of housing projects those programs assisted. As a result, those federal investments yield many fewer years of affordable housing for low-income tenants.

Finally, a sound state budget process should help the state maintain appropriate relationships with local governments. Lacking fiscal responsibility for major means-tested programs in most states, and more heavily reliant on relatively stable property-tax revenues, local budgets are somewhat less vulnerable to the business cycle than are those of states. Nonetheless, local governments depend on states for direct financing and legal authority to tax; they thus are vulnerable to aid cuts, shifts in programmatic responsibility, and preemption of revenue streams. A budget process that encourages state officials to shift their fiscal problems downward will engender mistrust between the levels of government as it produces chaos and political distortions at the local level. Conversely, one that forces a state to assume functions it would otherwise decentralize may humiliate, and undercut civic support for, local government. Budget-process rules, such as tax, spending, or debt limitations, should not weigh so heavily on state or local governments that their manipulation or evasion becomes an important objective in dividing functional responsibilities.

ii. Integration into National Policy

Although states are sovereigns in their own right, they can and should be expected to play constructive roles within our national system. Sound state budget processes will help them do so in at least two respects.

First, because state and local spending constitutes a considerable share of the gross domestic product, changes in state fiscal policy can have a significant stimulative or depressing impact. The interconnectedness of the national economy makes the concept of independent state economic management fanciful. States therefore should seek to support the national economic-management agenda formulated by the president, Congress, and the Federal Reserve. State budgetary rules should allow and encourage that support by relaxing pressure for balance during downturns and compelling operating surpluses during booms.

Second, just as state budgetary rules should not distort the political process's choices about allocating responsibilities between state and local governments, so too they should avoid artificially inducing or deterring the federal government from relying on states to perform functions legitimately within their competence in our federal system. This is particularly important in the current era, with devolution an active topic of debate. To be sure, states will simply lack the fiscal capacity to perform some functions: Franklin Roosevelt federalized much of the responsibility for relieving poverty during the Great Depression because state and local governments lacked the means to do so. It is a very different matter, however, when states' fiscal rules incapacitate them from assuming roles they would welcome and the federal government would gladly surrender. Simplistic definitions of annual balance, along with tax and expenditure limits, prevent states from relieving hardship during economic downturns.

iii. Modesty

Budget-process rules are fundamentally countermajoritarian. Just as guarantees of individual rights and structural rules of government occasionally deny political majorities the ability to work their will, so too budget-process rules intervene to block or void fiscal programs that otherwise would have been implemented. Unlike constitutional rights guarantees and structural provisions, however, budgetary rules depend on the political branches of government far more than the courts for enforcement. This enforcement typically requires officials to defy popular preferences for the principle of fiscal probity.

As with rules protecting individual liberties or delineating the structure of government, the argument for giving budgetary rules countermajoritarian force is extremely strong in the core areas of their responsibilities. We have great confidence in the wisdom of our judgment that transitory majorities should not be allowed to shut off political debate, to undermine the sovereignty of state or federal governments, or to abscond with public funds. The courts have learned, however, that their ability to safeguard core personal rights and principles of government depends on their restraint. If the courts intervened in too many routine political disputes, they would deplete their political capital and reduce the stigma associated with defying their orders. Eventually, they might lose the ability to compel obedience when truly fundamental principles are at stake. Nonetheless, the extent of caution required, and the particular problems the courts should leave unaddressed, however, can be intensely controversial.

Just as activists on the left and the right have shown great imagination in formulating arguments that the courts should address this or that social problem, so, too, activists of all persuasions have been tireless in identifying new substantive missions for budget-process rules. Some want to limit taxes and spending to levels below those political majorities might select on their own. Others want to give advantages to particular categories of spending in competition for scarce budgetary resources. Still others want to accomplish the same thing on the revenue side, steering policymakers away from types of taxation they particularly dislike. The merits of each of these proposals can be debated, but their collective impact is likely to be to expand the countermajoritarian footprint of budget-process law. The result could well be to reduce the political stigma of disregarding budget-process rules generally and to induce politicians and courts to accept devices for evading those rules.

Even within budget-process rules' core area of legitimacy, ensuring fiscal probity, overreaching can undermine effectiveness. Just as the Supreme Court's separation of powers doctrine has long accepted some adjudicatory and legislative functions being "misplaced" inside the executive branch because requiring a change would prove too disruptive, so, too, designers of budget-process rules should consider the consequences of demanding too radical a change in fiscal policy. A good example of this problem on the federal level was the Gramm-Rudman-Hollings deficit-reduction legislation. Meeting its annual deficit-reduction targets would have required such massive policy changes that the political costs of circumventing the targets kept proving far less than those of complying. By contrast, the Budget Enforcement Act of 1990 only required Congress to "pay as you go" in expanding entitlements or reducing taxes. Yet it proved remarkably successful in restraining fiscal excesses[7] and helped lay the groundwork for the first balanced budget in more than a generation later that decade.

The objective of modesty, then, counsels that budget-process rules be designed to husband their political capital, avoiding both interventions tangential to their core goals and making impractical demands on the political system.

II. THE PROBLEM OF CYCLICALITY

Probably the most fundamental source of instability in federal–state budgetary relations today is the business cycle. Governors of both parties and all political philosophies are portrayed as inept when an economic slowdown depresses their states' revenues, increases the costs of means-tested programs, and produces large deficits. Opponents run on platforms of "cleaning up the mess" in

---

[7] Ron Haskins et al., *Getting to Balance: Three Alternative Plans*, in Restoring Fiscal Sanity: How to Balance the Budget 15, 33–34 (Alice M. Rivlin and Isabel Sawhill eds., 2004).

the state capital. On the other hand, numerous profligate governors and legislatures have been saved from political accountability for their irresponsible behavior by economic booms. This tendency of the business cycle to distort political accountability for fiscal policymakers would merit attention standing alone. In a federal system, however, these recurring crises prevent states from being reliable fiscal partners with the federal government. Federal policies designed on the assumption that states will continue to perform as they are during booms will find themselves undercut when states' budgets go into cyclical crisis; these periodic collapses are perfectly predictable yet federal policy has done little to guard against them.

A. State Impact on Federal Macro-Economic Policy

The requirement that states balance their budgets, the centerpiece of state fiscal constitutions, dates from long before the modern understanding of the business cycle. Understood in light of today's economics, it proves inadequate as a guarantor of fiscal probity. This section considers the distortions this requirement can cause during economic downturns absent proper precautions. The converse also holds: even balanced budgets can be fiscally irresponsible during booms.

Cutting spending or raising taxes as the economy is slowing is likely to put state fiscal policies in direct opposition to federal macro-economic policy. Although the federal government can offset even the aggregate effects of state budgetary changes, it often takes some time to do so. Those states legally or politically obliged to make midyear adjustments when their budgets are going out of balance often will act before the federal government can agree upon and implement a countercyclical policy. In addition, state policy changes – disrupting settled expectations about service and taxation levels – may cause more harm than federal policies can offset.

B. State Impact on Federal Program Integrity

A prominent feature of states' responses to fiscal crises is gimmickry. Some gimmicks, such as timing shifts and accounting fictions, effectively displace costs onto future legislatures. Others burden local governments or private businesses, particularly those doing business with the state. A third group, however, displaces state costs onto the federal government. For example, Medicaid "maximization" plans allow states to draw down additional federal matching dollars without increasing their own contributions.

The availability of these gimmicks routinely is condemned as exemplifying a moral hazard. One could argue from a short-term perspective that not all of these gimmicks are objectionable: Future legislatures and the federal government likely are better equipped to supply the needed resources than the current legislature is. Once these gimmicks are legitimized, however, they become available to fund even more expansionary policies during the next boom. They also effectively demand federal legislation to close them off, and such legislation is rarely simple. Some maximization strategies can only be foreclosed by curtailing or eliminating otherwise valuable programmatic features. Moreover, once a maximization scheme has persisted for a few years, states may claim reliance interests in the continuation of the revenues it produces. Responding to these demands may slow corrective legislation, impair interstate equity, and ultimately increase programs' costs without concomitant improvement in services.

C. Substantive Instability in State Fiscal Policies

One logical response to a cyclical surplus would be to restore funding to programs cut, and rescind revenue increases, enacted during the preceding downturn. In practice, this is unlikely. Having fallen out of the baseline, those priorities generally enjoy no presumption of any kind in state budgetary processes.[8] Program employees and grant recipients who fought the initial cuts are likely to have become discouraged and scattered, with few feeling the same motivation to work for restorations. In addition, reversing these changes could be taken as an admission that the cuts and revenue increases were harmful, an argument many incumbent politicians will be reluctant to hand prospective challengers. Finally, politicians are likely to be able to attract far more favorable publicity, or to extract higher rents, for a new programmatic initiative or tax reduction than merely restoring an ancien régime.

The result, then, is likely to be the creation of new programs and newly designed tax cuts. Thus, not only do economic recoveries typically fail to prompt restorations of prior cuts, but they also often generate new policies that will compete for scarce resources with the cut programs in the next fiscal crisis. Programs and tax expenditures with more active interest-group support ratchet up at the expense of the maintenance of residual public obligations over the course of several business cycles. This suggests that booms are excellent times

---

[8] In theory, states could enact explicitly temporary budget cuts or revenue increases, with the underlying programs and taxes automatically reverting to pre-recession levels absent further legislation. In practice, this is relatively rare, particularly with spending programs. First, states enact one- or two-year budgets that set no policy for the out-years: States simply have no logical place to put any longer-term restoration. Second, and related, most state spending is controlled only by dollar figures in appropriations legislation. The prior year's number is all each legislature has to guide its future legislation. (The same is not true of taxes, which is why temporary tax increases are easier to legislate and more common than temporary program cuts.) Third, antilogrolling provisions in state constitutions commonly prohibit including substantive legislation in budget bills. Finally, state policymaking remains only haltingly aware of the business cycle; many policymakers appear to assume that a projected deficit in the current year is likely to continue in any future years in which current policies apply.

for the federal government to initiate new matching programs with states. On the other hand, it also suggests that existing federal–state matching programs will tend to ratchet down over the course of several business cycles.

This preference for new programs, to be sure, is not all bad. States are ideal laboratories of innovation in part because they periodically find themselves awash in huge surpluses. More innovative programs, as well as more foolish ones, are created when fiscal constraints are relaxed as improving economies produce sudden amounts of unbudgeted funds that the political process presumes should be spent or rebated to taxpayers. The practical value of these experiments, however, should not be exaggerated. States often fail to provide for the kind of objective evaluations that would help identify their merits. Initiatives that require several years to show effects – including many health, education, and other human-services programs – may be gutted or cancelled in the next fiscal crisis before they can demonstrate their promise. And even those programs recognized as worthy of emulation during an expansion may be forgotten over the course of the ensuing years of fiscal crisis. In short, the vision of states as laboratories assumes that the availability of ideas, rather than the capacity to provide consistent funding, is the primary limiting factor on state and local social policy.

III. FEDERAL BURDENS ON STATE FISCAL MANAGEMENT

Although federalism and decentralization play much greater roles in this country's public discourse now than they did a generation ago, their practical impact is intermittent. The former governors who have occupied the White House for all but four of the past 30 years have not hesitated to burden state budgets when doing so proved politically advantageous. Congress and Supreme Court majorities that on some occasions pay great fealty to states' role in the federal system similarly have imposed severe burdens on state fiscs.

These burdens have taken several forms. One of the most discussed, though not necessarily most important, is the unfunded mandate. In *Printz v. United States*,[9] the Supreme Court held that Congress may not directly order state or local governments to carry out federal policies. This ruling's impact is limited, however, because Congress can achieve similar results in most cases by conditioning federal funds on state compliance with federal requirements. The Court gave wide license to such conditions in *South Dakota v. Dole*.[10] With states receiving so many streams of federal funding, most of which vastly exceed the cost of complying with federal mandates, *Printz*'s effect is largely symbolic. Similarly, the Unfunded Mandates Reform Act of 1995 (UMRA) prohibits the same kinds of raw directives the Court struck down in *Printz* but does little to

---

[9] *Printz v. United States*, 521 U.S. 898 (1997).   [10] *South Dakota v. Dole*, 483 U.S. 203 (1987).

restrain costly conditions on federal grants-in-aid.[11] The restraints that UMRA and executive orders impose on unfunded regulatory mandates are similarly elastic.

At its core, the problem lies not with particular rules seeking to constrain unfunded mandates but with the concept of unfunded mandate control itself. With superior revenue-raising capacity and a more efficient tax system, federal-to-state revenue sharing is manifestly in the public interest. Pure gifts from politicians at one level of government to those at another, however, are rare and unsustainable. To justify the political capital required to secure revenues, federal lawmakers naturally will want recipient states to advance some policy priority of theirs. As long as these conditions are less burdensome than raising an equivalent amount of money themselves, states are likely to accept the conditional funding. Barring such conditions effectively would prevent the federal government from contracting with states to carry out federal policies, leaving both levels of government worse off; absent incompetence, barring two willing parties from entering into a mutually agreeable contract is generally inefficient. Indeed, such a rule would have the bizarre result of allowing the federal government to contract with private parties for the performance of public functions that it could not pay states to undertake.

The issue, then, is not mandates per se but rather conditions on federal funding. And with those conditions necessary to maintaining the beneficial flow of federal funding, the federal government's impact on states' fiscal position is best understood by comparing the impact of conditions with the value of funding provided. Ordinarily, little purpose is served by focusing on particular components of state budgets: A cut, or a net increase in conditionality, in one program may well balance out a change in burdens in another program. Thus, we should ask whether, in any given period, the impact of new or tightened funding conditions exceeded that of new or expanded federal funding. This, however, is but one of several ways in which the federal government can have an impact on state fiscs.

At least as important as conditions on federal funding are reductions in the amount of that funding. The extreme rarity of states refusing even heavily conditional federal funding suggests that the value of that funding exceeds the costs of compliance. Moreover, even where elimination of a funding stream absolves states of legal responsibility for complying with associated conditions, many functions that federal grants-in-aid support are ones states practically would have to perform in any event. This reveals a curious irony in the unfunded mandates argument: Although requirements affecting states' core functions

---

[11] UMRA also is not directly enforceable by state or local governments to void mandates. It allows members of Congress to raise points of order against bills containing unfunded mandates meeting its definition. A simple majority in either chamber, can override an UMRA point of order. Indeed, these points of order are raised only infrequently.

seem the most intrusive upon state sovereignty, they may be among the most important to maintain because loss of the underlying funding stream that those conditions justify would represent a pure cost shift to the states.

Although the level of federal grants-in-aid to states reflects many program-specific factors, some general patterns emerge. First and most obviously, the long-term imbalance in the federal budget poses a grave threat to states as well. Should Congress heed the calls elsewhere in this volume to rein in the structural federal deficit, grants-in-aid to states will be very much at risk. With large near-term savings in Social Security and Medicare unlikely, the Defense and Homeland Security budgets seemingly sacrosanct, and interest on the national debt growing, aid to state and local governments constitutes a large fraction of the remaining spending from which Congress is likely to seek savings. The Deficit Reduction Act of 2006, as well as other major spending reduction initiatives over the prior decade, relied heavily on cuts in aid to states.

Second, federal aid to states is largely insensitive to the business cycle. To be sure, Medicaid will match state expenditures for the additional people becoming eligible in a recession. It also, however, will reduce funding apace with states that cut Medicaid to relieve their fiscal imbalances in a slack economy. The Medicaid matching rate varies with state median income, but only slowly and from a fixed mean. Therefore, a state with a declining median income nonetheless may see its matching rate decline during an economic downturn if other states are harder hit; conversely, a booming state may receive a more generous match if other state economies are growing even faster. The unemployment compensation system does put money into state economies during recessions while siphoning off funds during booms, but it is best understood as a form of forced savings by states rather than true federal countercyclical aid. The federal government occasionally provides some ad hoc fiscal relief in response to recessions, but this typically has been small and has arrived too late to help states with the worst of their fiscal crises.

And, third, the very attack on funding conditions, under the banner of unfunded mandate reform, is likely to lead to further erosion in federal funding. The federal government funds state activities for three principle reasons: to compensate states for assuming responsibilities thought to be significantly those of the federal government; to enable the federal government to exercise policy leadership through the design of a program; and to take advantage of the federal government's superior revenue-raising capacity.[12] Only the third of these models is stable over the long term. When a program built on the leadership model loses support – either because of substantive disagreements with the content of that leadership or as part of a general reaction against federal conditions – the program may be abolished. Because the sudden loss of funding would cause chaos, and because the prior program had established an

---

[12] *See* David A. Super, *Rethinking Fiscal Federalism*, 118 Harv. L. Rev. 2544, 2571–2579 (2005).

implicit federal responsibility for funding that function, Congress will provide a new, relatively unconditioned, program based on the compensatory model. This may take the form of a block grant, revenue sharing, or a similar device. The basis for presuming federal fiscal responsibility in an area, however, will typically be contested. Over time, the parties to the original grand trade leave office or become engaged in other issues. The lack of a clear substantive purpose and detailed reporting requirements make the compensatory program's accomplishments difficult for new federal policymakers to discern, and the program falls down the priority list. State officials are likely to oppose reimposition of federal standards: The immediate burden of the standards is likely to outweigh in their minds the uncertain possibility that those conditions might improve the program's long-term funding prospects. The real value, and often the nominal value, of the block grant or revenue-sharing program thus is likely to decline steadily, perhaps eventually getting merged with remnants of programs that met similar fates. Just as President Reagan eliminated the revenue-sharing that President Nixon had substituted for an earlier round of categorical programs, the 104th Congress sought to merge or eliminate several Reagan-era block grants.

Yet despite this oft-repeated pattern, relatively little federal aid for states is justified explicitly in terms of the federal government's superior fiscal capacity. Reluctance to frame fiscal federalism in these terms helps explain the failure of the federal government to intervene more forcefully to address the problem of cyclicality, one of the clearest cases of impaired state fiscal capacity. It also helps explain the federal government's failure to help states struggling to find effective means of taxing interstate business activity.

In addition to mandates and funding cuts, a third way in which the federal government interferes with state fiscal management is the imposition of burdens of reenactment. With state constitutions largely mirroring the federal system of checks and balances, significant political capital is required to win passage of a revenue measure. A series of congressional and judicial policies, however, often has the effect of requiring proponents of revenue measures to amass this political capital multiple times, separated by some number of years, for their provisions to take effect. Congress has done this increasingly in recent years by preempting various state revenue measures. Even more significantly, Congress's cuts in federal taxes linked to state revenue systems – particularly the estate tax – have forced states to reenact their tax laws to "decouple" them from the federal system.

The courts, in turn, have applied complex and indeterminate standards for when a state tax will be deemed to discriminate unfairly against interstate commerce or to deny taxpayers equal protection of the laws. This leaves legislators with the unappealing choice of leaving significant amounts of economic activity untaxed – possibly putting in-state businesses at a disadvantage – or risking having to muster the political capital to reenact an alternative version of the legislation later. Because repealing tax measures and cutting spending continue to require only one-time majorities, these requirements of reenactment favor particular fiscal outcomes: spending reductions rather than revenue increases, and unpopular (and often regressive) sales and personal income taxes rather than corporate or business-activity taxes. States' caution in this area has led to steady erosion in their revenue bases as increasing shares of economic activity shift into interstate commerce and the difficult-to-tax service sector.

IV. REFORMING STATE FISCAL MANAGEMENT

The state budgetary process that cyclical pressures produce performs badly on the criteria described above for integrating budget-making with the state political environment. First, the budgets it produces are unlikely to represent the long-term preferences of the electorate. The political satisfaction lost when a nonessential spending program is expanded or an inoffensive tax is cut during a boom is far less than the dissatisfaction resulting from the cuts to more vital programs, or increases in burdensome taxes, necessary to balance state budgets during economic downturns. Current state budget processes, however, offer little opening for desirable deals to avoid this result. To be sure, many states contribute modest amounts to rainy-day funds, but these funds have little chance of prevailing against spending opportunities and tax cuts for available state funds during booms. Particularly in an era of term limits, politicians of one era are unlikely to defy interest groups competing for surplus dollars in order to ease the tasks of their successors during the next recession.

Second, the insensitivity of budget rules to the business cycle seriously distorts state political processes. The current rigid state budgetary rules, when subjected to cyclical pressures yield a welter of false positive and false negative evaluations of state officials. This produces an increase in the prevalence of disciplinary voting – and concomitant sacrifices of voters' policy preferences – and yet recaps no net improvement in the effectiveness of public management.

Third, cyclical pressures tend to produce a political dialogue that obscures rather than elucidates policy priorities. If the public believes these false positives and negatives to validate or discredit particular fiscal strategies, it will confound public discourse about budgetary priorities. Additional distortions arise when politicians are forced to defend budget cuts or tax increases they do not support, making them increasingly likely to misrepresent those policies' nature and effects. In particular, ordinal arguments are unsatisfying to make and easy to attack: Defenders of a program or tax-preference generally have little trouble persuading voters that "something else" (perhaps the venerable "waste, fraud, and abuse") is available as an alternative to budget cuts presented as the least of possible evils. Thus, politicians forced to cut programs or eliminate tax preferences commonly make cardinal, not ordinal, arguments: They condemn the target of their cuts as wasteful, inefficient, or "out of control." This delegitimizes claims of hardship resulting from the cuts, freeing the politician from criticism but also confusing the public and making restoration of the cut unlikely even when the state's finances improve.

Fourth, the combination of cyclical pressures and static budgetary procedures tends to separate state fiscal policies from their regulatory agendas. Swings in funding levels for state and local agencies can produce sharp changes in the intensity and content of the regulatory environment without any substantive policy decision to tighten or loosen pressure on regulated entities. Periods of recession-induced slack enforcement risk encouraging patterns of noncompliance that may be difficult to break even when the agency staffs up again. Moreover, a regulatory agency that must periodically lay off or overload its staff may have difficulty retaining quality personnel and may become more vulnerable to capture by private-sector interests on the other side of its "revolving door."

Fifth, the continual tidal pressures of budgetary processes insensitive to the business cycle tend to produce repeated changes in state spending programs unrelated to any changes in substantive policy preferences. As budgeteers struggle each year to achieve the required level of savings – but no more – from each program, they may impose successive layers of exotic and complex limiting rules. Although the complexities these rules create can be a nightmare for line administrators and program participants, top-level policymakers are unlikely to see much political advantage to cleaning up the complexity even once the state again can afford new spending.

Finally, extreme cyclical pressures on state governments tend to induce them to slight sincerely held principles about their proper relationships with local governments. Here again, principled champions of stable state–local fiscal relationships who are keenly aware of the consequences of sudden losses of state aid may nonetheless feel compelled to impose such cuts. Most aid to localities in many states results from a particular historical division of fiscal labor rather than from objectively derived principles. Thus, cutting local aid may prove politically safer than raising taxes or trimming some benefit the state provides directly. If reductions in local aid do lead to unpopular service reductions, the state politicians can hope that some of the public's anger will target their local counterparts.

Present state fiscal processes also engender undesirable tensions between state and federal governments. They require states to take money out of already weak economies during recessions while inviting expansionary tax cuts and spending increases during booms. State and local spending is a large enough share of the national economy that these policies have the potential to further slow an already ailing economy while contributing to inflationary pressures during expansions. Moreover, while deliberate federal policies to stimulate the economy often arrive too late to ease a recession, state and local governments commonly see falling revenues even before growth turns negative and thus may help tip a shaky economy into recession with spending cuts and tax increases. Even if the timing of federal and state fiscal policy could be synchronized, the benefits of artificial federal stimulative spending and tax cuts likely will be outweighed by the disruption that hurried state budget cuts and tax hikes cause.

State budgets' vulnerability to the business cycle also tends to skew the allocation of responsibility between federal and state governments. The past decade has seen determined efforts to devolve control over means-tested programs to the states. A significant group of devolution's opponents express concern over the ability of states to meet the needs of the newly poor during recessions. State performance during the early years of this decade bears out these concerns. Despite increases in the number of families in poverty every year from 2000 to 2004, cash-assistance caseloads under the Temporary Assistance to Needy Families (TANF) block grant remained static. Similarly, after the collapse of national health care reform in 1994, many states expanded health care coverage significantly with innovative policies. When the economy soured, however, many states curtailed or abandoned their programs. This seems likely to doom serious health care reform efforts in the states despite evidence that they can avoid the ideological gridlock that has stalled reform at the federal level.

Lastly, states' current fiscal rules fail the test of modesty. Their efforts to control the tidal pressures resulting from the business cycle burden budgetary rules with difficult tasks not essential to preserving states' long-term fiscal integrity. Governors and legislators sincerely committed to fiscal probity may be unable to tolerate the political cost of spending cuts and tax hikes when a cyclical downturn throws the state budget out of balance. And those willing to take hard measures may lose reelection to less responsible leaders. Either way, the result is likely to be a determined search for means of evading limits, with all major players facing strong pressure to acquiesce. Once accepted in a slump-induced fiscal crisis, however, these evasions become available to all policymakers at all points in the business cycle. Thus, explicit exceptions for economic downturns actually would enhance fiscal rules' long-term effectiveness by preserving their integrity for times when they are more important.

All of this suggests that reducing cyclical pressures is vital to improving the legitimacy and effectiveness of states' budget rules. Measures that relax fiscal pressures during economic downturns – but only then – and that limit policymakers' ability to dispose of cyclical surpluses will improve states' fiscal health and their constancy as programmatic partners for the federal government.

A. Equipping States to be Better Fiscal Partners for the Federal Government

Focusing on the intrastate goals of balance and limited government, most state budgetary processes to date have had their strongest impact when fiscal pressures were greatest. Obstacles to raising taxes or incurring debt bite when economic downturns throw state budgets into deficit. Spending limits or set-asides for perceived high-priority programs are most likely at issue when a recession drives up demand for Medicaid and other countercyclical programs states operate under formal or tacit divisions of responsibility with the federal government.

Even from an intrastate perspective, this structure has three fundamental defects. First, it imposes rules at precisely the wrong time in the business cycle. Rules whose legal and moral force could win widespread compliance at other times are thrust upon the political system precisely at the times when countervailing pressures are the strongest. This prevents development of a norm of compliance, indeed setting a precedent for egregious and unforced violations during better fiscal times later.

Second, it ignores the impact of decisions throughout the rest of the business cycle. No obvious reason argues that the ideal measure of spending restraint is the year rather than the decade or the business cycle. A dollar saved during a boom will have the same long-term value as a dollar saved during a recession. Moreover, profligate policies abound not in recessions but in booms, when natural political competition for funds abates. Containing wasteful excesses during booms would be a good in its own right and would moderate the pressures experienced during recessions.

And, third, the current regime has become discredited. Colorado's experience with TABOR widely is understood to have been an unhappy one, and a bipartisan coalition secured passage of a referendum in 2005 that repealed part of it and suspended the remainder. In 2006, well-funded petition drives failed to place it on the ballot in several states and, in the three where it did make the ballot, voters soundly rejected it.

More broadly, however, this focus on restraining state spending during economic downturns severely limits state reliability as a fiscal partner for the federal government and can lead to expansions of the federal role beyond what the political process would otherwise support. This section therefore proposes to shift the focus from imposing draconian restraints during recessions to imposing meaningful but more reasonable ones throughout the business cycle. In particular, it argues for reining in excesses during booms, when restraint is more politically feasible but, under current practices, rarely demanded.

i. Procedural Reforms

Several changes to state budgeting procedures, while lacking the demonstrative character of TABOR and other TELs, nonetheless could make important contributions to achieving the goals laid out above. Moreover, by adapting concepts from the federal budget process, some of these measures should facilitate communication between federal and state agencies involved with running joint programs while making gimmickry in these relationships easier to detect.

First, state budgets should be measured in terms of commitments as well as actual cash flow. In the federal budget, these concepts are known as "budget authority" and "outlays." Budget authority is a grant of legal authority to commit public funds. Thus, an appropriations bill empowering state officials to contract for the construction of a state office building should be scored as providing budget authority equal to the total cost of the building even though outlays under the contract may be minimal in the first budget year. Legislation postponing payments from the end of one year to the beginning of the next would reduce outlays in the first year but have no effect on budget authority. Budget authority thus is a useful device for assessing the full long-term impact of fiscal legislation – and an impediment to obscuring budgetary problems with artificial timing shifts.

Missing from the federal system, however, is a comparable measure of commitments with regard to revenues. Thus, legislation that induces individuals or businesses to prepay taxes at a deep discount is scored as increasing revenues even though it reduces the amount of revenue that will be received over the long term. This has led to absurd gimmickry in which one tax cut – such as a reduction in capital-gains tax rates or the opportunity to transfer funds to a tax-protected retirement account for a modest prepayment of taxes – pays for another. States are at least as vulnerable to tax changes with hidden long-term costs (e.g., long-term tax abatements to attract businesses to the state, whose revenue losses fall almost entirely in future years). Accounting for net reductions in the revenues payable to the state would expose the costs of those measures and allow more transparent debates on their merits.

Second, states should project the effects of governors' budget proposals and legislative amendments over at least five years into the future. This will further reduce the appeal of timing shifts. It also could reduce incentives to single out fast-spending programs, such as income transfers, for budget cuts.

Third, legislatures neither should be required nor allowed to make midyear adjustments once they have enacted a budget projected to be in balance. When the economy is improving relative to projections, allowing the legislature to increase spending or to cut taxes often will lead to ill-considered measures hurriedly passed at the behest of special interests. When the economy is sinking, requiring additional midyear cuts is likely to concentrate even more of the fiscal burden on the narrow range of programs in which outlays can be halted quickly.

Fourth, state rainy-day funds should be guaranteed contributions during periods of strong economic growth. If the rainy-day fund is given first claim on state funds after debt service and other contractual obligations, these contributions can become part of the baseline and, if the level is properly calibrated, not require the kinds of budget cuts or tax increases that motivate evasion. Calculating these contributions based on projected surpluses would be unwise: Doing so would increase incentives to manipulate projections and exacerbate the impacts of long-term spending commitments or tax cuts. Instead, the formula should depend on objective data on the functioning of the economy, with contributions beginning once the unemployment rate falls below the state's ten-year average and larger contributions required as the unemployment rate falls further.

Fifth, governors' budget proposals and legislative fiscal analysts should be required to report publicly on the nature and amount of tax expenditures.

Sixth, and in a similar vein, documents from both executive and legislative budget analysis offices should present a unified state budget. Ignoring or obscuring items of spending and their dedicated revenue streams again narrows the range of options available to correct cyclical budgetary imbalances, leading to disproportionate pressure on vulnerable programs and accentuating pressure to embrace gimmicks. Moreover, the existence of these specialized budgets tends to aggravate shortfalls: Any surpluses they may run are unavailable to cover shortfalls in the general fund, yet their deficits place additional demands on state finances and, in most cases, must be remedied.

Finally, states should continue to resist, as they did in the 2006 election cycle, the enactment of rigid limits on taxes and spending. Little evidence supports the notion that state spending is "out of control" or that state officials do not feel the electorate's resistance to new taxes. What may seem to be evidence of such insensitivity – revenue increases during recessions, when taxpayers can afford them least – is in fact an inevitable consequence of the cyclicality of budgets under current rules and the requirement of annual balance. The reforms proposed in this and the following subsection likely would reduce the need for such ill-timed revenue hikes – as well as ill-timed spending cuts – and bring aggregate spending and revenues over the course of the business cycle better in line with the electorate's preferences. States should, however, continue to seek to shut down devices for evading existing rules requiring transparency and annual balance in state budgets.

ii. Substantive Reforms

State governments have no capacity to repeal the business cycle or to immunize their budgets from cyclical fluctuations. Several concrete measures can, however, moderate their vulnerability to cyclical swings and hence allow more consistent administration of joint federal–state programs. Implementing these measures would allow state spending and revenues to rise less during booms and decline less during slumps, in both instances bringing them closer to the electorate's long-term preferences.

First, state budget rules should seek to shift spending whose timing is discretionary to periods of fiscal strength. In particular, this means that infrastructure projects should be initiated during booms and should be fully funded at the time the commitment is made. The current preference for financing major projects with revenue bonds is a striking example of the current rules' insensitivity to the cyclical stresses on state budgets. It implicitly assumes that each year's budget is equally capable of paying for projects of this nature and that a project's affordability in the year the project is authorized is a fair proxy for its affordability in subsequent years. This method of budgeting is likely to overcommit the state to expensive infrastructure projects during booms, when debt service on the bonds – if it has even begun – will consume a substantially smaller share of available funds than it will during the next recession. Requiring a legislature to fit the full costs of infrastructure projects within each budget it passes would subject possible infrastructure projects to more healthy competition rather than providing them an artificial advantage over other budgetary alternatives that are required to operate on a cash basis. By lessoning the states' debt-service load during recessions, eliminating bond financing of infrastructure projects would ease fiscal crises. It also would enlist proponents of those projects during booms to oppose increases in ongoing spending or permanent tax cuts that will undermine the state's long-term fiscal health.

Second, states should be permitted to issue bonds for operating expenses during periods when the economy, under a specified objective measure, is performing substantially below its historical average levels. The amount of such borrowing could be calibrated to readily available economic measures (e.g., an unemployment rate exceeding one level would allow borrowing up to a given percentage of the state's average real revenues over the preceding decade; a still higher unemployment rate would allow greater borrowing). If coupled with the elimination of bond financing for infrastructure projects, this might not require adjusting the amount of state debt limits.

Third, states should shift to less countercyclical revenue sources. In particular, the transition from income and business-activity taxes to sales taxes, in addition to being regressive, also is increasing states' vulnerability to the business cycle. It therefore should be reversed. Moreover, states should expand their sales taxes to cover more services.

Finally, states should adopt rules limiting off-budget financing and discretionary tax abatements. As already discussed, these are, in effect, opportunities for current legislatures to commit their successors' funds for projects inuring primarily to the political benefit of current officials. Here again, the relative cost of these initiatives in boom years will be far less than that during economic downturns, making in the ability to fit them into the budget for the year they are authorized a deficient measure of their long-term affordability. Removing these contractual and quasi-contractual commitments from the state budget will broaden policymakers' options in closing cyclical budget shortfalls.

B. Reforming Federal–State Fiscal Relations

Grants-in-aid to state and local governments form one of the largest categories in the federal budget. The federal government relies upon states and their subdivisions to carry out numerous important policies with political legitimacy, sensitivity to local conditions, and cost effectiveness that federal agencies could not match. Federal aid, in turn, is one of states' largest revenue sources. Its ebbs and flows go a long way to determining the fiscal climate for states. Moreover, the federal and state tax systems are linked closely; some changes in federal tax law automatically can raise or lower state revenues unless a state acts affirmatively to delink its tax system from its federal counterpart. Thus, the federal government has both substantial responsibility for, and a strong interest in, states' fiscal condition.

Current federal fiscal policy only intermittently considers impacts on states. Because it is free to pursue countercyclical policies largely forbidden to the states, the federal government has enormous unrealized capacity to shield states from cyclical pressures. Doing so would help states play a more consistent role in our federal system. It also would advance federal macro-economic policies by reducing the current procyclical behavior of states' budgets. In ensuring a more constant level of services in federal–state and federal–local programs, it would advance the federal policies behind those programs. Finally, reducing cyclical pressures on states would reduce the incentives to develop abusive "maximization" strategies to exploit matching programs.

i. Avoiding Federal Harm to State Budgets

The first and most basic change in federal policy needed to stabilize state budgets is the cessation of policies that destabilize states. During the fiscal crisis accompanying the recession of 2001, the federal government compounded states' difficulties severely. In particular, its tax cuts were structured in ways that reduced the revenues of numerous states automatically. When the federal government reduces tax rates, it has no effect on most state systems. The 2001 and 2003 tax cuts, however, changed definitions upon which state tax systems rely to reduce administrative burdens on taxpayers. Its elimination of the estate tax, if implemented, effectively would repeal the estate taxes of a number of states that base their levies on a share of federal liability. The timing of some of these cuts, coming after many states' legislative sessions had ended, made it particularly difficult for states to respond.

The federal government similarly should refrain from interfering directly in state revenue collections. Legislation during this period prohibited states from extending their sales taxes to transactions over the Internet, ensuring that state sales taxes will reach a steadily shrinking share of economic activity. Congress also considered legislation that would immunize significant amounts of business activity from state corporate income and related taxes.

In fiscal federalism as in medicine, the first principle should be to do no harm. Undermining state tax bases can cause far more harm than the more popularly debated "unfunded mandates."

ii. Restructuring Federal–State Funding Programs

A more affirmative step the federal government could take is to restructure federal–state matching programs to better account for the business cycle. The largest true matching programs, including Medicaid, foster-care assistance, and child-support enforcement, all implicitly assume that states have the same capacity to contribute throughout the business cycle. The federal government will provide more money to help meet the needs of beneficiaries newly qualifying for Medicaid in a recession, but only if the state can find additional funds, too. The federal government adjusts the Medicaid matching rate for changes in state median incomes, but because it measures states relative to the national median, these adjustments are a zero-sum game. A state with declining median income actually could see its matching obligations rise if other states are falling faster. Moreover, administrative and data limitations cause these adjustments to lag significantly behind changes in state conditions. This makes little sense.

The business cycle may have a greater impact on states' ability to fund federal–state programs than its relative median income some years previously. Moreover, no good reason supports current law's insistence that the average federal matching rate remain constant throughout the business cycle. Unemployment data, which are available far more rapidly than median incomes, could be used to adjust matching rates derived in the current manner. In a sour economy, the national average matching rate could be allowed to rise from the current 57 percent to perhaps 66 percent; in a boom, the average could be allowed to fall below 50 percent. This would ease pressures on states – and strengthen incentives to maintain commitments to matching programs – during economic downturns. It also would siphon off excess funds during expansions, reducing states' temptation to make unsustainable permanent policy changes. This also would make these programs much stronger automatic macro-economic stabilizers.

TANF is not a matching program in the usual sense in that it offers a fixed block grant to states on the condition that they contribute a largely fixed amount of "maintenance-of-effort" funding. Other block grants, with or without maintenance-of-effort requirements, fund other aspects of countercyclical aid. Fixed funding for highly cyclical needs makes little sense. During the boom economy of the late 1990s, state cash assistance caseloads fell rapidly, freeing up large amounts of TANF and maintenance of effort funds. Some of these were saved, and some went for innovative programming or expansions of child-care subsidies. A considerable amount, however, was diverted to other activities having little to do with TANF's purposes. When the recession increased poverty, TANF largely was unable to respond, in part because of the difficulty of dislodging entrenched interests that had become dependent on diverted TANF funds during the boom. Not all block grants for antipoverty programs are as vulnerable as TANF to diversion, but the problem of frozen funding is universal. By the time Congress considered increasing funding for some of these programs, much of the damage had been done.

Here again, varying the federal contribution automatically based on the economy's performance would ease states' distress during crises while heading off waste during periods of lesser need. TANF, a relatively new capped program and one with a more obviously countercyclical goal, has both a contingency fund and provision for loans to states in economic distress. Unfortunately, both are designed so badly that they provide little actual relief. For example, the contingency fund effectively requires states to increase their contributions by one-quarter to one-third before receiving any additional federal funds. Redesigning these devices and extending them to other programs would target benefits more closely to need; the increased federal cost could be offset by reducing the base funding for these programs (i.e., the funding provided during periods of strong economic growth).

iii. Reallocating Responsibilities Between Federal and State Governments

Although the policies recommended above significantly would ameliorate cyclicality in state budgets, they cannot bridge the gaps that recessions create between demand for countercyclical relief and declining revenues. Conversely, they are unlikely to absorb the windfalls that states receive when the economy surges. This raises serious questions about whether the current federal–state division of fiscal responsibilities makes sense.

Under current practice, state and local governments are the default funding source for aid to low-income people other than the elderly and people with disabilities. Since the New Deal, the federal government has helped with the cost of aid to many families with children, but most of this aid has been contingent on state and local contributions.

Funding this aid is a task that state and local governments singularly are ill-equipped to perform. Asking their cyclically mismatched revenue streams to bear this burden ensures that programs for low-income families will come under the greatest pressure precisely when they are needed most. Trading this responsibility for discontinuance of some routine operating subsidies for noncyclical functions of government would improve efficiency and keep spending closer to the electorate's preferred level over the course of the business cycle. Even within the realm of human services, states are far better equipped to support job training or child-support enforcement, both of which receive large federal subsidies despite their largely noncyclical character and broad political appeal. Indeed, the one major subset of low-income people for whom the federal government does assume primary responsibility – the elderly and persons with disabilities – is precisely the one with the *least* cyclical needs (and the strongest political position). States would be far better able to serve those populations than persons seeking public aid as a result of (often cyclical) unemployment or underemployment.

V. CONCLUSION

Although horizontal comparisons of state budgets are common, thoughtful longitudinal comparisons are far less so. Those that are attempted tend to focus on long-term substantive policy trends rather than the effects of the business cycle. This neglect has undermined states' fiscal performance in ways that should be objectionable across the political spectrum. It has left programs underfunded during recessions while leading to waste during booms. It repeatedly has defeated measures designed to ensure fiscal rectitude, with short-term effects that some might applaud but with serious long-term harm to states' role in fiscal federalism.

A proper appreciation of state budgets' cyclical character turns much presumed learning on its head. Leaders presiding over cyclical crises, even those that resort to gimmicks to balance their budgets, are not irresponsible threats to states' fiscal integrity. The beaming governor and appropriations chairs who announce that "the mess" has been "cleaned up" as the economy starts to grow again, in turn, may be more scoundrels than saviors. Moreover, the interstate equity concerns that to date have been the primary objection raised against states' fiscal responsibility for antipoverty programs may in fact be secondary concerns to the havoc countercyclical programs wreak on state budgets relying primarily on procyclical revenue sources. Our failure to place full responsibility for countercyclical fiscal policy on the federal government has imperiled states' effectiveness in performing many important functions.

Once these problems are understood, however, policymakers have several options for reining in excesses during economic expansions while applying a more realistic brand of fiscal discipline during downturns. These measures cannot eliminate cyclical pressures on states. They can, however, significantly improve state budgets' performance, integrity, and effectiveness in our federal system.

Questions for Chapter 12

1. In debate over budget policy, the states are often viewed as laboratories where a good deal of fiscal experimentation takes place and from which the federal government might learn lessons for reforming its own processes. As Professor Super notes, however, budgeting at the state level differs in some critical respects from what takes place in Washington. Most importantly for his analysis, states operate within fairly strict rules of mandatory fiscal balance and are especially vulnerable to fiscal difficulties in times of economic downturn both because their expenditures are likely to rise in such periods and because their revenues are apt to fall. Moreover, states operate under several additional constraints in that they are not fully free to tax all income generated within the boundaries, partially as a result of legal restrictions on taxing interstate commerce and partially from competitive concerns that tax increases will cause businesses and jobs to move out of states to more accommodating jurisdictions. While globalization has started to place the federal government under analogous constraints, the pressures are not yet as severe as those facing state budget makers. How severely does Professor Super's critique undermine the "laboratories of democracy" concept? In what ways might states' experiences still usefully guide policymaking elsewhere?

2. The role of the federal government in contributing to or resolving the fiscal problems of the states has been the subject of ongoing controversy. As recounted in Professor Super's chapter, the Supreme Court has often been called upon to consider the constitutionality of federal legislation imposing fiscal burdens on state governments. While the courts have limited the power of the federal government to impose direct mandates on state legislation, indirect mandates – typically in the form of conditional federal spending – are generally permissible and have generated considerable obligations for the states. These are obligations

that oftentimes rise in times of economic downturn.[13] In part to reduce the growth of these obligations, Congress enacted the Unfunded Mandates Reform Act of 1995 to make it more difficult – though by no means impossible – to create additional obligations of this sort.[14] Ordinarily, one would think that the same level of government that creates a public program should be the one that raises the revenue to finance the programs costs. Under what circumstances is it appropriate for the federal government to establish programs that the states must implement and finance? Does it solve the problem if the state is free to decline to participate in the program (and hence forego the partial federal funding that that program offers)?

3. In Section II.B of this chapter, Professor Super advances a list of goals which state budgetary procedures should achieve in order to ensure integration with state political processes These goals include reflecting the will of the people, maintaining transparent procedures that do not advantage special interests but do provide clear and accurate measures of the fiscal performance of political leaders, facilitating the setting of public priorities, allowing for coordination with other state programs, avoiding undue complexity, and maintaining an appropriate relationship with local governments. How well do the budget procedures of the federal government fulfill these goals? Are these the right goals for governmental budgeting, or would you propose other or different goals? Which of these goals are likely to prove the most difficult to achieve over the long run?

4. The federal–state relationship that Professor Super describes in this chapter is strikingly different than the relationship between the EU and member states that Professor von Hagen reviewed in an earlier chapter. As Professor Super notes, the American states typically operate under reasonably strict rules requiring balanced budgets, but then find their fiscal tasks complicated in economic downturns when tax receipts fall and the federal government may cut back on its sharing of revenues but does not relieve states of programmatic obligations that tend to rise in times of economic turmoil. In Europe, by contrast, it is community-wide treaty obligations that set standards of fiscal balance for the member states, but the member states have a considerable degree of freedom to ignore these obligations in times of economic downturns. While Professor Super advocates greater fiscal flexibility for U.S. states in times of economic

---

[13] For an overview of federal conditional spending, see Dan Klaff and Adam Lawton, Conditional Spending and Other Forms of Federal Cost Sharing, May 2, 2006 (Briefing Paper No. 18), *available at* http://www.law.harvard.edu/faculty/hjackson/ConditionalSpending_18.pdf.

[14] *See* Elizabeth Garrett, *Enhancing the Political Safeguards of Federalism? The Unfunded Mandates Reform Act of 1995*, 45 KAN. L. REV. 1113 (1997); *see also* Stacy Anderson and Russell Constantine, Unfunded Mandates, April 20, 2005 (Briefing Paper No. 7), *available at* http://www.law.harvard.edu/faculty/hjackson/UnfundedMandates_7.pdf.

downturns, Professor von Hagen laments the growing noncompliance of EU member states in meeting their fiscal treaty obligations. Can Professors Super's and von Hagen's positions be reconciled in light of the differences between the problems they are addressing, or do they seem to present fundamentally different visions of how government should respond to economic downturns?

5. In terms of dealing with the problem of economic cycles, would it be better for the states to relax their rules of fiscal balance along the lines that Professor Super propose or for the federal government to revise its revenue-sharing procedures to counteract state fiscal challenges caused by economic slowdowns? Which solution is more likely to be adopted?

6. Professor Super identifies a few programs, such as those providing relief for low-income families, for which he believes the federal government should have primary fiscal responsibility, and he identifies others, such as aid to the aged and persons with disabilities, that strike him as better suited to states' fiscal capacities. Do you agree with these recommendations? What other programs would you assign to one level of government or the other based on fiscal considerations?

7. Professor Super expresses concern about long-term fiscal harm caused by gimmicks that states rely upon to balance their budgets. For example, a legislature that sells a state office building and then leases back the space from the new owner will show a one-time revenue gain but saddle its successors with new long-term costs that likely more than offset those gains. Professor Super suggests that state courts are reluctant to strike these schemes down when the state is under fiscal duress in a recession, but that, once ratified, these gimmicks become available to fund extravagant spending increases and tax cuts once the crisis has passed. What approaches might be tried to rein in these devices? What are the strengths and weaknesses of each?

Bibliography

ARTICLES

James M. Buchanan, *Principles of Urban Fiscal Strategy*, 11 PUB. CHOICE 1 (1971).

Carter Goodrich, *The Revulsion Against Internal Improvements*, 10 J. ECON. HIST. 145 (1950).

Elizabeth Graddy and Ke Ye (2006). *When Do we "Just Say No"? Policy Termination Decisions in Local Hospital Services* (USC School of Policy, Planning, and Development Working Paper, 2007).

Robert P. Inman, *Federal Assistance and Local Services in the United States: The Evolution of a New Federalist Fiscal Order*, *in* FISCAL FEDERALISM: QUANTITATIVE STUDIES. (Harvey S. Rosen ed., 1988).

Louis D. Johnston and Samuel H. Williamson, *The Annual Real and Nominal GDP for the United States, 1790 – Present*, ECON. HIST. SERV., Apr. 1, 2006, *available at* http://eh.net/hmit/gdp/.

Kell Kelly, *TABOR is Unpatriotic*, DAILY OKLAHOMAN, Oct. 6, 2006, at 17A.

Brian Knight, *Legislative Representation, Bargaining Power, and the Distribution of Federal Fund Evidence from the U.S. Senate* (presented at the Fiscal Challenges: An Interdisciplinary Approach to Budget Policy conference, Feb. 10, 2006).

Wallace Oates, *Toward a Second-Generation Theory of Fiscal Federalism*, 12 INT'L TAX & PUB. FIN. 349 (2005).

James Poterba, *Balanced Budget Rules and Fiscal Policy: Evidence from the States*, 48 NAT'L TAX J. 329 (1995).

William J. Quirk and Lawrence E. Wein, *A Short Constitutional History of Entities Commonly Known as Authorities*, 56 CORNELL L. REV. 521 (1971).

Will Shanley, *Letter Warns States to Fight Initiatives*, DENVER POST, Aug. 3, 2006, at C1.

David A. Super, *Rethinking Fiscal Federalism*, 118 HARV. L. REV. 2544 (2005).

Charles Tiebout, *A Pure Theory of Local Expenditures*, 64 J. POL. ECON. 416 (1956).

John Joseph Wallis, *Constitutions, Corporations, and Corruption*, 65 J. ECON. HIST. 211 (2005).

John Joseph Wallis, *The Property Tax as a Coordinating Device: Financing Indiana's Mammoth System of Internal Improvements, 1835 to 1842*, 40 EXPLORATIONS IN ECON. HIST. 223 (2003).

John Joseph Wallis, Richard Sylla, and Arthur Grinath, *Sovereign Default and Repudiation* (Nat'l Bureau of Econ. Research Working Paper No.W-10753, 2004).

John Joseph Wallis and Barry R. Weingast, *Equilibrium Federal Impotence: Why the States and not the American National Government Financed Economic Development in the Antebellum Era* (Hoover Institution Stanford University Working Paper, 2005).

Barry Weingast, *A Rational Choice Perspective on Congressional Norms*, 24 Am. J. Pol. Sci. 245 (1979).

Barry R. Weingast, *Second Generation Fiscal Federalism: Implications for Decentralized Democratic Governance and Economic Development* (Hoover Institution Stanford University Working Paper, 2006).

Barry Weingast, Kenneth A. Shepsle, and Christopher Johnsen, *The Political Economy of Benefits and Costs: A Neoclassical Approach to Distributive Politics*, 89 J. Pol. Econ. 642 (August 1981).

BOOKS

Richard Briffault, Balancing Acts: The Reality Behind State Balanced Budget Requirements (1996).

Nancy Burns, The Formation of American Local Governments: Private Values in Public Institutions (1994).

Robin Einhorn, Property Rules (1991).

Carter Goodrich, Government Promotion of Canals and Railroads, 1800–1890 (1960).

Ron Haskins et al., *Getting to Balance: Three Alternative Plans, in* Restoring Fiscal Sanity: How to Balance the Budget 15 (Alice M. Rivlin and Isabel Sawhill eds., 2004).

Albert Miller Hillhouse, Municipal Bonds: A Century of Experience (1936).

Reginald C. McGrane, Foreign Bondholders and American State Debts (1935).

Wallace Oates, Local Government and the Property Tax (2001).

Paul Peterson, City Limits (1981).

B. U. Ratchford, American State Debts (1941).

Mark Schneider, The Competitive City: The Political Economy of Suburbia (1989).

Jon C. Teaford, The Unheralded Triumph: City Government in America, 1870–1900 (1984).

John Joseph Wallis, Richard Sylla, and John Legler, *The Interaction of Taxation and Regulation in Nineteenth Century Banking, in* The Regulated Economy: A Historical Approach to Political Economy 121 (Claudia Goldin and Gary D. Libecap eds., 1994).

CASES

Newell v. People, 7 N.Y. 9 (1852).

People v. Newell, 13 Barb. 86 (N.Y. Sup. Ct.), *rev'd*, 7 N.Y. 9 (1852).

Printz v. United States, 521 U.S. 898 (1997).

Rodman v. Munson, 13 Barb. 63 (N.Y. Sup. Ct.), *aff'd*, 13 Barb. 188 (N.Y. Sup. Ct.).

South Dakota v. Dole, 483 U.S. 203 (1987).

CONGRESSIONAL REPORTS

Census Office, Dep't of Interior, Report on Valuation, Taxation, and Public Indebtedness, The Tenth Census (1884).

Congressional Budget Office, Historical Budget Data, Table 5 (Jan. 26, 2006), *available at* http://ftp.cbo.gov/budget/historical.pdf.

The NBER/Maryland State Constitution Project, *available at* http://www.stateconstitutions.umd.edu.

National Conference of State Legislatures & National Governors' Association, Financing State Government in the 1990s 57–62 (Ronald K. Snell ed., 1993).

Report of the Debates and Proceedings of the Convention for the Revision of the Constitution of the State of Indiana 1850 676, Indiana Constitutional Convention (1850–1851).

U.S. Census Bureau, GC02(4)-5, Compendium of Government Finances: 2002, 4 2002 Census of Governments No. 5 (2002).

U.S. Census Bureau, GC02(1)-1, Government Organization, 1 2002 Census of Governments No. 1, 13–14 (2002).

LEGISLATION

Unfunded Mandates Reform Act of 1995, Pub. L. No. 104-4, 109 Stat. 48.

PART FIVE

JUDICIAL POWERS AND BUDGET POLICY

I n the world of budget policy, the primary government actors are the executive and legislative branches. The judiciary, however, also sometimes gets into the act. At the federal level, the courts occasionally are called upon to resolve disputes between the two other branches of government regarding the allocation of spending powers under the federal Constitution. So, for example, the Supreme Court has been called upon in recent times to rule on efforts of the executive to refrain from spending – either through impoundments[1] or through a line-item veto[2] – after the expenditures had been approved by Congress through authorizing legislation and appropriations. In both cases, the court ruled against the executive. On the other hand, the court also has invalidated provisions of the original Gramm-Rudman-Hollings Act, under which Congress had assigned to its own agent – the comptroller general – too great a role in the administration of the act's sequestration provisions.[3]

Separation-of-powers cases are, however, exceptional, and the overwhelming majority of federal cases dealing with spending decisions resolve much more individualized disputes. Each year, the federal courts hear a multitude of cases whereby private parties seek monetary awards from the federal government for benefits promised under various entitlement programs, torts committed by government agents, contractual disputes involving government contracts, and even unconstitutional takings proscribed under the Fifth Amendment. In all these contexts, the federal government has submitted itself to the jurisdiction of the federal courts, waiving sovereign immunity and enacting various appropriations to fund damage awards.[4]

---

[1] *Train v. City of New York*, 420 U.S. 35 (1975).

[2] *Clinton v. City of New York*, 524 U.S. 417 (1998).

[3] *Bowsher v. Synar*, 478 U.S. 714 (1986).

[4] *See* Stacy Anderson and Blake Roberts, The Capacity to Commit in the Absence of Legislation: Takings, Winstar, FTCA & the Court of Claims (May 2005), *available at* http://www.law.harvard.edu/faculty/hjackson/CapacitytoCommitt_12.pdf.

In the next two chapters, we present two different perspectives on the role of courts in budgetary policy. First, Professor John Harrison considers the extent to which Congress could strengthen the rights of Social Security beneficiaries by converting statutory rights to receive program benefits into property interests protected under the Takings Clause of the Fifth Amendment and associated anticonfiscatory provisions of the federal Constitution. Of critical interest here is the question whether subsequent Congresses would be barred from reneging upon these enhanced benefits. Professor Harrison's analysis explores challenging and largely unresolved questions regarding the capacity of one Congress to enlist judicial power to bind the spending decisions of future Congresses, and invites the reader to consider the vitality of traditional notions of sovereign immunity, which was once understood to give the government wide latitude to determine the scope of its own legal obligations and spending responsibilities.

In the next chapter, we return to the states, where constitutional provisions governing spending and budget policy are common. In a review of a series of recent state court decisions, Professor Richard Briffault reviews the records of state courts in enforcing constitutional provisions governing fiscal policy. The results are decidedly uneven. Some of these decisions involve constitutional provisions with ambiguous language, where the judicial branch understandably defers to the political branches. But even when faced with what appear to be fairly clear textual mandates, state courts have been reluctant to reverse spending decisions upon which the legislature and executive have agreed. Even when the courts nominally vitiate constitutional provisions dealing with fiscal matters, the holdings often leave plenty of wiggle room for politicians in future years, and the courts frequently acquiesce when the next dispute arises. Professor Briffault concludes his chapter with speculation as to why state courts are less likely to enforce constitutional provisions involving fiscal matters than they are to enforce provisions safeguarding individual rights.

13 New Property, Entrenchment, and the Fiscal Constitution

John Harrison

Taxation and spending are immensely important federal powers, and federal budgeting involves dealing with them together. Taxing and spending together are used to produce what often is called new property, which in its fiscal form consists of benefits provided by the government and funded by taxation. Old property, by contrast, consists of correlative claims and duties of private people, and associated private powers and their correlates. Old property has a substantial amount of stability deriving from the fact that legislation is required to change the legal relationships that create it, and legislation usually takes substantial political effort. In default of legislative action, the legal norms that create and protect old property remain in place. Moreover, to some uncertain extent, the Constitution itself limits changes with respect to old property through the Takings Clause (and its projection through the 14th Amendment) and sometimes through principles of substantive due process.[1]

This chapter is about the stability of new property and, in particular, of the most important form of new property created by the federal government, Social Security old-age benefits. It seeks to mine the analogies and disanalogies between old and new property. The first section discusses the statutory structure that governs the taxation and spending associated with Social Security, with a specific focus on the extent to which Congress has insulated it from legislative change. That insulation is substantial but does not equal the stability associated

---

[1] Although current judges may not recognize this when they distinguish between takings-based and due-process-based protections of property rights, the doctrine that now is called substantive due process originated in a reading of the state and federal Due Process Clauses that today would make them hard to distinguish from the Takings Clause. *See, e.g., Chicago, Burlington & Quincy R. Co. v. Chicago*, 166 U.S. 226 (1897) (taking private property without a public purpose is deprivation without due process).

John Harrison is the D. Lurton Massee, Jr., Professor of Law, University of Virginia. The author thanks the other participants in the symposium who reviewed this text, and he especially gives thanks to Elizabeth Garrett and Howell Jackson for their organizational and substantive contributions.

with old property because of the funding mechanism that Social Security uses. The first section describes the interlocked statutory provisions that create the system and endow it with its limited permanence, and then it discusses the possible consequences of that statutory arrangement if a time does come, as is now expected, at which the system will not be able to meet its obligations.

The second section, which addresses constitutional questions more directly, assesses the possibility of a stronger form of entrenchment for Social Security than Congress has created, one that would take advantage of constitutional protections that apply to old property. Thus far, Congress has gone out of its way to avoid making Social Security benefits property or contract rights for the purposes of the constitutional provisions that entrench such rights against future legislative interference.[2] I will ask whether Congress could provide such entrenchment if it wanted to, and then briefly assess the merits of doing so on the basis of the usual justifications for the entrenchment of constitutional rules.

I. STATUTORY STRUCTURE OF SOCIAL SECURITY TAXING AND SPENDING

The least controversial way in which Congress can entrench its decisions is simply by passing a statute. Repealing statutes is difficult, and the ordinary legislative process almost certainly amounts to a supermajority requirement, because of the bicameral nature of the federal legislature and the internal rules of each house, which enable minorities to block action even when they cannot act themselves. Any statute, then, is to some extent entrenched.[3] The extent of that entrenchment is, to a large extent, up to Congress. Laws can have sunset provisions or be contingent for their continued operation on future events.

Varying degrees of statutory permanence are especially common with respect to spending programs, and to a lesser but important extent with respect to taxation, and are thus a familiar feature of budgetary law and policy. These decisions about permanence and impermanence are of considerable importance when it comes to programs of combined taxation and spending that create new-property types of public benefits, so an exploration of the options and their consequences, and the actual decisions Congress has made in this regard, should

---

[2] The standard citation for the proposition that Social Security benefits are not property for purposes of the Fifth Amendment's substantive protections against confiscation is *Flemming v. Nestor*, 363 U.S. 603 (1960). The lower court in that case concluded that an act of Congress that terminated the Social Security benefits of a class of beneficiaries to which Nestor belonged deprived him of "an accrued property right." *Id.* at 608. The court concluded that Nestor's "right to Social Security benefits cannot properly be considered to have been of that order." *Id.*

[3] For present purposes I will adopt the orthodox position according to which Congress may not by legislation limit the statutes that it may pass in the future, including statutes that repeal prior acts of Congress. That orthodoxy is questioned powerfully in Eric A. Posner and Adrian Vermeule, *Legislation Entrenchment: A Reappraisal*, 111 YALE L.J. 1665 (2002).

help illuminate both the general subject matter and the important particular field of public benefits.

Any spending program requires a legislative decision to spend money and cash in the Treasury to be spent.[4] Cash to pay benefits comes largely from taxation and borrowing, both of which require exercises of Congress' constitutional power.

A Congress that wanted to commit its successors as little as possible to a program of public benefit would authorize or appropriate only for a limited period of time. This is quite common with respect to spending in general; a substantial fraction of federal expenditures every year are the result of annual appropriations, even when the programs funded in those appropriations are substantively authorized for an indefinite period.[5] Discretionary spending, as that concept is used elsewhere in this volume, comes mainly from annual appropriations. At the other extreme are spending programs that have temporally unlimited substantive authorizations and appropriations that are permanent in their duration and indefinite in their amount and that thereby provide for the expenditure for as much money as needed for the statutory purpose for as long as that purpose lasts.[6] Most of what is called mandatory spending comes from permanent, indefinite appropriations. Unless a future Congress musters a majority to the contrary, such programs commit the expenditure of federal funds for all future time (at least in principle).[7]

---

[4] The legal structure concerning the creation by Congress of power to spend money involves some fairly arcane distinctions. Congressional rules and practice often distinguish among three steps in the process, involving three different kinds of statutes: those that empower government agencies to carry out programs that involve spending money, those that authorize the appropriation of money to be spent, and those that actually appropriate the money. "Appropriations acts must be distinguished from two other types of legislation: enabling – or organic – legislation and appropriation authorization legislation." I GOVERNMENT ACCOUNTABILITY OFFICE, PRINCIPLES OF FEDERAL APPROPRIATIONS LAW 2–40 (3d ed. 2004). The distinction between substantive and appropriations legislation, which serves in part to keep distinct the functions of different congressional committees, makes considerable sense; whether the further distinction between enabling and appropriations-authorizing legislation is useful even for internal congressional purposes is less clear, but irrelevant here.

[5] For example, the United States Department of Justice is created by a standing statute that does not need to be renewed annually, 28 U.S.C. 501, and the attorney general is authorized to litigate on behalf of the United States by similar permanent substantive statutes, 28 U.S.C. 514–518. Funds to pay for federal litigation by the department, however, are provided by annual appropriations acts. *See, e.g.*, Consolidated Appropriations Act, 2004, Pub. L. No. 109–199, Div., B, tit. I, 118 Stat. 3, 46 (appropriation for salaries and expenses of the Department of Justice for fiscal year 2004).

[6] *See* PRINCIPLES OF FEDERAL APPROPRIATIONS LAW, *supra* note 4, *at* 2–14 (distinguishing between appropriations definite and indefinite in amount and current and permanent in time).

[7] Almost certainly the most important permanent indefinite appropriation currently in effect is that for paying principal and interest on the public debt; *see* 31 U.S.C. 1305(2). Another important permanent, indefinite appropriation provides for payment of judgments against the United States; *see* 31 U.S.C. 1304.

Power to draw money from the Treasury, though, is of limited use without money in the Treasury to be spent, so the permanence of funding affects the practical permanence of programs. The design of funding thus also affects the extent of entrenchment. For example, if Congress has not provided enough tax revenue and borrowing authority to provide the necessary cash, a shortfall will constrain even a program that has legal power to spend. Making sure that such shortfalls will not happen is thus another way to entrench a program.

One way to insulate a spending program from future shortfalls is to give it a statutorily dedicated revenue source that is available only to pay for that program, such as a tax that is earmarked for that purpose only. Social Security is currently funded by such a tax. Social Security benefits are paid from a separate account in the Treasury, the Social Security Trust Fund.[8] Amounts equal to the receipts of the Social Security payroll tax are appropriated specifically to that fund by a permanent appropriation.[9]

Right now the dedicated payroll tax is more than enough to pay the benefits mandated by law but, as other contributions to this volume discuss in detail, according to current projections a time will come when the expenditures called for by the spending laws will exceed the money raised by the associated taxes. A more thoroughly secured system of new property could be achieved by varying the associated tax so as to meet the needs of the program. Congress also could authorize the program to borrow an indefinite amount on the credit of the federal government.[10]

Congress has not gone that far with respect to Social Security. It has provided substantial permanence, with a substantive statute of indefinite duration and a permanent indefinite appropriation from the Social Security Trust Fund. With respect to legal power to spend, it is as fixed as Congress can make it (barring a possibility to be discussed in the next section). With respect to providing cash for the payment of benefits, however, the situation is a bit different. Rather than giving Social Security an indefinite call on federal cash, Congress has limited the funds available to pay benefits to the revenue produced by the payroll tax and certain other sources, although on a cumulative and not annual basis. Receipts from the payroll tax currently exceed the cash needs of the Social Security program. They are in effect kept within that system by being invested in government bonds that, along with the interest the bonds accrue, will later

---

[8] Section 401(a) of title 42 of the United States Code creates the Old Age and Survivors Insurance Trust Fund. Section 401(f) provides that benefits are to be paid from that fund, and Section 402(a) creates the basic entitlement to benefits.

[9] Amounts equal to the receipts of the Social Security payroll tax plus certain other specific funding sources are appropriated to the Old Age and Survivors Insurance Trust Fund of the Treasury by 42 U.S.C. 401(a).

[10] Although the secretary of the Treasury has broad authority to borrow on the credit of the United States, 31 U.S.C. 3102–3106, Congress imposes statutory limits on total borrowing, 31 U.S.C. 3101(b).

give the Social Security Trust Fund a claim on general tax revenues until the bonds are exhausted.[11] Once they are, the Social Security Trust Fund will, on current projections, face a shortfall.[12]

The arrangement the current statutes produce is sufficiently odd to be worth some thought. Congress has limited the permanence of Social Security, but has not done so with a sunset provision for the program itself or its appropriation; both are indefinite. Instead, by dedicating revenue sources and capping those revenue sources, Congress has set up a situation in which the program can, and on current projections will, run out of money without running out of legal authority and indeed legal obligation to spend. An obligation to spend that is not backed by actual cash is default, and it is virtually unheard of in federal fiscal history.[13] It would perforce mean a reduction in benefit payments.

By accident or design, this resembles the Gramm-Rudman-Hollings Act mechanism, with its automatic spending cuts, although it notably strikes at a category of spending that carefully was excluded from that act's automatic expenditure reductions.[14] One of the leading questions today is whether that prospect, as it comes closer, will do what the Gramm-Rudman-Hollings Act was designed to do, which is to lead to difficult but thought-through budgetary choices, most likely including benefit reductions.[15]

It may well be that the current arrangement is biased politically in favor of producing tax increases rather than benefit cuts or some combination of

---

[11] Pursuant to 42 U.S.C. 401(h), the balances of the Social Security Trust Funds that are not needed for current payments are invested in securities issued by the Treasury.

[12] Such a shortfall could come earlier if the government as a whole faced a cash shortfall at a time when the Trust Fund's bonds were being drawn on.

[13] Government shutdowns are not defaults. They occur when Congress has not passed annual appropriations needed to keep some parts of the government operating. Shutdowns result from a lack of legal authority to spend money, not from lack of cash to spend. (Sections 1341 and 1342 of title 31 preclude expenditures and the creation of obligations to spend in the absence of appropriations, and so force much of the government to shut down when Congress has not appropriated funds, as at the end of a fiscal year.) In recent history the government has come close to running out of cash when the debt ceiling has been approached, not when appropriations have not been adopted. The operation of the debt ceiling is discussed and defended in Anita S. Krishnakumar, *In Defense of the Debt Limit Statute*, 42 Harv. J. Legis. 135 (2005).

[14] The Gramm-Rudman-Hollings Act – less colloquially the Balanced Budget and Emergency Deficit Control Act of 1985, Pub. L. No. 99–177, 99 Stat. 1038 – which provided for automatic, broadly distributed spending reductions in Congress, did not meet the deficit-reduction targets set by the act. Social Security benefits were excluded from the automatic cuts. The legal mechanism for Social Security is different from that of the Gramm-Rudman-Hollings Act, which used reductions in appropriations, not in cash. In that regard the Social Security default outcome is even harsher.

[15] Congress statutorily could set the default the other way, so that taxes would go up in the absence of further action. It could give the Social Security Trust Fund authority to borrow to meet any shortfall and then provide for repayment of the debt by a subsequent increase in the payroll tax keyed to the debt that would have to be repaid. With some year-to-year slippage due to borrowing and incorrect estimates of payroll-tax collections, this would keep the Social Security Trust Fund in balance by raising taxes automatically.

the two. Because the authorizing and appropriating legislation will be in force when default arrives, it will be easy to say that Congress has promised payments in its statutes and is under an obligation to come up with the money. It also will be true that Congress implicitly has limited its promise to the funds generated by the payroll tax, but that response may seem inadequate, especially for those who think of current payroll taxes as the equivalent of pension contributions, rather than as the taxes that fund current expenditures. The current statutes thus may construct a self-binding mechanism that will politically coerce Congress into raising taxes by threatening to go off and cut benefits. If tax increases without benefit reductions will be desirable when the time comes, that is a desirable feature of today's statutes and a beneficial result of the limited form of entrenchment that Congress has provided. If not, it will have negative policy consequences.

The prospect of general reductions in benefits, reductions that would apply to all beneficiaries without regard to their level of need, likely will be one of the most fearsome aspects of the Social Security action-forcing structure. Those who would favor something other than just tax increases when the time comes might then think that a little tweaking now and, in particular, some provision for the contingency of default could be useful. I will offer a preliminary thought on that subject.

A political mountain as large as a Social Security shortfall can be seen a long way away and so is visible now even though it is more than a decade away. This unusual configuration is of special interest to constitutional theorists because it creates a situation in which an ordinary legislature, here the current Congress, can to some extent act like a constitution-maker with respect to future legislatures. Not only can choices made now significantly influence or constrain choices to be made if the crisis arises, but it also is at least possible that they can be made more coolly and with greater deliberation than will be possible when default is much closer in time. One standard justification for the constitutionalization of legal norms is that, through a constitution, the people in a calm moment can keep themselves from doing foolish things in less than calm moments, as when there is too little time for sound deliberation.[16] Moreover, although it is possible right now to see in broad outline the interests that will be affected by these choices, particular details have yet to emerge. As a result, Congress now operates with less information and, hence, perhaps with more neutrality, than in the future.[17] It might therefore be desirable for

---

[16] *See Home Building & Loan Ass'n v. Blaisdell*, 290 U.S. 398, 465 (1934) (Sutherland, J., dissenting) (Contracts Clause designed to limit states specifically in times of emergency).

[17] Adrian Vermeule has shown that a number of important constitutional provisions are alike in that they force decision makers to operate with limited information and, hence, behind a veil of ignorance. Adrian Vermeule, *Veil of Ignorance Rules in Constitutional Law*, 111 YALE L.J. 399 (2001). As he notes, prospectivity itself, which the Constitution often forces, puts decision makers behind a veil of ignorance. *Id.* at 408–411. One of Vermeule's main points is that

Congress right now to decide what to do about the possibility of a shortfall. The problem with operating behind a veil of ignorance, however, is ignorance: We know less now than we and our successors will know in the future. A more modest favor we could do our future selves and those who come after us would be to relieve them from some of the panic that imminent, total default is likely to bring. With that goal in mind, I suggest one possible reform that could be adopted now and that, rather than tying the hands of future decision makers, would enable them to decide more calmly. As I noted, current law would produce across-the-board default in case of a cash shortfall. The pain of default would fall on all beneficiaries. Congress today could provide that, in the case of a cash shortage, the reduction in payments would be means tested, with high-income recipients of benefits absorbing most or all of the reductions.

Were default to come, a provision like that would turn a catastrophe into a serious problem. It would prevent both harm to the truly needy and the hysteria that is likely to accompany it. Instead, there would be pain for the better off. Surely that pain would be felt by politicians, as the political self-awareness and influence of affluent retirees is a basic feature of American politics. But political exigency and panic are not the same thing. Moreover, a virtue of means-tested default as the (if the reader will pardon me) default option is that it would not strongly bias the ultimate outcome. It would be an action-forcing event that would force action by people perfectly capable of taking it: relatively well-off retirees and then-current taxpayers, two interest groups that are likely to be active and well represented. Perhaps that relatively level playing field, combined with the need for some kind of action, can produce a solution that reflects deliberation, rather than one that reflects the calamitous consequences of across-the-board default.

II. ENTRENCHMENT FOR SOCIAL SECURITY

So far I have discussed what could be called indirect constitutional entrench-ment: the ways in which Congress can use the standing rules about its own operations to influence future policy. One of the most interesting features of property, old and perhaps new, is that there are associated with it substantive limitations on the legislature that also may be empowerments of the legislature, the Takings Clause, and related anticonfiscation principles.[18] The constitutional

---

although constitutions themselves often are seen as enacted from behind a veil of ignorance, it is less common to focus on mechanisms through which they force subconstitutional decision makers so to operate. *Id.* at 399–401.

[18] Congress is constrained by the Takings Clause of the Fifth Amendment and the so-called substantive component of that amendment's Due Process Clause. The two can be hard to tell apart. In the *Eastern Enterprises* case, Congress had imposed on certain coal companies an effectively retroactive obligation to pay health benefits; a four-Justice plurality concluded that the statute violated the Takings Clause, *Eastern Enterprises v. Apfel*, 524 U.S. 498, 503 (1998)

principles that protect property rights allocate power among successive legislatures, and are thus both limiting and empowering because they enable one
legislature to make a decision that cannot be undone in the future or can be
undone only to a limited extent: the decision to provide a property right.[19]

To be sure, the Social Security Act as originally adopted specifically foreswore
any intention to create property rights or a contract between the government
and potential beneficiaries.[20] Yet a Congress that sought to protect its new
property from future limitation might do the opposite, explicitly stating that
it was creating property or contract rights in future beneficiaries. And with
respect to Social Security, at least, the analog to contract is reasonably strong;
by paying taxes during their working lives, Americans acquire at least a claim
in conscience to be paid when they retire. New legislation could seek to make
that claim legal and not just moral.

That Congress can by statute provide for the creation of contract rights
that are protected constitutionally is well established.[21] The Constitution thus
enables current legislatures, to some extent, to constitutionalize their own
decisions by creating private rights that then may not be dealt with freely
by future legislatures.[22] The classic instance of a private right that is protected
constitutionally and that runs against the government, as does the new property,
is government debt. Government bonds are property and are contracts with
the government.[23]

(plurality opinion of O'Connor, J.), while Justice Kennedy, who supplied the decisive fifth vote,
found that the statute violated the Due Process Clause, *id.* at 539 (Kennedy, J., concurring in the
judgment and dissenting in part). As Justice Kennedy noted in *Eastern Enterprises*, the court's
due process doctrine imposes some constraints on retroactive legislation, *id.* at 547–549; that
doctrine thereby resembles the constraints imposed on the states by the Contracts Clause, U.S.
Const., art. I, sec. 10.

[19] A classic example is *Trustees of Dartmouth College v. Woodward*, 17 U.S. (4 Wheat.) 518 (1819),
which held that the Contracts Clause blocked changes that the legislature of New Hampshire
attempted to make to the corporate charter of Dartmouth College. Under the Marshall Court's
Contracts Clause doctrine, one legislature could lock in at least some decisions with respect to
corporate charters and other contracts by creating private rights that a later legislature would
have to protect.

[20] Congress explicitly reserved its right to amend or repeal the Social Security Act. Social Security
Act, ch. 531, sec. 1104, 49 Stat. 620, 648.

[21] "[I]t is clear that the National Government has some capacity to make agreements binding
future Congresses by creating vested rights." *United States v. Winstar Corp.*, 518 U.S. 839, 876
(1996) (plurality opinion of Souter, J.) (citations omitted).

[22] Constitutional protections of property and contract thus not only are entrenched themselves
but also enable the entrenchment of subsidiary, particular decisions to create private rights.

[23] One of the few cases relevant here is the Court's remarkable decision in Perry v. United States,
294 U.S. 330 (1935), one of the Gold Clause Cases. Liberty Bonds issued by the United States
in 1917 provided for payment in gold of a specified fineness, as a hedge against inflation. In
1933 Congress repudiated the obligation to repay in gold and changed the gold value of the
dollar. Perry, a bondholder, sued in the Court of Claims for the loss he suffered from being paid
in depreciated dollars rather than gold. Chief Justice Hughes, for the Court, found that the
repudiation was unconstitutional but that the plaintiff's damages were zero because Congress,

Whether programs of government benefit are even eligible for treatment as Takings Clause property, or constitutionally protected contracts, is to my knowledge an open question. They are certainly property for purposes of the procedural due process doctrine but, as Merrill points out, it generally is accepted that the two clauses can diverge in their definitions of property.[24] The question here is whether they can converge. I believe that they can.

Certainly federal benefit programs can be and often are designed so that they have the basic features of private property. Social Security in particular has very high levels of determinacy in application, secures private control over resources, and, as already discussed, can be given indefinite duration. Moreover, as American politics routinely demonstrates, people come to rely on the control over resources that these legal norms create. For Congress to state that this collection of legal advantages that so much resembles property is to be treated as such for constitutional purposes is a recognition of a genuine affinity between old and new property, not just the arbitrary attachment of a label.[25]

Were Congress to seek to make Social Security into substantively protected property for constitutional purposes, the most serious technical obstacle it would face arises from the unique remedial mechanisms usually associated with new property, remedial mechanisms that in turn reflect the structure of such programs. Social Security does not tie any one recipient with any one payer of the associated tax, but instead puts the government between them. Because it does not create direct interprivate claims and duties, it is not enforced through direct interprivate actions. Instead, judicial enforcement of Social Security entitlements comes through suits against the government. By long-standing legal tradition, suits against the government require a waiver of sovereign immunity.[26]

Although the matter has not been much litigated in recent decades, a substantial body of 19th-century case law involves the ability of state legislatures to entrench waivers of sovereign immunity, specifically with respect to state bonds. Favoring entrenchment was the Contracts Clause, which in those days readily would invalidate future legislation repudiating bond obligations.

---

while it lacked authority to relieve the country of its debt obligations, did have the power to change the gold value of the dollar. It is difficult to know what to take away from that decision.

[24] Thomas W. Merrill, *The Landscape of Constitutional Property*, 86 VIRGINIA L. REV. 885, 955–960 (2000).

[25] According to the Supreme Court, the Due Process Clauses in their procedural aspect prevent Congress and state legislatures from creating bundles of entitlement that generally resemble property without attaching to them the status of property for constitutional procedural purposes. *Cleveland Board of Education v. Loudermill*, 470 U.S. 532 (1985).

[26] "It is a known maxim, justified by the general sense and practice of mankind, and recognized in the law of nations, that it is inherent in the nature of sovereignty not to be amenable to the suit of any private person without its own consent. This exemption is an attribute of sovereignty belonging to every State in the Union, and was designedly retained by the national government." 3 Joseph Story, COMMENTARIES ON THE CONSTITUTION OF THE UNITED STATES 538, sec. 1669 (1833).

Nineteenth-century courts, however, generally stopped short of saying that a state legislature could entrench a waiver of sovereign immunity, which of course limited the practical value of the nonrescindable promise to pay. The thinking seems to have been that sovereign immunity was one of those prerogatives that could not be given away and, hence, could not be subjected to entrenchment even by making a promise that the Contracts Clause would to some extent protect.[27]

If that aspect of old Contracts Clause doctrine were projected into modern Fifth Amendment anticonfiscation principles, then the entrenching effect of making government benefits nominally property would be quite limited, as there then would be a nonrescindable right with a rescindable remedy. It is quite possible, though, that 21st-century courts would not understand the relationship between sovereign immunity and government benefits as their predecessors did. Sovereign immunity is a baseline-dependent concept. In order to know whether it applies or not, it is necessary to know whether the government is plaintiff or defendant and that, in turn, depends on whether the stakes of the litigation belong at the outset to the government or the private individual litigating against the government. If new property really has been made into property or contract for constitutional purposes, then the baseline should be one in which the private person is in possession.

In any event, a Congress that sought strong entrenchment and faced courts that used a 19th-century baseline simply could imitate the Virginia coupon approach. During Reconstruction, Virginia issued coupon bonds to consolidate its debt. Knowing of the possibility of default and of the doctrine of sovereign immunity, ingenious participants in the legislative drafting process designed a mechanism by which Virginia was able to commit itself to its lenders despite its sovereign immunity. The legislation under which the bonds were issued provided that the interest coupons would be accepted in payment of taxes and fees due to the state. A coupon holder who owed taxes thus could turn in the coupons, and a bondholder who owed no taxes personally could sell them to a taxpayer.[28] Virginia soon repudiated the debt, adopting so-called coupon-killer legislation.[29] When the legislation came before it, the Supreme Court concluded that the repudiating legislation violated the Contracts Clause and that the state could not prevail in tax-collection actions against taxpayers who had paid in coupons.[30] Because the bonds could be used to pay taxes and thereby eliminate an otherwise existing obligation, it was not necessary to sue the state for nonpayment on the coupons. Instead, private people could litigate defensively, as in tax-collection actions by the government, in a context

[27] The 19th-century doctrine is described in penetrating detail in Ann Woolhandler, *The Common Law Origins of Constitutionally Compelled Remedies*, 107 YALE L.J. 77, 116–122 (1997).
[28] *Poindexter v. Greenhow*, 114 U.S. 270, 277–278 (1885).
[29] *Id.* at 275–277.   [30] *Id.* at 279–281.

in which sovereign immunity did not protect the government. The designers of the legislation creating the coupon bonds were able to defeat a baseline-dependent sovereign-immunity doctrine by shifting the baseline. If it needed to use this template to entrench Social Security, Congress could provide that accrued Social Security benefits, even if not paid in cash by the government, would constitute transferable credits that could be used to pay federal taxes. That in effect would give Social Security beneficiaries a claim against general revenues that could be made effective without suing the government.

The fundamental question here involves not technicalities of sovereign immunity but the content of constitutional anticonfiscation norms. The Takings Clause itself is certainly no absolute bar to redistribution by the government. If it were, much of the tax system would be unconstitutional. Perhaps, then, Social Security benefits that ostensibly had been granted status as property simply could be taxed away. Yet it is hard to believe that no tax would ever qualify as a taking or otherwise offend the Constitution because it amounted to a seizure of private property. A 100 percent tax on principal and interest payments on United States government bonds, which would amount to a rolling repudiation of the federal public debt, almost certainly would be found unconstitutional by the courts, perhaps most likely under the due process analog of the Contracts Clause.[31]

Somewhere, then, there must be a distinction between impermissible confiscation or repudiation and permissible redistribution. Without probing this difficult matter in depth, I will suggest that a substantial reduction in Social Security benefits as such, including a tax directed at those benefits specifically and not the total income of beneficiaries, likely would be analogized to a debt repudiation, had Congress earlier taken the step of explicitly characterizing benefits as property or its undertaking to pay them as a contractual obligation. And if I am correct that debt repudiation under any guise would be treated as violating some part of the Fifth Amendment, then Congress probably has the option of making this form of new property subject to significant constitutional protection.

The decision to lock in taxing and spending policies by creating property or contract rights can be evaluated on the same terms as other constitutionally

---

[31] It may seem likely that any set of circumstances that would lead Congress to repudiate the debt also would lead the courts to approve that repudiation. Certainly it is possible to imagine situations like that. But it is also possible to imagine situations in which a bitterly and closely divided Congress enacts debt repudiation, while the federal judiciary, indirectly selected and serving for life, holds the repudiation unconstitutional. To say that both the legislature and the judiciary are political institutions subject to political influences, or just that they are both composed of human beings who live in their own era, is not to say that they have identical incentives or that they behave identically. They do not. The important point for these purposes is that there likely is a significant set of possible situations in which Congress would approve and the courts would disapprove repudiation or some other form of large-scale expropriation.

enforced entrenchments, and thus on the same terms as constitutional provisions generally. American history suggests four main reasons for constitutional entrenchment. The first, which accounts for the constitutionalization of many structural rules, involves problems in the agency relationship between the people and their agents in government. Left to their own devices, members of a legislature might lengthen their own terms, or give themselves a handsome parting gift through a salary increase voted after an electoral setback.[32] While such concerns arise with respect to compensation and pension schemes that apply specifically to legislators, it is unlikely that spending policy concerning nationwide programs like Social Security involves major agency breakdowns between the people and their representatives. To the contrary, a standard criticism of policymaking in this field is that Congress is too responsive to the voters.

Government responsiveness to the voters, and possible excesses thereof, provide the second leading reason for constitutionalization: collective self-binding. As already noted, just as a rational person may put the alarm clock on the other side of the room, so rational people creating a constitution might use it to limit what they can do in irrational moments. The limitation in Article I, Section 9 on suspension of the privilege of habeas corpus probably falls into this category. It describes a limited set of emergencies in which the writ may be suspended, thereby ruling out that extreme step in emergencies that are real but less severe.[33] People in calm moments know that they panic, and people acting collectively in calm moments may believe that collective decisions in less calm moments are especially likely to reflect panic, as politicians compete in appealing to the fears of their constituents.

This rationale might support a constitutional lock-in for a major taxing and spending program, but the argument for it seems doubtful to me. The concern would be that during a fairly brief fiscal emergency, caused perhaps by a major economic shock or a war, funds would be diverted from the spending program in ways that are unwise in the long term. That is possible, but probably not very likely. Long-term spending programs are designed for the long term, and that central feature generally is borne in mind in making policy about them, even in straitened times. Maybe a retrenchment as severe as the government undertook in the early 1930s would call Social Security into question, but it is

---

[32] The fixed terms for House and Senate protect against the first form of misconduct, while the 27th Amendment deals with the second.

[33] Under Section 9, the privilege of the writ may be suspended only "in cases of Rebellion or Invasion, when the public Safety may require it." U.S. Const., art. I, sec. 9. A serious threat of domestic terrorism probably would not qualify. The court has noted the Suspension Clause's character as a collective self-binding measure: "Those great and good men [who framed the Constitution] foresaw that troublous times would arise, when rulers and people would become restive under restraint, and seek by sharp and decisive measures to accomplish ends deemed just and proper." *Ex parte Milligan*, 4 Wall. (71 U.S.) 2, 120 (1867).

hard to imagine that anything short of that would do so.[34] And nothing like that has happened for a while.

Third, and probably more relevant here, is the use of constitutional rules in a way that makes them genuinely like contracts. The ability to enter into a binding contract is valuable, even though it is a legal power to limit one's options in the future, because promises can induce performance from others. In the absence of enforceable promises, it would be more difficult to get others to begin long-term performance in return for a promise of payment when the performance was completed. Governments confront this problem when they borrow, and the various special devices that have been invented to guarantee sovereign performance in the face of sovereigns' special abilities to default demonstrate just how much is to be gained by making a truly binding promise to lenders. Several decades worth of Contracts Clause cases about government franchises involve the same problem. If a monopoly on bridge traffic, for example, is needed to induce investment in a bridge, some legal mechanism will be needed to make sure that the monopoly is respected by the government even when the voters are clamoring for another bridge.[35]

The applicability of this contract-like rationale to spending programs, especially programs like Social Security itself, is a sufficiently rich question that I can only touch on it here. One way to understand Social Security in contractual

---

[34] In the Legislative Appropriations Act of 1932, ch. 314, 47 Stat. 382, the applicable title of which is called the Economy Act, Congress adopted a number of major reductions in federal operating expenditures, including reductions in the salaries of judges that it believed were not protected by Article III. The Supreme Court concluded that judges of the Supreme Court of the District of Columbia were so protected, so that their salaries could not be reduced, *O'Donaghue v. United States*, 289 U.S. 516 (1933), but that judges of the Court of Claims were not, *Williams v. United States*, 289 U.S. 553 (1933). *O'Donaghue* in particular substantially muddied the already turbid waters of the distinction between so-called Article III and Article I courts.

[35] The best-known nugget of this rich lode of American legal, political, and economic history is probably *Charles River Bridge v. Warren Bridge*, 36 U.S. (11 Pet.) 420 (1837), which involved a grant by the Massachusetts legislature of a second corporate franchise to build a bridge over the Charles River. The court held that the state's contract with the first bridge company, which was protected from repudiation by the Contracts Clause, had not included an implicit term by which the state undertook not to charter another bridge company. Justice Story in dissent argued that the grant implied a monopoly for the first bridge. He asked "is there a man living of ordinary discretion or prudence, who would have accepted a charter" if the legislature were completely free to revise it and grant rights to competitors? *Id.* at 615 (Story, J., dissenting).

The same phenomenon can appear in contexts where it is less obvious. Suppose that one region of a state has resources the development of which would be valuable to everyone. People nevertheless may hesitate to move to that region if they fear that they then will become a distinct minority in the state legislature, subject to especially high taxes on their geographically identifiable products, for example. One way to induce that investment is to malapportion the legislature, giving those who live in sparsely settled but productive regions a greater proportionate vote with which to protect themselves. Current doctrine largely denies the states this option. *See Reynolds v. Sims*, 377 U.S. 533 (1964) (state legislatures must be elected from equipopulous districts); *Board of Estimates v. Morris*, 489 U.S. 688 (1989) (local legislatures must be elected from equipopulous districts).

terms is to think intergenerationally.[36] Current workers who pay the wage tax are supporting current beneficiaries. Their consent so to be taxed may be contingent on substantial satisfaction that they in turn will be supported. It may be in the interests of all parties, present and future generations, to induce that consent by giving current workers a strong promise that benefits will be paid them decades from now when they retire. That promise, of course, then will have to be redeemed by workers who are now too young to vote or are not yet born.

Because those future taxpayers are at best virtually represented, it is natural to wonder whether a constitutional entrenchment of Social Security actually would represent an instance of the fourth main reason for adopting inflexible rules, the most normatively dubious of the rationales. Sometimes constitutional rules are used to lock in the decisions of a current political majority, or those who have obtained a favor from a current political majority, simply because those now in power fear that their deal will be undone when political opinion changes. This kind of lock-in is especially troublesome when the fear of change in political opinion is based on the knowledge that the action of the current majority is self-interested.

Nineteenth-century courts routinely struggled to distinguish between examples of the third and fourth kinds of constitutional entrenchment. Was any particular grant a sound bargain by the state, so that future repudiation would be confiscation, or was the grant itself the product of a corrupt bargain that should be repudiated? A foundational Marshall Court case, *Fletcher v. Peck*,[37] is a fine example of the latter. A bribed Georgia legislature made a massive land grant, which a later legislature, the bums having been thrown out, repudiated.[38] The Supreme Court held that whatever the equities as between the people of Georgia and the initial grantees, subsequent purchasers were protected from repudiation by an implicit contract term that was in turn protected by the Contracts Clause.

Whether constitutionally protected status for Social Security benefits would fall into the third category or the fourth is a difficult question. The best argument that it would fall into the third rests on the participation in the current political process of current taxpayers who hope to become beneficiaries. Otherwise, it would just be a matter of current retirees making a promise to

---

[36] Other contributors to this volume, such as Howell Jackson, have addressed intergenerational issues more systematically than I will here. My purpose is to draw attention to the fact that intergenerational relations can include the kind of contracting by government that the Constitution facilitates by making possible the creation of private rights protected against future legislation.

[37] 10 U.S. (6 Cranch) 87 (1810).

[38] "In 1795, the Georgia legislature evidently was bribed to enact a statute directing the Governor to convey most of what is now Alabama and Mississippi for less than two cents an acre. The next year a new legislature irately repealed the grant." David P. Currie, THE CONSTITUTION IN THE SUPREME COURT: THE FIRST HUNDRED YEARS, 1789–1888, at 128 (1985).

themselves that would have to be paid for by the unrepresented. The beneficiaries of entrenchment probably mainly would be current workers, not current retirees, because Social Security's major imbalances will not arrive for a while yet. There is thus at least a plausible justification for giving current workers a reason to go along with the system by securing their future claims more than the current system does.

On the other hand, it has been suggested that the earth belongs to the living, and that constitutions should last no longer than the majority that creates them, a time once calculated at 19 years.

Questions for Chapter 13

1. Much of budget policy has a quasi-constitutional feel, in that past legislative actions have the effect of entrenching interests and restricting the latitude of future politicians and polities. Indeed, these rules sometimes are characterized in constitutional language.[39] As explored in the early chapters of this volume, congressional budget procedures include many provisions – points of order and procedures for adopting and enforcing budget resolutions – that steer future spending decisions. As Professor Harrison points out, mandatory spending programs with indefinite appropriations also have an element of entrenchment, as congressional procedures allow minority interests substantial power to block benefit reductions or adjustments in appropriations. Even discretionary expenditures have an element of entrenchment as there is often a presumption – reflected in Congressional Budget Office baseline projections – that discretionary programs typically will grow at the rate of inflation. The interesting question that Professor Harrison's analysis raises is under what circumstances might it make sense for the federal government to create a super-hardened form of entrenchments for certain kinds of spending. If we do want to create these enhanced property interests, can the judiciary be counted upon to safeguard them?

2. Somewhat in tension with Professor Harrison's line of inquiry are recent criticisms that existing levels of Social Security benefits are already too well entrenched. Today's Social Security benefit formulas, after all, were enacted into law nearly a quarter-century ago and have not been materially altered in the intervening years. Retirement benefits automatically are adjusted upward each year, rising not just with inflation but also with real-wage growth during the working lives of participants. In debates over Social Security reform, these indexed benefits are sometimes called "scheduled benefits" and are contrasted

---

[39] See, e.g., Kate Stith, *Rewriting the Fiscal Constitution: The Case of Gramm-Rudman-Hollings*, 76 Cal. L. Rev. 593, 640–641 (1988).

with the level of benefits that the Social Security trust funds can cover under current funding rules ("payable benefits"). While scheduled benefits have not yet been afforded the status of new property outlined in Professor Harrison's chapter, they have enjoyed a certain degree of reification in public discourse. For purposes of Social Security reform, one of the interesting features of Professor Harrison's commentary is his suggestion that the Social Security funding rules might be amended to favor certain beneficiaries (such as lower-income workers) over others. Under current law, if the trust fund resources are insufficient, all beneficiaries bear a pro rata cut in benefits. But, as Professor Harrison suggests, a priority should be given to low-income workers, and the costs of future funding shortfalls shifted to others. Would it make sense to enhance the entitlements of some beneficiaries in this way?

3. In thinking through issues of sovereign immunity, it is sometimes helpful to distinguish between the legal obligations of the government and the availability of funds to liquidate those obligations. As Professor Harrison's analysis suggests, the Takings Clause and associated anticonfiscatory provisions of the federal Constitution may inhibit the government from invoking sovereign immunity to effect certain policies (like rescinding public debt or reneging on duly created new property interests), but does that limitation authorize an aggrieved private party to get cash from the federal legislature? What is the relevance of the Appropriations Clause's requirement that no funds shall be withdrawn from the Treasury except as a result of an appropriation? Can the courts also order the Congress to enact such an appropriation? To raise taxes to finance the appropriation?

4. The authority of the federal courts to order spending and taxes is an issue that has arisen in cases brought against state actors for violation of constitutional provisions, mostly notably in the context of school desegregation cases. To remediate past violations of constitutional rights, the lower federal courts have entered into far-reaching injunctions requiring both specific expenditures and even the imposition of additional taxes. The practice, however, has been controversial, and recent Supreme Court opinions have raised questions about the appropriate scope of judicial power in this area, citing concerns of both separation of powers and federalism.[40]

---

[40] *See Missouri v. Jenkins,* 515 U.S. 70 (1995). *See also* Gerald E. Frug, *The Judicial Power of the Purse,* 126 U. PENN. L. REV. 715 (1978); Mark Champoux and John Lobato, The Limited Power of Courts to Order Spending (May 14, 2006), *available at* http://www.law.harvard.edu/faculty/hjackson/CourtOrderSpending_24.pdf.

14 Courts, Constitutions, and Public Finance

Some Recent Experiences from the States

Richard Briffault

I. INTRODUCTION

Unlike the federal Constitution, virtually all state constitutions give detailed attention to questions of public finance. State constitutions limit spending, mandate certain types of spending, constrain taxation and debt, and require special procedures for enacting a budget. One consequence of the constitutionalization of the state fisc is its judicialization, as these measures trigger litigation. Fiscal and political conflicts turn into legal disputes, with courts joining governors and legislatures in shaping state budgets and making state fiscal policy.

This chapter provides an early-21st-century snapshot of the state constitutional law of state finance through a survey of six recent state supreme court decisions – all handed down since the turn of the millennium – interpreting key provisions of their states' fiscal constitutions. Part II examines three cases concerning provisions intended to constrain the state fisc: a legislative supermajority vote for tax increases, a voter-approval requirement for new debt, and a balanced-budget requirement. In two cases, courts delivered decisions that aided the more political branches of government, but were sharply at variance with the constitutional text. In the third, the court followed the constitutional text and, in so doing, challenged a state's fiscal arrangements. Part III focuses on three cases dealing with the budgetary process: the executive budget, limits on the content of appropriations bills, and the item veto. These involved governor–legislature conflicts, debates over the programmatic reach of the special budgetary procedures, and questions about the scope of judicial intervention in these political–fiscal–constitutional matters.

Part IV considers some of the lessons of these recent state fiscal cases. State fiscal constitutional law is marked by inadequate definition of key fiscal

---

Richard Briffault is the Joseph P. Chamberlain Professor of Legislation at Columbia Law School, where he also is the Director of Columbia's Legislative Drafting Research Fund.

constitutional terms, tensions between different constitutional provisions, and conflicts between constitutional norms and ordinary politics. As a result, wide gaps often exist between constitutional text (or the principle the text was intended to enshrine) and judicial decisions, as well as broad differences across the states (and within states) in the interpretation and application of similar provisions. So, too, courts struggle with their proper place in what are often highly charged political conflicts. The difficulties of converting fiscal principles into workable legal rules and the uncertainty over the proper judicial role can make state fiscal constitutional law an uncertain, unpredictable enterprise.

II. OF DEBT AND TAXES (AND SPENDING): STATE CONSTITUTIONAL LIMITS ON THE STATE FISC

A. *Guinn v. Legislature of the State of Nevada*[1] and Supermajority Requirements for State Revenue Increases

Tax limitation has been an important component in the state fiscal constitution since the late 19th century, but it took on even greater salience in the aftermath of California's adoption of Proposition 13 in June 1978. Although known primarily for placing limits on the property tax, Proposition 13 imposed new voting rules for most forms of taxation in the Golden State, requiring a two-thirds vote in each house of the legislature for new or increased state taxes and supermajority approval by local voters of many new local taxes.[2] Proposition 13 had a catalytic effect, sparking tax revolts and antitax constitutional amendments around the country. The supermajority requirement for new taxes and tax increases proved particularly popular. Sixteen states now require legislative supermajorities – most commonly, a two-thirds vote – to raise some or all state taxes.[3]

Nevada mandated a two-thirds legislative vote for new or increased state taxes in the mid-1990s. The legislature considered, but voted down, such a constitutional amendment in 1993. Thereafter, the leading legislative proponent undertook a voter-initiative drive. Indeed, the voter initiative has been

---

[1] 71 P.3d 1269 (Nev. 2003) ("*Guinn I*"); 76 P.3d 22 (Nev. 2003) ("*Guinn II*").

[2] Four states – Arkansas, Florida, Louisiana, and Mississippi – had supermajority-vote rules for state taxes prior to Proposition 13. National Conference of State Legislatures, STATE TAX AND EXPENDITURE LIMITS – 2005, *available at* http://www.ncsl.org/programs/fiscal/tels2005.htm. The Florida limit applied only to the corporate tax, while Arkansas exempted the sales tax, which is an important source of state revenue.

[3] *Id.* In 13 states, the rule is applicable to all state taxes. In Arkansas, it does not apply to sales and alcohol taxes; the Florida requirement applies only to the corporate income tax; and Michigan's rule applies only to the state property tax, which is little used in practice. A two-thirds vote is required in eight states. Five states require a three-fifths vote. Three states – Arkansas, Michigan, and Oklahoma – require a three-fourths vote, although, as noted, the Arkansas and Michigan requirements do not apply to the principal state taxes.

the primary vehicle for constitutional tax limitations across the country. The measure was approved by the voters by a lopsided majority.[4] The legislature complied with the supermajority rule in enacting biennial state budgets in 1997, 1999, and 2001, but in 2003 things blew up. The combination of sharply rising service demands and shrinking revenues due to a depressed economy led Governor Guinn, a Republican, to propose significant tax and spending increases at the start of the regular 2003 legislative session.[5] The legislature raised spending but was unable to agree on tax increases. It reached the end of the constitutionally limited four-month session on June 3 and adjourned, having appropriated most of the available revenues without having passed the education budget. The governor immediately called the legislature back into a special session to take up school aid and taxation, but the legislature soon deadlocked and adjourned. The governor called a second special session but, once again, the legislature was unable to act. There was a two-thirds majority for revenue increases in the upper house, but only a 27–15 vote – or one vote shy of two-thirds – in the lower house. On July 1, at the start of the new fiscal biennium, the governor asked the state supreme court to declare the legislature in violation of its constitutional duty and to order it to approve a balanced budget with appropriations for education. The court agreed that judicial action was appropriate, but did far more than the governor had requested.

The Nevada Supreme Court suspended the two-thirds-vote requirement and ordered the legislature to apply a simple majority rule to the vote on the taxes necessary to fund the education appropriations and balance the budget.[6] The court found the two-thirds-vote rule in "tension" – if not "incompatible"[7] – with the state constitution's requirement that the legislature provide for the "support and maintenance" of public schools "by direct legislative appropriation."[8] The court sought to resolve this tension in what appeared to be a relatively mechanical way. Invoking "the same rules of construction used to interpret statutes,"[9] the court treated the case as involving a pair of conflicts – substance versus process, and specific versus general – whose outcomes could be resolved by general, objective legal principles. The court labeled the two-thirds-vote

---

[4] The Nevada Constitution requires that constitutional amendments be approved by the voters in two elections. The tax initiative was approved in 1994 and again in 1996, both times with roughly 70 percent of the vote. William D. Popkin, *Interpreting Conflicting Provisions of the Nevada State Constitution*, 5 Nev. L.J. 308, 316 note 44 (2004).

[5] *Guinn I*, 71 P.3d at 1273–1274.

[6] *Id.* at 1276. The court was nearly unanimous, with only Justice Maupin dissenting in part and concurring in part in Chief Justice Agosti's opinion. Justice Maupin found the governor's petition not ripe for action since the constitution does not require the budget to be completed by the start of the fiscal year. With the first quarterly distribution of state funds to local school districts not to occur until August 1, Justice Maupin would have deferred action until closer to that date. *See id.* at 1276–1277.

[7] *Id.* at 1274.   [8] Nev. Const., art. 11, § 6.

[9] *Guinn I*, 71 P.3d at 1274.

rule a mere "procedural requirement," while the education-funding provision was "a matter of substantive constitutional law," which "elevated the public education of the youth of Nevada to a position of constitutional primacy." Similarly, the two-thirds-vote rule was mere "general language" that must "give way" to the specific provisions concerning education. The court concluded that, "[i]f the procedural two-thirds revenue-vote requirement in effect denies the public its expectation of access to public education, then the two-thirds requirement must yield to the specific substantive educational right."[10]

The Nevada court's "interpretive" approach plainly is flawed. Even assuming the debatable presumption that substance trumps procedure, it is far from clear that the two-thirds rule is merely procedural. Surely, the intent and effect of such a requirement is substantive – to protect taxpayers by making it more difficult to increase taxes. So, too, even assuming that the specific trumps the general, either provision could be labeled specific or general. Arguably, the constitution's general commitment to education is qualified by the specific requirement that taxes need a two-thirds vote. Nor is it evident that the education-funding requirement and the tax-voting rule are truly in "irreconcilable conflict" given that the legislature managed to abide by both provisions during the three preceding budget cycles. Moreover, even if the tax-voting rule affected the legislature's ability to finance education, it is uncertain whether the funds available for education without a tax increase fell below the constitutional mandate. The only level of education specifically mandated by the constitution is that the schools be open at least six months per year, or far less than the standard school year.[11] It is possible that even without a tax increase the legislature could have funded the schools for just six months; it is certainly possible the legislature could have passed a budget, without judicial intervention, for the constitutionally mandated six-month school year. Finally, the court did not even mention a standard rule of interpretation – that a later law prevails over an inconsistent earlier one – which would have vindicated the two-thirds requirement.[12]

Perhaps aware of the limited persuasive value of its opinion, the court subsequently issued a second opinion that came close to a frontal attack on the two-thirds-voting requirement. Following *Guinn I*, 20 members of the legislature petitioned for rehearing. While that petition was pending, the second special legislative session took up the education and tax bills. The lower house again approved the necessary tax increases with one vote short of two-thirds, but this time the speaker gaveled the matter "passed." Just before final passage, one of the tax opponents switched his vote thus enabling the measure to pass with the constitutionally required two-thirds majority.[13] Instead of treating the

---

[10] *Id.* at 1275–1276.   [11] Nev. Const., art. 11, § 2.

[12] *See* Popkin, *supra* note 4, at 313.

[13] Steve R. Johnson, *Supermajority Provisions,* Guinn v. Legislature, *and a Flawed Constitutional Structure*, 4 NEV L.J. 491, 495 (2004).

case as moot and dismissing the petition, the court subsequently released a second opinion, taking credit for creating "a situation where the legislators were internally motivated to achieve a 2/3 consensus voluntarily,"[14] and providing a more emphatic and more substantive defense of its intervention.

First, the court reiterated the tension between the supermajority vote for taxation and the simple majority rule for appropriations. With these "two antagonistic constitutional provisions,"[15] "the stage was set for legislative impasse."[16] Second, the court found the two-thirds rule threatened "the democratic process." When a "majority of legislators, representing a majority of the citizens of this state, make decisions on the services to be provided and the future of the state – including transportation, social welfare, and paying the costs of law enforcement and regulation – the Constitution requires that the decision of the majority be respected."[17] Third, the court questioned the legitimacy of the electorate's approval of the two-thirds rule. The court noted that when the legislature considered the two-thirds rule, some legislators "expressed their concerns" that it would enable a minority to block the revenues necessary to fund the services approved by the majority. When the measure was put before the voters, however, its proponents did not address "the potential conflict that could result from requiring a simple majority for appropriations and a supermajority for new or increased public revenue" either in the initiative's language or in the ballot pamphlet distributed with the measure. As a result, Nevada's voters were uninformed about "the effect the proposal could have on other constitutional rights or the state's overall fiscal integrity."[18] Implicitly, such an uninformed decision was not entitled to compliance – at least not when it conflicted with other constitutional provisions.

Finally, the court minimized the value of the two-thirds rule. Proponents of the measure had argued it would "limit the influence of special-interest groups, ensuring that one group would not control changes in the tax structure" and "promote more efficiency in government."[19] Although "legitimate and important," these concerns were held to be less weighty than abiding by majority rule

---

[14] *Guinn II*, 76 P.3d at 25.   [15] *Id.* at 29.

[16] *Id.* at 27. Supermajority requirements to adopt appropriations are uncommon but not unknown. Since 1879, California has required a two-thirds vote for general-fund appropriations except for public schools. Since 1934, Arkansas has required a three-quarters vote for appropriations, except for education, highways, and paying down debt. (Both Arkansas and California require supermajorities for tax increases.) Rhode Island requires a two-thirds majority for appropriations for local or private purposes. "Because the state typically drafts all main appropriations for operations into a single bill, a two-thirds vote has been effectively necessary for all appropriations." National Conference of State Legislatures, SUPERMAJORITY VOTE REQUIREMENTS TO PASS THE BUDGET, *available at* http://www.ncsl.org/programs/fiscal/supmjbud.htm. Five other states require a supermajority vote under special circumstances – when the budget is enacted late (Illinois, Maine, Nebraska) or exceeds an expenditure ceiling (Connecticut, Hawaii).

[17] *Guinn II*, 76 P.3d at 32.   [18] *Id.* at 26.

[19] *Id.* at 32.

and effectuating the legislature's constitutional duties to fund education and balance the budget.

Guinn II's shift in reasoning is significant. *Guinn I* could rely on the constitution's education-funding article because the legislature already had acted on the rest of the state budget, and the governor had limited the special-session agenda to education and taxes and did not permit the legislature to reopen already-settled budget issues and transfer funds from other areas to education. Indeed, one commentator suggested the governor "hornswoggled" or "sandbagged" his legislative opponents – primarily his fellow Republicans – by limiting the fiscal impasse to education, which the court found enjoyed a special constitutional mandate.[20] In the future, legislative supporters of the two-thirds rule could insist on passing the education appropriations first, thereby reserving their minority veto for the rest of the budget, which does not share education funding's constitutional protection. *Guinn II* ended that possibility by reframing the issue as a conflict between the two-thirds rule and majority rule in budget-making across the board.[21]

The *Guinn* decisions are extraordinary. State courts frequently have trimmed tax limitations by, for example, narrow definitions of what constitutes a "tax" subject to limitation.[22] But state courts have rarely treated tax limitation or the supermajority vote as at odds with other constitutional commands. So, too, some state courts have suggested that some state constitutional provisions, including education requirements, can operate to require a state to appropriate a certain level of funding.[23] But state courts have rarely, if ever, changed the constitutional procedures governing appropriations to ensure that such constitutionally mandated appropriations actually are made.[24] Moreover, courts typically venerate voter-initiated measures as the voice of the people,[25] rather than call into question the legitimacy of the voters' assent.

---

[20] Jeffrey W. Stempel, *The Most Rational Branch: Guinn v. Legislature and the Judiciary's Role as Helpful Arbiter of Conflict*, 4 Nev. L.J. 518, 526 (2004) ("The Governor and his counsel choreographed a situation in which the [two-thirds] supermajority requirement was now in arguable conflict with another constitutional provision of similar stature and seeming clarity.").

[21] Two judges broke with the majority. Justice Shearing, concurring, would have denied the petition for rehearing and terminated the case. Justice Maupin, dissenting, would have vacated *Guinn I* since the Nevada legislature had complied with both the two-thirds voting rule and the education-funding requirement. Justice Maupin specifically disagreed with the majority's conclusion that the "supermajority initiative was flawed from its inception" and that the electorate did not understand what it was voting for. *Guinn II*, 76 P.3d at 34.

[22] *See* Richard Briffault, *The Disfavored Constitution: State Fiscal Limits and State Constitutional Law*, 34 Rutgers L.J. 907, 932–937 (2003).

[23] *See, e.g., White v. Davis*, 108 Cal. App. 4th 197 (Cal. Ct. App. 2002).

[24] *See White v. Davis*, 68 P.3d 74, 101–102 (Cal. 2003) (State constitution requires state employees who continue to work notwithstanding legislature's failure to enact state budget to be paid, "but actual payment is dependent on the existence of an available appropriation.").

[25] *See, e.g., Brosnahan v. Brown*, 651 P.2d 274, 277 (Cal. 1982) ("We are required to resolve any reasonable doubts in favor of this precious right."); *Amador Valley Joint Union High School Dist. v. Board of Equalization*, 583 P.2d 1281, 1283 (Cal. 1978) ("The power of initiative must be liberally construed . . . to promote the democratic process.").

Although about as "activist" a decision as can be imagined, the Nevada
Supreme Court's action actually placed it on the same political and fiscal side
as the governor and nearly two-thirds of the legislature. The court acted only
after the legislature repeatedly had deadlocked; moreover, after the court's
decision broke the impasse, the tax increase the legislature adopted actually
complied with the two-thirds rule. Nonetheless, despite the support from the
political branches and the decision's apparent success, the court's intervention
provoked intense public criticism.[26]

Considered in terms of the state fiscal constitution more broadly, *Guinn* flags
the structural tension that supermajority tax-voting rules create for the accom-
plishment of other fiscal goals, such as meeting service needs while balancing
the budget, even if it is doubtful whether a judicial directive to disregard the
voting rule is the most appropriate means to resolve that tension.

B. *Lonegan v. State* and the Demise of Constitutional Limitations on State Debt

Most state constitutions limit the ability of the state to borrow. A few bar state
debt outright[27] or impose very low limits on the amount of debt that may
be incurred.[28] Some cap debt or debt service at a specified fraction of state
taxable wealth or revenues.[29] Most often, state constitutions rely on special
procedures: Debt may not be incurred without the approval of a supermajority
in the legislature, the voters in a referendum, or both.[30]

These debt restrictions have much less bite in practice than state constitutional language would suggest. Debt limitations apply to debt backed by the "full
faith and credit" of the state. Stimulated in part by the desire to avoid those very
limitations, states have developed financial instruments – what I have elsewhere
referred to as "nondebt debts"[31] – that enable them to borrow without pledging
their full faith and credit, thus not committing the taxpayers to repaying the
debt. Instead, the debt is backed only by a specific revenue source. Bondholders
have a protected claim against that resource, but not against the state fisc more
broadly. Most state courts have held that these "nonguaranteed" or "revenue

---

[26] *See* Johnson, *supra* note 13, at 491 ("Criticism of the *Guinn* decision has exceeded praise of
it – probably in frequency, certainly in passion and rhetorical exuberance."); Stempel, *supra*
note 20, at 519 note 4 (Criticism of *Guinn* marked by an "ugly tone teetering on the brink of
violence."). The public outcry apparently led the chief justice, who authored *Guinn I*, not to
seek reelection. *See* Popkin, *supra* note 4, at 309 and note 9.

[27] *See, e.g.*, Ind. Const., art. X, § 5; W.Va. Const., art. X, § 4.

[28] *See, e.g.*, Ariz. Const., art. 9, § 5 (state debt limited to $350,000); Ky. Const., § 49 ($500,000
limit); R.I. Const., art. VI, § 16 ($50,000 limit).

[29] *See, e.g.*, Ga. Const., art. VII, § IV, ¶ II (state debt service limited to 10 percent of state revenue);
Nev. Const. art. IX, § 3 (state debt limited to 2 percent of assessed valuation of property in
state).

[30] *See, e.g.*, Mich. Const., art. IX, § 15 (state long-term debt requires approval of two-thirds of
each house of the legislature and a majority of state voters).

[31] *See* Briffault, *supra* note 22, at 918.

bond" debts are not subject to the constitutional limitations that apply to full-faith-and-credit debt. Today most state borrowing consists of nondebt debts not subject to constitutional debt limitations.

Initially, the revenue-bond exception applied only to obligations issued to finance a project that would generate the revenues used to pay off the debt incurred to finance the project. In addition to limiting state liability, these projects produced new revenues and thus did not threaten to divert older revenues from the general fund. Over time, the revenue-bond concept broadened. The new revenues component has been attenuated and sometimes has dropped out altogether, but the debt limits still may be avoided if the state does not give bondholders a legal claim on the general fund.

The best example of this is the "subject to appropriation" or "contract" bond. A public authority issues a bond and uses the borrowed funds to undertake some project for the state; the state contracts with the authority to pay for the annual debt service on the authority's bond. That payment is subject to annual appropriation by the legislature. The public authority is, in effect, a conduit for state borrowing. The whole purpose of the arrangement is to generate funds for the state while avoiding the constitutional limits on state debt. Virtually all state courts have held that the debts of public authorities are not debt in the constitutional sense, since the authorities lack the capacity to impose taxes or pledge the full faith and credit of the state.[32] As for the state's contractual commitment to pay the authority's debt service, so long as the obligation is subject to appropriation, it is not legally binding on the legislature – even though the state is virtually certain to make the appropriation. As a result, most state courts have concluded it is not "debt."[33]

The subject-to-appropriation device was subject to a significant challenge – and received a significant, albeit grudging, endorsement – in a pair of New Jersey Supreme Court decisions known as *Lonegan v. State*.[34] The case arose in reaction to New Jersey's plan to use subject-to-appropriation debt – and thereby avoid the need for voter consent – to finance an $8.6 billion bond program to repair and construct new public schools – the "largest, most comprehensive school construction program in the nation."[35] As the case unfolded, the plaintiffs expanded their attack to include the subject-to-appropriation financing provisions of 14 other statutes.[36] Indeed, as of the end of the 2001 fiscal year,

---

[32] *See, e.g., Schulz v. State of New York*, 639 N.E.2d 1140 (N.Y. 1994); *Dykes v. Northern Virginia Transportation District Comm'n*, 411 S.E.2d 1 (Va. 1991).

[33] *See, e.g., Carr-Gottstein Properties v. State*, 899 P.2d 136 (Ak. 1995); *In re Anzai*, 936 P.2d 637 (Hawaii 1997); *Wilson v. Kentucky Transp. Cabinet*, 884 S.W.2d 641 (Ky. 1994); *Employers Insurance Co. of Nevada v. State Bd. of Examiners*, 21 P.3d 628 (Nev. 2001); *Fent v. Oklahoma Capitol Improvement Authority*, 984 P.2d 200 (Okla 1999); *Dykes v. Northern Virginia Transportation District Comm'n*, 411 S.E.2d 1 (Va. 1991); *Schulz v. State of New York*, 639 N.E.2d 1140 (N.Y. 1994).

[34] 809 A.2d 91 (N.J. 2002) ("*Lonegan I*"); 819 A.2d 395 (N.J. 2003) ("*Lonegan II*").

[35] *Lonegan I*, 809 A.2d at 104.   [36] *Id.* at 94.

New Jersey authorities had issued $10.8 billion in subject-to-appropriation debt, which accounted for 73 percent of the state's total tax-backed debt.[37]

The New Jersey Supreme Court clearly was concerned by the enormous volume of non-voter-approved subject-to-appropriation debt, noting that the "substantial changes in the State's debt arrangements" reflected in the growth of subject-to-appropriation debt raised the "troubling question" of whether the voter-approval requirement "retains its fundamental approval and vitality."[38] However, some of the court's prior decisions appeared to approve of the subject-to-appropriation device. Moreover, the school-bond issue was being used to finance a capital improvement program that was the direct result of the court's own prodding in the state's multidecade school finance reform litigation, *Abbott v. Burke*.[39]

In *Lonegan I*, the court escaped from its dilemma by treating the use of debt to fund constitutionally mandated capital improvements for education as a special case. Like the Nevada court in *Guinn*, the New Jersey court determined that the state constitution's education article imposed a special spending requirement – in this case a "constitutional obligation . . . to provide safe and adequate school buildings in every school district in the State."[40] Moreover, the court apparently had signaled approval of something like the contract-debt-financing mechanism when it had upheld state legislation calling for significant state capital spending on local public schools. The combination of the state's reliance on the court's school finance decision and the "sui generis" nature of bonds "dedicated to the provision of constitutionally required facilities,"[41] led the court to approve the use of contract debt to pay for the public school program. The court, however, implicitly questioned the constitutionality of the other authorizations of subject-to-appropriation debt when it asked the parties to reargue the constitutional question outside the school construction context.[42]

Although apparently on the verge of a major decision curbing or invalidating the use of subject-to-appropriation debt, the court in *Lonegan II* drew back from the brink and sustained the general exemption of such debt from constitutional debt limitation. *Lonegan II* accepted plaintiffs' argument that subject-to-appropriation debt is the functional equivalent of full-faith-and-credit debt, agreeing that it is "most likely" that the state's failure to make an appropriation "would adversely affect the State's credit rating":[43] "We, too, acknowledge the realities of the marketplace."[44] Nonetheless, the court concluded that the formal distinction between the practical need to pay debt service and the legal obligation to do so provided an "objective and workable benchmark around

[37] *Id.* at 130.
[38] *Id.* at 93.
[39] See *Abbott v. Burke V*, 710 A.2d 450 (N.J. 1998).
[40] *Lonegan I*, 809 A.2d at 105.
[41] *Id.* at 105–107.
[42] *Id.* at 109.
[43] *Lonegan II*, 819 A.2d at 405.
[44] *Id.* at 406.

which to craft fiscal policy."[45] The court was also extremely wary of upsetting the rules of the fiscal game. Since the court had first approved contract-debt arrangements, the state had come to "rel[y] on the Court's precedents when crafting complex financing mechanisms.... We are well aware of the need to maintain stability in respect of the variety of financial instruments authorized by the Legislature."[46] For the court, "at this late date,"[47] to apply the debt-limitation clause to subject-to-appropriation debt would "disrupt the State's financing mechanisms."[48]

Lonegan II's deference to the legislature and narrow reading of the constitutional debt limitation is far from unusual. Courts in 32 other states have upheld some form of subject-to-appropriation debt,[49] and a 2001 statement issued by Standard & Poor's concluded that "this type of debt issuance is now common in at least 33 states."[50] Like the New Jersey court, most state courts have acknowledged that as a practical, fiscal matter subject-to-appropriation debt is as binding as full-faith-and-credit debt. As the California Supreme Court put it, "we are not naive about the character of this transaction."[51] A Colorado court recently acknowledged that failure to make an appropriation "would have a devastating effect on Colorado's credit rating."[52] Nonetheless, the formal disclaimer of the state's legal obligation to pay debt service is typically sufficient to exempt subject-to-appropriation debt from constitutional debt limitations.[53]

Indeed, in a 2004 decision, New York's highest court went one step further and upheld a measure intended to force, albeit still not quite require, the state to make a nonbinding debt-service appropriation. The state's Local Government Assistance Corporation (LGAC) can issue debt and use the proceeds to aid local governments. The LGAC bonds are backed by the state sales

---

[45] *Id.* at 401–402.
[46] *Id.* at 397.
[47] *Id.*
[48] *Id.* at 407.
[49] *Id.* at 404 note 2.
[50] Richard J. Marino and Colleen Waddell, *Revised Lease and Appropriation-Backed Debt Rating Criteria*, STANDARD & POOR'S RATING SERVICES, June 13, 2001.
[51] *Rider v. City of San Diego*, 959 P.2d 347, 358 (Cal. 1998). *See also Employers Insurance Co. of Nevada v. State Bd. of Examiners*, *supra* note 33, at 628, 632 (rejecting argument from "realism"); *Wilson v. Kentucky Transp. Cabinet*, 884 S.W.2d at 644 ("Practical, moral, or righteous claims do not pass the test of contract or constitutional law."). *But see Winkler v. School Building Authority*, 434 S.E.2d 420, 433, 435 (W.Va. 1993) ("Where the only source of funds for revenue bonds is general appropriations, it defies logic to say that the Legislature has no obligation to fund such bonds."); *State ex rel. Ohio Funds Management Bd. v. Walker*, 561 N.E.2d 927, 932 (Ohio 1990) (obligation to be considered "not only for what it purports to be, but what it actually is").
[52] *Colorado Criminal Justice Reform Coalition v. Ortiz*, 121 P.3d 288, 293–294. (Colo. Ct. App. 2005).
[53] Not all state judges are happy with this development. Many of the cases have been marked by close votes and sharp dissents. *Lonegan II* was decided by a 4–3 vote, with the dissenters emphatically asserting that the majority's decision "trespass[es] on the right of voters to approve or disapprove the State's ever-increasing contract indebtedness."

tax, subject to annual appropriation. To ensure that the annual appropriation is made, the legislation included what the court called a "trapping mechanism"[54] which barred the state from transferring any sales tax proceeds to the general fund until after the debt-service payment to LGAC had been made. The court had little difficulty sustaining the measure; indeed, it indicated that the "trapping mechanism" actually confirmed that the arrangement was not state debt because "[i]f the payments were meant to be mandated without the need for appropriation, there would have been no need to channel the payments through . . . the trapping mechanism."[55]

C. *Lance v. McGreevey* and the Balanced-Budget Requirement

Roughly two-thirds of the states have constitutional balanced-budget requirements,[56] but these requirements may be honored as much in the breach as in the observance. Some states with balanced-budget mandates run deficits, while many others achieve balance through such fiscal manipulations as unduly rosy revenue forecasts; accelerating revenues into one fiscal period while deferring expenses into another; reducing pension-fund contributions; and selling assets, refinancing debt, and raiding special funds.[57]

Balanced-budget requirements have received little judicial attention. Few courts have ever heard claims that a state budget fails to comply with the constitutional requirement and, in the few cases that have been brought, courts have been relatively deferential to the state.[58] A New York case, *Wein v. Carey*, involved a challenge to the state's plan to issue short-term debt to cover a year-end deficit. The state constitution permits such debt when the deficit is unanticipated and the notes will be paid in the coming fiscal year. Because the state had run deficits in the two preceding fiscal years, plaintiffs asserted the state's deficit was chronic and the budget not truly balanced, so that the notes were unlikely to be repaid without additional borrowing. The New York Court of Appeals, however, found that back-to-back year-end deficits did not show the budget was unbalanced: "The fact is that there may be an indefinite series of deficits honestly suffered. All that is necessary to produce the result are successive years of unpredictable shortfalls in revenues or rises in spending

---

[54] *Local Government Assistance Corp. v. Sales Tax Asset Receivable Corp.*, 2 N.Y.3d 524, 529 (2004).

[55] *Id.* at 538.

[56] *See* National Ass'n of State Budget Officers, Budget Processes in the States at 33 (2002). The state constitutions differ in what they require – 34 command their governors to submit balanced budgets, 33 direct their legislatures to pass balanced budgets, and 30 require their governors to sign balanced budgets.

[57] *See* Richard Briffault, Balancing Acts: The Reality Behind State Balanced Budget Requirements 16–27 (1996).

[58] *See Bishop v. Governor of Maryland*, 380 A.2d 220, 222–223 (Md. 1977).

beyond estimates."[59] Only if a plaintiff can show that the state's fiscal estimates were "dishonest" or patently unreasonable can a nominally balanced budget be challenged.

Against this backdrop, the decision of the New Jersey Supreme Court in *Lance v. McGreevey*[60] holding that the state failed to balance its FY 2005 budget comes as a shock. *Lance* appears to be the only time any state supreme court has ever held that a state failed to balance its budget as the state's constitution requires. It is doubly striking in that it came just 15 months after the extremely deferential *Lonegan II* decision upholding subject-to-appropriation debt.[61] Indeed, *Lance* involved the subject-to-appropriation mechanism. The state had authorized the Economic Development Authority to issue $1.9 billion in bonds; the proceeds would be turned over to the state to support "any lawful purpose," including the operating expenditures of the state government. Debt service would be paid by the state out of anticipated cigarette-tax revenues and motor-vehicle surcharges, subject to appropriation. In effect, the state sought to close its operating deficit by securitizing two ongoing revenue sources and borrowing against them.

The state defended the plan, arguing that the state constitution requires simply that "appropriations" not "exceed the total amount of revenue on hand and anticipated" during the fiscal year,[62] and that the bond proceeds can be treated as revenue. The constitution "does not define revenue," and the state contended that "in the absence of an explicit definition, the authority to define that term rests exclusively with the Governor, consistent with his expressed authority to 'certify' the amount of revenue available for each year." If "revenue" is any money taken in by the state, bond proceeds are revenue, and, counting the bond proceeds, revenues would fully balance expenditures.[63]

The court, however, found that treating bond proceeds as revenues "belies the common-sense notion of a balanced budget and is contrary to the framers' original intent. . . . [B]orrowed monies, which themselves are a form of expenditure when repaid, are not income (i.e., revenues) and cannot be used for the purpose of funding or balancing any portion of the budget pertaining to general costs without violating the" balanced-budget requirement.[64]

As *Lance* observed, the purpose of a balanced-budget requirement – to ensure that expenditures in a fiscal period do not exceed revenues in that same period – would be ignored if a state could use revenues borrowed from a future period to

[59] *Wein v. Carey*, 41 N.Y.2d 498, 504 (N.Y. 1977).

[60] 853 A.2d 856 (N.J. 2004).

[61] Chief Justice Poritz was the only member of the court who was in the majority in both *Lonegan II* and *Lance*. Of the three members of the four-justice *Lance* majority, two dissented in *Lonegan II* and the third joined the court after the *Lonegan* litigation. The sole *Lance* dissenter was in the *Lonegan II* majority. Two justices did not participate in *Lance*.

[62] N.J. Const., art. VIII, § 2, ¶ 2.   [63] *Lance v. McGreevey* 853 A.2d at 859–860.

[64] *Id.* at 860–861.

pay current operating costs. Nevertheless, given the dearth of judicial enforcement of balanced-budget requirements, the lack of a constitutional definition of "revenue," the widespread use of slippery budgetary devices to achieve nominal balance, and the New Jersey court's deference to the governor and legislature in other fiscal matters, the decision was clearly a surprise – to the state government, if not to the court itself. Having found that bond proceeds could not be used to balance the budget, the court nonetheless permitted the bond sales to go forward, partly, as in *Lonegan II*, to avoid "disruption" to the state and partly because the court was "satisfied that the legislative and executive branches acted in good faith, relying on an honest, albeit erroneous, belief that the budget properly was balanced under existing constitutional standards."[65] As a result, the balanced-budget ruling was prospective only. Almost as striking as the court's enforcement of the balanced budget itself is its finding that it was reasonable for the legislative and executive branches to have assumed that committing future revenues to pay for current operating expenses would create a balanced budget that satisfied the constitution.

Still, the New Jersey Supreme Court, apparently alone among state courts, actually found that a budget failed to satisfy the constitutional balanced-budget requirement. Perhaps the state's technique was more blatant than the unduly optimistic economic forecasts, revenue accelerations, expenditure deferrals, interfund transfers, and asset sales that other states often use to achieve nominal balance. Many of those devices surely would fail to satisfy generally accepted accounting principles, but even those devices do not on their face fail to provide new revenue or actually increase a state's costs, as New Jersey's plan to borrow against future revenues did. Moreover, whereas some challenges, like the one in *Wein v. Carey*, would "convert a courtroom into a super-auditing office to receive and criticize the budget estimates of a State,"[66] in *Lance* there was no forecasters' debate about the value of the bond proceeds, only the legal question of whether bond proceeds funded by future tax dollars could be used to achieve balance in the current fiscal period. In addition, unlike the taxes and debt at issue in *Guinn* and *Lonegan*, no specific, attractive, constitutionally mandated program like public education would suffer from the finding of imbalance. Indeed, by making the holding prospective only, the court ensured that no one would suffer at all. Whatever the reason, although state courts frequently read fiscal limits narrowly to minimize their impact on state finances, it is worth noting that sometimes a court actually will interpret a fiscal limit as the constitution's text and history suggest.

III. BUDGET PROCESSES AND POLITICS

State constitutions give detailed consideration to the procedures for making a state budget. Three elements stand out as departures from the federal

---

[65] *Id.* at 861.   [66] *Wein v. Carey*, 41 NY.2d at 504–505.

Constitution and as fonts of litigation: the executive budget, the item veto, and limits on appropriations bills.

Either by constitutional provision or by statute, many states give the governor the leading role in developing the budget.[67] State courts have found that the executive budget was intended to promote a balanced budget[68] and to control logrolling and pork-barrel spending.[69] The framers of these measures saw the governor as the officer with the broadest perspective on state finances, and thus the one most likely to "secure an economical and systemic plan for the annual budget of the state."[70]

Forty-three state constitutions further bolster the executive by authorizing the item veto.[71] By striking out individual items in appropriations bills, the governor can protect the executive budget by undoing changes passed by the legislature without having to forfeit the rest of the budget.[72] The item veto also advances the balanced budget and anti-pork-barrel goals of the executive budget by enabling the governor to eliminate – and in some states reduce[73] – items of appropriation, and to disentangle the appropriations packages put together by legislative logrolling.[74]

One-third of state constitutions bar the inclusion of substantive legislation in appropriations bills.[75] As the one bill that absolutely has to pass, the budget is a tempting target for legislators seeking to move policy proposals that might not be able to make it on their own. The opportunity to trade votes for policy matters also may facilitate pork-barrel spending. The appropriations-only clause, thus, may damp down logrolling and control spending. It also can promote deliberation, debate, and transparent decision making. Although it does not directly enhance executive power, governors sometimes have sought

---

[67] National Conference of State Legislatures, Legislative Budget Procedures: A Guide to Appropriations and Budget Processes in the States, Commonwealths, and Territories, *available at* http://www.ncsl.org/programs/fiscal/lbptabls/index.htm ("Most states follow the executive budgeting model."). In some states, the legislature wields considerable budgetary autonomy. *See id.* (citing Arizona, Colorado, and Texas).

[68] *See Judy v. Schaefer*, 627 A.2d 1039, 1048 (Md. 1993) (The "main objective" of the executive budget system is a balanced budget.).

[69] *See Pataki v. New York State Assembly*, 4 N.Y.3d 75, 81 (2004) (reviewing the statements of executive budget proponents at the 1915 constitutional convention).

[70] *Id. See also Judy v. Schaefer*, 627 A.2d at 1042–1048. *Cf. Washington State Legislature v. Lowry*, 931 P.2d 885, 889 (Wash. 1997) (The governor, "who is elected statewide rather than from a particular district," is more likely "to advance statewide rather than parochial fiscal interests" including the exclusion of unneeded pork-barrel spending.).

[71] *See* Richard Briffault, *The Item Veto in State Courts*, 66 Temple L. Rev. 1171, 1175 (1993).

[72] All states with the item veto permit legislative overrides, usually by the same two-thirds majority necessary to override other gubernatorial vetoes. *See id.* at 1176 and note 18.

[73] Twelve states permit governors to reduce, as well as strike, items from appropriations. *See* National Conference of State Legislatures, *supra* note 67.

[74] *See, e.g., Washington State Legislature v. Lowry*, 931 P.2d at 885; *Rios v. Symington*, 833 P.2d 20, 23 (Ariz. 1992).

[75] *See* Daniel S. Strouse, *The Structure of Appropriations Legislation and the Governor's Item Veto Power: The Arizona Experience*, 36 Ariz. L. Rev. 113, 126 (1994). *See also Apa v. Butler*, 638 N.W.2d 57, 61 (S.D. 2001); *Washington State Legislature v. State*, 985 P.2d 353 (Wash. 1999).

to justify the item veto of substantive language inserted by the legislature into an appropriation as an enforcement of the "nothing-but-appropriations" principle.[76]

The executive budget, the item veto, and the nothing-but-appropriations clause raise two cross-cutting cleavages – between definitions of executive and legislative power, and between "appropriations" and "substantive" or "policy" matters. Both the executive budget and the item veto break from the traditional idea that the legislature is the initiator and source of legislation, with the executive limited to vetoing the legislature's work product, subject to legislative override. The executive budget gives the governor the initiative, while the item veto enables the governor to pick bills apart, and, in effect, make a law that the legislature never passed. These departures from the traditional model of executive–legislative relations have been a source of difficulty for the courts, with some courts striving to minimize the change and others willing to read executive power over fiscal matters more broadly. The scope of executive power also is connected closely to the distinction between appropriations and substantive law. The item veto nearly always is limited to appropriations bills,[77] while the executive budget is, of course, limited to the budget. In many cases the scope of gubernatorial power will turn on whether the matter in question involves spending or policymaking – and whether, how, and by whom those matters are to be distinguished. That distinction, of course, is central to the appropriations-only clause. The cases in this section address how courts have struggled with these overlapping questions of executive power and the meaning of "appropriations."

A. *Pataki v. New York State Assembly*: The Governor as the "Constructor" of the Budget

The New York constitution creates one of the most executive-centered budget processes in the nation. Not only does the governor set the budgetary agenda, but he or she may include a substantive law change in a budget bill if the change "relates specifically to some particular appropriation in the bill."[78] On the other hand, the legislature is limited in how much it can depart from the governor's proposal: It "may not alter an appropriation bill submitted by the governor except to strike out or reduce items therein." The legislature may add new items, but these must be stated separately and distinctly from the original items of the governor's proposal and are subject to the governor's item veto.[79] In recent years, the governor and legislature repeatedly have clashed over the meaning of these provisions, with legal battles over the 1998 and 2001 state

---

[76] *See, e.g., Chiles v. Milligan,* 659 So.2d 1055 (Fl. 1995).

[77] The exception is the state of Washington; *see* Briffault, *supra* note 71, at 1175 and note 14.

[78] N.Y. Const., art. VII, § 6.   [79] N.Y. Const., art. VII, § 4.

budgets culminating in the landmark 2004 decision of the New York Court of Appeals in *Pataki v. New York State Assembly*.[80]

In the 1998 budget, the legislature passed the governor's appropriation bills, with some constitutionally permissible strikeouts or reductions but without alterations. Thereafter, it amended the accompanying nonappropriations bills to change the appropriations it had just enacted, not by changing the amounts appropriated but by changing the conditions under which the money would be spent. The governor, claiming the legislature's actions violated the "no-alterations" clause, item vetoed 55 changes. The legislature sued, contending the governor could not item veto textual conditions on appropriated items without vetoing the underlying appropriations. In the 2001 budget, the governor included significant substantive law changes in his appropriations bills. The school-aid appropriation bill contained a provision for "school-wide performance payments" and "17 pages of provisos and conditions, determining (based on pupil population, services provided, and many other factors) how much money would go to each school district." "In previous budgets, such extensive material had not been contained in appropriations bills";[81] rather, the school-aid formula was contained in a separate statute. Another appropriations bill included a modification of the method – previously codified in state law – of computing the Medicaid rates payable to residential health care facilities.[82] The legislature struck some of the substantive provisions without touching the appropriations to which they were attached. In other instances, it struck whole items of appropriations and then enacted its own appropriations bills, spending identical amounts of money for similar purposes but subject to different conditions and restrictions. The governor signed the bills but then sued, contending the legislature had again violated the no-alterations clause.

New York's top court found for the governor with respect to both the 1998 and 2001 budgets, holding he had the constitutional authority to include policy changes related to the budget in his budget bills and that the legislature's changes violated the no-alterations clause. The court found "the original purpose of the executive budgeting system was to change the roles of the Governor and the Legislature" and centralize budgetary planning in the governor in order to eliminate the "extravagance, waste, and irresponsibility" that had marked legislative budgeting. Quoting the principal proponent of the executive-budget plan at the 1915 state constitutional convention, the court found the constitution made the governor the "constructor" of the budget, and reduced the legislature to no more than a "critic," albeit a critic whose assent was necessary to enactment.[83]

---

[80] *Pataki v. New York State Assembly*, 4 N.Y.3d at 75.
[81] *Id.* at 86–87.   [82] *Id.*
[83] See *id.* at 82–83. The executive budget was part of the constitution submitted by the 1915 convention to the electorate, but the voters turned down that constitution. In 1926, the voters approved constitutional amendments similar to the 1915 executive-budget proposals. *Id.*

The harder question for the court was the scope of executive power to make substantive law changes through the budget. A plurality of three judges broadly hinted that there are no judicially enforceable limits – other than a weak germaneness constraint – on the governor's ability to include policy language in the budget. They acknowledged that "the Governor's power to originate appropriation bills is susceptible to abuse," providing a string of hypotheticals that nicely illustrate the kind of abuse that could occur.[84] But they expressed sharp skepticism about the ability or wisdom of any judicial effort to draw a substantive–fiscal distinction to cabin the governor's power: "The line between 'policy' and 'appropriations' is not just thin, but essentially nonexistent: every dollar the State spends is spent on substance, and the decision of how much to spend and for what purpose is a policy decision. Thus all appropriations are substantive, and all appropriations make policy."[85]

As the plurality opinion found the school-aid formula and Medicaid reimbursement changes were essentially fiscal, it declined to say what it would do when faced with the inclusion of clearly nonbudgetary matters in a budget bill. It stressed the legislature's political option to reject the governor's budget, create a "political stalemate," and force negotiations, and it condemned the idea of "judicial budgeting."[86] But it stopped short of concluding that there are no legal constraints on the governor's power to place nongermane substantive law changes in his budget bills.[87]

The two concurring judges agreed that the nonbudget language at issue had sufficient budgetary implications to be included in the budget bills but, unlike the plurality, they insisted on the need for judicially enforceable limits on the governor to prevent him from "trespassing on legislative turf." The concurring judges would look to "the effect on substantive law" as well as "the durational impact of the provision, and the history and custom of the budget process" in determining whether an appropriation is "impermissibly legislative."[88]

Although divided over the scope of the governor's power to insert substantive policy changes in the budget, the five-judge majority agreed that the legislature lacked power to modify the governor's budget bills either by amending the policy conditions before enactment, or by passing them and then amending with new appropriations bills. Such action constituted an impermissible effort by the legislature to set itself up as a "rival constructor."[89]

---

[84] *Id.* at 92–93. For example, the governor might make an appropriation to local fire departments contingent on an increase in the retirement age for firefighters, or exempt appropriations for state construction projects from certain worker-safety laws. *See id.* at 93.

[85] *Id.* at 93.   [86] *Id.* at 97–99.

[87] There was no disagreement that, consistent with art. VII, § 6 of the state constitution, all provisions in the budget bill must be germane to the budget, that is, they must "relate specifically to some particular appropriation in the bill." However, as the plurality conceded, that is no test at all "because it is quite possible to write legislation that plainly does not belong in an appropriation bill, and yet 'relates specifically to' . . . an appropriation." *Id.* at 93.

[88] *Id.* at 100–101.   [89] *Id.* at 89.

The two dissenters, like the concurrence, emphasized the constitutional limits on the governor's power to include substantive law changes in his budget bills', and, indeed, they found that the governor's 2001 budget submission had gone too far. The dissenters, however, looked to the legislature to control the governor. Notwithstanding the no-alterations clause, they would have permitted the legislature to strike out or amend the governor's nonfiscal conditions.[90]

The opinions in *Pataki* nicely lay out some of the central tensions of the executive-budget model: What substantive law changes with budgetary consequences can the governor include in the executive budget? How much can the legislature modify the governor's proposals? And who should decide those questions – the political branches themselves or the courts? As the plurality explained, budget and policy are profoundly intertwined. The budget is certainly a policy document. As a practical matter, it may make sense to include the substantive law changes on which the budget depends in the budget bills. If, after the budget passes, those changes are never made, then the budget may prove unworkable. Moreover, as the plurality noted, it is uncertain whether a judicially enforceable line can be drawn between policy or program on the one side and the budget on the other. The relatively open-ended criteria listed by the concurring opinion only underscore the difficulty of the question – although, as noted in the next section, courts in states whose constitutions bar the inclusion of substantive matters in appropriations bills have had to make that distinction.

On the other hand, the combination of broad executive power to include substantive law in the budget with limits on the legislature's power to alter or amend those substantive law proposals gives the governor authority not just to construct the budget, but also to make policy beyond the budget. Under *Pataki*, the governor can fast-track and force action on policy initiatives that the legislature otherwise might ignore. Although the governor cannot literally compel the legislature to approve these measures, the legislature's only alternative is to reject the spending to which these initiatives are attached, even if the legislature supports the spending and even though rejection of appropriations for major spending programs like school aid or Medicaid can be both politically and substantively devastating.[91] True, as the court observes, the legislature can refuse to act and thereby force the governor to negotiate. But relying on impasse is a high-risk strategy for the state.

The dissent's position that the legislature should be able to amend the governor's programmatic conditions is attractive. This would enable the governor to

[90] *Id.* at 118–119. The dissent also would have held that the line-item veto could not be used to strike out conditions imposed by the legislature on appropriations. In the dissent's view, the item veto was intended solely as a "check on government *spending*," *id.* at 121 (emphasis in original), and thus could not be deployed against conditions that do not spend money.

[91] As the Washington Supreme Court observed in a similar dispute, "an operating budget bill is essentially a compulsory outcome of a legislative session." *Washington State Legislature v. State*, 985 P.2d at 353, 362 note 6.

continue to include related policy matters in the budget, and to enable the legislature to approve those gubernatorial initiatives it finds acceptable – thereby avoiding the cumbersome alternative of requiring separate consideration of related fiscal and policy matters. By providing for political, rather than legal, enforcement of the limits on budget bills, it would free the courts of the difficulty of coming up with a legal standard for distinguishing budgetary from nonbudgetary matters. This approach would maintain executive–legislative balance through symmetry – whatever the governor could put in, the legislature could take out. The dissent's "political" solution, however, has a legal precondition – that it is constitutional for the legislature to strike out programmatic conditions while accepting the attached appropriation. The executive-budget provisions of the New York constitution give the legislature the power only to "strike out or reduce *items*" in the governor's budget bills.[92] The dissent's approach would require that programmatic language and policy conditions be treated as distinct "items" separable from the appropriated dollars to which they are attached. The question was raised in *Pataki* but not addressed by the court.[93] As will be discussed in the next section, whether such conditions are separable from the appropriations to which they are attached has been a hotly contested issue in item-veto litigation.

B. *Alaska Legislative Council v. Knowles*: The Limits of the Item Veto and the Appropriations Bill

Courts have differed sharply over whether a governor may item veto restrictions or conditions on an appropriation without vetoing the underlying appropriation. A significant number of courts have held that the condition cannot be separated from the appropriation; the two together constitute an "indivisible"[94] item.[95] These courts are uncomfortable with the law-making power the veto gives the governor "in derogation of the general plan of state government."[96] They have construed the item veto narrowly to minimize the departure from the traditional separation of powers.[97]

At the other extreme, the Wisconsin Supreme Court held that the governor can veto not just text but also individual phrases and words, even if they are expressed as conditions on an appropriation, and even if the result of the

---

[92] N.Y. Const., art. VII, § 4 (emphasis supplied).

[93] Ironically, the issue was addressed by the dissent, which determined that conditions added by the legislature were not vetoable items apart from the appropriations to which they are attached. *Id.* at 120–122. It is difficult to see how gubernatorial text can be an alterable "item" for the legislature but legislative text is not a vetoable "item" for the governor.

[94] *Colorado General Assembly v. Lamm*, 704 P.2d 1371, 1385 (Colo. 1985).

[95] *See generally* Richard Briffault, *supra* note 71, at 1185–1189.

[96] *Colorado General Assembly*, 704 P.2d at 1383.

[97] *Id.*; *Drummond v. Beasley*, 503 S.E.2d 455, 456 (S.C. 1998) (item veto to be "strictly construed").

governor's action is to change legislative policy completely. In one case, the legislature had authorized a system for the public financing of election campaigns and funded it by allowing taxpayers to "add on" to their tax liabilities an additional dollar that would be placed into the state campaign fund. The governor, by artful use of the veto, converted the add-on to a "check-off" in which taxpayers could commit a dollar of their existing tax liabilities to the campaign fund.[98] The Wisconsin court upheld this maneuver. Indeed, at one point, the Wisconsin court went so far as to hold that a governor could veto word fragments and individual letters from words[99] – although a constitutional amendment subsequently denied the governor to power to "create a new word by rejecting individual letters."[100] The only limitation the Wisconsin court has placed on the item-veto power is that "what remains after the veto must be a complete and workable law" and the result must be "germane" to the bill originally passed by the legislature.[101] The Wisconsin approach takes the change in the separation of powers created by the item veto to an extreme well beyond the fiscal purposes of the veto. Unsurprisingly, no other court has gone as far as Wisconsin in enabling a governor to pick apart and remake legislation.[102]

Several courts have struggled to find a middle position, permitting the veto of some but not all nonfiscal language attached to an appropriation. The Iowa Supreme Court, for example, has drawn a distinction between nonvetoable conditions on an appropriation and vetoable "riders." Thus, in one case, the governor vetoed language attached to an appropriation to the State Department of Health directing the department to relinquish authority over certain federal grants to the State Family Planning Council. Although the directive expressly stated it was "a condition of the appropriation," the Iowa court found that, as the language did not "limit or direct the use of that appropriation," it was not a "condition" at all but a "rider," which the governor could treat as a discrete item vetoable apart from the attached appropriation.[103]

In *Alaska Legislative Council v. Knowles*,[104] the Alaska Supreme Court combined a narrow reading of the item veto with an activist reading of the state

[98] *State ex rel. Kleczka v. Conta*, 264 N.W.2d 539 (Wis. 1978). As passed by the legislature, the bill read, "Every individual filing an income tax statement may designate that their income tax liability be increased by $1 for deposit into the Wisconsin Election Campaign Fund." The governor lined out the words "that their income tax liability be increased by" and the words "deposit into," thereby creating a check-off program. *Id.* at 545.

[99] *State ex rel. Wisconsin Senate v. Thompson*, 424 N.W.2d 385 (Wis. 1988).

[100] Wisc. Const., art. V, § 10(1)(c).

[101] *State ex rel. Wisconsin Senate v. Thompson*, 424 N.W.2d at 393.

[102] *See Washington State Legislature v. State*, 985 P.2d at 353, 360–361 (governor may item veto a legislative proviso, but must veto the whole proviso in order for the item veto to be constitutional), but *cf. Management Council of the Wyoming Legislature v. Geringer*, 953 P.2d 839 (Wyo. 1998) (governor may veto "any portion" of any bill making appropriations).

[103] *Colton v. Branstad*, 372 N.W.2d 184, 190–92 (Ia. 1985). *Accord, Welsh v. Branstad*, 470 N.W.2d 644 (Ia. 1991). *See also Opinion of the Justices*, 582 N.E.2d 504, 510 (Mass. 1991).

[104] *Alaska Legislative Council v. Knowles*, 21 P.3d 367 (Ak. 2001).

constitution's appropriations-only clause – known in Alaska as the "confinement clause" – to reach a result similar to Iowa's, albeit based on very different reasoning. *Knowles* involved five vetoes of textual conditions. Three vetoes deleted provisos making appropriations to the Alaska Seafood Marketing Institute (ASMI) contingent on the ASMI having all senior employees located within Alaska. The fourth struck out language added to an appropriation for community residential centers, requiring the facilities not to be owned or controlled by municipalities. In the fifth, the governor vetoed language attached to the appropriation for a therapeutic community treatment program that stated the program's cost per inmate "will not exceed the statewide average cost per inmate day for correctional institutions." The legislature sued, claiming the vetoes were unconstitutional since the vetoed passages were not "items." The governor counterclaimed, contending the provisos violated the constitutional requirement that "bills for appropriations shall be confined to appropriations."[105]

The Alaska court rejected the governor's broad reading of the item-veto power. Although it framed its opinion in part on the need to maintain traditional executive and legislative roles,[106] it also provided a more functional justification, stressing that "[p]ermitting a governor to strike descriptive language would not limit expenditures or help balance the budget."[107] Nor would allowing the item veto of provisos advance the antilogrolling goal of the veto: "Although striking language that is only descriptive might reduce logrolling, doing so would only alter purpose, not amount."[108] The court thus viewed the antilogrolling purpose as an aspect of the fiscal limitation goal, without considering that logrolling also could entail vote-trading of budgetary amounts with policy objectives. The court conceded that "[a]n approach more favorable to the executive would certainly advance the item veto's historic purposes. But our definition of 'item' does not prevent the governor from using the item veto for those purposes."[109]

The court also rejected the governor's argument that the vetoes were justified by the confinement clause's goal of keeping nonbudgetary matters out of appropriations.[110] Again viewing the item veto through a fiscal lens, the court concluded that the fiscal purposes of the item veto would not be advanced by the veto of nonfiscal language.[111]

---

[105] Ak. Const., art. II., § 13.

[106] The court emphasized that the power to appropriate is vested in the legislature, with the governor's power only one of limitation. *Alaska Legislative Council v. Knowles*, 21 P.3d at 371. As "an executive exercise of legislative power," the item veto should be strictly construed." *Id.* at 372.

[107] *Id.* at 373.   [108] *Id.*

[109] *Id.* at 374.

[110] The Washington Supreme Court has held that the governor can use the item veto to strike out provisos that violate that state's counterpart to Alaska's confinement clause. *Washington State Legislature v. Lowry*, 931 P.2d at 885.

[111] *Alaska Legislative Council v. Knowles*, 21 P.3d at 374. *Accord, Brown v. Firestone*, 382 So.2d 654 (Fla. 1980); *Chiles v. Milligan*, 659 So.2d 1055.

Having limited the governor's power, the court expanded its own – and curbed the legislature's. Developing a fiscal–substantive distinction of the sort rejected by the *Pataki* plurality, it applied the confinement clause directly to the legislature's provisos. The three provisos mandating the in-state location of the ASMI senior staff were invalidated for going beyond the "minimum necessary"[112] to specify how the appropriated funds would be spent, while imposing "new substantive law." Inserting such a substantive policy measure in the appropriations bill "would reduce the public scrutiny and debate which accompany policy making, and could encourage logrolling and free-riders to achieve results not politically attainable in non-appropriation bills."[113] The court upheld the other two vetoed provisos on the theory that they did not affect substantive law. It reached the debatable conclusion that the language restricting the appropriation for new community residential centers to facilities "not owned or controlled by municipalities" did not change substantive law. As current law permitted the state to contract with both municipalities and private providers but did not require contracting with municipalities, the proviso assertedly did not change the statutory mandate and thus did not violate the confinement clause.[114] The court found it unclear whether the fifth proviso dealing with the inmate therapeutic treatment program simply described the program or imposed a condition. Preferring to avoid finding a constitutional violation, the court determined the language was merely "descriptive and non-binding" and upheld it.[115]

Knowles places Alaska firmly in the camp of those state courts that have taken a narrow approach to the item veto; however, more clearly than many other limited-item-veto courts, it also provided a functional account for its action by stressing the fiscal purpose of the item veto. The court did not wholly give up on the antilogrolling goal of the item veto, but looked to judicial enforcement of the confinement clause to vindicate that value by preventing the legislature from piggybacking substantive matters onto the budget process. With the executive and the legislature both constrained, *Knowles* gives the court an important role in policing the budget process. The court's confidence in its ability to distinguish the fiscal from the programmatic is in sharp contrast with the skepticism expressed by the *Pataki* plurality. However, as the court's analysis of some of the legislative conditions indicates, deciding whether a budget provision actually changes substantive law often will be difficult – which has been the experience of other state courts that have sought to enforce comparable provisions.[116]

---

[112] *Alaska Legislative Council v. Knowles*, 21 P.2d at 377–378.
[113] *Id.*
[114] *Id.* at 382. One justice dissented, finding the proviso amended existing law and, thus, violated the confinement clause. *See id.* at 385.
[115] *Id.* at 383. Two justices dissented on this point, finding that even nonbinding language would violate the confinement clause. *See id.* at 384–385.
[116] *See Washington Legislative Council v. Lowry*, 931 P.2d 885; *Chiles v. Milligan*, 659 So.2d 1055.

C. *Bennett v. Napolitano*: Judicial Modesty Produces Executive Power

In June 2003, Governor Janet Napolitano item vetoed 35 provisions from the
FY 2004 Arizona operating budget. The legislature did not attempt to override
her vetoes; instead four legislative leaders[117] sued, claiming that 11 of the vetoes
were unconstitutional. In nine of the 11 vetoes, involving the vast majority of
the funds affected, the governor lined out legislative language reducing appropriations. In some cases, the legislature had approved departmental allocations
and then added a directive requiring the governor to make a lump-sum reduction for the department – leaving to her the determination of which programs
would be subject to particular reductions; in other cases, the legislature had
added language ordering the reduction of funding for certain programs.[118] The
legislators argued that the language deleted did not constitute "items." Moreover, given that the language ordered a reduction in spending, it was not clear
the vetoes could be justified in terms of the item veto's fiscal limitation and
balanced-budget goals.

The governor relied heavily on an earlier Arizona Supreme Court decision,
Rios v. Symington,[119] which upheld vetoes of legislative language that would
have transferred money from certain special funds to the general fund, thus
reducing the money available for the programs supported by the special funds.
Rios acknowledged that "[v]iewed in isolation, the fund transfers themselves
are not clearly 'items of appropriation,'" but emphasized that the transfers
effectively reduced the funds available for a "previously-made appropriation."
To permit such an action to escape the item veto "would seriously limit the
Executive's constitutional role in the appropriation process."[120] The fact that the
"net effect of the Governor's vetoes is to increase state spending" was dismissed
as irrelevant.[121] In *Rios*, however, the vetoed transfers were made in a special
session many months after the budget had been passed, whereas Governor
Napolitano's 2003 vetoes applied to reductions embedded in the measures
making the appropriations. Thus, upholding those vetoes would extend *Rios*
beyond the setting of a "two-step, veto-proof legislative manipulation."[122]

This time the Arizona court dismissed the case, concluding that in the
absence of formal legislative authorization, the individual legislators lacked
standing to assert the interest of the legislature as a whole. The court relied
heavily on prudential concerns. The "dispute is political," the court noted,
and "we are reluctant to become the referee of a political dispute." The court

---

[117] The plaintiffs were the president of the Senate, the speaker of the House of Representatives, and the majority leaders of both chambers. *See Bennett v. Napolitano*, 81 P.3d 311, 313
(Az. 2003).

[118] *See id.* at 313–315.   [119] *Rios v. Symington*, 833 P.2d at 20.

[120] *Id.* at 26.   [121] *Id.* at 28.

[122] Daniel S. Strouse, *The "Item Veto" Case, Bennett v. Napolitano: What About the Merits?*, 37 ARIZ.
ST. L.J. 165, 170 (2005). *See also* Daniel S. Strouse, *The Structure of Appropriations Legislation*,
supra note 75, at 158–161 (criticizing *Rios*).

emphasized that the legislature had failed "to exercise available political means by seeking to override the veto." Although "not fatal per se," the lack of an override attempt made the court especially wary about hearing the case.[123]

The *Bennett* outcome is surprising in several respects. The Arizona court previously had entertained numerous challenges to the item veto, including *Rios*; moreover, *Rios* had been brought by an individual legislator. To be sure, the governor in *Rios* had not raised the standing question,[124] but the contrast between the court's handling of standing in *Rios* and *Bennett* is noticeable. Courts in other states have recognized legislator standing in similar item veto litigation.[125] Moreover, the plaintiffs were the four leading members of the legislature. Nor was the significance of the legislature's failure to seek an override entirely clear. If the legislature had overridden, there would have been no case. But what if the override had failed? Would that constitute legislative "ratification" of the vetoes, thereby barring a subsequent suit?

Still, there is something to the point that before calling for judicial resolution of a difficult, politically loaded question, the legislature should have at least tried to handle the matter politically, as well as formally authorized the action. The denial of individual legislator standing sensibly limits item-veto litigation to matters the legislature as a whole deems important. Requiring the legislature to "exhaust" its political remedies also seems sensible – provided that failure to override because of inability to muster a supermajority does not stop a majority from pursuing its claim.

Surely, in the future the legislature will dot its *i*'s and cross its *t*'s by first trying to override a veto and then formally authorizing a suit. Moreover, the "unusual method" deployed by the legislature to cut appropriations, with the item veto used to restored spending, "is likely a non-recurring event."[126] Nevertheless, the case is worth noting for its striking display of judicial modesty. Given the significant role courts in many states (including Arizona) play in interpreting the fiscal constitution, and their frequent willingness to address politically charged fiscal issues, it is important to recognize that sometimes the opposite occurs, and courts look for reasons to stay out. Of course, judicial passivism – like judicial activism – has consequences. In *Bennett*, judicial modesty in the form of judicial nonreview of an item veto upheld the governor's action and strengthened her political position.

IV. CONCLUSION: IN SEARCH OF LESSONS

What, if anything, can be learned about state fiscal constitutional law from these six cases? Certainly not much as a matter of social scientific proof, given the limited nature of the data. Still, a handful of themes do emerge.

---

[123] *Bennett v. Napolitano*, 81 P.3d at 317–318.
[124] *See id.* at 316, citing *Rios*, 833 P.2d at 22 note 2.
[125] *See, e.g., Pataki v. Silver*, 96 N.Y.2d 532 (2001).
[126] *Bennett v. Napolitano*, 81 P.3d at 319.

First is the high level of inconsistency in judicial decision making. In our sample of six, one court, *Lance v. McGreevey*, enforced a constitutional provision according to its terms and its spirit. *Lonegan* basically ignored a constitutional provision. *Guinn* directed another branch of government to ignore a constitutional provision. *Knowles* read one constitutional provision relatively narrowly, but vigorously enforced another provision. *Bennett* opted out of adjudication altogether. This inconsistency may affect broad categories of cases, as in the varying approaches to the definition of "item" for the item veto. This inconsistency also can be found within the same state, given *Rios* and *Bennett* in Arizona, or, over a much shorter period of time, *Lonegan* and *Lance* in New Jersey.

Doctrinal inconsistency is hardly unique to the fiscal constitution, but a second theme – the undefined nature of many of the basic terms of the state fiscal constitution – runs through the cases and contributes to the first theme. The "debt" limited by debt limitations; the "revenue" that can be used to balance the budget; the "appropriations" to which appropriations bills may be confined; and the "item" subject to veto almost never are defined in the constitution. These may seem like relatively dry, technical terms with relatively determinate, coherent, and consistent meanings, unlike the essentially contested concepts of "equal protection, "due process," "free speech," or "privacy" that bedevil other domains of constitutional law. But, it turns out that these essential elements of the fiscal constitution are open to multiple interpretations, with different political and institutional consequences. The absence of constitutional definitions makes the fiscal constitution a breeding ground of doctrinal uncertainty.

Third, many conflicts arise because of the clash between constitutional norms and ordinary politics. The supermajority requirement for tax increases does not fit easily with the powerful political pressures to spend money on public services, much as the substantive and procedural limitations on debt are often in tension with the need to finance new infrastructure. It often seems there is a structural gap – indeed, a chasm – between what the public wants from government and what it is willing to pay for, a gap that produces constitutional provisions that make it hard for elected officials to get the public to pay for the services that the public demands. So, too, there is often a disconnect between the idealized version of the legislative process that imposes rules intended to promote deliberation, accountability, and transparency and the reality of legislative politics. Budgets, policymaking, and substantive law change overlap in ways that may not respect the separation of appropriations from other legislative matters enshrined in many state constitutions. These tensions between constitutional constraints and aspirations and the practices and demands of politics generate difficult disputes. Given the political context, it is not surprising that courts disagree as to just how aggressive they ought to be in enforcing fiscal constitutional norms.

To be sure, constitutional provisions generally constrain the political process. That is why rules are made constitutional – to take them out of ordinary politics. But the fiscal provisions look and feel different from the fundamental rights, due process, and equal protection requirements that are the focus of constitutional jurisprudence. Although these cases deal with state constitutional provisions that have no federal analogues, state courts still may be influenced by a federal constitutional jurisprudence that has determined that economic and social matters that do not affect fundamental rights or involve discrimination against discrete and insular minorities are for the political process and not for the courts. Thus, neither the Nevada court in *Guinn* nor the New Jersey court in *Lonegan II* gave any hint that it thought the tax and debt limitations at issue vindicated a fundamental constitutional norm. On the other hand, the *Lance* court did enforce the balanced-budget requirement.

Fourth, a central issue in nearly all these cases was the judicial role in dealing with fiscal and political matters. The courts often seemed uncomfortable in addressing the issues raised by the state fiscal constitution even though, as provisions embedded in their constitution, they presented legal questions. Even in the most activist case, *Guinn*, the Nevada court sought to justify itself, initially, by claiming to do no more than apply relatively mechanical legal rules, and by emphasizing that its role was thrust upon it by the constitution and the failure of the political branches. The courts in *Lonegan*, *Pataki*, and *Bennett*, justified their decisions in terms of the need for judicial nonintervention, of leaving what they considered political matters to the political process. Even the *Lance* court made its obeisance to the dominance of the political process in budgeting by making its decision prospective only.

Finally, many cases involved conflicts between constitutional norms. *Guinn* treated the tax supermajority requirement as in conflict with the education spending mandate and the simple majority rule for appropriations. In the executive budget and item-veto cases, courts regularly noted the tension between the usual model of legislative primacy over legislation and the enhanced power these constitutional provisions give the executive in the budget arena. Sometimes, as in *Pataki*, the fiscal constitution's departure from other constitutional norms was used to justify an expansive reading of the enhanced gubernatorial power. Alternatively, as in many of the item-veto cases, the differences lead to a narrow reading of the governor's expanded authority. But either way, the special powers of the governor with respect to the budget generate uncertainty. When combined with the lack of definition of the basic terms that are the focus of that conflict – "appropriation" and "item" – doctrinal messiness seems likely to follow.

The lessons of these cases, thus, should be sobering to those who want to reform fiscal practices – federal or state – through constitutional revision. To succeed, such reforms would require careful definition of key terms, close attention to potential conflicts with other constitutional provisions or norms, and the crafting of rules capable of judicial enforcement. Even then, these examples drawn from state constitutional law caution against assuming that fiscal constitutional amendments necessarily will lead to the changes in fiscal practices sought by their proponents.

Questions for Chapter 14

1. The complexities facing state courts in the decisions that Professor Briffault reviews here are reminiscent of difficulties documented through-out this volume. The definitional problems of fiscal policy are ubiquitous. What is spending? What is debt? As recounted in Professor Block's chapter, Congress, when faced with budgetary constraints over the past few decades, has devised numerous and ingenious ways to reclassify expenditures so that they do not count toward binding constraints on annual spending and to gen-erate cash flows that can be used to meet deficit targets. Professor Jackson's discussion of budgetary measures demonstrates that even accountants have trouble deciding exactly when the federal government should recognize lia-bilities. And, in their historical study of 19th-century public works projects, Professors Wallis and Weingast document how special-purpose local financ-ing vehicles were used to evade the literal requirements of state constitutional provisions adopted. We, therefore, should not be surprised that the courts in recent years have had difficulties interpreting the meaning of debt and rev-enues for purposes of vindicating constitutional provisions involving fiscal matters.

2. But, of course, more is going on with these cases than just interpretative difficulties. As Professor Briffault's analysis emphasizes, states courts are often quite candid in admitting that they are trying to avoid political decisions that fall beyond the competence of the judicial branch either to fully understand or to adequately oversee. The federal courts often express similar sentiments when invoking judicial doctrines that permit them to avoid ruling on the merits of fiscal policies made by Congress and the executive.[127] Should we therefore think of fiscal provisions written into constitutions as a form of public right that

---

[127] *See* Drew McClelland and Sam Walsh, Litigating Challenges to Judicial Spending Decisions: The Role of Standing and Political Question Doctrine (May 1, 2006), *available at* http://www.law. harvard.edu/faculty/hjackson/LitigatingChallenges_33.pdf.

routinely should not be amenable to judicial vindication? If so, what exactly is the purpose of such a right?

3. Where constitutional provisions are clear and courts choose to reach the merits of a case before them, why shouldn't we expect more of the judiciary than we see in the cases reported in this chapter? Professor Briffault explains the rulings of the *Guinn* cases as judicial acquiescence to political processes when the taxes in question were endorsed by a majority of legislators, but not by the two-thirds supermajority required by a citizen's initiative. Is it acceptable for a court to ignore the supermajority requirements of an initiative on the pragmatic grounds that some sort of state budget must be enacted? Or is a court bound in such a context to strike down the legislation in question and leave it to the political branches to pick up the pieces? As we have seen in previous chapters, the representative branches often fail to keep their fiscal promises and even the general public has been known to go back on initiatives designed to enforce budgetary constraints. Is it unreasonable to expect the judiciary to do better? Or is it simply yet another political branch?

4. In the previous chapter, Professor Harrison explored how one Congress might use legal devices to protect property interests in an enhanced form of Social Security benefits should a subsequent Congress seek to pare back those benefits. Having read Professor Briffault's analysis of the tenacity of state courts in resisting the enforcement of constitutional provisions on fiscal matters, how confident are you of the viability of Professor Harrison's program? Does it matter that his strategy was to create individual property rights in Social Security benefits? Is it possible to recharacterize the constitutional provisions discussed in Professor Briffault's chapter as individual rights not to be taxed without supermajority votes or not to endure the debts associated with unbalanced budgets?

5. Notwithstanding the decidedly spotty record of state courts in enforcing state constitutional provisions, proposals for similar constitutional requirements are advanced periodically at the federal level. Bowen presents an interesting effort to structure a federal balanced-budget amendment that addresses some of the weaknesses observed at the state level.[128]

---

[128] James W. Bowen, *Enforcing the Balanced Budget Amendment*, 4 SETON HALL CONST. L.J. 565 (1994).

Bibliography

ARTICLES

Stacy Anderson and Blake Roberts, *The Capacity to Commit in the Absence of Legislation: Takings, Winstar, FTCA & the Court of Claims* (May 2005), *available at* http://www.law.harvard.edu/faculty/hjackson/CapacitytoCommitt_12.pdf.

James W. Bowen, *Enforcing the Balanced Budget Amendment*, 4 SETON HALL CONST. L.J. 565 (1994).

Richard Briffault, *The Disfavored Constitution: State Fiscal Limits and State Constitutional Law*, 34 RUTGERS L.J. 907 (2003).

Richard Briffault, *The Item Veto in State Courts*, 66 TEMPLE L. REV. 1171 (1993).

Mark Champoux and John Lobato, *The Limited Power of Courts to Order Spending* (May 14, 2006), *available at* http://www.law.harvard.edu/faculty/hjackson/CourtOrderSpending_24.pdf.

Gerald E. Frug, *The Judicial Power of the Purse*, 126 U. PENN. L. REV. 715 (1978).

Steve R. Johnson, *Supermajority Provisions*, Guinn v. Legislature, *and a Flawed Constitutional Structure*, 4 NEV L.J. 491 (2004).

Anita S. Krishnakumar, *In Defense of the Debt Limit Statute*, 42 HARV. J. LEGIS. 135 (2005).

Richard J. Marino and Colleen Waddell, *Revised Lease and Appropriation-Backed Debt Rating Criteria*, STANDARD & Poor's Rating Services, June 13, 2001.

Drew McClelland and Sam Walsh, *Litigating Challenges to Judicial Spending Decisions: The Role of Standing and Political Question Doctrine* (May 1, 2006), *available at* http://www.law.harvard.edu/faculty/hjackson/LitigatingChallenges_33.pdf.

Thomas W. Merrill, *The Landscape of Constitutional Property*, 86 VIRGINIA L. REV. 885 (2000).

William D. Popkin, *Interpreting Conflicting Provisions of the Nevada State Constitution*, 5 NEV. L.J. 308 (2004).

Eric A. Posner and Adrian Vermeule, *Legislation Entrenchment: A Reappraisal*, 111 YALE L.J. 1665 (2002).

Kate Stith, *Rewriting the Fiscal Constitution: The Case of Gramm-Rudman-Hollings*, 76 CAL. L. REV. 593 (1988).

Jeffrey W. Stempel, *The Most Rational Branch: Guinn v. Legislature and the Judiciary's Role as Helpful Arbiter of Conflict*, 4 NEV. L.J. 518 (2004).

Daniel S. Strouse, *The "Item Veto" Case, Bennett v. Napolitano: What About the Merits?*, 37 ARIZ. ST. L.J. 165 (2005).

Daniel S. Strouse, *The Structure of Appropriations Legislation and the Governor's Item Veto Power: The Arizona Experience*, 36 ARIZ. L. REV. 113 (1994).

Adrian Vermeule, *Veil of Ignorance Rules in Constitutional Law*, 111 YALE L.J. 399 (2001).

Ann Woolhandler, *The Common Law Origins of Constitutionally Compelled Remedies*, 107 YALE L.J. 77 (1997).

BOOKS

Richard Briffault, BALANCING ACTS: THE REALITY BEHIND STATE BALANCED BUDGET REQUIREMENTS (1996).

David P. Currie, THE CONSTITUTION IN THE SUPREME COURT: THE FIRST HUNDRED YEARS, 1789–1888 (1985).

CASES

Apa v. Butler, 638 N.W.2d 57 (S.D. 2001).

Abbott v. Burke V, 710 A.2d 450 (N.J. 1998).

Brown v. Firestone, 382 So.2d 654 (Fla. 1980).

Alaska Legislative Council v. Knowles, 21 P.3d 367 (Ak. 2001).

Amador Valley Joint Union High School Dist. v. Board of Equalization, 583 P.2d 1281 (Cal. 1978).

Bennett v. Napolitano, 81 P.3d 311 (Az. 2003).

Bishop v. Governor of Maryland, 380 A.2d 220 (Md. 1977).

Board of Estimate v. Morris, 489 U.S. 688 (1989).

Bowsher v. Synar, 478 U.S. 714 (1986).

Brosnahan v. Brown, 651 P.2d 274 (Cal. 1982).

Carr-Gottstein Properties v. State, 899 P.2d 136 (Ak. 1995).

Charles River Bridge v. Warren Bridge, 36 U.S. (11 Pet.) 420 (1837).

Chicago, Burlington & Quincy R. Co. v. Chicago, 166 U.S. 226 (1897).

Chiles v. Milligan, 659 So.2d 1055 (Fl. 1995).

Cleveland Board of Education v. Loudermill, 470 U.S. 532 (1985).

Clinton v. City of New York, 524 U.S. 417 (1998).

Colorado Criminal Justice Reform Coalition v. Ortiz, 121 P.3d 288 (Colo. Ct. App. 2005).

Colorado General Assembly v. Lamm, 704 P.2d 1371 (Colo. 1985).

Colton v. Branstad, 372 N.W.2d 184 (Ia. 1985).

Drummond v. Beasley, 503 S.E.2d 455 (S.C. 1998).

Dykes v. Northern Virginia Transportation District Comm'n, 411 S.E.2d 1 (Va. 1991).

Eastern Enterprises v. Apfel, 524 U.S. 498 (1998).

Employers Insurance Co. of Nevada v. State Bd. of Examiners, 21 P.3d 628 (Nev. 2001).

Fent v. Oklahoma Capitol Improvement Authority, 984 P.2d 200 (Okla. 1999).

Flemming v. Nestor, 363 U.S. 603 (1960).

Guinn v. Legislature of the State of Nevada, 71 P.3d 1269 (Nev. 2003) ("*Guinn I*").

Guinn v. Legislature of the State of Nevada, 76 P.3d 22 (Nev. 2003) ("*Guinn II*").

Home Building & Loan Ass'n v. Blaisdell, 290 U.S. 398 (1934).

Judy v. Schaefer, 627 A.2d 1039 (Md. 1993).

Lance v. McGreevey, 853 A.2d 856 (N.J. 2004).

Local Government Assistance Corp. v. Sales Tax Asset Receivable Corp., 2 N.Y.3d 524 (2004).

Lonegan v. State, 809 A.2d 9130 (N.J. 2002) ("*Lonegan I*").

Lonegan v. State, 819 A.2d 395 (N.J. 2003) ("*Lonegan II*").

Management Council of the Wyoming Legislature v. Geringer, 953 P.2d 839 (Wyo. 1998).
Missouri v. Jenkins, 515 U.S. 70 (1995).
O'Donaghue v. United States, 289 U.S. 516 (1933).
Opinion of the Justices, 582 N.E.2d 504 (Mass. 1991).
Pataki v. New York State Assembly, 4 N.Y.3d 75 (2004).
Pataki v. Silver, 96 N.Y.2d 532 (2001).
Poindexter v. Greenhow, 114 U.S. 270 (1885).
Reynolds v. Sims, 377 U.S. 533 (1964).
Rider v. City of San Diego, 959 P.2d 347 (Cal. 1998).
Rios v. Symington, 833 P.2d 20 (Ariz. 1992).
Schulz v. State of New York, 639 N.E.2d 1140 (N.Y. 1994).
State ex rel. Kleczka v. Conta, 264 N.W.2d 539 (Wis. 1978).
State ex rel. Ohio Funds Management Bd. v. Walker, 561 N.E.2d 927 (Ohio 1990).
State ex rel. Wisconsin Senate v. Thompson, 424 N.W.2d 385 (Wis. 1988).
Train v. City of New York, 420 U.S. 35 (1975).
Trustees of Dartmouth College v. Woodward, 17 U.S. (4 Wheat.) 518 (1819).
United States v. Winstar Corp., 518 U.S. 839 (1996).
Washington State Legislature v. Lowry, 931 P.2d 885 (Wash. 1997).
Washington State Legislature v. State, 985 P.2d 353 note 6 (Wash. 1999).
Wein v. Carey, 41 N.Y.2d 498, 504 (N.Y. 1977).
Welsh v. Branstad, 470 N.W.2d 644 (Ia. 1991).
White v. Davis, 108 Cal. App. 4th 197 (Cal. Ct. App. 2002).
Williams v. United States, 289 U.S. 553 (1933).
Wilson v. Kentucky Transp. Cabinet, 884 S.W.2d 641 (Ky. 1994).
Winkler v. School Building Authority, 434 S.E.2d 420 (W.Va. 1993).

CONGRESSIONAL REPORTS

Government Accountability Office, Principles of Federal Appropriations Law (3d ed., 2004).
National Ass'n of State Budget Officers, Budget Processes in the States at 33 (2002).
National Conference of State Legislatures, Legislative Budget Procedures: A Guide to Appropriations and Budget Processes in the States, Commonwealths and Territories (2006), *available at* http://www.ncsl.org/programs/fiscal/lbptabls/index.htm#dveloprb.
National Conference of State Legislatures, State Tax and Expenditure Limits – 2005 (2005), *available at* http://www.ncsl.org/programs/fiscal/tels2005.htm.
National Conference of State Legislatures, Supermajority Vote Requirements to Pass the Budget (1998), *available at* http://www.ncsl.org/programs/fiscal/supmjbud.htm.
Joseph Story, Commentaries on the Constitution of the United States (1833).

LEGISLATION

Ak. Const., art. II., § 13.
Ariz. Const., art. 9 § 5.
Consolidated Appropriations Act, 2004, Pub. L. No. 109-199, Div., B, tit. I, 118 Stat. 3, 46.

Emergency Deficit Control Act of 1985, Pub. L. No. 99-177, 99 Stat. 1038.
Ga. Const., art. VII, § IV, ¶ II.
Ind. Const., art. X, § 5.
Ky. Const., § 49.
Legislative Appropriations Act of 1932, ch. 314, 47 Stat. 382.
Mich. Const., art. IX, § 15.
Nev. Const., art. 11, § 2–6.
N.J. Const., art. VIII, § 2.
N.Y. Const., art. VII, § 4–6.
R.I. Const., art. VI, § 16.
Social Security Act, ch. 531, sec. 1104, 49 Stat. 620, 648.
28 U.S.C. 501–518.
31 U.S.C. 3102–3106.
42 U.S.C. 401.
U.S. Const., art. I, sec. 9–10.
10 U.S. (6 Cranch) 87 (1810).
W.Va. Const., art. X, Sec.§ 4.
Wisc. Const., art. V, § 10(1)(c).

Index

accountability, 75, 80, 89, 376. *See* transparency
accounting methodologies, 54, 63, 142, 158, 185, 212, 216, 218, 367, 386
   accrual method, 52–53, 140, 142, 186, 202, 206, 208, 215, 219
   cash-flow accounting, 56, 60–61
Alaska, 437–439. *See Alaska Legislative Council v. Knowles*
Alaska Legislative Council v. Knowles, 439, 442
alternative minimum tax (AMT), 151, 177, 179
anchoring and underadjustment, 224, 230, 235
appropriations, 1, 12, 20, 26, 47, 55, 62, 81, 183, 254, 399, 403, 404, 420, 422, 423, 425–427, 429, 431, 432, 434–438, 440, 442, 443
appropriations bills, 24–26, 74, 83, 418, 431–434, 439, 442
Appropriations Clause, 417, 432
Appropriations Committees, 5, 6, 16, 19, 24, 26, 81, 199
   House Appropriations Committee, 23
   Senate Appropriations Committee, 23
Arizona, 440–442. *See Bennett v. Napolitano*

Baby Boomers, 35, 168, 176, 177, 183
back loaded accounts, 60
balanced budget, 144, 160, 182, 191, 221, 226, 228, 230, 232, 237–238, 424, 431, 438, 440, 442, 445
balanced budget requirements, 172, 249, 252, 258, 260, 267, 269, 271, 272, 274, 276–278, 329, 365, 367, 371, 372, 377, 384, 393, 418, 420, 430, 443
Barro, Robert, 164
Base Realignment and Closure Acts, 94

baseline projections, 193–196
behavioral economics, 223, 225, 240, 241
Bennett v. Napolitano, 441–443
bonds, 153–155, 329, 332, 335, 339, 340, 344, 356–362, 387, 388, 404, 408, 410, 411, 425, 426, 429, 430
Budget and Accounting Act of 1921, 6
budget authority, 28, 55, 200, 214, 370, 386
budget baseline, 16, 19, 20, 41, 47, 49, 55, 57–60, 62, 184, 255, 302, 377, 386
budget committees, 7, 9, 15, 17, 21, 28, 44, 63, 73, 80, 81, 97, 273
   budget resolution, 19, 21, 28
   budget resolution consequences, 20
budget deficits, 12
Budget Enforcement Act of 1990, 13, 20, 41, 50, 104, 375
budget gimmicks, 2, 40, 45, 49, 51, 59, 61–63, 309, 386, 395
   impact, 40
budget obligations, 370
budget outlays, 10, 27, 28, 31–33, 44, 45, 47, 54, 140, 143, 149, 173, 189, 191, 196, 198–200, 202, 203, 211, 216, 217, 335, 336, 370, 386
budget periodicity, 252, 254, 258, 259, 263, 269, 372, 381, 384, 387–389, 395, 421
   annual budget, 263, 273
   biennial budget, 263, 273
   business cycle, 142, 143, 373, 378, 384, 385, 387, 390, 392
budget policy, 13, 69, 127, 139, 183, 185, 197, 329, 400, 402, 416, 433
   economic effects of budget policy, 144, 155
budget process history, 15
   Appropriations Committees, 6
   early Constitutional period, 5
   founding period, 5

budget summits, 83, 89, 92, 98. *See*
    transparenc
budget surplus, 142, 147, 149, 154, 169, 172,
    177, 179, 187, 189, 191, 209, 228, 231,
    232, 235, 367, 384, 386, 387
budget window, 12, 39, 43, 51, 54, 55, 58, 59,
    151
budgetary aggregate, 191
budgetary aggregates, 103, 140, 195, 200–204,
    207, 209, 211–212, 215, 216, 218
budgetary projections, 183, 194, 197, 210,
    214
Bureau of Economic Analysis, 170
Bush, George H. W., 147
Bush, George W., 13, 40, 44, 65, 145, 149, 150,
    183, 189, 194, 195, 202, 226, 238
Byrd Rule, 9, 10, 30, 31, 34, 58, 65
Byrd, Robert, 9

capital assets, 170
cash flow, 179, 386, 444
Census, 48, 251, 297, 299, 300, 302, 307, 308,
    310, 328, 332, 334, 347, 350
civil government employee benefits, 204, 211,
    213, 215
Civil War, 5, 42, 349, 350
Clinton, Bill, 13, 48, 147, 194
closed-group liability, 207, 209
collective action problem, 286
common pool externality, 117, 120, 338, 361
concurrent budget resolution, 8, 18, 70, 73,
    80–82, 87, 96
conditional spending, 330
Congressional Budget and Impoundment
    Control Act of 1974, 1, 7
Congressional Budget Office, 1, 7, 10, 17, 31,
    43–46, 50–52, 54, 56, 58, 60, 61, 63, 147,
    149–151, 160, 183, 185, 186, 188, 189,
    193–196, 416
congressional budget resolutions, 41, 55
consumption tax, 166, 168
contracts approach, 117–118, 121, 123, 128
contracts clause, 409–411, 413, 414
counter-majoritarianism, 374, 375
crowding out, 141, 158, 160, 164, 180, 191,
    192, 194

debt limits, 266, 272, 274, 277–278, 329, 347,
    349–350, 353, 355–360, 373, 388, 426,
    427, 442
debt to GDP ratio, 114, 124, 147, 149, 153,
    172, 177, 180, 181
default bias, 224
deficit, 139, 142–143, 145, 151, 153–155, 157,
    159, 162, 164, 168, 169, 172, 176, 177,
    181–182, 185, 187, 194, 196, 198, 209,
    223, 226, 230–231, 235, 237, 238, 240,
    241, 444
delayed disclosure, 93, 97
    budget summits, 89
    federal advisory committees, 93
delegation approach, 117, 121, 123
Department of Defense, 48, 67, 189, 196
deposit insurance, 143, 147, 171
depreciation, 57, 65, 143, 145, 166, 170, 179
Desert Storm, 143
direct democracy, 371, 419–420, 422
directed scorekeeping, 44, 50
directed scoring, 46
discretionary spending, 24, 41, 48, 62, 64, 104,
    151, 189, 193, 199, 200, 214–216, 403

earmarks, 24, 46, 47, 215, 404
earned-income tax credit (EITC), 168
Economic Growth and Tax Relief Act of 2001,
    56, 58
Electoral Count Act of 1887, 94
emergency spending, 48
endogeneity, 258–259, 262, 266, 269, 273, 277,
    288, 296, 349
endowment effect, 226, 237
entitlement programs, 139, 140, 179, 183,
    184, 195, 216, 218, 399
entrenchment, 402, 404, 406, 415–416
European fiscal policies, 166, 168, 179
European Monetary Union, 3, 105, 116,
    124–125, 127
European Union, 3, 104–106, 127, 128, 132,
    134, 193, 394. *See* European Monetary
    Union. *See* The Stability and Growth
    Pact. *See* Excessive Deficit Procedure
    Economic and Financial Committee, 106
    EU governments debt and deficit, 109, 111,
    122, 125
    European Commission, 105–108
    European Council of Economics and
    Finance Ministers, 105–108, 127
    Treaty on European Union, 105, 106
Excessive Deficit Procedure, 104, 107
executive power, 72, 268, 272, 274
    veto power, 268–269, 272
exogeneity, 277, 305

Federal Accounting Standards Advisory
    Board, 219
federal advisory committees, 69, 89, 91, 93, 98.
    See transparency. *See* delayed disclosure
federal aid to states, 381, 389, 392
federal constitutional limits on states' taxing
    authority, 370

federal debt, 139, 142, 150, 153–156, 162, 164, 169, 170, 179, 188, 203
federal mandates, 255, 330, 378
Federal Reserve System, 84, 374
filibuster, 8, 11, 13, 15, 21, 25
Financial Reports of the United States Government, 185, 186, 200, 202, 203, 212, 217
fiscal drag, 165
fiscal federalism, 256, 330, 362, 389, 392
fiscal gap, 144, 167, 173, 174, 176, 179–181, 208, 219
    California, 167
fiscal limits, 279, 280, 285, 293, 295, 438, 440
fiscal outcomes, 279, 293, 295, 296, 305
fiscal policies, 182, 183, 194, 197, 209, 223, 226, 366, 392, 400, 444
    relationship between federal and state fiscal policies, 371, 374, 378, 382–385, 392–394
fiscal rules, 105, 116, 126, 191, 295, 296, 330–331, 342, 355, 373–375, 384. See Maastricht Treaty
    Australia, 104
    Austria, 109, 112
    Belgium, 109, 111, 113, 123, 124
    Canada, 104
    Denmark, 109, 111, 113, 123
    Finland, 112, 123
    France, 109, 112, 119, 125
    Germany, 103, 108, 109, 112–113, 119, 125
    Greece, 109, 112, 119, 121
    Ireland, 109, 112, 119, 123, 124
    Italy, 109, 112, 119, 121, 125
    Japan, 103, 105
    Luxembourg, 109, 112, 123, 124
    Netherlands, 109, 124
    New Zealand, 104
    Portugal, 109, 112, 123
    Spain, 109
    Sweden, 109, 112, 119, 123
    Switzerland, 104
    United Kingdom, 109, 112, 119, 123, 124
    United States, 104, 105
    West African Economic and Monetary Union, 104
fiscal rules index, 123–124
framework laws, 1, 105, 116
    objective, 2
framing, 225

Gann Limit, 291, 313
General Accounting Office, 6, 259
generational accounting, 66, 144, 173, 219
generational equity, 165, 174, 179, 180
global capital markets, 159

Government Accountability Office, 6, 10, 45, 52. See General Accounting Office
government shutdowns, 366
government sponsored enterprises, 46, 171, 214
government structure, 332, 336, 359
    local governments, 329, 335, 353, 355–356, 359–362, 364, 373, 383
    state governments, 334, 349, 355, 359–361, 364
Gramm-Rudman-Hollings Act, 11–12, 104, 128, 191, 241, 375, 399, 405
Great Depression, 153, 176, 335, 374
gubernatorial budget power, 254, 268, 275–276, 429, 431–432, 436, 439, 441, 443. See line-item veto
Guinn v. Legislature of the State of Nevada, 424, 430, 442, 443, 445

home rule, 355
House of Representatives Armed Services Committee, 45
House of Representatives Rules Committee, 19, 25, 28
House of Representatives Ways and Means Committee, 27–28
human capital, 154, 167

identified-victim effect, 224, 231, 232, 237
impoundments, 7, 266, 399
inconsistent discounting, 225
incremental budgeting, 256–257, 273
indexes of budget institutions, 121
individual retirement accounts, 59, 60, 170
industrialization, 330, 350
infinite horizon, 176, 183
inflation, 143–145, 149, 151, 153, 160–162, 169, 179, 191
infrastructure, 162, 192, 329, 330, 332, 334–336, 340, 347, 357–364, 367, 371, 387, 388, 442
interest payments, 172, 189, 196, 197, 210, 276, 309, 411
intergenerational transfers, 162, 366, 369, 371
isolation effect, 224, 226, 228, 231
item reduction, 252–253

Jobs and Growth Tax Relief Reconciliation Act of 2003, 58
Joint Committee on Taxation, 34, 43

Kahneman and Tversky, 222

Lance v. McGreevey, 430, 442, 443
Leviathan model, 271, 273, 283, 286, 288

line-item veto, 252, 253, 267, 271, 272,
    276–277, 284, 365, 399, 431, 432, 435,
    439–443
loans and guarantees, 201, 204, 213, 214
Lobbying Disclosure Act, 88, 92
lobbyists, 198, 199
local fiscal institutions, 329, 362
Lonegan v. State, 428–430, 442, 443

Maastricht Treaty, 104–105, 109, 112,
    119–121, 123, 125, 128
macro-economic indicators, 142, 192, 211
mandatory spending, 6, 26, 49, 189, 193, 196,
    200, 206, 215, 216, 403, 416
median-voter model, 271, 273, 281, 286, 288
Medicaid, 6, 26, 44, 151, 194, 195, 199, 272,
    336, 369, 376, 380, 385, 390, 433–435
Medicare, 6, 14, 18, 26, 44, 46, 50, 53, 54, 56,
    62, 140, 144, 151, 164, 171, 173, 174, 176,
    177, 180, 181, 183, 186, 195, 209, 211,
    213, 215, 216, 219, 223, 239, 240, 336,
    369, 380
military and veteran benefits, 204, 213, 215
monetary policy, 141, 145, 160, 181, 285
multi-year appropriations, 218
myopic, 11, 12, 50, 154, 156, 223, 228, 230,
    238

National Conference of State Legislatures,
    252, 260, 293
national debt, 141, 153–154, 162, 170, 171
Nevada, 419, 421, 422, 424, 426, 443. *See
    Guinn* v. *Legislature of the State of
    Nevada*
New Jersey, 425, 426, 429, 430, 442, 443. *See
    Lance v. McGreevey* . *See Lonegan v. State*
New York, 427, 428, 432, 436. *See Pataki v.
    New York State Assembly*
Nixon, Richard, 7, 381

off budget accounts, 47, 49
Office of Management and Budget, 6, 7, 10,
    11, 16–17, 41, 43–45, 48, 50–52, 61, 72,
    170, 183, 192
omission bias, 224
optimism bias, 228, 230, 238
overlapping generations model, 169

parliamentarian, 81
    Senate, 9, 13, 20, 31–32
Pataki v. New York State Assembly, 436, 443
PAYGO, 12–14, 20, 41, 49, 62, 164, 257,
    375
Pension Benefit Guaranty Corporation
    (PBGC), 171, 201, 203, 212–214

point of order, 11, 13, 19–20, 22, 24, 25,
    30–32, 34, 41, 72
political culture, 212, 260, 262, 297, 301, 313,
    314, 316
political economy, 211, 260, 271, 283
political economy literature, 116, 249, 279,
    292, 297
political psychology, 140, 223, 226, 240
President's Tax Reform Panel, 90, 93
primary budget, 143, 147
principal-agent problem, 256, 264, 282, 291,
    292, 318, 320
Printz v. United States, 378
property, 400, 402, 407–411, 417, 445
property tax, 344, 360, 369, 373
Proposition 111, 19, 294, 301, 302, 304, 305,
    310, 312
Proposition 13, 3, 291, 302, 419
Proposition 4, 1, 291, 294, 301–306, 310,
    313
public choice, 256, 263, 281
public debt, 139, 153, 159, 163, 164, 182, 185,
    188, 191–194, 198, 200, 201, 203, 204,
    207, 209, 213, 411, 417

rainy-day funds, 365, 367, 382, 386
rational expectations, 223
Reagan, Ronald, 9–11, 147, 192, 225, 238, 241,
    381
reconciliation bills, 74
reconciliation process, 4, 8–10, 13–14, 19, 26,
    27, 30–32, 42, 49, 62–63, 88
reconstruction, 350, 410
referendum, 276, 284, 326, 343, 344, 357, 359,
    360, 370, 385, 424
rescission, 7, 252, 254, 266, 269
research and development tax credit, 58
reserve requirements, 254, 257, 258, 260
revenue estimate, 40–41, 43, 46, 55, 59, 61, 63,
    194
Ricardian equivalence, 156, 164, 179

sales taxes, 388
Senate Finance Committee, 28
separation of powers, 399, 417, 436
sequestration, 10, 12, 41
social insurance, 209, 213, 216, 218, 219
Social Security, ii, 6, 12, 26, 34, 43, 46, 47, 53,
    90, 140, 144, 151, 164, 171–174, 176, 177,
    180, 181, 183, 184, 186, 195, 209, 211,
    213, 215, 216, 219, 223, 239, 240, 336,
    369, 380, 400–402, 405, 415–416, 445
South Dakota v. Dole, 378
sovereign immunity, 213, 399, 400, 409–411,
    417

special purpose districts, 331, 332, 334, 347, 359, 362–364
Stability and Growth Pact, 104, 108, 125, 128, 132
starve the beast strategy, 140, 221, 225, 226, 230, 235, 238, 241
state budgetary practices, 251, 254–255, 273, 370, 375, 384, 387–388, 394, 432, 434
   size and growth of government, 273, 290, 314
state constitutions, 418–424, 428–430, 438, 442–445
state debt, 330, 334, 335, 344, 349–350, 424, 428
   debt limitations, 329, 424, 428
   defaults on debt, 342, 362
state fiscal institutions, 255, 268, 271, 273, 286, 295, 301, 329, 355, 362
state fiscal policies, 251, 258, 297, 330, 364, 366, 371, 375, 378, 382
state legislatures, 294, 427, 430, 432, 433, 438, 440, 441, 445
status quo bias, 224–226, 235–237
Stockman, David, 10, 192, 225
substantive due process, 401
sunsets (expiring provisions), 34, 59, 402, 405
supermajority vote requirements, 252, 254, 258–259, 265, 267, 274, 275, 302, 316, 402, 418–420, 422–424, 442, 443, 445

takings clause, 400, 401, 407, 409, 411, 417
tax and expenditure limits, 249, 250, 252, 254, 258, 266–267, 269, 271, 272, 274–275, 277, 278, 283, 293, 295, 301, 319–320, 329, 365, 368, 371, 374, 375, 385, 387
   California, 292, 294, 299, 313
   Colorado, 292, 313, 316
   Utah, 292, 313, 316
   Washington, 292, 313, 318
tax cuts, 149, 150, 155, 156, 183, 221, 226, 230, 235–237, 239
tax expenditures, 37, 49
tax policy, 153, 155, 165–168, 223, 402, 411
tax rate, 42, 53, 56, 58, 110, 111, 142, 143, 152–154, 158, 161, 165, 167–169, 180, 181, 259, 284, 306, 344, 389

tax revolt, 369
Taxpayers' Bill of Rights (TABOR), 265, 272, 275, 281, 313–315, 368, 385
Temporary Assistance to Needy Families (TANF), 384, 391
The Economic Growth and Tax Relief Act of 2001, 56
The National Conference of State Legislatures, 293
Tiebout, Charles, 358, 359, 367
timing gimmicks, 61
transparency, 3, 24, 70, 86, 118, 127, 239, 257, 360, 365, 372, 387, 394, 442
   accountability, 75, 80, 89
   budget summits, 83, 89, 92, 98
   collective action problem, 78–79
   federal advisory committees, 98
   federal budget process, 75
   institutional and political constraints to optimal structure, 98
   interest group pressure, 79–80, 86, 89, 91
   motivations of Congress members, 74, 77, 83, 87, 95–96
   open meeting requirements, 69, 73, 93
   optimal structure, 93
transportation infrastructure, 331, 335, 337, 340, 342, 358
Treasury Department, ii, 52, 63

U.S. Constitution Article I, §9, 1, 4
U.S. Supreme Court, 7, 10, 11, 175, 213, 280, 330, 369, 375, 378, 393, 399, 410, 414, 417
unfunded mandate, 239, 275, 330, 378, 379, 389
Unfunded Mandates Reform Act, 330, 378, 394

Virginia, 411
voters, 78, 84, 86, 221, 240, 241, 372, 412, 422

West African Economic and Monetary Union, 104
Wildavsky, Aaron, 255
World War II, 10, 143, 149, 152, 153, 176, 191, 192, 335